Imperial Germany
and a
World Without War

Imperial Germany and a World Without War

*The
Peace Movement
and
German Society,
1892-1914*

Roger Chickering

PRINCETON UNIVERSITY PRESS
PRINCETON, NEW JERSEY

Copyright © 1975 by Princeton University Press
Published by Princeton University Press, Princeton and London
ALL RIGHTS RESERVED

Library of Congress Cataloging in Publication Data will
be found on the last printed page of this book

This book has been composed in Linotype Janson

Printed in the United States of America
by Princeton University Press, Princeton, New Jersey

For Wendy

Contents

PREFACE — xi

ABBREVIATIONS — xiii

1. INTRODUCTION: THE PEACE MOVEMENT,
   PACIFISM, AND POLITICAL CULTURE — 3
   The Development of the International
   Peace Movement — 4
   Pacifism and Internationalism — 14
   The Peace Movement and Political Culture — 26

2. THE GERMAN PEACE SOCIETY — 38
   Early Pacifist Organizations in Germany — 39
   The Establishment of the German
   Peace Society — 44
   The Stuttgart Years — 59
   Portrait of the Pacifists — 72

3. THE IDEOLOGY OF GERMAN PACIFISM — 89
   Alfred Fried and the Development of
   a Scientific Pacifism — 94
   The Route to World Peace — 109
   Pacifism and Modernization — 116

4. THE EXPANSION OF THE GERMAN
   PEACE MOVEMENT — 122
   Pacifists and Other Prophets of Progress — 122
   Pacifism and the Academic Disciplines — 135
   The *Verband für internationale
   Verständigung* — 148

5. THE PEACE MOVEMENT AND THE POLITICAL
   EDUCATION OF GERMAN SOCIETY — 163
   The Political Education of German
   Children: Family and Youth Groups — 165

vii

The Educational System 170
The Military 181
The Press 184
The Churches 192

6. THE PEACE MOVEMENT AND GERMAN POLITICS 218
The Imperial Government 218
Political Parties and Politicians 239
The Interparliamentary Union in Germany 253
The Social Democrats 259

7. THE GERMAN PEACE MOVEMENT AND
INTERNATIONAL POLITICS 286
Alsace-Lorraine and Rapprochement
with France 290
Colonialism and Conciliation with England 305
War, 1914 317

8. EXCURSUS: THE PEACE MOVEMENT IN FRANCE 327
The Contours of the French Peace Movement 331
The Peace Movement and French Politics 351
Agencies of Political Education:
Schools, the Press, Churches 372

9. THE PEACE MOVEMENT IN IMPERIAL GERMANY:
THE NATURE OF THE OPPOSITION 384
The Feasibility of War: The Confutation
of Bloch 387
The Indispensability of War:
Extreme Antipacifism 392
The Likelihood of War:
Moderate Antipacifism 403
The Indispensability of the Likelihood of War 410

BIBLIOGRAPHY 421

INDEX 467

List of Figures and Maps

FIGURE 1. Pacifism and Internationalism 26

FIGURE 2. Frankfurter Friedensverein Membership,
1888–1911 64

FIGURE 3. Occupations of Members in Three
Local Peace Societies 73

Map, Local Groups of the German Peace
Society, 1911–1912 60

Map, French Peace Societies in 1913 342

Preface

THIS study belongs to the genre of peace research. The principal characters in it are pacifists; its principal theme is their campaign to eliminate violent conflict from international politics. However, the study is ultimately more concerned with the society and political system within which this campaign took place.

I was originally drawn to study the German peace movement by my curiosity about attitudes toward war in Europe prior to the First World War. For an era that did not know of the public opinion poll, the peace movement seemed to be one possible vehicle to get at this problem. It was particularly attractive to me because of the presence, at the Hoover Institution, of the library of Alfred Fried, one of the leaders of the peace movement in Germany. Largely on the basis of the material in this collection, I wrote my dissertation. I concluded that the peace movement had, with remarkable accuracy, foreseen the disastrous impact of general war, but that its predictions and the reforms it proposed for making war unnecessary were overwhelmingly rejected in Germany.

Partially because of the limitations of the available documentary evidence, my dissertation did not adequately explain why the opposition to the peace movement was so widespread in Germany, nor was I able to determine conclusively whether it was any less widespread elsewhere. In 1970–71 I continued my research into the problem in Europe, using the private papers of many of those who had been active in the German movement, as well as the archives of the secretariat of the international peace movement, which enabled me to investigate the campaign of the movement in other countries. I also rethought the problem. I began to recognize that attitudes about war cannot be analyzed in isolation, that they are intimately bound up in perceptions of the whole complex of international relations, and that these perceptions in turn play an important role in the functioning of political systems. As a result, I began to view the pacifists' campaign in a somewhat different light, in the context of the attitudes that composed the political culture of imperial Germany. This analytical framework drew my attention to features in the German political system that accounted for the fact, which I could now demonstrate, that the peace movement was significantly weaker in Germany than elsewhere.

While preparing this study I have had a great deal of help, both financial and intellectual. I wish at this point to thank the individuals and agencies that have come to my aid. My benefactors include the National Endowment for the Humanities, the North Atlantic Treaty Organization, and the Office of Scientific and Scholarly Research of the Graduate School of the University of Oregon. Numerous people have offered bibliographical suggestions or made comments about the manuscript at various stages of its growth. They include Gordon Craig, who directed my dissertation and subsequently made valuable suggestions, Gordon Wright, Ivo Lederer, Walter Sokel, Karl Holl, Adolf Wild, Dorothee Stiewe, Friedrich-Karl Scheer, Val Lorwin, Stanley Pierson, Robert Berdahl, Thomas Brady, John Perrin, Lloyd Sorenson, James Shand, Dieter Buse, and John Conway. I would like as well to thank the staffs of the Hoover Institution on War, Revolution and Peace, especially Agnes Peterson, the Bayerische Staatsbibliothek in Munich, and the United Nations Library in Geneva for their kind help.

Eugene, Oregon
September 1974

Abbreviations

AA   Politisches Archiv des Auswärtigen Amtes, Bonn. ACP and UC numbers refer to microfilm designations: see American Historical Association, Committee for the Study of War Documents, *A Catalogue of Files and Microfilms of the German Foreign Ministry Archives, 1867–1920* ([Washington, D.C.], 1959).

AStA   Bayerisches Hauptstaatsarchiv, Munich: Allgemeines Staatsarchiv

BA   Bundesarchiv, Coblenz

BIP   Archives of the Bureau international permanent de la paix, United Nations Library, Geneva

CBM   *Correspondance bi-mensuelle*

CW   *Christliche Welt*

DDF   *Documents diplomatiques français (1871–1914).* First and Second Series. Paris, 1929–55

DWN   *Die Waffen nieder!*

ER   *Ethische Rundschau*

FB   *Die Friedens-Blätter*

FW   *Die Friedens-Warte*

GP   Johannes Lepsius, *et al.*, eds., *Die Grosse Politik der europäischen Kabinette 1871–1914.* Berlin, 1926–27.

GStA   Bayerisches Hauptstaatsarchiv, Munich: Geheimes Staatsarchiv

HB (1)   Alfred H. Fried, *Handbuch der Friedensbewegung.* Vienna and Leipzig, 1905

HB (2)   Alfred H. Fried, *Handbuch der Friedensbewegung.* 2d ed. Berlin and Leipzig, 1911–13

xiii

HStASt	Hauptstaatsarchiv Stuttgart
JPC	David Starr Jordan Collection, Peace Correspondence, Hoover Institution, Stanford University
KA	Bayerisches Hauptstaatsarchiv, Munich: Kriegsarchiv
KVfiV	*Korrespondenz des Verbandes für internationale Verständigung*
MFK	*Monatliche Friedenskorrespondenz*
MVfiV	*Mitteilungen des Verbandes für internationale Verständigung*
NL	Nachlass
NZ	*Neue Zeit*
PD	*La paix par le droit*
PM	*The Peace Movement*
SFC	Suttner-Fried Correspondence, United Nations Library, Geneva
StAH	Staatsarchiv Hamburg
StBR	*Stenographische Berichte über die Verhandlungen des Reichstages.* Berlin, 1871–1933
StOb	Bayerisches Hauptstaatsarchiv, Munich: Staatsarchiv für Oberbayern
VF	*Der Völker-Friede*

Imperial Germany
and a
World Without War

"Is there any point to which you would wish to
     draw my attention?"
"To the curious incident of the dog in the night-time."
"The dog did nothing in the night-time."
"That was the curious incident," remarked Sherlock Holmes.

1

Introduction: The Peace Movement, Pacifism, and Political Culture

AMONG the documents of that tangle of events in 1914 known to historians as the July crisis, one of the least controversial has been the Serbian reply to the Austrian ultimatum. Convinced that the Austrians were determined to go to war regardless of how the Serbs answered the ultimatum, and convinced that the Serbs knew this, historians have not ascribed much importance to the substance of the Serbian reply, except to note that it was a clever piece of dissimulation designed to win for Serbia the support of world opinion. No doubt this interpretation is correct, and one ought to regard with skepticism any concessions the Serbs made in the document. This skepticism ought certainly to extend to the remarkable offer contained in the second paragraph of Article X of their reply: "In the event the Austrian government is not satisfied with this response, the Serbian government . . . is prepared, as always, to accept a peaceful agreement, by submitting the question . . . to the decision of the International Tribunal at The Hague."[1]

However disingenuous, the Serbian offer was not altogether implausible. There was in fact a tribunal at The Hague, which had on several occasions successfully arbitrated international disputes submitted to it. In the years prior to 1914 numerous international agreements had been negotiated, binding signatory states to arbitrate certain kinds of disputes either at The Hague or before some other suitable agency. There was, moreover, a considerable body of world opinion which believed that arbitration repre-

[1] G. P. Gooch and Harold Temperley, eds., *British Documents on the Origins of the War* (11 vols., London, 1926–38), XI, 367–71 (Appendix B).

3

sented a realistic alternative to war and that the competence of bodies like the Hague tribunal ought to be enlarged.

Historians who have studied the origins of the First World War have shown little more interest in the development and popularization of arbitration than the diplomats in Vienna showed in the Serbian offer to resolve the July crisis at The Hague. Only recently have general studies of the prewar years begun to acknowledge that arbitration appeared to many Europeans as a feasible solution to the problem of international violence.[2] The historical questions that remain unanswered about this possible alternative are legion. Given the political and social tensions in Europe at the turn of the twentieth century, was arbitration in fact a feasible alternative to war? Did the men who formulated government policy regard arbitration as feasible or desirable? What was the nature of popular support for arbitration? Did it influence political decisions? What resistance did the concept of arbitration encounter?

No single volume can deal adequately with this complex of questions, at least not at the present stage of historical research into the problem. Obviously, the concept of arbitration was international in scope; this meant that discussion of the concept took place in all countries in Europe, in different circumstances and with significantly different results. Nonetheless, an analysis of this discussion in any single country must begin with a brief consideration of a movement in which there had by the turn of the century developed a strong sense of international solidarity.

The Development of the International Peace Movement

There has been no dearth in western history of thinkers who have envisaged the definitive elimination of violence

---

[2] Two examples: Fritz Klein, *et al.*, *Deutschland im ersten Weltkrieg* (3 vols., Berlin, 1968–70), I: *Vorbereitung, Entfesselung und Verlauf des Krieges bis Ende 1914*; Oron J. Hale, *The Great Illusion, 1900–1914* (New York, 1971), esp. pp. 16–21.

4

from international affairs and have made specific proposals to this end.[3] As a rule, however, these thinkers—men such as Crucé, Sully, St. Pierre, and Kant—were isolated intellectuals, officials, or clerics, who spoke for no articulate group but relied on the benevolence and insight of the sovereign heads of state for the realization of their projects. Only in the nineteenth century did proposals to do away with war begin to attract a politically active popular following.

The immediate stimulus for the creation of peace societies in the early nineteenth century was revulsion over the Napoleonic wars.[4] The first such society was established in New York in August 1814, while the first in Europe, the Society for the Promotion of Permanent and Universal Peace, was founded in London in June 1815. Most of the societies that appeared subsequently in the first half of the nineteenth century were located in England, but one was established in Paris in 1821 and another in Geneva in 1830. Tied together by little more than personal acquaintances and a common commitment to working against war, this early peace movement represented the outgrowth of three dif-

[3] For general surveys see: Roland H. Bainton, *Christian Attitudes toward War and Peace: A Historical Survey and Critical Reevaluation* (New York and Nashville, Tenn., 1960); Adda B. Bozeman, *Politics and Culture in International History* (Princeton, 1960), esp. pp. 238–97; F. H. Hinsley, *Power and the Pursuit of Peace: Theory and Practice in the History of Relations between States* (Cambridge, 1963), pp. 13–149; Elizabeth V. Souleyman, *The Vision of World Peace in Seventeenth and Eighteenth Century France* (New York, 1941); Kurt von Raumer, *Ewiger Friede: Friedensrufe und Friedenspläne seit der Renaissance* (Freiburg and Munich, 1953); Sylvester John Hemleben, *Plans for World Peace through Six Centuries* (Chicago, 1943).

[4] On the international peace movement in the nineteenth century see especially August Schou, *Histoire de l'internationalisme*, III: *Du Congrès de Vienne jusqu'à la première guerre mondiale (1914)* (Oslo, 1963); A. C. F. Beales, *The History of Peace: A Short Account of the Organised Movements for International Peace* (London, 1931), pp. 45–277; F. S. L. Lyons, *Internationalism in Europe, 1815–1914* (Leyden, 1963), pp. 309–61.

ferent, though not unrelated traditions.[5] The most important of these was Quakerism, a denomination whose unique
blend of doctrinal precepts would make it the most active
of all Christian groups in organized efforts to secure peace.
Like many Christian sects, Quakers repudiated all forms of
warfare, whether aggressive or defensive, as unbefitting a
Christian life, and refused to participate in military service.
In the case of most sectarian groups this repudiation was
part of a general rejection of secular concerns; in Quakerism it was coupled with constructive political activism, a
commitment to achieving the reforms that would eliminate
the need for war. In this connection it was significant that
the authors of two of the most important peace projects of
the seventeenth and eighteenth centuries, William Penn and
John Bellers, were Quakers. In the early nineteenth century
Quakers were the leading element in most English and
American peace societies.

The second major tradition underlying the early peace
movement was free-trade liberalism. Secular and utilitarian
in its assumptions, this school of thought condemned warfare, to use the words of one of its principal figures, James
Mill, as "the pestilential wind which blasts the property of
nations" and "the devouring fiend which eats up the precious treasure of national economy."[6] As the most effective
guarantee of a durable peace, these liberals prescribed un-
impeded international trade, which would tie the peoples
of the world together in a network of commercial interdependence. The most renowned champions of this liberal
case against war were Richard Cobden and John Bright,
whose stature and influence made the peace movement an
important factor in English politics.[7]

[5] See Pierre Renouvin and Jean-Baptiste Duroselle, *Introduction to
the History of International Relations* (New York, 1967), p. 219.

[6] Quoted in Edmund Silberner, *The Problem of War in Nineteenth
Century Economic Thought* (Princeton, 1946), p. 41; cf. Helen Bosanquet, *Free Trade and Peace in the Nineteenth Century* (Kristiania,
1924), esp. pp. 71–79.

[7] Gavin B. Henderson, "The Pacifists of the Fifties," *Journal of
Modern History* IX (1937), 314–41.

Throughout the first half of the nineteenth century the peace movement remained much stronger in England than on the European continent, where neither Quakerism nor free-trade liberalism was as deeply rooted. The continental peace societies managed to attract primarily liberals, such as the Frenchmen Frédéric Bastiat and Joseph Garnier. Toward the middle of the century, however, an alliance began to form between the peace movement and a tradition indigenous to the continent. One of the articles of faith of nationalists inspired by Mazzini was that warfare would persist only as long as reactionary statesmen frustrated the national aspirations of the peoples of Europe. Lasting peace, they argued, would be the natural product of the division of mankind into harmonious, responsibly governed, national groups.

Largely a middle-class phenomenon, the early peace movement was more homogeneous socially than doctrinally. Although all elements in it agreed that war was reprehensible, they were severely at odds about conditions in which war might be permissible. Quakers argued that war was legitimate in no circumstances, while liberals approved of wars of self-defense, and Mazzinian nationalists even condoned revolutionary wars of national unification. There was, however, one point on which all could agree. Arbitration appealed to Quakers as a means to remove the need for wars of any kind; liberals regarded it as the appropriate device for resolving misunderstandings in the community of trading partners, and nationalists endorsed it as a useful tool for settling disputes that might occasionally arise in the great sisterhood of nations they envisaged. A principal activity of peace societies everywhere was, accordingly, the popularization of the concept of arbitration and the elaboration of plans for some kind of international arbitral agency.

The first phase of the peace movement's history culminated in a series of international peace congresses in the middle of the century. In 1843 delegates from the existing peace societies gathered in London for the first General

Peace Convention. Then, amidst the euphoria of the mid-century revolutions on the continent, peace congresses convened in Brussels in 1848, in Paris in 1849, in Frankfurt in 1850, and in London in 1851. Although they created the impression of international solidarity, these congresses, like the peace movement itself, were overwhelmingly dominated by the English; 292 of the 324 delegates to the convention in 1843, and 670 of the 850 delegates to the congress in Paris were from Great Britain.[8]

Even as this series of congresses was drawing to a close, the peace movement began to enter an eclipse that extended almost until the 1870s. The onset of reaction on the continent made it impossible for peace societies to work in public. The Crimean War and then the wars of national unification on the continent badly discouraged the Quakers, who made up much of the English movement. The American Civil War likewise created serious difficulties for the peace movement in the United States.

Measured by the numbers of people associated with it, the range of its activities, and the influence it enjoyed, the peace movement experienced its golden age in the period between the Franco-Prussian War and the outbreak of the First World War. This was both a result and a symptom of the significant developments that were changing the face of European society and politics. The most important of these was the accelerated internationalization of western life at the end of the century. The development of an international economy, unprecedented in its degree of interdependence, seemed to confirm the expectations of liberals that the nations of the world would tie themselves together in a vast commercial and financial network. To make this economic internationalization possible, an international communications and transportation network developed, overseen in part by international agencies such as the Universal Postal Union and the Telegraphic Union. In the wake of economic developments numerous cultural, humani-

---

[8] Beales, *History of Peace*, pp. 67, 78.

tarian, professional, and religious organizations appeared. Between 1870 and 1914 over four hundred such nongovernmental organizations were created, and in 1910 representatives of 137 of them met in Brussels to found the Union of International Associations, which was designed to serve as a coordinating agency for what was becoming known as the "international movement."[9]

The late nineteenth century also saw a marked increase in the international coordination of political activity. The Second International provided the most conspicuous example; less dramatic, but no less political in implication, was the response of governments to the internationalization of communications, transportation, and the economy. Through a network of treaties, conventions, and agencies, governments regularized their relations in such important areas as the navigation of international waterways, consular jurisdiction, extradition, and some categories of commercial legislation. The product was a growing body of international law, which in turn stimulated scholarly and professional interest in its continued development. In 1873 two private organizations were founded to study and promote the expansion of international law. The *Institut de droit international*, with headquarters in Ghent, was an elite group of statesmen and scholars, while the more widely based International Law Association in London appealed to lawyers, politicians, and professional people with a more practical interest in the development of international law.

From one perspective the expansion of the peace movement after 1870 represented an aspect of this internationalization. Peace societies sought to capitalize on the growth of international interdependence and to push it through to what they believed was its logical conclusion—the regulation by law of all critical aspects of international affairs, including the kinds of disputes that had routinely led in the past to war.

[9] See *Annuaire de la vie internationale* (Brussels and Monaco, 1905–11). The best general survey of late nineteenth century internationalization is Lyons, *Internationalism in Europe*.

The growth of the peace movement at the end of the century was also a response to a paradoxical development: the same period in which international ties multiplied so rapidly also witnessed the transformation of Europe into an armed camp.[10] The adoption of universal military service in the aftermath of the Franco-Prussian War and the development and deployment of efficient new weaponry, such as the small-caliber rifle, the machine gun, and siege artillery, portended war of unprecedented scale. The revolution in military equipment and organization also provoked popular alarm over the likely consequences of such a war and over the cost, both fiscal and moral, of maintaining vast armies and navies in peace time. From another perspective, then, the expansion of the peace movement represented an attempt to articulate this concern and make it politically effective.[11]

One final factor contributed to the growth of the peace movement at this time. This was the very fact of a long period of peace in Europe—a phenomenon the peace movement tended to ascribe to internationalization rather than to the deterrent effect of large armies. Despite sporadic colonial wars and a series of increasingly ominous international crises after the turn of the century, peace societies could point to more than three decades of peace in Europe as evidence that war had become an anachronism.

The recovery of the peace movement from its mid-century decline can be dated from 1867, when two of the most durable peace societies on the continent were founded.[12] Created in Paris by Frédéric Passy, the *Ligue*

[10] The best short survey of these developments is Michael Howard, "The Armed Forces," *The New Cambridge Modern History*, xi: *Material Progress and World-Wide Problems, 1870–1898* (Cambridge, 1967), pp. 204–42.

[11] William L. Langer, *The Diplomacy of Imperialism, 1890–1902* (2d ed., New York, 1965), p. 581.

[12] For an extensive account of the peace movement in the late nineteenth century see Irwin Martin Abrams, "A History of European

internationale et permanente de la paix represented a continuation of the liberal tradition in calling for international political cooperation on the basis of free trade. The other new organization, the *Ligue internationale de la paix et de la liberté*, emphasized the more radical Mazzinian vision of a peaceful community of democratic nations, and after its creation in Geneva by Charles Lemonnier, it became a haven for disaffected republicans throughout Europe. Both new organizations stressed secular considerations in opposing war and were more successful in finding support on the continent than English Quakers had been earlier in the century.

After a brief relapse occasioned by the Franco-Prussian War, the peace movement's expansion began in earnest. By the middle of the 1870s new peace societies had been founded in Italy, Belgium, and the Netherlands. In 1878 an international peace congress convened in Paris, attended by delegates from thirteen countries. In the 1880s peace societies underwent further expansion and reorganization. Plans began to take shape for some kind of international apparatus to coordinate activities among peace societies in different countries. In 1880 Hodgson Pratt established the International Arbitration and Peace Association of Great Britain and Ireland, an organization whose secular orientation appealed to those who were uncomfortable in the religious atmosphere that still prevailed in most English peace groups. Pratt was also a tireless agitator and set up several peace societies on the continent. At the same time a vigorous peace movement developed in Scandinavia.

In 1889 the development of the peace movement entered a new phase. In that year both of the institutions that would become the focal points of the prewar peace movement appeared. In June the first Universal Peace Congress met in Paris. There representatives from peace societies in western

---

Peace Societies, 1867–1899" (Ph.D. dissertation, Harvard University, 1938).

Europe and America decided to coordinate their campaign through a series of regular international congresses. They agreed as well that this campaign should emphasize the need for obligatory arbitration of international disputes. Immediately after this congress adjourned, the first Interparliamentary Conference convened, likewise in Paris. There, some one hundred parliamentarians, principally from France and England, also agreed to launch a series of regular international meetings and to exert pressure within their respective parliaments for negotiation of permanent treaties of arbitration.[13]

The third event in 1889 of major significance for the peace movement was the publication of Bertha von Suttner's antiwar novel, *Die Waffen nieder!* Although (or perhaps because) its polemical value exceeded its literary merit, it was an immense popular success. By 1905 the book, which was hailed as the *"Uncle Tom's Cabin* of the peace movement," had gone through thirty-seven editions and had been translated into more than a dozen languages.[14] Far more than the annual international congresses, *Die Waffen nieder!* mobilized popular support for the peace movement; many, if not most, of those who found their way into peace societies after 1889 probably did so after reading this book.

During the last decades before the First World War the peace movement continued to grow and enlarge the scale of its operations. While the parliamentarians sought to utilize the political channels open to them in order to promote arbitration and international conciliation, peace societies

[13] On the Interparliamentary Union see Chr. Lange, *et al., The Interparliamentary Union from 1889 to 1939* (Lausanne, 1939); Richard Eickhoff, "Die Interparlamentarische Union (1889–1914)," *Zeitschrift für Politik* VIII (1915), 452–93.

[14] Beatrix Kempf, *Bertha von Suttner: Das Lebensbild einer grossen Frau* (Vienna, 1964), pp. 29–30; cf. Bertha von Suttner, *Memoirs of Bertha von Suttner: The Records of an Eventful Life* (2 vols., Boston and London, 1910), I, 294–311; Bertha von Suttner, *Aus der Werkstatt des Pazifismus* (Leipzig and Vienna, 1912), pp. 7–14.

attempted to mobilize public opinion to the same end. In the 1890s existing peace societies expanded and new ones appeared, notably in Austria-Hungary and Germany. To add more international direction to their efforts both facets of the peace movement, the Universal Peace Congresses and the Interparliamentary Conferences, established permanent secretariats in Berne in 1892. Thereupon the International Peace Bureau and the Interparliamentary Bureau began to serve as general supervisory agencies for their respective groups, publishing journals, protocols, and statistics. The convocation of the two Hague conferences, in 1899 and 1907, worked to the further advantage of the peace movement; with diplomats now debating projects for a court of international arbitration, apparently in earnest, it became more difficult to dismiss the peace movement as a group of dreamers who were not to be taken seriously. Although the actual results of the Hague conferences were minimal, peace societies benefitted from the popular interest they created in arbitration.

By the first years of the twentieth century the peace movement had become a prominent feature in political affairs. Universal Peace Congresses and Interparliamentary Conferences were noteworthy events, and leaders of the movement, such as William Stead, Frédéric Passy, Henri La Fontaine, Albert Gobat, and Bertha von Suttner, commanded wide respect. In 1910 the peace movement acquired a benefactor, which enabled it to expand its operations further. Through its European bureau in Paris, the Carnegie Endowment for International Peace sent annual subsidies to selected peace groups, journals, and the International Peace Bureau.

The peace movement remained a middle-class phenomenon that harbored a diversity of outlooks, although by the turn of the century the secular, humanitarian, and liberal doctrines of the continental societies had begun to predominate over the religious antiwar thinking of most of the Anglo-American groups. And, in an era enchanted with science, this liberal opposition to war took on the accents of positivism: the development of a community of nations, linked by economic, cultural, and ultimately by political ties, was now characterized as the natural product of social evolution. Although there remained severe philosophical tensions, which surfaced whenever the problem of defensive war was raised, all elements in the peace movement continued to agree on the need for arbitration and, particularly with the acceleration of the arms race at the turn of the century, on the urgency of some kind of comprehensive arms agreement. Interparliamentary Conferences and Universal Peace Congresses were devoted to studying ways to implement these measures, as well as to discussion of more long-range projects, notably the creation of a world federation with its own judicial, executive, and legislative agencies.[15]

Pacifism and Internationalism

Throughout most of the nineteenth century people who joined peace societies and attended international peace congresses referred to themselves simply as "peace workers," "peace advocates," or, most commonly, "friends of peace." With the expansion of the peace movement in the 1890s dissatisfaction grew over these conventional labels, which, it seemed, did not adequately distinguish members of peace societies from others who held that war was objectionable but were unwilling to do anything about it. Labels like "friends of peace" had the added disadvantage of sounding a little silly and seemed inappropriate for a movement that aspired to bring about major international reforms. After considerable discussion among leading personalities in the movement, a Frenchman, Émile Arnaud, contrived the term "pacifism" to describe the doctrine and program of the

[15] For an analysis of the proposals studied by these congresses see Sandi E. Cooper, "Peace and Internationalism: European Ideological Movements behind the Two Hague Conferences (1889 to 1907)" (Ph.D. dissertation, New York University, 1967).

peace movement. As an ism, the word suggested a well-developed and coherent body of thought, and it could be integrated with relative uniformity into different languages. In 1901 this designation was officially adopted at the Tenth Universal Peace Congress in Glasgow, whereupon those active in the peace movement began to refer to themselves, and were referred to by others, as pacifists.[16]

Almost immediately problems arose over the scope and application of the word. Debates raged over whether to use the label to describe a statesman who was pursuing peaceful policies, or whether someone deserved the label if he only advocated voluntary but not obligatory arbitration, or if socialists, who called for arbitration but generally avoided the peace societies, should be regarded as pacifists.[17] These problems seemed academic in retrospect, however, once the peace movement split in 1914 between those who supported the war efforts of their respective countries and those, principally in England, who did not. After the war, amidst considerable recrimination within the movement, it became common to reserve the label pacifist for those who unconditionally opposed all forms of international violence. Those who proposed to eliminate war through arbitration and international organization, but who countenanced defensive warfare or the use of collective sanctions, became known as "internationalists," "world federalists," or even, more recently, as "pacificists."[18] Since Pro-

16 BIP (viiiAi), Richard Grelling to Élie Ducommun, Berlin, 11 May 1896; BIP (iH), Commission du Bureau, Séance, 18 May 1896; "Die Geschichte eines Wortes," FW, xii (1920), 60–61; HB (2), ii, 317.

17 NL Alfred Fried, United Nations Library, Geneva (cited hereafter as NL Fried), Fried to Nippold, Vienna, 22 December 1913; Fried, "Neo-Pazifisten," FW, v (1903), 89; "Ich bin kein Pazifist," FW, xiv (1912), 347–48; VF, xv (1914), 81.

18 Norman Angell, "Pacifism," Encyclopedia of the Social Sciences (New York, 1933), xi, 527. For the unfortunate term "pacificist" we are indebted to A. J. P. Taylor, The Trouble Makers: Dissent over Foreign Policy, 1792–1939 (London, 1957), p. 51. He has the support of Fowler.

fessor Beales adopted this distinction in his pioneering study of the peace movement in 1931, historians too have tended to use the term pacifist in a restricted sense, to refer to someone who repudiates all forms of international violence.[19]

This distinction is important, and it reflects significant differences between varieties of opposition to war. But it is also troublesome, since it excludes from the category of pacifist the very people who invented the term as a self-designation. For this reason, and because I shall be centrally concerned with these same people, my conceptualization of the pacifist will be broad enough to comprehend both unconditional repudiation of violence and advocacy of international political organization. I shall define the pacifist simply as one who holds war to be wrong and has made a personal commitment to pursuing the kinds of activity he believes will lead to its systematic elimination from international affairs. Pacifism, then, is a doctrine or body of thought that postulates the reprehensibility of war and prescribes a course of action designed to make it impossible or unnecessary. The concept includes two elements, an assertion and a precept. By itself, asserting that war is bad is not enough to distinguish the pacifist from anyone who, like the apologist for the balance of power, prefers peace to war but accepts conflict as a normal feature of international relations. Pacifism holds not only that war is an evil, but that it is, to quote R. C. Stevenson, "an evil sufficiently serious under present conditions to warrant effort and a reasonable sacrifice of group interests to establish a stable international order."[20] It entails, that is, a relatively high degree of en-

---

[19] Beales, *History of Peace*, pp. 5–8, 332–34; cf. Mulford Q. Sibley, "Pacifism," *International Encyclopedia of the Social Sciences* (New York, 1968), XI, 353; Sibley, *The Political Theories of Modern Pacifism* (Philadelphia, 1944).

[20] R. C. Stevenson, "The Evolution of Pacifism," *International Journal of Ethics* XLIV (1934), 444. Max Scheler's definition of pacifism is basically the same: "not just the sentiment of peaceableness, love of peace, but rather the belief in . . . systematic methods of directing

gagement in activity that will presumably contribute to the definitive removal of violence from international relations.

This general definition comprehends a rich variety of assumptions, analyses of international conflict, and prescriptions for action, which pacifists have historically brought to bear in trying to do away with warfare. Their condemnation of war has derived from a wide range of considerations, including the incompatibility of war with the Christian ethic, the material waste it causes, or the outrage it does to humanitarian values. Pacifists have located the basic causes of war on different levels of analysis. Some have found them in human nature, others have put the blame on the social or political structure of states, still others have cited factors at the level of international relations.[21] Finally, depending upon their assumptions and analyses of the causes of war, pacifists have prescribed numerous different methods to deal with the problem. Some have called for nonresistance to all forms of violence, others have advocated the democratization of the world, still others international organization.

In an attempt to lend some coherence to this complexity, historians have undertaken to classify the varieties of pacifism, usually according to the methods by which pacifists propose to eliminate war or according to the considerations for which they condemn it.[22] Among the more common types cited are "religious pacifism," "humanitarian pacifism," "political pacifism," "economic pacifism," "revolutionary pacifism," and "juridical pacifism." There are two basic

---

wills, techniques, [or] arrangements, with which immediately to approach the problem of bringing about 'perpetual peace' in some way or the other." *Die Idee des Friedens und der Pazifismus* (Berlin, 1931), p. 11.

[21] On this "level of analysis" problem see Kenneth N. Waltz, *Man, the State, and War* (New York, 1959).

[22] See Marcel Merle, ed., *Pacifisme et internationalisme XVIIe–XXe siècles* (Paris, 1966), esp. pp. 12–41; Scheler, *Die Idee des Friedens und der Pazifismus*, pp. 31–61; Renouvin and Duroselle, *Introduction*, pp. 214–24.

drawbacks to these systems of classification, apart from the fact that there are as many systems as there are systematizers. In the first place, by classifying varieties of pacifism according to methods advocated for securing peace, or according to considerations that lead to the condemnation of war, these systems focus upon a single component of pacifist thought, overlooking the integrated complex of assumptions, analyses, and prescriptions that composes each pacifist doctrine. Analysis of the entire complex reveals that many of the common distinctions are peripheral or, conversely, that some of these common categories obscure more basic distinctions. For example, the doctrines commonly called "economic pacifism" and "juridical pacifism" are basically alike, in that they locate the roots of war in the insufficient development of bonds among naturally peaceful nations; one doctrine merely emphasizes the need for economic ties while the other stresses legal ties, and in fact, each also endorses the work of the other. On the other hand, "religious pacifism," in the sense of opposition to war out of considerations of Christian morality, comprehends both constructive activism and withdrawal, two fundamentally dissimilar approaches to the problem of war.

The most serious drawback of these systems of classification is not that they present an incomplete intellectual picture of the varieties of pacifism; it is that they present only an intellectual picture. They neglect the sociological dimension of pacifism, the fact that every pacifist doctrine is rooted in a social and political context, which in turn vitally affects its character, development, and its relative success.

In an effort to isolate the central distinction among varieties of pacifism, a distinction based upon their socio-political context as well as their integrated intellectual content, I shall suggest two basic categories, for which I am indebted to Karl Mannheim for more than just the terminology.[23] Us-

[23] See Karl Mannheim, *Ideology and Utopia: An Introduction to the Sociology of Knowledge* (New York, 1936), esp. pp. 33–108.

ing the orientation of a pacifist doctrine toward politics and society as the basic criterion of differentiation, it is useful to distinguish between pacifism as utopia and pacifism as ideology. Utopian pacifism conceives of war as an inseparable aspect of a social and political order that is utterly corrupt and beyond rehabilitation. Ideological pacifism rejects war because of the threat it poses to a social and political order that is basically sound and praiseworthy. Differences in nuance and emphasis among varieties of pacifism are subordinate to this central distinction.

Basic to utopian pacifism is an analysis of war and violence that regards these as intrinsic features of a social and political order whose perversity is fundamental and incorrigible. Whether this perversity derives from human nature or the corruptive effects of political society, and whether it is conceived in religious or secular terms, it creates an absolute antagonism between the pacifist, struggling to maintain his own purity, and the society which he regards as the source of perdition. This antagonism in turn severely restricts the range of action available to the pacifist in coping with the problem of warfare. He may, on the one hand, withdraw from society in order to preserve his own virtue in uncorrupted and transcendent isolation, adopting a posture of nonresistance to those agencies of society that would have him commit acts of violence in their name. Since society does not, in the eyes of the pacifist, admit of reform, his only alternative to continued withdrawal is a revolutionary assault on society in order to reconstruct it on a totally new and virtuous foundation.[24]

Utopian pacifism has been a sectarian and chiliastic phenomenon.[25] It has typically appealed to lower-class or mar-

[24] On this pacifist tradition see especially the provocative essay by David A. Martin, *Pacifism: An Historical and Sociological Study* (New York, 1966).

[25] See Wilhelm Mühlmann, ed., *Chiliasmus und Nativismus: Studien zur Psychologie, Soziologie und historische Kasuistik der Umsturzbewegungen* (Berlin, 1961); Norman Cohn, *The Pursuit of the Millen-*

ginal sectors of society, whose disposition to repudiate the existing social and political order has been nurtured by their own minimal stake in it. Most prominent manifestations of utopian pacifism have been sectarian derivatives of early Christian pacifism; in the modern period, though, these have been largely supplanted by the secular religions, anarchism and revolutionary socialism.[26] All hold war to be an integral and necessary aspect of political society as they find it; the Christian pacifist regards war as a symptom of the corruption of temporal existence, the revolutionary socialist views it as a product of the ineluctable antagonisms in capitalism, and the anarchist sees it as the necessary result of the very fact of political society. All are profoundly disturbed by the phenomenon of warfare, and all assume a radically negative posture toward existing society, either by withdrawing from it and maintaining this isolation, or by undertaking an assault on it in order to establish a fundamentally new order devoid of factors that give rise to warfare.

Utopian pacifism seeks to solve the problem of war by transcending society or repudiating it. Ideological pacifism seeks to use factors immanent in society to do away with war. While utopian pacifism anticipates a radical personal or collective solution to the problem, ideological pacifism calls for moderate, constructive reform within the framework of political society. While one rejects existing society because of the violence it spawns, the other seeks to preserve society from the potentially destructive effects of that violence.

Ideological pacifism proceeds from a much more positive evaluation of political society than does utopian pacifism.

nium: Revolutionary Messianism in Medieval and Reformation Europe and Its Bearing on Modern Totalitarian Movements (New York, 1961).

[26] For a survey of these groups see Peter Brock, Pacifism in Europe to 1914 (Princeton, 1972) and his earlier Pacifism in the United States: From the Colonial Era to the First World War (Princeton, 1968).

Ideological pacifism assumes that the features of society that give rise to warfare are, while admittedly significant, remediable. Ideological pacifism postulates the basic goodness and rationality of man and denies that political society is necessarily corrupt or corruptive. It assumes that men are by nature peace loving and that a society that conforms, as it should, to the needs and aspirations of men will likewise be peaceful. Accordingly, ideological pacifism holds peace to be the natural or normal condition in international relations; deviations from this norm it ascribes to popular ignorance and the conspiracies of a few selfish men. Imputing to states as well as to individuals the capacity for ethical behavior, ideological pacifism calls for the creation of conditions in which such behavior will be possible. Typically this entails the education and moral enlightenment of society and the establishment of agencies to facilitate the peaceful settlement of international misunderstandings.

The increasing secularization of European politics made ideological pacifism the dominant variety in Europe after the sixteenth century. Ideological pacifism informed the peace projects of Sully, Crucé, St. Pierre, Kant, and others in the seventeenth and eighteenth centuries. In the eighteenth and nineteenth centuries it assumed the character of a middle class reform movement and constituted an important facet of the major bourgeois ideologies of the era. Liberalism and, in its classical formulations, nationalism both assumed that the infusion of society with their principles would bring the lasting reign of international peace.

It should be noted that neither utopian nor ideological pacifism entirely excludes the instrumental use of violence. Ideological pacifism contemplates both wars of national defense and the use of collective sanctions by international agencies. Utopian pacifism fluctuates between extreme passivity and extreme, often violent activism. Beyond this similarity, the two pacifist traditions are fundamentally divergent sociologically and philosophically, although, as the combination of nonresistance and reform-oriented activism in Quakerism demonstrates, it is possible to bring the two traditions into a fairly stable synthesis. In addition, groups can undergo a transition from one to the other, a process that reflects either the growing integration of a group into the dominant social order or, conversely, its growing estrangement from that order. Such a transition was one of the issues in the revisionist controversy within the Second International.

Unless I specify otherwise, I shall henceforth use the terms "pacifism" and "pacifist" in the sense of the ideological tradition, for the program of the organized peace movement at the end of the nineteenth century was clearly informed by ideological pacifism. The people who gathered at peace congresses believed it was possible to exploit the forces at work in society to create international institutions to guarantee the peace. Moreover, they were confident that this could be done without fundamentally altering the existing social order; indeed, much of their aversion to war derived from their fear of what a general war might do to the fabric of European society.

These pacifists called specifically for the settlement of international disputes through legal channels, through arbitration. In itself deceptively simple, this demand rested upon a number of crucial assumptions about the nature of international relations. Most obviously, the call for arbitration presupposed the feasibility of regulating international affairs by law. This in turn presupposed the existence *in potentia* of a body of law, international in scope, analagous to public law in the domestic realm. But the assertion that such a body of law existed, needing only to be articulated for arbitral application, rested upon another assumption: that there existed a source for this law.

Political theorists today are generally agreed that there are two prerequisites for the successful functioning of a political system in which behavior is regulated by law. The more basic is the existence of a community of interest or purpose among the constituents of the system—"an unconditional consensus on cooperation, a belief in a common good (however vague) and in the precedence of this common good over particular interests."[27] The second prerequisite, an institutionalized source of power and law, then represents the formal expression and focus of this community. From the perspective of the mid-twentieth century it seems clear that the absence of both these prerequisites has prevented the emergence of a binding system of legal relationships among the nations of the world and that, barring imposition of an institutionalized source of law through conquest, the emergence of an effective international political system must await the development of a genuine sense of international community. To quote the words of Hans Morgenthau, "a world community must antedate a world state."[28]

Pacifists at the turn of the century were gifted—or plagued—by no such insight. They believed in an international community and predicted that out of it would emerge the institutions necessary for legal settlement of all international disputes. This international community, which was the central postulate of late nineteenth century pacifism, had two dimensions, one ethical, the other material. By virtue of their views on the nature of man, pacifists assumed the existence of an ethical and rational community among all men, a union in which all men partake because of their very humanity and their innate disposition to rational and ethical conduct.[29] By itself, however, belief in an ethical community only supported the assertion that war should be eliminated; it could not justify the expectation that the elimination of war was imminent or even possible. Yet nine-

[27] Stanley Hoffmann, "International Systems and International Law," *The State of War: Essays on the Theory and Practice of International Politics* (New York, 1965), p. 89.

[28] Hans J. Morgenthau, *Politics among Nations: The Struggle for Power and Peace* (4th ed., New York, 1967), pp. 499–500.

[29] See Walter Schiffer, *The Legal Community of Mankind: A Critical Analysis of the Modern Concept of World Organization* (New York, 1954), esp. pp. 142–54.

teenth century pacifism was confident that the problem of warfare could be resolved. This optimism derived from the belief that the international community was acquiring a material infrastructure; in the ongoing social and economic internationalization of European life pacifists perceived a process that would link men in a community of interests, as well as one of ethical disposition, and would make the elimination of warfare a question of economic utility, as well as one of moral precept. In one sense, then, the community the pacifists envisaged transcended politics; in it men were bound together by ethical and material ties irrespective of the political units into which they were organized. Yet in another sense the international community was profoundly political, since both its ethical and material dimensions implied norms or patterns of behavior binding upon the state as well as the individual. Specifically, pacifists believed that these norms prescribed harmony, cooperation, and peaceful competition and interchange for mutual benefit among the constituent political groups in the international community; conversely, they proscribed national prejudice, hostility, and violent conflict.

The pacifists' goal was to infuse politics with the spirit and ethics of international community—to elevate international politics into a realm governed by law and morality. To make this possible they called for the political institutionalization of the international community, a process that would entail both the translation of the community's ethical norms into a code of international justice and the establishment of an arbitral agency to adjudicate international disputes on the basis of this code.

Pacifists at the end of the nineteenth century were a fractious group of people. They disagreed with one another, for example, about whether to emphasize the ethical or material aspects of international community. They argued over the composition and prerogatives of the arbitral agency they hoped to create. And they were at odds over whether, in an era in which politics would be governed by ethics, an executive agency would be necessary to enforce arbitral decisions.[30] Yet however great their differences, pacifists were at one in their belief in international community. Whether this belief derived from an *a priori* assumption of an ethical community of man, or from confidence in the progressive development of a community of material interests, or from both, pacifists urged the promotion and elaboration of this community and its translation into politics.

Emphasizing the centrality of international community in pacifist ideology raises another problem of definition, for it suggests that equating this variety of pacifism with "internationalism," as some authors have done, is justified. However, I prefer to view internationalism, as a credo, more broadly than pacifism and to define it as an attitude or doctrine that affirms the systematic growth of international ties. It includes revolutionary doctrines such as Marxism, in which internationalization is the prelude to fundamental social change, as well as liberal credos, like ideological pacifism, in which the development of international ties is interpreted as a healthy feature of the existing social order. Internationalism is as multifaceted as the internationalization process itself; it comprehends doctrines that call for no more than reduction of tariffs, as well as those that promote the extension of international law.

The ideological pacifism of the late nineteenth century might thus be called an extreme political variety of liberal (as opposed to revolutionary) internationalism.[31] Pacifism and internationalism are generically similar concepts, which lie, so to speak, on different concentric levels of generality, separated by an intermediate concept, which can be labeled liberal political internationalism (figure 1).

All three connote a positive orientation toward international interchange and cooperation. Internationalism is the

[30] On these disagreements see Cooper, "Peace and Internationalism."

[31] See Max Huber, *Die soziologischen Grundlagen des Völkerrechts* (Berlin, 1928), pp. 3, 85; Sandi E. Cooper, "Liberal Internationalists before World War I," *Peace and Change* 1 (1973), 11–19.

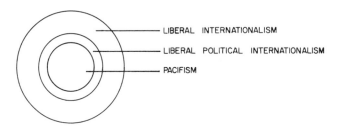

PACIFISM AND INTERNATIONALISM

FIGURE 1

most general concept and refers to the growth of international ties of all kinds. Liberal political internationalism is a doctrine or orientation that affirms that the growth of such ties will or ought to have political repercussions in the extension of international law and regular recourse to arbitration; however, it does not necessarily specify how far these developments should lead, though it expects international conciliation to result. Ideological pacifism, then, is an extended form of liberal political internationalism, a doctrine which, while it does not reject the nation-state as a political unit, calls for the subordination of the nation to the international community and the comprehensive legal regulation of international relations.

These conceptual distinctions might well appear to be arbitrary, overelaborate, or even pedantic. In fact they reflect the complexity of the doctrines and organizations spawned by internationalization at the end of the nineteenth century. They are also necessary for an understanding of the character of the peace movement.

The Peace Movement and Political Culture

I have used the term "peace movement" to refer collectively to peace societies that were established in Europe and America during the nineteenth and early twentieth centuries. For most of this period this is a reasonably accurate designation, but the problem of delimiting the peace movement after 1889 becomes more complicated. During this late period peace societies began to find allies in two different kinds of internationalist organizations. The first were those which, like societies to promote an international language or certain feminist groups, were not peace societies in the first instance, though their programs included working for arbitration and world peace. The second kind of allied organization included those like the American Association for International Conciliation or the Interparliamentary Union, which were founded to promote arbitration and international conciliation, but did so with more restraint and caution than the peace societies and, for this reason and in order not to compromise their respectability, generally disdained the term pacifist.

Contemporary descriptions of the peace movement frequently included all these groups. Moreover, although pacifists and peace societies were the most conspicuous proponents of peace and arbitration, some of the most effective work was undertaken by persons and organizations that refused to call themselves pacifist. For purposes of analytical clarity, and in order to remain as consistent as possible with contemporary descriptions, I shall define the peace movement by correlating it not with pacifism, but rather with the more general concept of liberal political internationalism. The peace movement, then, was the aggregate of all organizations and individuals that sought to promote the growth of international law and the practice of international arbitration.

The correlation with liberal political internationalism also helps clarify the relationship between the peace movement and two other kinds of organizations whose programs resembled that of the peace societies in some respects. The first included a number of friendship societies that were founded around the turn of the century in order to improve relations between two or more countries; in some instances, however, they did so for dubious reasons that had little to do with world peace. Unless these organizations were internationalist, in the sense of favoring general international conciliation, I shall not include them in my definition of the peace movement. I shall also in general exclude the socialist movement from my definition of the peace movement, in keeping with the views of most socialists themselves. As a pacifist credo, orthodox Marxism was more in the utopian than the liberal, ideological tradition, and discussion of the problem of war and its elimination was conducted in quite different categories at socialist meetings than at peace congresses. As long as they held that the only effective way to prevent war was to overthrow capitalism, socialists remained suspicious of efforts to promote international arbitration and were deaf to pleas for their cooperation from bourgeois peace organizations.

The peace movement, as it was generally known at the turn of the century, and as I shall define it, was thus a bourgeois phenomenon which typically comprehended, in each country in which it operated, a number of elements. The most dedicated, visible, and articulate sector comprised the pacifists in the peace societies. Less outspoken, but often more influential, were the politicians and notables gathered in more prestigious organizations, such as the Interparliamentary Union, which usually maintained some distance from the peace societies. Finally, the peace movement included assorted reform organizations, many of which were led by pacifists or had international ties themselves, and which promoted arbitration as an aspect of the causes they championed.

With the exception of several groups that attempted to work directly through parliamentary channels, all sectors of the peace movement conceived of their mission in terms of the enlightenment and education of society. They did this because they believed that the most effective, as well as the most accessible means to influence political decisions was to work through public opinion. They reasoned that the mobilization of popular support for arbitration would compel politicians and statesmen to negotiate international agreements setting up the institutions necessary for the peaceful settlement of international disputes.

Mobilizing popular support for international arbitration seemed to the pacifists to be a multifaceted, though eminently feasible undertaking; it would entail convincing public opinion of the reality of a harmonious international community whose precepts ruled out resort to war. Pacifists proposed to do this through a concerted campaign designed to awaken the ethical sense of community that resided in all men, to educate the public about the internationalization process and its implications, and to acquaint people in different countries with one another. In addition, pacifists set out to eradicate all popular attitudes incompatible with the norms of international community, such as exclusive nationalism, hostility, and the willingness to accept war as a legitimate feature of international affairs.

The pacifists were students of the processes by which public opinion was created and influenced. They concluded early that some sectors of society were, by virtue of their prestige, visibility, or power, particularly important in shaping the attitudes of the masses about international relations. As early as 1850, when an international congress met in Frankfurt, one delegate called upon peace societies to "work for the eradication of popular hate and the political and commercial prejudices that have so often led to the most lamentable wars." The channels he identified for this work included "careful education of youth . . . instruction from the pulpit and the speakers platform, [and] . . . the public press."[32] As the peace movement underwent its major expansion at the end of the century, in an era marked by the growing intrusion of the masses into European politics, Universal Peace Congresses devoted numerous sessions to studying how best to mobilize this new political force. As principal targets for their agitation and propaganda, pacifists isolated schools, youth groups, the press, political par-

[32] Quoted in HB (2), II, 68–69.

ties, religious associations, and labor organizations.[33] They calculated that if they succeeded in convincing these articulate sectors of society that the international community was a reality, the masses would soon accept its validity.

The study of the formation of political attitudes has progressed a long way since the peace movement attempted to win popular support for arbitration; concepts developed by sociologists and political scientists have made possible a much better understanding of this complex process. These concepts can in turn be employed in an historical analysis of the peace movement's activities. For seen in this analytical perspective, the peace movement's campaign to educate public opinion represented an attempt to refashion political culture.

Political culture, as defined by the two foremost students of the concept, is "the particular distribution of patterns of orientation toward political objects among the members" of a political system.[34] The key words in this definition are "orientation" and "political objects." "Orientation" connotes the knowledge, concepts, beliefs, feelings, and judgments which make up the political outlook of every member of a political system. Orientations suggest "deeply-rooted patterns of thought" rather than the more ephemeral attitudes implied by the word "opinion."[35] Orientations may be rationally or irrationally based; they involve cognitive perceptions, emotions, and evaluations. The "political objects" to

[33] *Proceedings of the Universal Peace Congress . . . London, 14–19 July, 1890* (London, 1890), pp. 82, 85, 98; *Troisième Congrès international de la paix, Rome, Novembre 1891* (Rome, 1892), p. 39; *Bulletin officiel du IVme Congrès universel de la paix tenu à Berne du 22 au 27 août 1892* (Berne, 1892), pp. 141–67.

[34] Gabriel A. Almond and Sidney Verba, *The Civic Culture: Political Attitudes and Democracy in Five Nations* (Boston and Toronto, 1965), pp. 12–14; cf. Almond, "Comparative Political Systems," *Journal of Politics* XVIII (1956), 391–409.

[35] Sidney Verba, "Comparative Political Culture," in Lucian W. Pye and Sidney Verba, eds., *Political Culture and Political Development* (Princeton, 1965), p. 514.

which these orientations refer include the political system itself and all its component parts: attitudes about the legitimacy of the system as a whole, about the role of the individual within it, about the purposes or function of government, and about specific policies and political figures.

The existence of a political culture or, in the case of developing nations, the desire to create a new one raises the question of how political orientations are formed. The answer given by theorists of political culture is that these are learned, through the process known in modern parlance as political socialization.[36] Political socialization refers chiefly to the transmission of orientations from one generation to the next, both through direct teaching of political attitudes (political or civic education) and by more subtle and indirect means, such as exposure to authority patterns in the family. As such, the process is principally concerned with the learning of political concepts by young people; the most important institutions of political socialization are, accordingly, the family, peer groups, and schools. In a stable and established political culture, the process tends to have a conservative bias, perpetuating dominant orientations by passing them on to each succeeding generation of citizens.

However, in circumstances of rapid political change, and when this change involves the transformation of a political culture, socialization becomes an integral part of the process of political mobilization into new orientations and goals.[37] The process of creating political orientations is now generated more directly by conscious political decision, and it takes place on many different levels, actively affecting adults as well as children. A wide range of institutions, of

[36] Gabriel Almond and G. Bingham Powell, Jr., *Comparative Politics: A Developmental Approach* (Boston and Toronto, 1966), pp. 64–65; Herbert Hyman, *Political Socialization: A Study in the Psychology of Human Behavior* (New York, 1959); Richard E. Dawson and Kenneth Prewitt, *Political Socialization: An Analytic Study* (Boston, 1969); Almond and Verba, *Civic Culture*, pp. 269–74.

[37] See J. P. Nettl, *Political Mobilization: A Sociological Analysis of Methods and Concepts* (New York, 1967).

secondary socializing importance in a stable culture, are recruited into the mobilizing process in order to resocialize citizens into new patterns of orientation.[38] Variously called "formative institutions," "communications channels," or "institutions for countersocialization," these agencies, whose importance stems from their power, visibility, and accessibility to political control, typically include the military, schools and universities, newspapers, political parties or movements, and religious organizations.[39]

I wish to emphasize two points in drawing the connection between the work of the peace movement and the processes that relate to the formation of political culture. The first has to do with international relations as "political object." Although the literature on political culture has not emphasized this aspect of the subject, orientations about the way political systems interact with one another are among the most important an individual acquires during socialization, and they directly color his attitudes toward his own political system. Prevailing attitudes about a system's legitimacy and identity, the proper role of authority and government, and the validity of specific policies reflect orientations about the world at large: ideas about the role of the country in the world, perceptions of foreign countries, and views about the nature of the international system itself—whether conflict or harmony is the norm and whether the outside world is hostile or benign.[40]

[38] Robert LeVine, "Political Socialization and Culture Change," in Clifford Geertz, ed., *Old Societies and New States: The Quest for Modernity in Asia and Africa* (New York, 1963), p. 301; cf. James S. Coleman, "Introduction: Education and Political Development," in James S. Coleman, ed., *Education and Political Development* (Princeton, 1965), pp. 3, 13.

[39] See Richard R. Fagen, *Politics and Communication* (Boston, 1966), p. 37; Sidney Verba, "Germany: The Remaking of Political Culture," in Pye and Verba, *Political Culture and Political Development*, p. 136.

[40] Lucian Pye, "Identity and the Political Culture," in Leonard Binder, *et al., Crises and Sequences in Political Development* (Prince-

The second point I wish to emphasize concerns the peace movement's understanding of the concept of public opinion. Although pacifists did—increasingly after the turn of the century—attempt to influence popular beliefs about specific policies, issues, and disputes, they thought of public opinion in a more general sense, akin to what Leonard Doob has called "enduring public opinion."[41] To pacifists public opinion connoted basic views about the whole complex of international politics; it referred, in fact, to those orientations toward international affairs which are inculcated during socialization and constitute a fundamental part of any political culture. "Winning over public opinion" thus meant entering directly into the socialization process in order to promote popular attitudes and beliefs conducive to peace and arbitration. It meant creating positive orientations toward an international community and the corollary propositions that peace and cooperation were the normal conditions in international relations and that conflict was pathological, unethical, and detrimental to the interests of all. The pacifists' goal was tantamount to modifying national political cultures everywhere in order to create the cultural foundations of an international political system. This entailed promoting orientations within existing national cultures which were compatible with the concept of international community, and extirpating those which were not.

The peace movement was a paradoxical political phenomenon, difficult to categorize because the implications of its program were both revolutionary and basically conservative. The changes pacifists proposed would have revolutionized the system of international politics, substituting

---

ton, 1971), p. 102; Robert A. LeVine, "Socialization, Social Structure, and Intersocietal Images," in Herbert C. Kelman, ed., *International Behavior: A Social-Psychological Analysis* (New York, 1965), p. 47; cf. William Buchanan and Hadley Cantril, *How Nations See Each Other: A Study in Public Opinion* (Urbana, 1953), esp. pp. 60–67.

[41] Leonard W. Doob, *Public Opinion and Propaganda* (2d ed., Hamden, Conn., 1966), pp. 50, 54.

law for power as the regulatory principle of international political behavior. Yet pacifists insisted that these changes would not threaten the social or political foundations of existing nation states, whose validity all pacifists recognized; such changes would merely alter the mode in which these individual political systems interacted. Indeed, pacifists everywhere regarded themselves as patriots and believed that the implementation of their international reforms would make the social and political order in existing nation-states more secure. They thus tended to compartmentalize the international and national systems of politics, arguing that far-reaching changes in the one would require no substantial changes in the other. Without commenting at this point on the validity of this expectation, I would emphasize the social conservatism of the international peace movement, and the fact that pacifists affirmed the legitimacy of their respective national political systems, by eschewing the label "social movement" to refer to them.[42] As this term is generally used by sociologists, it refers to a movement that "aims at fundamental and comprehensive alterations in the total social order."[43] It would thus be a more accurate description of a movement inspired by utopian pacifism. For the late nineteenth century peace movement, however, a more suitable designation would be a "movement with limited goals," to use Rudolf Heberle's term, or a "norm-oriented"—as opposed to a "value-oriented"—movement, to use Neil Smelser's.[44]

One of the great advantages of using concepts drawn from political sociology to analyze the history of the peace movement is that it immediately throws into perspective the staggering dimensions of what the pacifists were trying to

[42] See Dorothee Stiewe, "Die bürgerliche deutsche Friedensbewegung als soziale Bewegung bis zum Ende des Ersten Weltkrieges" (Inaugural dissertation, Freiburg, 1972).

[43] Rudolf Heberle, *Hauptprobleme der politischen Soziologie* (Stuttgart, 1967), pp. 9–15.

[44] *Ibid.*; Neil J. Smelser, *Theory of Collective Behavior* (New York, 1963), esp. pp. 270–312.

do. Studies of nation-building have documented the tenacity with which traditional cultural patterns have withstood the attempt to impose orientations and values of a new political culture, even when this attempt involves a systematic assault on the social foundations of that cultural tradition and is supported by all the political, economic, and military resources at the regime's disposal. These lessons certainly apply to orientations about international relations. As one study has concluded, "When one considers the variety of sources of resistance . . . deriving both from group norms and from personality motives—one is left with a rather bleak picture."[45] This is particularly true when one considers that the peace movement had only very limited political resources with which to work and that it had to contend with established systems of socialization which in every country counteracted its efforts to some extent. Indeed, even if one is able to suspend an acute sense of skepticism about the pacifists' view of international politics, the enormous incongruity between their aspirations and the resources they commanded casts an air of unreality about their whole campaign.

This air of unreality makes it difficult to treat the history of the peace movement without abandoning one's sense of political proportion. It also raises the question of whether the history of this movement, whose goals seemed nearly as extravagant then as they do now, is worth recounting at all. The answer is that the history of the peace movement can be justified on a number of compelling grounds. Like other movements that never witnessed the complete realization of their goals (and most never do), the peace movement left a mark in the form of some notable partial successes. The Hague tribunal, the League of Nations, and ultimately the United Nations can be traced back to the inspiration and persistent agitation of this movement. Moreover, the

[45] Irving L. Janis and M. Brewster Smith, "Effects of Education and Persuasion on National and International Images," in Kelman, *International Behavior*, p. 211.

pacifists did succeed in making some minor inroads into systems of political socialization in countries where they operated, and it is important to note the extent of both their success and failure.

Finally, and for this study most importantly, the history of the peace movement has heuristic value for the historical study of political culture. Pacifists in every country attempted to refashion indigenous political cultures by working through agencies of socialization to inculcate the view that the nations of the world formed a harmonious community. Their success in this campaign varied significantly from country to country. This variation reflected in the final analysis significant differences in the national political cultures the peace movement encountered—the fact that prevailing orientations toward international relations were more congenial in some countries than in others to the concept of international community and its implications. And even where the movement experienced almost no success, the history of its campaign provides a revealing glimpse into the processes by which orientations toward international relations were created and fostered in Europe before the First World War.

All this suggests the need for systematic comparative analysis of the peace movement in different countries on the eve of the war. As my own contribution to such a project, I have undertaken to study the history of the peace movement in imperial Germany and have added only enough of a comparative dimension to indicate roughly how the German example differed from others. I have three principal objectives in this study. The first is to survey the organizations and ideologies of the peace movement in Germany. The second is to describe the activities of the German peace movement, treating them as a more or less systematic attempt to modify an important facet of German political culture. Finally, I propose to analyze the significance of the peace movement's experience in imperial Germany, first by comparing it briefly with the experience of the peace movement in France and then by isolating elements in the German political culture that influenced the reception of the peace movement. My argument, in brief, will be that the peace movement was substantially weaker and less successful in Germany than elsewhere in the west, in part because the domestic peculiarities of the German political system fostered a pattern of orientations toward international affairs that emphasized the likelihood or desirability of international conflict.

The study is organized into three parts, which correspond to my objectives. The first part, consisting of chapters two, three, and four, deals with the internal history of the German peace movement—the organizations that composed it and the doctrines they espoused. The second part, which includes chapters five, six, and seven, analyzes the interaction between the peace movement and German society, concentrating on the movement's efforts to convert socializing agencies and leading political groups, as well as its direct attempts to promote the peaceful resolution of international tensions. The third part consists of the final two chapters and is an attempt to assess the meaning of the peace movement's experience in imperial Germany.

2

The German Peace Society

GERMANS contributed significantly to the articulation and development of pacifist ideologies.[1] Several thinkers of the *Aufklärung*, including Leibniz and Christian Wolff, addressed themselves to the problems of war and international organization. But the most important of them was Immanuel Kant, who can indeed with little exaggeration be called the single most influential pacifist thinker in German history. In his treatises, *Idea for a Universal History* and *Perpetual Peace*, he observed that international relations were naturally characterized by conflict and violence. From this observation, which typically underlay either utopian pacifism or a fatalistic acceptance of war, Kant concluded that overcoming this natural state was both feasible and morally imperative; it would accompany the triumph of man's reason and moral consciousness over his baser instincts. Kant went on to propose an elaborate system of international law that would make possible the rule of reason and morality among independent states.[2] Kant's optimism, his insistence that the elimination of war was at the core an ethical problem, and his assertion that ethical norms should govern the conduct of states and individuals alike were all

[1] I do not intend to treat any of these thinkers in detail. For more extended analyses see: Veit Valentin, *Geschichte des Völkerbundgedankens in Deutschland* (Berlin, 1920); Jacob ter Meulen, *Der Gedanke der internationalen Organisation* (2 vols., The Hague, 1929-40), II; Samuel Max Melamed, *Theorie, Ursprung und Geschichte der Friedensidee: Kulturphilosophische Wanderungen* (Stuttgart, 1909), pp. 225-50.

[2] See Hinsley, *Power and the Pursuit of Peace*, pp. 62-80; Leo Gross, *Pazifismus und Imperialismus: Eine kritische Untersuchung ihrer theoretischen Begründungen* (Leipzig and Vienna, 1931), pp. 166-86.

to exert a powerful influence in the late nineteenth century peace movement, most conspicuously in Germany and Austria.

During the nineteenth century German writers developed other themes that related to pacifism. Romantics, such as Novalis and Friedrich Schlegel, wrote of the religious foundations of universal peace. In the writings of the philosophers Friedrich von Schelling and Jacob Wagner, the realization of a world community was portrayed as the culmination of the inexorable movement of history. As Friedrich Meinecke has shown in his classic study of the subject, early German nationalism emphasized that the organization of mankind into national political units was desirable as a means to a higher, more universal end—the perfection of humanity in the full expression of its creative variety.[3] Although particularly pronounced in the works of Herder and Karl Christian Friedrich Krause, this vision appeared in the writings of many articulate German nationalists in the early nineteenth century.[4] German liberals of the early and mid-nineteenth century also emphasized a community of humanity, which they proposed to realize through free trade, national self-determination, and responsible government.[5]

Early Pacifist Organizations in Germany

Despite this rich intellectual heritage, Germans did not play a prominent role in the development of pacifist organizations in the nineteenth century. Not until 1886 did a peace society of any significance or durability appear in Germany,

[3] Friedrich Meinecke, *Weltbürgertum und Nationalstaat* (Munich, 1962).

[4] See Hans Kohn, "Nationalism and Internationalism in the Nineteenth and Twentieth Centuries," xiie Congrès international des sciences historiques, Vienne, 29 août–5 septembre 1965, *Rapports* (Horn and Vienna, n.d.), I, 210–18.

[5] Theodore S. Hamerow, *The Social Foundations of German Unification, 1858–1871: Ideas and Institutions* (Princeton, 1969), pp. 140–42.

and it proved impossible to establish a peace organization on a national scale until the 1890s. Prior attempts to organize pacifists in Germany met only with official hostility and popular indifference.

The first peace society in Germany was founded in September 1850 in Königsberg. Its inspiration came from Julius Rupp, a local clergyman, and Robert Motherby, a physician who had attended the international peace congress which met in 1850 in the Paulskirche in Frankfurt. By the beginning of 1851 the group had attracted a membership of 141 and had begun to publish a modest journal. Its activities were short-lived, however, for in the aftermath of the 1848 revolutions the political atmosphere in the city of Kant was not conducive to the growth of unorthodox organizations. The police had from the start viewed the peace society with suspicion, and in May 1851 they dissolved it.[6]

There was no further organized pacifist activity in Germany until the end of the next decade. In the meantime the unification of the German states was taking place in a way hardly designed to encourage opposition to war.

An antiwar movement working within a political system born of a brilliant series of wars was bound, almost by definition, to be politically eccentric. Located on the fringes of the German peace movement there would be, moreover, a number of remarkable individuals whose eccentricity might well have invited clinical study. It is no doubt significant that the first of these figures constituted virtually the entire German peace movement for nearly twenty years.

Eduard Löwenthal was born in 1836. After taking a doctorate in philosophy and law in Tübingen in 1859, he became active in the nascent German socialist movement, serving as editor of a number of radical newspapers and even working for a time with Ferdinand Lassalle in Berlin.

[6] Carl Ludwig Siemering [Oskar Schwonder], *Von der ersten deutschen Friedensgesellschaft* (Frankfurt, 1909), pp. 12–15; FW, VIII (1906), 64–65; FW, XI (1909), 47–49; Alexander Dietz, *Franz Wirth und der Frankfurter Friedensverein* (Frankfurt, 1911), p. 18.

After Lassalle's death Löwenthal lost interest in socialism and dedicated himself instead to creating a world organization to guarantee international peace. He did so with an intensity that was uncommon even among devoted pacifists, but he added to this passion an obstinacy which made cooperation with others impossible. In 1869 he established the first of a series of organizations with which he proposed to bring peace to the world. His *Europäischer Unionsverein* attempted to popularize the idea of a European political system modeled after the North German Confederation.[7] In 1874 he reconstituted his society as the *Deutscher Verein für internationale Friedenspropaganda* and under its auspices issued a circular calling for regular meetings of European parliamentarians to promote peace. The only result of the circular was that Löwenthal was henceforth to style himself as the father of the Interparliamentary Union; his peace society itself quietly disappeared when he was sentenced to five months imprisonment for publishing an indelicate critique of the German military tradition. He then spent fourteen years in exile, returning to Berlin in time to watch the peace movement finally take hold in Germany. In 1894 he revived his old organization, this time unconditionally committed to the principle of obligatory arbitration of all international disputes. Since the rest of the peace movement was willing to endorse optional arbitration, at least in the short run, Löwenthal disdained cooperation with it and in 1896 reconstituted his society, this time as the *Deutscher Verein für obligatorische Friedensjustiz*. Despite the fact that this society, like all his others, consisted of little more than Löwenthal himself, he never wavered in the conviction that his was the only proper avenue to peace—a

[7] Valentin, *Völkerbundgedanken*, pp. 136–37. On Löwenthal's career see: Eduard Löwenthal, *Mein Lebenswerk auf sozialpolitischem, neureligiösem, philosophischem und naturwissenschaftlichem Gebiete* (Berlin, 1912); Löwenthal, *Geschichte der Friedensbewegung: Mit Berücksichtigung der zweiten Haager Friedenskonferenz* (Berlin, 1907).

view shared neither by the Reichstag, to which he appealed, nor by the other pacifists in Germany.[8] In later years he made himself an occasional nuisance to the rest of the peace movement and devoted his energies to a pathetic attempt to have himself nominated for the Nobel Peace Prize.[9] However, in this attempt—indeed, throughout his entire career—no one, not even the pacifists, took the poor man seriously.

If one disregards the organizations Löwenthal founded, there was no organized pacifism in Germany until the middle of the 1880s, although (for the record) Rudolf Virchow proposed international disarmament in a speech in the Reichstag in 1869, and several issues of a *Friedensblatt* appeared at the end of the same year in the Lusatian town of Ebersbach.[10] But these "events" led to nothing. Bismarck himself regarded the international peace movement as a communist conspiracy with Marx at its head, and his distaste for it was an apt reflection of public opinion in Germany.[11]

When peace societies did finally appear in Germany, the initiative came from the outside. In 1884 the English pacifist, Hodgson Pratt, undertook a tour of German cities in order to breathe life into a peace movement in Germany. In Stuttgart he conferred with local notables from the left-liberal German People's party, who agreed to form a committee to establish a peace society. Upon his departure,

[8] StBR, xiii L.P., 1 Session (29 April 1914), cccv, 3263; DWN, iv (1895), 394–96; DWN, vi (1897), 34–35; DWN, vii (1898), 453.

[9] BIP (vB6), Löwenthal to International Peace Bureau, Berlin, 12 January 1912; NL Alfred Fried, United Nations Library, Geneva (cited hereafter as NL Fried), Fried to Frederik Bajer, Vienna, 2 November, 3 November 1906; Hans Wehberg to Fried, Düsseldorf, 30 October 1909.

[10] "Eine deutsche Friedenszeitschrift aus den Jahren 1869–70," FW, xxxiv (1934), 269.

[11] Frédéric Passy, "Les origines et le but de la Ligue internationale de la paix, selon M. de Bismarck," *Revue de la paix* (December 1902), pp. 392–93.

however, the committee fell apart and remained dormant until Pratt returned the next year to renew his efforts. This time he succeeded in organizing a public meeting which was attended by some six hundred persons, including the mayor. In repeated visits between 1884 and 1886 Pratt attempted, by using similar techniques, to set up peace societies in Darmstadt, Berlin, and Frankfurt am Main. Although he enlisted the cooperation of Virchow in Berlin and the philosopher Ludwig Büchner in Darmstadt, his efforts in these two cities resulted in little more than an occasional meeting and an ephemeral committee of local notables.[12]

Of these early groups, the one in Frankfurt became the most vigorous. In 1886 more help arrived in Frankfurt from abroad when the Danish pacifist, Frederik Bajer, pulled together the local committee Pratt had set up and recruited as its chairman one of the city's leading democrats, Franz Wirth, a son of J. A. G. Wirth, the organizer of the Hambach festival. Late in 1886 the two men officially founded the *Frankfurter Friedensverein*, which was to remain one of the most active groups in the German peace movement throughout the prewar years.

In January 1887 delegates from Frankfurt met with members of the local committees in Stuttgart and Darmstadt and agreed to form a loose confederation, with the committee in Darmstadt handling relations with peace societies abroad. However, the confederation dissolved as soon as the Germans learned that Pratt wanted the problem of Alsace-Lorraine debated at an international peace congress. They quickly severed relations with Pratt's organization in England, after which the committees in Stuttgart and Darmstadt collapsed.

---

[12] Gustav Rühle, "Zum 25.-jährigen Jubiläum der Deutschen Friedensgesellschaft," in Georg Grosch, ed., *Deutsche Pazifisten: Eine Sammlung von Vorkämpfern der Friedensbewegung in Deutschland* (Stuttgart, 1920), p. 27; Dietz, *Franz Wirth*, pp. 18–26; Frederik Bajer, "Zur Vorgeschichte der deutschen Friedensvereine," FB, IX (1908), 87; Abrams, "European Peace Societies," pp. 213–18.

Had the Germans consented to discuss the legality or justice of the annexation of Alsace-Lorraine, it would have exacerbated the unfavorable atmosphere in which the peace societies found themselves anyway. Even in the liberal city of Frankfurt the reception of a peace society was not warm. With the exception of the left-liberal *Frankfurter Zeitung* (whose editor was Franz Wirth's brother, Max), the press either greeted the founding of the *Friedensverein* with derision or ignored it. Although the group carefully avoided activity that might be construed as political, the police promptly classified it as a political organization and supervised it accordingly. Under these circumstances many were reluctant to join, and in 1890 the membership of the only real peace society in Germany stood at sixty-nine.[13]

The Establishment of the German Peace Society

This inauspicious climate had not improved significantly when, in the early 1890s, efforts began to organize a national peace society in Berlin. However, the major events of the year 1889 drew enough public attention to the international peace movement that it seemed possible to establish a peace society even in the city that Bertha von Suttner called "the citadel of militarism."[14]

Germans were conspicuously underrepresented at both the early Universal Peace Congresses and Interparliamentary Conferences. The only German delegate to the first Universal Peace Congress was a south German industrialist, Adolf Richter, a cousin of the left-liberal political leader, Eugen Richter. By 1892 the German delegation had grown to only three. German Reichstag deputies were likewise sparse at international peace conferences; when several of them attended the second Interparliamentary Conference

[13] Dietz, *Franz Wirth*, pp. 19, 67; M. Höltzel, "Die moderne Friedensbewegung," *Pazifismus und Internationalismus* (Nuremberg, 1911), p. 14; DWN, IV (1895), 387.

[14] SFC, Suttner to Fried, Harmannsdorf, 12 June 1892.

in London in 1890, their presence was announced as "the most gratifying feature of the meeting."[15] Germans who did attend these international congresses were embarrassed by their isolation. Partially, then, for patriotic reasons, they moved to establish some form of organizational backing to ensure a more creditable German showing.[16] After the third Interparliamentary Conference met in Rome in November 1891, a group of some sixty Reichstag deputies created the Parliamentary Committee for Peace and Arbitration, which was designed to lobby for the passage of treaties of arbitration and to lend direction to German participation at Interparliamentary Conferences. Among the more prominent members were Max Hirsch, Karl Baumbach, Rudolf Virchow, Heinrich Dohrn, Ludwig Bamberger, Heinrich Rickert, Ludwig von Bar, and Theodor Barth, all of whom belonged to the left-liberal Progressive party (*Deutsche Freisinnige Partei*).[17] Attempts to interest other parties failed, and the committee remained almost exclusively a left-liberal organization. This did not prevent its members from acting with some success; the arbitration clauses appended to Caprivi's commercial treaties in December 1891 were the direct result of pressure from Barth and other members of the Arbitration Committee.[18]

Several members of the committee, including Barth, Hirsch, and Dohrn, attempted early in 1892 to create, as an adjunct to their parliamentary group, a peace society in

---

[15] Ludwig Quidde, "The Creation of the Interparliamentary Union," in Lange, *The Interparliamentary Union*, pp. 23–24.

[16] Adolf Richter, "33 Jahre im Dienste der Friedensbewegung," in Grosch, *Deutsche Pazifisten*, p. 12; Alfred H. Fried, "Die moderne Friedensbewegung in Deutschland und Frankreich, I: Die Bewegung in Deutschland," *Der Continent* 1 (1907), 696–97.

[17] DWN, 1 (March 1892), 27–28.

[18] *Ibid.*; NL Bertha von Suttner, United Nations Library, Geneva (cited hereafter as NL Suttner) (Mrii, 2), Max Hirsch to Suttner, Berlin, 27 January 1892.

Berlin drawn from the populace at large. They soon concluded that there was not enough popular enthusiasm to justify the effort and abandoned the idea.[19]

When the politicians lost interest, the initiative passed to an aspiring young journalist and publisher who had recently set himself up in business in Berlin. When in the fall of 1891 Alfred Fried learned that Bertha von Suttner had just founded a peace society in Vienna, he immediately approached the baroness with an offer to publish a peace journal for her. She agreed, and the first issue appeared in January 1892, named after Suttner's now-famous novel.[20] Inspired and encouraged by Suttner, Fried then set out to find support among prominent figures in Berlin in order to assemble a respectable executive committee for a peace society. In March 1892 he arranged for Suttner to speak in Berlin before a gathering of liberal journalists and politicians at the *Verein Berliner Presse*, but although she was well received, there was little enthusiasm for establishing a peace society.[21] Throughout the spring and summer of 1892 Fried continued to approach left-liberal politicians, newspaper editors, distinguished authors (Gustav Freytag and Friedrich Spielhagen), journalists, professors at the University of Berlin, and countless others. From Vienna Suttner sent letters to influential people, including Bismarck who, to nobody's great surprise, was not interested.[22]

In August 1892 the German delegation to the Universal Peace Congress in Berne issued a public appeal for "the establishment of local organizations to propagate the idea of peace" in Germany.[23] This gave the signal for renewed

---

[19] SFC, Suttner to Fried, Harmannsdorf, 2 January 1891 [*sic*], 29 January 1892; NL Suttner (MrII, 2), Hirsch to Suttner, Berlin, 27 January 1892; Ludwig Quidde, "Zum vierzigjährigen Bestehen des Internationalen Friedensbureaus und der Deutschen Friedensgesellschaft," FW, xxxII (1932), 340.

[20] SFC, Suttner to Fried, Harmannsdorf, 7 December 1891.

[21] DWN, I (March 1892), 39–43.

[22] SFC, Suttner to Fried, Harmannsdorf, 13 July 1892.

[23] NL Fried, Franz Wirth, *et al.*, Aufruf [August 1892].

activity in Berlin and other cities. Wirth contacted people in Constance, Munich, Nuremberg, and Hanover, while a peace society was actually founded in Wiesbaden in October.[24] In Berlin, where the political atmosphere was charged by controversy over Caprivi's new arms bill, Fried began at last to receive commitments. Indeed, by November his confidence had become boundless, and he even approached Friedrich Krupp, who, like Bismarck, showed no interest in a peace society.[25] Nevertheless, on 9 November 1892 Fried was able to organize a committee that included Hirsch, Barth, Spielhagen, Hermann Pachnicke, Karl Schrader, Adolf Richter, Wirth, and Wilhelm Foerster, the director of the Berlin Observatory.[26] With some difficulty he then persuaded Josef Kohler, a professor of law at the University of Berlin, to serve as chairman.[27] Late in November the committee drafted an appeal to Germans "publicly to give notice of their peace-loving disposition by joining the German Peace Society."[28] Finally, on 21 December, a general meeting convened officially to found the German Peace Society.[29]

The international peace movement was jubilant over the incursion of pacifism into the very heart of militarism. On 21 December Suttner wrote to Fried: "How my heart throbs at it. How I rejoiced over your *Habemus Papam!* Yes, this is a Christmas deed."[30] But this ecstasy was pre-

[24] BIP (vB6), Wirth to Élie Ducommun, Frankfurt, 25 October 1892.

[25] NL Fried, Friederich Krupp Direktorium to Fried, Essen, 21 November 1892.

[26] DWN, 1 (November 1892), 36.

[27] SFC, Suttner to Fried, Harmannsdorf, 4 April 1892, 18 December 1892; NL Suttner (Nk 1), Josef Kohler to Suttner, Berlin, 23 December 1892.

[28] FW, xxvi (1926), 325–26.

[29] On the founding of the German Peace Society see: Abrams, "European Peace Societies," pp. 261–66; Alfred Fried, *Jugenderinnerungen* (Berlin, 1925), pp. 18–38; Suttner, *Memoirs*, 1, 372–73, 389–99, 440–48; FW, xiv (1912), 361–63; FW, xxviii (1928), 7.

[30] Suttner, *Memoirs*, 1, 448.

mature, for no sooner had the German Peace Society been founded than it was beset by internal problems. The most fundamental controversy involved divergent conceptions of the peace society's mission, and it had begun even before the organization was founded. Earlier in 1892 a jurist in Dresden, Eugen Schlief, had published a provocative book in which he proposed the negotiation of an international treaty, of limited duration, which would bind its signators to respect the territorial *status quo* and then to settle all disputes among one another by legal means.[31] The book appeared at the time Fried was recruiting people for his prospective peace society, and Schlief soon received inquiries. It rapidly became clear, though, that his ideas about how to secure the reign of international law differed significantly from those of Fried and Bertha von Suttner. While they envisaged a broadly based popular movement which would mobilize public opinion in support of arbitration, Schlief insisted that such an organization would be incapable of any effective political action. He proposed instead to create an elite pressure group with parliamentary connections to lobby for treaties of arbitration.[32] Because of this disagreement, Schlief refused to join Fried's committee, but several of the Reichstag deputies who did join inclined toward Schlief's view and advocated creating a group to function both as lobbyist and political faction in the Reichstag.[33] Fried's thinking prevailed, however. As the peace society's first public appeal made clear, the organization was designed to educate the populace at large: "We pursue [our] goals by practical means, the most powerful of which is public opinion; once the number of members in the peace societies has grown to the point that the expression of their

---

[31] Eugen Schlief, *Der Friede in Europa: Eine völkerrechtlich-politische Studie* (Leipzig, 1892).

[32] NL Fried, Schlief to Fried, Dresden, 6, 9, 15 November 1892, 19 December 1892.

[33] NL Fried, Deutsche Friedensgesellschaft, Vorstandsprotokoll, 21 December 1892; [Fried] "Pro Domo," *Der Friede* (February 1895).

will is the expression of the popular will, no power will be able to unleash a war."[34] The immediate result of the decision to adopt this approach was that most of the Reichstag deputies, who were too busy for this kind of agitation, soon lost interest in the peace society.

Trouble also arose in the peace society over less refined matters. Many of the committee members were uncomfortable around Fried, who combined an insufferable zeal with no tact whatsoever. His continued presence on the committee became intolerable when it came to light that, in addition to publishing Bertha von Suttner's peace journal, his firm had been dealing in morally disreputable books and magazines, which would not reflect at all well on the peace society.[35] Humiliated and indignant, Fried was forced to resign from the committee at the beginning of January 1893. This deprived the new peace society of its main source of energy, and without Fried it quickly became apathetic and ineffectual. Although it could claim a membership of over two hundred and branch sections in six cities by the end of 1893, the society in Berlin proved unable to provide any direction to the movement it nominally led.[36] Kohler soon resigned in disgust, to be followed as chairman by a series of figures who had little more success than he in developing a program of concerted action. Not until late 1893 could the Berlin committee even issue another public appeal for membership, and its failure to oppose Caprivi's arms bill with any energy caused dismay among pacifists elsewhere.[37]

[34] BIP (vB6), Deutsche Friedensgesellschaft, "An das deutsche Volk"; cf. DWN, II (1893), 402–403.

[35] SFC, Suttner to Fried, Vienna, 27 December 1892; Suttner to Fried, Harmannsdorf, 31 December 1892; NL Suttner (If 7), Albert Südekum to Suttner, Berlin, 8 January 1893.

[36] DWN, III (1894), 29.

[37] SFC, Suttner to Fried, Harmannsdorf, 7 May 1893. There is no reason to believe that Kohler resigned under official pressure, since he subsequently became involved in the peace movement again: cf. Walter Bredendiek, *Der ewige Friede—Traum, Hoffnung, Möglichkeit: Friedensideen und Friedensbewegungen der Vergangenheit* (Berlin, 1960), p. 26.

Because of this inactivity in Berlin, the expansion of the peace movement into the rest of Germany took place under the supervision of a different group of people. Even as Fried was seeking support for a peace society in Berlin, Franz Wirth, Adolf Richter, and others had been engaged in a campaign to set up peace groups elsewhere. In fact, one of the considerations that had lent urgency to the founding of a national society based in the capital was the fear that with no central coordination, the appearance of numerous small organizations would cause the fragmentation of the peace movement in Germany.[38] The incapacity of the central committee in Berlin soon made these apprehensions academic, and the focus of the expanding movement shifted to the south and west, where it would remain until the First World War.

In 1893 peace societies began to appear throughout Germany in a pattern that remained typical throughout the decade. Wirth, Richter, or other prominent pacifists contacted leading citizens in target cities, urging them to establish a provisional committee for a peace society. If the committee then generated enough local interest, it called a public meeting and founded a peace society.[39] In most cases the notables who cooperated were local leaders of the Progressive party, and many peace societies originated around a core of the local *Demokratischer Verein* or a similar organization.[40] Success in founding a society often depended upon the influence of the man who agreed to lead it. In

[38] BIP (vB6), Wirth to Ducommun, Frankfurt, 9 April 1892, 25 October 1892; SFC, Suttner to Fried, Harmannsdorf, 19 September 1892. For accounts of the expansion of the German peace movement see: Alfred H. Fried, *Die Ausgestaltung der Friedensaktion in Deutschland* (Berlin, 1903); FW, iv (1902), 145–60; Eduard de Neufville, "Franz Wirth und die Friedensbewegung," FW, xiv (1912), 420–22; Dietz, *Franz Wirth*, pp. 30–41; Abrams, "European Peace Societies," pp. 267–75.

[39] Franz Wirth, "Die Gründung von Friedens-Ortsgruppen," DWN, iv (1895), 94–95.

[40] NL Fried, Wirth to Fried, Frankfurt, 18 February 1895.

Königsberg the mayor became the chairman, while in other localities the presence in the committee of a *Landgerichtsrat* or a deputy in the Landtag or Reichstag made possible the founding of a peace society.[41] Most of the peace societies established in this way consisted of a handful of men and women, whose activities did not extend much beyond an occasional discussion of pacifist literature. Otto Umfrid, a pastor in Stuttgart who was to play a leading role in the German peace movement, recalled that the peace society in his city originated when "eight men and two women sat in a local club and talked about world peace."[42] Many of the new groups were really no more than reading circles and were so designated.[43]

In 1896 Richter, Wirth, and Richard Reuter, a lawyer from Naumburg, toured the Palatinate and Hesse, where they established seven new peace societies. Wirth founded seven more in Franconia in 1897, and by the time of his death later in 1897 he had personally created thirty-seven local peace societies.[44] Otto Umfrid was scarcely less active, as he brought more than twenty groups to life in Württemberg.[45] In other areas the pattern was similar. In the area around Ulm, for instance, a music teacher by the name of Cyprian Eberle contacted prospective leaders, spoke before public meetings, and established several peace societies.

The most remarkable of the agitators who founded local societies in Germany in the 1890s was Richard Feldhaus, a

---

[41] NL Fried, S. Habruner to G. Haberland, Schweinfurth, 30 March 1897; DWN, IV (1895), 423-24; DWN, V (1896), 22-23.

[42] Otto Umfrid, "Meine Erlebnisse in der Friedensbewegung," ER, I (1912), 144; Hans Wehberg, *Die Führer der deutschen Friedensbewegung (1890 bis 1923)* (Leipzig, 1923), p. 41.

[43] AStA, MInn 66321, Die politischen Vereine auf dem Stande des Jahres 1895; NL Fried, Wirth to Fried, Frankfurt, 7 May 1894; Eberle, "Friedens-Lesekreise," MFK, I (May 1894).

[44] BIP (vB6), Wirth to Ducommun, Frankfurt, 4 March 1897; Dietz, *Franz Wirth*, pp. 37-38. On Wirth's role see also Wehberg, *Führer*, pp. 13-15.

[45] Grete Umfrid, ed., *Zum Gedächtnis von Otto Umfrid* (Stuttgart, n.d.), p. 10.

professional actor with the municipal theater in Königsberg. Early in the decade he read Bertha von Suttner's
novel and decided to place his dramatic talents at the service of the peace movement. So successful did he become
as an itinerant lecturer that it would be no exaggeration to
say that a majority of Germans who joined peace societies
before the war did so after hearing Feldhaus speak. Fried
once likened him to Peter the Hermit—an unfortunate comparison—but Feldhaus was unquestionably a powerful personality.[46] Typically, his performances involved dramatic
renditions of scenes from Suttner's novel and readings from
other antiwar literature. By the turn of the century he had
refined his techniques and supplemented his descriptions
of combat with slides showing the most grisly aspects of
warfare. Many who emerged shaken from these presenta-
tions willingly signed the registers of the local peace society.[47] Feldhaus soon began to attract large audiences,
sometimes over a thousand at a single meeting. At the turn
of the century he moved to Switzerland but returned to
Germany for protracted tours. By 1914 he had delivered
over six hundred lectures and undertaken tours to the
United States, Scandinavia, and England.

Owing principally to the efforts of Feldhaus, Wirth,
Reuter, Richter, and Umfrid, the peace movement made
impressive gains in Germany. In 1893 there were six peace
societies, in 1895 there were twenty-six, and by 1898 this
figure had increased to fifty-six local groups, which were
situated in cities and towns of all sizes, though a large proportion were in small towns in the southwest.[48] Not all of
these societies were small; in 1898 the group in Hamburg
numbered eight hundred, Stuttgart had six hundred, and
the *Frankfurter Friedensverein* had grown to over three

[46] FW, xxxvi (1936), 203; Wehberg, *Führer*, pp. 25–26.

[47] NL Fried, Richard Feldhaus to Fried, Bottmingermuble, 27 February 1905; Wehberg to Fried, Düsseldorf, 20 March 1913; PM, iii
(1914), 53, 55.

[48] FW, xxvi (1926), 257.

hundred.[49] By 1900 more than five thousand Germans had joined peace societies.[50] Indeed, so impressive was the growth of the German peace movement that foreign pacifists, who had tended to regard Germany as a lost cause, found it difficult to believe.[51]

The fact that foreign pacifists were impressed by the German movement was of the utmost importance to the leading German pacifists, but it was also the key to some of the weaknesses of the peace societies established in Germany. The patriotic considerations that had originally motivated the Germans to set up a national society in Berlin continued to influence them in the period of expansion, often with unfortunate results. Wirth and the others were more interested in having a great number of peace societies on paper, with which to impress the international movement, than they were in ensuring any durability in the organizations they created. They made few demands on the notables they recruited to lead the local societies, so that the leadership was uninspired and many of the peace societies quickly became defunct—a fact conveniently overlooked in compiling statistics.[52] The *Friedensvereinigung München*, for example, carried on activities for several months after its establishment in 1894 and then quietly expired; in 1897 the group was reconstituted, but with an entirely different membership.[53] The experience in Munich was atypical only insofar as the group actually acknowledged that it had dissolved and reconstituted itself; the short-lived enthusiasm

[49] G. Haberland, "Ein Friedenswort zur Jahreswende," *Friedens-Correspondenz* (January 1898).

[50] FW, IV (1902), 145.

[51] Gaston Moch, "De l'organisation du mouvement de la paix en France," PD, VI (1896), 233.

[52] BIP (vB6), Wirth to Ducommun, Frankfurt, 20 May 1892; NL Fried, C. Eberle to Fried, Neu-Ulm, 12 November 1897; DWN, IV (1895), 94–95.

[53] StAOb, RA 3784/57791, Polizeidirektion München to Kgl. Staatsministerium des Innern, Munich, 27 January 1898, number 47769/98; MFK, IV (April 1897), 5.

and transitory interest of its members were characteristic of most local societies. When Fried spoke in 1899 of "Potemkin societies," he had in mind most of the German movement, including some of the supposedly stronger groups.[54] Wirth and the other national leaders also had to live with the financial consequences of their organizing techniques. In order to attract as many members as possible, they required only minimal dues and seldom demanded that even these be paid. This left most of the local groups in such dire financial straits that it was impossible to carry on any effective activity. The organizers themselves were forced to finance their agitation out of their own pockets; fortunately Wirth and Richter were men of substantial wealth, but even they were hard pressed.

The need to impress the international movement also dictated that a Universal Peace Congress eventually meet in Germany. The leaders of the German movement viewed this prospect with some apprehension, for they could not count on governmental support and they feared that popular hostility might provoke an incident. Nevertheless, representatives from leading German peace societies decided in June 1896 to apply to the International Peace Bureau for permission to play host to the Universal Peace Congress in 1897. Berlin was a logical place to hold the congress, but in view of the lamentable condition of the peace society there, the German leaders decided instead on Hamburg, where the local peace society was the largest in the country.[55] Despite the reservations of some French pacifists, the Germans convinced the International Peace Bureau with the argument that a peace congress would benefit the German movement by dispelling the popular notion that "the peace movement [was] an exotic plant, perhaps suited for other countries, but not for Germany."[56]

---

[54] NL Suttner (BbII, b35), Fried MS, "Los von Berlin!" Berlin, 1899; NL Fried, Eberle to Fried, Neu-Ulm, 4 November 1898.
[55] MFK, III (August 1896), 4.
[56] BIP (IIIL), Reuter to International Peace Bureau, Naumburg, 4

It was an apt indication of the coordination within the German peace movement that when the peace society in Hamburg began making arrangements for the congress, it received no support whatsoever from Berlin or any other society.[57] When they approached the government of the *Hansestadt*, leaders of the Hamburg group were relieved to find the mayor and senate cooperative, if not enthusiastic.[58] The senate gave the pacifists a modest subsidy, and when the peace congress convened in August 1897, a senator officially welcomed the pacifists with the appropriate courtesies.[59] The congress itself, although poorly attended, ran smoothly. The only incident occurred when one of Eduard Löwenthal's friends briefly threw the congress into consternation by protesting the pacifists' failure to send greetings to the German emperor. Nonetheless, everyone went home pleased over what a leading French pacifist called "a definitive consecration for the German peace movement."[60]

The German movement profited from the congress in Hamburg, but the events of the next two years brought more significant gains. When in August 1898 the Russian tsar proposed an international disarmament conference, pacifists in Germany (and everywhere else) were jubilant. Fried expressed the pacifists' sense of satisfaction when he observed that "we utopians of yesterday have become the

---

March 1897; Richter to Ducommun, Pforzheim, 27 December 1896; Reuter, "Der erste internationale Friedenskongress auf deutschem Boden," *Correspondenz für die Friedensbewegung*, number 3, March 1897.

[57] NL Fried, Lorenzen to Fried, Hamburg, 1 July 1897.

[58] BIP (IIIL), Otto Ernst to Bajer, Hamburg, 4 March 1897.

[59] *Bulletin officiel du VIIIᵉ Congrès universel de la paix tenu à Hambourg du 12 au 16 août 1897* (Berne, 1897), p. 17.

[60] Gaston Moch, "Le VIIIᵉ Congrès universel de la paix," *Questions diplomatiques et coloniales* 1 (15 October 1897), 345; BIP (IIIL), Lorenzen to Ducommun, Hamburg, 28 August 1897; DWN, VI (1897), 281, 299–301.

Realpolitiker of today."[61] In the hope that the conference would reach effective agreements on arms limitation and a court of international arbitration, the German peace movement began to act with renewed vitality. The Russian proposal made the peace movement's goals the subject of lively public debate, and meetings sponsored by peace societies were well attended.[62] In an effort to coordinate action in support of the conference, several pacifists in Munich, led by a young historian, Ludwig Quidde, founded a special committee to circulate resolutions and petitions. In Munich itself the committee enlisted the support of important notables, including the mayor, and sponsored public meetings attended by over fifteen hundred persons.[63] Mass meetings in support of the conference were also held in Frankfurt, Stuttgart, and throughout Württemberg. This activity even extended to Berlin, where the peace society sent a petition to the Reichstag. To promote the conference Fried also organized a special committee in Berlin, which included the left-liberal Reichstag deputy Adolf Jacobsen, Hirsch, Barth, Virchow, Hans Ullstein, Rudolf Mosse, and Prince Schönaich-Carolath.[64]

The achievements of the Hague conference in 1899 consisted of a few rules of war and an arbitration tribunal to which recourse was to be entirely voluntary. Despite these

[61] Fried, "Victoria!" MFK, v (September 1898), 103.

[62] The Prussian representative in Dresden reported that the Russian proposal was "the alpha and omega of political discussion" in the press: AA, Eur. Gen. 37 number 1, Bd. 2, AS2425 (ACP 102), Wedel to Hohenlohe, Dresden, 2 September 1898.

[63] *Ibid.*, Bd. 7, A2992 (ACP 103), Monts to Hohenlohe, Munich, 12 March 1899; NL Ludwig Quidde, Bundesarchiv, Coblenz (cited hereafter as NL L. Quidde), Quidde MS, "Aus den Erinnerungen eines alten Pazifisten," pp. 2–3; DWN, VIII (1899), 60–61, 97.

[64] AA, Eur. Gen. 37 number 1, Bd. 10, A5745 (ACP 103), Derenthall to Hohenlohe, Stuttgart, 12 May 1899; NL Fried, Komitee für Kundgebungen der Friedenskonferenz; DWN, VIII (1899), 73; see for comparison Marianne Liedtke, "Die Entwicklung des Pazifismus in Deutschland und Frankreich" (Inaugural dissertation, Cologne, 1953), pp. 52–154.

minimal results, pacifists in Germany and elsewhere were encouraged, since the conference itself seemed to represent an advance in the direction of peaceful settlement of international disputes, and its achievements were at least a foundation on which to build. Within Germany the convocation of the Hague conference unquestionably had an important effect on the peace movement, not so much in terms of giving rise to a few new local peace societies or stimulating the growth of existing ones, as in provoking extensive discussion in Germany, really for the first time, of the peace movement and its program. As a result of the Hague conference and the fact that statesmen had now begun to discuss arbitration and arms limitation, the German pacifists were in a better position to claim that their program was feasible.

In view of the expansion of the peace movement in the 1890s and the increasing political currency lent to it by the Hague conference, the weakness of the central committee in Berlin posed a distinct liability, and the pacifists concluded that the leadership would have to be invigorated if the movement were to capitalize on its recent gains. The situation in Berlin had scarcely improved during the 1890s. Although most of the local societies that were founded during the decade were officially affiliated with Berlin, the German Peace Society as a whole had no effective coordination; virtually the only tie between the committee in Berlin and the local groups was the society's journal, the *Monatliche Friedenskorrespondenz*, which Wirth and Fried edited.[65] Constant bickering within the Berlin committee emphasized the lamentable state of affairs.[66] Although the Berlin group was really no less active than most of the other peace societies, its failings were magnified because of its central location and because it had to contend with Alfred Fried. Instead of withdrawing from the peace movement in 1893, Fried set himself up as critic-in-residence and began pub-

[65] NL Fried, Fried to Bothmer, Berlin, 8 June 1899; K. F. Reichel, *Die pazifistische Presse* (Würzburg, 1938), pp. 5–6.

[66] BIP (vB6), Richter to Ducommun, Pforzheim, 8 June 1899.

licly to berate the Berlin committee for its incompetence. The committee attempted on several occasions to neutralize him by asking him to rejoin the peace society, but Fried preferred his independence and could not forget the circumstances of his expulsion.[67] He even contemplated setting up a rival peace society and joined forces briefly with Löwenthal, before it became obvious that two such personalities could not possibly cooperate.[68] A series of unedifying disputes ensued between Fried and the Berlin committee over the editorship of the *Monatliche Friedenskorrespondenz* and other affairs.[69] The final crisis came in 1899 when Max Hirsch, who had become chairman of the committee and who was just as querelous as Fried, fired him as editor of the journal and had him barred as a reporter from the Interparliamentary Conference that met that year in Christiania.[70] In the eyes of leading pacifists in the rest of Germany, who had watched the quarrels in Berlin with growing dismay, this clash was terminal, and they resolved to act.

As early as 1895 Fried himself had called publicly for removal of central headquarters of the society from Berlin to Frankfurt. In ensuing years others concluded that a move ought to be made to a city, such as Hamburg or Munich, where the peace movement was stronger, and in 1898 the beleaguered Berlin committee itself reached the same conclusion.[71] In December 1899 delegates from the local soci-

[67] NL Fried, Richard Grelling to Fried, Berlin, 26 April 1895.

[68] NL Fried, Löwenthal to Fried, Berlin, 5 September 1895; Grelling to Fried, Berlin, 18 March 1896; "Deutscher Verein für internationale Friedenspropaganda von 1874," DWN, IV (1895), 457–58; MFK, III (December 1895), 5.

[69] NL Fried, Deutsche Friedensgesellschaft to Fried, Berlin, 20 September 1897; *Mitteilungen der Deutschen Friedensgesellschaft* v (April 1898).

[70] NL Fried, "An die Ortsgruppen der Deutschen Friedensgesellschaft," Berlin, May 1899; NL Suttner (Bb1, b22), Fried to Reinhardt Schmidt, Berlin, 4 September 1899.

[71] [Fried] "Pro Domo," *Der Friede* (February 1895); SFC, Suttner

eties met in Frankfurt and, after reviewing the alternatives, decided to remove the headquarters to Stuttgart. It was a logical choice. The growth of the movement in Württemberg had been one of the most gratifying aspects of the expansion of the 1890s; by the end of 1898 there were twenty-four local societies in the kingdom, and in 1899 these federated into the *Landesverein Württemberg*.[72] Otto Umfrid and the other leaders of the Stuttgart society were reluctant to accept what seemed to be a thankless assignment but relented under pressure in January 1900.[73]

The Stuttgart Years

The organization over which the Stuttgart committee agreed to preside was a loose collection of local societies with very little cohesion. These societies were concentrated overwhelmingly in the liberal-democratic southwest part of the country, most notably in Württemberg, where by 1913 over one-half of the groups, with more than a quarter of the German Peace Society's membership, were located (see map).[74] Baden and Rhineland-Hesse were also well represented with local peace societies, as was Alsace-Lorraine, where sympathy for the peace movement was widespread because of the likelihood that any future Franco-German war would be fought there.[75] Northern and eastern

---

to Fried, Harmannsdorf, 8 January 1895; NL Fried, Wirth to Fried, Frankfurt, 2 March 1895; *Mitteilungen der Deutschen Friedensgesellschaft* v (April 1898).

[72] "Die Gründung des Württembergischen Landesvereins," FW, I (1899), 115; DWN, VIII (1899), 33.

[73] NL Fried, Kundgebung der Geschäftsleitung der Deutschen Friedensgesellschaft in Stuttgart [January 1900]; Hartmann to Fried, Stuttgart, 7 January 1900; FW, II (1900), 16; CBM, v (1900), 3; Dietz, *Franz Wirth*, p. 42.

[74] VF, XIV (1913), 7; HB (2), II, 288–89.

[75] Friedrich Curtius, *Deutsche Briefe und elsässische Erinnerungen* (Frauenfeld, 1920), p. 239; Gilbert Ziebura, *Die deutsche Frage in der öffentlichen Meinung Frankreichs von 1911–1914* (Berlin, 1955), pp. 22–23.

Groups in Württe

Altensteig
Backnang
Baisingen
Balingen
Bietigheim
Bönningheim
Calw
Creglingen
Ebingen
Esslingen
Freudenstadt
Geislingen
Gmünd
Hall
Heidenheim
Heilbronn
Kornwestheim
Laichingen
Laupheim
Mergentheim
Metzingen
Nagold
Nürtingen
Reinsbronn
Reutlingen
Rottweil
Schorndorf
Schwenningen
Stuttgart
Tailfingen
Tübingen
Ulm
Vaihingen
Waiblingen
Weikersheim
Weinsberg
Winnenden

LOCAL GROUPS
OF THE
GERMAN PEACE SOCIETY
1911-1912

Germany remained hostile to pacifism, and the only groups
of any significance in the north or east were those in Hamburg, Königsberg, and Breslau. In the state of Prussia in
1913 there were only eighteen local peace societies, and of
these only nine were located east of the Elbe River. In the
rest of Germany there were seventy-eight.[76] Local groups
generally varied in size between thirty and several hundred
members. The largest and most active were located in Ham-

[76] [Walter Kloss], *Das Friedensjahrbuch* (Stuttgart, 1913), p. 41.

burg, Königsberg, Stuttgart, Frankfurt, Mannheim, Nuremberg, Munich, and Wiesbaden.

The meeting in Frankfurt in December 1899, which presented Stuttgart with a mandate to lead the German Peace Society, also attempted to add some cohesion to the organization by formalizing its administrative structure.[77] With several exceptions, all the local groups that had been founded were incorporated as *Ortsgruppen* of the German Peace Society.[78] The national society was in turn to be governed by a board of directors (*Hauptvorstand*), composed of fifteen to twenty leading pacifists from all over the country, and the central committee (*Geschäftsleitung*) in Stuttgart. Adolf Richter became president of the board of directors and Otto Umfrid vice-president. The board of directors was responsible for all matters pertaining to the administration of the peace society, and the Stuttgart committee was technically only its executive arm. The board was accountable to annual general meetings of the society, which became known after 1907 as national peace congresses. At these congresses delegates from the branch groups voted resolutions, made changes on the board of directors, and endorsed a resolution that was annually sent to all countries by the International Peace Bureau in Berne.

The German Peace Society was thus adorned with all the administrative trappings required by the dictates of respectability, as well as by law. In fact, however, whatever leadership the society received came almost exclusively from Stuttgart, more specifically from the three men who directed the local peace society there. In addition to

[77] HStASt, E 130 I, Bü. 457, Program und Satzung der Deutschen Friedensgesellschaft (3 December 1899 and 19 February 1905).

[78] The *Friedensvereinigung München* remained independent until 1902. The *Frankfurter Friedensverein* and the *Wiesbadener Friedensgesellschaft* also remained nominally independent, although they contributed money to Stuttgart: FW, IV (1902), 72; FB, VI (1905), 48; VF, XII (1911), 49.

61

Umfrid, who was president of the Stuttgart group, Wilhelm Hartmann, a civil servant, became secretary to the German Peace Society, and Paul Alber became its treasurer. Besides collecting dues, compiling membership lists, and distributing materials to the local groups, the Stuttgart committee was responsible for a wide range of activities connected with the peace society's attempt to carry on an effective propaganda campaign in Germany. It executed the resolutions of the annual meetings, coordinated lectures by Feldhaus and others, watched the press in order to rebut chauvinistic articles, and regularly sent a communiqué to some five hundred German newspapers. The committee also directed the distribution of a monthly journal, *Die Friedens-Blätter* (after 1909 called *Der Völker-Friede*), which was edited by Martin Kohler, a school inspector in Esslingen.

In addition to these activities, the Stuttgart committee oversaw the German Peace Society's relations with the international movement, although it did not act as an official German representative at international peace congresses, largely because Umfrid could not speak French.[79] Richter's primary role in the peace society was to serve as representative of the Germans abroad, but as his health began to fail after 1904, this role fell increasingly to Ludwig Quidde from Munich. Quidde also served as a German delegate on the executive commission of the International Peace Bureau, along with Richter, Eduard de Neufville of Frankfurt, and Adolf Heilberg from Breslau.

During the years in which the headquarters were located in Stuttgart the membership of the German Peace Society continued to grow. In 1902 there were sixty local groups with a membership of six thousand; by 1914 this figure had risen to ninety-eight groups with a membership of just under ten thousand.[80] As in the 1890s, however, these figures

[79] NL Fried, Umfrid to Fried, Stuttgart, 23 November 1907; Hans Wehberg, ed., *Ludwig Quidde: Ein deutscher Demokrat und Vorkämpfer der Völkerverständigung* (Offenbach a. M., 1948), p. 34.

[80] FW, IV (1902), 145; VF, XV (1914), 75; FW, XXVI (1926), 257.

were misleading, for the concept of membership in the German Peace Society was nebulous, and no one could be certain how many people actively belonged.[81] This ambiguity continued to reflect the situation of the local groups. Those that appeared after the turn of the century bore all the characteristics of the ones that had been set up in the 1890s. Once called to life at a public meeting that featured Feldhaus or another *Wanderredner*, most of the local peace societies continued to exist on paper only. Fried once estimated that no more than a third of the local groups carried on any activity at all, and even this was probably a liberal estimate.[82] Fried's description of the typical local peace society underlined the tenuous commitment of most members: "The overwhelming majority consists of people who do no more than affirm the pacifist doctine in principle and belong to some local group because it seems suitable to support, with fifty pfennings or a mark a year, a society that works for something good. Most of the members think they have done all they need to when they pay their dues, and they indignantly reject all requests for their effective participation in the cause, claiming that they are already too busy in their *Weihnachtsbescherungsverein* . . . or some such humanitarian organization."[83] Umfrid shared this view of his constituents, comparing them to "sleepy parishioners who nod their heads at everything the pastor says, but do not do anything."[84]

Because most members were not seriously committed, the size of the local groups fluctuated erratically (figure 2).[85]

[81] See for instance *Bulletin officiel du XIe Congrès universel de la paix tenu à Monaco du 2 au 6 avril 1902* (Berne, 1902), pp. 201–202; cf. *Official Report of the Thirteenth Universal Peace Congress, Boston, Massachusetts, October 3–8, 1904* (Boston, 1904), pp. 39, 245.

[82] NL Fried, Fried to Reuter, Vienna, 9 September 1904; cf. FW, IV (1902), 149.

[83] *Ibid.*

[84] FW, IV (1902), 174; cf. Umfrid, "Wurzelechte Pazifisten," VF, XIV (1913), 125.

[85] Source for figure 2: Dietz, *Franz Wirth*, p. 67.

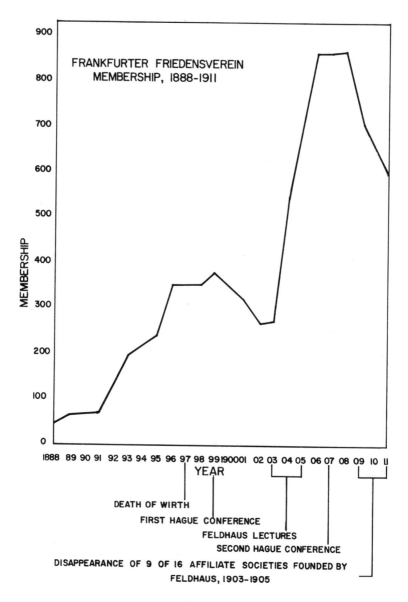

FIGURE 2

Where societies already existed, the Feldhaus lectures swelled the registers with new members, who promptly lost interest in the work of the peace society. Most groups continued to count their membership as the aggregate of those who had once signed up, and chose to disregard the fact that most of these either failed to renew their memberships by paying dues or otherwise played no meaningful role in the activities of the society. Even when a group did survive, the activity of its members was frequently another source of concern. When one of Fried's correspondents moved to Jena in 1911, she discovered that the local peace society consisted of about ten people who occasionally enjoyed each other's company over a glass of beer.[86] Such conditions were fairly widespread, and even when the activities of peace societies involved more than an evening at the *Stammtisch*, they were often little more than social affairs, only incidentally devoted to a serious discussion of world peace.[87] In these circumstances it was rare that local societies became excited about anything; indeed, some of them remained entirely ignorant of the goals for which the peace movement stood.[88]

As a general rule, peace societies were active only when there was a dedicated individual in the locality. People like Count Bothmer in Wiesbaden, Adolf Heilberg in Breslau, Friedrich and Elsbeth Friedrichs in Königsberg, and Friedrich Bloh in Hamburg provided the foundation not only of their local organizations, but of the national society as well. They were responsible for recruiting members and supervising all activities, and the local organizations continued to function only as long as they were present.[89]

[86] NL Fried, Elsbeth Friedrichs to Fried, Jena, 17 September 1911, 15 November 1911.

[87] NL Fried, Fried to Otfried Nippold, Vienna, 5 April 1910; cf. MFK, IV (April 1897), 8.

[88] SFC, Suttner to Fried, Harmannsdorf, 2 December 1896; NL Fried, Umfrid to Fried, Stuttgart, 11 April 1911, 27 November 1911; DWN, VIII (1899), 72–73.

[89] NL Fried, Jacob Wolff to Fried, Hamburg, 22 December 1903;

The situation in Berlin continued to cause special concern, for the pacifists had hoped that the move to Stuttgart would be only temporary. In 1902, after the Berlin organization collapsed entirely, Richter and Quidde were dispatched to salvage the situation; they soon discovered that the indispensable element, a dedicated person to lead the group, was lacking.[90] As a result, the Berlin peace society continued to vegetate until the war. Indeed, so bad were conditions in Berlin that in 1913 the International Peace Bureau thought it appropriate to congratulate a French pacifist for having had the courage to deliver a lecture there.[91]

It is difficult to determine how many active pacifists there were in the peace society, but in view of the condition of most *Ortsgruppen*, the national organization's claim to a membership of ten thousand was a patent misrepresentation. Attendance at annual national peace congresses, probably a more accurate reflection of the actual state of affairs, rarely exceeded fifty, most of whom were perennial delegates.[92] German delegations to Universal Peace Congresses generally consisted only of a handful of the same people. Even conceding the danger of relying on indices such as these, it is clear that there were not many dedicated pacifists in Germany. Indeed, as an educated guess, there were probably no more than two to three hundred men and

---

H. Weihinger to Fried, Gera, 1 October 1904; G. Hönnicke to Fried, Görlitz, 17 November 1905; Elsbeth Friedrichs to Fried, Königsberg, 15 January 1910, 30 April 1910; cf. Rennie Smith, *Peace Verboten* (London, 1943), pp. 19–20.

[90] NL Margarethe Quidde, Stadtbibliothek München (cited hereafter as NL M. Quidde), Einladung zur Generalversammlung der Deutschen Friedensgesellschaft, Ortsgruppe Berlin, 13 November 1902; NL Fried, Quidde to Fried, Munich, 1 November 1902.

[91] PM, II (1913), 133–34; cf. VF, XIII (1912), 46; NL Fried, Rudolf Breitscheid to Fried, Berlin, 20 December 1909.

[92] CBM, VI (1901), 46; CBM, IX (1904), 49; CBM, X (1905), 27; CBM, XV (1910), 64; FB, IX (1908), 55; ER, II (1913), 150–55.

women in Germany willing to sacrifice any significant amount of time or money for the peace movement.

The German Peace Society's financial misery also continued after the turn of the century. Although income from various sources did increase during the Stuttgart years, a chronic lack of funds hampered activities and prevented the implementation of reforms that might have made the peace society more financially efficient. The local groups were tied to Stuttgart by little more than the peace society's journal, and Umfrid and Alber found it impossible to enforce the collection of dues. On paper the locals were to contribute a quarter of the dues they received in return for subscriptions to the journal for their members; in practice the branches rarely delivered their quotas.[93]

With the major source of its income so unreliable, the peace society was forced back onto other expedients in order to finance its operations. The International Peace Bureau contributed subsidies to peace societies in all countries, and after the Carnegie Endowment came to the aid of the bureau, these funds became more substantial. In addition, German pacifists could draw on the estates of several friends of the international peace movement, notably the Russian financier, Ivan Bloch, and the French painter, Narcissus Thibault. When Franz Wirth died in 1897, his estate was placed at the disposal of the *Frankfurter Friedensverein*, and this enabled the group to carry on a relatively active campaign as long as the money held out.[94] Since even these resources were hardly adequate, however, the pacifists were literally reduced to begging.[95] They could per-

[93] NL M. Quidde, Ludwig Quidde MS, "Die Lage der Deutschen Friedensgesellschaft, ihre nächsten Aufgaben und ihre Finanzen," Easter 1915.

[94] NL Fried, Elsbeth Friedrichs to Bertha von Suttner, Neu Insenburg b. Frankfurt, 30 April 1912.

[95] When the announcement was made in 1905 that Bertha von Suttner had won the Nobel Peace Prize, Umfrid promptly sent, along with

suade neither the Reichstag nor the Württemberg Landtag to subsidize their operations, but there were a few sympathetic individuals of means in Germany.[96] Eduard de Neufville in Frankfurt gave a large share of his considerable wealth to the peace movement. In addition to making regular contributions to Stuttgart and Berne, he financed a lecture tour for Feldhaus into the Frankfurt area in 1903 and paid Bertha von Suttner's expenses at the second Hague conference in 1907.[97] Another wealthy and generous pacifist in Frankfurt was Heinrich Rössler, who directed a firm that processed precious metals. But the pacifists' most important benefactor, in terms of both the money and the financial advice he gave, was Georg Arnhold, a director of the *Dresdner Bank*, who combined an active interest in the peace movement with membership on the board of directors of the *Deutsche Kolonialgesellschaft*.[98] Arnhold not only bailed out the peace society on numerous occasions, but served as Fried's business manager and made possible the publication of his major works, including his journal.[99] By issuing a special appeal for money to its members, the peace society was finally able in 1911 to hire a full-time national secretary to relieve the overworked leaders of the

---

his congratulations, an appeal for some of the prize money: NL Suttner (Fk 7), Umfrid to Suttner, 10 December 1905.

[96] StBR, XII L.P., 1 Session (1907-1909), CCLIII, number 1162; Otto Umfrid, "Die Bitte der Deutschen Friedensgesellschaft um eine Subvention vor der württembergischen Kammer der Standesherren," *Der Beobachter* (Stuttgart), 11 May 1909.

[97] Dietz, *Franz Wirth*, p. 46; PD, XX (1910), 150-51; Wehberg, *Führer*, pp. 44-46.

[98] Hans Jaeger, *Unternehmer in der deutschen Politik (1890-1918)* (Bonn, 1967), pp. 142, 185. These interests were not contradictory: see below, chapter 7, pp. 305-309.

[99] "Georg Arnhold als Pazifist," FW, XVII (1915), 14-15; NL Fried, Arnhold to Fried, Dresden, 4 January 1908; NL Hans Wehberg, Bundesarchiv, Coblenz (cited hereafter as NL Wehberg) (54), Arnhold to Wehberg, Dresden, 24 September 1910; UN Library, Geneva, MSS Coll., Fried, "Wer ist's" (Georg Arnhold).

Stuttgart committee, who had scarcely been able to afford a typist.[100] Although the budgetary situation did improve somewhat in the years just prior to the war, owing to the Carnegie money and special appeals, the pacifists continued to find their program frustrated by the scant resources at their disposal, and they looked with envy at the funds available to nationalist organizations, which by comparison were lavish.

Despite the persistence of financial problems and grave deficiencies in the local groups, the peace society did make some progress after the turn of the century, in large part because the men in Stuttgart gave some direction to the work of the organization. As evidence of the progress they were making, German pacifists could point to the fact that when a Universal Peace Congress met for a second time in Germany, it was a great success.

The Universal Peace Congress in Hamburg in 1897 had gone well, in the sense that nothing disastrous had happened, and the Germans looked forward to hosting another. As early as 1902 the Munich group suggested that their city, which had been the headquarters of agitation in Germany in favor of the Hague conference, would be a suitable location for a Universal Peace Congress.[101] In the spring of 1906 Ludwig Quidde, who was the leader of the Munich group, began to inquire about the possibility of holding a peace congress in Munich in 1907. The mayor responded favorably with the promise of a subsidy, and the Bavarian state government raised no objections, although it was cautioned by the German foreign office to be discreet.[102] Quidde took

[100] NL Georg Gothein, Bundesarchiv, Coblenz (22), Deutsche Friedensgesellschaft, Rundschreiben, 20 September 1910.

[101] CBM, VII (1902), 64.

[102] BIP (IIIU), Quidde to Ducommun, Munich, 2 April 1906; GStA, MA 93657 (5), Auswärtiges Amt to Bayerisches Staatsministerium des Aeussern, Berlin, 19 October 1906, number 1329. For an account of the congress and its preliminaries see Utz-Friedebert Taube, *Ludwig Quidde: Ein Beitrag zur Geschichte des demokratischen Gedankens in Deutschland* (Kallmünz, 1963), pp. 153-56; FW, IX (1907), 186-87.

on responsibility for preparing the congress. By the summer of 1907 he had put together an impressive honorary committee, consisting of over one hundred prominent local figures, including the Bavarian prime minister, Clemens von Podewils, Ernst Müller-Meiningen, Lujo Brentano, and Ludwig Thoma. As president of the congress he recruited Henrich Harburger, a member of the Bavarian *Oberstes Landgericht*.[103] When the congress convened in September, it was an immense success. The city fathers and Bavarian officials welcomed the more than three hundred pacifists—nearly half of them German—with utmost courtesy, and even the Bavarian prince-regent sent his greetings.[104] The week of the congress was filled with banquets and social gatherings, including an excursion at city expense to the Chiemsee. Even the normally hostile press in Munich treated the peace congress cordially and published detailed reports on all the proceedings. The pacifists were dazzled by this reception. The leader of the Belgian peace movement, Henri La Fontaine, remarked that everything "seemed to run on wheels," and Bertha von Suttner sang the praises of the German peace movement.[105] The Munich congress subsequently became known in pacifist circles as the "model congress" in recognition of Quidde's flawless management.

After 1907 Ludwig Quidde became increasingly prominent in the movement, and many looked logically to him

[103] BIP (IIIU), Quidde MS, "Von der Organisation des Friedenskongresses in München."

[104] GStA, MA93657 (5), Neufville to Podewils, Frankfurt, 16 September 1907; Richter, "33 Jahre," in Grosch, *Deutsche Pazifisten*, p. 15; *Bulletin officiel du XVIe Congrès universel de la paix tenu à Munich de 9 au 14 septembre 1907* (Berne, 1908). The pacifists did not repeat their Hamburg mistake; they sent greetings to the Kaiser.

[105] Walter Schücking, "Ludwig Quiddes Lebenswerk," FW, XXVIII (1928), 2; Bertha von Suttner, *Der Kampf um die Vermeidung des Weltkrieges: Randglossen aus zwei Jahrzehnten zu den Zeitereignissen vor der Katastrophe (1892–1900 und 1907–1914) von Bertha von Suttner*, edited by Alfred Fried (2 vols., Zurich, 1917), II, 58; FW, IX (1907), 187.

when, on the eve of the war, it was necessary to find a new president for the German Peace Society. By 1914 Richter and Umfrid had both become incapacitated, and this raised the uncomfortable prospect of having to move central headquarters prematurely back to Berlin. After several expedients had been proposed to keep the headquarters in Stuttgart, Quidde agreed in May 1914 to become president of the peace society and commute from Munich to Stuttgart for business meetings.[106]

Quidde's acceptance of office coincided with the outbreak of the war. Both events marked the end of an era in the history of German pacifism. Although Quidde remained president of the German Peace Society until 1929, its focal point shifted back to Berlin and its character changed radically in response to the war.[107] The prewar peace society was

[106] NL Fried, Quidde to Fried, Munich, 18 February 1914; G. Grosch, "VII. Deutscher Friedenskongress," ER, III (1914), 116–17; cf. NL L. Quidde, Quidde MS, "Der deutsche Pazifismus während des Weltkrieges," pp. 3–5.

[107] The literature on the German peace movement after 1914 is sparse, but see: Richard Barkeley, *Die deutsche Friedensbewegung 1870–1933* (Hamburg, 1948); Gustav Fuchs, *Der deutsche Pazifismus im Weltkrieg* (Stuttgart, 1928); James D. Shand, "Doves among the Eagles: German Pacifists and their Government during World War I," *Journal of Contemporary History* x (January 1975), 95–108; Ursula Fortuna, *Der Völkerbundsgedanke in Deutschland während des Ersten Weltkrieges* (Zurich, 1974); Erwin Gülzow, "Der Bund 'Neues Vaterland': Probleme der bürgerlich-pazifistischen Demokratie im Ersten Weltkrieg (1914–1918)" (Inaugural dissertation, East Berlin, 1969); Karl Holl, "Die 'Vereinigung Gleichgesinnter': Ein Berliner Kreis pazifistischer Intellektueller im Ersten Weltkrieg," *Archiv für Kulturgeschichte* LIV (1972), 364–84; Karl Holl, "Europapolitik im Vorfeld der deutschen Regierungspolitik: Zur Tätigkeit proeuropäischer Organisationen in der Weimarer Republik," *Historische Zeitschrift* CCXIX (1974), 33–94; Henri Burgelin, "Le mouvement pacifiste dans l'Allemagne de Weimar," *Cahiers de l'Association interuniversitaire* (Strassbourg, 1961), pp. 57–88. In addition, several important studies are in progress. Friedrich-Karl Scheer in Bochum is completing a dissertation on the German Peace Society between 1892 and 1933. Karl Holl of the University of Bremen is working on the relations between the peace movement and the DDP in the Weimar years.

largely a south German phenomenon, which subsisted on the dedication of a small group of people in Stuttgart. However immodest, Otto Umfrid's observation in 1913 that "without the activity of those of us in Stuttgart the German peace movement would probably have disappeared," was hardly an exaggeration.[108]

Portrait of the Pacifists

What kinds of people joined peace societies in Germany? Were there any significant correlations between social background and a commitment to ideological pacifism? These questions are difficult to answer, in large part because the archives of the German Peace Society were destroyed shortly after the First World War, and with them any registers that might have made possible a systematic analysis of the social composition of the organization's membership. Any conclusions must therefore be based upon fragmentary statistics and supplementary evidence.

In the graphs in figure 3 I have broken down by occupational categories the only three fairly complete membership lists I could locate—those for the *Frankfurter Friedensverein* in 1911, the peace society in Königsberg in 1910, and the local group in Danzig in 1906.[109] The limitations of these statistics are very great: I found that many members listed no occupation, the categories are imprecise, and there are no figures for groups south of Frankfurt, which is particularly unfortunate in view of the German Peace Society's geographical concentration. Even these statistics, however, suggest some patterns. By far the largest single category in all the groups was commercial. Although there was a sprin-

---

Brigitta Ludwig in Cologne is doing a dissertation on the peace movement and the SPD between 1919 and 1933.

[108] NL Wehberg (88), Umfrid to Wehberg, Stuttgart, 4 June 1913.

[109] Dietz, *Franz Wirth*, pp. 68–73; Deutsche Friedensgesellschaft, Ortsgruppe Königsberg, *Jahresbericht 1910* (Königsberg, 1911), pp. 13–16; FB, VII (1906), 45; cf. VF, XV (1914), 61.

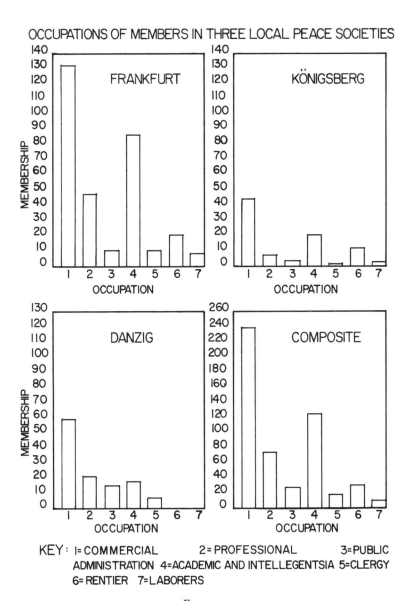

OCCUPATIONS OF MEMBERS IN THREE LOCAL PEACE SOCIETIES

KEY: 1=COMMERCIAL   2=PROFESSIONAL   3=PUBLIC
ADMINISTRATION 4=ACADEMIC AND INTELLEGENTSIA 5=CLERGY
6=RENTIER 7=LABORERS

FIGURE 3

kling of people in this category who listed their occupations as banker or owner of an industrial firm, the great preponderance were those who designated themselves *Kaufmann*. Even this is not very precise, but in view of the minimal support the peace movement found among chambers of commerce and other larger merchant associations, and since there were evidently not many wealthy people in the peace societies, the bulk of these *Kaufleute* consisted in all likelihood of merchants or independent entrepreneurs doing business on a small scale. The next largest category, "academic and intelligentsia," included a few writers and journalists, but the great majority were *Volksschullehrer* and school officials who worked in the lower echelons of the educational system; there were very few professors, for institutions of higher education were quite hostile to the peace movement. The most common in the professional group were physicians, lawyers, and pharmacists. The people who were connected with public administration were generally drawn from the lower ranks of municipal bureaucracies; there were few state or national officials involved in the peace movement.[110] Clergymen and blue-collar workers were conspicuous chiefly in their absence.

This general pattern, particularly the prominence of independent entrepreneurs and primary school teachers, is confirmed by a list of the occupations of leaders of the *Ortsgruppen* in 1913.[111] Here the largest single category, fifteen out of the seventy-nine who reported, consisted of teachers. The next largest group (thirteen out of seventy-nine) were those who designated their occupations as *Kaufmann*.

Some other features of the peace societies' membership are worth noting. Many of the pacifists were women—near-

[110] VF, XIV (1913), 127.

[111] HB (2), 288–89; Fritz Köhler, "Deutsche Friedensgesellschaft (DFG) seit 1892," in Dieter Fricke, *et al.*, *Die bürgerlichen Parteien in Deutschland: Handbuch der Geschichte der bürgerlichen Parteien und anderer bürgerlicher Interessenorganisationen vom Vormärz bis zum Jahre 1945* (2 vols., Leipzig, 1968–70), I, 365.

ly a third of the members of the peace society in Königsberg and a quarter of the *Frankfurter Friedensverein.* Although the fact does not show up in the statistics, the peace societies also tended to attract the elderly a great deal more than young people.[112]

Leaders of the German Peace Society frequently pointed out—and complained—that the organization was largely a *kleinbürgerlich* phenomenon.[113] The available statistics are not inconsistent with this conclusion. They suggest that the bulk of the membership in the peace society was drawn from a nonrural, middle to lower-middle class constituency —that it consisted of people who, in the words of one police report, "belong to the middle *Bürgerstand* but occupy no prominent position in society."[114]

It is not immediately clear, however, why these kinds of people were the most prone to join the peace society. Some of the businessmen who belonged were no doubt reliant upon foreign trade, though probably not many. A more plausible explanation, which is born out in the history of the pacifists' campaign in Germany, is a negative one: these people were the least unlikely to join a peace society. The key is the fact that they were not, as a rule, highly situated socially or politically. This meant, in the first place, that their education stopped short of a university degree and they did not hold reserve commissions in the army. Consequently they had not been exposed to the influences inimi-

[112] See "Bei den Friedensfreunden," *Süddeutsche Zeitung,* 2 April 1914.

[113] Fried, "Die moderne Friedensbewegung in Deutschland und Frankreich, I," p. 699; FW, xv (1913), 365.

[114] StAH, Polizeibehörde (Politische Polizei), S4930, Bd. 2, Präsidial-Abteilung B to Lappenburg, Hamburg, 21 April 1900; cf. FB, vi (1905), 41; Köhler, "Deutsche Friedensgesellschaft," pp. 364–66. Istvan Deak's description of the prewar peace society as an "intellectually refined association of professors, journalists, and Jewish businessmen" is inaccurate: *Weimar Germany's Left-Wing Intellectuals: A Political History of the Weltbühne and Its Circle* (Berkeley and Los Angeles, 1968), pp. 50–51.

cal to the peace movement that prevailed in the officer corps and universities. Furthermore, the fact that they were not among the elites of their professions, and in most cases had no prospects for joining these elites, made it easier for them to belong to the peace society without fearing that membership in the organization, which many Germans regarded as unpatriotic, would damage their careers. Their social position was such that most of them were democrats, yet it was not so low that they felt any attraction for the revolutionary pacifism of social democracy.

In any event, social factors are not enough to explain why some people committed themselves to ideological pacifism, particularly considering that membership in a peace society was in most cases hardly a sign of commitment. And a survey of the most dedicated members of the peace society, the small group of people in the national leadership, reveals that they were drawn from the very social sectors that were underrepresented in the rank and file; they included an aristocrat, a wealthy industrialist, a Protestant clergyman, and an academic historian. These were in fact unusual people, courageous idealists, whose commitment to pacifism probably derived from psychological idiosyncrasies, about which the available evidence does not even justify speculation.

Wilhelm Foerster, one of the few active members of the peace society in Berlin, was fond of telling about one of his friends who, by the end of a lecture he had been delivering to some reform group, was trembling with rage, at which point he screamed at his audience, "We must preach reason everywhere!"[115] In the company of dedicated pacifists Foerster must have been reminded of this story often, for while most of the rank and file of the German Peace Society remained indifferent, the activists in the leadership were generally quite the opposite. The devoted pacifist was a mil-

---

[115] NL Fried, Foerster to Fried, Charlottenburg, 26 April 1907. On Foerster see his *Lebenserinnerungen und Lebenshoffnungen (1832 bis 1910)* (Berlin, 1911).

itant crusader, convinced of his own righteousness and intolerant of criticism. His world was black and white, a morality play in which the forces of peace, justice, and morality did battle with militarism and ignorance. "In fact it is a simple problem," Umfrid wrote in 1910, "either war is beneficial, in which case it must be promoted, or it is not beneficial, in which case it must be fought just like the plague or cholera."[116] This crusading mentality, which lent itself well to caricature, gave rise to a smug elitism in the pacifist leadership, which viewed itself as a vanguard bringing peace to humanity.[117] The men and women who dedicated themselves to the peace movement were as a rule intense, volatile people, who fought with each other a great deal more than with their political enemies. Fried's tactless intolerance was legendary and a constant source of exasperation to leaders of the German Peace Society, who were not themselves always graceful in their dealings with him. Theodor Heuss has noted that Walther Schücking, one of the few professors active in the peace movement, was a man "easily made enthusiastic and easily annoyed."[118] Heinrich Weinel, a pacifist theologian in Jena, was, in the words of one of his colleagues, "an impulsive hot-head (*Stürmer*)," and Hans Wehberg, one of Fried's close associates, has been recalled as "a battler."[119]

The two most internationally prominent figures in the German peace movement were Austrians. After they cooperated in founding the German Peace Society in 1892, Bertha von Suttner and Alfred Fried maintained a close

---

[116] VF, XI (1910), 15; cf. Wilhelm Unseld, "Zwei Lager," DWN, VII (1898), 64; Werner Bellardi, "Bekennt Farbe!" FW, XIV (1912), 296–97.

[117] VF, XIV (1913), 48; cf. "Die Friedensfanatiker," FW, VIII (1906), 176–77.

[118] Theodor Heuss, *Erinnerungen 1905–1933* (Tübingen, 1963), p. 315.

[119] Friedrich Rittelmayer, *Aus meinem Leben* (Stuttgart, 1937), p. 257. For the reference to Wehberg I am indebted to his wife, with whom I spoke in Geneva in May 1971.

association during the prewar years and exerted an influence throughout German-speaking Europe. For their efforts in the peace movement they both received the Nobel Peace Prize.[120]

Bertha von Kinsky was born in Prague in 1843.[121] After her mother had gambled away most of the family's money, she was hired in the early 1870s as a tutor to the Suttner family, itself confronted with severe financial problems and intent upon a brilliant marriage for its son, Arthur. When Bertha and Arthur fell in love, Arthur's alarmed parents spirited her off to Paris in 1876, where she served briefly as secretary to Alfred Nobel before returning to elope with Arthur von Suttner. After spending nine years in semiexile in Russia, the couple returned to Austria as authors of some distinction. With the publication and success of the novel *Die Waffen nieder!* the two devoted the rest of their lives to the peace movement.

After founding the Austrian Peace Society in 1891, Bertha von Suttner became a central figure in the international peace movement, appearing regularly at Universal Peace Congresses and as guest of honor at Interparliamentary Conferences. With Fried she edited the journal *Die Waffen*

[120] See Ferdinand G. Smekal, *Oesterreichs Nobelpreisträger* (Vienna, 1961), p. 37.

[121] The best biography of Bertha von Suttner is Beatrix Kempf, *Bertha von Suttner: Das Lebensbild einer grossen Frau* (Vienna, 1964). Others include Ann Tizia Leitich, "Bertha von Suttner," *Grosse Oesterreicher* (Vienna, 1957), x, 66–75; Ilsa Reicke, *Bertha von Suttner: Ein Lebensbild* (Bonn, 1952); Hertha Pauli, *Nur eine Frau: Biographischer Roman* (Vienna, 1937); Carolyn E. Playne, *Bertha von Suttner and the Struggle to Avert the World War* (London, 1936); Leopold Katscher, *Bertha von Suttner, die "Schwärmerin" für Güte* (Dresden, 1903); Alfred H. Fried, *Bertha von Suttner* (Charlottenburg, n.d.); see also Walter Bredendiek's perceptive appreciation, "Stimme der Vernunft und Menschlichkeit," in Internationales Institut für den Frieden, *Vermächtnis und Mahnung zum 50. Todestag Bertha von Suttners* (Vienna, 1964), pp. 13–44. An edition of her memoirs has recently been published in the DDR: Bertha von Suttner, *Lebenserinnerungen*, edited with an introduction by Fritz Böttger (Berlin, 1968).

nieder! until 1899, after which she contributed to the new journal that Fried edited. She published an immense amount of fictional and nonfictional material for the peace movement and in 1905 received the Nobel Peace Prize, an award she had herself inspired in her continuing contacts with Nobel.[122]

At the height of her career Bertha von Suttner was a woman of great eminence. A poll by the *Berliner Tageblatt* in 1903 showed her to be the most famous woman in Europe, running ahead of such contemporaries as Carmen Sylva, Sarah Bernhardt, and Eleonora Duse.[123] She prided herself on her social prominence and actively cultivated her contacts with members of European high society; her Viennese peace society became a chic social circle for liberal aristocrats and wealthy businessmen.[124] The pacifists in Germany acknowledged her as their leader, and the fact that they shared her pretensions for social and political influence only magnified the reverence with which they treated her. But her prominence also had its disadvantages. Her pacifism tended to be sentimental; in her efforts to make peace among her bickering disciples in Germany she often became excessively moralistic, and this hardly supported the German pacifists' claim that they were political realists. Her incantations to justice and humanity also made her the target of vicious satire, which extended to those in Germany who called her their leader.[125] Bertha von Suttner insulated herself against these attacks by taking refuge in a naive optimism, from which she only occasionally escaped.[126]

[122] Irwin Abrams, "Bertha von Suttner and the Nobel Peace Prize," *Journal of Central European Affairs* xxii (1962/63), 286–307.

[123] CBM, viii (1903), 56.

[124] Kempf, *Bertha von Suttner*, pp. 114–15; cf. AA, Eur. Gen. 37 number 5, Bd. 2, A2853 (ACP 107), Brockdorff-Rantzau to Wedel, Vienna, 17 February 1907.

[125] NL Suttner (Vi i–ii). These files contain press clippings with attacks on her.

[126] See Stefan Zweig, *Die Welt von gestern: Erinnerungen eines Europäers* (Berlin, 1962), pp. 194–95.

In one of the great mercies of history, she died one week before the assassination of the Austrian archduke in 1914.

Bertha von Suttner's prestige derived in part from her pose as the great conciliator of the peace movement, which enabled her to disdain petty rivalries and the more unpleasant aspects of political agitation. No one could have been less suited for such a role than Alfred Hermann Fried.[127] Born in Vienna in 1864, the son of a Jewish merchant of Hungarian descent, Fried had neither the money nor the scholastic record to continue his education beyond the *Gymnasium*. In 1887 he established himself as a journalist and proprietor of a *Verlagsbuchhandlung* in Berlin. There he also joined the German Social Democratic party, and like many other articulate and rootless young Jews, might well have found a career in the party, had he not become associated with Suttner. As a boy of fifteen he had viewed an exposition of the macabre war paintings of the Russian artist Vereshchagin. This left him with an abiding horror of war, and when he learned of the founding of the Austrian Peace Society in 1891, he immediately decided to dedicate himself to the peace movement.

After his break with the German Peace Society in 1893 Fried remained in Berlin as a writer for the Ullstein papers *Welt am Montag* and *Berliner Zeitung*. In 1899 he began to edit his own peace journal, *Die Friedens-Warte*, which by 1914 was recognized as one of the best in the world and, with the aid of a subsidy from the Carnegie Endowment, enjoyed a circulation of close to ten thousand.[128] In the wake of the dissolution of the second of his three marriages

[127] Hans Wehberg, "Alfred Hermann Fried," *Neue Deutsche Biographie* (Berlin, 1961), v, 441–42; Wehberg, "Alfred Fried," *Deutsches Biographisches Jahrbuch*, III, 105–106; Doris Dauber, "A. H. Fried und sein Pazifismus" (Inaugural dissertation, Leipzig, 1923); Rudolf Goldscheid, ed., *Alfred H. Fried: Eine Sammlung von Gedenkblättern* (Leipzig, 1922); Wehberg, *Führer*, pp. 19–23.

[128] NL Fried, Fried to N. M. Butler, Vienna, 20 September 1913; Carnegie Endowment for International Peace, *Year Book for 1913–1914* (Washington, D.C., 1914), p. 66.

he left Berlin in 1903 for Vienna, where he was forced to live entirely by his pen. His literary activity was staggering; in addition to editing his journal, he had by 1914 published over seventy books and several thousand articles.[129] Although his intellect was by no means outstanding, and most of his ideas were unoriginal, Fried was a gifted popularizer and polemicist with an incisive style. He was also an extremely difficult man. Unable to balance his intensity and dynamism with any tact, he was the center of countless quarrels, from which even the venerable Bertha von Suttner was not entirely exempt.[130] Adding to his irascibility was the fact that he was also an insecure and unhappy man, who felt surrounded by people who did not understand or appreciate him. He was obsessed by the accusation that, as a pacifist, he was a utopian dreamer, and he spent his career trying to develop a theory of pacifism that would have the authority of a scientific discipline. Significantly, the real apex of his career did not come with his reception of the Nobel Peace Prize in 1911, but rather with the award of an honorary doctorate from the University of Leyden in 1913, a distinction that seemed at last to confirm the legitimacy of his life's work.[131]

Although he left Germany in 1903, Fried continued to exert an overbearing influence on the German peace movement. He never forgave the German Peace Society for expelling him, and fought with nearly everyone who was prominent in it; the Stuttgart leadership found it just as difficult to live up to his expectations as the Berlin committee had in the 1890s. In order to shape the German peace movement according to his own ideals, Fried sought disciples in leaders of the *Ortsgruppen*, most importantly in Hamburg, and he was not above fostering revolt against the Stuttgart

[129] See *Verzeichnis von 1000 Zeitungs-Artikeln Alfred H. Frieds zur Friedensbewegung (Bis März 1908)* (Berlin, 1908).

[130] Kempf, *Bertha von Suttner*, pp. 95–98.

[131] NL Wehberg (59a), Fried to Wehberg, Vienna, 15 February 1912; NL Fried, Wehberg to Fried, Düsseldorf, 20 June 1913; cf. FW, XXV (1925), 50.

committee.[132] He also cultivated the friendship of several young jurists, who became interested in the peace movement and promised to bring to it the more rigid discipline of their profession. In particular, he was drawn to a young lawyer and publicist in Düsseldorf, Hans Wehberg, whom he groomed as his successor in Germany by warning him to avoid close association with the German Peace Society.[133] In spite of his incessant criticism of the German peace movement, Fried more than anyone else was responsible for what little success it enjoyed in German society, and even the German pacifists admitted his indispensability. Fried was not fortunate enough to die before the war that signalled his complete failure broke out. Forced into exile in Zurich during the war, he continued to publish his journal, but his life had really ended years before his sudden death in 1921.[134]

"Fried is very active and enthusiastic," Adolf Richter wrote in 1902, "but unfortunately he has so many disagreeable qualities that he has been unable to win friends among us."[135] Richter was in a good position to appreciate the antagonisms between Fried and other German pacifists, since it was frequently his lot to resolve them. Having made a modest fortune in gold and silver processing in Pforzheim, Richter devoted himself to politics, serving as local coordinator of the German People's party and holding numerous local offices.[136] In 1879 he joined Lemonnier's *Ligue inter-*

[132] NL Fried, Jacob Wolff to Heinrich Harder, Hamburg, 19 November 1903; Fried to Harder, Vienna, 14 April 1905.

[133] NL Wehberg (59a), Fried to Wehberg, Vienna, 15 December 1911; NL Wehberg (59b), Fried to Wehberg, Vienna, 8 March 1913.

[134] NL Wehberg (51), Neufville to Wehberg, Blonay, 31 December 1926.

[135] BIP (vB6), Richter to Ducommun, Pforzheim, May 1902.

[136] On Richter see Adolf Richter, "33 Jahre im Dienste des Weltfriedens," in Georg Grosch, ed., *Deutsche Pazifisten: Eine Sammlung von Vorkämpfern der Friedensbewegung in Deutschland* (Stuttgart, 1920), pp. 8–16; cf. ER, I (1912), 119–22; NL Fried, Richter to Fried, Pforzheim, 3 November 1892; Wehberg, *Führer*, pp. 11–13.

nationale de la paix et de la liberté; for years he was the only German to attend international peace congresses, and he continued until the turn of the century to be the principal representative of the German pacifists abroad. In 1905, however, he suffered a heart attack and was forced to confine his activities. Thereafter his role as president of the German Peace Society was largely symbolic.

With Richter incapacitated, leadership of the German Peace Society devolved onto Otto Umfrid, in some ways the most remarkable figure in the German peace movement.[137] Born in 1857 in the small town of Nürtingen, Umfrid was exposed by his father to the philosophy of Karl Christian Planck, who was to be the dominant intellectual influence in his life. In a series of treatises, whose turgidity rivalled those of his fellow Swabian Hegel, Planck developed a system that purported to transcend the dualism of matter and spirit in a great pantheistic unity. The social implications of this system pointed toward corporativism, but for Umfrid the central aspect of Planck's thought was its affirmation of the unity of all existence. From this Umfrid derived his commitment to working for the international political reforms that would reflect the unity of mankind.

For a German Evangelical pastor to hold such views was difficult, even in the politically liberal kingdom of Württemberg, and Umfrid was constantly in trouble with his superiors in the church. Nonetheless, his activity in the service of the peace movement was so prodigious that Fried once remarked that it would be an understatement to call

---

[137] The East German historian Walter Bredendiek is preparing a biography of Umfrid. See also Bredendiek, "Otto Umfrid—ein vergessener Vorkämpfer für eine Welt ohne Krieg: Zu seinem fünfzigsten Todestag," *Stimme* (Stimme der Gemeinde zum kirchlichen Leben, zur Politik, Wirtschaft und Kultur, 13) XXII (1970), 394–402; Umfrid, "Meine Erlebnisse in der Friedensbewegung," ER, 1 (1912), 144–46; Mathilde Planck, "Otto Umfrid," FW, XXII (1920), 206–208; Grete Umfrid, ed., *Zum Gedächtnis von Otto Umfrid*; Wehberg, *Führer*, pp. 41–44.

Umfrid indefatigable.[138] In addition to his professional commitments, which included editing a regular leaflet for a parish of six thousand in Stuttgart, Umfrid found time to administer the German Peace Society and to compose disputatious tracts and articles for pacifist journals and left-liberal newspapers, such as the *Beobachter* in Stuttgart.[139]

A courageous and persistent man, Otto Umfrid could almost be cast as an heroic figure, the "militant pacifist" struggling undaunted in the face of overwhelming odds, were it not for the underlying element of pathos in his personality and career. "I am neither a scholar nor a born journalist," he once wrote, "neither a brilliant speaker nor a magnetic agitator."[140] This self-characterization was entirely apt. An aggressive polemicist, he took pride in engaging opponents of the peace movement in debate, but he was not very effective. Throughout his career in the movement he lived in the shadow of Fried, whom he alternately adulated and vilified. In his dealings with others, too, he combined belligerence with a severe self-depreciation that made him uncomfortable to be around.[141] In 1908 an incurable disease destroyed the retina of one eye and began to attack the other. As his health deteriorated, he was plagued by self-doubts and spells of profound depression, in which he despaired of the peace movement and his own failure to win adequate recognition. In an act of genuine compassion, as well as a tribute to Umfrid's essential contribution to pacifism in Germany, Fried nominated him in 1913 and again in 1914 for the Nobel Peace Prize, but the outbreak of the war prompted the Nobel Committee to suspend the award of any peace prize.[142] Although the war deprived him of the

[138] FW, XII (1910), 78; PD, XX (1910), 142.

[139] NL Wehberg (88), Umfrid to Wehberg, Stuttgart, 29 July 1912, 10 June 1913, 19 February 1914.

[140] NL Wehberg (88), Umfrid to Wehberg, Stuttgart, 27 May 1913.

[141] NL M. Quidde (380/59), Ludwig Quidde to Margarethe Quidde, London, 19 May 1908.

[142] NL Fried, Fried to Nobelkomitee des norwegischen Storthing,

recognition he deserved, Umfrid's efforts did not go unappreciated, for his fellow pacifists regarded him on a level with Suttner and Fried.[143] Indeed, Otto Umfrid was the German Peace Society's principal asset during the period before the war, and in many respects his career epitomized the futility of the pacifist crusade in imperial Germany. By 1914 he was totally blind and withdrew during the war to contemplate the meaning of Planck's philosophy. After learning that his only son had been wounded in combat and captured by the British, he suffered a nervous breakdown and finally died in 1920, like Fried, a broken man.

Of scarcely less importance than Umfrid for the German peace movement was Ludwig Quidde.[144] A student of Hermann Baumgarten, Julius Weizsäcker, and Gustav Schmoller, Quidde seemed destined for a brilliant career as an historian. Under the sponsorship of Weizsäcker and Heinrich von Sybel he was installed in the early 1880s as principal editor of the Imperial *Reichstagsakten* for the Bavarian Academy of Sciences. By the end of the decade he had established a considerable reputation and became the editor of the new *Deutsche Zeitschrift für Geschichtswissenschaft*. Between 1890 and 1892 he served as director of the Royal Prussian Historical Institute in Rome, before returning to work on the *Reichstagsakten* in Munich.

A democrat by persuasion, Quidde became interested in politics in the early 1890s. In 1893 he published an anonymous critique of Caprivi's arms bill, in which he warned of the pervasive influence of the German military.[145] The next

---

Vienna, 17 January 1913, 7 January 1914; Alfred H. Fried, *Mein Kriegs-Tagebuch* (4 vols., Zurich, 1918–20), I, 213.

[143] Goldscheid, *Fried Gedenkblätter*, p. 65.

[144] Taube, *Ludwig Quidde*; Wehberg, *Ludwig Quidde*; NL L. Quidde, Quidde MS, "Aus den Erinnerungen eines alten Pazifisten" (1935); Wehberg, *Führer*, pp. 26–31; Wehberg, "Ludwig Quidde, ein deutscher Pazifist," *Die Wage* xxv (1922), 61–63.

[145] *Der Militarismus im heutigen deutschen Reich: Eine Anklageschrift* (Stuttgart, 1893).

year he brought out a small book that committed him irre-
vocably to politics, as it destroyed his academic career. Os-
tensibly a historical sketch of the Roman emperor Caligula,
the pamphlet was quickly recognized as an irreverent
parody of the German emperor William II.[146] Publication
of the pamphlet was an act of professional suicide, and it
attached a stigma to Quidde that survived into the 1920s.
Although the authorities were unable to demonstrate that
the book was libelous, Quidde stood with one foot in jail
throughout the prewar era and did in fact spend three
months in prison in 1896 on charges of *Majestätsbeleidi-
gung*.[147] He was quickly removed from the editorship of the
Reichstagsakten and was forced to abandon any hope of
securing a university chair. Officials treated him like a
pariah; in the German foreign office he was known as "the
infamous Dr. Quidde," and people of prominence were hesitant to deal with him politically or socially.[148] The pacifists
were also touched by Quidde's ostracism. When he was preparing for the Universal Peace Congress in Munich in 1907,
Quidde experienced extreme difficulty in finding people to
serve with him on the executive committee.[149] Association
with him became so compromising that when a replacement
had to be found for Richter as president of the German
Peace Society, Quidde, though a logical choice, was selected
only with reluctance and after others had declined.

Fortunately, the publication of *Caligula* did not bring
financial ruin too, for Quidde was a man of some means and
had married well. He was consequently able to devote himself to politics and the peace movement, in addition to pursuing his historical studies as a private scholar in Munich.
During the 1890s he emerged as a leader of the *Süd-*

[146] *Caligula: Eine Studie über römischen Cäsarenwahnsinn* (Leipzig,
1894).

[147] Taube, *Ludwig Quidde*, pp. 99–101.

[148] AA, Eur. Gen. 37 number 1, Bd. 7, A2992 (ACP 103), Monts to
Hohenlohe, Munich, 12 March 1899.

[149] NL Fried, Quidde to Fried, Munich, 27 May 1907; FW, xxxviii
(1938), 86.

deutsche Volkspartei in Bavaria and served in the Bavarian Landtag continuously after 1903, although his candidacy for the Reichstag in 1907 was unsuccessful. After 1900 he devoted himself increasingly to the peace movement, serving as German representative on the International Peace Bureau, as a member of the board of directors of the German Peace Society, and as a participant in virtually every committee the peace society established. Fluent in four languages, he replaced Richter as the leading German delegate at Universal Peace Congresses. In view of his many services to the peace movement, the pacifists were not altogether reluctant to have him president of the German Peace Society.

Quidde was reputed to be the great organizer and strategist of the German peace movement, the man who understood politics and could make pacifism more effective in high circles. While his skills as an administrator and organizer were considerable, his reputation among the pacifists as an adroit politician was an interesting comment on the general level of political intelligence in the German peace movement. Ernst Müller-Meiningen, who had frequent political contact with Quidde, used to refer to him as *"Ludwig das Kind,"* and one scholar has recently called him aptly an *"anima candidissima."*[150] Compared to his pacifist colleagues, Quidde might have been a man of uncommon political sense, but he remained an idealist, whose willingness to make sacrifices in the service of his cause was occasionally reckless and exasperated the seasoned politicians with whom he worked.

Not even the outbreak of war in 1914 could deter this *Parzifalnatur.*[151] Throughout the war he agitated in favor

[150] Joachim Reimann, "Der politische Liberalismus in der Krise der Revolution," in Karl Bosl, ed., *Bayern im Umbruch: Die Revolution von 1918, ihre Voraussetzungen, ihr Verlauf und ihre Folgen* (Munich and Vienna, 1969), p. 182; Karl Holl, "Ludwig Quidde," *Liberal* XIII (March 1971), 228.

[151] Wehberg, "Ludwig Quidde 80 Jahre alt!" FW, XXXVIII (1938),

of a moderate peace, and though the war failed to bring the justice in international relations he had hoped for, he continued his efforts at the head of the German Peace Society until 1929, when internal dissensions forced his resignation. His services to world peace were recognized in 1927 when he received the Nobel Peace Prize, the first *Reichsdeutscher* to be so honored. In 1933 he fled to Switzerland. By now a poor man, he survived by gardening and doing other odd jobs in Geneva, where he died in 1941 at the age of eighty-three.

Quidde, Umfrid, Richter, Fried, Suttner, and a small group of others constituted the foundation of the German Peace Society. Their endorsement of international arbitration and arms limitation was unqualified, and their dedication to pursuing these goals was intense. Yet their power and influence were negligible. The peace society they led was confined to a narrow geographical and social base, and the commitment of most of its nominal adherents was minimal. The peace society's failure to expand beyond this restricted base demonstrated the extravagance of the pacifists' expectation, announced at the founding of the German Peace Society, that they could mobilize German society directly by convincing a majority of Germans to join the peace society. This failure was also symptomatic of the tensions between the peace movement and the German political system—tensions that became more clearly defined as the pacifists set out, with whatever meager human and financial resources they could find, to exert an influence on German political culture. Indeed, the character of these tensions became manifest as soon as the pacifists attempted to systematize and clarify their ideology in order to make their campaign in Germany more persuasive.

---

62. Not even the Nazi *Machtergreifung* caused him to abandon his optimism: see Quidde, "Der deutsche Pazifismus in nationalsozialistischer Beleuchtung," FW, xxxiv (1934), 150–53.

3

The Ideology of German Pacifism

By even the most compassionate standards of literary criticism, the artistic value of Bertha von Suttner's novel, *Die Waffen nieder!* is not very high. The plot concerns an Austrian countess who, during the wars of 1859–71, successively loses two husbands, most of her immediate family, a fortune, and her pet dog. She emerges chastened from the ordeal, and when she learns of the work of Hodgson Pratt, she devotes the rest of her life to the cause of universal peace. The prevailing tone of the novel is melodramatic sentimentality, despite the fact that much of the book consists of war scenes described in lurid detail. The characters are shallow representations of various points of view, and the dialogue is declamatory and tedious. In view of these considerable literary failings, it is difficult to argue with the judgment of one reviewer who called it "an extremely bad novel."[1]

However, as no less a critic than Benno von Wiese has pointed out, to judge the novel on these terms would be to miss the point.[2] It was conceived as a polemic, designed to draw the attention of the public to realities of warfare too often overlooked in literature. Judged on its own terms, the novel was one of the most successful and effective pieces of antiwar literature ever written.

[1] Karl Bleibtreu, "Der falsche Friedenspreis der Nobelstiftung," *Die Gegenwart* LXXIV (1908), 418. Many pacifists considered Bertha von Suttner one of the great luminaries of world literature: see VF, XIV (1913), 64. Fried, however, did not: see Fried, *Jugenderinnerungen*, p. 19.

[2] Benno von Wiese, *Politische Dichtung Deutschlands* (Berlin, 1931), pp. 10–11, cited in P. B. Wiener, "Bertha von Suttner and the Political Novel," in Siegbert S. Prawer, *et al.*, *Essays in German Language, Culture and Society* (London, 1969), pp. 162–63.

The historical significance of the novel derives not only from its immense popular appeal, but from the fact that it was the principal ideological document of the German peace movement until after the turn of the century. The book was a compelling protest against the outrage done by warfare to common standards of human decency. The pacifism that informed this protest assumed that men were gifted by nature with the capacity for rational and ethical conduct; hence there existed a community of moral consciousness among all men, the dictates of which not only proscribed warfare, but imposed an ethical obligation to work actively against it.

As an expression of moral protest and a statement of precept, *Die Waffen nieder!* was effective. As an analysis of the causes of war and a proposal for constructive reform it was not very compelling. The most extended discussion of ways to eliminate war comes in the last chapter of the novel and concludes when the son of the heroine proclaims:

> as long as we cling to the past we shall remain savages. But we are already standing at the threshold of a new era —gazes are directed forward, everything is pushing powerfully on to another, a higher condition [*Gestaltung*]. . . . Savagery, with its idols and weapons—these are already repelling people. If we are still closer to barbarism than most people think, we are perhaps also closer to ennoblement than many hope. *The prince or statesman is perhaps already alive* who will accomplish what will be regarded in the future as the most glorious and brilliant of all deeds—who will bring about general disarmament. . . . The realization is already dawning that justice should serve as the foundation of all social existence . . . and from such a realization human nature, the nobility of humanity, shall bloom forth.[3]

This passage is a distillation of Bertha von Suttner's pacifism. It reveals the eloquence as well as the limitations of an

[3] Bertha von Suttner, *Die Waffen nieder! Eine Lebensgeschichte* (38th ed., 2 vols., Dresden, n.d.), II, 322-23 (italics in the original).

approach that emphasized ethical ennoblement as the solution to the problem of war.

Bertha von Suttner was first and foremost a moralist. Because she refused to exclude politics from the purview of morality, she regarded both warfare and its elimination as intrinsically ethical problems. She ascribed the existence of war, as well as the willingness to countenance its use, to moral ignorance. As she wrote in 1912, "War continues to exist not because there is evil in the world, but because people still hold war to be a good thing."[4] Her solution to the problem was education and enlightenment to awaken the ethical consciousness that resided in all men. The result would not be a transformation of human nature, but rather the realization of human potential, or, to paraphrase her own words, "the blooming forth of the nobility of humanity."

She believed further that the translation of this noble ethic into international reform would follow naturally, as soon as moral consciousness had become so pervasive that it compelled a "prince or statesman [who] is perhaps already alive" to take the initiative in negotiating treaties of disarmament and arbitration. Political change merely required the moral enlightenment of heads of state. "William II wanted his warships," she wrote to Fried in 1898, "so he demanded them and now he has them. If he wanted peace and disarmament just as much, he could have them too."[5] As this assertion suggests, Bertha von Suttner's view of politics and society was fundamentally conservative. Just as the ethical awareness of which she spoke entailed no change in human nature, the political reforms she envisaged presupposed no basic change in the existing social or political order and could in fact be realized virtually overnight. Capacity for moral insight was not the product of any particular social or political system; it inhered in all political leaders, be they democrats or autocrats, by virtue of their being human.

Bertha von Suttner was also an optimist. The inspiration

[4] FW, xiv (1912), 112.
[5] SFC, Suttner to Fried, Vienna, 10 March 1898.

of Comte, Darwin, Spencer, Buckle, and other theoreticians of progress was evident in her major novels, though less in *Die Waffen nieder!* than in *Das Maschinenzeitalter.*[6] While her pacifism rested on no specific analysis of patterns of social or political change, contemporary theories of progress served as philosophical corroboration for her almost intuitive confidence that the human condition was bound to improve, and that the growth of moral awareness and the definitive elimination of warfare were to be aspects of this process.

The strength of Bertha von Suttner's pacifism lay less in its intellectual precision than in the emotive power of its idealism. She paid little attention to the deterministic implications of the theories to which she appealed and emphasized the need for moral commitment in overcoming war. Nor was she concerned by the fact that her pacifism made political action irrelevant by assuming a more or less automatic transition from moral awareness to international reform. Indeed, the humanitarian crusade she envisaged was to transcend politics, religious divisions, and class conflict.

The German peace movement was animated by Suttner's crusading idealism, but the history of the early peace societies demonstrated the practical drawbacks of her approach. The movement's program was little more than an affirmation of the desirability of peace and arbitration. Since they eschewed politics and did not wish to antagonize anyone, pacifists emphasized concepts like "humanity," "justice," and "harmony." Peace meetings were devoted to protesting the immorality of war and militarism, and they often consisted of poetry readings and dramatic sketches, followed by concerts or dances—all of which exuded, as Carl von Ossietsky later recalled of Bertha von Suttner, "a gentle perfume of absurdity."[7] Such activities hardly enhanced the

[6] See Stiewe, "Die bürgerliche deutsche Friedensbewegung," pp. 249–53.

[7] Quoted in Deak, *Left-Wing Intellectuals*, pp. 113–14; cf. NL Fried, Quidde to Fried, Munich, 5 November 1894; Fried to Wirth, Berlin, 9 November 1895; Fried to Grosch, Vienna, 10 January 1914.

public image of the German Peace Society, and it soon acquired a reputation of being "a comical sewing bee composed of sentimental aunts of both sexes."[8]

A further liability of Bertha von Suttner's pacifism was that its emotional moralism repelled many people who were seriously interested in arbitration and might otherwise have become involved in the peace society. One incident in the 1890s pointed this out clearly. Although Eugen Schlief's disagreements with Suttner and Fried over the organization and mission of the German Peace Society had prevented him from participating in the founding of the organization, he did subsequently become active for a short time in the Berlin committee. During this period he concluded that the peace society, as it was then set up, would be unable to accomplish anything. His repeated pleas that incantations to peace and humanity be replaced with politically oriented agitation provoked Bertha von Suttner to chide him for his want of humanitarian idealism.[9] When he realized that his attempts to realign the peace movement according to his own ideas were bound to fail, he resigned from the German Peace Society. As he did so, he published another exposition of his theories on international law and added some gratuitous observations on the "apostles of peace," whose approach, he noted, was given to "such phenomenal lack of conceptual clarity, such enormous naiveté . . . and such receptivity for entirely empty, utopian fantasies that public opinion must regard any improvement in the present [international] situation as impossible."[10]

The categories in which Bertha von Suttner's pacifism was conceived invited such criticism from friends and enemies of the peace movement alike. An ideology of moral protest, it was vacuous as a constructive theory of interna-

---

[8] Kurt Hiller, *Leben gegen die Zeit* [*Logos*] (Reinbek, 1969), p. 148.
[9] Suttner to Schlief, 25 November 1893, in DWN, II (1893), 491–95.
[10] Eugen Schlief [pseud. B. O. T. Schafter], *Hohe Politik: Kritische Randbemerkungen zum internationalen Leben der Gegenwart* (2d ed., Berlin, 1902), p. 9; see SFC, Suttner to Fried, Vienna, 26 November 1898.

tional relations. Her pacifism inspired an intense commitment from the small group of pacifist leaders, but it severely limited the ability of the German peace movement to attract wider support. Her proposals for ending war seemed hopelessly superficial and naive. She called for arbitration and arms limitation on the basis of moral principle, but she could adduce little convincing evidence, beyond her own faith, that morality and law could in fact regulate international politics. As long as pacifists approached the problems of war and peace in these terms, it was difficult for anyone important to take them seriously, which made negligible their chances of mobilizing public opinion in Germany. No one was more sensitive to these limitations than Alfred Fried, who shortly after the turn of the century began to publicize a more intellectually rigorous and credible doctrine, which, he hoped, would make pacifism more appealing and influential in Germany.

Alfred Fried and the Development of a Scientific Pacifism

Alfred Fried was drawn into the peace movement by Bertha von Suttner, and his pacifism was originally inspired by her views on the problems of war and its elimination. In 1894 he published a catalogue of aphoristic propositions about the peace movement, which he later characterized as a "silly work of youth," but which clearly showed Suttner's influence both in its tone and its emphasis on ethical insight as the key to peace.[11] However, as his frustrations with the German Peace Society grew, he increasingly questioned the efficacy of the ideology it espoused. He concluded that German pacifism was little more than an affirmation of faith that morality would govern international relations, but that unsupported by empirical evidence, this affirmation was hardly credible in an era marked by international tension.

In the later 1890s Fried began to read widely in an effort

[11] Fried, *Friedens-Katechismus: Ein Compendium der Friedenslehre* (Dresden and Leipzig, 1894); NL Wehberg (59a), Fried to Wehberg, Vienna, 1 March 1910; cf. FW, xxv (1925), 47.

to formulate a pacifist ideology more consistent with the apparent realities of international relations. It is difficult to determine exactly what he read, for his subsequent writings reflected the influence of many sources, including the pacifist liberalism of Richard Cobden, the writings of the utopian socialists, and the theories of progress that colored Bertha von Suttner's pacifism. However, the influence of certain figures was particularly marked and can be documented.

Fried found the conceptual framework for his new ideology in an unlikely place, the writings of Marx. Although he was a member of the SPD throughout the 1890s and occasionally served as a correspondent for *Vorwärts*, Fried did not read Marx closely until the end of the decade, and even then his understanding was rather shallow. Nevertheless, his reading of Marx convinced him of the futility of Bertha von Suttner's expectations and suggested to him an alternative approach. In a letter to the baroness in March 1898, which announced his intellectual parting of ways, Fried wrote:

> You still believe that all progress in the world can be decreed, that any individual who happens to find himself in power could bring about a great revolution and refashion the world according to our ideas. No, he cannot do that, for that would mean placing himself beyond the limits of his power. . . . William II cannot convoke an international disarmament conference, even if he wanted to, because the interested circles of industry and commerce, who possess power, need the division rather than the consolidation of nations in order to carry on their despoilation to greater advantage.[12]

Fried's debt to Marx was limited, however, and he stopped far short of Marx's conclusion that only the revolutionary overthrow of capitalism would bring world peace. In fact, Fried extracted from Marx only the basic insight that social

---

[12] NL Fried, Fried to Suttner, Berlin, 8 March 1898; see Goldscheid, *Fried Gedenkblätter*, p. 22.

and economic forces, and not moral consciousness, determined political behavior and that these forces developed
according to regular patterns.

In the work of the contemporary Russian sociologist,
Jacob Novikow, Fried found an analysis of socio-economic
developments that was much more cordial than Marxism
to his own ideas about peace.[13] A disciple of Montesquieu,
Adam Smith, Comte, and Spencer, Novikow predicted that
world federation would result from the natural development of society—a process he held to be governed by predictable rules. Specifically, Novikow believed that social relationships were dominated by struggle and competition,
but instead of concluding that this condemned mankind to
perpetual violence, he demonstrated how struggle was being sublimated into peaceful economic and cultural competition, as societies became increasingly interdependent. The
growth of international economic interdependence, the
spread of political and intellectual contacts across national
frontiers, and the biological evolution of humanity into an
undifferentiated organism were all preparing the way for
the realization that world federation should be the product
of social evolution.[14] Fried was so impressed by the scholarly sobriety of Novikow's work that he became his German
translator, as well as his regular correspondent.

Fried also studied the legal ramifications of the developments Novikow described. Here his principal source was
Ludwig Quidde. As a prelude to his possible *Habilitation*
Quidde had begun work in the early 1880s on the Peace of
God movement during the thirteenth and fourteenth centuries.[15] After he became involved in the peace movement
in the 1890s, he was struck by the parallel between the
gradual elimination of the *Fehderecht* toward the end of

[13] On Novikow see Cooper, "Peace and Internationalism," pp. 34–
105; Langer, *Diplomacy of Imperialism*, pp. 86–87.

[14] Novikow, *Die Föderation Europas* (Berlin and Berne, 1901).

[15] Quidde, *Studien zur Geschichte des Rheinischen Landfriedensbundes von 1259* (Frankfurt, 1885).

the Middle Ages and the process that he and other pacifists believed would lead to the end of violence among nations. In 1900 he composed a lecture for delivery at peace meetings, which emphasized this parallel and suggested a regular pattern of historical development marked by the replacement of violence by law in increasingly comprehensive political units.[16]

Fried's legal education also included study of the writings of Eugen Schlief, who insisted that the source of international law was to be the sovereign state rather than the abstract norms of morality. Although he never fully accepted or understood the implications of this legal positivism, Fried's reading of Schlief contributed to his determination to rid pacifism of its ethical *motif* and concentrate on material factors underlying the development of international law.[17]

Finally, Fried's belief that material factors would make possible the end of warfare was nurtured by the publication, in 1898, of a remarkable set of volumes that seemed to demonstrate conclusively that under modern conditions war had become impossible. Entitled *The War of the Future in Its Technical, Economic and Political Significance*, the study was written by Ivan Bloch, a Polish banker who had amassed such a fortune in railway construction that he was known as the "Polish Rothschild."[18] He was also a pacifist, and his concern over the likely consequences of a modern

[16] NL Fried, Quidde to Fried, Munich, 8 April 1901; *Münchner Freie Presse*, 26 November 1900.

[17] NL Fried, Fried to Schlief, Vienna, 1 November 1903; cf. Fried, *Jugenderinnerungen*, pp. 32–33.

[18] Johann von Bloch, *Der Krieg: Uebersetzung des russischen Werkes des Autors: Der zukünftige Krieg in seiner technischen, volkswirtschaftlichen und politischen Bedeutung* (6 vols., Berlin, 1899). For a brief biographical sketch of Bloch see Edwin D. Mead's introduction to the English condensation: Jean de Bloch, *The Future of War* (Boston, 1914). For an interesting discussion of Bloch and this genre see I. F. Clarke, *Voices Prophesying War, 1763–1984* (London, 1966), esp. pp. 107–61.

war caused him to write this enormous study, which was said to have contributed to the tsar's decision to convoke the first Hague conference.

In six volumes Bloch explored all aspects of war under modern conditions. He devoted single volumes to weaponry and munitions, strategy and tactics in land warfare, war at sea, economic dislocation and material losses, and the problem of casualties. He embellished the study with all manner of illustrations, statistics, graphs, maps, and diagrams. From this mountain of data Bloch concluded, in the first place, that the development of weaponry since the Franco-Prussian War dictated that any future war would entail the unprecedented slaughter of combatants. He then demonstrated that in any confrontation between modern fighting forces an immense advantage would accrue to those on the defense. Provisioned with rapid-firing, long-range firearms and employing the latest entrenching techniques, troops manning defensive positions would be virtually invulnerable; altogether Bloch estimated that the advantage of the defensive forces would be roughly eight to one. The formidability of the defense would in turn make swift offensive campaigns and decisive victories impossible. Thus, Bloch concluded that the war of the future would result in a stalemate, with both sides exhausting themselves in futile attacks. Moreover, such a prolonged military encounter would inevitably have disastrous repercussions on the home front. Since the most productive sectors of society would have been conscripted, the economies of the belligerents would soon collapse under the titantic logistical requirements of modern field armies. Bloch then concluded his prophetic vision with a picture of general chaos, with privation, dislocation, and resentment leading to political collapse and social revolution.[19]

Bloch wrote this study explicitly to demonstrate that war

[19] Novikow had earlier come to similar, though less alarming conclusions: see Novikow, *Der Krieg und seine angeblichen Wohltaten* (Leipzig, 1896). Fried also translated this study into German.

had become a practical impossibility and that the only alternative was international arbitration. In the final volume he summarized his observations with a rhetorical question: "even in the leading circles of Europe hardly anyone will dare deny that it will be possible to bring our means of annihilation to such a degree of perfection that war must become completely impossible. But the question is: have we not already reached such a stage of development in military apparatus, does that sum total of conditions not already exist under which we must eliminate war, since it has not only become a shattering experience, but also politically fruitless?"[20] Despite its admitted partiality, Bloch's study was an impressive *tour de force* and attracted widespread attention in military circles. To Alfred Fried it was of particular importance, for it seemed to provide unimpeachable scientific evidence in support of his aversion to warfare.

Hans Wehberg has suggested that the meager results of the Hague conference prompted Fried to develop a theory of pacifism that emphasized the gradual evolution of society toward international organization.[21] The Hague conference did undoubtedly influence Fried's outlook, insofar as it confirmed his view that the world would not change overnight. However, it is clear from his correspondence and published writings that the transformation of his thought had begun several years before. As early as 1897, for instance, he had claimed that technological advances were making possible the rule of law in international affairs.[22] By the turn of the century he had assembled a large inventory of intellectual fragments, from which he proceeded eclectically to construct a new pacifist ideology.

[20] *Der Krieg*, vi, 360; see also *ibid.*, i, ix–xviii; vi, 315–33.

[21] Wehberg, "Alfred Hermann Fried," *Neue Deutsche Biographie*, v, 441–42; Wehberg, "Alfred Fried," *Deutsches Biographisches Jahrbuch*, iii, 105–106; NL Wehberg (59a), Fried to Wehberg, Vienna, 1 March 1910.

[22] Fried, "Die moderne Friedensbewegung," *Unter der weissen Fahne: Aus der Mappe eines Friedensjournalisten* (Berlin, 1901), pp. 21–26.

The product of Fried's *Bildungsjahre* was his *Handbuch der Friedensbewegung*, published in 1905, in which he sought to sever all ties with moralism and to found pacifism on principles whose validity would stand the test of scientific scrutiny.[23] He began with the assertion, drawn from Novikow and confirmed, Fried believed, by empirical observation, that struggle (*Kampf*) dominated all human relationships: "From the great struggles of the political parties down into the smallest subgroupings of social life, the home, the workshop, even the children's room, there is nothing but bitter, unremitting struggle."[24] Fried's characterization of primitive culture was Hobbesian: here human struggle appeared in its most savage form, as unrestricted physical conflict (*Krieg*). The need for survival and security in this state of universal war caused individuals to band together in the earliest forms of social organization—the tribe and family. These groups then became the units among which physical conflict was waged, but within each, struggle was moderated in the interests of group survival. Gradually, by conquest and cooperation, social communities expanded, enlarging the area in which physical conflict was no longer tolerated. The communities' need for survival then led to the adoption of a new device for ensuring internal harmony: "There appeared law; it became increasingly established in social intercourse and increasingly comprehensive. In the same measure as the social community expanded and law became more powerful, physical conflict, war, was restricted, so that it only came into play in dealing with those outside the community."[25] The growth of social communities, both in complexity and expanse, made the rule of law increasingly comprehensive in human affairs. This process, which in Fried's view represented the main theme in western history, had reached its highest stage to date with the appearance of the modern nation-

[23] Fried, *Handbuch der Friedensbewegung* (Vienna and Leipzig, 1905).

[24] *Ibid.*, p. 12.   [25] *Ibid.*, p. 11.

state. War was now possible only among sovereign states; within each state law had proscribed physical conflict, and struggle had been sublimated into civilized, legal outlets, such as economic competition and electoral contests.

Fried believed that the expansion of the purview of legal relationships was a natural and inexorable process, analogous to the biological evolution of higher organisms. He was also convinced that the process had not culminated in the nation-state and that the material foundations were being laid for an international social and legal community. As evidence he pointed out that the ongoing internationalization of transportation, communications, industry, commerce, science, and culture was giving rise to a completely new style of life: "We citizens of the twentieth century have achieved a kind of omnipresence which would have seemed like a fairy tale to our forefathers. We are everywhere, we converse everywhere with one another, we trade everywhere, and we are universally dependent."[26] In fact, the internationalization of society had already bound the people of the civilized world into a community of interest: "We have become citizens of the world, true cosmopolitans who . . . owe [our] allegiance to the great goals of all humanity. This organization can no longer be torn apart, pushed back, or restrained. Its furious [rasend] development proceeds every day and ties the bond of interests ever tighter, so that we can justifiably say that the point has been reached where the common interests of the civilized nations will, by their very multitude, overwhelm and settle the small divisive issues that still exist."[27]

On the basis of these observations, Fried predicted the definitive end of war. Drawing directly from Ivan Bloch, he noted that internationalization, and the technological advances that had stimulated it, had made warfare unfeasible; war in modern conditions would destroy the delicate network of international ties, resulting in the economic ruin of

[26] *Ibid.*, p. 46.   [27] *Ibid.*, p. 47.

all countries involved. However, internationalization was at the same time making war progressively less likely. Using the historical parallels suggested to him by Quidde, Fried asserted that the development of an international social community was the prelude to an international legal and political community. The outlines of an international legal system, including an international court of justice, had already appeared, and Fried was confident that law would soon regulate all international disputes. The result would be the elimination of physical conflict within the international community and its replacement with peaceful competition among the nations for the ultimate benefit of mankind.

Fried's "scientific pacifism" was almost entirely unoriginal. It was a restatement of the traditional liberal argument that free trade would create an international community of interests and make war impossible. To Cobdenism Fried added some other theories of progress, gleaned principally from Novikow, and arrived at the conclusion that the growth of international community, though slow, was inevitable, guaranteed by the laws of society and historical development.

The determinism in this ideology was for Fried its most appealing feature. It would enable those who espoused scientific pacifism to style themselves as realists whose program merely affirmed the inevitable. Fried believed that he had purged all ethical considerations and vestiges of sentimentality from his system. He claimed that scientific pacifism rested exclusively on objective, scientifically valid evidence. The establishment of an international organization to settle disputes did not depend upon a moral commitment to reshape society and politics; it would come inexorably into existence because of the natural forces already at work in society.

In the belief that scientific pacifism held the key to success for the peace movement, Fried began to purvey his theories among the German pacifists. He disparaged appeals to sentiment and idealism in opposing war. He condemned ethical aversion to warfare as intuitive and hence scientifically unsound. Opposition to war for reasons that did not emphasize the natural evolution of society he labeled romantic or utopian.[28] He even recommended to the German Peace Society that it eliminate poetry from all its activities, since poetry appealed to the emotions and was inappropriate for a scientific movement.[29] Fried's hostility toward nonscientific varieties of pacifism ran the risk of being construed as an attack on Bertha von Suttner, but so immense was her prestige and so deep was Fried's own respect for her, that his attacks on idealism and sentimentality always stopped short of the baroness. Instead, he found a convenient object for attack in Lina Morgenstern, an old feminist crusader active in the Berlin peace society, whom he portrayed as the epitome of the sentimental pacifist, "the lunatic enthusiast with the olive branch, who yearns for a world in which little lambs graze at the side of a babbling brook."[30]

Despite animosities between Fried and pacifist leaders in Germany, scientific pacifism rapidly became orthodox in the German peace movement. Leaders of the peace society were impressed by the logic of the scientific approach and the credibility it seemed to lend their cause. Umfrid recommended Fried's *Handbuch der Friedensbewegung* to German pacifists as an "indispensable tool."[31] Manifestoes issued by the peace society now emphasized that natural forces would give rise to international organization. Thus, in an appeal to German students in 1909, Richter and Umfrid announced: "If you familiarize yourselves with our

[28] FW, IV (1902), 146; FW, XII (1910), 222; VF, XII (1911), 91; cf. Hans Wehberg, "Les vingts premiers années du mouvement pacifiste en Allemagne," PD, XXII (1912), 234–36; Walther Nithack-Stahn, *Völkerfriede? Ein Streit-Gespräch* (Stuttgart, n.d.), p. 5.

[29] "Friedensbewegung und Lyrik," FW, V (1903), 21.

[30] FW, V (1903), 3; NL Fried, Lina Morgenstern to Fried, Berlin, 26 February 1906.

[31] VF, XII (1911), 84.

literature you will soon discover that what we are working for is only a natural development of human civilization, which must lead uninterruptedly to its appointed goal."[32] Even Bertha von Suttner succumbed, albeit with some misgiving, to scientific pacifism. In a letter of May 1907 she wrote that the peace movement "is a phenomenon which, based entirely on the law of evolution, endeavors to bring human society up to a higher level of development."[33]

The transformation of pacifism from a "critical theory" and an expression of moral protest into what Fried claimed was a *Wissenschaft* recalled earlier changes in Marxist socialism. Indeed, despite the fact that Fried's intellectual debt to Marx was limited, there were distinct parallels between scientific socialism and scientific pacifism.[34] Both were products of an era enchanted by science, and both repudiated antecedent doctrines that had relied on good will or moral conviction to bring reform. Both bodies of thought looked instead to the material factors at work in society, and although they disagreed radically about the *dénouement* of social development, both insisted that the processes they described were scientifically determined. Finally, this determinism raised in both systems serious tactical and philosophical issues, which focused upon the role of free will in effecting political change and the relationship between theory and empirical reality. And several years after these issues had provoked the revisionist crisis in the Socialist International, they gave rise to a similar controversy within the German peace movement.

Although most German pacifists welcomed scientific pacifism, it posed problems that had not been apparent as long as the dominant impulse in pacifism was ethical. Scientific pacifism clearly implied that the inexorable growth of inter-

[32] FW, XI (1909), 100.
[33] BA, Kl. Erw., number 311, Bertha von Suttner an den Herausgeber einer Zeitschrift betr. Pazifismus, 3 May 1907; cf. Suttner, *Memoirs*, II, 403; Goldscheid, *Fried Gedenkblätter*, pp. 34–35.
[34] See Gross, *Pazifismus und Imperialismus*, pp. 52–56, 151–60.

national community would make resort to warfare progressively less frequent. Reality, however, belied this expectation, as Europeans continued to wage war in the twentieth century. Indeed, skeptics pointed out that the Hague conference in 1899 had, if anything, encouraged war.[35] It was particularly distressing to find Nicholas II, who had convoked the Hague conference and was consequently known as the *Friedensczar* in pacifist circles, at war in the far east, while England and the United States, the other principal champions of arbitration and arms limitation, showed no reluctance to go to war as soon as important interests were at stake. The recurrence of minor wars in the years before 1914 was thus a continual source of embarrassment to Fried and those who shared his beliefs, and it made necessary some doctrinal acrobatics.[36] Fried most commonly took refuge in the observation that history worked slowly and that there were still residues of the past that might occasionally cause wars.

A more serious drawback of scientific pacifism was its repudiation of idealism, which threatened to rob pacifism of its critical power.[37] The logic of Fried's arguments seemed to demand a passive acceptance of the forces at work in society, which would, entirely unaided by human volition, bring the end of warfare. However, many in the peace society, for whom ethical considerations were paramount, could not accept this proposition; nor were they made receptive to scientific pacifism by Fried's smug deprecation of their idealism.

Growing dissatisfaction over scientific pacifism led shortly before the war to what might be described as a neo-Kantian revival within the German Peace Society. In Kant's

---

[35] Karl von Stengel, "Die Idee des ewigen Friedens und die sogenannten Friedenskonferenzen," *Die Umschau*, XI (1907), 151; FB, VI (1905), 77; FW, XIV (1912), 151.

[36] FB, V (1904), 89–90; cf. FB, VI (1905), 23.

[37] Stiewe, "Die bürgerliche deutsche Friedensbewegung," pp. 185, 197, 212–13.

treatises on politics, the relationship between ethical freedom and natural necessity was subtle and intimately tied
to the whole of his epistemology. In sum, Kant both affirmed the moral obligation to work for peace and predicted that natural forces, such as man's inherent "asocial
sociability," would necessarily lead to peace. It is clear,
though, that the ethical *motif* was primary; for Kant the
significance of natural developments or propensities lay in
making the free exercise of man's moral judgment possible
and, indeed, eventually necessary. In the "First Supple-
ment" in his essay, *Perpetual Peace*, Kant concluded his discussion of the "Guarantee of Perpetual Peace" by describing the convergence of nature and moral will in these
terms: "In this way Nature guarantees the coming of perpetual peace, through the natural course of human propensities; not indeed with sufficient certainty to enable us
to prophesy the future of this ideal theoretically, but yet
clearly enough for practical purposes. And thus this guarantee of Nature makes it a duty that we should labor for
this end, an end which is no mere chimera."[38] Fried's thesis
that natural forces alone were sufficient to cause the end of
war upset the Kantian balance between nature and moral
duty. Significantly, two of Fried's principal sources, Novikow and Quidde, had preserved this balance in their own
theories, calling attention to the manner in which historical
developments were facilitating the growth of moral awareness of the perversity of warfare.[39] Quidde in particular
was disturbed at what Fried had done with historical evidence, for he was too good a historian to place any confidence in historical inevitability; he approached the prob-

[38] Quoted in John Herman Randall, Jr., *The Career of Philosophy*,
II: *From the German Enlightenment to the Age of Darwin* (New
York and London, 1965), pp. 190–91. The text of Kant's treatise on
perpetual peace appears in Carl Joachim Friedrich, *Inevitable Peace*
(Cambridge, Mass., 1948), pp. 245–81; also see above, chapter 2, n. 2.
[39] See Gross, *Pazifismus und Imperialismus*, p. 137; Cooper, "Peace
and Internationalism," p. 41.

lem of peace rather with an attitude of cautious optimism, which reflected his own deep commitment to Kantianism.[40] As he became more prominent in the peace movement, Quidde grew increasingly critical of scientific pacifism, insisting that the basic impulse in the pacifist doctrine was ethical and that, even with the propitious effects of social evolution, war would disappear only when men actively worked for its elimination. In the years immediately prior to the war Quidde emerged as the leader of a campaign to reaffirm the importance of ethics in pacifism.[41] In this connection his election to the presidency of the German Peace Society in 1914 was particularly significant, for it suggested that the revival of the ethical *motif* had become widespread in the peace society even before the war seemingly demonstrated the bankruptcy of scientific pacifism. In his speech to the congress that elected him president, Quidde sought to balance science and ethics, but he made it clear that he, like Kant, believed in the primacy of the latter: "Some claim they have overcome sentimental pacifism and that they represent a scientific variety. It is true that pacifism has developed and that today we possess a ramified literature that stands far above the old. But to distinguish between old and new pacifism harbors the danger that idealism will be sold short, or even repudiated altogether. Pacifism today has a scientific foundation which it utilizes, but it is not itself a science; it is a matter of orienting one's will [*Willensrichtung*]."[42] Referring then to the writings of Norman Angell, who had echoed Fried in claiming that there existed such economic and financial interdependence among civilized nations that war would be ruinous to all, Quidde pointed to the basic issue in the controversy over scientific pacifism: "Wars can break out, unfortunately, at any time, and peace will not emanate out of the factors Norman Angell

[40] Taube, *Ludwig Quidde*, pp. 68–69, 130.
[41] NL Fried, Paul Alber to Fried, Stuttgart, 18 August 1912; FB, XI (1910), 22; VF, XIII (1912), 102; VF, XIV (1913), 8, 17–18.
[42] VF, XV (1914), 81.

cites; it must instead, as the great Kant said, be founded [*gestiftet*]."[43]

German pacifists devoted a great deal of time to this ideological debate, but the philosophical cleavage between the idealists and the "scientists" was more apparent than real, or rather, it was less philosophical than psychological. While Fried's theory was more systematic and possessed more intellectual appeal than moralistic pacifism, the two were basically the same. Fried's intellect, like Bertha von Suttner's, was neither profound nor rigorous, and he failed to comprehend the problems involved in trying to predict the future on the basis of an allegedly scientific analysis of the past.[44] Robert Nisbet's comment on all developmentalist theories applies with particular force to Fried's scientific pacifism: "To believe that the vast, plural, and infinitely particular history of mankind can somehow be worked into ordered frameworks of either cyclical or linear development, that somehow progress (or degeneration) can be made endemic processes, fixed parts of reality, calls plainly for a gigantic act of faith. More, it calls for gigantic acts of compression of diversity into unity, of reduction of incredible complexity into simplicity, and transposition of the moral into the existential."[45] Despite an imposing array of evidence that he mustered in support of his contention that the triumph of pacifism would come as a product of history, Fried disregarded or dismissed as insignificant equally imposing indications that events might be leading toward a

[43] *Ibid.*

[44] For penetrating critiques of Fried's "scientific pacifism" see: Heinrich Rogge, *Nationale Friedenspolitik: Handbuch des Friedensproblems und seiner Wissenschaft* (Berlin, 1934), pp. 4–12; Gross, *Pazifismus und Imperialismus*, pp. 47–50; Liedtke, "Die Entwicklung des Pazifismus," pp. 206–20. Such criticism has not, however, prevented subsequent attempts to devise a "science of peace": see J. G. Starke, *An Introduction to the Science of Peace (Irenology)* (Leyden, 1968).

[45] Robert A. Nisbet, *Social Change and History: Aspects of the Western Theory of Development* (New York, 1969), p. 223.

major European war. In the final analysis, his vision of the future was based on his own assumptions about what the world ought to be like—assumptions he held in common with Suttner and Quidde. Afraid lest he seem naive, Fried was drawn to the apparent certainties of science because of the cogency they lent to his moral convictions. Despite his pretensions that he was a cool, objective scholar, Fried was, in Wehberg's words, "more than anything else, a man with a warm heart."[46] If all the scientific embellishments had never been contrived, Fried would still have been working for world peace, for the simple reason that he held it to be a good thing.

The ideology of German pacifism before the war was thus basically uniform. Differences among the German pacifists were rhetorical and involved questions of emphasis or nuance. Even Fried, in his conciliatory moments, argued that ethical considerations had an important contribution to make and that pacifism had to comprehend both the ethical and scientific approaches. This, of course, was also Quidde's contention. Indeed, it was the consensus among the German pacifists, all of whom were idealists, though many, like Fried, chose to accentuate scientific themes in an effort to portray themselves as realists. The clearest indication of this basic consensus was the widespread agreement among pacifists about how to proceed in bringing about a world without war.

The Route to World Peace

Bertha von Suttner paid little attention to the problem of what specific action pacifists were to undertake. She assumed that criticism of the immoral aspects of contemporary international politics would have a didactic effect and would eventually bring an enlightened statesman to initiate reforms. Thus, the function of the pacifists themselves was to serve as moral educators, condemning war and other

[46] Wehberg, *Führer*, p. 22.

objectionable features of international relations, while encouraging arbitration, arms limitation, and international conciliation.

Fried was troubled by the enormous gap in Suttner's thought between moral enlightenment and political reform. However, his scientific pacifism, which represented an attempt to close that gap with a more detailed and reasoned analysis of the process by which war would be eliminated, only aggravated the problem. Suttner's pacifism assumed that an act—education through moral criticism—would lead more or less automatically to peace. Scientific pacifism implied that peace would come so automatically that pacifist action was entirely superfluous. As early as 1901, for instance, Fried wrote that "we [pacifists] are not the motive forces in the course of history, but rather the modest mileage indicators from which one can tell how wonderfully far we have already gone."[47] And writing in 1911, Hans Wehberg, who was one of the most outspoken devotees of scientific pacifism, put it even more explicitly: "The gradual attenuation of warfare . . . is a completely natural phenomenon, which would occur even were there no peace movement."[48]

Fried's *Handbuch der Friedensbewegung* was conspicuously silent on the subject of pacifist action. Not until 1908, when he published an elaboration of his theories, did Fried deal systematically with the problem of how pacifists could or should act in the process of social evolution.[49] He began by emphasizing the inexorability of the process: "We do not have to change the course of things; we have merely to explain it, to discover the direction of events. We do not say boldly, 'Let it be!' We say modestly, 'It will be!' "[50] Active

[47] NL Fried, Fried to Friedrich Goldschmidt, Berlin, 6 August 1901.

[48] Wehberg, *Die internationale Friedensbewegung* (Moenchen Gladbach, 1911), p. 12.

[49] Alfred H. Fried, *Die Grundlagen des revolutionären Pacifismus* (Tübingen, 1908).

[50] *Ibid.*, p. 39.

involvement by pacifists was justified then, in Fried's view, on aesthetic grounds: making people aware of the process would heighten their appreciation of it:

> Our job consists . . . in the first instance only in sharpening the visual capabilities of our contemporaries. They should learn to recognize the course of developments in order to coordinate their activities with it. . . . As long as men act blindly, driven simply by the force of things, they will not get to enjoy the higher values that grow out of the organization of states. They will be like the blind, for whom the splendor of nature does not exist even though they live in the middle of it. . . . Pacifism is thus basically nothing other than a problem of intellectual optics.[51]

However, Fried also conceded that it was possible to accelerate the process of international organization: "We face —as a secondary goal—the necessity of promoting all those factors that benefit the development of the process through which mankind becomes organized, and of impairing all those factors that can appear to hinder this process."[52] Despite the fact that he assigned only secondary importance to this point, all the specifics of Fried's program revolved around it. Under the heading of impairing factors that obstructed the process, Fried called upon pacifists to "immunize the masses" against the plots of selfish leaders to start wars, chiefly by breaking down the national prejudices these leaders exploited.[53] Under the rubric of accelerating the process, Fried defined the program of the pacifists as 1) promoting international commerce, 2) adapting law to international commerce, and 3) adapting politics to international law.[54]

Once Fried was pinned down on the specifics of pacifist action, the differences between scientific and ethical pacifism dissolved. His admission that the development of inter-

---

[51] *Ibid.*, pp. 39–40.   [52] *Ibid.*, pp. 41–42.
[53] *Ibid.*, p. 51.   [54] *Ibid.*, p. 59.

national organization was a process that could be affected by human intervention reintroduced the element of moral imperative into pacifism. And although he pointed to the social forces promoting world peace, Fried's prescription for the pacifists differed from Suttner's only in terminology. What she called moral enlightenment became "immunization of the masses" in Fried's pseudoscientific jargon. What Fried referred to as the process of international organization corresponded in Suttner's language to the ennoblement of mankind.

Whatever the terminology they used, German pacifists defined their mission in terms of popular education. Taking for their precept either an ethical or a material community of nations, these latter-day *philosophes* proposed to enlighten the masses about the improprieties of contemporary politics and to show how the situation might be improved. This emphasis on educating the masses stemmed from the pacifists' belief that the masses were at the same time the most dangerous and the most promising factor in international politics. Though the seeds of war were planted by conspiracies of evil or misguided leaders, war could not break out without the consent of the masses. The masses in turn were vulnerable to deception and manipulation by these leaders, and therein, the pacifists reasoned, lay the greatest threat to peace. Since they believed further that the malleability of the masses was directly proportional to their ignorance—whether it be moral ignorance or ignorance of their real interests—pacifists concluded that education was the key to peace. However, enlightenment would merely awaken a potential that already existed in the masses, whom the pacifists held to be naturally peace-loving.

Thus the German pacifists set out to do battle on all fronts with the forces of ignorance and deception. Their principal enemies were militarism and chauvinism, as well as the most obvious symptom of these, the arms race. Militarism was an inclusive epithet in the pacifists' vocabulary, and it referred to the view that war was desirable, necessary, or unavoidable. Chauvinism connoted the belligerent and exclusive fostering of the power or interests of a single nation. Both concepts, in denying the fundamental harmony of all nations, were incompatible with international community.

The arms race presented the pacifists with special problems. They deplored it for several reasons: it aggravated international tensions, diverted resources better employed in international commerce, and the security afforded by spiraling armaments was illusory.[55] Yet the pacifists also recognized that until an international organization could guarantee the security of all nations, armies would be necessary for defense. They also feared—and their fears were substantiated—that advocacy of disarmament would be misconstrued to mean that they were calling for the unilateral disarmament of Germany.[56] Like pacifists elsewhere, who encountered similar difficulties, German pacifists emphasized that they wished only a simultaneous limitation of arms among all the powers and that full disarmament would await the creation of an international organization.[57] Even so, they found it prudent to avoid the sensitive problem of armaments as much as possible and to stress other aspects of their program.

The reform most consistently promoted by pacifists was international arbitration. They called for the conclusion of treaties of arbitration, the enlargement of the jurisdiction of the Hague court, making recourse to it obligatory in as many instances as possible, and giving the court's verdicts the force of law. Yet they also emphasized that arbitration

[55] See Gustav Maier, "The Economic Significance of the Peace Movement," PM I (1912), 154–56.

[56] NL Suttner (MnI, I), Heilberg to Suttner, Breslau, 20 April 1907; FW, IV (1902), 91.

[57] NL Suttner (PQaI, 4), Quidde to Suttner, Munich, 22 April 1902; Eickhoff, "Die interparlamentarische Union," pp. 485–86; Otto Umfrid, *Die Formel der Abrüstung mit besonderer Berücksichtigung des englischen Abrüstungsvorschlags* (Stuttgart, n.d.); HB (I), pp. 27–28.

was for them only a short-range goal, or rather only a symptom of growing international organization.

The German pacifists' final goal was a federation among the civilized states of the world—an international political organization equipped with the powers necessary to settle peacefully all disputes among its members. The pacifists did not say a great deal about how the transition to this federation would be made, but on the subject of the organization itself their speculation was abundant. Most agreed that the central agency of the federation would be a court of international law to adjudicate disputes on the basis of a code of international justice. Some pacifists envisaged a legislative body to draft supplementary international law, but such a body would be of secondary importance since pacifists believed that the norms of international justice were unchanging and could be defined with relative precision in the initial code.

More controversial was the problem of how to enforce the judgments of the international court and whether the federation should include an executive agency empowered to use force. Those who, like Ludwig Quidde, opposed sanctions pointed out that the use of force would confront pacifists with the absurdity of waging war for the sake of peace.[58] Fried, on the other hand, insisted that force might be necessary in the federation, either against deviant members or to defend against attack from uncivilized nonmembers.[59] Nor did the lines in this debate coincide with the divisions between scientists and moralists. Otto Umfrid, who stood ideologically closer to Quidde than to Fried, shared Fried's views on the possible use of force.[60]

However, even this disagreement was of minor impor-

[58] FW, VIII (1906), 117; FB, VIII (1907), 73–75; cf. *Bulletin officiel du XVme Congrès universel de la paix tenu à Milan du 15 au 22 septembre 1906* (Berne, 1906), pp. 39–40, 80, 85–86.

[59] HB (1), pp. 20–23.

[60] Umfrid, "Lebensfragen," FW, XIV (1912), 410–12; Umfrid, *Friede auf Erden! Betrachtungen über den Völkerfrieden* (Esslingen, 1897), p. 85.

tance, for no one thought that force would be used often. German pacifists of all persuasions believed that the creation of a world federation would lead to the metamorphosis of international politics, a great *Aufhebung* from a Hobbesian system of conflict, power, and interests, to one in which law, justice, and morality would govern all behavior. Even Alfred Fried could not maintain the guise of scientific objectivity to deny this. "It will occasion some amusement in subsequent generations," he wrote in his *Handbuch*, "to find out that in 1899 people still distinguished between politics and morality. A change [in this] is likely to take place soon, because of purely material factors [*sic*]."[61] The rule of justice and morality in international politics would make the question of forcible sanctions academic; nations would, as a matter of course, accede to the just verdicts of the court.

Similar considerations lay behind the insistence of Fried and others that the organization they contemplated would require only a minimal sacrifice of each member's sovereignty.[62] Membership in the federation would entail relinquishing the unrestricted right to make war, but the federation would make such a right altogether superfluous. Beyond that, the state would function entirely as before, with sovereign jurisdiction over its own citizens. By the same token, the federation would not presuppose any specific domestic social or political system.

It would be easy to criticize the pacifists for their naiveté in looking forward to the transformation of international politics, their facile transition from Hobbesian assumptions to Kantian conclusions.[63] However, such criticism would be

[61] HB (1), p. 183; cf. Martin Rade, "Machtstaat, Rechtsstaat und Kulturstaat," FB, IX (1908), 101–103, 105–108.

[62] HB (1), pp. 85, 87–88, 90; H. Michelis, *Geschichte und Ziele der modernen internationalen Friedensbewegung* (Königsberg, 1906), p. 10.

[63] See G. Grosch, "Völkerrecht und die Weltfriedensbewegung," *Zeitschrift für die gesamte Staatswissenschaft* LXVII (1911), 179–217.

idle, and would rest upon a great deal of cynical hindsight. It is more legitimate to question their neat separation of domestic and international politics, their assertion that their international reforms required no substantial social or political changes in the domestic realms of member states. Indeed, there is ample evidence that many pacifists themselves suspected that, particularly in the case of imperial Germany, far-reaching domestic changes would be unavoidable.

Pacifism and Modernization

The concept of modernization has recently come under fire from political scientists and sociologists.[64] Among other things, critics object to the ethnocentricity and normative judgments implicit in the assertion that all societies tend to approach the western model of extensive industrialization, social differentiation, rationalized cultural patterns, and a high level of interaction between the political system and society.

To go into the controversy over modernization would be beyond the scope of this essay. Here it is germane only to point out that these criticisms apply also to pacifism, which, particularly in its scientific variation, was preeminently a theory of modernization—even to the point of terminology.[65] The pacifists styled their international reforms as the political counterpart of the "modern" economic, social, and cultural developments that were revolutionizing the

[64] See Nisbet, *Social Change and History*; J. P. Nettl and Roland Robertson, "Industrialization, Development or Modernization," *British Journal of Sociology* XVII (1966), 274–91; Nettl and Robertson, *International Systems and the Modernizaiton of Societies: The Formation of National Goals and Attitudes* (New York, 1968), pp. 17–61.

[65] Eg. Anonymous [Alfred Fried], *Kaiser werde modern!* (Berlin, 1905). In 1898, when Fried attempted to draw Suttner's attention to the economic foundations of political change, he wrote: "If I could bring you over to this point of view . . . the lack of which makes you so unmodern." SFC, Fried to Suttner, Vienna, 10 March 1898.

world.[66] The federation they envisaged was to represent the culmination of political change, and as less developed nations became more modern and civilized, they too could look forward to becoming members. Beyond that, the pacifists' program of international organization clearly implied the inevitability or desirability of a specific pattern of political and social development within each nation. Any protestations to the contrary resulted from the pacifists' naiveté, unsystematic thinking, or disingenuousness for the sake of public relations.

The theory that the origins of war lay in the conspiracies of willful leaders and that the masses were by nature peaceful led logically to democracy. Indeed, Kant himself followed this line of reasoning but was inhibited by the excesses of the French Revolution from advocating democracy as a prerequisite for perpetual peace; instead he called for republican government, by which he meant government responsible to the desires of the governed: "If . . . the consent of the citizens is required in order to decide whether there should be war or not, nothing is more natural than that those who would have to decide to undergo all the deprivations of war will very much hesitate to start such an evil game."[67] At the turn of the twentieth century it was clear to most of Kant's successors in Germany that democracy would best translate the ethical consciousness inherent in all men into political decisions. Statesmen who were responsible to the masses would of necessity deport themselves peacefully. Quidde once remarked that pacifism was "nothing other than the application of the fundamentals of democracy to international relations."[68] And Umfrid had the same point in mind when commenting in 1906 on the Moroccan crisis: "If someone asked the peoples themselves

[66] HB (1), p. 47.
[67] Quoted from Friedrich, *Inevitable Peace*, p. 251.
[68] Quidde, "Wie ich zur Demokratie und zum Pazifismus kam," *Frankfurter Zeitung*, 4 January 1928.

whether they wanted war over Morocco, he would perhaps to the astonishment of many find an aversion to warfare about which statesmen dare not dream."[69] The political implications of Fried's pacifism were the same, although the rationale was couched in different terms. Fried held democracy to be the modern system of government, best suited to enable the masses, who were the beneficiaries of internationalization, to express their interests politically. He also regarded democratization, like internationalization, as a natural and inexorable process.[70] The pacifists' conception of their mission further implied a democratic bias: popular enlightenment made little sense if governing bodies were not responsible to public opinion.

The social implications of the pacifist ideology were scarcely less evident. The process that Fried described as the guarantee of the peace was the internationalization of capitalism. Indeed, a more emphatic affirmation of the forces at work in capitalism would be difficult to find: "The volume of world trade increased yearly. . . . Great amounts of capital, the red blood of international trade, have for a long time had no home. Capital, particularly the capital of the great trusts and commercial institutions, is working in all countries and seeking profits everywhere there is an opportunity. National loans, which were earlier covered by 'patriots,' must now be floated on the international market, and one frequently finds national enemies seizing upon the certain prospect of profit and supporting one another financially."[71] This view of capitalism had important corollaries. In the first place, pacifists looked with approval upon attempts to promote the international expansion of capitalism, which, they reasoned, could only have a propitious impact on international relations. Foremost among the measures they endorsed was the systematic reduction of tariffs. "Free

[69] Umfrid, "Die Konferenz in Algeciras und die Kriegsgefahr," FB, VII (1906), 42; cf. FB, IX (1908), 145; VF, XIII (1912), 135.

[70] "Zu den deutschen Wahlen," FW, V (1903), 74; cf. Fried, Grundlagen des revolutionären Pacifismus, p. 56.

[71] HB (1), p. 43.

trade stimulates progress through unhindered competition," wrote one pacifist in 1904. "What God hath joined let no man put asunder."[72] The converse of the pacifists' confidence in the expansion of capitalism was their concern over those with a vested interest in impeding the process. Their analysis of the roots of war would subsequently be called Schumpeterian; it emphasized the deleterious influence of premodern, illiberal sectors of society, whose social survival was being threatened by the very processes the pacifists sought to encourage.[73] Dependent upon tariffs to sustain their outdated agrarian economic base and upon large armies for their occupations and prestige, aristocrats represented a major threat to peace, as they conspired to keep international relations agitated and the masses deceived. The pacifists' program would consequently entail the social and political demise of this class.

The pacifists' vision culminated in a liberal paradise: a peaceful world of capitalist, democratic nations, in which leadership devolved naturally onto the progressive bourgeoisie. And here the process of social change would stop. Pacifists were convinced that no social system was as well suited to ensure the peace as capitalism, which, in addition to tying the nations together in a community of interests, made possible the sublimation of man's aggressive drives into peaceful competion. Further social change was unnecessary; poverty and social injustice, the existence of which the pacifists acknowledged, were not, as claimed by socialists, necessary products of capitalism, but derived rather from the wasteful effects of military spending.[74] Moreover,

[72] Opitz, "Freihandel und Zollkriege," FB, v (1904), 109; cf. Fried, *Grundlagen*, pp. 60, 65.

[73] See the provocative discussion of this in Stiewe, "Die bürgerliche deutsche Friedensbewegung," esp. pp. xiv, 56, 114, 184, 235–36; see also FW, iv (1902), 179.

[74] Franz Wirth, "Die soziale Bedeutung der internationalen Friedensbewegung," *Berichte des Freien Deutschen Hochstiftes zu Frankfurt* xi (1895), 185–88; Richard Reuter, "Sociale Reform und die Friedensbewegung," *Correspondenz für die Friedensbewegung*, number 2

revolution to secure social change was no less objectionable to pacifists than war. Thus, the pacifists called for the peaceful integration of the working classes into the fabric of bourgeois society—a process they themselves hoped through their reforms to promote.[75]

In its affirmation of democracy, free-trade capitalism, bourgeois society, and the peaceful accommodation of the working classes, German pacifism was similar to pacifist ideologies elsewhere in western Europe and in the United States. In these other countries the pacifists' domestic social and political ideals seemed largely to have been realized, and pacifism did not conflict with prevailing social and political systems or values. In Germany, however, where the influence of the Junker aristocracy was enormous, where the constitutional system was undemocratic in numerous crucial respects and excluded parliament from the control of foreign and military policy, and where most of the working classes espoused a militant ideology that repudiated bourgeois society, the domestic ideals of pacifism clashed directly with social and political reality. Herein lay the anomalous position of the German pacifists. As patriots, they affirmed the legitimacy of the empire and professed themselves loyal subjects of the emperor. Yet their ideology implied a challenge to the foundations of the imperial system and to the elites who were its beneficiaries. Writing in 1911, Fried specified the problem with complete candor: "If Germany were to develop into a democracy and carry on a democratic foreign policy, we would have peace in Europe. . . . The problem of peace is therefore a problem of domestic German politics. It lies in the conquest of Junkerdom, in the victory of liberalism and democracy."[76]

(February 1897); C. Simon, "Friedensfrage und soziale Frage," VF, XII (1911), 79; DWN, V (1896), 166–67; DWN, VI (1897), 50–52, 319–20; FB, IX (1908), 76.

[75] CBM, IX (1904), 34; VF, XIV (1913), 46; FB, VIII (1907), 8.

[76] FW, XIII (1911), 219–20.

Whether or not "the victory of liberalism and democracy" in Germany would in fact have brought peace to Europe—and the evidence is at best equivocal—the domestic implications of the pacifists' ideology were as important as the international reforms they advocated in determining the reception of the peace movement in Germany. The connection between arbitration and arms limitation, on the one hand, and liberalism and democracy on the other was manifest. It was thus no coincidence that the attempt by the dominant elites in imperial Germany to fend off the domestic reforms implied by pacifism prominently included resistance to arbitration and arms limitation, as well as a systematic attempt to discredit the attitudes and orientations toward international relations that the pacifists hoped to propagate.

Finally, it was a measure of this situation that the range within which the pacifists could look for support and allies was severely circumscribed. With but a few exceptions, all the groups in Germany that attempted to promote arbitration and arms limitation were, like the German Peace Society, drawn from the ranks of those who were opposed to the illiberal aspects of the empire and who also rejected social revolution. For all intents and purposes, this confined the German peace movement to small groups of ardent liberals, who had not succumbed to the Bismarckian political legacy and abandoned their commitment to democracy.

4

The Expansion of the German
Peace Movement

ALTHOUGH the philosophical distance between Alfred Fried and Bertha von Suttner was a great deal less than Fried himself realized, the practical results of his formulating a scientific pacifism were considerable. Fried attempted to portray pacifism as the logical, indeed inevitable, outgrowth of internationalization. The results were not altogether convincing, but he did succeed in adducing a body of observable evidence on which to base his assertions. He also provided pacifism with a coherent sociological theory and philosophy of history, which were more credible and admitted of more dispassionate consideration than Bertha von Suttner's raptures.[1] Largely as a result of Fried's recasting the credo, pacifism began to receive favorable attention in wider sectors of German society, among groups that had also been impressed by the process of internationalization and were inclined to draw at least some of the same political consequences that the pacifists foresaw. It was thus testimony to Fried that the German peace movement came to comprise more than just the pacifists in the German Peace Society.

Pacifists and Other Prophets of Progress

Carlton J. H. Hayes has referred to the last three decades of the nineteenth century as the climax of the Enlightenment, noting in particular a widespread confidence in science and progress.[2] While H. Stuart Hughes and others

[1] See Hans Wehberg, "Alfred Hermann Fried und seine Bedeutung für die pazifistische Wissenschaft," ER, III (1914), 10–12.
[2] Carlton J. H. Hayes, *A Generation of Materialism, 1871–1900* (New York, 1963), pp. 328–32.

have shown that positivism came under increasing attack after 1890, the general faith in progress, founded on the writings of Comte, Darwin, and Spencer, had by no means been dethroned prior to the First World War.[3] In 1907, as if to illustrate the continuing vitality of this confidence, an institute was established in Paris that published a journal in three languages devoted entirely to the theme of progress. The journals, entitled respectively *Dokumente des Fortschritts, Les documents du progrès,* and *The International,* appeared regularly until 1914 and boasted as contributors such prominent figures as Ramsay MacDonald, William Stead, Émile Durkheim, Max Nordau, Marcel Sembat, Werner Sombart, Bruno Wille, Ferdinand Tönnies, and Georg Simmel.[4] Articles drew attention to a wide variety of social, cultural, and scientific advances. One of the topics frequently discussed was the peace movement, for as the work of Jacob Novikow, Norman Angell, and Alfred Fried clearly showed, pacifism had by the beginning of the twentieth century sunk deep roots into the positivist tradition.[5]

In Germany this tradition was weaker than in England or France. The influence of Comte in intellectual circles was negligible, and while social Darwinism enjoyed wide popularity in Germany, it tended to connote an emphasis on the necessity of social or political conflict, rather than confidence in the ameliorative aspects of social evolution by natural laws.[6] The positivist tradition survived chiefly on the

[3] H. Stuart Hughes, *Consciousness and Society: The Reorientation of European Social Thought, 1890–1930* (New York, 1958).

[4] NL Fried, Institut des Documents du Progrès, Programm.

[5] See R. Moe, *Le prix Nobel de la paix et l'institut Nobel norvégien: Rapport historique et descriptif accompagné d'une histoire du mouvement pacifiste de 1896 à 1930* (Oslo, 1932), pp. 220–69; Oscar J. Falnes, *Norway and the Nobel Peace Prize* (New York, 1967), p. 33.

[6] W. M. Simon, *European Positivism in the Nineteenth Century: An Essay in Intellectual History* (Ithaca, N.Y., 1963), pp. 262–63; Fritz Bolle, "Darwinismus und Zeitgeist," in Hans-Joachim Schoeps, ed., *Zeitgeist im Wandel,* I: *Das Wilhelminische Zeitalter* (Stuttgart,

fringe of German intellectual and political life, among a remarkable cluster of reform-oriented thinkers and organizations commonly known as the monist movement. Far from united on doctrinal specifics, the movement was characterized above all by its faith in progress through science, or, to use Hermann Lübbe's expression, its *Fortschritts-Pathos*.[7] Its leaders were Ludwig Büchner, Friedrich Jodl, Ernst Haeckel, and Wilhelm Ostwald. All shared the belief, most popularly expressed in Haeckel's *Die Welträtsel*, that the progress of mankind depended upon the triumph of a secular ethic based on scientific principles, specifically the propositions that the universe was monistic in character and governed in all its aspects by immutable scientific laws. In the name of science and reason, then, the movement set out to regenerate society, most centrally by purging it of the influence of organized religion, though the reforms advocated by monists also included political democracy and a vague kind of socialism.[8]

In 1881 Büchner founded the *Deutscher Freidenkerbund*, the first German organization dedicated to propagating a scientific ethic. This group was joined in 1892 by a German branch of the international ethical culture movement, the *Gesellschaft für ethische Kultur*, which was established in Berlin by Georg von Gizycki, Wilhelm Foerster, Jodl, and Büchner, with the goal of enlightening society about the "scientific perception of ethics."[9] These two groups were

---

1967); Hans-Günter Zmarzlik, "Der Sozialdarwinismus in Deutschland als geschichtliches Problem," *Vierteljahrshefte für Zeitgeschichte* XI (1963), 246–73.

[7] Hermann Lübbe, *Politische Philosophie in Deutschland: Studien zu ihrer Geschichte* (Basel and Stuttgart, 1963), pp. 129–30.

[8] Niles Robert Holt, "The Social and Political Ideas of the German Monist Movement, 1871–1914" (Ph.D. dissertation, Yale University, 1967).

[9] DWN, III (1894), 295–96. See also Wilhelm Foerster, *Die ethische Bewegung in Deutschland* (Berlin, 1903); Foerster, *Lebenserinnerungen*, pp. 225–36, 244–57, 277–80, 286–96, 313–18; Lily Braun, *Memoiren einer Sozialistin* (Munich, 1909), pp. 501–651; Peter Gilg, *Die Erneue-*

but the most prominent of a number of related organizations that appeared in Germany at the end of the nineteenth century, including a *Deutsche Positivistische Vereiningung* in Munich and several "free religious communities"— groups that had originally broken off from the established Protestant churches in the 1840s in order to teach a rationalized Christianity, but had by the end of the century gradually severed all ties with Christianity. Drawn largely from a moderately educated middle-class constituency, these reform groups occasionally ran afoul of the authorities for their unabashed attacks on organized religion and for political views that seemed to border on socialism or even anarchism.[10]

After the turn of the century the movement acquired more coherence and national prominence as Haeckel became its leading figure. In 1906 he founded the *Deutscher Monistenbund*, which attracted many free-thinkers and members of ethical culture societies. The next year he attempted to give more cohesion to the movement by sponsoring the so-called Weimar Cartel, a loose cover organization that included the *Monistenbund*, the branches of the Ethical Culture Society and *Freidenkerbund*, and assorted other reform groups. By the outbreak of the war, leaders of the cartel claimed a membership of some eighty thousand persons.[11]

Throughout its sometimes bizarre history the monist movement was one of the principal sources from which the pacifists drew support. Monism was ideologically akin to pacifism—particularly to scientific pacifism: both were con-

---

rung des demokratischen Denkens im Wilhelminischen Deutschland: Eine ideengeschichtliche Studie zur Wende vom 19. zum 20. Jahrhundert (Wiesbaden, 1965), pp. 246–49.

[10] AStA, MInn 73551, Kgl. Polizeidirektion München to Kgl. Staatsministerium des Innern, number 54462 II, Munich, 14 July 1902; Staatsministerium des Innern, Confidential Report, Munich, 8 January 1914; cf. Ulrich Linse, "Die Anarchisten und die Münchner Novemberrevolution," in Bosl, *Bayern im Umbruch*, pp. 39–43.

[11] Holt, "Social and Political Ideas," pp. 163–64.

fident that scientific laws would provide for the felicity of mankind. The monist movement was recruited from the same social sectors as the peace society.[12] Indeed, there was considerable interpenetration between the two movements, as many monists were members of the peace society.

The pacifism in monism derived from the beliefs that scientific laws did not distinguish among national groups and that international violence was a relic of the unscientific past. In a lecture to the Ethical Culture Society in Berlin in 1892, Georg von Gizycki called war mankind's "most serious infantile disease" and observed that "wars will certainly be made eternally impossible once we attain a higher level of civilization."[13] Most of the leading figures in the monist movement shared Gizycki's expectation that the triumph of monism would bring the end of warfare. Büchner had been one of the notables around whom Hodgson Pratt tried to form a peace society in Darmstadt in the 1880s. Wilhelm Foerster, one of the leading pacifists in Germany, was Jodl's brother-in-law, and repeatedly stressed the generic relationship between pacifism and "ethical culture." Both Foerster and Gizycki were members of the executive committee of the German Peace Society in Berlin, as was Rudolf Penzig, another leader of the Berlin Ethical Culture Society. Several local chapters of Ethical Culture Society were also corporate members of the German Peace Society.[14] In 1908 the *Freidenkerbund* resolved that all its members should actively participate in propagating peace.[15] Two of them, Arthur Westphal and Fritz Röttcher, did so by serving as national secretaries of the German Peace Society.

[12] Köhler, "Die deutsche Friedensgesellschaft," p. 365; see also Heinz Herz, *Alleingang wider die Mächtigen: Ein Bild vom Leben und Kämpfen Moritz von Egidys* (Leipzig, [1970]), p. 78; Holt, "Social and Political Ideas," p. 7.

[13] DWN, 1 (December 1892), 33.

[14] BIP (vB6), Penzig to International Peace Bureau, Berlin, 10 August 1907; cf. Liedtke, "Die Entwicklung des Pazifismus," p. 39.

[15] FW, x (1908), 136–37.

Ernst Haeckel's views on politics were thoroughly eccentric, and any attempt to systematize them would be misleading.[16] Like many others who sought to apply Darwinism to politics, Haeckel believed that struggle was natural among nations and races, but in his later writings, such as *Die Welträtsel*, he anticipated scientific pacifism by insisting that this struggle was to be cultural and not physical. Yet he did not find it inconsistent to support a large navy with which to protect a high level of German culture. An anti-Semite, he belonged to the *Kolonialgesellschaft* and the Pan-German League, as well as the Navy League. Were this the whole of Haeckel's political profile, it would be a fairly unambiguous picture of an ardent German nationalist.[17] Shortly after he joined the Pan-German League, however, he sent his greetings to the Universal Peace Congress which was meeting in Rome in November 1891.[18] After the turn of the century he joined the German Peace Society and described himself as a "convinced pacifist," drawing attention to the fact that war gave rise to a kind of reverse natural selection, by killing off the fittest of all races at the battle front.[19]

The views of Wilhelm Ostwald, who succeeded Haeckel as leader of the *Monistenbund* in 1911, were characterized by no such inconsistency. Ostwald's monism was cast in terms of applying universally what he called "the energetic

[16] This is particularly true of Daniel Gasman's recent attempt to portray Haeckel as one of the fathers of Nazism: *The Scientific Origins of National Socialism: Social Darwinism in Ernst Haeckel and the German Monist League* (London and New York, 1971). Haeckel's philosophical views were also eccentric: see Niles Holt, "Ernst Haeckel's Monistic Religion," *Journal of the History of Ideas* XXXII (1971), 265–80; Holt, "Social and Political Ideas," pp. 124–35.

[17] This is just the picture that has been commonly drawn. See, in addition to Gasman's book, Karl Kupisch, "Bürgerliche Frömmigkeit im Wilhelminischen Zeitalter," in Schoeps, *Zeitgeist im Wandel*, p. 40.

[18] DWN, 1 (February 1892), 19.

[19] "Ernst Haeckel zum 80. Geburtstag," FW, XVI (1914), 110–11.

imperative," according to which society should be made scientifically efficient and happy. Since he believed that war was contrary to the dictates of this imperative, Ostwald became interested in pacifism; in fact, his pacifism antedated his activity in the *Monistenbund*.[20] A friend of Wilhelm Foerster, Heinrich Rössler, and Bertha von Suttner, Ostwald was also a member of the German Peace Society and was present at several major pacifist gatherings.[21] During his tenure as head of the *Monistenbund* pacifism was accentuated as a facet of the organization's program. Ostwald's journal, *Das Monistische Jahrhundert*, became a forum for pacifist views and regularly solicited articles from Fried about the peace movement.[22]

Ostwald's enthusiastic endorsement of pacifism was not unopposed in the *Monistenbund*. The monists shared with the pacifists a propensity for frequent quarrels, one of which arose in 1913, when Ostwald's journal ran a series of articles that were so critical of nationalism that they provoked an outcry within the ranks against the spread of pacifism in the organization. However, Ostwald was hardly the man to alter his views under pressure. Dismissing his critics as *Gefühlsmonisten*—a term of severe opprobrium in his vocabulary—he rallied support for his own position and weathered the crisis as the dissidents resigned.[23]

Neither the existence of opposition to pacifism within the movement nor the support most monists—including Ostwald himself—gave to the German war effort in 1914

[20] HB (2), II, 385; Grete Ostwald, *Wilhelm Ostwald: Mein Vater* (Stuttgart, 1953), p. 130.

[21] NL Suttner (Cf1), Ostwald to Suttner, Grass Bothen, 8 October 1909; Wilhelm Ostwald, *Lebenslinien: Eine Selbstbiographie* (3 vols., Berlin, 1926–27), III, 329–35.

[22] NL Fried, W. Blossfeldt to Fried, Leipzig, 3 October 1912, 15 March 1913.

[23] NL Walther Schücking, Bundesarchiv, Coblenz (cited hereafter as NL Schücking) (38), Deutscher Monistenbund, Geschäftsstelle an die Ortsgruppen des Deutschen Monistenbundes, Munich, 3 December 1913; cf. Ostwald, *Lebenslinien*, II, 230–31.

should obscure the fact that before the war monism and pacifism were closely allied on a number of levels. In this connection it is significant that the *Bund Neues Vaterland*, one of the important groups that emerged during the war to urge a moderate peace, originated around a core of monists.[24]

The influence of pacifism was also strong among a number of other reform groups, which were usually spinoffs from the monist movement addressing themselves to specific ills in German society. Prominent among the progressive causes they championed were sex education, cremation, temperance, natural healing, and vegetarianism, as well as opposition to capital punishment, vivisection, duelling, and vaccination. Many pacifists, including Fried, Quidde, and Martin Rade, were active in such groups; these organizations in turn frequently sent representatives and greetings to peace congresses and sponsored joint meetings with peace societies.[25]

Of these progressive reforms, the one that interested the pacifists the most was the attempt to popularize an international language, a device they believed would facilitate the growth of international community. Although there was an inevitable quarrel among pacifists over the comparative virtues of the various possible universal languages, most preferred Esperanto.[26] They found, however, that an international language, like disarmament, was a sensitive issue

[24] Otto Lehmann-Russbüldt, *Der Kampf der Deutschen Liga für Menschenrechte, vormals Bund neues Vaterland, für den Weltfrieden 1914–1927* (Berlin, 1927); Ostwald, *Lebenslinien*, III, 259–60.

[25] NL Fried, M. Schwantje to Fried, Berlin, 2 November 1911; Eberle to Fried, Neu-Ulm, 12 November 1897; Fried MS, "Umfrage über die Todesstrafe," Berlin, January 1898; FB, V (1904), 81–83; CBM, 2 March 1902 Annex, p. 2; CBM, XV (1910), 45; VF, XII (1911), 49; FW, XXXVIII (1938), 82; Johannes Rathje, *Die Welt des freien Protestantismus: Ein Beitrag zur deutsch-evangelischen Geistesgeschichte. Dargestellt an Leben und Werk von Martin Rade* (Stuttgart, 1952), p. 177.

[26] NL Fried, Heinrich Molenaar to Fried, Kochel, 5 November 1908.

in Germany; advocating the use of Esperanto threatened to raise protests from nationalists that the pacifists were subverting the German language and culture. Accordingly, pacifists were cautious in supporting Esperanto and did not publicly advocate teaching it in German schools.[27] They were nevertheless prominent in Esperantist organizations in Germany.[28]

Freemasonry, another internationalist organization dedicated to the progress of mankind, was closely allied with pacifism in many countries, and international Masonic congresses regularly passed resolutions calling for arbitration.[29] In Germany, however, Masons did not entirely share this orientation, despite the expectations of Fried and other pacifists who were Masons that they would. When pacifists sought the active support of German lodges they were frequently told that Masons believed that world peace was good, but that agitation for arbitration or arms limitation would be a political activity, which the lodges were supposed to avoid.[30] It was more likely that the nationalism of most German lodges kept them away from the peace movement; it was, for instance, a curious reflection of both the lodges' purported apolitical stance and their support for world peace that the *Deutscher Grosslogenbund* persistent-

[27] FB, v (1904), 51–52.   [28] FB, viii (1907), 83.

[29] *Bulletin officiel du IXe Congrès universel de la paix tenu à Paris du 30 septembre au 5 octobre 1900* (Berne, 1901), p. 122; Alfred Fried, "Freimaurerei und Friedensfrage," *Zwanglose Mitteilungen aus dem Verein Deutscher Freimaurer*, ii (June 1914), 273–74; Wolfgang Krämer, "Zum ewigen Frieden," *Pazifismus und Internationalismus*, pp. 3–6; "Die Freimaurer als Friedensförderer," VF, xi (1910), 24; Robert Parsons Baker, "The Belgians and the European Peace Movement, 1889–1914" (Master's thesis, Stanford University, 1962), p. 46.

[30] NL Wehberg (59a), Fried to Wehberg, Clarens, 10 September 1912; Fried, "Friedensbewegung und Freimaurerei," *Zwanglose Mitteilungen* ii (June 1914), 275–76; DWN, vi (1897), 421; August Horneffer, *Deutsche und ausländische Freimaurerei* (Munich, 1915), pp. 44–45; cf. Johannes Tiedje, "Die Friedensfrage: Eine Gewissensfrage für die deutschen Freimaurer," *Zwanglose Mitteilungen* ii (June 1914), 268–71.

ly refused to resume relations with lodges in France, which had been severed since 1870.[31] Nevertheless, overtures from the peace society did produce some results. Particularly in southern and western Germany, lodges were sympathetic to the peace movement, even to the extent that some joined the German Peace Society *in corpore*.[32] Of all the German lodges, the *Freimaurerbund "Zur Aufgehenden Sonne,"* based in Nuremberg, was the most active in progressive causes, and it enthusiastically endorsed the work of the pacifists.[33] On the national level, pacifists found support in the Masonic journal, *Der Herold*, and in the *Verein Deutscher Freimaurer*, a central agency set up to promote closer ties among the German lodges and to conduct research on aspects of the Masonic movement.[34]

Another category of internationalist organizations within which the pacifists failed to find as much support as they had anticipated were those designed to promote free trade. Believing their two causes to be eminently compatible, pacifists approached a number of free-trade groups in hopes of enlisting them in the campaign for arbitration and arms limitation. Some of these groups, such as the *Verband reisender Kaufleute* and, more significantly, the *Internationale Handels-Union*, responded favorably.[35] The far more influ-

[31] NL Fried, C. Barthel to Fried, Frankfurt, 22 July 1904.

[32] NL Fried, Ludwig Wagner to Suttner, Kaiserslautern, 26 February 1912; G. Grosch to Fried, Stuttgart, 26 February 1914; [Kloss], *Das Friedensjahrbuch 1911*, p. 42; Dietz, *Franz Wirth*, pp. 45, 71; FW, VIII (1906), 157; PM, III (1914), 172.

[33] *Pazifismus und Internationalismus* (Veröffentlichungen des F. Z. A. S., number 1) (Nuremberg, 1911); Grete Ostwald, *Wilhelm Ostwald*, p. 141; AStA, MInn 73551, *Neues Münchener Tageblatt*, 25 June 1912.

[34] NL Fried, Stephan Kekulé von Stradonitz to Fried, Gross-Lichterfelde, 12 December 1911; Bischoff to Fried, Leipzig, 9 January 1914; J. C. Schwabe to Fried, Jena, 28 January 1914, 13 May 1914; Ludwig Bangel to Fried, Frankfurt, 23 March 1914.

[35] NL Fried, Ludwig Ullmann to Fried, Berlin, 25 December 1909; H. Bothmer to Fried, Leipzig, 25 June, 10 July 1910. The *Handels-Union* tried to make Andrew Carnegie its honorary president.

ential *Hansabund*, however, flatly refused to have anything to do with the peace movement, despite the fact that its chairman, Jakob Riesser, had served along with Jacob Novikow, Albert Gobat, and Bertha von Suttner on an international commission to study European federation.[36] The lesson of the pacifists' encounters with free-trade groups was that most of them were interested in reducing trade barriers, but were reluctant to get involved in what Heinrich Flinsch, the president of the *Handelsvertragsverein*, referred to as "friendly rhetoric [*Freundschaftsphrasen*] and expressions of sentiment."[37] Even some of the endorsements the peace movement received were dubious. In 1906 Julius Wolf, the president of the *Mitteleuropäischer Wirtschaftsverein*, suggested the possibility of utilizing peace societies to promote closer commercial ties between Germany and France, and he underlined his belief that political *rapprochement* would ultimately be the result. The extent to which the *Wirtschaftsverein* actually wished to cooperate with the pacifists was perhaps best indicated by the fact that the organization's board of directors included Hermann Paasche and Heinrich Class, neither of whom was noted for his pacifism.[38]

This survey of progressive organizations and causes within which pacifism found some resonance can conclude by

[36] NL Fried, Georg Kossak to Fried, Königsberg, 21 January 1913; BIP (JG), 1er Congrès de la Fédération Européenne, Compte-rendu sommaire des séances du 16 au 20 mai 1909; see also Dirk Stegmann, *Die Erben Bismarcks: Parteien und Verbände in der Spätphase des Wilhelminischen Deutschlands* (Cologne and Berlin, 1970), esp. pp. 176–95.

[37] NL Fried, Deutsch-französischer Wirtschaftsverein, Bericht über die Gründungsversammlung, 28 March 1908; Walther Borgius to Fried, Gross-Lichterfelde-Ost, 28 November 1908; cf. FW, x (1908), 56.

[38] NL Fried, Julius Wolf to Fried, Breslau, 8 February 1906; Hartmut Kaelble, *Industrielle Interessenpolitik in der Wilhelminischen Gesellschaft: Centralverband Deutscher Industrieller 1895–1914* (Berlin, 1967), pp. 155–58.

noting parenthetically that several important German literary figures also supported the pacifists' campaign. It would be tempting to view Gerhart Hauptmann's pacifism as an outgrowth of literary naturalism, the attempt to apply science to art, and thus to show the affinities between scientific pacifism and Hauptmann's artistic theories. Such a relationship cannot be documented, however, for Hauptmann outgrew naturalism before Fried began to publicize scientific pacifism. As early as 1893, though, Hauptmann had satirized aspects of Prussian militarism in *Der Biberpelz*, a play pointedly set during the struggle over the *Septennat* in 1887 and featuring, as the brunt of the satire, a disagreeable Prussian official named Wehrhahn. In the years immediately prior to the war Hauptmann's pacifism became outspoken. When he accepted the Nobel prize for literature in 1912 he alluded to the significance of all the Nobel prizes in promoting peace.[39] His views on war and militarism were evidently unknown to the city fathers of Breslau, who commissioned him to write a play to commemorate the centenary of the Wars of Liberation in 1913. The play, which Hauptmann entitled *Festspiel in deutschen Reimen*, enraged German nationalists by parodying the heroes of the *Völkerschlacht*, including the venerable Marshall Blücher, as puppets. The play was hardly the product of caprice. Shortly before it was produced, Hauptmann wrote to Bertha von Suttner: "If you draw upon the *Festspiel* to strengthen the idea of world peace, it will represent the most noble utilization of my national [*sic*] work. May it continue in this sense."[40]

Gerhart Hauptmann's brother, Carl Hauptmann, was also a devoted pacifist. His play, *Krieg*, which Max Reinhardt produced early in 1914, owed more than a little to the in-

[39] FW, xv (1913), 24; cf. VF, xiv (1913), 24.

[40] NL Suttner (D12), Gerhart Hauptmann to Suttner, Hermsdorf Kynast, 24 December 1912; cf. Josef Gregor, *Gerhart Hauptmann: Das Werk und unsere Zeit* (Vienna, n.d.), pp. 292–97.

fluence of Fried and Suttner, both of whom intervened, at Hauptmann's request, to urge Reinhardt to produce it.[41] Other German writers shared the Hauptmanns' sympathy for pacifism. Friedrich Spielhagen was one of the original members of the German Peace Society. Ludwig Fulda was Fried's regular correspondent, and the pacifists classified him as "*ein Gesinnungsgenosse*," a category into which they also placed Hermann Hesse.[42] On the other hand, the pacifists were critical of Karl May, whose popular adventure stories seemed to glorify violence; nonetheless, May informed Bertha von Suttner in 1905 that "your spirit animates all my books."[43]

By no means all German writers regarded the pacifists so favorably. Heinrich Mann, before he became a leading critic of German militarism, assailed the pacifists in an unabashed defense of war in *Das Zwanzigste Jahrhundert*, the right-wing journal he edited briefly in the 1890s.[44] When Detlev von Lilienkron was asked for his opinion about the peace movement in 1906, he was moved to compose a short poem:

> Der ewige Fried ist für Kinder ein Gedicht
> Werft nur die Waffen weg, ich tu' es aber nicht.[45]

Felix Dahn, too, expressed his sentiments about the pacifists best in verse:

> Die Waffen hoch! Das Schwert ist Mannes eigen,
> Wo Männer fechten, hat das Weib zu schweigen,

[41] NL Fried, Carl Hauptmann to Fried, 19 April 1914, 15 May 1914.

[42] VF, XIV (1913), 43; DWN, I (February 1892), 19; FW, X (1908), 5; VF, XIV (1913), 24.

[43] NL Suttner (Ai5), Karl May to Suttner, Radebeul-Dresden, 17 October 1905; cf. Richard Henning, "Randbemerkung zur kgl. preussischen Pädagogik," DWN, III (1894), 437–41.

[44] DWN, IV (1895), 367–69, 404–406; cf. David Gross, "Heinrich Mann and the Politics of Reaction," *Journal of Contemporary History* VIII (January 1973), 125–45.

[45] "Perpetual peace is a poem for children/Just throw your weapons away, but I'm not going to." FB, VII (1906), 142.

Doch freilich, Männer gibt's in diesen Tagen,
Die sollten lieber Unterröcke tragen.[46]

Pacifism and the Academic Disciplines

While the German pacifists were willing to accept almost anyone as an ally, they recognized that some allies were more important than others. They welcomed monists, vegetarians, antivivisectionists, and other such reformers, despite the fact that these people were commonly regarded as harmless eccentrics. The pacifists were far more elated when Fried's scientific pacifism began to open doors into a much more significant sector of German society.

At the turn of the twentieth century the attitude of German academics toward pacifism was almost universally negative, and Theodor Mommsen's remark that the first Hague conference was a "misprint in world history" was a widely shared view.[47] As long as pacifism represented little more than moralistic indignation over war, there seemed to be no compelling reason for the academic community to take the peace movement seriously. Fried's attempt to transform pacifism into a *Wissenschaft*, for all its shortcomings, had important repercussions in this respect, as it provided the ideology with a degree of credibility and intellectual rigor. And despite the fact that scientific pacifism was based on positivistic and materialistic assumptions that most German academics disdained, Fried's revision of the credo led to an earnest and sympathetic discussion of the peace movement in some academic circles.[48]

Sympathy for the peace movement was most uncommon

---

[46] "Raise high your weapons! The sword belongs to the man,/ Where men fight, women have to keep quiet./Yet there are, to be sure, men around these days,/Who ought rather to be wearing petticoats." FB, IX (1908), 26.

[47] FW, V (1903), 85; cf. Arthur Kirchhoff, ed., *Männer der Wissenschaft über die Friedenskonferenz* (Berlin, 1899).

[48] See Fritz Ringer, *The Decline of the German Mandarins: The German Academic Community, 1890–1933* (Cambridge, Mass., 1969), esp. pp. 295–304.

in the traditional academic disciplines, such as history, economics, and philosophy. As has been thoroughly documented, the dominant historiographical tradition in Germany was diametrically opposed to the pacifists' belief that material forces shaped history and that the nation would become subordinate to a political organization founded on universally valid moral principles.[49] When in 1915 Walther Schücking chided Hans Delbrück for the failure of German historians to alert the country to the historical significance of the Hague conferences, Delbrück's response betrayed both the historical assumptions and the political orientation that led most of his colleagues to deprecate pacifism. "The failure was intentional," he replied, "for we Germans were a young people which still had a great future and did not believe that it could seize upon what the future offered through institutions like a court of arbitration."[50] The historians who shared Delbrück's view and denied that universal norms could bind the nation in fulfilling its historical mission included most of the luminaries of the profession, among them Erich Marcks, Hermann Oncken, and Friedrich Meinecke, whose *Weltbürgertum und Nationalstaat* was particularly alarming to the pacifists as a tribute to power politics at the expense of morality.[51]

With the exception of Martin Spahn, the Catholic historian in Strassburg who later became an outspoken conservative, the historians who looked favorably on the pacifists' campaign came from the isolated group of left-liberals in the profession.[52] Quidde was one; Max Lehmann was an-

[49] See, for instance, George C. Iggers, *The German Conception of History: The National Tradition of Historical Thought from Herder to the Present* (Middletown, Conn., 1968).

[50] NL Wehberg (43), Protokoll über die Sitzung des 1. Unterausschusses des Parlamentarischen Untersuchungsausschusses . . . 24 March 1922, pp. 4–5.

[51] NL Fried, Schücking to Fried, Marburg, 13 May 1911; see, for example, Erich Marcks, "Die imperialistische Idee in der Gegenwart," *Männer und Zeiten* (2 vols., Leipzig, 1911), II, 265–91.

[52] Martin Spahn, *Der Friedensgedanke in der Entwicklung des*

other.[53] However, the most prominent of the academic historians in the peace movement was Karl Lamprecht, a man whose political eccentricity rivaled Ernst Haeckel's. In the 1890s Lamprecht was, like Haeckel, one of the few professors to join the Pan-German League.[54] After the turn of the century he underwent a complete transformation and lent his wholehearted support to numerous internationalist causes, only to return to aggressive nationalism in 1914. The roots of his internationalism lay in his concepts of history and historical method, which in the 1890s aroused the concerted opposition of the great names in the profession in the so-called *Methodenstreit*. Lamprecht held that history was governed by certain fundamental "sociopsychological" laws, and he proposed to write history from a comparative, transnational perspective, which would reflect the universal working of these laws.[55] Thus, he sought to transcend the limitations imposed by the dominant school of idealist, na-

---

deutschen Volkes zur Nation (Stuttgart, 1913); see also Martin Spahn, "Selbstbiographie," in Hans von Arnim and Georg von Below, eds., *Deutscher Aufstieg: Bilder aus der Vergangenheit und Gegenwart der rechtsstehenden Parteien* (Berlin, 1925), pp. 479–88.

[53] Veit Valentin became a dedicated pacifist during the First World War: FW, LXVII (1947), 275. As a curious footnote, Theodor Schiemann, who was something of an historian but hardly a pacifist, agreed in 1911 to serve on a study commission on national economy and history for the Carnegie Endowment. Quidde's reaction was: "How did Saul arrive among the prophets?" NL Lujo Brentano, Bundesarchiv, Coblenz (cited hereafter as NL Brentano) (254), Carnegie-Stiftung zur Förderung des internationalen Friedens . . . Studienprogramm; NL Brentano (44), Quidde to Brentano, Kreuth, 26 August 1911.

[54] Alfred Kruck, *Geschichte des Alldeutschen Verbandes 1890–1939* (Wiesbaden, 1954), pp. 18, 254.

[55] See Georg Jahn, "Karl Lamprecht als Wirtschafts- und Kulturhistoriker . . ." *Schmollers Jahrbuch* LXXVI (1956), esp. 133–38; Adolf Kuhnert, *Der Streit um die geschichtswissenschaftlichen Theorien Karl Lamprechts* (Gütersloh, 1906); Herbert Schönebaum, "Karl Lamprecht," *Archiv für Kulturgeschichte* XXXVII (1955), 269–305; Simon, *European Positivism*, p. 244; Ringer, *German Mandarins*, pp. 302–304; Iggers, *German Conception of History*, pp. 197–200.

tional history, by showing that the history of all cultural groups conformed to demonstrable evolutionary patterns and that the history of Germany could be only a prelude to a universal history of humanity. While this perspective kept Lamprecht in professional disrepute, it made him receptive to the theories of Alfred Fried, who was also trying to show the existence of international developmental patterns that would eventually lead to the unification of mankind. As he began to correspond regularly with Fried, Lamprecht became a warm supporter of pacifism, which he called in 1910 "the most sublime blossom of European political culture."[56] He also made it clear that he thought that historical science should aid in securing world peace. In his view, German historians had performed great services for the unification of the nation in the nineteenth century, and he called on them to "intercede no less gloriously and decisively in the movement for the unity of mankind, which is becoming ever more manifest in the development of international relations."[57] At the University of Leipzig he founded an institute for comparative international history, which, as he explained to Bertha von Suttner, was "completely designed to contribute to peace and the progress of the nations."[58] Along with Wilhelm Ostwald, his colleague in Leipzig, Lamprecht sponsored several internationalist student organizations and promoted international exchange of students and professors.[59] Some of Lamprecht's students, who shared his professional isolation, also drew the implications

[56] FW, XII (1910), 41–44; cf. Karl Lamprecht, *Die Nation und die Friedensbewegung* (Berlin, 1914), p. 7.

[57] "Auswärtige Kulturpolitik und Geschichtswissenschaft," MVfiV, I (1913), 8; cf. Lamprecht, *Europäische Expansion* (Ullsteins Weltgeschichte, Vol. 6) (Berlin, 1908), p. 621; HB (2), II, 254.

[58] NL Suttner (Ch17), Lamprecht to Suttner, Leipzig, 30 September 1909; NL Fried, Lamprecht to Fried, Thierke (Harz), 4 January 1912.

[59] Lamprecht, *Rektoratserinnerungen*, edited by Arthur Köhler (Gotha, 1917), pp. 15–16, 40–41; NL Fried, Edgar Herzog to Fried, Leipzig, 31 August 1912; NL Wehberg (59a), Fried to Wehberg, Vienna, 30 June 1910.

of his historical theories and endorsed the work of the pacifists.[60]

The isolation of Lamprecht and other historians who were close to the pacifists reflected the situation in other academic disciplines as well. The study of economics in Germany, significantly called *Nationalökonomie*, was principally concerned with the relationship between the economy and the power of the nation-state. Sympathy for the pacifists was consequently very sparse, limited for the most part to free-trade liberals such as Lujo Brentano. However, not even Brentano was willing to join an organization associated with the peace movement, although he did consent to speak before peace meetings and allow his name to be placed on innocuous honorary committees like the executive committee for the 1907 Universal Peace Congress in Munich.[61] One economist who did actively oppose what he called the "incredible narrow-mindedness" of his colleagues was Bernhard Harms in Kiel, who in his publications and as editor of the *Weltwirtschaftliches Archiv* attempted to draw the attention of scholars to the developments in international economics on which Fried based his pacifism.[62]

Although neo-Kantianism pervaded German academic philosophy prior to the war, few philosophers adopted Kant's views about applied ethics and perpetual peace along with his epistemological insights. Among those who did, however, were two of the most illustrious figures in the neo-Kantian movement. Hermann Cohen and Paul Natorp,

[60] Rogge, *Nationale Friedenspolitik*, pp. 22–23; see Karl J. Weintraub, *Visions of Culture: Voltaire, Burckhardt, Lamprecht, Huizinga, Ortega y Gasset* (Chicago and London, 1966), p. 175.

[61] NL Schücking (58), Brentano to Schücking, Munich, 10 December 1909; NL Brentano (44), Nippold to Brentano, Oberursel, 9 September 1913; Brentano, "The Chief Causes of War Today," PM, 1 (1912), 96–98; cf. James J. Sheehan, *The Career of Lujo Brentano: A Study of Liberalism and Social Reform in Imperial Germany* (Chicago and London, 1966), p. 186.

[62] NL Fried, Harms to Fried, Kiel, 1 May 1912; Harms, *Volkswirtschaft und Weltwirtschaft: Versuch der Begründung einer Weltwirtschaftslehre* (Jena, 1912).

who formed the so-called "Marburg school," were both out-spoken pacifists.[63] A more peripheral figure in the neo-Kant-ian movement, Ludwig Stein, was also active in the peace movement. Professor of philosophy in Berne until 1910, Stein served along with Eduard Zeller and Wilhelm Dilthey as editor of the *Archiv für die Geschichte der Philosophie*. Stein's own philosophical works were devoted to reconcil-ing Kant's critical theory with natural selection, as he tried to demonstrate that the categories of man's cognition were a critical advantage in the struggle to survive.[64] Stein's reading of Kant and Darwin also convinced him, like Fried, that man had reached an evolutionary stage at which ethics would govern all facets of human behavior, including inter-national relations. Thus Stein became a pacifist and was for many years a Swiss representative on the International Peace Bureau. In 1912 he moved to Berlin to succeed Paul Lindau as editor of the journal *Nord und Süd*, in which capacity he continued to advocate international organiza-tion and conciliation.[65] In Berlin, however, he found it pru-dent to tone down his pacifism, even to the point of a public recantation, once he became involved as a diplomatic con-tact between Bethmann Hollweg and Richard Haldane, whom he had previously known as a philosophy student in Zurich.[66]

[63] NL Fried, Guido Edler von Goutta to Fried, Freiburg, 4 Feb-ruary 1912; Otto Koester, "Hermann Cohen und der kritische Idealis-mus," VF, XVIII (1918), 80–82; FW, XXIX (1929), 68. Wilhelm Windel-band, the other major figure in the neo-Kantian movement, did not share this orientation: Paul Honigsheim, *On Max Weber* (New York and East Lansing, 1968), p. 16.

[64] Ludwig Stein, *Aus dem Leben eines Optimisten* (Berlin, 1930), esp. pp. 102–106.

[65] Gerald Deckart, "Deutsch-englische Verständigung: Eine Dar-stellung der nichtoffiziellen Bemühungen um eine Wiederannäherung der beiden Länder zwischen 1905 und 1914" (Inaugural dissertation, Munich, 1967), pp. 165–80.

[66] Stein, *Leben eines Optimisten*, pp. 194–95; "Ich bin kein Pazifist," FW, XIV (1912), 347–48.

In the well entrenched disciplines in German universities, both academic tradition and political conservatism contributed to the distaste or indifference with which most professors viewed pacifism. It was in the newer disciplines, which were themselves objects of political and academic suspicion, that pacifism found its most significant scholarly support.

One can only speak in a qualified sense of sociology as an academic discipline in Germany before the war. Most of those who devoted themselves to the "science of society" had been trained in other disciplines and lectured on the subject as a peripheral facet of economics, psychology, or philosophy. Academic hostility to sociology was widespread. Prior to the war there was no chair of sociology at a German university, for it was commonly held that the discipline was based upon positivism and tainted with political radicalism.[67]

This belief was not altogether unfounded. Sociology was in many cases pursued by men with left-liberal political views who subscribed to progressive evolutionism. Georg Simmel and Ferdinand Tönnies, for instance, were members of ethical culture societies, as was Werner Sombart.[68] That a majority of German sociologists approached their work with an optimistic faith in progress became apparent in the history of the German Sociological Association, the organization perhaps best known as the forum in which Max Weber fought for the principle of scientific objectivity.[69] Weber's opponents in this organization have been largely overlooked. Their principal spokesman was Rudolf Goldscheid, the leader of the Austrian *Monistenbund*, a

[67] Anthony Oberschall, *Empirical Social Research in Germany, 1848–1914* (The Hague, 1965), pp. 140, 145.

[68] DWN, v (1896), 353; Foerster, *Ethische Bewegung*, cover.

[69] Marianne Weber, *Max Weber: Ein Lebensbild* (Tübingen, 1926), pp. 425–31; Guenther Roth, "Max Weber's Empirical Sociology in Germany and the United States: Tensions between Partisanship and Scholarship," *Central European History* II (1969), 201–204.

close friend of Wilhelm Ostwald, and a man entirely convinced that the inexorable progress of mankind could be scientifically documented. Weber, who recognized in this view an extension of Goldscheid's ethical assumptions, was successful at the founding of the association, in 1909, in having the principle of *Wertfreiheit* affirmed in the group's statutes. At subsequent meetings, however, it was clear that most of the members of the association sympathized with Goldscheid. As a consequence, Weber left the organization in 1912, complaining of Goldscheid's "so-called *Weltanschauung* . . . with scientific pretensions, the nature of which makes it altogether impossible for me to work with him."[70]

Rudolf Goldscheid was a devout pacifist, an intimate friend of Fried and Suttner in Vienna. His pacifism was axiomatic in his sociological system, which he called *Menschenökonomie* and which was virtually the same as the sociology of Fried's scientific pacifism.[71] Many of the others in the German Sociological Association who supported Goldscheid against Weber also derived pacifism from sociology. Robert Michels corresponded regularly with Fried, who was himself a member of the association. Simmel and Georg Gothein belonged to organizations close to the peace movement, as did Alfred Vierkandt, who in 1912 confessed to Fried that he had often thought about how his theories would justify pacifism.[72] Although Tönnies was unable to subscribe unequivocally to the cultural optimism of Goldscheid and Fried, he shared their commitment to working

---

[70] Weber, *Weber*, p. 430; Paul Honigsheim, "Die Gründung der deutschen Gesellschaft für Soziologie in ihren geistesgeschichtlichen Zusammenhängen," *Kölner Zeitschrift für Soziologie* XI (1959), 8–9; Honigsheim, *On Max Weber*, pp. 60–61; Leopold von Wiese, "Die deutsche Gesellschaft für Soziologie: Politische Eindrücke in den ersten fünfzig Jahren (1909 bis 1959)," *Kölner Zeitschrift für Soziologie* XI (1959), 11.

[71] Rudolf Goldscheid, *Friedensbewegung und Menschenökonomie* (Berlin and Leipzig, 1912).

[72] NL Fried, Vierkandt to Fried, Lichterfelde, 4 May 1912; cf. FW, XIV (1912), 152–53.

for world peace.[73] Franz Müller-Lyer, another prominent member of the German Sociological Association, was convinced that sociology would play a role in the triumph of the peace movement and regarded pacifism as "one of the main indices of cultural progress."[74]

If the sociological analysis that formed the basis of Fried's scientific pacifism found resonance within one new academic discipline, the fact that he utilized this sociology to develop a theory of legal evolution suggested that the peace movement might find allies in another. The study of international law had traditionally been suspect within the legal faculties of German universities. The fact that it was a new discipline, whose most conspicuous advocates in Germany were the pacifists, brought both academic and political prejudices into play. Perhaps even more important was the fact that the implications of international law seemed inconsistent with the dominant tradition of German legal theory. In Germany, *Rechtswissenschaft* remained into the twentieth century founded on a tradition of legal positivism, according to which the function of the jurist or legal theorist was strictly confined to the analysis and application of existing law. Legal positivism held further that the only source of law was the sovereign state, whose will was embodied in legislation, and that existing law provided the only valid foundation for legal norms. The theory consequently rejected all antecedent norms for legislation, be they rooted in divine prophesy, natural law, or moral precept; it likewise denied the possibility of predicting desirable goals for legal evolution. In fact, German scholars were willing to admit a departure from textual analysis only for historical study of the origins of legislation, and they resisted the assertion that any source of law outside the state,

[73] Arthur Mitzman, "Tönnies and German Society, 1887–1914: From Cultural Pessimism to the Celebration of the *Volksgemeinschaft*," *Journal of the History of Ideas* XXXII (1971), 519.

[74] NL Suttner (Fa8), Müller-Lyer to Suttner, Munich, 5 March 1912; NL Fried, Müller-Lyer to Fried, Munich, 20 October 1910.

whether a general principle or an agency, could legally bind the state.[75]

An accommodation between legal positivism and international law was theoretically possible. As long as international legal obligations were the explicitly defined products of freely negotiated agreements, they could be regarded as expressions of the will of the sovereign state.[76] However, neither German jurists nor the pacifists were interested in such a compromise. The pacifists advocated the wholesale extension of international law as the foundation for a world federation, and they posited antecedent principles of justice as the basis of that law. They thereby violated the cardinal tenets of German legal philosophy and called for a return to the tradition of natural law, which had fallen into disfavor in German universities early in the nineteenth century. Just as alarming, from the standpoint of the jurists, was the politicization of the law that the pacifists envisaged; once international law had been extended to the limits advocated by the pacifists, the control of the state over matters vital to its own interests, most obviously the decision to go to war, would be circumscribed, if not eliminated. To German jurists, trained to regard the law as unpolitical, such an extension was patently unthinkable from both a professional and a patriotic standpoint, and in practice they viewed the very concept of international law, especially international public law, with apprehension.[77]

Because most German jurists rejected the implications of international law, the study and teaching of the subject remained until the end of the nineteenth century no more

[75] See Detlev Acker, *Walther Schücking (1875–1935)* (Münster, 1970), pp. 38–39; Max Huber, "Walther Schücking und die Völkerrechtswissenschaft," FW, xxxv (1935), 197–201; William O. Shanahan, "Liberalism and Foreign Affairs: Naumann and the Pre-War German View," *Review of Politics* xxi (1959), 191–92.

[76] See Schiffer, *Legal Community*, pp. 165–86.

[77] FW, xxxviii (1938), 235–36; Josef Kohler, "Die Friedensbewegung und das Völkerrecht," *Zeitschrift für Völkerrecht und Bundesstaatsrecht* iv (1909–10), 129–39.

than a peripheral concern, as professors of law lectured only occasionally, and then unenthusiastically, about it. The few scholars who believed that the development of international law was a positive feature of modern life included the left-liberal jurist Ludwig von Bar in Göttingen, Georg Jellinek in Heidelberg, and the noted penologist, Franz von Liszt.[78] But these men remained isolated amidst the general academic hostility that made it impossible to establish a chair in international law at a German university until 1912.[79]

Given the formidability of the barriers that separated jurists and pacifists in Germany, the developments of the first decade of the twentieth century, which culminated in a tentative alliance, were quite remarkable. The event that marked the beginning of the process was the first Hague conference. However minimal its results, the conference did set up a court of international arbitration; this fact in itself suggested to some German legal scholars that arbitration and the growth of international law were more than the chimera of *Friedensschwärmer*. As a result, important voices within the German legal profession began to take international law seriously and to confront its potentialities with some sympathy. As they were doing so, German pacifism was itself beginning to reflect the salutary effects of the Hague conference, particularly in Fried's reformulation of the credo. Indeed, Fried's contribution to the dialogue between legal scholars and the pacifists was decisive, as

[78] BIP (vB6), Franz von Liszt to Ducommun, Halle, 14 January 1898; Georg Jellinek, *Der Kampf des alten mit dem neuen Recht* (Heidelberg, 1907); Chr. de Boeck, "Ludwig von Bars Lebenswerk," *Zeitschrift für Völkerrecht* VIII (1914), 420–36; Wehberg, *Führer*, pp. 34–37.

[79] Theodor Niemeyer, *Erinnerungen und Betrachtungen aus drei Menschenaltern* (Kiel, 1963), pp. 143, 156; Max Huber, "Lebensgeschichte und Zeitgeschichte," in Walther Schätzel and Hans-Jürgen Schlochauer, eds., *Rechtsfragen der internationalen Organisation: Festschrift für Hans Wehberg zu seinem 70. Geburtstag* (Frankfurt, 1956), pp. 18–19.

scientific pacifism provided scholars with a plausible and suggestive sociological theory of international law, which succeeded to a modest degree in overcoming the parochialism of legal positivism.

In the aftermath of the Hague conference, especially after the publication of Fried's *Handbuch der Friedensbewegung* in 1905, there appeared a series of scholarly commentaries which were very favorable not only toward arbitration and its development, but toward the peace movement as well. In 1905 Theodor Niemeyer, a leading legal scholar in Kiel, who in 1894 had vigorously rejected the validity of normative principles in international private law, spoke out in favor of the peace movement as he praised Fried's *Handbuch*: "The practical and scientific cultivation of international law is no longer in a position to dismiss the peace movement as utopian. It must now be respected as a developing factor."[80] The same year Christian Meurer, who taught at the University of Würzburg, published the first of two volumes of commentary on the Hague conference.[81] Drawing prominently from Fried's writings and other pacifist literature, he concluded that the conference pointed the way toward a legitimate expansion of the scope of international law. In 1906 Philipp Zorn, a professor of law in Bonn who had been the legal advisor to the German delegation at the Hague conference and an outspoken critic of the pacifists, published a significant article which reflected the reassessment that many German scholars were making about the peace movement: "Simply to dismiss the modern peace movement with a derisive shrug of the shoulders, as is perhaps still customary in Germany, will not do. Their ideas have spread throughout the world and constitute a significant factor in contemporary international life. We

[80] Quoted in FW, VIII (1906), 88; cf. NL Fried, Niemeyer to Fried, Kitzeberg bei Kiel, 5 November 1909.

[81] Meurer, *Das Friedensrecht der Haager Konferenz* (Munich, 1905). A second volume appeared two years later: *Das Kriegsrecht der Haager Konferenz* (Munich, 1907).

must therefore pay careful attention to them."[82] In 1907 Otfried Nippold, who taught law in Berne, published a detailed study of the Hague conference, in which he, like Meurer, relied heavily on pacifist literature and concluded that elaboration of international legal ties, even to the point of obligatory arbitration in some instances, was both necessary and desirable.[83]

The convocation of a second Hague conference in 1907 lent momentum to the growing interest of German jurists in international law. A new generation of legal scholars, less encumbered by their mentors' positivism, were more willing to admit that ethical and social factors could influence the evolution of international law.[84] Particularly notable was the work of Walther Schücking, a student of Ludwig von Bar and professor of law in Marburg. In 1907 he published a short article in *Die Zukunft*, in which he urged his colleagues to reconsider the applicability of natural law and devote themselves to the study of goals for the development of international law.[85] Even more remarkable was Schücking's publication in 1909 of a volume in which he surveyed the history of the idea of universal peace and concluded, like Fried, that historical evolution pointed clearly in the direction of a world federation.[86] Hans Wehberg, who was one of Zorn's students, was equally outspoken in his support of the pacifists and emphasized the contribution they had

[82] Quoted in HB (2), II, 247; cf. FW, IV (1902), 66; FW, IX (1907), 215.

[83] Otfried Nippold, *Die Fortbildung des Verfahrens in völkerrechtlichen Streitigkeiten: Ein völkerrechtliches Problem der Gegenwart speziell im Hinblick auf die Haager Friedenskonferenzen* (Leipzig, 1907).

[84] See Max Huber, "Beiträge zur Kenntnis der sozialen Grundlagen des Völkerrechts und der Gesellschaft," *Jahrbuch des öffentlichen Rechts* IV (1910), 56–134.

[85] Schücking, "Modernes Weltbürgertum," *Die Zukunft* LX (1907), 244–45. On Schücking see the recent biography by Detlev Acker, *Walther Schücking (1875–1935)* (Münster, 1970).

[86] Schücking, *Die Organisation der Welt* (Leipzig, 1909); cf. FW, XXXV (1935), 197–201.

made to the Hague conferences and to the development of a *Völkerrechtswissenschaft*.[87] With the establishment of the *Zeitschrift für Völkerrecht und Bundesstaatsrecht* in 1906 under the editorship of Josef Kohler, the former chairman of the German Peace Society, the views of progressive young scholars like Schücking, Wehberg, Nippold, Karl Strupp, and Max Huber found a regular outlet.[88]

Fried was ecstatic over the favorable reaction his theories had evoked from the German academic community, for it exceeded the bounds of his most optimistic expectations. His description of the academic response as the *"Kapitulation der Wissenschaft"* can be dismissed as a characteristic hyperbolism, but the interest and sympathy shown by German professors, especially the jurists, were indeed impressive.[89] It was no less impressive that Fried was able to capitalize on this reaction and establish an organization drawn largely from German academics, designed to promote international conciliation through the extention of international law.

The VERBAND FÜR INTERNATIONALE VERSTÄNDIGUNG[90]

Fried had long been considering the possibility of reorganizing the German peace movement. His dissatisfaction with the German Peace Society was far too profound for him to believe that transferring the headquarters

[87] Wehberg, "Friedensbewegung, Völkerrechtwissenschaft, Haager Friedenskonferenz," *Deutsche Revue* xxxv (1910), 349–54.

[88] NL Wehberg (63), J. Kohler to Wehberg, Berlin, 17, 19 June 1913.

[89] Fried, "Die moderne Friedensbewegung in Deutschland und Frankreich, I: Die Bewegung in Deutschland," *Der Continent* I (1907), 703; cf. Fried, "Le développement récent du pacifisme allemand," PD, xx (1910), 398–410.

[90] Parts of this and the preceding section have appeared in article form: Roger Chickering, "A Voice of Moderation in Imperial Germany: The 'Verband für internationale Verständigung,' 1911–1914," *Journal of Contemporary History* viii (January 1973), 147–64.

from Berlin to Stuttgart could make pacifism appreciably more effective in Germany. He began almost immediately after the move to Stuttgart to plan a new peace organization, possibly based upon an alternative approach. The German Peace Society remained founded on the belief that it would be possible to win the massive support of public opinion and thereby to put pressure on political elites. By the turn of the century, though, it was clear that the peace society, as it was then constituted, would be unable to mobilize that kind of popular support. This suggested the alternative, which Eugen Schlief had advocated in the early 1890s, of an elite organization to work directly with political leaders. But Fried was also skeptical about whether a peace organization could have any direct appeal or influence among elite sectors of German society. Thus he reverted to the idea that a mass organization was preferable and formulated a proposal for a new peace society, modeled after the Anti-Corn Law League, which could mobilize what he believed was widespread latent support for the peace movement in Germany.[91]

The sudden rise of academic interest in pacifism made Fried change his mind once again. It now seemed that there was in fact potential support for an elite committee, such as the one proposed by Schlief, composed of scholars to study and make recommendations about treaties of arbitration. Accordingly, Fried began to lay plans for a new, independent peace organization, whose members would enjoy the prestige to make the idea of international arbitration politically respectable in Germany. To coordinate the establishment of the new organization he sought an individual relatively untainted by prior association with the peace movement. Schlief himself seemed to be the logical choice,

[91] Fried, *Die Ausgestaltung der Friedensaktion in Deutschland* (Berlin, 1903); FW, IV (1902), 145–60; NL Fried, Quidde to Fried, Munich, 27 April 1902; Fried to Rogalla von Bieberstein, Berlin, 27 September 1902; Fried to Eugen Schlief, Vöslau, 23 June 1904.

but he proved to be interested only in an organization to promote his own specialized theories of international law.[92] Instead, Fried turned to Otfried Nippold, a man whose progressive views on arbitration seemed to correspond closely with his own and who shared Fried's desire to enlist academic support for arbitration.[93]

In Nippold, Fried found a man gifted with a penetrating legal mind, as well as immense energy. Born in 1864, he spent his early years without putting down roots. After receiving his doctorate in law in Jena, where his father was professor of religious history, he spent three years lecturing in Japan and then worked for two years in Berlin at the German foreign office, before settling in Berne as a *Privatdozent*.[94] In 1907 he agreed to Fried's proposal, and the two began to plan the new organization. The next year they were joined by Walther Schücking, who was also enthusiastic about Fried's project.[95]

In 1909 Nippold accepted an editorial position with the *Frankfurter Zeitung* and moved to Germany, whereupon he and Schücking, with Fried in the background, began to look for support among professors and selected politicians. Seeking as wide a range of support as possible, in order to avoid charges of political parochialism, they experienced

[92] NL Fried, Fried to Schlief, Vienna, 8, 21 January 1908; Schlief, "Die Partei der internationalen Ordnung," FW, XI (1909), 25–28.

[93] NL Fried, Nippold to Fried, Berne, 16 December 1906; Fried to Nippold, Vienna, 29 May 1911.

[94] NL Wehberg (67), Otfried Nippold, "Erklärung"; *Volksstimme* (Saarbrücken), 25 March 1926; see also Otfried Nippold, *Meine Erlebnisse in Deutschland vor dem Weltkriege (1909–1914)* (Berne, 1918). Nippold spent the war years in Switzerland working with peace groups in the pay of the Allies. After the war the French installed him as president of the *Oberstes Landgericht* in the Saar, where his Swiss background and his ties to the Allies made him unpopular: NL Conrad Haussmann, Hauptstatsarchiv Stuttgart (cited hereafter as NL Haussmann) (4), D. Cohnstedt to Robert Haussmann, 24 January 1925. There is a Nippold *Nachlass* in Berne, which I was unable to use.

[95] NL Fried, Schücking to Fried, Marburg, 2 March 1908; cf. Acker, *Walther Schücking*, pp. 50–58.

considerable success.[96] In May 1910 they announced the projected organization in a public appeal, which ran in part: "We must strive for a new political system of international relations, specifically by seeking to extend international arbitration and to promote treaties with other nations to proliferate guarantees of world peace. . . . [Germans] must come to the realization that in the final analysis the common interests of competing states are larger than their rivalries, and, therefore, that international understanding is possible."[97] The appeal, which concluded by calling for the creation of a *Verband für internationale Verständigung* to promote these goals, bore the endorsement of many of the leading scholars in Germany; among them were Karl von Amira, Hermann Cohen, Max Fleischmann, Ernst Haeckel, Adolf Harnack, Georg Jellinek, Karl Lamprecht, Franz von Liszt, Paul Natorp, Friedrich Naumann, Robert Piloty, Martin Rade, Ernst Troeltsch, and Max Weber.[98]

In the summer of 1910 Nippold elaborated on his conceptions about the new organization in an article he published in the *Deutsche Revue*. Drawing directly from Fried, he pointed out that legal ties had come to regulate all aspects of international life except politics, which remained founded on armed force. The correction of this anomaly was the most urgent problem of the day: "We must prepare the way for impending progress in politics. That means primarily enlightening public opinion in the advanced nations about existing inadequacies in international political relations, about the proper legal interpretation of future conflicts, [and the establishment of] a more substantial ordering of international relations through the negotiation of treaties of international law."[99]

[96] NL Rade, Schücking to Rade, Marburg, December 1909; NL Fried, Schücking to Fried, Marburg, 4 March 1910.

[97] NL Wehberg (67), Aufruf zur Begründung eines Verbandes für internationale Verständigung.

[98] *Ibid.*

[99] Nippold, "Kulturentwicklung und Weltpolitik," *Deutsche Revue* XXXV (1910), 190–202.

The recruiting of members for the organization that would take on this assignment continued throughout the year, as Nippold awaited an appropriate moment, when domestic issues were tranquil, to convoke an assembly to found the group.[100] On 11 June 1911 forty-one delegates met in Frankfurt and officially constituted the *Verband für internationale Verständigung*, with Emmanuel von Ullmann, a professor of law in Munich, as chairman, Nippold and Schücking as vice-chairmen, and Hermann Maier, a director of the *Deutsche Bank* in Frankfurt, as treasurer. The delegates also selected an executive committee, which included Richard Eickhoff and Prince Schönaich-Carolath from the Reichstag, Christian Meurer, Piloty, Liszt, Lamprecht, and the pacifists Ludwig Quidde and Heinrich Rössler.[101]

As defined in its statutes, the goal of the *Verband* was "to spread understanding of the significance of mutually beneficial contacts among nations . . . [and] especially an understanding of questions of international law."[102] In the eyes of its founders the organization was designed to do for the development of foreign policy what the *Verein für Sozialpolitik* had done for social policy.[103] By studying and

[100] NL Schücking (58), Nippold to Schücking, Frankfurt, 19 April 1910. Other early supporters included Julius Bachem, Wilhelm Foerster, Heinrich Weinel, Wilhelm van Calker, Theodor Lipps, and Heinrich Sieveking: NL Schücking (58), Entwurf zu einem Aufruf zur Begründung eines Verbandes für internationale Verständigung.

[101] On the background and founding of the *Verband* see: Hans Wehberg, "Der Verband für internationale Verständigung," FW, XIII (1911), 171–74; Nippold, *Erlebnisse*, p. 9; *Schulthess' Europäischer Geschichtskalender 1912* (Munich, 1913), pp. 12–13; Carnegie Endowment for International Peace, *Year Book for 1912* (Washington, D.C., 1912), p. 78; "Zur internationalen Verständigung," *Kölnische Zeitung*, 12 June 1911; "Verband für internationale Verständigung," *Frankfurter Zeitung*, 12 June 1911.

[102] *Statuten des Verbandes für internationale Verständigung* (Frankfurt, n.d.), p. 3.

[103] NL Brentano (56), Schücking to Brentano, Marburg, 7 December 1909. On other occasions leaders of the *Verband* stressed its simi-

popularizing bold new concepts, notably the extension of international law, the *Verband* would, it was hoped, nurture attitudes more conducive to international understanding and relieve statesmen of pressure from an uninformed and excitable populace. "We desperately need public opinion that is not vulnerable to the power of suggestion," Nippold declared in 1912. "As long as mistrust persists, nations must be armed, but the *Verband* hopes that education of public opinion . . . will make possible a gradual disappearance of this mistrust."[104] Thus, the founders of the organization conceived of it as an antidote to chauvinist groups such as the Pan-German League.[105] The *Verband für internationale Verständigung* was to be an elite group, which through its moderating influence on the press, its informed commentary on international disputes, and through the very prestige of its members would promote friendly relations among the powers.

After the founding congress in June 1911 recruiting continued. The Moroccan crisis in the summer of 1911 retarded the campaign, but by the time a new public appeal appeared early in 1912, the *Verband's* membership had grown significantly.[106] When the group's first general congress met in October 1912, membership stood at two hundred, a figure that had grown to over three hundred by the outbreak of war in 1914.[107] Among the people who had

---

larities to the *Nationalverein*: NL Schücking (58), Entwurf zu einem Aufruf . . . ; Carl Strimberg to Schücking, 2 February 1910.

[104] Nippold, "Auswärtige Politik und öffentliche Meinung," MVfiV, 1 (1913), 2.

[105] Friedrich Curtius, *Deutsche Briefe und elsässische Erinnerungen* (Frauenfeld, 1920), p. 124.

[106] NL Haussmann (4), Verband für internationale Verständigung, Aufruf. Among the new members were Rudolf von Bennigsen, Arthur von Gwinner, Friedrich von Payer, Peter Spahn, Robert Gyssling, Conrad Haussmann, Ernst Müller-Meiningen, Rudolf Oeser, Hermann Pachnicke, and Hans Vaihinger.

[107] NL Haussmann (4), Verband für internationale Verständigung, 2. Verbandstag zu Nürnberg; FW, XIV (1912), 381. Several organiza-

joined were Karl Trimborn, Rudolf Breitscheid, Georg Gothein, Max Lehmann, Georg Simmel, Bernhard Harms, Eduard Cassirer, Paul Laband, Hugo Preuss, Alfred Vierkandt, and Alfred Weber.

Despite the aspirations of some leaders that the *Verband* would attract a mass following, it remained an elite group in which academics, particularly the jurists, predominated.[108] Led by Conrad Haussmann, a small group of Reichstag deputies belonged, drawn primarily from the left-liberal *Fortschrittliche Volkspartei* and the left wing of the Catholic Center party; efforts to stimulate interest in the *Verband* among the other parties met with little success.[109] Since the *Verband* conceived of its mission in educational terms, it made a special effort to recruit student groups and did succeed in bringing in several *Burschenschaften* as corporate members.[110] In an attempt to gain support from the economic elite of the country, whose interests would presumably profit from a more secure international peace, the *Verband* tried to enlist chambers of commerce, business firms, and prominent industrialists and financiers. While a few prominent firms and business leaders, such as *Nord-*

---

tions held corporate memberships, which enabled leaders of the *Verband* to claim a larger number of adherents: see Nippold, *Erlebnisse*, p. 23; NL Fried, Wehberg to Fried, Düsseldorf, 13 September 1912; Adolf Wild, *Baron d'Estournelles de Constant (1852–1924): Das Wirken eines Friedensnobelpreisträgers für die deutsch-französische Verständigung und die europäische Einigung* (Hamburg, 1973), p. 404.

[108] Friedrich Curtius, "Die ethische Aufgabe des Verbandes für internationale Verständigung," KVfiV, 1 (1 July 1912); NL Fried, Nippold to Fried, Frankfurt, 15 November 1909, 7 April 1910.

[109] NL Haussmann (117), Schücking to Haussmann, Marburg, 16 March 1912; NL Fried, Schücking to Fried, Marburg, 4 March 1910.

[110] NL Wehberg (67), Nippold to Wehberg, Oberursel, 21 February 1911, 28 July 1913; NL Wehberg (36), Burschenschaft Marchia to Wehberg, Bonn, 20 June 1913. There was, however, no rush of student corporations to join the *Verband*: NL Wehberg (67), Wehberg to Nippold, Düsseldorf, 12 March 1910.

deutscher Lloyd and Arthur von Gwinner, did join, there was no great enthusiasm on the part of chambers of commerce or other interests to affiliate with the new organization.[111]

The *Verband für internationale Verständigung* was administered by a five-man board of directors and an executive committee, which was composed of some twenty members. The most important activities of the organization were coordinated by special commissions for education, legal questions, the press, and propaganda. The preponderance of international lawyers in the organization was reflected foremost in the fact that they chaired these commissions. Headquarters of the *Verband* were in Frankfurt, with local chapters in Strassburg and Munich. Soon after its founding, the group became an affiliate of *Conciliation internationale*, an international association of statesmen and scholars, founded in 1905 by the French politician Paul Henri d'Estournelles de Constant (an organization to which a handful of Germans, in including Haeckel, Schönaich-Carolath, Foerster, and Ludwig von Bar, had already belonged). The affiliation brought the *Verband* to the attention of *Conciliation internationale*'s benefactor, the Carnegie Endowment, which ended the new German group's financial anxieties with a healthy annual subsidy.[112]

Although a succession of prominent figures served as chairmen of the new organization, the real power remained in the hands of Nippold.[113] Indeed, he made himself into a virtual autocrat, supervising the administration, controlling the disbursement of funds, and even censoring the contents

[111] "Die deutschen Handelskammern," KVfiV, 1 (1 May 1913); NL Wehberg (77), Schücking to Wehberg, 7 June 1912.

[112] NL Fried, American Association for International Conciliation, Quarterly Report to the Council of Direction (June 1912); Wild, *Baron d'Estournelles de Constant*, pp. 220–40, 388.

[113] Chairmen were Emmanuel von Ullmann (1911–13); Ludwig von Bar (1913); and Friedrich Curtius, president of the directory of the Alsatian Evangelical church (1913–1914).

of speeches to be delivered at official meetings.[114] It soon became evident that Nippold, who was obstinate and devoid of tact, was a very ambitious man, and that he regarded the *Verband* as a vehicle to advance his own career in the new field of international law. However, since he was also the organization's primary source of energy, and everyone knew it, the other leaders had to endure countless affronts and incidents, until Nippold's continued presence became an intolerable financial burden as well.[115] In 1913 he installed himself as salaried executive secretary of the *Verband*, with a pension included in the event his contract should be terminated for any reason. This proved to be more than the group's finances could support, and a revolt within the board of directors on the eve of the war forced him into premature retirement, subsidized by the Carnegie Endowment.[116]

Any thoughts that the *Verband* might be able to exert direct pressure on political leaders were dispelled by the group's inability to find support among more than a handful of progressive deputies in the Reichstag. Thus, like the German Peace Society, the *Verband* concentrated on educating public opinion, though its general approach to this problem differed somewhat from that of the peace society, which emphasized active agitation among agencies of opinion for-

[114] JPC, John Mez to David Starr Jordan, Munich, 11 June 1914; FW, xxxviii (1938), 238. In 1913 Lujo Brentano was asked to deliver a speech to the second general congress of the *Verband* on the subject of *"Weltpolitik und Weltwirtschaft."* He agreed and dutifully sent a copy of what he intended to say to Nippold, who replied that Brentano's hostile references to Russia would have to be eliminated for the speech to be acceptable. Brentano did not speak: NL Brentano (44), Nippold to Brentano, Oberursel, 9 September 1913.

[115] NL Fried, Fried to d'Estournelles, Vienna, 25 July 1912; Wild, *Baron d'Estournelles de Constant*, p. 389.

[116] NL Fried, Wehberg to Fried, Düsseldorf, 19 February 1914; NL Wehberg (77), Schücking to Wehberg, Marburg, 7 February 1914; NL Schücking (58), [Hermann Maier] Entwurf eines Schreibens an Professor Nippold [June 1914].

mation. While the *Verband* did engage in some such activity, notably with regard to the press, the organization was founded on the assumption that the very spectacle of prestigious people speaking and writing knowledgeably about international understanding would have a favorable impact on public opinion. Consequently, the emphasis in the *Verband*'s activities fell on exposing the German public to the views of its elite membership, by such means as a series of pamphlets written by members of the organization on various aspects of international relations.[117] The major facet of the *Verband*'s activity was the convocation of congresses; it was instrumental, for instance, in calling the Anglo-German conciliation conference in London in 1912 and the meeting of French and German parliamentarians in Berne in 1913. But the real highlights of the *Verband*'s existence were its own two national congresses, in Heidelberg in October 1912 and in Nuremberg in October 1913. Attended by several hundred people, both were impressive spectacles and featured lectures by leading members on the problems of international conciliation.[118]

The pacifists in the German Peace Society were elated over the founding of the *Verband für internationale Verständigung*, for it seemed to them, and not altogether without justification, that the intellectual elite of the country

[117] The titles included: Martin Rade, *Der Beitrag der christlichen Kirchen zur internationalen Verständigung* (Stuttgart, 1912); and Martin Spahn, *Der Friedensgedanke in der Entwicklung des deutschen Volkes zur Nation* (Stuttgart, 1913). Probably the most noteworthy was Nippold's *Der deutsche Chauvinismus* (Stuttgart, 1913), an impressive compilation of extracts from nationalist newspapers. One of Fritz Fischer's students has rediscovered the pamphlet as "exhaustive evidence of how radical German imperialism was": Stegmann, *Bismarcks Erben*, p. 281; cf. Fritz Fischer, *Krieg der Illusionen: Die deutsche Politik von 1911 bis 1914* (Düsseldorf, 1969), p. 362.

[118] FW, xiv (1912), 380–85; FW, xv (1913), 363–68; Conciliation internationale, *Bulletin*, number 1, 1913, pp. 16–48; number 4, 1913, pp. 63–85; *Kölnische Zeitung*, 9 October 1912; PD, xxii (1912), 656–71; PD, xxiii (1913), 629–36.

had endorsed the essentials of their program. As corroboration for this view they noted that many pacifists were members of the new organization and that leaders of the *Verband* participated in activities sponsored by the peace society.[119] Their elation was premature, however. Indeed, there was ample evidence as early as 1911 that the *Verband* did not regard the peace society with anything like unreserved approval. Alfred Fried, the man to whom the organization owed its inspiration, was not present when the *Verband* was officially constituted. In his desire to avoid all possible allegations that the group was merely a new haven for pacifist *Schwärmer*, as well as to eliminate potential rivals to his own power, Nippold had made it clear to Fried that he, as a man too closely identified with pacifism, was not wanted in Frankfurt.[120] The mood at the congress itself was also hostile to the German Peace Society, as Nippold emphasized that the *Verband* would be an eminently practical and realistic undertaking, which by clear implication the peace society was not.[121] Then, in the summer of 1911, Nippold removed the two pacifists, Quidde and Rössler, from the group's executive committee.[122]

What might have been justified as maintaining a tactical distance from the peace society soon became the source of a most unedifying antagonism among the Germans who advocated international arbitration and conciliation. Leaders of the *Verband* soon discovered that despite their tactics, nationalists were unable to distinguish between the *Verband* and the more conventional pacifists, whom they had been ridiculing for years. The *Deutsche Tageszeitung*, for exam-

[119] FW, XIV (1912), 171–72; NL Fried, Fried to Umfrid, Vienna, 11 October 1913.

[120] NL Wehberg (59a), Fried to Wehberg, 31 May 1911; cf. FW, XXV (1925), 47; NL Schücking (58), Nippold to Schücking, Frankfurt, 10 May 1910.

[121] NL M. Quidde, Ludwig Quidde to Margarethe Quidde, Frankfurt [11 June 1911]; NL Fried, Quidde to Fried, Bad Kreuth, 21 August 1911.

[122] NL Fried, Quidde to Fried, 15, 21 August 1911.

ple, responded to the *Verband*'s public appeal in January 1912 with the remark that "all things considered, we will be pleased if the group only becomes a public concern when it dissolves itself out of boredom."[123] In June 1912 Paul Dehn, writing for the Pan-German League, pointed out that the money behind the *Verband* was foreign and that the group could only encourage ill-calculated belligerence in England and France. "Are these gentlemen blind," he asked, "or have they closed their eyes intentionally?"[124]

If pacifists were accustomed to this kind of criticism, Nippold and the other leaders of the *Verband* were not. In response, they attempted to underscore their realism and patriotism by deprecating disarmament, announcing their approval of defensive war, and by gratuitously disparaging the peace society.[125] At the *Verband*'s congress in Nuremberg in 1913 Nippold announced that "the *Verband* has nothing to do with either the political alcoholism of the Pan-Germans or the abstinence of the pacifists."[126] And in a pamphlet he published shortly thereafter, Nippold again spoke uncharitably of the pacifists. In his view it was necessary to found the *Verband* because there had been no other organizations that adequately analyzed the problems of international understanding: "The few groups that do occasionally deal with pertinent questions do so unfortunately in a way that hardly merits approval."[127]

The German Peace Society was enraged over this treatment. It responded with sharp criticism of the *Verband*, and the dispute quickly escalated. Eventually even the International Peace Bureau entered the fray on the side of the

---

[123] Quoted in FW, XIV (1912), 179; cf. MVfiV, II (1914), 22.

[124] Dehn, "Für internationale Verständigung," *Alldeutsche Blätter* XX (22 June 1912), 217–18.

[125] NL Haussmann (4), Verband für internationale Verständigung, Aufruf; NL Fried, Quidde to Fried, Munich, 6 March 1914; NL Suttner (Fc6), Nippold to Suttner, Oberursel, 14 February 1912.

[126] Quoted in FW, XV (1913), 364.

[127] Nippold, *Ziele und Aufgaben des Verbandes für internationale Verständigung* (Stuttgart, 1913), esp. pp. 7–10.

peace society, before the intervention of d'Estournelles himself brought an uneasy truce at the end of 1913.[128] In the meantime, within the peace society itself the quarrel with the *Verband* had lent encouragment to the reaction against scientific pacifism, as Nippold's organization seemed to represent the offspring of Fried's theories as well as his disparagement of ethical pacifism.

Fried, who was himself hurt in the dispute, was correct when he emphasized the role played by Nippold in determining the *Verband*'s posture toward the peace society.[129] But while the dimensions of the antagonism were exacerbated by Nippold's indelicacy, most of the members of the organization sympathized with the tactical intent, if not the tone of Nippold's criticism of the pacifists. Jurists such as Schücking and Wehberg, who advocated closer cooperation with the peace society, remained isolated among their more conservative colleagues who dominated the *Verband*.

The cautious attitude of most of the law professors in the *Verband* was aptly put by Theodor Niemeyer in 1910: "Even if one does not hold the goals espoused by the pacifists to be empty fantasies, one must still concede that these goals represent the extreme degree of human perfection, the highest and farthest goals of international socialization —perhaps the culmination of the development of international law. . . . We are [however] only in the first stages of this development."[130] The jurists who subscribed to this view remained skeptical about the assumptions on which pacifism was based, for in spite of their increased interest in international law, they had hardly abandoned legal positivism in favor of normative abstractions like justice and

[128] MVfiV, I (1913), 4; FW, xv (1913), 364–65; PM, II (1913), 435–40; NL Fried, d'Estournelles de Constant, Note personnelle pour quelques uns de mes amis, Paris, 22 November 1913.

[129] NL Wehberg (59b), Fried to Wehberg, Vienna, 12 October 1913; NL Fried, Fried to d'Estournelles, Vienna, 25 July 1912.

[130] Niemeyer, "Vom Wesen des internationalen Rechtes," *Zeitschrift für internationales Recht* xx (1910), 9.

morality. The tension between legal positivism and international law they tried to resolve by insisting that the only international disputes appropriate for legal settlement were those that were nonpolitical, and hence that international law was itself nonpolitical in nature—this despite their avowed hope that the cautious growth of an international legal community would lead to political conciliation.[131] In sum, they hoped that the *Verband für internationale Verständigung* could promote the legal settlement of certain minor kinds of disputes and that this would in turn contribute to reducing international tensions. Such a modest conception of the *Verband's* role also enabled the group to appeal beyond a circle of specialists to other notables, such as Naumann and Max Weber, who were relatively indifferent to international law and were interested only in introducing some moderation into German foreign policy.[132]

Historians differ about the significance of the *Verband für internationale Verständigung*. George Hallgarten has dismissed it as "a brilliant gathering of officers without an army," which was incapable of doing "anything visible and positive for peace."[133] On the other hand, d'Estournelles de Constant's recent biographer has emphatically rejected Hallgarten's view, pointing out (with some exaggeration) that the "most prominent and most brilliant figures in the intellectual, economic, and parliamentary life of Germany were represented almost without exception" in the organization.[134] The two views are actually not hard to reconcile, for the significance of the organization varies largely according to one's perspective. From the standpoint of its im-

---

[131] Nippold, "Vorfragen des Völkerrechts," *Jahrbuch des öffentlichen Rechts* VII (1913), 20–48; FW, XXXVIII (1938), 235–43.

[132] See Honigsheim, *On Max Weber*, p. 13; Wolfgang J. Mommsen, *Max Weber und die deutsche Politik 1890–1920* (Tübingen, 1959), pp. 52–54, 75.

[133] George W. F. Hallgarten, *Imperialismus vor 1914* (2d ed., 2 vols., Munich, 1963), II, 393–94.

[134] Wild, *Baron d'Estournelles de Constant*, pp. 389–90.

pact on German society and politics, the importance of the *Verband* was indeed minimal, and Nippold only betrayed an exaggerated sense of his own importance when he later claimed that "had the *Verband* had a few more years in which to make an impression, it would in all probability have been able to overcome a great many of the obstacles it faced."[135] Its membership and appeal limited to progressive academics and politicians, the organization was unable to exert any pressure on those who formulated German foreign policy, nor did its genteel congresses have any appreciable influence on public attitudes about international relations.

From the standpoint of the German peace movement, however, the founding of the *Verband für internationale Verständigung*, and the growth of academic interest in pacifism that made it possible, were unquestionably the most important developments of the prewar period. Because of these, the peace movement managed for the first time to expand beyond the narrow social and geographical confines of the peace society and gain a foothold in one of the most prestigious sectors of German society. Yet even in this success there was cause for concern. The fact that the *Verband* was unwilling to espouse anything more extreme than a cautious political internationalism was a measure of how much pacifism would have to be diluted in order to find any significant support. Moreover, even with its eminently moderate goals, the *Verband* was able to exert almost no influence in German society and politics. In this respect, the experience of the *Verband für internationale Verständigung* was no different than that of the other sectors of the peace movement in Germany, which were enencountering enormous resistance to the concept of an international community of any kind.

---

[135] NL Wehberg (67), Nippold, "Erklärung"; see also Nippold, *Erlebnisse*, p. 24; Nippold, "Vom gegenseitigen Verstehen der Völker," *Durch Wahrheit zum Recht: Kriegsaufsätze* (Berne, 1919), p. 69.

5

The Peace Movement and the Political Education of German Society

"In truth . . . different nations do not represent hostile antagonists, but rather complementary and mutually edifying members of that entity which is humanity; their genuine and lasting interests are accordingly harmonious."[1] This proposition, which recalled the vision of the humanitarian nationalists of the early nineteenth century, must have sounded curiously out of date when it appeared in the program of the German Peace Society in 1897—the year in which Tirpitz began to lay the foundations of the German battle fleet. Yet it constituted the core of the pacifists' ideology, and the activities in which they engaged all revolved around the attempt to make Germans accept it and its political consequences.

The pacifists in Germany, like pacifists elsewhere, were thus centrally concerned with the formation of political attitudes, or, as they themselves referred to the process, the shaping of public opinion. "Lasting success," one German pacifist wrote in 1912, "the definitive elimination of war and militarism, will only be secure when the movement has won public opinion over to its ideas."[2] While their own expectations were more modest than the pacifists', leaders of the *Verband für internationale Verständigung* shared the belief that Germans should be taught to view international affairs in a new light, to recognize the growth of an international

[1] *Statut und Programm der Deutschen Friedensgesellschaft* (n.p. [1897]), p. 7; cf. FW, XXVI (1926), 326.
[2] NL Fried, Ludwig Wagner, "Errichtung eines Friedensseminars im Anschluss an die Ferienkurse für Ausländer in Kaiserslautern . . ." (September 1912).

legal community. Enlightened by this realization, public opinion would be made, in Emmanuel von Ullmann's words, "independent of tendencies that disturb the peace: chauvinism and similar psychological phenomena."[3]

In its attempt to create popular attitudes conducive to international community, the peace movement proceeded from the assumption that certain sectors of society played a critical role in shaping public opinion. In Germany, leaders of the movement isolated the educational system, the press, the churches, political parties, and the imperial government itself. They reasoned that any attempt to reorient popular attitudes about international relations would have to succeed first in these influential agencies, which meant that articulate spokesmen within them would have to be convinced to join the peace society or *Verband*, to endorse specifics of the peace movement's program, or at least to lend their moral support by publicly acknowledging the validity of the peace movement.

The German peace movement did not appreciate the enormity of what it was trying to do. The attitudes that it hoped to influence were fundamental components of the German political culture; they involved basic orientations about the nature of the entire system of international relations—orientations that have historically proved to be extremely resistant, in Germany as elsewhere, to conscious change of any kind. In retrospect it seems clear that both the German Peace Society and the *Verband für internationale Verständigung* set impossible goals for themselves, particularly in view of the resources at their disposal and the character of prevailing orientations about international politics.

Nevertheless, the significance of their undertaking ought not to be minimized. In the first place, they did experience some modest successes among the agencies they approached, and while these accomplishments had little im-

[3] MVfiV, I (1913), 2.

pact on popular attitudes, they are important to note. More significantly, the peace movement correctly perceived that agencies of socialization on many levels of the German political system were fostering attitudes about international relations utterly incompatible with the concept of international community. However naive their appreciation of politics, leaders of the peace movement identified many of the grave problems in Wilhelmine society; indeed, the response their campaign evoked in Germany was itself symptomatic of these problems.

The Political Education of German Children: Family and Youth Groups

The pacifists appreciated the importance of an individual's childhood in the formation of his basic attitudes about war and international affairs. They consequently devoted much of their effort to exposing "innocent youth" to their ideas before it could be "inoculated with the military spirit."[4] In this respect, pacifists were chiefly concerned with agitation in the educational system, but they also attempted to intervene in the earliest stages of political education in the home.[5]

The pacifists hoped to gain access to political socialization in the home by appealing indirectly to mothers, through the growing movement for women's rights. They reasoned that women were more naturally opposed to warfare than were men; gentle and moderate by nature, women could expect from war only anxiety and deprivation of their loved ones. In fact, according to the pacifists' analysis, the social and

[4] Umfrid, "Kriegerischer Geist," VF, XIV (1913), 36; Müller-Lyer, "Friedensbewegung und Schule," FW, XV (1913), 368–69; FB, IX (1908), 28.

[5] NL Fried, Feldhaus to Fried, Lörrach, 30 December 1903; Elsbeth Friedrichs to Fried, Schwetzingen, 23 January 1914; Curtius, "Ueber militärische Suggestion," KVfiV, II (6 December 1913), 6; H. Brück and E. Triebel, *Erziehe zum Frieden! Eine ernste Mahnung an Eltern und Lehrer* (Frankfurt, 1905).

political subordination of women was itself the product of the state's having to prepare for war by cultivating manly virtues.[6] The pacifists believed that more emphasis on feminine virtues and prerogatives, both within the home and in society at large, would ultimately work to the benefit of the peace movement. And in order to ensure that the emancipation of women would contribute to the progress of pacifism, they attempted to cultivate an alliance with the feminist movement.[7]

This was a logical approach. The movement for greater political and civil rights for women, which had grown rapidly in western Europe and North America at the end of the nineteenth century, was generally a close ally of the international peace movement. Many of the prominent leaders of the international feminist movement were outspoken pacifists, and national sections of organizations such as the International Council of Women and the International Women's Union officially endorsed arbitration as a means to world peace.[8]

In Germany a branch of the International Council of Women, the *Bund Deutscher Frauenvereine*, was established in 1894 to coordinate the numerous local groups that had been founded in the late nineteenth century to agitate for more educational opportunities, higher pay, and other benefits for women.[9] Unlike most of the movements in other countries, however, German feminists were as a rule politically timid and avoided the issue of women's suffrage in favor of more immediate and seemingly practical reforms,

[6] Deutsche Friedensgesellschaft, Frauenbund, *Flugblatt*, numbers 1–2; FW, VI (1904), 110; VF, XI (1910), 52.

[7] Liedtke, "Die Entwicklung des Pazifismus," pp. 437–40.

[8] *Ibid.*, pp. 442–43; *Bulletin officiel du XIIᵉ Congrès universel de la paix tenu à Rouen et Le Havre, 1903* (Berne, 1903), pp. 238–39; BIP (vQ4), International Women's Union.

[9] See Hiltrud Bradter and Imgard Weber, "Bürgerliche Frauenbewegung," in Fricke, *Die bürgerlichen Parteien* I, 201–16. I have confined my discussion to the bourgeois facet of the German feminist movement; socialists were also active proponents of women's rights.

such as opening German universities to women.[10] Political activism was confined to a vocal faction on the left wing of the movement, led by Minna Cauer, Helene Stöcker, Lina Morgenstern, and Lily von Gizycki (the wife of the leader of the Ethical Culture Society).

This left-wing group was the principal locus of pacifism within the German feminist movement. Leaders of the faction attempted to incorporate agitation for international arbitration into the program of the entire movement by promoting pacifism in the organizations they controlled, such as the *Deutscher Verein für Frauenstimmrecht*, and in progressive feminist journals such as the *Frauen-Tageszeitung*, *Frau der Gegenwart*, and Minna Cauer's *Die Frauenbewegung*.[11] For their own part, the pacifists tried to encourage these feminists. They endorsed the political emancipation of women.[12] Bertha von Suttner, though not an active feminist, often spoke at feminist meetings, where she emphasized the role women could play in eliminating war.[13] In 1914 a group of women established a *Frauenbund* within the German Peace Society in order to promote an alliance between feminism and the peace movement.[14]

The ties between the feminist movement and the peace movement remained considerably looser in Germany than in other countries. In 1897 the *Bund Deutscher Frauenvereine* sent greetings to the Universal Peace Congress in

10 Amy Hackett, "The German Women's Movement and Suffrage, 1890–1914: A Study of National Feminism," in Robert J. Bezucha, ed., *Modern European Social History* (Lexington, Mass., 1972), pp. 354–86.

11 CBM, v (1900), 44; CBM, vi (1901), 75; CBM, x (1905), 15; CBM, xii (1907), 62; VF, xi (1910), 51.

12 FB, vi (1905), 106–107; Walther Schücking, *Neue Ziele der staatlichen Entwicklung* (Marburg, 1913), p. 66.

13 Kempf, *Bertha von Suttner*, p. 10.

14 NL Fried, Elsbeth Friedrichs to Fried, Schwetzingen, 27 July 1913; VF, xv (1914), 83–84; NL. Quidde, Protokoll der Deutschen Friedensgesellschaft Vorstandssitzung, Stuttgart, 12 July 1914; Protokoll der Deutschen Friedensgesellschaft Ortsgruppe Stuttgart Sitzung, 24 June 1914.

Hamburg, and the next year, at the behest of Lina Morgen-stern, the organization resolved to incorporate agitation for world peace into its "sphere of activity."[15] But these innocuous expressions of sympathy could not disguise the fact that most German feminists were not interested in the peace movement. Indeed, many opposed it because it seemed unpatriotic, and on at least one occasion a woman was expelled from a feminist group because she belonged to a peace society.[16] Even within the more politically active faction around Cauer, which was itself not very large, sympathy for the peace movement was not strong; in 1909, for instance, Cauer explained to Fried that given the nationalist views of most of those who read her journal, she could proceed only gradually in teaching them about pacifism.[17] Nor were all pacifists happy about the prospect of an alliance with the feminists, since they feared—with good reason—that nationalists would brand the peace movement a haven for sentimental women.[18]

However shrewd the pacifists' reasoning in trying to reach German mothers through the feminist movement, it was improbable that even the closest alliance would have enabled them to exert much influence in the German home. Their chances of intervening in the process of political education as it continued in youth groups were even more remote. The peace movement appealed much less to young people than it did to activistic women, so the pacifists could do little more than protest publicly the militarization of German boys in a system of semiofficial youth organizations, most blatantly in the *Jungdeutschlandbund* and the network of *Wehrkraftvereine*.[19] Pacifists did not object to

---

[15] Moch, "Le VIIIe Congrès de la paix," p. 346.

[16] NL Fried, Feldhaus to Fried, 9 August 1911.

[17] NL Fried, Cauer to Fried, Berlin, 6 July 1909; Elsbeth Friedrichs to Fried, Eberstadt, 30 July 1912.

[18] NL Fried, Fried to A. Mehlisch, Vienna [1903]; cf. *Leipziger Neueste Nachrichten*, 12 June 1904.

[19] NL Fried, Müller-Lyer to Fried, Munich, 9 August 1913; *Das*

the idea of organized physical training for young Germans; they were disturbed rather by the military emphasis in this training, which fostered an uncritical willingness to accept war as a natural or attractive feature of international relations.

The pacifists did in fact endorse the activity of groups such as the *Wandervögel*, in which, they believed, there prevailed "a spirit of the freedom and self-determination of youth."[20] However, such a spirit did not make these groups open to pacifism. Attitudes about war seem to have been amorphous within the *Wandervögel*, but any aversion to warfare or belligerent nationalism was not a reflection of the peace movement's influence, but rather the product of a general disdain for politics.

It is worth noting, though, that Gustav Wynecken, the guru of the prewar youth movement, was a pacifist.[21] Wynecken's enormous appeal in the movement derived from his progressive theories of education, which seemed to articulate the *ethos* of the *Jugendbewegung*. By emphasizing the independence and integrity of the student, and by synthesizing physical and intellectual training, he hoped to create a spirit of genuine community among students and teachers.[22] In 1906 he founded a model school based on his pedagogical theories in the Thuringian town of Wickersdorf, where the experiment attracted the attention of the leading progressive thinkers in Germany, including

Friedensjahrbuch 1913, p. 42; VF, XIII (1912), 100; VF, XIV (1913), 36, 73; ER, III (1914), 116.

[20] Carl Ludwig Siemering, "Gegen die Militarisierung der Jugend," ER, II (1913), 207.

[21] NL Fried, Müller-Lyer to Fried, Munich, 18 January 1912.

[22] Walter Z. Laqueur, *Young Germany: A History of the German Youth Movement* (London, 1962), pp. 53–55; Harry Pross, *Jugend, Eros, Politik: Die Geschichte der deutschen Jugendverbände* (Berne, 1964), pp. 130–37; cf. Zwi Erich Kurzweil, "Gustav Wynecken, sein Werk und seine Auseinandersetzung mit Hermann Lietz," *Paedagogica historica* XI, 1 (1971), 31–59.

Haeckel, Jodl, Ostwald, and Lamprecht. Wynecken also planned that his model school would become "a light-house for the newer ideals of peace and education among German youth"—a hope that the pacifists shared.[23] He attempted as well to turn the attention of the youth movement toward the universal humanitarianism that underlay his own philosophy. The speech he delivered at the gathering of youth groups at the Hohe Meissner in 1913 was an eloquent plea against an exclusive nationalism, the danger of which he, like Gerhart Hauptmann, had perceived in the celebrations taking place in connection with the centennial of the Wars of Liberation.[24] However, this particular aspect of his theories did not find much resonance in the youth movement; and apart from an occasional member of the *Wandervögel* who later became involved in the peace movement, there is no evidence that pacifists exercised any influence in the *Jugendbewegung*.[25]

The Educational System

The schools were a much more frequent target of the peace movement's propaganda than youth groups or the home, largely because the educational system was more accessible, and entreaties could be directed at ministries of public instruction and teacher organizations. The primary and secondary school systems were a source of great concern to the pacifists, who harbored no illusions about the attitudes and concepts German children were learning about international politics. They perceived early what scholars have subsequently confirmed: that curricula in primary and secondary schools were designed to educate obedient patriots, steeped

[23] Wynecken, "The Free School and the Peace Movement," *Advocate of Peace* LXXV (1913), 232–33; NL Fried, Aufruf (Den Herren Unterzeichnern des Aufrufes zur gefälligen Kenntnisnahme ihrer bisher abgegebenen Unterschriften), 1913.

[24] Pross, *Jugend, Eros, Politik*, pp. 158–59.

[25] NL Fried, Hans Vogel to Fried, Berlin, 25 May 1911; cf. Reichel, *Die pazifistische Presse*, pp. 15–16.

in the military heroics of the German past, convinced of the inferiority of other nations, and prepared to accept war as a positive aspect of international affairs.[26] In 1904 one exasperated pacifist reported on what was being presented in German schools as history: "As he leafs through the texts that are being used today, the question must strike the perceptive observer: 'Is this a history book or a manual of war?' All the accomplishments of a ruler center upon the wars he waged, so that even when the laudatory remarks about bravery, courage, and intrepidity in battle are not there, every student has to come to the conclusion that the primary duty of the ruler is to wage as many wars as possible."[27] Other pacifists pointed out that readings from classical literature were selected to illustrate bravery and military skill, that poems to be memorized were usually those of Arndt, Körner, or some other militant nationalist, and that literature with cosmopolitan overtones was virtually excluded from the curriculum until the higher forms, by which time the student was presumably immune to subversive ideas.[28] The education of children in Germany thus fell far short of the ideals of the pacifists, who believed students should learn that war was terrible, that arbitration was the proper way to resolve international disputes, and

[26] Horst Schallenberger, *Untersuchungen zum Geschichtsbild der Wilhelminischen Aera und der Weimarer Zeit: Eine vergleichende Schulbuchanalyse deutscher Schulgeschichtsbücher aus der Zeit von 1888 bis 1933* (Ratingen bei Düsseldorf, 1964), esp. pp. 53–54, 102–104, 127–29; Jürgen Heinel, *Die deutsche Sozialpolitik des 19. Jahrhunderts im Spiegel der Schulgeschichtsbücher* (Braunschweig, 1962), esp. pp. 26–27; Walter Consuelo Langsam, "Nationalism and History in the Prussian Elementary Schools under William II," in Edward Mead Earle, ed., *Nationalism and Internationalism: Essays Inscribed to Carlton J. H. Hayes* (New York, 1950), pp. 241–60.

[27] "Schule und Friedensbewegung," FB, v (1904), 144.

[28] Ludwig Bräutigam, "Die Kriegsdichtung in den Schulen," DWN, I (September 1892), 5–8; Richard Henning, "Randbemerkung zur kgl. preussischen Pädagogik," DWN, III (1894), 437–41; FB, VI (1905), 64–65.

that genuine patriotism was compatible with an international community.[29]

In an effort to reorient political education in the German schools, the pacifists directed their attention both to teachers and the books from which they taught. Teachers in *Volksschulen* made up one of the more politically progressive sectors of German society.[30] It was a reflection of this that the literature, lectures, and appeals the pacifists addressed to teacher organizations produced some success.[31] A significant proportion—perhaps as much as twenty percent—of the German Peace Society's membership consisted of primary school teachers and lower level educational administrators. Several local *Lehrervereine* joined the peace society *in corpore*, while a number of pedagogical journals, including the *Pädagogisches Wochenblatt* and *Die Volksschule*, endorsed the peace movement's campaign.[32] Yet seen in perspective, even these accomplishments were not very impressive; the membership of the *Deutscher Lehrerverein*, the national teachers' organization, was in excess of one hundred thousand, so the number of teachers who did not re-

[29] Ernst Böhme, *Friedensbewegung und Lebenserziehung* (Gautzsch b. Leipzig, 1913); Richard Reuter, "Die Erziehung zum Rechts- und Friedensbegriff," DWN, vii (1898), 185–89, 226–28; Leopold Katscher, "Friedenspädagogik," VF, xiv (1913), 107–108; CBM, x (1905), 73; VF, xiv (1913), 127.

[30] HB (2), ii, 235; Liedtke, "Die Entwicklung des Pazifismus," pp. 249, 426–27; cf. Thomas Nipperdey, *Die Organisation der deutschen Parteien vor 1918* (Düsseldorf, 1961), p. 187.

[31] Ludwig Wagner, *Warum muss der Lehrer Stellung zur heutigen Friedensbewegung nehmen?* (Stuttgart, 1914); Brück and Triebel, *Erziehe zum Frieden!*; BIP (viiiB6), Deutsche Friedensgesellschaft, Ortsgruppe Königsberg, "An die Lehrerschaft Königsbergs," April 1911; DWN, ii (1893), 425–26; DWN, vi (1897), 382–83; CBM, vi (1901), 68.

[32] NL Fried, W. Hartmann to Fried, Stuttgart, 15 September 1897; Ludwig Bräutigam, "Die Kriegsdichtung in den Schulen," *Pädagogisches Wochenblatt*, viii (1898–99), 187–89, and replies, pp. 251–54, 299, 343; PM, iii (1914), 215–16; Liedtke, "Die Entwicklung des Pazifismus," pp. 426–27.

spond to the pacifists' appeals far exceeded the number of those who did.

Even had the pacifists' most optimistic expectations about converting school teachers been fulfilled, they would still have faced the problem of a curriculum that even the most dedicated pacifist teacher would have found difficult to counteract. Thus, the most concerted—and certainly the most publicized—aspect of the pacifists' work in the German educational system was their attempt to eliminate, or at least to moderate, the militaristic tenor of the textbooks used in German schools. In 1895 the International Peace Bureau called on peace societies everywhere to scrutinize texts for objectionable passages.[33] When the branches of the German Peace Society in Baden examined the books issued by the state's *Oberschulrat*, they found that these heavily emphasized war and contained repeated references to the "hereditary enemy," "French covetousness," and other such aspersions in describing foreign countries.[34] The Baden peace societies accordingly submitted a petition to the Landtag in 1897, calling for the elimination of the "chauvinistic trappings [*Beiwerk*]" from the texts, less extensive treatment of war, and more emphasis on cultural history, both of Germany and other nations.[35] To the amazement of the pacifists, who had already learned not to expect much from this kind of appeal, first the Landtag's committee on petitions, and then the Landtag itself voted favorably on the petition.[36]

The pacifists' jubilation was exceeded only by the disbelief and consternation of the nationalist press. To the *Deutsche Tageszeitung* the action of the Baden Landtag

---

[33] BIP (vQ3a), Rapport sur une réforme des manuels scolaires, 10 September 1895.

[34] MFK, v (March 1898), 37.

[35] BIP (vB6), Richter to Ducommun, Pforzheim, 19 December 1897; DWN, vi (1897), 349–50; DWN, vii (1898), 57–58.

[36] *Ibid.*; MFK, v (January/February 1898), 2–15; DWN, vii (1898), 89–97.

conjured up visions of a "prematurely tired and old, sickly and apathetic race," while the semiofficial *Norddeutsche Allgemeine Zeitung* was no less alarmed: "The naive 'peace makers' in Pforzheim and Lörrach demand more 'cultural' history in the schools; in reality they are serving the purposes of the sworn, irreconcilable enemies of our people and our German culture."[37] The nationalist reaction, in which most of the major German newspapers participated, was altogether out of proportion to the significance of the Landtag's decision. Passage of the pacifists' petition was a partisan move, designed by the Catholic Center opposition to embarrass a National Liberal cabinet, and the measure was passed on to the cabinet only "for its information [*zur Kenntnisnahme*]"; there was no explicit recommendation for action. The kind of attention the petition was going to receive from the cabinet was apparent even during the debate in the Landtag, as the government spokesman for education professed complete confidence in the quality of his textbooks, noting that the government would conduct the examination the pacifists called for, but that he "could not promise significant results."[38]

As the examination of textbooks proceeded in Baden as predicted, pacifists elsewhere in Germany were encouraged to submit similar petitions. In 1898 the *Frankfurter Friedensverein* sent one to the Prussian Landtag, but despite its endorsement by the *Preussische Lehrerzeitung*, the petition was rejected by both the committee on petitions and the Landtag as a whole. Max Hirsch's efforts to salvage it could not allay the apprehensions of those like the Free Conservative deputy Walter von Tzschoppe, who believed it "dangerous to interject among the immature children in the *Volksschulen* the idea that courts of arbitration could replace wars."[39] The pacifists were not easily discouraged,

---

[37] "Der Beschluss der Badischen Kammer und die gegnerische Presse," MFK, v (March 1898), 35–37; DWN, vii (1898), 71–73, 98–99.

[38] MFK, v (January/February 1898), 3.

[39] *Verhandlungen des Hauses der Abgeordneten*, 19 L.P., 1 Session

however, and they continued throughout the period before the war to scrutinize textbooks and send petitions to the state diets, despite the fact that these appeals were routinely ignored.[40]

Another aspect of the pacifists' campaign in German elementary schools was their attempt to stop the annual celebration in September of the German victory at Sedan in 1870, which they condemned as being calculated only to enflame old antagonisms. Leaders of the peace society repeatedly sent appeals to ministries of public instruction, suggesting that school children celebrate instead an annual peace day, on May 18, the anniversary of the opening of the first Hague conference.[41] They had little more success here than in their campaign with the school books, and they provoked almost as much criticism. In 1895 Heinrich Rössler did convince the city council in Frankfurt that money earmarked for the *Sedanfeier* could be better spent on charity, but more typical was the experience of Otto Umfrid, who had to endure attacks from nationalists whenever he questioned the propriety of the celebration.[42]

Whatever minimal successes the pacifists could claim in working with the schools were limited for the most part to the lower echelons of the educational system. People who taught in *Gymnasia* were as a rule very hostile to the peace movement.[43] Indeed, it often seemed to the pacifists that the more education a German had, the less likely he was to be sympathetic.[44] One of the roots of this problem was the

(23 March 1899), pp. 1703-13; NL Suttner (MrlI5), Hirsch to Suttner, Berlin, 21 April 1899; DWN, VIII (1899), 175-80.

[40] FW, IV (1902), 117-18, 166; FW, VI (1904), 143; FB, VI (1905), 41; CBM, XVI (1911), 117.

[41] Otto Umfrid, *Friede auf Erden! Betrachtungen über den Völkerfrieden* (Esslingen, 1897), p. 76; FB, IV (1903), 139; CBM, XII (1907), 70; VF, XI (1910), 53.

[42] BIP (vB6), Umfrid to Peace Bureau, Stuttgart, 5 September 1910; DWN, IV (1895), 342; cf. DWN, V (1896), 22-23.

[43] NL Fried, Alber to Fried, Stuttgart, 8 January 1903.

[44] FB, VI (1905), 41.

enormous hostility toward the peace movement at German universities.

In 1913 the French journalist Georges Bourdon published a series of essays in which he tried to analyze what he called "the German enigma."[45] In discussing German universities he spoke of the traditional image of the professor as a raging nationalist and noted that "this image is no doubt accurate, but it is not complete."[46] What made him hedge was the existence of the *Verband für internationale Verständigung*, whose impact he accurately gauged when he refused to challenge the basic validity of the traditional image of the German professor. Drawn from only a few disciplines, the professors in the *Verband* were by no means representative of university faculties, for on the whole universities were centers of some of the most extreme resistance the pacifists encountered in Germany.

This hostility stemmed from the well-documented belligerent nationalism which pervaded German universities. The common image of the peace movement was a *"vaterlandsloses Gesindel,"* whose program was either treacherous or criminally naive.[47] It was symbolic of this that repeated attempts by Schücking and Wehberg to secure an honorary doctorate for Fried at a German university were rejected everywhere, as was Quidde's attempt on behalf of Bertha von Suttner; yet Gros von Schwartzhoff, the soldier who had distinguished himself as an opponent of disarmament while serving as military attaché to the German delegation

[45] Georges Bourdon, *L'énigme allemande: Une enquête chez les Allemands* (Paris, 1913).

[46] *Ibid.*, pp. 94–95.

[47] Karl Heinrich Höfele, "Selbstverständnis und Zeitkritik des deutschen Bürgertums vor dem ersten Weltkrieg," *Zeitschrift für Religions- und Geistesgeschichte* VIII (1956), 50–56; see also Ringer, *German Mandarins*, p. 139; Klaus Schwabe, "Ursprung und Verbreitung des alldeutschen Annexionismus in der deutschen Professorenschaft im I. Weltkrieg," *Vierteljahrshefte für Zeitgeschichte* XIV (1966), 108–109; FB, IX (1908), 63; FW, XIV (1912), 111.

at the first Hague conference, quickly received an honorary doctorate of laws in Königsberg.[48]

Both the German Peace Society and the *Verband für internationale Verständigung* attempted to promote international understanding among professors and students at German universities. Lacking adequate financial resources and members with academic credentials, the peace society could do little more than circulate appeals, which were usually ignored. Fried was able to send his journal free of charge to university libraries and selected professors once the Carnegie Endowment began to subsidize his activities.[49] The professors in the *Verband* were better situated, but even they encountered formidable resistance.

Just how formidable this resistance could be was illustrated in the ordeal of Walther Schücking. An ambitious scholar, Schücking was appointed professor of law in Marburg at the early age of twenty-eight. A series of publications, in which he successively protested against the dispossession of Poles in West Prussia, predicted world government, and advocated a number of radical domestic reforms, soon resulted in his ostracism both from the faculty and the community.[50] His criticism of Prussian policy in Poland led to the supervision of his lectures and then to his removal from the state commission that certified appli-

[48] Schücking was told in Marburg that an honorary degree for Fried would be interpreted as a manifesto against the imperial regime: NL Fried, Schücking to Fried, Marburg, 27 February 1909; Wehberg to Fried, Düsseldorf, 18 February 1912; Quidde to Fried, Munich, 15 July 1913; Goldscheid, *Fried Gedenkblätter*, p. 66.

[49] NL Wehberg (59a), Fried to Wehberg, Vienna, 18 March 1912; "Die Friedenswarte an den Universitäten," FW, xiii (1911), 1–2. In Freiburg the university librarian refused to accept the journal: NL Fried, A. Flemmich to Fried, Freiburg, 30 January 1911.

[50] Schücking, *Das Nationalitätenproblem: Eine politische Studie über die Polenfrage und die Zukunft Oesterreich-Ungarns* (Dresden, 1908); *Die Organisation der Welt* (Leipzig, 1909); *Neue Ziele der staatlichen Entwicklung* (Marburg, 1913).

cants for the civil service.[51] The other pacifists on the faculty, Martin Rade, Hermann Cohen, and Paul Natorp, befriended him, but he was nevertheless most uncomfortable in Marburg. "I am not only the youngest on the faculty," he wrote to Fried in 1909, "but I am also completely isolated because of all my ideas."[52] He was even the brunt of local humor, as it became common to feign sympathy for "*die arme Frau Schücking*"—a woman married to a fool.[53] In spite of all this, Schücking attempted to bring Hans Wehberg to Marburg for a *Habilitation* and then, along with him, to establish a seminar on international law. However, the rector of the university rejected the project out of hand, and he took the occasion to express his satisfaction that Germany was at last manufacturing enough machine guns.[54]

Schücking's plight was extreme in degree, but hardly unique. The attempts of other professors in the *Verband* to popularize instruction in international law met with little more success. In Heidelberg, in fact, the university administration forced Georg Jellinek to cancel his lectures on the subject.[55] Others whose internationalism was indiscreet found that promotions were slow and positions for their students hard to find.

Students at German universities were no more receptive to the peace movement than were faculties and administrators. Attempts to establish peace societies among students at a number of universities proved abortive.[56] The fact that several *Burschenschaften* agreed to join the *Verband* is difficult to explain (particularly since these were duelling fraternities), for as a rule there was no sym-

[51] FW, x (1908), 217.

[52] NL Fried, Schücking to Fried, Marburg, 22 January 1909.

[53] Wehberg, *Führer*, p. 54.

[54] NL Wehberg (77), Schücking to Wehberg, Marburg, 25 June 1912; Umfrid, *Zum Gedächtnis*, p. 5; JPC, John Mez to Jordan, Munich, 8 February 1914.

[55] Honigsheim, *On Max Weber*, p. 72; see also NL Fried, Nippold to Fried, Oberursel, 29 January 1911.

[56] FB, iv (1903), 91, 117.

pathy for the peace movement among the traditional student corporations, which pursued, as one official explained to Wehberg, "strictly national goals."[57] Only among the organizations of unincorporated students, the *Freie Studentenschaften*, did the pacifists find any support. Because they were active in progressive political causes, these *Finkenschaften* (as they were known) were the object of disdain from fraternities and university administrators, and their image was not enhanced by the fact that they invited pacifists to speak at their meetings.[58]

Shortly before the war, the pacifists announced what appeared to be a major advance among university students: the formation of *Internationale Studentenvereine* at seven German universities.[59] Modeled after the Cosmopolitan Clubs at American universities, these groups were designed to promote cultural interchange and friendship among students of all nationalities. The fact that the peace movement took them so seriously—Nippold tried to recruit them *en masse* into the *Verband*—was an interesting comment on the opportunities for promoting international harmony at German universities.[60] For not only were these groups very small, but they were composed predominantly of foreign students, especially Russians and Americans. The

[57] NL Wehberg (67), Wehberg to Nippold, Düsseldorf, 12 March 1910; NL Wehberg (59a), Fried to Wehberg, Vienna, 20 February 1913; "Die deutsche Burschenschaft und internationale Verständigung," FW, XIII (1911), 285; FW, XI (1909), 170; VF, XII (1911), 16.

[58] BIP (vA3), K. Peters to Peace Bureau, Leipzig, 17 May 1908; NL Fried, Walter Berendsohn to Fried, Kiel, 3 January 1910; FW, X (1908), 66; VF, XI (1910), 67; PM, II (1913), 74; cf. Lamprecht, *Rektoratserinnerungen*, pp. 40–45; Helene Tompert, *Lebensformen und Denkweisen der akademischen Welt Heidelbergs im Wilhelminischen Zeitalter: Vornehmlich im Spiegel zeitgenössischer Selbstzeugnisse* (Lübeck, 1969), p. 55.

[59] "Die internationale Studentenbewegung in Deutschland," FW, XIV (1912), 271.

[60] NL Schücking (57), George Nasmyth to Schücking, Berlin, 19 November 1912; Friedrich Depkan, "Internationale Bestrebungen in der deutschen Studentenschaft," KVfiV, II (20 June 1913), 14–16.

group in Marburg, for instance, had nine members, of whom three were German; only one of the twelve students who founded the group in Munich was a German.[61] However, neither their insignificance nor the fact that they barely survived in Germany made them immune to attacks on their *Deutschfeindlichkeit*.[62]

In sum, hostility to the peace movement at German universities was intense. Pacifists who spoke before university audiences, usually at the invitation of the local *Finkenschaft* or *Internationaler Studentenverein*, could expect to contend with administrative harassment and ill-humored students.[63] This hostility did not even observe the limits of courtesy to foreign visitors, as Norman Angell discovered in 1913, when he toured a number of German universities under the sponsorship of the *Verband für internationale Verständigung*. In Göttingen the police interrupted his lecture after students objected to his lecturing in English, which they claimed (wrongly) was illegal; the official university-wide student organization then staged a mass rally to protest against Angell's visit. In Berlin the mood at his lecture was even uglier, and it culminated in a full-scale riot.[64]

Angell returned to England encouraged by the interest his theories had stimulated among students in Germany,

[61] Staatsarchiv Marburg, Univ. Marburg/L., Rektor u. Senat, Acc. 1950/9, number 192; StOb, AR 3187/401; NL Fried, Hans Vogel to Fried, Berlin, 25 May 1911; *Die Eiche*, I (1913), 180.

[62] NL Fried, Karl Brunner to Fried, Berlin, 2 July 1912; JPC, Mez to Jordan, Munich, 11 June 1914.

[63] NL Fried, Feldhaus to Fried, Frankfurt, 3 December 1912; Feldhaus to Fried [Giessen], 20 December 1912; JPC, Mez to Jordan, 8 February 1914; "Friedenspropaganda unter den Studenten," VF, xi (1910), 67.

[64] Ball State University, Muncie, Indiana, Norman Angell Papers (C78–13), "Norman Angell's Tour of the German Universities, February 1–14, 1913" (General Report of George W. Nasmyth); Norman Angell, *After All: The Autobiography of Norman Angell* (London, 1952), p. 172; see also Paul David Hines, "Norman Angell: Peace Movement, 1911–1915" (Ed.D. dissertation, Ball State Teachers' College, 1964); FW, xv (1913), 109.

but he was blind to the conditions at German universities. After years of frustration, leaders of the German peace movement could hold no illusions about the immediate possibility of reforming attitudes about war and world politics at the university level. Indeed, there were few sectors of German society where the peace movement was more loudly denounced.

The Military

In imperial Germany the army was, by design, an active agency of political socialization. The influence of this "school of the nation" was, as recent studies have shown, by no means limited to the period of a recruit's active service.[65] The military sponsored numerous youth groups, which served to train both the body and the mind of the potential recruit, while a network of reserve organizations enabled the army to continue its educational role once the recruit had been discharged.[66] The principal purpose of this political education was to counteract socialist subversion, both within the army and society at large. To this end, potential recruits, recruits, and dischargees learned about the virtues of Christian deportment and about the international menaces that made loyalty to the Kaiser necessary. Although the soldiers were far less concerned about the bourgeois pacifists than about socialists, they rejected (one is tempted to say out of occupational necessity) the assumptions of the pacifists' ideology, and occasionally articulated

[65] See Reinhard Höhn, *Die Armee als Erziehungsschule der Nation* (Bad Harzburg, 1963).

[66] Klaus Saul, "Der Kampf um die Jugend zwischen Volksschule und Kaserne: Ein Beitrag zur 'Jugendpflege' im Wilhelminischen Reich, 1890–1914," *Militärgeschichtliche Mitteilungen*, number 1 (1971), pp. 97–143; Saul, "Der 'Deutsche Kriegerbund': Zur innenpolitischen Funktion eines 'nationalen' Verbandes im kaiserlichen Deutschland," *Militärgeschichtliche Mitteilungen*, number 2 (1969), pp. 95–159; Hansjoachim Henning, "Kriegervereine in den preussischen Westprovinzen: Ein Beitrag zur preussischen Innenpolitik zwischen 1860 und 1914," *Rheinische Vierteljahrsblätter* XXXII (1968), 430–75.

their goals in terms of combating pacifist influence. In 1911, for instance, the program of a Bavarian youth group sponsored by the military suggested that "a soft and careful appeal to the martial spirit of the nation may serve as a counterweight to the prevailing [sic] fantasy about 'perpetual peace.' "[67]

Leaders of the peace movement were alarmed that the army played such an important role in educating Germans about world politics; indeed, their analysis of how military attitudes were fostered in German society was quite perceptive.[68] However, since even the pacifists believed that armies would be necessary until the establishment of international government, they had some difficulty in defining the proper role of the military. The compromise they most frequently suggested was to replace professional armies with popular militias geared for defensive war.[69] This alternative, which seemed justified by Bloch's predictions about future wars, promised both national security and the diminution of the social influence of the officer corps. However, the pacifists made no concerted effort to influence the army, though some soldiers who were interested in Bloch's theories attended lectures by Feldhaus on the subject. Feldhaus in fact occasionally received invitations to lecture about Bloch before veterans' organizations.[70]

In general, the military establishment viewed the peace movement with indifference. Several reserve officers actually joined the peace society or the *Verband*, but they were not bothered as long as they remained discreet; those who did not ran the risk of losing their commissions.[71]

[67] Quoted in Saul, "Kampf um die Jugend," pp. 116–17; see also FW, XIII (1911), 304–305.
[68] Curtius, "Ueber militärische Suggestion," KVfiV, II (6 December 1913), 4–6; FW, VII (1905), 215–16; FB, IX (1908), 143.
[69] VF, XV (1914), 15; FW, II (1900), 135.
[70] NL Fried, Feldhaus to Fried, Frankfurt, 24 October 1903; Harder to Fried, Hamburg, 15 May 1904; DWN, VI (1897), 390–91; FW, V (1903), 171.
[71] NL Fried, Richard Gädke to Fried, Berlin, 29 June 1912; Weh-

There is no evidence of any systematic attempt by the army to harass the pacifists, aside from its general prohibition on participation by soldiers in political organizations, which applied to the peace society and *Verband*. The military's attitude about the peace movement was distilled in the wry reply of the Bavarian war minister to Nippold's invitation to attend the general congress of the *Verband* in Nuremberg. "The war ministry," he noted, "has no *particular* interest in attempts to secure world peace."[72]

The fact that the army was not alarmed by the peace movement accounts for the lack of consensus among military writers about its significance. While some prominent authors, such as Albrecht von Boguslawski and Friedrich von Bernhardi, denounced the peace movement as part of a conspiracy to sap Germany of its military power, culture, and virility, other officers were not entirely unsympathetic.[73] In 1894, for example, one officer in the Bavarian general staff gently criticized Boguslawski's fulminations and suggested that the pacifists were right, that internationalization would some day lead to the unity of mankind. However, he added one critical reservation: "The entire course of our development points to the fact that the nations of Europe will only be forged together in a comprehensive alliance after great new battles. . . . We, however,

---

berg to Fried, Düsseldorf, 25 December 1912, 31 March 1913; KA, MKr. 11521, number 4866, Agitation des Oblts. v. Bay. Inft. I. Aufg. *Molenaar als Sekretär der deutsch-französischen Liga*, 22 May 1905; KA, MKr. 11521, number 2732, Gen. Cde. d. I. Bay. A Corps. Eing. to Kriegsministerium, 18 February 1913; DWN, VI (1897), 405–406.

[72] KA, MKr. 228, Randbemerkung des Kriegsministeriums zu Nr. 24700, betreff: Tagung des Verbandes für internationale Verständigung, 20. 9. 1913.

[73] Albrecht von Boguslawski, *Der Krieg in seiner wahren Bedeutung für Staat und Volk* (Berlin, 1892); Friedrich von Bernhardi, *Unsere Zukunft: Ein Mahnwort an das deutsche Volk* (Stuttgart and Berlin, 1912); NL Fried, Fried to Generalleutnant z. D. Pelet-Narbonne, Vienna, 22 May 1907; Quidde to Fried, Munich, 31 December 1912.

are still in the middle of the period of battle."[74] Many other soldiers were impressed by Bloch's work, and some military writers, such as Ferdinand Rogalla von Bieberstein, publicly endorsed the concept of arbitration.[75] In fact, shortly before he became war minister in 1896, Heinrich von Gossler went on record in favor of an international treaty to preserve the peace—a proposal for which he was castigated by the *Kreuzzeitung*.[76]

Not even the pacifists could seriously believe that occasional expressions of interest in arbitration or the peace movement meant that the army would cease to promote an orientation toward international relations that emphasized antagonism and conflict. The dispassion of military writers in analyzing the peace movement was merely a reflection of indifference. The military establishment rejected the peace movement and its ideas about the nature of international politics as completely as other sectors of German society. Yet it is interesting to note that basic though it was, antipathy toward the peace movement was less exuberant among the soldiers than it was elsewhere in Germany.

The Press

"Of all the factors that determine the relations of nations to one another," wrote one member of the *Verband für internationale Verständigung*, "the press undoubtedly has the greatest significance."[77] This view was shared by the pacifists, who attributed much of the tension in international relations to the machinations of irresponsible editors, who,

[74] E. Hagen, "Ist der Krieg unabänderliches Völkergeschick?" *Militär-Wochenblatt* LXXIX (1894), 2075–78; MFK, II (November 1894).

[75] NL Fried, Fried to Rogalla von Bieberstein, Berlin, 27 September 1902; FW, I (1899), 56–57; cf. Generallt. a. D. Karl Ritter von Landmann, "Die heutige Friedensbewegung," *Hochland* V (January 1908), 465–74.

[76] MFK, I (May 1894).

[77] Arthur Bönninger, *Die Presse und die internationale Verständigung* (Munich, 1911), p. 5.

often for no better reason than to sell their newspapers, emphasized international antagonisms and the threat of war.[78] Umfrid once called newspaper editors "public enemies who pull the strings of public opinion," noting that "the public has for the most part surrendered itself to them without resistance, since it reads its newspapers uncritically and feels obligated to swarm into the frenzy the editors instigate."[79]

There is much to suggest that the pacifists' concern was well founded and that most German newspapers did little to disorient Germans who had learned to accept violent conflict as an integral aspect of international relations.[80] Nor did the pacifists have far to look in documenting the baleful influence of the German press; they could point to the way newspapers treated the peace movement itself. The overwhelming majority of the German papers was hostile.[81] It was difficult to find a newspaper in which accounts of pacifist activities were not couched in derisive terms of *Friedensschwärmerei, Friedensfanatiker, Friedensapostel,* or *Friedensduselei.* The list of papers habitually ill-disposed toward the peace movement was geographically comprehensive, and it transcended party lines, although papers with leftist leanings were generally less outspoken critics. Denunciations and mockery of the pacifists appeared regu-

[78] C.A. Flügge, *Gegenwartsnöte: Aus dem Zeitenspiegel der Tagespresse* (Kassel, n.d.), esp. p. 36; FB, vi (1905), 65; FB, viii (1907), 120; VF, xv (1914), 2; CBM, viii (1903), 64.

[79] Umfrid, "Fanatismus," VF, xiv (1913), 25-26.

[80] See Klaus Wernecke, *Der Wille zur Weltgeltung: Aussenpolitik und Oeffentlichkeit im Kaiserreich am Vorabend des Ersten Weltkrieges* (Düsseldorf, 1970); Isolde Rieger, *Die wilhelminische Presse im Ueberblick* (Munich, 1957); E. Malcolm Carroll, *Germany and the Great Powers, 1866-1914: A Study in Public Opinion and Foreign Policy* (New York, 1938); Oron James Hale, *Publicity and Diplomacy, with Special Reference to England and Germany, 1890-1914* (New York, 1940).

[81] Richard Reuter, "Presse und Publikum in Deutschland gegenüber der Friedensbewegung und ihren neuesten Triumphen," FW, vi (1904), 81-85.

larly in Conservative papers close to ruling circles, such as the *Norddeutsche Allgemeine Zeitung*, the *Kreuzzeitung*, the *Berliner Lokal-Anzeiger*, and the *Deutsche Tageszeitung*.[82] Newspapers with National Liberal ties were, if anything, even more intense in their condemnation and ridicule. The *Hamburger Nachrichten* and *Münchner Neueste Nachrichten* were the two most dedicated pacifist-baiters in the country, but they differed only in degree from other National Liberal papers, such as the *Rheinisch-Westfälische Zeitung*, the *Tägliche Rundschau*, the *Magdeburgische Zeitung*, the *Berliner Neueste Nachrichten*, the *Berliner Börsen-Zeitung*, and the *Schwäbischer Merkur*.[83] While attacks from the Conservative and National Liberal press were the most vicious (and did not stop short of libel or conscious misrepresentation), criticism of the peace movement also appeared in the nominally nonpartisan papers of the *General-Anzeiger* chain, as well as those associated with the progressive bourgeois left, including such eminent democratic papers as the *Vossische Zeitung*.[84] The Catholic and socialist press also failed to support the peace movement, though for special reasons.[85]

Even more disturbing than the scurrilous attacks, to which the pacifists soon became inured, was the indifference they encountered in the German press. Pacifists could not get newspapers to take note of their activities. Articles

[82] "Die Presse und die Friedensidee," DWN, II (1893), 46–47; DWN, III (1894), 427–30; NL Fried, Fried to Redaktion der "Neuen Preussischen Zeitung," Vienna, 27 February 1913.

[83] NL Fried, Fried to A. J. Mordtmann, Berlin, 20 January 1903; Harder to Fried, Hamburg, 19 July 1905; DWN, III (1894), 427–30; FW, VI (1904), 55, 173; cf. E. Baasch, *Geschichte des Hamburgischen Zeitungswesens vom Anfang bis 1914* (Hamburg, 1930), p. 143.

[84] NL Fried, Fried to Umfrid, Vienna, 24 May 1909; Fried to Heinrich Arnhold, Vienna, 20 October 1913; Fried to Alexander Meyer, Berlin, 4 November 1904; Fried to Eduard Bernstein, Vienna, 24 October 1911; FW, I (1899), 81–84; FW, VI (1904), 91; FW, IX (1907), 97, 217.

[85] See below, chapter 5, pp. 202–204; chapter 6, pp. 259–82.

they submitted, even to papers known to harbor some good will, were rarely published, and few German correspondents ever attended peace congresses.[86] The pacifists attributed this indifference to an obscurantist conspiracy among bellicose editors (which was unlikely) or to the nationalist bias of most of the German press (which was more likely).[87] They could not, however, appreciate the fact that to anyone but the most devout pacifist, peace congresses did not make good press, or they did so only if satirized. An editor once told to Fried not to file a report on a peace congress "unless something exciting happens—like a riot."[88] Even left-liberal papers found it difficult to justify much coverage of the peace movement on the basis of reader interest.[89] Moreover, press coverage of the peace movement was severely restricted because the official German wire service, the Wolff Telegraphic Bureau, was reluctant to send correspondents to peace congresses, for reasons of nationalist distaste and sheer boredom.[90]

German papers persisted in their ways despite many attempts by pacifists to enlighten them. Fried, Umfrid, and others sent a steady stream of articles and other materials to papers of all persuasions. Fried regularly offered to serve for numerous papers as a correspondent to peace congresses, but his services, like his articles, were in most cases turned down. Leaders of the peace society besieged editors

[86] NL Fried, Wirth to Fried, Frankfurt, 24 May 1894; Fried to Rogalla von Bieberstein, Berlin, 27 September 1902; Wehberg to Fried, Düsseldorf, 28 October 1911.

[87] FW, II (1900), 22–23; FW, VI (1904), 82; PM, I (1912), 15; PM, II (1913), 156.

[88] FW, II (1900), 22.

[89] NL Fried, Redaktion der Berliner Zeitung to Fried, Berlin, 11 November 1896; Ullstein & Co. to Fried, Berlin, 16 August 1900; Redaktion der Breslauer Zeitung to Fried, Breslau, 25 January 1904.

[90] NL M. Quidde (349/59), Ludwig Quidde to Margarethe Quidde, Bad Kreuth [24 September 1907]; Marschall to Bülow, Scheveningen, 28 July 1907, GP, XXIII, 264–72, number 7961; Nippold, *Erlebnisse*, p. 14.

and publicists with appeals for more understanding and coverage.[91] Since the press figured prominently in its own diagnosis of international tensions, the *Verband für internationale Verständigung* tried to publicize its views in the press. One of its special commissions watched the press and regularly sent a correspondence sheet to newspapers with commentary on aspects of international relations.

Himself a journalist by profession, Fried was especially interested in cultivating better press coverage for the peace movement in Germany. In 1904 he published an "Appeal to the German Press of the Left," in which he scolded liberal editors for failing to educate Germans about the significance of arbitration and the peace movement. He called on them to "arouse and enlighten German public opinion in favor of an organization for peace among the civilized nations" and to join him in a new "Union of the German Press Friendly to Arbitration."[92] His plans did not bear fruit, however. Martin Rade, the editor of *Christliche Welt*, editors from a few minor left-liberal papers, and Arthur Dix of the *National-Zeitung* (whose principal stockholder was the pacifist Georg Arnhold) consented to join, but when important figures like Arthur Levysohn of the *Berliner Tageblatt*, Alexander Meyer of the *Vossische Zeitung*, and Otto Hörth of the *Frankfurter Zeitung* did not, Fried was forced to abandon the project.[93]

Undiscouraged, Fried then accompanied leading German editors and journalists on a tour to England in 1906, hoping to win friends for the peace movement through personal

[91] BIP (vQ2h), Aufruf der Deutschen Friedensgesellschaft an Publizisten, Stuttgart, 1903.

[92] "Ein Aufruf an die deutsche Presse der Linken," FW, vi (1904), 90–92.

[93] NL Fried, Fried to Dix, Vienna, 7 November 1904; Fried to Arnhold, Vienna, 3 February 1905; Fried to Rösch, Vienna, 18 November 1904; see also "Die Nationalzeitung und die Friedensbewegung," FW, vi (1904), 156; Stegmann, *Die Erben Bismarcks*, p. 170, n. 225.

contacts.[94] In 1909 he attempted to establish another organization of friendly journalists and editors, this time on an international scale, but like his earlier project, his "International Union of the Pacifist Press" failed for want of interest, especially in Germany, where he could not find a single editor to participate.[95] Fried then proposed, among other things, to create an international press directory to catalogue the bias and reliability of newspapers, negotiation of a "Black Cross" convention to outlaw journalistic malpractices, such as provoking public opinion, and setting up an international wire service more sensitive than the Wolff Bureau to the importance of the peace movement.[96]

Owing partially to Fried's persistence, the pacifists did find sympathy in a few German newspapers. The paper unquestionably closest to the peace movement was the democratic *Frankfurter Zeitung*; indeed, it was virtually the only major German newspaper the pacifists could call a consistent friend, as it regularly published appreciative commentary and sent correspondents to national and international peace congresses.[97] Several members of its editorial staff, including Nippold, Alexander Dietz, and Theodor Curti, were close friends of pacifists or belonged to groups associated with the peace movement.[98] Another important, if

[94] NL Fried, Fried to Felix Moschelles, Vienna, 14 May 1906; see below, chapter 7, p. 314.

[95] BIP (1), Procès verbal de l'assemblé générale des délégués des sociétés de la paix, Brussels, 1909, pp. 32–36; *Bulletin de l'Union internationale de la presse pour la paix*, number 1 (July 1909); NL Fried, Richter to Fried, Pforzheim, 24 January 1910; FW, xi (1909), 88–89.

[96] Fried, *The Peace Movement and the Press* (Berne, 1913); NL Hans Delbrück, BA (34), Organisation Potentia (1904); Foerster to Delbrück, Berlin, 29 November 1904; Dotation Carnegie pour la paix internationale, Centre européen, Procès-verbal des séances de la commission de la presse, 22–23 janvier 1914, pp. 15, 26–27.

[97] NL Wehberg (69), Quidde to Wehberg, Munich, 9 July 1910; NL Fried, Umfrid to Fried, Stuttgart, 25 May 1911; DWN, iv (1895), 387; DWN, v (1896), 74.

[98] NL Schücking (58), Nippold to Schücking, Frankfurt, 9 May

less consistent, supporter of the peace movement was the *Berliner Tageblatt*. When Arthur Levysohn was editor, the paper accepted articles from pacifists, though its commentary on the peace movement frequently provoked Fried's outrage.[99] In 1906, when Theodor Wolff became editor of the paper, he brought to it a strong idealism and commitment to international conciliation, and under his tutelage the *Tageblatt* became one of the peace movement's most outspoken advocates.[100]

The peace movement enjoyed a relatively good press in Berlin, aside from the Conservative and semiofficial papers that were published there. Both the reigning press lords in Berlin, Hans Ullstein and Rudolf Mosse (who published the *Tageblatt*), supported international arbitration, and their papers reflected their views.[101] While living in Berlin, Fried was a correspondent for the Ullstein papers *Welt am Montag*, *Berliner Morgenpost*, and *Berliner Zeitung*. In Vienna he continued to provide the *Morgenpost* with material about the peace movement, but he was dropped by the *Berliner Zeitung* in 1904 when Hellmut von Gerlach, who at that time was still an ardent nationalist, became editor.[102] Fritz Auer, however, who in 1907 became political editor

---

1910; NL Fried, Opinion de M. Th. Curti, Frankfurt, 6 September 1913; Nippold, *Erlebnisse*, pp. 10, 13; Taube, *Ludwig Quidde*, p. 80.

[99] NL Fried, Fried to Levysohn, Vienna, 3 November 1904; Fried to Richard Fischer, Röhrbach, 14 July 1905; MFK, I (February 1894); DWN, IV (1895), 149.

[100] NL Fried, Wolff to Fried, Paris, 18 February 1903; PD, XX (1910), 609-10; see also Gotthard Schwarz, *Theodor Wolff und das "Berliner Tageblatt": Eine liberale Stimme in der deutschen Politik 1906 bis 1933* (Tübingen, 1969).

[101] Both Mosse and Ullstein were members of the Munich-based committee to promote the first Hague conference: NL Fried, Komitee für Kundgebungen der Friedenskonferenz [1899].

[102] NL Fried, Redaktion der Berliner Morgenpost to Fried, Berlin, 24 October 1903; Fried to Redaktion der Berliner Zeitung, Vienna, 18 November 1907; see also Hellmut von Gerlach, *Von Rechts nach Links* (Zurich, 1937), p. 261.

of Ullstein's *B.Z. am Mittag* and *Berliner Morgenpost*, was one of Fried's admirers.[103]

Fried's most notable accomplishment was his "conversion" of Ernst Posse, the editor of the *Kölnische Zeitung*. The pacifists had long recognized the importance of this paper, which had ties to the German foreign office, but they had found very little sympathy among its editorial staff.[104] Posse was among the editors with whom Fried toured England, and as a result of the discussions between the two, the treatment of pacifists in the columns of the *Kölnische Zeitung* improved after 1906, and the paper began to publish some of the articles pacifists submitted to it.[105]

The *Verband für internationale Verständigung* likewise succeeded in publicizing its views in several papers, most of them with left-liberal leanings. The *Frankfurter Zeitung* served almost as the group's official organ. Editors of several small newspapers also belonged to the organization, as did Julius Bachem of the *Kölnische Volkszeitung*.[106] In 1913 the *Verband* acquired another sympathetic organ when it came to the financial rescue of the left-liberal literary review, *März*.[107] Aside from these, both the peace society and the *Verband* could expect generally favorable treatment in a number of other left-liberal journals and newspapers, including the *Deutsche Revue*, the *Weser-Zeitung* in Bremen, the *Kieler Zeitung*, the *Breslauer Zeitung*, the *Königsberger Hartungsche Zeitung*, and the *Münchner Allgemeine Zeitung*.[108]

---

[103] NL Fried, Auer to Fried, Berlin, 2 May 1907.

[104] DWN, III (1894), 36.

[105] NL Fried, Fried to Posse, Vienna, 16 July 1906; Posse to Fried, Cologne, 19 July 1906. Fried had less success with Heinrich Rippler of the *Tägliche Rundschau*, whom he also met in London: Rippler to Fried, Berlin, 29 September 1906.

[106] NL Haussmann (4), Verband für internationale Verständigung, II. Verbandstag zu Nürnberg.

[107] NL Haussmann (4), Herman Maier to Haussmann, Frankfurt, 17 October 1913.

[108] NL Wehberg (59a), Fried to Wehberg, Vienna, 17 August

These few sympathetic papers did not significantly alter the dominant pattern in the German press, and Fried's note to Bloch in 1902 that "Newspapers are resisting our enlightenment" remained an accurate, if understated, characterization of the peace movement's experience with the press throughout the prewar period.[109] Whatever their differences on other issues, newspapers of all political persuasions, and even those with no pronounced political leanings, were very nearly at one in their rejection of the peace movement. The only exceptions were scattered left-liberal papers, most notably the *Frankfurter Zeitung* and the *Berliner Tageblatt*, which were themselves suspect among nationalists for their views on foreign affairs.[110] As a rule, what little the Germans read in the newspapers about the peace movement was not designed to heighten their appreciation either of the movement or of its view of international relations.

The Churches[111]

Late in 1890 a remarkable little book was published in Leipzig. Entitled *Ernste Gedanken*, it issued a challenge to the German churches and called for a wholesale revitalization of Christianity:

> Is the church in its present form fulfilling its calling—to promote the activation and spread of Christianity? . . . I say no. . . . By religion I understand the preservation of

---

1912; NL Fried, Fried to Mohr, Vienna, 3 March 1904; Georg Peterson to Fried, Kiel, 13 November 1907; see also Reichel, *Die pazifistische Presse*, pp. 84–86.

[109] FW, IV (1902), 120.

[110] See Bernhard Guttmann, *Schattenriss einer Generation, 1888–1919* (Stuttgart, 1950), p. 223; August Eigenbrodt, *"Berliner Tageblatt" und "Frankfurter Zeitung" in ihrem Verhalten zu den nationalen Fragen 1887–1914* (Berlin, 1917).

[111] Parts of this section have appeared in article form as "The Peace Movement and the Religious Community in Germany, 1900–1914," *Church History* XXXVIII (1969), 300–11.

the divine spark that initially exists in every man. "God created man in his image," and since God is love, the divine spark planted in us is a seed of love. . . . It is clear to every thinking man that the church's only purpose is the education of man to religiosity, the stimulation [of man] to a Christian way of life. . . . God reveals himself in every man, and for me he revealed himself in the most recognizable way in Jesus Christ, the human being in whose soul the divine spark glowed most brightly and who was the First to set forth the Essence of Divinity when he called it "love."[112]

The book was unusual, not so much because of the heterodoxy of its theology, as because of its author, who was a colonel in the Prussian army. As an officer, Moritz von Egidy had given no outward indication of unconventionality or the religious crisis that prompted him to write this book.[113] Its publication predictably forced his retirement from the army and brought attacks from alarmed Protestant theologians. Egidy then moved to Berlin, where he began to elaborate his religious ideas and seek allies for a Christian crusade to convert mankind to love. His overtures to leading liberal Protestant theologians, among them Adolf Harnack and Martin Rade, drew encouragement along with criticism of his Christology.[114] His encounters with the Protestant bureaucracy were less encouraging, and so vicious were Adolf Stöcker's attacks that the two men only narrowly averted a duel.

Because of his failure to find any appreciable support within the churches, Egidy concluded that the regeneration of humanity could only take place outside the bounds of

[112] Moritz von Egidy, *Ernste Gedanken* (Leipzig, 1890). Passages quoted in Heinz Herz, *Alleingang wider die Mächtigen: Ein Bild vom Leben und Kämpfen Moritz von Egidys* (Leipzig, [1970]), pp. 163–64.

[113] On Egidy see, in addition to Herz, Heinrich Driesmans, ed., *M. von Egidy: Sein Leben und Wirken* (Dresden, 1900); Wehberg, *Führer*, pp. 37–40.

[114] Herz, *Alleingang wider die Mächtigen*, pp. 316–17, 319–20, 272–74.

organized religion. In his search for allies he then gravitated toward the ethical culture movement, which was calling for roughly the same kind of moral reform, though on decidedly non-Christian terms. Egidy's refusal to renounce Christianity made lasting cooperation with this movement impossible, and his only real constituency remained a dedicated circle of what one admirer described as some two hundred "eccentrics of every sort"—anarchists, students, nature freaks, and old ladies—who made up his salon.[115] Undiscouraged, Egidy continued his crusade, delivering innumerable lectures, publishing a journal called *Die Versöhnung*, and running twice unsuccessfully for the Reichstag. The frantic tempo at which he worked left him exhausted, and in 1898, shortly after the failure of his second candidacy, he died at the age of fifty-one.

During his crusade on behalf of applied Christianity— what he called "the religion of action"—Egidy also came into contact with the peace movement. In 1891 he began a correspondence with Bertha von Suttner that continued until his death. He argued that world peace would result from the triumph of mutual love, but since he was less interested in arbitration than in making people love one another, his association with the peace movement, like his dealings with the ethical culture movement, remained at a distance.[116] In 1897, though, he spoke before the Universal Peace Congress in Hamburg and left the assembled pacifists entranced by the power of his vision of an "era without violence."

"Egidy is without a doubt the most powerful individual his country currently has in the service of the cause of peace," a leading French pacifist wrote in 1897.[117] Bertha von Suttner called him an *"Edelmensch."*[118] Obsessed by a

[115] *Ibid.*, pp. 90–98; Braun, *Memoiren*, p. 506.

[116] NL Suttner (Di3), Egidy to Suttner, Berlin, 6 February 1892; NL Fried, Egidy to Fried, 19 October 1894; Egidy, "Zur Friedensbewegung," in Driesmans, pp. 530–40.

[117] Moch, "viie Congrès de la paix," p. 414.

[118] BIP (iiiL), Suttner to Ducommun, Vienna, 9 July 1899.

vision in which mankind would be permeated with love, Egidy was convinced that he himself would live to see its realization, and he conveyed this confidence with a charisma unusual among the pacifists, who were not as a rule very exciting people.[119] Yet few appreciated his message, and while unfair and probably inaccurate, the observation by the chief of police in Berlin that the man was "more or less insane" typified the popular reaction to his crusade.[120]

What is interesting about Moritz von Egidy, however, is not his emotional balance, but rather the fact that he explicitly made the correlation between Christianity and world peace and sought to translate it into action. In this respect, his career anticipated many of the themes that marked the experience of the peace movement with the Christian churches in Germany: the theological controversy, the places where the pacifists could expect to find opposition and support, and the danger of having the wrong kind of friends.

If the relationship between Christian churches and the peace movement in other countries were any indication, the prospects for a close alliance between pacifists and churchmen in Germany were good. In England and the United States the initial impulse for creating peace societies in the early nineteenth century had come from religious organizations, and clergymen continued to play an active role in the peace movement into the twentieth century. Many European Catholics showed an interest in the peace movement after two popes, Leo XIII and Pius X, endorsed its goals in official greetings to Universal Peace Congresses. In 1910 a group of Frenchmen founded the International Catholic Peace League with branches in France, Spain, Switzerland, and Belgium.[121]

[119] NL Suttner (Di8), Egidy to Suttner, Berlin, 23 September 1894.
[120] Herz, *Alleingang wider die Mächtigen*, p. 339.
[121] A. Vanderpol, "Les sociétés catholiques de la paix," *Almanach de la paix* (1911), pp. 61–64; Martin Rade, *Der Beitrag der christlichen Kirchen zur internationalen Verständigung* (Stuttgart, 1912), pp. 5–6; Baker, "Belgians and the Peace Movement," pp. 49–50; Abrams, "Eu-

The German pacifists expected that similar cooperation would develop in their own country. Like pacifists elsewhere, they argued that the precepts of Christianity, as articulated principally in the Sermon on the Mount, demanded that Christians actively pursue world peace.[122] Thus, they anticipated that both Catholics and Protestants would join the campaign to reeducate German society about international relations by promoting internationalism and humanitarian patriotism.[123]

These expectations remained unfulfilled, for in Germany the situation was quite different from that in other western countries. Far from supporting the peace movement, the German churches actively opposed it, in many instances with a truculence unparalleled even in other sectors of German society.[124] Otto Umfrid, for example, who was the most outspoken of the pacifist pastors in Germany, was subjected to constant harassment and calumny from his colleagues, and on one occasion his agitation earned him a reprimand from his consistory.[125] In 1911 the chairman of the local peace society in Berlin, who was also a pastor, resigned his chairmanship under official pressure.[126] Journals with ties to the Evangelical churches, such as the *Tägliche Rundschau*, *Der Reichsbote*, the *Allgemeine Evangelische-Lu-*

---

[122] J. Lucht, *40 Erwägungen über Religion und Weltfrieden* (Berlin, 1908); Walther Nithack-Stahn, *Völkerfriede? Ein Streit-Gespräch* (Stuttgart, n.d.); *Bulletin du XVIe Congrès universel*, pp. 151–52; Otto Umfrid, *Völkerevangelium* (Esslingen, 1913); Ernst Böhme, "Der Krieg und die christliche Kirche," DWN, III (1894), 282–85, 365–69; DWN, IV (1895), 121–25.

European Peace Societies," p. 286; Joseph Muller, *L'oeuvre de toutes les confessions chrétiennes (églises) pour la paix internationale* (Paris, 1931); FB, IV (1903), 132; VF, XIII (1912), 117–18.

[123] W. Nithack-Stahn, *Kirche und Vaterland* (Berlin, 1914).

[124] See Ernst Böhme, *Die Unterlassungssünde der Kirche vor dem Kriege* (Stuttgart, 1919).

[125] SFC, Suttner to Fried, Vienna, 27 March 1897; DWN, VI (1897), 110; FW, XXII (1920), 88.

[126] NL Fried, W. Foerster to Fried, Berlin-Charlottenburg, 26 December 1911.

theranische Kirchenzeitung, and the *Deutsch-Evangelische Blätter,* denounced the pacifists. Although German Catholic clergymen were not as intense in their criticism of the peace movement, they were just as disinclined to associate with it, and Germans were conspicuously absent from the International Catholic Peace League.[127] Participation by German clerics in the peace movement was limited to scattered individuals, while the only organized religious support the peace societies received came from isolated sects such as the Moravian Brethren or small branches of non-indigenous denominations, such as Methodists and Baptists.[128] By 1912, despite concerted attempts by the pacifists to recruit members from the religious community in Germany, only one hundred seventeen of the over thirty-five thousand Protestant and Catholic clergymen in the country belonged to the German Peace Society.[129]

Several factors contributed to the hostility of German Protestant churchmen toward the peace movement. The most critical, since it had both a political and a theological dimension, was the fact that the Evangelical churches were constitutionally tied to the state. As state supported public servants, Protestant clerics were reluctant to embrace a cause which, in advocating international institutions, appeared to deprecate the state's sovereignty and criticize its policies. Thus, throughout the prewar period political conservatism in ecclesiastical bureaucracies made clergymen look askance at the pacifists.[130]

[127] A. Vanderpol, "Mes pérégrinations: Impressions d'un propagateur du pacifisme dans les milieux catholiques," *Almanach de la paix* (1912), p. 59; "Die Katholiken und der Friede," VF, XIII (1912), 118; VF, XIV (1913), 127; cf. VF, XI (1910), 44.

[128] BIP (VA7–8), Stephan van Bohr to Peace Bureau, Oldenburg, 17 June 1910; VF, XV (1914), 88; CBM, IX (1904), 18; VF, XII (1911), 40; CBM, XIV (1909), 109.

[129] Rade, *Beitrag,* p. 14; VF, XIII (1912), 109.

[130] Rade, "Wege zum Pazifismus: Protestantische Kirche," in Kurt Lenz and Walter Fabian, eds., *Die Friedensbewegung: Ein Handbuch der Weltfriedensströmungen der Gegenwart* (Berlin, 1922), pp. 67–70.

On another level the alliance between *Thron und Altar* was even more ominous for the pacifists, since its ultimate effect was to endow even the most belligerent nationalism, and hostility to the peace movement with a theological sanction.[131] Protestant theological criticism of the pacifists was heterogeneous, but it generally postulated a strict dualism between the *Weltreich*, the realm of man's debased temporal existence, and the transcendent *Gottesreich*, the Kingdom of Heaven, in which man and God were finally reconciled and where Christian ideals found their realization. This dualism implied another: the distinction between the personal and collective contexts of human behavior, between having to endure the social and political depravities inherent in the *Weltreich* and the struggle to achieve Christian piety in one's personal life. It followed that Christian ethics were appropriate for orienting one's personal life in the search for salvation, but that they had no general social or political validity in the temporal world.

This distinction had important ramifications for the problem of war, and nowhere were these more consequentially developed than in the writings of the jurist Rudolf Sohm, whose influence in Protestant theological circles in Germany was extensive.[132] Rejecting the proposition that the Christian ethic was relevant for statecraft, Sohm characterized international politics in terms of power and unremitting conflict. In his analysis, war represented the generative force of all political life, both domestically, in creating

[131] See Walter Bredendiek, "National-Protestantismus und christliches Friedenszeugnis," in *Irrwege und Warnlichter: Anmerkungen zur Kirchengeschichte der neueren Zeit* (Hamburg, 1966), pp. 10–34; Wolfgang Huber, "Evangelische Theologie und Kirche beim Ausbruch des Ersten Weltkrieges," in Huber, ed., *Historische Beiträge zur Friedensforschung* (Stuttgart and Munich, 1970), pp. 139–46; Fritz Fischer, "Der deutsche Protestantismus und die Politik im 19. Jahrhundert," *Historische Zeitschrift* CLXXI (1951), 473–518; Kupisch, "Bürgerliche Frömmigkeit," in Schoeps, *Zeitgeist*, pp. 47–48.

[132] See Andreas Bühler, *Kirche und Staat bei Rudolf Sohm* (Zurich, 1965), esp. pp. 33–36, 311–15.

and maintaining the state, and externally, in the perpetual struggle among nations for survival and self-assertion. Nor was his emphasis on conflict in international relations apologetic or resigned. Since he accepted Luther's belief that political order was an essential condition for man's leading a Christian life, Sohm concluded that war, because it was vital to the survival of political order in the state, was by its very nature a Christian undertaking. "Christianity, the Christian life of the individual," he wrote in 1900, "has as its *precondition* existence in the state and nation; for the sake of the *individual's* religious life there *must be* the state and thus also war, so that Christianity can prosper in our hearts."[133]

Other Protestant thinkers also justified the role of war in international affairs, if not like Sohm, with emphatic affirmation, then in the fatalistic recognition that international conflict represented a part of the burdens prescribed for man by God's inscrutable plan.[134] The practical effect of either point of view was the same. In restricting the applicability of Christian ethics to the confines of the individual's search for personal salvation, Protestant churchmen adopted a kind of theological social Darwinism, which deduced the inevitability or desirability of war from the doctrine of original sin and the depraved character of the *Weltreich*.[135]

Theological criticism of the peace movement followed directly from this analysis of the dynamics of international relations. Theologians pointed out that the pacifists' program challenged the distinction between *Weltreich* and *Gottesreich*, between political behavior and personal piety, by calling for the application of Christian ideals in world

---

[133] Quoted *ibid.*, p. 313. The italics are Sohm's.

[134] Mahr, "Christentum und Weltfrieden," CW, xxviii (1914), 995; DWN, iv (1895), 56–59; FB, vi (1905), 56.

[135] Otto Koester, "Theologische Gegner der Friedensbewegung," *Nord und Süd* xxxviii (August 1914), 160–61; cf. ER, iii (1914), 165; Huber, "Evangelische Theologie," p. 149.

affairs.[136] This, they claimed, overlooked the corruption of temporal existence and the fact that the ideal of perpetual peace was unattainable prior to the moral regeneration of mankind, which would occur only with the coming of the Kingdom of Heaven. In sum, the theological objection to the peace movement recalled the soldier who predicted that world peace would come only after a period of great battles; world peace was admittedly a desirable Christian ideal, but to advocate its implementation prior to the coming of the *Gottesreich* was premature and evidence of muddled thinking.

Protestant theologians reinforced their critique of the pacifists by drawing from the Bible, ecclesiastical history, and the Protestant tradition to show that war did not contradict Christian principles. They pointed out that the Old Testament was hardly a pacifist document and that Jesus himself never explicitly condemned warfare. They cited crusades, holy wars, Luther's commentaries on the Peasant War, and Schleiermacher's role in the resistance to Napoleon as evidence of the perversity of the pacifists' campaign to do away with war.[137] Indeed, so commonplace did these theological criticisms become that Martin Rade was forced to confess in 1899 that "it is nearly a matter of Christian orthodoxy [*nahezu für christlich-korrekt gilt*] to be against the peace movement."[138]

Protestant churchmen also frowned upon the kinds of allies the pacifists attracted. The fact that scientific pacifism appealed to philosophical materialists, whose principal enemy was organized Christianity, hardly enhanced the

[136] O. Umfrid, "Das Evangelium und der Krieg," VF, XII (1911), 9–11; Th. Rohleder, "Der Pietismus und die Friedensvereine," VF, XIV (1913), 132; FB, IV (1903), 117; FB, VII (1906), 15.

[137] See Karl von Stengel, *Der ewige Friede* (3rd ed., Munich, 1899), pp. 11–12; Rogge, "Nochmals geistlicher Antimilitarismus," in Deutscher Wehrverein, *Die Friedensbewegung und ihre Gefahren für das deutsche Volk* (Berlin, 1914), pp. 15–16; Rade, *Beitrag*, p. 13; FB, VI (1905), 56; VF, XV (1914), 89–90.

[138] CW, XIII (1899), 661.

prospects for cooperation between the peace movement and the churches. The pacifists experienced the gravity of this problem first hand. Arthur Westphal, the man whom the German Peace Society hired as its national secretary in 1911, was a convinced monist. Relations between him and Umfrid were strained from the start, and when Westphal then became active in the *Komitee "Konfessionslos,"* an organization founded in 1911 by Ostwald and other monists to promote mass secessions from the established churches, Umfrid drove him out of his job with the peace society.[139] This incident brought to a head tensions that had been lying latent for years in the peace movement between progressive materialists and the small group of religiously inspired pacifists around Umfrid.[140] It also symptomized the difficulty of finding common ground between such hostile groups as monists and clergymen; indeed, to most of the Protestant clergy in Germany, the thought of cooperating with the likes of Ostwald was probably itself repugnant enough to keep them away from the peace movement, regardless of their views on war and peace.

The product of philosophical, theological, and political considerations, the antagonism of Protestant clergymen toward the peace movement was one of the most intense the pacifists encountered, since it was played out in religious terms. Protestant churchmen excoriated the pacifists for their ill-informed theological views and defended with passion the moral probity of war.[141] They also attended pacifist meetings in order to defend the nation against arbitration and disarmament. In view of the general situation pacifists

[139] NL Fried, Umfrid, "Verehrliche Ortsgruppe," Stuttgart, December 1913; JPC, Jordan to Jesse Knight Jordan, Stuttgart, 16 December 1913; see also Otto Lehmann-Russbüldt, *Der geistige Befreiungskreig durch Kirchenaustritt* (Berlin, 1914); FB, v (1904), 54.

[140] NL Fried, Harder to Fried, Hamburg, 14 August 1908; Fried to Alber, Vienna, 2 December 1913; FW, x (1908), 17.

[141] Koester, "Gegner der Friedensbewegung," p. 166; VF, xiv (1913), 126; see also Ferdinand Kattenbusch, *Das sittliche Recht des Krieges* (Giessen, 1906).

found among the Protestant clergy in Germany, the indictment issued by an irate pastor in 1912 cannot be dismissed as unrepresentative: "We must protest against the peace movement in the name of Christianity, for it does not present the truth, but a lie, which is all the more captivating because it is covered with a froth of Christian-sounding phrases."[142]

The attitude of German Catholics toward the peace movement was also negative, though less outspoken, since it was the product of a somewhat different set of circumstances. As papal endorsements of the peace movement made clear, theological considerations were no obstacle to cooperation with the pacifists. The concept of the just war was the controlling doctrine, but Catholic thought did not reject, as did the more fatalistic and individualistic Protestant orthodoxy, the possibility of applying Christian ethics to politics in order to reduce or eliminate recourse to violence.[143] The posture of German Catholics toward the peace movement was determined, rather, by more strictly political considerations. Recent studies have shown that in the aftermath of the *Kulturkampf*, German Catholics attempted to reach an accommodation with the empire, with the result that beginning in the 1890s, but with increasing visibility after the turn of the century, they became outspoken patriots.[144] Reversing their earlier position, Catholic politicians now supported military appropriations in the Reichstag. Led by Cardinal Kopp, whose national enthusiasm made him an intimate of the Kaiser, the Catholic clergy

---

[142] Quoted in FW, XIV (1912), 429-30.

[143] Franz Xaver Eberle, *Krieg und Frieden im Urteile christlicher Moral* (Stuttgart, 1914).

[144] Rudolf Morsey, "Die deutschen Katholiken und der Nationalstaat zwischen Kulturkampf und Erstem Weltkrieg," *Historisches Jahrbuch* XC (1970), 31-64; see also Heinrich Lutz, *Demokratie im Zwielicht: Der Weg der deutschen Katholiken aus dem Kaiserreich in die Republik 1914-1925* (Munich, 1963); Heinrich Missalla, *Gott mit uns: Die deutsche katholische Kriegspredigt 1914-1918* (Munich, 1968).

and lay officials likewise left little doubt about their national loyalty, and by the eve of the war it had become difficult to criticize German Catholics for want of nationalist fervor. At the annual German Catholic congress in 1912, one official announced, reportedly to stormy applause: "We are prepared, when the Kaiser calls us, to sacrifice our possessions and our blood for our fatherland. We will let ourselves be surpassed by no one in love and loyalty to monarch and fatherland, and our patriotism will expire [only] with our last breath."[145]

This determination to emphasize their patriotism prompted German Catholics to avoid all association with organizations, such as the peace society, whose national credentials were in any way suspect. The pacifists' attempts to organize a Catholic peace society, or even to have Catholic clergymen speak at peace meetings elicited polite, but persistent refusals.[146] The Catholic press was likewise indifferent to the peace movement; the only significant exception was Bachem's *Kölnische Volkszeitung.*

In addition, German Catholics were no more fond of progressive materialists than were Protestants. Many Catholic commentators were convinced that these types—Catholics always called them Freemasons—controlled the peace movement for their own ends.[147] But this consideration merely reinforced the impulse toward accommodation in the nation-state which governed the Catholic position toward the peace movement. Having tried unsuccessfully to

---

[145] Quoted in Morsey, "Die deutschen Katholiken," p. 62.

[146] NL Fried, Decker to Fried, Cologne, 29 May 1905; Decker to Fried, Düsseldorf, 20 July 1914; *V. Deutscher Friedenskongress am 26. und 27. Oktober 1912 in Berlin* (Esslingen, n.d.), p. 8; ER, II (1913), 153–54; PM, III (1914), 172.

[147] Karl Fruhstorfer, "Treibende Kräfte und Charakter der Friedensbewegung," *Theologisch-praktische Quartalsschrift* LXIV (1911), 85; DWN, III (1894), 383; DWN, IV (1895), 24; DWN, V (1896), 526; see also Hermann Josef Dörpinghaus, *Darwins Theorie und der deutsche Vulgärmaterialismus im Urteil deutscher katholischer Zeitschriften zwischen 1854 und 1914* (Freiburg, 1969).

enlist the support of Catholic clergymen, one German pacifist observed that they seemed "to be taking their lead from above and did not think it opportune to participate in a cause not particularly popular and esteemed by those currently in positions of temporal power."[148] After his attempts had failed to find Germans for the International Catholic Peace League, a French pacifist concluded that "Catholics in Germany more or less share the ideas of a majority of their compatriots."[149] The Catholic response to the peace movement thus differed from the Protestant only insofar as the refusals of Catholics to cooperate were not as a rule accompanied by the theological vituperation pacifists came to expect from Protestants.

In part because one of its most prominent figures was himself a clergyman, the German peace movement devoted a great deal of attention to the churches. Pacifists sent appeals to churchmen, wrote articles for theological journals, and delivered lectures on the subject of Christianity and peace. Convinced that the constitutional structure of the Protestant churches was one of the main obstacles to their work, some pacifists advocated cutting the link between church and state, democratizing the ecclesiastical organization, or creating some kind of independent clerical office to promote pacifism among churchmen.[150]

The pacifists also attempted repeatedly to persuade the religious community to devote one Sunday each year to services based on the theme of world peace.[151] They were inspired by the success of the peace movement in England, where by 1901 over three thousand parishes had, at the behest of the pacifists, begun observing peace Sundays.[152] The

[148] ER, II (1913), 153–54.
[149] Vanderpol, "Mes pérégrinations," p. 59.
[150] BIP (vA7–8), Rohleder to Gobat, Post Wolpertshausen, 29 December 1907; Schücking, Neue Ziele, pp. 72–73, 78.
[151] Elsbeth and Friedrich M. Friedrichs, Der Völkerfriede und die Religion (Gautzsch b. Leipzig, 1910); DWN, v (1896), 204–205.
[152] BIP (vA7), Communication faite par M. le Dr. Evans Darby au viiie congrès; PD, xi (1901), 86.

Germans, however, were far less successful. Their only noteworthy accomplishment came in 1913, when the *Oberkonsistorium* of the Evangelical *Landeskirche* in Alsace-Lorraine agreed to institute special prayers for peace and to recommend that sermons be devoted to peace on the second Sunday of Advent each year.[153] Elsewhere establishment of the churches had brought more deference to the nation, and every *Landeskirche* the pacifists approached rejected the appeals for a peace Sunday.[154]

On several occasions pacifists sent special appeals to clerics, urging them to join the German Peace Society or to express their support publicly for world peace. One such appeal for membership, sent in 1903 to one thousand Protestant clergymen in Württemberg, received three (3) positive responses.[155] In 1907, as part of a campaign undertaken by pacifists in all countries, the peace society approached another thousand Evangelical theologians throughout the country and called for their support. This time the results were a little more encouraging, as more than one hundred responded favorably and some sixty even agreed to join the peace society.[156] Finally, in 1913 Umfrid and several other pacifist pastors sent another appeal to three thousand of their colleagues, drawing their attention to the futility of

[153] "Die Einrichtung eines Friedenssonntags in Elsass-Lothringen," VF, xv (1914), 50–53; ER, ii (1913), 232–33. Friedrich Curtius of the *Verband für internationale Verständigung* played an important role in setting up the peace Sunday as a member of the Directory of the Alsatian *Landeskirche*: Curtius, *Deutsche Briefe*, p. 239.

[154] BIP (vA7–8), Deutsche Friedensgesellschaft, Ortsgruppe Königsberg to Komitee-Sitzung des Berner Bureaus, Königsberg, 22 April 1910; Umfrid to Peace Bureau, Stuttgart, 3 December 1909; *Herald of Peace*, 1 March 1909, pp. 237–38.

[155] BIP, (vB6), Aufruf der Deutschen Friedensgesellschaft an Geistliche, Stuttgart, 1903; Hoeltzel to Ducommun, Stuttgart, 13 March 1905.

[156] On the appeals of 1907 and 1913 see Walter Bredendiek, "Die Friedensappelle deutscher Theologen von 1907/08 und 1913," in *Irrwege und Warnlichter*, pp. 40–60; CBM, xiii (1908), 34; FB, ix (1908), 72, 136.

the arms race and urging them to "regard it as an important part of their mission to proclaim with their words and in their writings the brotherhood of all men and nations."[157] They requested that the pastors acknowledge their support by signing the appeal and returning it. Of the three thousand whom the pacifists approached, the vast majority ignored the appeal, while about four hundred endorsed it. Umfrid's judgment that the appeal represented a "startling success" was dubious, for the statistics compiled on those who signed revealed that nearly one-third of the endorsements came from Alsace-Lorraine.[158] A number of the clergymen responded by denouncing the appeal, the peace society, and pastors active in it. One found the appeal a "personal insult" and a "contamination of his Lutheranism." Another regarded the appeal's confusion of the temporal world with the Kingdom of Heaven as evidence of its authors' "spiritual lunacy." Still another admonished Umfrid for making proposals that smacked of treason.[159]

The only significant exception to the general pattern of clerical repudiation of the peace movement, apart from Alsace-Lorraine, where the political situation was unique, was a group of liberal Protestants who denied that the Christian ethic was limited to the realm of personal piety and insisted that Christianity implied precepts for social and political action in the temporal world. The inspiration for this liberal Protestantism was Adolf Harnack's historical study of the Christian dogma. Most notably in his *Das Wesen des Christentums*, Harnack located the essential articulation of the dogma in the Gospels, and he concluded that before it underwent centuries of exegetic obfuscation,

---

[157] FW, xv (1913), 209.

[158] NL Fried, Umfrid to Fried, Stuttgart, 29 May 1913; "Für und wider den Friedensruf der deutschen Geistlichen," *Die Eiche* I (1913), 141–43.

[159] PM, II (1913), 146; VF, xiv (1913), 63; Wagner, "Friedensbewegung und Kirche," in Umfrid, *Der Wehrverein*, pp. 24–25; Umfrid, "Mobilmachung der Kirchen gegen den Krieg," FW, xv (1913), 210.

the message of Jesus Christ was that the Kingdom of God was immanent in the soul of man, even during his temporal existence, disposing him to love and lead an active life in the service of his fellow man. In addition to the theological problems it raised for Protestant orthodoxy, Harnack's interpretation had important social and political ramifications. In construing the essence of Christianity as the active disposition to love, he denied the dualism between the *Gottesreich* and *Weltreich* that had bred fatalism among Protestant theologians about the existence of evil in the world. In practice, like Moritz von Egidy (whose conception of Christianity was close to Harnack's in important respects), many of those who subscribed to this view became involved in organizations working for political and social reform, among which the Evangelical-Social movement was the most celebrated.

This liberal Protestantism was most closely identified with the circle around Harnack's close friend and former student, Martin Rade, who edited the journal *Christliche Welt*.[160] Rade's own career as theologian, politician, social reformer, and journalist reflected his belief that Christianity should serve as a guide for social and political reform. His journal, as its title indicated, was dedicated to making the world Christian, and its contributors, who included Friedrich Naumann, Ernst Troeltsch, Paul Göhre, Wilhelm Bousset, and Harnack himself, dealt with a wide range of contemporary problems.[161] Although there was no consensus about the solutions these problems demanded, the "Friends of the *Christliche Welt*" agreed that they existed and that a Christian should confront them.

One such problem was war. Here, too, the implications

---

[160] See Johannes Rathje, *Die Welt des freien Protestantismus: Ein Beitrag zur deutsch-evangelischen Geistesgeschichte. Dargestellt an Leben und Werk von Martin Rade* (Stuttgart, 1952).

[161] Emil Fuchs, "Christliche Welt," in Hermann Mulert, ed., *Vierzig Jahre "Christliche Welt": Festgabe für Martin Rade* (Gotha, 1927), p. 73.

of Harnack's work were seminal. In finding the essence of Christianity embodied in the Gospels, Harnack depreciated the significance of the bellicose passages in the Old Testament that supported the orthodox justification of warfare. More importantly, by correlating the essential Christian message with the experience of the early church, Harnack implied that pacifism was central to Christianity. Indeed, in his small volume, *Militia Christi*, which he published in 1905, he made this explicit. He demonstrated that early Christians had tried to realize the adjurations of the Gospels by adopting a posture of nonresistance to force and refusing to serve in Roman armies, an endeavor in which they were generally successful until the third century, after which the conversion of the emperor Constantine brought a basic transformation in the church's attitude about military activity and a doctrinal accommodation of warfare.[162]

However clearly Harnack's conclusions seemed to vindicate the peace movement, they did not lead directly to an acceptable pacifist position, for no responsible theologian— particularly no Lutheran theologian—could advocate nonresistance as a policy for statesmen charged with guiding the nation's destiny.[163] Beginning in 1899, on the occasion of the Hague conference, a protracted controversy took place in the *Christliche Welt* over the problems of Christian pacifism, and out of this debate emerged the clearest statement of what might be called liberal Protestant pacifism.[164] The most important figure in the controversy, which cen-

[162] Harnack, *Militia Christi: Die christliche Religion und der Soldatenstand in den ersten drei Jahrhunderten* (Tübingen, 1905).

[163] See Umfrid, "Die Stellung der alten Kirchen zum Kriegsdienst," FB, IX (1908), 33–36, 47–48, 62–63; H. Weinel, "Christentum und Patriotismus," FB, IX (1908), 83.

[164] For instance, Friedrich Paulson, "Politik und Moral," CW, XIII (1899), 385–92, 415–23; Paul Göhre, "Der Friedensgedanke und das Christentum," *ibid.*, pp. 547–50; Paul Sander, "Christentum und Krieg," *ibid.*, pp. 660–62; Wilhelm Koppelmann, "Nochmals Politik und Moral," *ibid.*, pp. 674–78; Johannes Gottschalk, "Die christliche Moral und die Politik," CW, XIV (1900), 74–78, 98–102, 122–25, 147–52.

tered upon the problem of reconciling Christian ethics and international politics, did not actually participate, but his specter was always in the background. Leo Tolstoy was the foremost advocate of a radical, utopian Christian pacifism. Paradoxically, he accepted the premise of Sohm and other Protestant thinkers who denied the compatibility of politics and the Christian ethic, one being based on the use of force, the other prescribing forbearance and humility. However, Tolstoy rejected Sohm's resolution of this problem, which was to exclude Christian morality from politics; instead, he concluded that leading a Christian life required the repudiation of politics (and political order) in favor of a Christian anarchism.[165]

The problem faced by liberal Protestants, who accepted the legitimacy of the nation-state, was to break the restrictions imposed on Christian morality by Sohm's position without being forced to Tolstoy's radical conclusion, which itself seemed fully justified by Harnack's historical research. The chief protagonists of an alternative were Rade and Otto Umfrid (whose Christian activism owed less to the influence of Harnack than to Planck). Their solution was to reject the premise that Sohm and Tolstoy held in common, that politics and morality were necessarily incompatible. Instead, they asserted that the implementation of certain political reforms, notably international arbitration, would enable statesmen to live professionally by the Christian ethic and make it possible for states to coexist according to Christian principles.[166]

The theologians close to Rade who accepted this position

---

[165] See Moe, *Le prix Nobel*, pp. 269–79; Sibley, *Political Theories*, pp. 12–13; NL Fried, Umfrid to Fried, Stuttgart, 21 December 1910; Curtius to Fried, Strassburg, 11 December 1913.

[166] Rade, "Ein Schlusswort über Krieg und Frieden," CW, XIII (1899), 972–74; Umfrid, "Der nationale Interessenkrieg—Das Widerspiel der christlichen Gesinnung," CW, XVII (1903), 33–38; Umfrid, "Die theologische Gegnerschaft gegen die Friedensbewegung und die Rechtswidrigkeit des heutigen Krieges," CW, XX (1906), 867–70.

became supporters of the peace movement. Harnack himself was well aware of the relevance of his theology for the contemporary problems of war and national prejudice. In an article in the *Christliche Welt* on the lessons to be learned from the early church, he wrote: "We are happy when a noble patriotism is fostered in this world dominated by material interests; but how wretched is the man who sees in patriotism his highest ideal, or honors the state as the epitome [*Zusammenfassung*] of everything good in life! What a relapse after we have experienced Jesus Christ in this world!"[167] In 1909 he praised the role of the pacifists in articulating a new political ethic and noted "that the peace societies are highly significant and certainly are not premature in their anticipatory work."[168] Harnack was also active in the peace movement. He was one of the initial members of the *Verband für internationale Verständigung* and was one of the leaders of the campaign to improve relations with England through closer contacts between German and English churchmen. In addition to Harnack and Rade, who was himself prominent in several peace-oriented groups, Heinrich Weinel and Hans Wendt, who were both professors of theology in Jena, Ernst Troeltsch, Paul Göhre, Friedrich Curtius, Walther Nithack-Stahn, Karl Jatho, and Gottfried Traub were all among the "Friends of the *Christliche Welt*" actively supporting the peace movement.[169]

Of all the Christian activists in the circle around Rade, probably the most committed was Friedrich Siegmund-Schultze. A student of Harnack and Rade, he was only twenty-nine when the war broke out, but he had already distinguished himself as a man of enormous energy in dedicating his life to solving the problems of society through Christianity. He was active in promoting Christian youth groups, working with the urban indigent, and fostering

[167] Quoted in Rathje, *Die Welt des freien Protestantismus*, p. 59.
[168] Quoted in HB (2), II, 256–57.
[169] NL Fried, Decker to Fried, Cologne, 20 May 1905; Lothar Schücking to Fried, Dortmund, 23 September 1910.

world peace through Christian ecumenicism. Although he was critical of some of the leaders of the peace society, whom he accused of disregarding national sensitivities, he subscribed without qualification to the pacifist ideals of Rade and Umfrid. As he wrote in 1910 to an English friend, "The same relations which we demand to be between man [sic], should also be between nations. . . . Christian ethics must be appreciated not only by the single person, but also to [sic] even the largest communities."[170] In his efforts to promote observance of the Christian ethic in international politics he joined both the German Peace Society and the *Verband für internationale Verständigung*, but more important was his role in the attempt to establish closer ties between German and English churchmen.

In 1907, in conjunction with the second Hague conference, a group of English Quakers circulated an appeal in favor of arbitration as an alternative to war. The document, which had the endorsement of leading religious figures in England and the United States, was then presented to the conference by a delegation led by the Quaker M.P., J. Allen Baker. Baker was convinced that the most solid foundation for world peace was cooperation among the Christian churches, particularly the churches in England and Germany. At The Hague he discussed his ideas with Siegmund-Schultze and Eduard de Neufville, who were there as observers, and the three agreed that increased Christian cooperation might well promote Anglo-German *rapprochement*.

These discussions encouraged Baker to form a committee of English churchmen, which early in 1908 invited more

[170] NL Friedrich Siegmund-Schultze, Evangelische Kirche in Deutschland Archiv, Berlin (cited hereafter as NL Siegmund-Schultze) (B IV b 2), Siegmund-Schultze to Alan Baker, Sansoucci, 1 August 1910; Siegmund-Schultze to Umfrid, Sansoucci, 2 September 1911. See also Siegmund-Schultze, "Religion und Friede," *Monatsschrift für Pastoraltheologie* VII (1910–11), 101–106.

than one hundred leading German churchmen to visit England.[171] After an approving nod from the German government, which was itself trying to improve relations with the English, a German delegation including top officials from the Prussian Evangelical church spent two weeks in England during the spring of 1908.[172] Upon their return the Germans formed a committee to coordinate a return visit from the English churchmen, which took place in June 1909.

The benevolence of the German government made it possible in 1910 to transform the committees in England and Germany into a permanent organization, the Associated Councils of Churches in the British and German Empires for Fostering Friendly Relations between the Two Peoples (the German title was scarcely more manageable: *Das kirchliche Komitee zur Pflege freundschaftlicher Beziehungen zwischen Grossbritannien und Deutschland*). In England, where its leaders were Baker and the Liberal M.P., Willoughby Dickinson, the committee found considerable support among clergymen. The Archbishop of Canterbury became honorary president, and by the outbreak of the war its membership stood at over eleven thousand laymen and clergy.[173] In Germany the organization was less vigorous, despite official patronage which brought the support of the Protestant general synod in Prussia and the participation of the major figures in the Prussian church, including Bodo Voigts, Wilhelm Faber, Dieter Lahusen, Ernst Dryander, and Albert Spiecker.[174] From the beginning, though, the

---

[171] On the visits and the founding of the Associated Councils see Elizabeth Balmer Baker and P. J. Noel Baker, *J. Allen Baker, M.P.: A Memoir* (London, 1927), pp. 169–205; Ruth Rouse and Stephan Charles Neill, eds., *A History of the Ecumenical Movement, 1517–1948* (Philadelphia, 1954), pp. 511–12; Daril Hudson, "The Ecumenical Movement and World Order" (Ph.D. dissertation, London School of Economics and Political Science, University of London, 1965), pp. 24–52; Deckart, "Deutsch-englische Verständigung," pp. 90–108.

[172] See Fischer, *Krieg der Illusionen*, p. 104.

[173] Hudson, "Ecumenical Movement," p. 52.

[174] NL Siegmund-Schultze (B IV b 3), [Siegmund-Schultze] Bericht

Prussians were not enthusiastic about the committee and insisted that it eschew all political activity. German Catholic officials were even less excited about cooperating in a committee with German and English Protestants, and they could only with difficulty be persuaded to participate at all.[175] Altogether, the German branch was able to attract only three thousand members.[176]

The principal source of energy in the German committee was Siegmund-Schultze, who served as its secretary and presided over all its activities. These included promoting cultural exchanges between Germany and England, sending a correspondence sheet to religious journals, and, after 1912, publishing a journal, *Die Eiche*, which the Carnegie Endowment subsidized.[177] Siegmund-Schultze was also the most active proponent of closer ties between the German committee and the peace movement. But despite the presence of pacifists—Neufville, Rade, and Umfrid—on the committee's executive, the conservative Prussians determined the group's posture. They restrained Siegmund-Schultze whenever he tried to extend the scope of the committee's operations in a way that might imply endorsement of the peace movement, and this applied to his attempts to broaden the Anglo-German committee into a world alliance of churches.[178] The German committee was thus unrespon-

---

über die Arbeit des Kirchlichen Komitees . . . [July 1911]; *ibid.* (B 1 c), Siegmund-Schultze to Baker, Sansoucci [April 1911]; *ibid.* (B iv b 3), Siegmund-Schultze to Hentig, Sansoucci, 19 August 1911; *ibid.* (B iv c 1), Protokoll der Sitzung, 7 October 1910.

[175] *Ibid.* (B iv b 1), Spiecker to Dickinson, Berlin, 31 October 1910; *ibid.* (B 1 c), Spiecker to Baker, 19 August 1911; cf. Baker, *Baker*, p. 178.

[176] Hudson, "Ecumenical Movement," p. 52.

[177] NL Siegmund-Schultze (B iv a 1), Protokoll der constituierenden Sitzung des Kirchlichen Komitees . . . 9 December 1909; *ibid.* (B iv b 1), Siegmund-Schultze to Dickinson, Berlin, 13 September 1910.

[178] *Ibid.* (B 1 c), Siegmund-Schultze to Baker, Sansoucci [March 1911]; *ibid.* (F 1 d), Siegmund-Schultze to Lahusen, Berlin, 7 December 1911; *ibid.* (B 1 d), Siegmund-Schultze to Baker, Berlin, 17 April

sive to suggestions from the English branch that the two cooperate in promoting treaties of arbitration.[179] It likewise rejected a proposal to establish a working agreement with the German Peace Society and the *Verband für internationale Verständigung*.[180]

This conservative definition of the committee's mission was clearly to the taste of the German government. Shortly after its establishment, Bethmann Hollweg expressed his satisfaction that the committee was serving the peace (only) by promoting "mutual acquaintance and understanding between two great nations."[181] The Kaiser, too, demonstrated his approval of the committee's work by appearing at several meetings with Baker and other council leaders.[182]

In the final analysis, the existence of the *Kirchliches Komitee* hardly challenges the generalization that the German churches were extremely hostile toward the peace movement. Nor should one overestimate the impact of the pacifist impulse in liberal Protestantism. Siegmund-Schultze, for instance, had no success in stimulating interest in the peace movement among the other groups in which he was active, including the German Y.M.C.A. movement and the allied *Deutsche-Christliche Studenten-Vereinigung*, both of which were politically conservative and nationalist in spite of their international affiliations.[183] Even within the small

---

1912; *ibid*. (B ɪv b 6), Siegmund-Schultze to Umfrid, Berlin, 4 June 1914; Rouse and Neill, *Ecumenical Movement*, p. 514.

[179] NL Siegmund-Schultze (B ɪv b 1), Spiecker to Dickinson, Berlin, 11 April 1911.

[180] *Ibid*. (B ɪv d 4 c), Lübke to Kirchliches Komitee, Hamburg, 30 May 1913.

[181] *Ibid*. (B ɪv b 2), Bethmann Hollweg to Lahusen, Hohenfinow, 14 August 1910.

[182] NL Fried, Neufville to Fried, Frankfurt, 30 June 1910; Baker, *Baker*, pp. 185, 189.

[183] NL Fried, E. Vierow to Fried, Griefswald, 27 May 1912; VF, xɪɪɪ (1912), 100; Theophil Mann, "Die Christliche Studentenweltbund und der Friede unter den Nationen," *Die Eiche* 1 (April 1913), 98–

group around Rade there was no consensus in favor of the peace movement.[184] Liberal Protestants were especially concerned about the prominence of monists in the peace society, for having subjected the sacrosanctity of the dogma to historical criticism themselves, they were if anything more vulnerable than conservative Protestants to attacks from progressive materialists.[185] Harnack's celebrated condemnation of Ostwald at the Evangelical-Social congress in 1912 was symptomatic of this tension between Protestant liberals and the peace society, and even Siegmund-Schultze deplored the fact that the leadership of the peace movement was in the hands of those who were "not in every respect upholders of moral idealism."[186]

Moreover, the political implications of liberal Protestant theology itself were ambiguous, and it was not unusual for a theological liberal to be a political conservative who despised the peace movement. Liberal Protestant pacifism rested on Harnack's conclusion that the Gospels posed an ethical absolute which implied world peace. However, Harnack's views were themselves the object of repeated attack even among his own followers—from those who, like Ernst Troeltsch, employed historical criticism to question the ab-

102; Karl Kupisch, *Der deutsche CVJM: Aus der Geschichte der Christlichen Vereine Junger Männer Deutschlands* (Kassel-Wilhelmshöhe, 1958), pp. 37–59; Kupisch, *Studenten entdecken die Bibel: Die Geschichte der Deutschen Christlichen Studenten-Vereinigung (DCSV)* (Hamburg, 1964), pp. 63, 94–95; cf. Siegmund-Schultze, "Der christliche Studentenweltbund als internationale Kraft," FW, xvi (1914), 91–94.

[184] NL Martin Rade, Universitätsbibliothek, Marburg (cited hereafter as NL Rade), Nithack-Stahn to Rade, Berlin, 28 April 1910, 26 September 1910; Rathje, *Die Welt des freien Protestantismus*, p. 41.

[185] NL Schücking (57), Josef Munk to Schücking, Mainz, 13 March 1914; NL Rade, Pechmann to Rade, Munich, 27 February 1909; Otto Lehmann-Russbüldt, "Der kirchliche Liberalismus und die Kirchenaustrittsbewegung," *Das Monistische Jahrhundert* 1 (1912–13), 641–44.

[186] Ostwald, *Ostwald*, pp. 151–52; Siegmund-Schultze, "Warum wir unsere deutsch-britische Freundschaftsarbeit treiben," *Die Eiche* 11 (1914), 3.

solute status of the Christian religion itself, and from those who used historical analysis to challenge Harnack's interpretation of the substance of the Gospel message.[187] Troeltsch supported the peace movement, but the principal figure in the other group of Harnack's critics, Ferdinand Kattenbusch, did not. Like Harnack, a student of Albrecht Ritschl and a member of Rade's circle, Kattenbusch published a reply to Harnack's *Militia Christi* in 1906, in which he accepted the legitimacy of Harnack's historical approach, his interpretation of the centrality of the Gospels, and even the binding character of Jesus' call to love one's enemy. Nonetheless, he concluded that war was morally justified, as he depreciated the significance of specific Gospel passages as moral injunctions and noted that since love can entail punishment, "war and love of one's enemies do not contradict one another."[188] However perverse his logic, Kattenbusch demonstrated that it was possible to deny the orthodox dualism between the personal and collective contexts of human behavior and still to view war as an entirely legitimate undertaking.

In his survey of nationalism in the German Protestant churches, the East German historian Walter Bredendiek has concluded that the churches "contributed to the fact that the middle sectors [of German society] . . . did not choose the anti-imperialist alternative that was developed by the working class movement and also by the peace movement."[189] It is impossible to quarrel with the basic accuracy of this conclusion, at least as it pertains to the churches and the peace movement. The German churches were overwhelmingly opposed to the proposition, which the peace movement sought to popularize, that it was morally imperative for the nations of the world to coexist in a peaceful

---

[187] Rathje, *Die Welt des freien Protestantismus*, pp. 92–93, 102–103, 106, 211.

[188] Ferdinand Kattenbusch, *Das sittliche Recht des Krieges* (Giessen, 1906), esp. pp. 24–28; cf. CW, xx (1906), 515–20, 532–36, 553–58.

[189] Bredendiek, "National-Protestantismus," p. 13.

community. Bredendiek's conclusion applies as well, though, to the other sectors of German society which the pacifists approached in hopes of changing popular attitudes about war and international relations. Except for isolated pockets of support, everywhere the pacifists turned they discovered not only that agencies of opinion formation rejected their concept of an international community, but that these agencies were actively fostering attitudes incompatible with it, emphasizing the antagonisms inherent in international relations and the role of violence in resolving international disputes.

In imperial Germany most of these agencies of political socialization—schools, churches, the army, the press, and youth groups—were accessible to direct political control, either through their constitutional ties to the state or, as in the case of the press, through more subtle means of political persuasion.[190] Most of the pacifists did not appreciate the implications of this situation for their campaign. They continued to insist that theirs was a humanitarian crusade that transcended politics; they failed to see that changing popular attitudes about war was at the core a political problem. Nor did they recognize that the situation in Germany virtually negated the assumptions on which their campaign rested, for it was unlikely that popular attitudes about international affairs could force changes in the views of political elites, as long as these elites themselves controlled the processes by which popular attitudes were formed. In any event, the control of the state over agencies of opinion formation made the peace movement's attempt to influence the German government and political parties especially important.

[190] Wernecke, *Der Wille zur Weltgeltung*, p. 312.

6

The Peace Movement
and German Politics

THE ULTIMATE goal of the peace movement's campaign in Germany was to influence political decisions that affected international relations. Both the German Peace Society and the *Verband für internationale Verständigung* emphasized an indirect—one is tempted to say unpolitical—approach, by trying to saturate all the agencies that shaped German public opinion with attitudes consonant with international community. At the same time, both organizations did attempt, as part of their wider campaign, to work with those sectors of society most immediately involved in making political decisions in Germany, in order to enlighten them on matters of international politics. The reception of the peace movement among political agencies and organizations was much the same as it was elsewhere in German society. Only among groups on the periphery of German politics did the peace movement find any support or sympathy; the closer the pacifists got to the real centers of power the more determined was the resistance they encountered.

The Imperial Government

"In looking back on the events of the concluding years of the nineteenth century, I must not omit to mention the Hague Peace Conference."[1] That Bernhard von Bülow recalled the Hague conference in his memoirs as little more than an afterthought well bespoke the minimal importance the German government had attached to it—as well, perhaps, as the fact that Bülow himself, though foreign secre-

[1] Bernhard von Bülow, *Memoirs of Prince von Bülow* (4 vols., Boston, 1931), I, 404.

tary at the time, was on vacation during much of the period the conference met.[2] Yet however unimpressed German officials remained over the importance of arbitration and arms limitation, the two Hague conferences did provide the occasions on which the government most systematically articulated its position with regard to the peace movement and the cardinal tenets of its program.[3]

When in August 1898 the Russian tsar issued a circular calling for an international conference to put limits on the arms race, it made the international peace movement jubilant, but it was less happily received in governmental circles. This was particularly true in Berlin, where, behind Bülow's effusive public support for the conference, officials reacted with skepticism and apprehension to the proposal, calculating, in all probability correctly, that the Russians had been moved less by love of international peace than by anxiety over the costs of keeping their armaments competitive.[4] Because he did not wish to offend the tsar, the Kaiser agreed to German participation, but he and the foreign office were determined to oppose unconditionally any international disarmament agreement. It soon became clear, though, that the Russians were alone among the major powers in seriously wanting to limit the arms race, so the

[2] Hans Wehberg, *Gutachten: Deutschland und die Friedensbewegung. Sonderabdruck aus Das Werk des Untersuchungsausschusses des Verfassungsgebenden Deutschen Nationalversammlung und des Deutschen Reichstages 1919–1930*, Erste Reihe, *Die Vorgeschichte des Weltkrieges* v, 2 (Berlin, n.d.), 31.

[3] For more complete accounts of the German position at The Hague see: Andrej Józef Kamiński, *Stanowisko Niemiec na pierwszej Konferencji Haskiej 1899* (Poznan, 1962); Philipp Zorn, *Deutschland und die beiden Haager Friedenskonferenzen* (Stuttgart and Berlin, 1920); Wehberg, *Gutachten*. W. D. Curtsinger of the University of Maryland has been working on a dissertation on this subject.

[4] Boutiron to Delcassé, Berlin, 3 September 1898, DDF (1), XIV, 505–509, number 322; see also Dan L. Morrill, "Nicholas II and the Call for the First Hague Conference," *Journal of Modern History* XLVI (1974), 296–313.

Germans could await the conference confident that they would not be too embarrassed.

In January 1899, however, complications arose, as the Russians supplemented their original proposal with a memorandum calling for discussion at the conference of ways to implement arbitration in international disputes. To the German government this posed a much more troublesome problem, as during the months prior to the conference the possibility of setting up a court of arbitration became the focus of popular interest and enthusiasm. It became apparent as well that the other powers were willing to make concessions to this enthusiasm by creating a court of international arbitration with obligatory jurisdiction in certain minor kinds of disputes. However, the more the Germans studied arbitration, the more convinced they became that it was no less objectionable than disarmament.

For the public record, the German government opposed arbitration because it would entangle the question of responsibility for international disputes in legal technicalities, thereby making it possible for a would-be aggressor to escape condemnation; this, the Germans pointed out, would endanger rather than promote world peace.[5] However, in the series of discussions that the Russian proposal provoked in the privacy of the foreign office, it was clear that considerations of a quite different nature were really at the root of German hostility toward international arbitration. In a memorandum he drew up in May 1899, which was then incorporated *verbatim* into the instructions issued to the German delegation to the first Hague conference, Friedrich von Holstein expressed the Germans' fundamental objection with complete candor: "the state regards itself as an end in itself [*Selbstzweck*]—the greater the state the more this is true—not as a means to attaining higher, ulterior objectives. For the state there is no higher objective than the protection of its own interests. These, however, will not, in the

[5] AA, Eur. Gen. 37 number 2a, Bd. 1, A6530I (ACP 104), Bülow to Münster, 3 June 1899 (GP, xv, 242–44, number 4280).

case of the great powers, necessarily be identical with maintaining the peace."[6] Since Holstein and Bülow attributed to other states the same motives that guided their own policy, they viewed arbitration as vexatious at best. A fully disinterested international court was, in their opinion, inconceivable, so that arbitration would in practice "represent the principle of regulated intervention" in international disputes.[7] This in turn would only delay in legal complications the actual outbreak of armed hostilities, to the disadvantage of the power capable of the most rapid mobilization. "We would thus give up our political independence," wrote one of the German delegates at the first Hague conference, "and if it came to questions that could finally lead to war, we would lose the advantage given to us by rapid mobilization, which no other power can come close to matching." To this the Kaiser noted: "Quite right! That is what the whole fraud is designed to do."[8]

An inability to believe that statesmen could act for altruistic reasons and the suspicion that arbitration was *ipso facto* directed against German mobilization formed the bases of German policy at The Hague. There were, however, additional considerations that contributed to the government's fear of arbitration. In a penetrating critique of the second Hague conference, Alfred Marschall von Bieberstein, who led the German delegation, pointed out the uncomfortable implications of the concept:

> For great powers, and especially those with small or middle-sized states as neighbors, an international treaty of arbitration, since it is founded on the principle of the absolute equality of states, would be tantamount in many

[6] AA, Eur. Gen. 37 number 1, Bd. 10, A5514 (ACP 103), Holstein Memorandum, 9 May 1899 (GP, xv, 188–89, number 4255).

[7] AA, Eur. Gen. 37 number 2a, Bd. 1, zu A6900 (ACP 104), Holstein, Zu der heutigen Mittheilung des Grafen Lanza, 9 June 1899 (GP, xv, 267–68, number 4298).

[8] Münster to Hohenlohe, The Hague, 28 May 1899, GP, xv, 234–47, number 4276.

cases to a renunciation of the factor of power, by which the stronger governs the weaker. In other words, relationships based upon power would be transformed into legal relationships, and a kind of spiderweb would be created, in which even the smallest states would feel like spiders—and perhaps here and there the great powers will become the flies in the web. One need not, therefore, subscribe to the motto "might makes right" in order to oppose the kinds of leveling schemes that abound at all [these] international conferences.[9]

Arbitration was, in short, a democratic principle. If carried to its logical conclusion, it would fully revolutionize the foundations of international relations, making all states equal in the eyes of international law. If such a system did not destroy the category of great power altogether, it would fundamentally alter the character of relations among the larger states in a way the Germans did not contemplate favorably. Unable to foresee the end of interest politics under any circumstances, German officials anticipated the transformation of the arms race into competition among the great powers for the support of the small countries, which would, by virtue of their numbers, constitute a majority on any court and thus preside over the development of international law.[10] In view of Germany's low esteem in international opinion, German statesmen preferred to rely on their army.

Not only did arbitration portend the triumph of demo-

[9] AA, Eur. Gen. 37 number 6, Bd. 1, A17473 (ACP 106), Marschall to Bülow, Neuershausen, 10 November 1907, pp. 7-8 (GP, XXIII, 289-95, number 7965).

[10] AA, Eur. Gen. 37 number 2, Bd. 1, A6825 (ACP 104), Münster to Hohenlohe, Scheveningen, 7 June 1899; *ibid.*, 37 number 2a, Bd. 1, A7078I (ACP 105), Hellwig, Zu der Frage des permanenten Schiedsgerichts, 13 June 1899 (GP, XV, 274-75, number 4303); *ibid.*, 37 number 2a, Bd. 2, Zu A7314 (ACP 105), Bülow to Radolin, Berlin, 17 June 1899 (GP, XV, 286-90, number 4314); *ibid.*, 37 number 5, Bd. 2, A2002 (ACP 107), Tschirschky, Runderlass an die kaiserlichen Botschafter . . . Berlin, 4 December 1907.

cratic principles to the exclusion of national power in international relations; equally ominous, if not more so, was the fact that arbitration, like disarmament, had democratic implications for domestic politics. During both Hague conferences German opposition to arbitration and disarmament was dictated in part by what Bülow referred to as "the fundamental principles of a conservative monarchy."[11] A glance at the kind of popular support disarmament and arbitration had attracted convinced ranking German officials, from the Kaiser on down, that the implementation of these reforms could only work to the benefit of socialists and democrats, who advocated parliamentary control over foreign and military policy.[12] Nor was it difficult to see just how this would happen. As Heinrich von Tschirschky, the foreign secretary, explained it in 1907: "supported by an eventual disarmament treaty, or even by negotiations on this subject at a conference, a parliamentary body would easily be inclined to involve itself in an undesirable way in the state's foreign relations, as well as in matters pertaining to armaments, with the result that the monarch would be restricted in implementing the measures he holds necessary for the security of the empire."[13] An international arms agreement would, for example, make the Reichstag more recalcitrant in scrutinizing requests from the government for defense appropriations.[14]

11 AA, Eur. Gen. 37 number 1, Bd. 10, A5795 (ACP 103), Bülow Memorandum, 14 May 1899 (GP, xv, 193–96, number 4257, Anlage).

12 William's initial reaction to the tsar's proposal for a peace conference was: "He has presented our democrats and opposition with a brilliant weapon for agitating." GP, xv, 143–45, number 4216; AA, Eur. Gen. 37 number 1, Bd. 1, AS2350 (ACP 102), William II to Nicholas II, Berlin, 29 August 1898 (GP, xv, 151–52, number 4222); ibid., 37 number 2, Bd. 2, A7635 (ACP 104), Münster to Hohenlohe, Scheveningen, 24 June 1899 (cf. GP, xv, 311–12, number 4326).

13 AA, Eur. Gen. 37 number 5, Bd. 3, A3803/3935/393_ (ACP 107), Tschirschky to Schoen, Berlin, 9 March 1907 (GP, xxiii, 149, number 7871).

14 AA, Eur. Gen. 37 number 1, Bd. 2, A10291 (ACP 102), Eulenburg to Hohenlohe, Vienna, 4 September 1898 (GP, xv, 154, number

Underlying these apprehensions was a more basic fear. The official rationalization for unrestricted monarchical control over foreign and military policy was that a threatening international climate put a premium on efficient coordination of the country's diplomatic and military forces—the kind of coordination the Reichstag could not provide. The concepts of arbitration and disarmament threatened to deflate this argument by promoting the illusion in public opinion that peace was secure. Thus, German officials feared that the "pressure of misled public opinion" could conceivably force the government to arbitrate, thus undermining the emperor's power in the realms of foreign and military policy, and threatening the entire political system whose pillars rested on the monarch's prerogatives.[15]

Altogether, these considerations led German officials to conclude that arbitration and disarmament were designed principally to limit German power.[16] An arms agreement would merely allow other countries to catch up in the arms race. Arbitration was calculated to neutralize a swift German mobilization and to subject German policy to the scrutiny of a gaggle of small nations. Moreover, both disarmament and arbitration would undermine German power by abetting the spokesmen for parliamentary control over German foreign and military policy.

Because the Germans were inalterably opposed to arbitration and arms limitation, their policy at The Hague in

4224); *ibid.*, 37 number 5, Bd. 2 (no number) (ACP 107), Aufzeichnung über das von der Russischen Regierung vorgeschlagene Programm der zweiten Haager Friedenskonferenz, pr. 17 July 1906; *ibid.*, 37 number 5, Bd. 3, A3706 (ACP 107), Wedel to Foreign Office, Vienna, 5 March 1907 (GP, XXIII, 141–43, number 7864).

[15] See AA, Eur. Gen. 37 number 2a, Bd. 1, zu A6900III (ACP 104), Hellwig, Zu der Frage des permanenten Schiedsgerichts, 10 June 1899 (GP, XV, 268–69, number 4300).

[16] In May 1899 the Kaiser observed that "The whole conference [is] more or less directed against our military development." AA, Eur. Gen. 37 number 1, Bd. 10, A5795 (ACP 103), Bülow Memorandum, 14 May 1899 (GP, XV, 193–96, number 4257, Anlage).

1899, and again in 1907, was to sabotage both projects as thoroughly as possible without becoming the isolated object of popular censure or, more importantly, overly antagonizing the Russians, who had staked their prestige on the success of the conferences. From the start, however, the Germans made tactical errors. As the chief of their delegation to the first Hague conference they dispatched Count Georg zu Münster, the German ambassador in Paris. A crusty old career diplomat, Münster made no secret of his disgust over the entire conference, which he believed was part of a Russian plot against Germany.[17] Nor was he the only unfortunate personality in the German delegation. At the urging of the Bavarian government, the foreign office agreed to include a Bavarian in the delegation and selected as legal consultant Karl von Stengel, a professor at law at the university in Munich.[18] Immediately prior to being named, Stengel had published a pamphlet, entitled *Der ewige Friede*, in which he condemned disarmament, arbitration, and the peace movement in the strongest terms.[19] His views were fully known to the Kaiser and the foreign office, and his selection was properly interpreted by both the peace movement and the Russians as evidence of German disdain for the conference.[20] The other two members of the German delegation, Colonel Gros von Schwartzhoff, the military attaché, and Philipp Zorn, another legal consultant, were also known not to favor disarmament or arbitration. The personal views of all four were entirely consistent with the instructions they received from the foreign office, according

[17] AA, Eur. Gen. 37 number 1, Bd. 12 (ACP 104), Münster to Hohenlohe, Scheveningen, 30 July 1899.

[18] AA, Eur. Gen. 37 number 1, Bd. 4, A325 (ACP 102), Klehmet, Bemerkungen zu A11632/98, pr. 9 January 1899; *ibid.*, Bd. 8, A3464 (ACP 103), Bülow to Geschäftsträger München, Berlin, 25 March 1899.

[19] Karl von Stengel, *Der ewige Friede* (Munich, 1899).

[20] AA, Eur. Gen. 37 number 2, Bd. 1, A6178 (ACP 103), Münster to Hohenlohe, The Hague, 23 May 1899; DWN, VIII (1899), 207–208; cf. Wehberg, *Gutachten*, p. 8.

to which they were to avoid all commitments in the matter of arbitration and to make no concessions to disarmament.[21]

When the conference opened in May 1899, disarmament was the less controversial issue, since all the other powers, except the Russians, were no more willing to discuss it than the Germans. Nonetheless, Schwartzhoff gratuitously took the initiative in opposing the Russian proposals by announcing, to the consternation of the other delegates, that Germany could quite easily afford the arms race.[22] The military delegates then devoted themselves to discussing less objectionable matters than disarmament, such as codifying the rules of war and extending the 1864 Geneva convention.

Arbitration threatened to become a major problem. With Russia, England, and the United States in the lead, the major powers were prepared to establish a permanent international court and to assign certain kinds of minor disputes to its obligatory jurisdiction. The Germans, however, persisted in their unconditional opposition to arbitration and soon found themselves isolated. Zorn, who was the chief German spokesman in the commission on arbitration, attempted to build assorted loopholes into the court and its jurisdiction, in order to "make the project as harmless as possible" and thus acceptable in Berlin.[23] But the Kaiser and foreign office rejected even the product of Zorn's modifications, which would have been a court bereft of any obligatory jurisdiction, and by the middle of June the conference was on the verge of collapse.[24] Faced with a crisis,

[21] AA, Eur. Gen. 37 number 1, Bd. 10, A522/5514 (ACP 103), Bülow to Münster, Berlin, 12 March 1899 (GP, xv 189–92, number 4256).

[22] Délégation française à la Conférence de La Haye to Foreign Office, The Hague, 2 July 1899, DDF (1), xv, 384–85, number 228; cf. A. Fonck, "Deutschlands Haltung zur Abrüstungsfrage auf der Friedenskonferenz im Haag 1899," Berliner Monatshefte vii (1929), 1091–95.

[23] AA, Eur. Gen. 37 number 2a, Bd. 1, A7088 (ACP 105), Zorn, Bericht über die Arbeiten der iii. Kommission (Subkomité), v, 12 June 1899 (GP, xv, 275–78, number 4304).

[24] AA, Eur. Gen. 37 number 2a, Bd. 1, A7078III (ACP 105), Bülow

both Zorn and Münster concluded that they should approve a court of arbitration as "the lesser evil."[25] When Holstein remained intransigent despite the prospect of major complications, Zorn rushed back to Berlin to confer with Bülow, who was known to be less opposed to arbitration than either Holstein or the Kaiser.[26] Zorn persuaded Bülow of the wisdom of concessions, and Bülow finally prevailed upon the Kaiser to accept the court. William's approval, however, was not exactly enthusiastic: "Lest [the tsar] make a fool of himself in front of Europe I shall go along with this nonsense. But in practice I shall continue to rely on and appeal to only God and my sharp sword. And shit on all their decisions!"[27] It now fell to Zorn and Münster to dilute the project even further, by insisting that the court not sit permanently and that in any given dispute it be composed of judges selected from a long list by the interested parties.[28] In the end they succeeded in pushing through what Münster decribed as a "net with many holes."[29] Lacking any obligatory jurisdiction, the court was enough to preserve the illusion of a breakthrough without committing the

---

to Münster, Berlin, 15 June 1899 (GP, xv, 281–83, number 4308); see also Andrew Dickson White, *Autobiography of Andrew Dickson White* (2 vols., New York, 1905–1907), II, 299.

[25] AA, Eur. Gen. 37 number 2a, Bd. 2, A7302 (ACP 105), Münster to Hohenlohe, Scheveningen, 16 June 1899 (GP, xv, 284–85, number 4311).

[26] AA, Eur. Gen. 37 number 2a, Bd. 2, A7311 (ACP 105), Holstein Memorandum, 17 June 1899; *ibid.*, 37 number 1, Bd. 10, A5795 (ACP 103), Bülow Memorandum, 14 May 1899 (GP, xv, 193–96, number 4257, Anlage). On Zorn's role, see NL Wehberg (9), Folder 1.

[27] AA, Eur. Gen. 37 number 2a, Bd. 2, A7382/number 4984 (ACP 105), Bülow to William, Berlin, 21 June 1899 (GP, xv, 300–306, number 4320).

[28] AA, Eur. Gen. 37 number 2a, Bd. 2, A7429II (ACP 105), Bülow to Münster, Berlin, 22 June 1899 (GP, xv, 307–308, number 4321); *ibid.*, 37 number 2, Bd. 2, A7858 (ACP 104), Bülow to Münster, Berlin, 2 July 1899 (cf. GP, xv, 317–18, number 4331).

[29] AA, Eur. Gen. 37 number 1, Bd. 12, A9099 (ACP 104), Münster to Hohenlohe, Scheveningen, 30 July 1899.

German government—or any other government—in any way whatsoever.

The German government expressed official satisfaction that the Hague conference had "brought its work to a happy conclusion," and it sought to convince public opinion that the German delegation had "attempted with its sincere cooperation to promote the humanitarian endeavor to the best of its ability."[30] Stengel again proved to be an embarrassment to the foreign office, as he publicly denounced the Hague convention, but Bülow felt safe in recommending ratification to the Kaiser, since he was convinced that the court of arbitration was of "small practical significance."[31] Ever mindful of the domestic political implications of the projects discussed at The Hague, the government decided that it was neither constitutionally necessary nor politically wise to submit the Hague convention to the Reichstag for ratification.[32]

No official expressions of satisfaction could conceal the fact that the Germans had been badly embarrassed by the Hague conference. While none of the other major powers was seriously interested in exploring the potentialities of arbitration, they were at least willing to make gestures to public opinion.[33] The Germans, however, believed that any tentative step toward binding arbitration would be dangerous, and, unlike representatives of the western democracies, they feared the domestic repercussions of both disarmament

[30] AA, Eur. Gen. 37 number 2, Bd. 2, A9205 (ACP 104), Bülow Memorandum, pr. 1 August 1899.

[31] AA, Eur. Gen. 37 number 2a, Bd. 4, A9245 (ACP 105), Richthofen to Pr. Gesandte [Munich], Berlin, 10 August 1899; ibid., 37 number 2, Bd. 4, A14843/10574 (ACP 104), Bülow to William, Berlin, 20 December 1899 (GP, xv, 360–62, number 4354); Stengel, "Die Frage der internationalen Schiedsgerichte," Münchner Neueste Nachrichten, 2, 4, 5 August 1899.

[32] AA, Eur. Gen. 37 number 2, Bd. 4, A9418/A12243/10435 (ACP 104), Bülow to Staatssekretär des Innern, et al., Berlin, 13 November 1899.

[33] Wehberg, Gutachten, pp. 90–92; GP, xv, 191 n.

and arbitration. As a result, they found themselves playing just the role they had hoped to avoid and emerged as the international *Störenfried*. Their candid and arrogant opposition to any meaningful agreement on arbitration or arms limitation enabled other powers to follow the German lead and avoid responsibility for the failure of the conference.[34]

That the Germans did not find themselves in this unhappy situation again during the second Hague conference in 1907 was due to the fact that popular expectations were not so high and because the German representatives were more adroit. German policy toward arbitration and arms limitation had not changed when preparations began for the second conference. As before, the foreign office was resolutely opposed to any obligatory arbitration, and it refused even to discuss arms limitation.[35] The chief German delegate in 1907 was Alfred Marschall von Bieberstein, the ambassador to Constantinople and a man who distrusted peace conferences just as much as Münster (though Marschall was convinced that the English, rather than the Russians, were behind the plot against Germany). Marschall, however, was gifted with patience and grace.

Because disarmament had been excluded from the conference agenda at German insistence, the dangerous issue, from the German standpoint, was once again arbitration. The principal item of business was an international treaty of arbitration proposed by the Americans, which would provide for some categories of obligatory jurisdiction. The speech that Marschall delivered at the beginning of the deliberations on the treaty was a masterpeice of dissimulating eloquence. Heaping praise on the ideals that underlay the concept of arbitration, he went on to caution the other dele-

[34] Langer, *Diplomacy of Imperialism*, pp. 591–92.

[35] AA, Eur. Gen. 37 number 5, Bd. 2 (no number) (ACP 107), Aufzeichnung über das von der Russischen Regierung vorgeschlagene Programm der zweiten Haager Friedenskonferenz, pr. 17 July 1906; *ibid.*, A2002 (ACP 107), Tschirschky Runderlass, Berlin, 4 February 1907.

gates to proceed with the greatest care and to guide its development as one would watch over a child. Accordingly, he concluded, Germany was acting only in the ultimate interest of the ideal in rejecting the still premature concept of obligatory arbitration. Marschall later confessed that he was not sure whether he had spoken for or against arbitration, but his speech made German opposition to obligatory arbitration irreproachable and effectively quashed the American proposal, prompting a Belgian delegate to remark that "he wished he could die as painlessly as Baron Marschall had killed the court of arbitration."[36]

The German government's hostility toward arbitration and arms limitation extended to the popular movement that sought to promote these reforms. In their correspondence in connection with the Hague conferences, German officials spoke of the pacifists in the same contemptuous terms found in the Conservative and National Liberal press. The peace movement consisted of *Friedensschwärmer* and *Friedensdamen*; the projects they advocated were *Friedensphantasien*.[37] Münster was particularly annoyed by Fried, Suttner, Bloch, and the other pacifists who had congregated at The Hague and denounced the Germans for their opposition to arbitration: "The conference has attracted the worst political rabble in the world—newspapermen of the worst sort like [William] Stead, baptized Jews like Bloch, *Friedensweiber* like Frau von Suttner, who yesterday feted the entire Russian delegation. . . . This whole mob (young Turks and Armenians are working with them—socialists too) is working completely and openly under Russian protection."[38] Bülow regarded the pacifists as "unsophisticated,

[36] AA, Eur. Gen. 37 number 6, Bd. 1, A17473 (ACP 106), Marschall to Bülow, Neuershausen, 10 November 1907 (GP, xxiii, 289–95, number 7965); *Frankfurter Zeitung*, 6 October 1907.

[37] AA, Eur. Gen. 37 number 1, Bd. 10, A5745 (ACP 103), Derenthall to Hohenlohe, Stuttgart, 12 May 1899; Bülow to William, Berlin, 26 July 1907, GP, xxiii, 261–63, number 7960.

[38] AA, Eur. Gen. 37 number 2, Bd. 2, A7858 (ACP 104), Münster

and occasionally dishonest fanatics."[39] The Kaiser, too, viewed the pacifists with contempt. The suggestion that the tsar was sincerely interested in the ideal of perpetual peace prompted William to comment, "Holy Bertha!"[40] And when Bülow mentioned that the first Hague conference would consider the possibility of setting up a peace bureau to co-ordinate future conferences, William responded, "*O herrje! Vorstand Frau von Suttner?!*" ("Oh wow! Board of direc-tors Frau von Suttner?!")[41]

The German government was under no illusions about the influence or appeal of the peace movement in Germany; it regarded the pacifists as a nuisance, but hardly a threat. Thus, throughout the prewar period the policy of German officials toward the peace movement was characterized by negative indifference. The government initially watched Universal Peace Congresses with some apprehension, but soon lost all interest.[42] Unlike the French, English, and American governments, which sent official representatives to these congresses, the imperial government refused to associate with them in any way, although it raised no objec-tions when the state governments of Hamburg and Bavaria agreed officially to greet the two Universal Peace Con-gresses that met in Germany before the war. While the Prussian government occasionally checked on peace societ-ies, officials of the imperial government took no special in-terest in their activities, aside from noting that these were "for the most part not in harmony with the current goals of

---

to Bülow, Scheveningen, 26 June 1899 (GP, xv, 312–14, number 4327).

[39] Bülow, *Memoirs*, ii, 329.

[40] AA, Eur. Gen. 37 number 1, Bd. 12, A8561/number 6894 (ACP 104), Bülow to William, Berlin, 25 August 1899.

[41] AA, Eur. Gen. 37 number 1, Bd. 10, A5795 (ACP 103), Bülow Memorandum, 14 May 1899 (GP, xv, 193–96, number 4257, Anlage).

[42] GStA, MA93657 (5), Ortenburg to Ministerium des Aeussern [Munich], Berlin, 15 September 1906, number 7910; Wehberg, *Gutach-ten*, pp. 87–89.

the government's policy and only make the realization of these goals more difficult."[43]

If government officials did on occasion display a more active interest in groups in which pacifists were active, it was only because they were either unusually annoyed or expected tangible political benefits. The support given by the government to the Associated Councils of Churches and the committee that coordinated the exchange visits of English and German journalists was designed to serve the specific goal of promoting better relations with England.[44] The government's position toward the *Verband für internationale Verständigung* was dictated by similar considerations. The foreign office could not endorse the views of the organization about the potentialities of international law, but it saw in the *Verband* an opportunity to neutralize some of the embarrassing excesses of the Pan-German League.[45] Thus, the government offered the organization mild encouragement. It agreed to Zorn's entering the *Verband's* executive committee and allowed the colonial secretary, Wilhelm Solf, to be recruited as a speaker at one of the group's national congresses.[46] Nippold was well known, if not well liked, in the Wilhelmstrasse, and he retained some of the contacts he had made while serving earlier in the foreign office.[47]

On only a very few occasions did the government feel compelled to take measures against the peace movement. Early in 1900 pacifists established a *Friedenscentrale* in

[43] StAH, Polizeibehörde (Politische Polizei), S4930, Bd. 2, Schöneberg to Burchard, Hamburg, 12 March 1900, number 368; Wehberg, *Gutachten*, p. 87; PD, xxi (1911), 318–19.

[44] See below, chapter 7, pp. 314–15.

[45] NL Fried, Niemeyer to Fried, Kitzeberg bei Kiel, 5 November 1909; Nippold, *Erlebnisse*, p. 25; Curtius, *Deutsche Briefe*, p. 124.

[46] NL Fried, Zorn to Fried, Bonn, 2 February 1907; Wehberg to Fried, Düsseldorf, 6 June 1911; Wehberg to Fried, The Hague, 14 June 1911; Nippold, *Erlebnisse*, p. 34.

[47] AA, Eur. Gen. 37, number 4, Bd. 1, A2904 (ACP 106), Richthofen to Ratibor, Berlin, 15 March 1900; NL Wehberg (67), Nippold, "Erklärung"; Nippold, *Erlebnisse*, p. 25.

Munich to organize protests against the war in South Africa. Through the Prussian embassy in Munich the government, which feared complications with England, convinced the committee to dissolve quietly.[48] In 1909 the government became interested in the German Peace Society after the pacifists had issued a manifesto condemning the financial reform bill pending before the Reichstag, the unconcealed purpose of which was to fund increased military spending. The Prussian representative in Stuttgart began observing the peace society's activities and encouraged the Württemberg government not to send an official representative to the national peace congress in 1909, which met in Stuttgart to reaffirm opposition to the financial reform.[49] These incidents were not, however, part of any systematic campaign by the government to harass the peace movement, just as patronage of the *Verband* and other peace-oriented groups did not signify general endorsement of their goals. The German government in fact had no systematic policy toward the peace movement and, feeling no immediate threat, was for the most part content to leave it alone.

Had they been so inclined, the pacifists could easily have discerned how the Kaiser and other officials viewed the peace movement. That they did not can be ascribed to their unbounded optimism, as well as to the Kaiser's own eccentricity, which fed the pacifists' gullibility. In the eyes of the pacifists, William was a man guided by lofty principles, certainly "one of us," who was prevented only by his reactionary advisers from announcing his support for the peace movement.[50] As evidence for this view they cited speeches

---

[48] GStA, MA93657 (4), A. Monts to Crailsheim, Munich, 2 February 1900.

[49] HStASt, E 130 I, Bü 457 (p. 78), St. M. 763, Staatsministerien Cirkulation, 10–12 May 1909; GStA, MA93657 (6), Below-Rutzau to Bülow, Stuttgart, 18 May 1909; cf. Taube, Ludwig Quidde, pp. 180–81.

[50] HB (2), II, 194; FW, IX (1907), 84, 88; PD, XX (1910), 601; Alfred Fried, *The German Emperor and the Peace of the World* (London, 1912), pp. 62, 213–14; Karl Lamprecht, *Der Kaiser: Versuch einer Charakteristik* (2d ed., Berlin, 1916).

he had made which seemed to endorse their views. In 1904, for example, William stated in Hamburg: "I think . . . that every objective observer will be forced to the conclusion that solidarity among the peoples of the civilized world is making gradual but incontestable progress in various areas."[51] The Kaiser seemed to be most friendly to the peace movement during his annual excursions to Kiel, where he made remarks that the pacifists construed as "approval of our efforts" and entertained figures prominent in the peace movement, notably d'Estournelles de Constant, on his yacht.[52] William's close friend, King Albert of Monaco, was a celebrated patron of the international peace movement, and the pacifists were confident that he, too, was exercising a benevolent influence on the Kaiser.[53]

This uncritical adulation extended to all the high officials in the German government who had ever said anything positive about international conciliation, including Caprivi, Bülow, Bethmann Hollweg, Kiderlen-Wächter, and even the war minister, Karl von Einem.[54] In fact, the only one around the Kaiser whom the pacifists could identify as an opponent was the crown prince, who publicly called the peace movement un-German and criticized "schemes for internationalization which threaten to efface our healthy national distinctiveness [deutschnationales Volkstum]."[55]

Even though they believed they had many friends in high places, the pacifists attempted to enlighten the government.

[51] Quoted ibid., pp. 100–101; cf. Fried, "Kaiser Wilhelm und der Weltfriede: Zum Regierungsjubiläum des Kaisers," FW, xv (1913), 201–204.

[52] BIP (1C2), Ducommun to Suttner, et al., Berne [July 1895]; MFK, III (December 1895), 2; FB, vi (1905), 12; PM, III (1914), 192–94; Wild, Baron d'Estournelles de Constant, pp. 202–19.

[53] See 3. Beiblatt des 8. Uhr-Abendblatt der National Zeitung, 19 November 1928.

[54] Fried, German Emperor, pp. 64–69; FB, vii (1906), 140; FW, xii (1910), 22; PD, xx (1910), 603–605; FW, xv (1913), 22, 93; HB (2), II, 242–44.

[55] Suttner, Randglossen, II, 261, 485–86; VF, xii (1911), 110; FW, xv (1913), 175–76.

Generally this took the form of direct appeals to the chancellor, urging support of arbitration or offering advice on how to deal with some international crisis.[56] Occasionally these appeals contained gentle criticism, especially when the subject was defense spending, but only in 1909 was it strong enough to bring a reaction. Most leaders of the German Peace Society recognized that their appeals had virtually no impact, but Fried was not so easily convinced.[57] Believing that the Kaiser needed only to be made aware of the internationalization of the world and his own potential role in the process, Fried set out to educate him. In 1905 he published a pamphlet entitled *Kaiser werde modern!*, in which he asserted that since William was obviously a friend of world peace, he should "become modern" by aligning himself with the growing forces of international solidarity.[58] In 1910 Fried published another volume, *Der Kaiser und der Weltfriede*, in which he developed the same theme at more length in order to show William "what the world expects of him"—that he should lead all peacefully inclined states into an *entente cordiale*.[59] Fried's attempt to flatter the Kaiser's sense of destiny proved abortive, though, when the foreign office returned the complimentary copy Fried had sent to him.[60] Undiscouraged, Fried then tried to persuade Andrew Carnegie, who also believed that William held the key to world peace, to use his influence on the Kaiser.[61]

[56] See Wehberg, *Die internationale Beschränkung der Rüstungen* (Stuttgart and Berlin, n.d.), pp. 407-15.

[57] NL Wehberg (88), Umfrid to Wehberg, Stuttgart, 10 June 1913; Abrams, "European Peace Societies," p. 387.

[58] *Kaiser werde modern!* (Berlin, 1905). Aware of what happened when Quidde had criticized the Kaiser, Fried published this pamphlet anonymously.

[59] *Der Kaiser und der Weltfriede* (Berlin, 1910); English ed., *The German Emperor and the Peace of the World* (London, 1912).

[60] FW, XII (1910), 213.

[61] NL Wehberg (59b), Fried to Wehberg, Vienna, 18 June 1913; cf. FW, XXV (1925), 49; Joseph E. Johnson and Bernard Bush, "An-

Fried also attempted to educate Bethmann Hollweg, a man whose potential the pacifists rated high after he agreed in 1910 to grant a government subsidy to the Interparliamentary Union and expressed the hope that "the friends of peace and disarmament" would be able to counterbalance the forces that were enflaming popular passions.[62] The avenue through which Fried attempted to exert influence on Bethmann was the chancellor's friend, Karl Lamprecht. Lamprecht himself found merit in Fried's idea, for he believed that Bethmann's appointment as chancellor represented an important gain for the peace movement.[63] Early in 1912 Lamprecht began to discuss international affairs with Bethmann and presented him with copies of some of Fried's writings. In January, after a long interview with the chancellor, he wrote to Fried to express his confidence that "the peace movement has in him a *Bundesgenosse* who will in practice be absolutely reliable for years. We only spoke a little at the end of our conversation about the position of the chancellor toward the organized peace movement, because after all the assurances he had already given me, it seemed completely superfluous to clarify this point, which is really only secondary. This much is certain: within the present framework of European politics, which he is convinced is firmly established, he approves of the peace movement's goals."[64] Thus encouraged, though without consider-

---

drew Carnegie: Apostle of Peace," in Carnegie Endowment for International Peace, *Perspectives on Peace, 1910–1960* (London, 1960), p. 8; David S. Patterson, "Andrew Carnegie's Quest for World Peace," *Proceedings of the American Philosophical Society* CXIV (1970), 374–75.

[62] StBR, XII L.P., II Session (30 March 1911), CCLXVI, 6001–6002; Fried, "Die Friedensbewegung im Berichtsjahr 1912," *Jahrbuch des Völkerrechts* I (1911–12), 1308–1309; Ernst Jäckh, *Der Völkerbundgedanke in Deutschland während des Weltkrieges* (Berlin, 1929), pp. 24–25.

[63] NL Fried, Lamprecht to Fried, Leipzig, 1 March 1910.

[64] NL Fried, Lamprecht to Fried, Leipzig, 13 January 1912; cf. Lamprecht to Fried, Leipzig, 22 January 1912, 23 February 1912.

ing whether the goals of the peace movement were in fact compatible with "the present framework of European politics," Lamprecht continued his efforts. The celebrated public exchange of letters between him and Bethmann in 1913, in which he urged the chancellor to adopt what he called *Kulturpolitik*, represented another phase in this campaign.[65] By *Kulturpolitik* Lamprecht meant a policy of cultivating appreciation abroad for the finer, idealistic aspects of German culture. While such a policy would, to be sure, serve Germany's interests, it would also, as Lamprecht assured Fried, direct the attention of German statesmen toward more idealistic goals, such as leading the nations of the world to international organization.[66]

It is, of course, most unlikely that these overtures had any significant influence on Bethmann. It is not improbable, though, that he gave them some thought and that Fried was ultimately responsible for some of the remarks Bethmann made in the Reichstag in 1912: "Much is happening to reduce the possibilities of [international] conflict—not only at peace congresses, but also through arrangements among states, arbitration agreements and similar measures. By these means the possibility of war will be reduced, but not eliminated. Relations among nations are becoming increasingly extensive all over the globe. Undoubtedly this will increase the peaceful points of contact, but at the same time new possibilities for conflict appear in the competition of material interests."[67]

The fact that Bethmann made these remarks while introducing a major increase in military spending underscores

---

[65] See Kurt Stenkewitz, *Gegen Bajonett und Dividende: Die politische Krise in Deutschland am Vorabend des ersten Weltkrieges* (Berlin, 1960), p. 110; Wernecke, *Der Wille zur Weltgeltung*, p. 306.

[66] NL Fried, Fried to Lamprecht, Vienna, 15 December 1913; Lamprecht to Fried, 19 December 1913; Herbert Schönebaum, "Karl Lamprechts Mühen um innere und äussere Kulturpolitik," *Die Welt als Geschichte* xv (1955), 137-52.

[67] StBR, xii L.P., 1 Session (22 April 1912), CCLXXXIV, 1300.

the naiveté of Lamprecht and Fried, who interpreted such utterances as evidence that they had an inside track to the chancellor and that Bethmann was in reality a warm supporter of the peace movement. Bethmann and other high officials in the government might publicly announce their support for world peace, but their actions and statements in private left little doubt about how they regarded the peace movement and its program. At a time when it had become fashionable to negotiate treaties providing for arbitration of minor disputes, the German government concluded only one, with England, and rejected assorted arbitration proposals from other governments.[68] With the exception of a few isolated figures, such as Johann von Bernstorff, the German ambassador in Washington, and the colonial secretary Bernhard Dernburg (who was actually a member of the German Peace Society), there were no high governmental officials who regarded either arbitration or the peace movement with any sympathy whatsoever.[69] What William himself thought about his role as *Friedenskaiser*, who would lead the nations to world federation, was much less ambiguous in private than in his public pronouncements. In 1911 Andrew Carnegie's assertion in the New York *Times* that William was an ardent "disciple of peace" brought from the Kaiser the comment, "*Schaaf!*"[70] And on New Year's day in 1912 the New York *World* wrote to the Kaiser that "The World would de[e]ply appreciate a noble sentiment from Your Majesty on President Taft's efforts to make 1912 the arbitration year." The noble sentiment that William penned (in English) in the margin epitomized the attitude of the German government toward the peace movement: "May the devil take arbitration and all

[68] See James W. Gerard, *My Four Years in Germany* (New York, 1917), pp. 60–61; GP, xxxix, 317–18, n.; HB (2), 1, 185–88.

[69] NL Fried, Quidde to Fried, Munich [June 1914]; Wehberg, *Gutachten*, pp. 93–94.

[70] AA, Eur. Gen. 37 Secr., Bd. 2, A21083 (UC 68), Bernstorff to Bethmann, 5 December 1911.

who prate about it!"[71] Indeed, in this appreciation of the peace movement William spoke not only for the government, but for most of the German political parties as well.

Political Parties and Politicians

The German Peace Society was officially a nonpartisan organization. Since its leaders believed that their organization represented, in the words of one manifesto, "an all-encompassing concept of humanity," it seemed inappropriate for the group to become involved in partisan politics.[72] Considerations of a more practical nature also contributed to the peace society's desire to remain nonpartisan. Designation as a political organization by the government of a German state entailed severe restrictions. Not only did a group so designated have to undergo the petty annoyances of registering with the police, but in most German states women could not belong to political organizations. Given the character of the German Peace Society's membership, this would have been a critical handicap.[73] Since state governments defined political activities rather broadly and did not hesitate to use the political designation against organizations whose goals they did not approve, the pacifists were careful not to antagonize the authorities with overt partisan activity or involvement in domestic political issues. Nonetheless, the Bavarian government routinely classified peace societies as political organizations; Löwenthal's *Deutscher Verein für internationale Friedenspropaganda* in Berlin acquired the label in 1896, but the German Peace Society itself escaped blanket designation as a political organization in Prussia.[74]

The threat of the political designation placed severe lim-

[71] AA, Eur. Gen. 37 Geheim, A 60 (UC 68), New York *World* to William, New York, 1 January 1912.

[72] FW, III (1901), 143.

[73] Fried, *Jugenderinnerungen*, pp. 36–37.

[74] NL Fried, Quidde to Fried, Munich, 5 November 1894; DWN, v (1896), 422–23.

its on the activities the peace society could undertake when approaching the Reichstag or state diets. In practice the pacifists were content with innocuous appeals to the parliaments, which urged arbitration or international conciliation but were couched in such general language that the deputies could piously recommend them to the consideration of the government with no fear of the consequences.[75] After 1908, when passage of the imperial *Vereinsgesetz* removed the prohibition on participation by women in political organizations, the peace society could afford to be less circumspect, and their appeals and manifestoes to parliament occasionally became more pointed. In addition to its criticism of the finance reform in 1909, the German Peace Society officially came out in 1913 against the arms bill before the Reichstag.[76]

The other result of the peace society's need to avoid partisanship was that it went through the motions of appealing to politicians of all parties for support. Conservatives and socialists alike received petitions and interpellations from pacifists, and Fried made a point of sending copies of his journal to all members of the Reichstag irrespective of their political affiliations.[77] This was a charade. By virtue of their ideology the pacifists were situated far to the left on the German political spectrum. They believed that all civilized people were predisposed to peace and that wars could not break out if statesmanship were made responsible to enlightened public opinion. It was idle, though, to pursue this logic while maintaining the guise of political neutrality, for in imperial Germany advocacy of government responsible to public opinion meant *nolens volens* adopting major

[75] StBR, ix L.P., 4 Session (1895–97), v, 3726–27; *ibid.*, x L.P., 1 Session (1898–1900), vi, 175; cf. Wehberg, *Internationale Beschränkung*, pp. 407–15.

[76] *Ibid.*, pp. 411–12; PM, ii (1913), 144–46; cf. Liedtke, "Die Entwicklung des Pazifismus," p. 315.

[77] NL Fried, Fried to N. M. Butler, Vienna, 20 September 1913; VF, xi (1910), 53; VF, xii (1911), 17–18; FW, x (1908), 104; FW, xi (1909), 184.

points of the program of the democratic left. Indeed, like the parties of the left, the pacifists called for reforms calculated to bring more popular control over the conduct of foreign and military policy; they advocated giving the Reichstag the power to determine foreign policy, to supervise comprehensively the military establishment, and to declare war.[78]

Because it advocated such reforms, the peace movement became widely known as a *Parteisache* of the left-liberals.[79] Writing in 1902, Fried confessed that "When we remain neutral, it goes without saying that this should only be taken with a grain of salt, for we work within a certain area that begins with the left wing of the Center party."[80] The range of the political spectrum within which the peace movement found any resonance was indeed very narrow, and it corresponded for all practical purposes to the progressive bourgeois left. Further to the right (and to the left) the pacifists found little but condemnation and ridicule.

As one of the pillars of the illiberal political system whose transformation pacifists held to be a vital prerequisite for lasting peace, the Conservative party could hardly be expected to approve of the peace movement. In the eyes of many pacifists the party represented everything the peace movement opposed; it spoke for the elements whose very social and political survival demanded a large army.[81] "A genuine conservative," as Fried once pointed out, "has to be opposed to us."[82] The Conservative party was in fact very ill-disposed toward the pacifists, and the remarks in the Reichstag made by the Conservative deputy, Georg Oertel,

---

[78] Michelis, *Geschichte und Ziele*, pp. 8–9; FB, VII (1906), 139; FB, IX (1908), 145; VF, XI (1910), 3; VF, XIII (1912), 100; FW, VII (1905), 215.

[79] Umfrid, "Meine Erlebnisse in der Friedensbewegung," ER, I (1912), 146.

[80] FW, IV (1902), 173.   [81] FB, VIII (1907), 45.

[82] FW, IV (1902), 173; FW, VI (1904), 27–28; FW, VIII (1906), 65.

on the subject of the pacifists' "song of general world peace" may be taken as a representative view in the party: "Sometimes the song may sound good, [but] in these cacaphonous times it seems quite strange to me, something very childish, something hyperchildish, something very fantastic, hyperfantastic."[83] At the same time, though, the Conservatives were the government's party, so their behavior toward the peace movement, or groups close to it, was frequently a more reliable index of official policy than of the Conservatives' own inclinations. Thus, on more than one occasion prominent Conservatives found their way into organizations in which pacifists were conspicuous.[84]

National Liberals were under no such pressure to observe the dictates of political expediency, and their policy toward the peace movement was one of undisguised contempt. Ernst Bassermann was one of the loudest critics of the Baden Landtag's decision to scrutinize the school books, and he did nothing in later years to improve relations between his party and the peace movement.[85] In 1907 in the Reichstag he prefaced his remarks on the international situation by expressing his confidence that Germany would soon "successfully have *survived* the Hague conference."[86] In 1912 the National Liberal Reichstag delegation met in Heidelberg at the same time the *Verband für internationale Verständigung* was holding its annual congress. When Nippold suggested that the National Liberals send representatives to the congress, they refused.[87]

One major figure in the National Liberal party was a friend of the peace movement. Prince Heinrich zu

---

[83] StBR, XIII L.P., 1 Session (15 April 1913), CCLXXXIX, 4765.

[84] In addition to the *Kirchliches Komitee*, leading Conservatives turned up in the Interparliamentary Union and the *Deutsch-französisches Annäherungskomitee*: see below, chapter 6, p. 256; chapter 7, pp. 303–304, 314.

[85] DWN, VII (1898), 280.

[86] StBR, XII L.P., 1 Session (30 April 1907), CCXVIII, 1247 (italics added).

[87] Nippold, *Erlebnisse*, p. 16.

Schönaich-Carolath can be fairly described as a political eccentric, or, as his biographer has put it, "a political character in an era not rich in characters."[88] The National Liberal party was as far to the left as this "Red Prince" could respectably drift, and he occupied important positions of leadership in the party, but his political views were really those of a left-liberal. An advocate of widening the prerogatives of the Reichstag, Schönaich-Carolath dabbled in several progressive causes, including the peace movement. His progressive views were already common knowledge in the early 1890s, when Fried asked him to help in founding the German Peace Society. Although he refused, calling the venture "hopeless at this time," he did subsequently join the executive of the peace society for a while in the later 1890s.[89] He was also an active supporter of arbitration in the Reichstag, a leader of the German branch of the Interparliamentary Union, and a member of the *Verband für internationale Verständigung*. However, Schönaich-Carolath's activity in the peace movement was the product of his own political idiosyncrasy; it was certainly not indicative of any significant sentiment within the National Liberal party.

In its broad contours the position of the Catholic Center party toward the peace movement reflected the increasing emphasis German Catholics placed on their patriotism. Under the leadership of Ernst Lieber, the Center remained into the 1890s an opponent of increased military appropriations and a champion of international conciliation; Lieber

[88] Ludwig Maenner, *Prinz Heinrich zu Schönaich-Carolath: Ein parlamentarisches Leben der wilhelminischen Zeit* (Stuttgart and Berlin, 1931), p. 7; see also Bourdon, *L'énigme allemande*, pp. 133–39; Richard Eickhoff, *Politische Profile* (Dresden, 1927), pp. 129–33. Rudolf von Bennigsen was a member of the *Verband*, but did not play a prominent role.

[89] NL Fried, Schönaich-Carolath to Fried, Amtitz, 2 November 1892; NL Suttner (Ec6), Schönaich-Carolath to Suttner, Palsgaard, 13 August 1896; *ibid.* (Ec8), Schönaich-Carolath to Fried, Haseldorf, 19 July 1897; DWN, v (1896), 417.

even spoke in the Reichstag of a United States of Europe.[90]
Georg Haberland, another Reichstag deputy in the Center
party, served briefly as chairman of the German Peace Society in the 1890s. By the turn of the century, however, the
party had come to regard arbitration and arms limitation
with a derisive skepticism more befitting a nationalist outlook. In 1899 the Catholic deputy Peter Spahn dismissed the
Hague conference by noting that it had accomplished nothing and that the court of arbitration was built on sand—all
of which was probably true, but friends of the peace movement were not proclaiming it.[91] In 1907 Georg von Hertling
sided with Conservatives and National Liberals in deprecating disarmament as a subject for discussion at the second
Hague conference. "At the very best," he said, "I hold disarmament to be a question of academic interest [*eine aka-
demische Doktorfrage*]."[92] Such views, which provoked one
pacifist to call the Center party "the most influential enemy
of pacifism in Germany," remained dominant in the party
until the war, accentuated by Matthias Erzberger's enthusiastic support of military bills.[93]

The attitude of the Catholic Center party was not entirely
consistent, however, for as a group, liberal Catholic politicians were second only to left-liberals in joining organizations
associated with the peace movement. Erzberger himself
was a member of the Interparliamentary Union, as were
over forty other Catholic deputies in the Reichstag.[94] Lib-

[90] StBR, IX L.P., 2 Session (28 February 1894), II, 1483; NL Fried,
Fried to ten Brink, Vienna, 3 November 1904; Morsey, "Die deutschen
Katholiken," p. 49.

[91] "Das Centrum täuscht uns!" FW, I (1899), 69.

[92] StBR, XII L.P., I Session (30 April 1907), CCXVIII, 1237.

[93] NL Fried, Seufert to Fried, Süchteln, 30 November 1913; see also
Klaus Epstein, *Matthias Erzberger and the Dilemma of German Democracy* (Princeton, 1959), pp. 75–76; FW, VI (1904), 29; FB, VIII
(1907), 3; FB, IX (1908), 55; VF, XII (1911), 32.

[94] NL Haussmann (3), Deutsche Gruppe der Interparlamentarischen
Union, pp. 14–19; NL Fried, F. Decker to Fried, Cologne, 21 February
1907.

eral Catholics also made up one of the most prominent political groups in the *Verband für internationale Verständigung*. Among others, Karl Bachem, Karl Trimborn, Michael Sir, August Trendel, and Richard Müller were members.

The most consistent political support the peace movement enjoyed came from the left-liberal parties of the Progressive coalition. Both ideologically and socially, these parties most resembled the peace movement, and it is reasonably certain that most pacifists voted for Progressive candidates in elections. Conversely, deputies in the Reichstag and state diets who belonged to the peace society or *Verband*, or who publicly spoke out in favor of the peace movement, were generally members of one of the Progressive parties—men such as Rudolf Oeser, Heinrich Rickert, Karl Schrader, Ernst Harmening, Heinrich von Dove, Leonhard Hoffmann, Georg Pflüger, Conrad Haussmann, Friedrich von Payer, and Georg Gothein.

During the attempt to establish a peace society in Germany in the early 1890s, the Progressive party was alone in showing an interest. Among the Progressives, sympathy for the peace movement was particularly warm in the circle around Theodor Barth and his journal, *Die Nation*. Barth's internationalism derived primarily from his faith in free trade, and many of his political friends, such as Baumbach, Rickert, and Schrader, shared his views.[95] Others in the *Nation* group, like Hugo Preuss and Alexander Meyer, emphasized ethical or juridical themes in advocating international solidarity.[96] Barth's pacifism seemed at first to be genuine, as he attended the Universal Peace Congress in 1891 and was an important figure in establishing the German Peace Society late the next year.[97] But the sincerity of

[95] Konstanze Wegner, *Theodor Barth und die Freisinnige Vereinigung: Studien zur Geschichte des Linksliberalismus im Wilhelminischen Deutschland (1893–1910)* (Tübingen, 1968), pp. 32–33.
[96] Gilg, *Die Erneuerung des demokratischen Denkens*, pp. 98–100.
[97] DWN, I (January 1892), 4; DWN, II (1893), 43; Abrams, "European Peace Societies," p. 395.

his convictions was severely discredited when, in 1893, he and other members of his group defected from the Progressive party to vote in favor of Caprivi's arms bill. Thereafter, to the dismay of the pacifists, they regularly supported expansion of both the army and navy.[98] By the early years of the twentieth century it had become clear that Barth's *Freisinnige Vereinigung* had abandoned pacifism in order to enhance its influence in domestic politics.[99]

Only in the twilight of his career did Barth begin to return to the peace movement. In 1908 he again contributed to the decimation of the left-liberal forces by founding the *Demokratische Vereinigung* for those of his followers who could not join the Bülow bloc. In writing the program of the new organization, Barth reverted to pacifism and called for arbitration of all international disputes and an international agreement to regulate the size of land and naval forces.[100] Several people who followed Barth into the *Demokratische Vereinigung* also became pacifists. Barth's disciple, Rudolf Breitscheid, was active in the peace society in Berlin.[101] Hellmut von Gerlach, who split from Friedrich Naumann on the issue of joining the Bülow bloc, also repudiated the nationalism of Naumann's group, and by the eve of the war he had become an outspoken pacifist. By his own testimony his conversion was inspired by the old Barth, Norman Angell, and Walther Schücking, with whom he had been active in local politics in Marburg.[102] It was an ironic com-

[98] DWN, iv (1895), 138; DWN, vii (1898), 34.

[99] As Rickert put it in 1898, in connection with the Hague conference: "But we also demand, in conjunction with sound finances and a strong army, a national [*volksthümliche*] domestic policy." StBR, x L.P., 1 Session (14 December 1898), clxv, 80.

[100] Wegner, *Theodor Barth*, p. 136; cf. FW, xi (1909), 117; PD, xvii (1907), 297; NL Fried, Georg Arnhold to Fried, Dresden, 30 April 1908.

[101] NL Fried, Breitscheid to Fried, Berlin, 16 July 1906, 20 December 1909; VF, xi (1910), 100.

[102] Gerlach, *Rechts nach Links*, pp. 261–62; see also Ruth Greuner, *Wandlungen eines Aufrechten: Lebensbild Hellmut von Gerlachs* (Berlin, 1965), pp. 73–75.

ment on the radical nature of Gerlach's metamorphosis that Fried saw fit in 1913 to include him in his "Who's Who of the Peace Movement," for Gerlach was the man who had earlier driven Fried off the *Berliner Zeitung* because of his pacifism.[103]

When Barth defected in 1893, it fell to the two other left-liberal parties, Eugen Richter's *Freisinnige Volkspartei* and the *Süddeutsche Volkspartei*, to support the peace movement in parliament. When Richter reconstituted his forces in 1894, his new party's program called for "support of efforts to secure international peace [and] the general application of arbitral procedures in disputes involving international law."[104] Unlike Barth, Richter continued to enjoy the praise of pacifists for his opposition to increases in defense spending.[105]

Of all the left-liberal parties, the closest to the peace movement was the *Süddeutsche Volkspartei*. In addition to the ideological and social affinities that drew pacifists to the Progressive parties generally, geographical factors contributed to the relative intimacy between the peace movement and the *Süddeutsche Volkspartei*. Like the peace movement, the party drew most of its support from Württemberg, Baden, and the Frankfurt area.[106] Among the leaders of the party, Franz Wirth, Heinrich Rössler, Friedrich von Payer, Conrad Haussmann, and Adolf Richter were active in the peace society or the *Verband*.[107] Quidde was the leader of the Bavarian branch of the party and was instrumental in drawing up the section of the party's program that dealt with international policy: "The *Volkspartei* is a party of peace. It regards war and militarism as the most serious injury to popular welfare, as well as to culture and

[103] HB (2), II, 353.   [104] DWN, III (1894), 344.

[105] DWN, VII (1898), 236; FW, IV (1902), 150.

[106] Nipperdey, *Organisation der deutschen Parteien*, p. 231.

[107] BIP (vA5), Extrait d'une lettre de M. Richter, September 1897; NL Fried, Rössler to Fried, Königstein i.T., 6 October 1902; NL Haussmann (116), Payer to Haussmann, Stuttgart, 27 December 1905.

the interests of freedom. It strives for an alliance of peace and freedom among the nations."[108] The party was unique, even among the left-liberals, in its willingness to be associated publicly with the peace movement, and the pacifists could count on it for accommodating responses to their various appeals.[109]

In 1910 the three left-liberal parties reunited to form the *Fortschrittliche Volkspartei*. The program of the new party carried on the Progressives' traditional endorsement of the peace movement's goals. It called for arms limitation and "extension of international law and establishing an international court of arbitration for the peaceful compromise of disputes that arise."[110]

The Progressive fusion created some unlikely political alliances. One of the most anomalous was the bringing together of pacifists, such as Quidde, Haussmann, and Payer, with Friedrich Naumann, a man who had devoted his career to enhancing the power of the nation-state. This combination was not as unlikely as it seemed, though, for Naumann's relationship to the peace movement changed significantly in the years just before the war. An associate of Martin Rade, as well as his brother-in-law, Naumann spent his early career trying to solve the social problems of a modern industrial state through the application of Christian principles; like many liberal Protestants, though, he saw nothing inconsistent in denying at the same time that Christian morals could regulate international politics. His

[108] Quoted in Taube, *Ludwig Quidde*, p. 77; NL M. Quidde, [L. Quidde] Entwurf zu einem Programm der deutschen Volkspartei.

[109] HStASt, E 130 I, Bü 457, *Schwarzwälder Bote*, 1 *Beilage*, 19 May 1909; FW, VIII (1906), 66; CBM, x (1905), 141–42; Michelis, *Geschichte und Ziele*, p. 10; cf. Klaus Simon, *Die Württembergischen Demokraten: Ihre Stellung und Arbeit im Parteien- und Verfassungssystem in Württemberg und im Deutschen Reich 1890–1920* (Stuttgart, 1969), pp. 98–103.

[110] Wilhelm Mommsen, *Deutsche Parteiprogramme: Eine Auswahl vom Vormärz bis zur Gegenwart* (Munich, 1952), p. 57; VF, XI (1910), 34.

celebrated encounters with Rudolf Sohm and Max Weber reinforced and made more systematic his belief that the nation-state was bound by no normative standards save considerations of its own power. The exuberance with which Naumann's *National-Sozialer Verein* embraced the national cause determined its attitude toward the peace movement, but Naumann's own dignity prevented its commentary from degenerating into vituperation. Nonetheless, his rejection of pacifism was unconditional. When Bertha von Suttner approached him for a kind word about the peace movement, Naumann responded: "As a political party we have quite different tasks than to concern ourselves with good heart and good will. For us the decisive question is: does this movement contribute to, or detract from German power? And it is my position that it detracts."[111] The pacifists in turn took a dim view of Naumann. In 1897 Bertha von Suttner called him "a horrible man," while others condemned his *Kanonen-Sozialismus* and spoke of him as the epitome of the militarist churchman.[112] Some perceptive pacifists were even more disquieted by the implications of Naumann's manifesto, *Demokratie und Kaisertum*, in which he proposed to stimulate the enthusiasm of the masses for the monarchy by means of an aggressive foreign policy; since the peace movement proposed the converse, to bring about a more conciliatory foreign policy by means of pressure from the enlightened masses, the gulf between Naumann and the pacifists could scarcely have been wider.[113]

The Naumann organization was not totally impervious to the peace movement. Because they subscribed to his so-

---

[111] Quoted in Theodor Heuss, *Friedrich Naumann: Der Mann, das Werk, die Zeit* (Stuttgart and Tübingen, 1949), pp. 122–23; cf. Naumann,"Der Krieg in der Zukunft," *Die Hilfe* v (1899), 4–5; Naumann, "Was ist der Friede?" *Süddeutsche Monatshefte* I (1904), 453–59; DWN, vi (1897), 5–7; DWN, vii (1898), 419–23.

[112] SFC, Suttner to Fried, Vienna, 26 March 1897; DWN, vi (1897), 5–7, 158–59; Gottfried Traub, "Friedensbewegung," *Die Zeit* II (1902–3), 752.

[113] Michelis, *Geschichte und Ziele*, p. 9.

cial views, both Rade and Schücking were active in the National Socialist group in Marburg, and at least one other of Naumann's local leaders described himself as a pacifist.[114] But the peace movement had little to hope from Naumann, even when he joined forces in 1903 with Barth, Rickert, and Schrader, who had once supported the cause. Then, after he entered the Reichstag in 1907, Naumann's views apparently began to change. In 1909 he spoke of the "interdependence of all modern nations" in terms that suggested scientific pacifism.[115] In 1911 he became one of the charter members of the *Verband für internationale Verständigung* and voted in the Reichstag in favor of a resolution urging the government to explore the possibility of arms negotiations.[116] When he returned to the Reichstag in 1913 he joined the Interparliamentary Union and participated in several other organizations designed to promote international conciliation. In 1913 he even praised the peace society, noting that "we cannot value the work of the German Peace Society highly enough—as a counterbalance to those who agitate for war."[117]

The change in Naumann's appreciation of the peace movement is not difficult to explain. He had originally rejected pacifism because he believed it would weaken Germany, as the country pursued its goals in an international arena where power was the only valid consideration. Naumann never really departed from this view of international politics, but during the first decade of the twentieth century he watched Germany's international position deteriorate and the anti-German *rapprochement* among England, France, and Russia become stronger, encouraged by the

[114] NL Fried, Gallert to Fried, Rheinfeld in Holstein, 3 May 1908; FW, xxxv (1935), 193–95.

[115] "Friedrich Naumanns Wandlung zum Pazifismus [*sic*]," FW, xi (1909), 215.

[116] Heuss, *Naumann*, pp. 304–305.

[117] Deutsche Friedensgesellschaft, Ortsgruppe Königsberg, *Auf dem Weg zum Weltfrieden in Ostpreussen (Dritter Jahresbericht 1912–Februar 1913)* (Königsberg, 1913), p. 11.

ineptitude of German statecraft. In these circumstances it impressed Naumann that a crescendo of nationalist sentiment would only increase the country's isolation, but that attempts to promote international conciliation might help alleviate the situation. Thus, for reasons of power politics —because he thought the peace movement would in fact strengthen Germany's international position—he consented to join the *Verband* and other internationalist organizations.

Yet it is tempting to speculate that there might have been more to the shift in Naumann's views than that. As Richard Nürnberger has pointed out, Naumann was never able to sever politics from Christianity, national interest from universal norms, with the assurance of Sohm and Weber; in Naumann the relationship between the two realms was always an "unsatisfactory juxtaposition."[118] The program of the *National-Sozialer Verein* itself contained an indication of the latent discord between the two. Having called for *"eine Politik der Macht nach aussen,"* it closed with the equivocal assertion that Christianity "ought to hold true in public life, too, as a force of peace and solidarity."[119] The universalist motif surfaced again when, after the turn of the century, Naumann began to read widely in economics, exploring the implications of growing international interdependence and organization, which he concluded were among the most important features of modern economic development. Fried noticed the new accents that began to appear in Naumann's writings after 1906 and attempted to steer him toward scientific pacifism. In 1910 Naumann confessed to Fried that "it is certain that our thinking has in recent years occasionally run along the same lines," but his conception of international relations remained too power-oriented for him to draw the political, much less the ethical implications from economic interdependence that Fried

[118] Richard Nürnberger, "Imperialismus, Sozialismus und Christentum bei Friedrich Naumann," *Historische Zeitschrift* CLXX (1950), 533–34.
[119] Mommsen, *Parteiprogramme*, pp. 52–54.

did.[120] Yet Fried did probably exert some influence on Naumann's thinking and contribute to his willingness to be associated with the peace movement.[121] By the eve of the war, although he had by no means abandoned the conviction that armed force was the basis of international politics, Naumann had come to the conclusion that social, economic, and intellectual internationalization was the harbinger of an—albeit distant—"Organization of Humanity" and that it behooved Germans to "have an ear for the future music of humanity."[122]

The significance of statements such as this from left-liberal politicians ought of course not to be overestimated, nor should the endorsements of arbitration that regularly appeared in the programs of their political parties. Indeed, with the exception of the *Süddeutsche Volkspartei*, most left-liberal politicians were unwilling to go even as far as Naumann in demonstrating their support for the peace movement.[123] Eugen Richter had little use for the peace movement, despite the role of his cousin in it.[124] After the Progressive fusion in 1910, Quidde's political position in Munich became precarious. Although he was the logical choice to lead the local Progressive organization, he was,

[120] NL Fried, Naumann to Fried, Schöneberg-Berlin, 30 January 1908, 13 December 1910; Fried to Naumann, Vienna, 10 December 1910.

[121] "Friedrich Naumanns Stellungnahme zum Pazifismus," FW, xiv (1912), 389–90.

[122] *Ibid.*; Heuss, *Naumann*, pp. 304–305; cf. Naumann, "Der Zwang zum Frieden," *Die Hilfe* xviii (1912), 258–59; Shanahan, "Liberalism and Foreign Affairs," pp. 212–13; FW, xv (1913), 66–67. Naumann's associate and foreign policy adviser, Ernst Jäckh, became involved in pacifist groups during the First World War: Ernst Jäckh, *Der goldene Pflug: Lebensernte eines Weltbürgers* (Stuttgart, 1954), pp. 348–55.

[123] NL Suttner (PQA14), Quidde to Suttner, Munich, 22 April 1902; NL Fried, Quidde to Fried, Lucca, 4 October 1905; Reuter "Zur Rückständigkeit der Friedensbewegung in Deutschland, insbesonderheit das Verhalten der Freisinnigen Partei," FW, iii (1901), 142.

[124] FW, vi (1904), 29; FW, viii (1906), 66; NL Wehberg (44), Untersuchungsausschuss Protokoll, 20 June 1923.

because of his pacifism and his indiscretions in criticizing the Kaiser, only elected chairman of the *Fortschrittlicher Verein* after protracted negotiations, and he found himself surrounded by "people of a vigorous militaristic and nationalistic disposition," who kept a close eye on what he did in public.[125] In all, one can safely say that the Progressives were the political group most willing to experiment with arbitration and that they looked the most favorably upon the prospect of arms negotiations. Unlike the pacifists, however, the Progressives gave no indication, as one pacifist noted wryly, "that they are so imbued with the idea of peace and arbitration that they expect it to bring international salvation."[126] Just how little they and other German politicians were imbued with the idea of arbitration was apparent in the singularly uninspired record of the German branch of the Interparliamentary Union.

The Interparliamentary Union in Germany

In the years before the war parliamentarians in Europe and America who were interested in promoting international law, arbitration, and arms limitation were generally members of the Interparliamentary Union, the body that Bertha von Suttner called "the really important branch of the peace movement," whose international conferences met almost annually to deliberate on these and other problems of international conciliation.[127] The German Parliamentary Committee for Peace and Arbitration, which Barth and other Progressives had set up in 1891 as the German branch of the Interparliamentary Union, continued to function sporadically into the early years of the twentieth century. The group consisted of about sixty-five members, including most of the Progressives in the Reichstag and a few scat-

---

[125] NL Fried, Quidde to Fried, Munich, 12 September 1912, 14 April 1913; NL Gothein (28), Quidde to Gothein, Munich, 14 April 1913.
[126] FB, VI (1905), 9.
[127] Suttner to Egidy, 8 August 1897, quoted in Herz, *Alleingang wider die Mächtigen*, pp. 296–97.

tered members from the state diets.[128] After Barth's defection in 1893 leadership fell to Max Hirsch, who remained the most active man in the committee until his death in 1905. Under his direction it led an existence not much more vigorous than that of the German Peace Society, of which Hirsch was also chairman. The German contingents to international conferences were regularly the smallest, often only two or three people, and their contribution to the deliberations consisted of "quiet propaganda," as one German delegate described it, or opposition to the proposals of other delegations.[129] Nor was the behavior of the committee any more encouraging at home. In the Reichstag, members voted in favor of army and navy appropriations and failed to promote the Hague conference with any enthusiasm. In the Prussian Landtag several members of the committee voted in 1898 against the peace society's petition to examine the school books.[130] Despite the organization's timidity and the fact that the Interparliamentay Union had no official status, the German government regarded its activities with suspicion and instructed German delegates that they were to attend the international conferences in a strictly private capacity.[131]

It should be noted in Hirsch's defense that he was a very busy man, whose job was made no easier after he lost his seat in the Reichstag in 1893, or by the fact that he had to

[128] MFK, 1 (June 1894); DWN, v (1896), 190; cf. Schlief, *Hohe Politik*, pp. 73–74.

[129] NL Fried, Fried to Reuter, Vöslau bei Wien, 16 July 1904; DWN, vi (1897), 33; FB, v (1904), 155; Suttner, *Memoirs*, ii, 56–57, 332.

[130] Reuter, "Der Friedensgedanke in Deutschland: Regierung und Reichstag," FW, vi (1904), 143–44; FW, ii (1900), 104; DWN, vii (1898), 34.

[131] In Holstein's words, "The mention of the Interparliamentary Union is distasteful. Needless to say, it will in all cases be ignored by our side." GP, xxiii, 60–61, number 7793; Wehberg, *Gutachten*, pp. 87–88; BIP (vB6), Reinhardt Schmidt to Umfrid, Elberfeld, 19 January 1903.

contend with the incessant criticism of Alfred Fried.[132] Hirsch was succeeded in 1905 by Richard Eickhoff, one of Eugen Richter's protégés from the Ruhr town of Remscheid.[133] Because Eickhoff was able to devote more time and energy to the committee, it began to grow and attract members from outside left-liberal circles, most notably from the left wing of the Center party. Eickhoff also succeeded in winning the confidence of the German government; however, the price paid was the subversion of whatever little integrity the group had previously possessed. For Eickhoff, although a firm believer in free trade, was also a colonial and naval enthusiast and did not let his sympathy for arbitration impair the interests of his constituents, who happened to manufacture side arms. In the Reichstag in 1902, for example, he thanked the war minister on their behalf for a recently awarded defense contract and took the occasion to request more of the same, pointing out that *"l'appetit vient en mangeant."*[134] Bülow was naturally pleased to have him at the head of the Parliamentary Committee on Peace and Arbitration and in fact supported Eickhoff's reelection in 1907 with all the resources at his disposal, including the *Flottenverein* and the man who led it, August Keim, who at the time was quite possibly the least pacifistic man in the country.[135]

This situation had its advantages for the committee, as it at last became possible to hold an Interparliamentary Conference in Germany. At the conclusion of the conference in 1906, which met in London, Eickhoff and Conrad Haussmann approached the German ambassador to England, Count

[132] NL Suttner (MrII 1), Hirsch to Suttner, Berlin, 4 January 1900.

[133] See Richard Eickhoff, *Politische Profile* (Dresden, 1927); Wehberg, *Führer*, pp. 47–48.

[134] StBR, x L.P., 2 Session (21 February 1902), v, 4387; Ludwig Elm, *Zwischen Fortschritt und Reaktion: Geschichte der Parteien der liberalen Bourgeoisie in Deutschland 1893–1918* (Berlin, 1968), pp. 144, 154; FW, VIII (1906), 5–6; NL Fried, Eickhoff to Fried, Berlin, 22 February 1906.

[135] Elm, *Zwischen Fortschritt und Reaktion*, p. 181.

Paul Wolff-Metternich, and inquired about the prospects for official patronage at an Interparliamentary Conference in Berlin. Wolff-Metternich was receptive to the idea and raised the matter with the foreign office. Such patronage, he explained, would "win friends for us abroad and dispel the mistrust of others about our purportedly aggressive tendencies, without committing the imperial government in any way whatsoever."[136] Bülow, too, was taken with the idea of emulating other countries who understood how "to drape themselves with the cloak of modern, humane and liberal views."[137] The Kaiser was initially opposed to the idea, but relented late in 1906, remarking "In general I hold the whole thing to be nonsense! But I have nothing against their playing their stupid games here. But under one condition— that the idiots guarantee in advance that there will be no abusing the Prussian army or the German navy or our military system."[138]

Bülow, to whom responsibility for the conference fell, recognized the importance of making it succeed. "We have every interest," he wrote, "in harnassing the peace movement—and the Interparliamentary Union—to the cart of our (peace) policy, rather than letting others use them against us."[139] In playing host to the conference, which met in Berlin in September 1908, Bülow adopted a policy that compensated in thoroughness for what it lacked in credibility. To ensure that the German delegation would be respectably large he coaxed Conservatives into it, and he prompted the press to take an active interest in the event.[140] When the delegates arrived he had them meet in the

[136] Wolff-Metternich to Bülow, London, 2 August 1906, GP, XXIII, 78–79, number 7811.

[137] Bülow Aufzeichnung, Norderney, 5 August 1906, GP, XXIII, 79–80, number 7812.

[138] GP, XXIII, 80–81; Wehberg, *Gutachten*, p. 89.

[139] GP, XXIII, 81–82 n. (the parentheses are Bülow's); Bülow, *Memoirs*, II, 83.

[140] FB, IX (1908), 122; FW, X (1908), 182. On the background of the conference see also Stein, *Leben eines Optimisten*, pp. 127–28, 187–90.

Reichskanzlerspalais, where he greeted them with praise: "You have achieved far more than was at first considered possible, and your success has increased from year to year. ... 'May your labors be fruitful; may they be to the good of all the nations whose representatives have done us the great honor, and given us the great pleasure of [their] coming to Berlin.' "[141] There were several minor incidents. D'Estournelles de Constant did not attend in protest against Germany's opposition to arbitration at the second Hague conference, and the German government snubbed Bertha von Suttner by refusing to accord her the status of honored guest, although this gesture had become traditional at Interparliamentary Conferences.[142] On the whole, though, the delegates were most impressed by the hospitality of the German government, as was Fried, who called the conference "a success that exceeded all expectations."[143]

As a result of the conference the German Parliamentary Committee became more politically respectable. In 1910 the German government followed the lead of other countries and gave the Interparliamentary Union an annual subsidy.[144] Nonetheless, the German branch of the Interparliamentary Union remained comparatively anemic. German parliamentarians were never as well represented as politicians from other countries. All one hundred members of the Danish Chamber of Deputies belonged to the organization, as did nearly one-third of the English House of Commons and well over half of the French Chamber of Deputies.[145] In Germany the number of Reichstag deputies in the committee was never much more than one hundred, and nearly

[141] Bülow, *Memoirs*, II, 384–85.

[142] NL Wehberg (44), Untersuchungsausschuss Protokoll, 2 May 1923; NL Fried, Eickhoff to Fried, Remscheid, 22 July 1908; Suttner, *Randglossen*, II, 128, n.1; FW, XXIII (1923), 45; Wild, *Baron d'Estournelles de Constant*, pp. 323–24.

[143] Ch. Beauquier, "Impressions de Berlin," PD, XVIII (1908), 422–26; FW, X (1908), 181; cf. Bülow, *Memoirs*, II, 384.

[144] HB (2), II, 242.

[145] PD XVII (1907), 36; VF, XV (1914), 15.

two-thirds of these belonged to the Center or Progressive parties.[146]

The growth of the German branch of the Interparliamentary Union after 1905 was the product of the government's benevolence, Eickhoff's energy, and, certainly not least, the success of the group's leaders in disavowing all association with the peace society.[147] It did not, however, reflect any growth of genuine interest in arbitration or arms limitation within the Reichstag. In order to maintain the cohesion of the committee, Eickhoff had to avoid taking positions on controversial issues; the fact that Ernst von Heydebrand and Hermann Paasche were members is an apt indication of his success.[148] Indeed, the German committee had little more than ceremonial significance. Quidde, who belonged by virtue of his membership in the Bavarian Landtag, was completely isolated in his efforts to mobilize the group and could only look on in dismay at the inanity of most of its activities.[149] Quidde was not the only one who learned not to expect much from the Interparliamentary

[146] NL Haussmann, Deutsche Gruppe der Interparlamentarischen Union, pp. 15–19. A statistical breakdown in 1911:

	In Reichstag	In Interparliamentary Union
Conservative	60	10
Reichspartei	24	12
Center	105	42
National Liberal	54	6
Progressives	49	29
Social Democratic	43	—
Poles	20	8
Alsatian	7	5

[147] StBR, xii L.P., 2 Session (15 March 1910), CCLX, 2113; NL Fried, Eickhoff to Fried, Berlin, 15 April 1913; "Die interparlamentarische Union in ihrem Verhältnis zur Friedensbewegung," FW, x (1908), 183; VF, xi (1910), 47, 63.

[148] NL Haussmann (2), Eickhoff to Haussmann, Berlin, 15 April 1913; NL Wehberg (58), Eickhoff to Wehberg, Baden-Baden, 8 September 1913.

[149] NL Haussmann (3), Quidde to Haussmann, Munich, 23 November 1910; NL Fried, Quidde to Fried, Munich, 19 October 1912, 23 October 1912.

Union, for the whole undertaking soon acquired the not un-
deserved reputation of being a pretext for a relaxing, state-
subsidized vacation.[150] As August Bebel put it as early as
1900: "That is what is sad and at the same time comical
about all these demonstrations by the bourgeois parties.
People congregate, give nice, sentimental speeches, amuse
themselves well, eat well, drink well too, and depart assuming that they have accomplished something earth-shaking;
but when they come back home to parliament they promptly
vote for all the army and navy appropriations."[151] Bebel's
description was accurate, and it pointed to one of the principal reasons why no Social Democrats belonged to the German branch of the Interparliamentary Union. It also touches
upon some of the wider problems that characterized the
relationship between Social Democracy and the peace
movement in Germany.

The Social Democrats

Socialists occupied a special place in the calculations of the
international peace movement before the war. Pacifists
found much to admire in the socialist movement—its opposition to war, its apparent solidarity, its exemplary organization, and the fact that it represented the pacifists' most
important potential ally.[152] In Germany the Social Democrats were of particular importance, because they were the
only factor that lent even a faint aura of credibility to the
pacifists' expectations. "We will succeed as soon as the
masses are converted to our ideas," Umfrid wrote in 1904.
"The prospects of this are bright; the best evidence is, in
spite of all its surliness, German Social Democracy."[153]

---

[150] Fried, *Die moderne Friedensbewegung in Deutschland und
Frankreich* (Gautzsch b. Leipzig, 1908), p. 4; cf. Wernecke, *Der Wille
zur Weltgeltung*, p. 28.

[151] StBR, x L.P., 1 Session (10 February 1900), v, 4018–19.

[152] BIP (vQ9–13), A. Gobat, "Développement du Bureau international permanent de la paix (B.I.P.P.)," Berne, May 1910.

[153] FB, v (1904), 125.

Leaders of the peace society reasoned that the victory of their cause would be assured once the German socialist movement, with its wide popular support and growing political power, had entered into an active alliance with the peace movement in support of arbitration and arms limitation.

The evidence on which pacifists everywhere based their hopes in the socialist movement was somewhat ambiguous. The position of the Second Socialist International toward the bourgeois peace movement and its goals was not entirely consistent, for it reflected the ideological equivocation of socialists about the role of international violence under capitalism. Resolutions passed during the 1890s at congresses of the International vacillated between uncompromising assertions that warfare would continue as long as capitalism survived and endorsements of arbitration and disarmament, which implied that nonviolent settlement of international disputes was possible even prior to socialist revolution.[154] In the first decade and a half of the twentieth century, when prevention of war became, in Professor Joll's words, "almost the reason for existence of a Socialist International," socialists appeared to have resolved this ambiguity and openly endorsed the proposition that disarmament and arbitration could contribute to peace, even within the context of capitalist society.[155] However, commitment to working for disarmament and arbitration did not lead the International to

[154] For summaries of the attitude of the Socialist International toward the bourgeois peace movement and its program see: Moe, *Le prix Nobel*, I, 200–19; Carl Grünberg, *Die Internationale und der Weltkrieg* (2 vols., Leipzig, 1916–28), I, 5–13; Milorad K. Drachkovitch, *Les socialismes français et allemand et le problème de la guerre 1870–1914* (Geneva, 1953), esp. pp. 313–44; Hans-Josef Steinberg, *Die Stellung der II. Internationale zu Krieg und Frieden* (Trier, 1972); Karl Kautsky, *Sozialisten und Krieg: Ein Beitrag zur Ideengeschichte des Sozialismus von den Hussiten bis zum Völkerbund* (Prague, 1937).

[155] James Joll, *The Second International, 1889–1914* (New York, 1966), p. 70.

commend the activities of the bourgeois peace movement. Although the international socialist congress in Zurich in 1893 resolved that "the whole of the socialist movement should lend its support to all associations that have universal peace as their goal," this resolution was unique in its favorable orientation toward the work of the peace movement. On every other occasion when socialists at international congresses passed resolutions that pertained to the bourgeois pacifists, they dismissed the peace movement with contempt. In Brussels in 1891 the delegates announced that "all efforts to eliminate militarism and institute peace that do not take into consideration the economic causes of the problem are impotent, however noble their motives may be." In 1896 the international congress in London declared, alluding to Bertha von Suttner's novel, that "like every other appeal to the humanitarianism of the capitalist class, the cry, *'Die Waffen nieder!'* dies fruitlessly out." In 1900 the congress in Paris condemned "more or less platonic demonstrations of international solidarity" and protested against the Hague conference, which it characterized as "fraud and deception." Finally, in Copenhagen in 1910 socialists dismissed peace congresses as ineffective.

Despite these regular ideological expressions of contempt, a pattern of guarded cooperation between socialists and bourgeois pacifists began to emerge after the turn of the century in some countries. In England labor leaders openly supported the peace movement and sent delegations to national and international peace congresses; leaders of the labor movement in Parliament joined the Interparliamentary Union.[156] In France, where Jean Jaurès was an eloquent advocate of international arbitration and common

[156] BIP (vA5), Hodgson Pratt, "The Best Methods of enlisting the cooperation of the working classes on behalf of International Arbitration and Peace," Draft Report, 1895; Pratt to Ducommun, Le Pecq, 27 August 1903; *Official Report of the Thirteenth Universal Peace Congress*, pp. 134–36, 140–43; *Bulletin officiel du XVme Congrès universel*, pp. 68, 230.

action with the bourgeois pacifists, the peace movement enjoyed extensive socialist support. In 1902 French socialists began to participate in national peace congresses, and by 1912 over two-thirds of the socialists in the Chamber of Deputies belonged to the Interparliamentary Union.[157] In 1903 the entire Swiss Social Democratic Party officially affiliated with the International Peace Bureau.[158] The president of the International Socialist Bureau, Émile Vandervelde, was active in the bourgeois peace movement and attended Interparliamentary Conferences and Universal Peace Congresses with Belgian delegations.[159]

At first it appeared as if a pattern of cooperation would also develop in Germany, as in 1892 *Vorwärts* published a *Volksausgabe* of Bertha von Suttner's antiwar novel.[160] Subsequently, however, German socialists refused all overtures for further cooperation with the bourgeois peace movement, and by the turn of the century the SPD had in fact become one of the pacifists' most outspoken critics. The socialist press ridiculed the *Schwärmer* in the peace society with as much enthusiasm as did nationalist papers. *Vorwärts* denounced the Hague convention as *"ratifizierter Friedensschwindel"* and called Bertha von Suttner a "Madame Krüdener *rediviva*."[161] Socialists in the Reichstag persistently declined to join the Interparliamentary Union.[162] The party refused to send representatives to peace congresses, to respond to the pacifists' inquiries, or to participate in any of the exchange visits to other countries which pacifists helped

[157] See below, chapter 8, pp. 357–64.

[158] BIP (vA5), Geschäftsleitung der Sozialdemokratischen Partei der Schweiz to Peace Bureau, Biel, 9 July 1903.

[159] Baker, "Belgians and the Peace Movement," pp. 111–12.

[160] NL Suttner (Fd6), W. Liebknecht to Suttner, Charlottenburg, 24 April 1892.

[161] Fried, "Die Sozialdemokratie und die Friedensbewegung," FW, II (1900), 133–35; FW, v (1903), 101; DWN, VIII (1899), 290.

[162] In 1906 the Germans vetoed a resolution of the International Socialist Bureau calling on socialists in all countries to join the Interparliamentary Union: FB, VII (1906), 105.

to arrange.[163] The few socialists who did associate with the peace movement did so on a strictly individual basis, for as a whole the party even refused as a gesture to admit the constructive value of the peace movement.[164]

The gulf between socialists and the peace movement was the product of tactical, ideological, and social factors in both camps. A lower-middle class phenomenon, the peace movement was liberal-democratic politically but conservative socially, and the implications of the pacifist ideology for the "social question" reflected this social bias. Particularly in scientific pacifism, the inexorable tendency of modern capitalism toward more ramified forms of organization and greater international interdependence was portrayed as the guarantee of both international peace and social justice. In the pacifists' analysis both the international political system and the existing social system represented potentially harmonious entities. The existence of disharmony in each could be traced to the same problem, which was militarism. Pacifists denied, however, that militarism was a function or necessary aspect of capitalism or international relations among capitalist states; it was rather an extraneous and pathological element in an otherwise healthy system, deriving from the conspiracy of a few evil men. The definitive elimination of international conflict through arbitration would undermine militarism and solve the social question, by which pacifists understood the existence of urban poverty, because in the final analysis this was merely one of the more perverse effects of military spending.[165]

For the pacifists this was an attractive proposition. It

[163] Goldscheid, *Fried Gedenkblätter*, p. 14; FW, III (1901), 142; FW, VI (1904), 29; FW, VIII (1906), 63; FW, IX (1907), 37.

[164] One of the socialists who belonged to a bourgeois peace society was Wilhelm Liebknecht, who was a member of Frederik Bajer's Danish Peace Society: Abrams, "European Peace Societies," p. 395; StBR, VIII L.P., 1 Session (26 March 1892), VII, 5012. While a student in Berlin, Albert Südekum was active in the German Peace Society: SFC, Suttner to Fried, Harmannsdorf, 1 November 1892.

[165] See above, chapter 3, n. 74.

enabled them in good conscience to deprecate social revolution, the prospect of which they abhorred, to style their program as an alternative to revolutionary socialism, and to portray themselves as mediators among all classes of German society.[166] But it also limited their ability to appeal to the labor movement for support, since they could do little more than counsel the working classes to accommodate themselves to capitalism, strive for self-improvement, and discard the revolutionary aspects of their program.

In practice support for the peace movement within the German labor movement was restricted to the nonsocialist *Deutsche Gewerkvereine*, whose ideas about the vitality of capitalism and its capacity to accommodate the worker corresponded to the pacifists'. Founded in 1869 by Max Hirsch and Franz Duncker, these unions comprised at the turn of the century some one hundred thousand members, principally skilled workers and artisans. Politically they stood close to the left-liberal parties, and while they did not rule out resort to the strike, they emphasized self-improvement and peaceful negotiations with employers as the means to higher wages.[167] The similiarity of their social and political views made the Hirsch-Duncker unions close allies of the pacifists, as did the prominence of Max Hirsch in the peace movement. Pacifists frequently spoke at meetings of local Hirsch-Duncker unions and *Arbeiterbildungsvereine*, and published articles in Hirsch-Duncker journals.[168] The unions in turn sent greetings and official representatives to

[166] Fried, *Grundlagen*, p. 1; Opitz, "Deutschland und Frankreich angesichts der sozialen Gefahr der Gegenwart," FB, IX (1908), 21; FB, V (1904), 144; FB, VII (1906), 8; VF, XII (1911), 4.

[167] W. Kulemann, *Die Berufsvereine*, Erste Abteilung, *Geschichtliche Entwicklung der Berufsorganisationen der Arbeitnehmer und Arbeitgeber aller Länder* (Jena, 1908), II, 4–32; Gerhard Bry, *Wages in Germany, 1871–1945* (Princeton, 1960), pp. 30–32.

[168] Fried, "Die Friedensbewegung und die Arbeiter," FW, VIII (1906), 162; FW, VIII (1906), 179; DWN, V (1896), 32; CBM, XI (1906), 74; CBM, XII (1907), 6; FB, VIII (1907), 22.

peace congresses.[169] The national Hirsch-Duncker organization seriously considered becoming a corporate member
of the German Peace Society, and although it eventually
decided not to commit itself, several local Hirsch-Duncker
organizations did affiliate with the peace society.[170]

The same factors that favored an alliance between the
peace movement and the Hirsch-Duncker unions partially
accounted for the hostility displayed by the socialists toward the pacifists. The claim that the natural evolution of
capitalism would bring either domestic or international
peace was anathema to a movement committed ideologically to class conflict and the proposition that capitalism
and war were functionally related. Yet it is significant that
socialists in England, France, Switzerland, Belgium, and
elsewhere found it possible to cooperate with pacifists of
the same social background and ideological persuasion as
those in Germany. This suggests that factors within the German Social Democratic Party itself contributed to its hostile
attitude toward the peace movement.

The sources and internal functions of the SPD's ideology
have been the object of lively interest and debate among
historians.[171] In his massive attempt to synthesize the work
of these historians, Dieter Groh has recently labeled the
party's ideology as "revolutionary *Attentismus*," which
might be characterized as a doctrine of passively waiting

[169] *Bulletin officiel du XVme Congrès universel*, pp. 217-18.

[170] NL Fried, Goldschmidt to Fried, Berlin, 5 April 1906, 16 August
1906.

[171] See Erich Matthias, "Kautsky und der Kautskyanismus: Die
Funktion der Ideologie in der deutschen Sozialdemokratie vor dem
ersten Weltkrieg," in Iring Fetscher, ed., *Marxismusstudien* (2. Folge)
(Tübingen, 1957), pp. 151-97; Gerd Irrlitz, "Bemerkungen über die
Einheit politischer und theoretischer Wesenzüge des Zentrismus in
der deutschen Sozialdemokratie," *Beiträge zur Geschichte der
deutschen Arbeiterbewegung* VIII (1966), 43-59; Hans-Josef Steinberg,
*Sozialismus und deutsche Sozialdemokratie: Zur Ideologie der Partei
vor dem I. Weltkrieg* (Hannover, 1967), esp. pp. 75-86.

for a revolution thought to be foreordained by the forces at work in capitalist society.[172] Simply stated, socialist ideologues, led by Karl Kautsky, insisted that the proper strategy for the party to pursue was to insulate itself as far as possible from capitalist society, mobilizing the working masses electorally while the inevitable demise of capitalism proceeded according to its own logic and laws. Kautsky thus condemned attempts from whatever quarter to persuade the party to abandon this "inheritor" role, be they from those who claimed that the laws of capitalism were not going to produce a revolution and that the party ought therefore to collaborate with bourgeois progressives, or from those who urged the party to intervene actively in order to hasten the day of revolution.[173] Kautsky's continued success in ideologically beating back these challenges, first from the one group and then from the other, was the controlling factor in the SPD's attitude toward the bourgeois peace movement.

As a pacifist credo, the doctrine espoused by the SPD leadership was in the utopian tradition, inasmuch as it held that the antagonisms in capitalist society were the basic cause of international conflict and that nothing short of socialist revolution would do away with the problem of war. In keeping with this analysis, and in line with a general refusal to cooperate politically with bourgeois organizations, the party rejected overtures for cooperation from the German Peace Society throughout the 1890s, citing the resolution passed by the International in Brussels to the effect that only socialism would bring world peace.[174] In truth, the

[172] Dieter Groh, *Negative Integration und revolutionärer Attentismus: Die deutsche Sozialdemokratie am Vorabend des Ersten Weltkrieges* (Frankfurt, 1973).

[173] See Peter Nettl, "The German Social Democratic Party 1890–1914 as a Political Model," *Past and Present*, number 30 (April 1965), pp. 65–95.

[174] Fried, "Die deutsche Sozialdemokratie und die Friedensbewegung," FW, v (1903), 101. The German protocol of the Zurich congress of the International omitted the passage in the resolution calling

party was generally indifferent at this time to problems that pertained to foreign policy, so the party's ideologues did not analyze the matter of arbitration and the bourgeois peace movement at all extensively until the end of the decade, when the first Hague conference invited a more thorough ideological appraisal. Significantly, the convocation of the Hague conference coincided with the outbreak of the revisionist crisis within the party. This in turn led to accentuated intransigence in party commentary on the peace movement, for it was not difficult for party leaders to recognize the affinity between bourgeois pacifism and the views of revisionists on international politics.[175] Indeed, even before the Hague conference convened, revisionist leaders such as Eduard Bernstein, Richard Calwer, and Max Schippel had begun to suggest that the development of capitalism could lead to international conciliation and political solidarity.[176]

In part a reflection of party leaders' anxiety about the revisionist threat, what emerged after the turn of the century as the semiofficial socialist position on the bourgeois peace movement was ironically a secular variation of the position held by Protestant theologians. Both socialists and churchmen assured the pacifists that although world peace was a praiseworthy ideal, it could be realized only in the wake of apocalyptic changes, by which the theologians understood the arrival of the Kingdom of God and the socialists meant proletarian revolution. Kautsky and other party spokesmen responded to the peace movement's calls for cooperation by inverting the pacifists' thesis that the so-

for cooperation with bourgeois groups: Kautsky, *Sozialisten und Krieg*, p. 310.

[175] Fried, "Die Amsterdamer Kongress und die Friedensbewegung," FW, VI (1904), 164–65.

[176] Gerhard Schulz, "Die deutsche Sozialdemokratie und die Idee des internationalen Ausgleichs," in Alfred Hermann, ed., *Aus Geschichte und Politik: Festschrift zum 70. Geburtstag von Ludwig Bergsträsser* (Düsseldorf, 1954), pp. 98–104.

cial question was a function of the problem of international peace.[177] They insisted that the elimination of militarism and international conflict would come with—and only with —the definitive solution of the social question, by which they meant the revolutionary overthrow of capitalism. For militarism was not, as pacifists insisted, a phenomenon extraneous to capitalism, but was rather an intrinsic aspect of the system, and its symptoms would become exacerbated, not attenuated, as capitalism continued to develop naturally. Given this analysis of international conflict, the call for arbitration that appeared in the SPD's Erfurt program took on the character of a precept for a future socialist society, for as socialist commentary on the first Hague conference made clear, party leaders believed that negotiations for arbitration and arms limitation, if conducted by capitalist statesmen, were at best a harmless chimera; but these reforms also harbored the danger of enabling capitalist governments to pursue a less expensive kind of militarism, concentrating their armed forces on the repression of domestic opposition.

The bourgeois pacifists who championed arbitration appeared then in the eyes of socialist ideologues as a curious anomaly, a group of naive dreamers whose approach to the problem of war rested upon a basic misapprehension of the forces at work in capitalist society. The pacifists' idealism, their appeal to humanity, and the uncritical confidence they placed in reactionary statesmen such as the Russian tsar were all evidence of a faulty understanding of politics, which ignored or refused to accept as valid the role of class conflict. "And so," observed *Vorwärts* in 1900, "everything dissolves in harmony—within the German Peace Society that is!"[178] Toward these feckless idealists the party as-

---

[177] Karl Kautsky, "Demokratische und reaktionäre Abrüstung," NZ, XVI (1898), 740–46; StBR, x L.P., 1 Session (30 April 1907), CCXXVIII, 1243–44; Heinrich Ströbel, "Wege zum Pazifismus: Sozialismus," in Lenz and Fabian, *Die Friedensbewegung*, p. 104; cf. DWN, v (1896), 41–43; VF, XIII (1912), 101.

[178] "Sonderbare Schwärmer," *Vorwärts*, 4 April 1900.

sumed an attitude of bemused, frequently derisive indifference. They were at best a group of innocuous visionaries
who were given, in August Bebel's words, to "superficial
dilettantism."[179] The socialists' advice to them was to divest
themselves of their illusions and join forces with the revolutionary socialist movement. As Wilhelm Liebknecht wrote
to Bertha von Suttner, "What you are trying to achieve,
peace on earth, *we* will attain—I mean social democracy,
which in truth is a great international peace league."[180]

The pacifists were well aware of how the SPD viewed
their activities, but since they believed the socialist movement had a critical role to play in the success of their own
cause, they persisted in the face of all obstacles in sending
resolutions, interpellations, and appeals to leading socialists
and trade union officials. Fried dispatched letters to Bebel,
whom he addressed as *Parteigenosse*, and other socialists in
the Reichstag to urge them to join the Interparliamentary
Union.[181] But if socialists replied at all, their responses were
ritual repetitions of the party's critique of the peace movement. In 1906, for instance, Fried sent out questionnaires
to all major German unions soliciting their participation at
peace congresses. Carl Legien's answer on behalf of the
Free Trade Unions came as no surprise: "No. For this purpose we have international workers' congresses. The delegates to Interparliamentary Conferences vote for disarmament but turn around and approve all the demands of their
governments for more weapons. Nothing goes on at peace
congresses except hypocrisy [*Friedensheuchelei*]."[182]

---

[179] NL Fried, Decker to Fried, Cologne, 29 May 1905; cf. Goldscheid, *Fried Gedenkblätter*, p. 14; DWN, v (1896), 34; FW, III
(1901), 142; FW, VI (1904), 29; FW, VIII (1906), 163.

[180] NL Suttner (Fd6a), Liebknecht to Suttner, Berlin, 2 May 1892;
cf. Friedrich Stampfer, "Der erste Mai und die Friedensbewegung,"
DWN, III (1894), 157–59; Stampfer, *Erfahrungen und Erkenntnisse:
Aufzeichnungen aus meinem Leben* (Cologne, 1957), pp. 19–20.

[181] NL Fried, Fried to Bebel, Berlin, 28 April 1898.

[182] *Bulletin officiel du XVme Congrès universel*, p. 217; FW, VIII
(1906), 162–63.

After years of hearing nothing but this kind of criticism from the socialists, the pacifists had little reason for optimism. They were dismayed at their inability to find even token sympathy within a movement likewise committed to world peace, but their experience showed that the gulf separating the two pacifist traditions, each with its own characteristic social analysis of the causes of war, was very broad in Germany.

All the more surprising was the transformation in the SPD's attitude toward the peace movement which began not long after Legien had contemptuously turned the pacifists away. This change owed practically nothing to the continued exertions of the pacifists themselves, but arose rather as an aspect of the SPD's response to another internal crisis.

Socialist leaders had long shied away from confronting the problem of imperialism, but found it more difficult to avoid after a series of crises on the periphery of Europe, beginning with the Russo-Japanese War in 1904, raised the distinct possibility of general war. After the SPD fared poorly in the "Hottentot" elections to the Reichstag in 1907, during which the issue of colonial policy had figured prominently, the need became acute for the party to articulate an official position on imperialism and deal with basic questions about its significance, implications, and its relationship to the growing threat of war.[183] This was particularly true since

[183] On this general problem see: Max Victor, "Die Stellung der deutschen Sozialdemokratie zu den Fragen der auswärtigen Politik," *Archiv für Sozialwissenschaft und Sozialpolitik* LX (1928), esp. 164–67; Erwin Dörzbacher, *Die deutsche Sozialdemokratie und die nationale Machtpolitik bis 1914* (Gotha, 1920), pp. 222–30; Kurt Mandelbaum, "Die Erörterungen innerhalb der deutschen Sozialdemokratie über das Problem des Imperialismus (1895–1914)" (Inaugural dissertation, Frankfurt a. M., 1926); Walter Wittwer, *Streit um Schicksalsfragen: Die deutsche Sozialdemokratie zu Krieg und Vaterlandsverteidigung 1907–1914* (Berlin, 1964); Hans-Christoph Schröder, *Sozialismus und Imperialismus: Die Auseinandersetzung der deutschen Sozialdemokratie mit dem Imperialismusproblem und der "Weltpolitik" vor 1914*, Erster Teil (Hannover, 1968), esp. pp. 183–98; Wolfram Wette,

discussion of the problem had begun to endanger the organizational cohesion of the party itself. On the party's right wing Bernstein, Eduard David, and other revisionist leaders argued that colonial acquisitions by a capitalist power worked ultimately to the material benefit of the working class; they consequently advocated that the party abandon its traditional opposition to colonialism.[184] Even more disquieting to the party leadership was the analysis of imperialism developed by a vocal faction on the party's left wing around Rosa Luxemburg, Paul Lensch, and other contributors to the *Leipziger Volkszeitung*. These radicals proceeded from what seemed to be the unobjectionable proposition that imperialism was an intrinsic, symptomatic aspect of the process by which the contradictions and antagonisms in capitalism were becoming more critical. But from there they went on to argue that if these tensions were allowed to develop, war among the capitalist powers was soon inevitable. With a sense of urgency born of this conclusion, the radicals called for heightened revolutionary activism, ultimately to take the form of a mass strike, to bring about the overthrow of capitalism. This they held to be the only alternative to general war, for they denied the possibility of finding any accommodation between imperialist capitalism, and its consequences, and revolutionary socialism. Specifically, they repudiated arbitration and disarmament as concepts that predicated the possibility of ameliorating tensions among capitalist powers; such an assumption, they believed, betrayed a misunderstanding of imperialism and

---

Kriegstheorien deutscher Sozialisten—Marx, Engels, Lassalle, Bernstein, Kautsky, Luxemburg: Ein Beitrag zur Friedensforschung (Stuttgart, 1971), pp. 125–90; Carl E. Schorske, *German Social Democracy, 1905–1917: The Development of the Great Schism* (New York, 1955), pp. 59–87, 241–50.

[184] See Abraham Ascher, "Imperialists within German Social Democracy prior to 1914," *Journal of Central European Affairs* xx (1961), 397–422.

nourished counterrevolutionary illusions about the capacity of capitalism for reform.[185]

At first it appeared that Kautsky shared this evaluation of imperialism. It was he who in 1907 had devised the slogan, "imperialism or socialism," to which the radicals appealed while deprecating measures short of revolution to combat imperialism. His manifesto, *Der Weg zur Macht*, which appeared early in 1909, likewise cited the growing danger of imperialist war as evidence that the socialist revolution was near. But Kautsky and the party central were unprepared to pursue the implications of these premises as far as the radicals, for they realized that the radical position was unacceptable to most of the party, particularly to the unions, which opposed resort to the mass strike. Kautsky was also alarmed over the revolutionary activism of the radicals because it threatened to undermine the strategy of "waiting for the revolution" by precipitating a premature showdown with the forces of counterrevolution. Unable to endorse the radicals' cataclysmic analysis of imperialism, Kautsky and the "Centrists" attempted to formulate a compromise position on imperialist expansion which would be consistent with the party's established strategy and its anti-war tradition.

The debate within the party on imperialism raged for several years and was not tentatively resolved until the party congress in Chemnitz in 1912 (nor definitively until 1917). But the emergence of an official compromise position can be documented with some precision from, among other things, the attitude of the party toward the bourgeois peace movement and its program.[186] As late as 1908 *Vorwärts* was still mocking the peace movement: "The breed of dreamers

[185] Annelies Laschitza, "Karl Liebknecht und Rosa Luxemburg über die Dialektik von Frieden und Sozialismus," *Zeitschrift für Geschichtswissenschaft* XIX (1971), 1117–38.

[186] See Ursula Ratz, "Briefe zum Erscheinen von Karl Kautskys 'Weg zur Macht,'" *International Review of Social History* XII (1967), 432–77.

of perpetual peace has not yet died out in the bourgeoisie. Do we not still have the bourgeois peace movement? It exists and is nourished on illusions. . . . Its view does not extend into the economic substructure of political events. The legend of the historical 'great man' is so fundamental to the movement that it hopes to see the cart of human progress pushed forward by the bloody hand of the Russian autocrat."[187] Then, in March 1909, to the amazement of the pacifists, the SPD Reichstag delegation introduced a resolution that proposed international negotiations to limit the naval race and, in so doing, called attention to the Hague conferences.[188] The doctrinal justification for such proposals began shortly to appear in the party press, in the form of a new theory of imperialism. By 1911 Kautsky, whose views had evidently undergone a dramatic change, had become the official spokesman for the new position.[189] In a series of important articles in his journal, *Neue Zeit*, Kautsky developed a theory of imperialism that anticipated Joseph Schumpeter's analysis of the phenomenon by denying the functional relationship between war and capitalist expansion.[190] Kautsky distinguished between two distinct modes

[187] *Vorwärts*, 1 May 1908, cited in FW, x (1908), 92–93.

[188] StBR, xii L.P., 1 Session, ccLIX, number 1311; *ibid.* (29 March 1909), ccxxxvi, 7822; Fried, "Zeichen und Wunder," FW, xi (1909), 82.

[189] Ursula Ratz, "Karl Kautsky und die Abrüstungskontroverse in der deutschen Sozialdemokratie," *International Review of Social History* xi (1966), esp. 216, n. 1; Irrlitz, "Bemerkungen über die Einheit politischer und theoretischer Wesenzüge," pp. 53, 59; cf. Groh, *Negative Integration*, p. 350, n. 275. On Kautsky's role and the debate on the problem of imperialism, both in Germany and in the International, see Georges Haupt, *Socialism and the Great War: The Collapse of the Second International* (Oxford, 1972), esp. pp. 135–60.

[190] Kautsky, "Krieg und Frieden: Betrachtungen zur Maifeier," NZ, xxix, 2 (1911), 97–107; "Der erste Mai und der Kampf gegen den Militarismus," NZ, xxx, 2 (1912), 97–109; "Nochmals die Abrüstung," NZ, xxx, 2 (1912), 841–54; cf. Mandelbaum, "Die Erörterungen," p. 37. On the similarities between Kautsky's theory and Schumpeter's see: John H. Kautsky, "J. A. Schumpeter and Karl Kautsky:

or components of capitalist expansion. It was indisputable, he believed, that industrial capital became expansive as it developed and was forced to seek new markets and sources of raw material abroad; but he denied that this mode of expansion, which did inhere in the nature of capitalism, harbored the seeds of war. Indeed, its consequences were more likely to lead in the opposite direction, toward greater international interdependence, organization, and cooperation. The bellicose aspects of expansion were rooted elsewhere: "the spirit of imperialism [i.e. of bellicose expansion] does not grow out of the seeds of industrial development [and] the expansion of capital. It arises instead because, as this development continues, the military, the bureaucracy, and high finance become increasingly powerful and dominant in all aspects of a society's life. As they do so, they promote the spirit of violence in both foreign and domestic politics."[191] Kautsky insisted that this bellicosity, though it grew out of capitalist expansion, was not the product of any economic necessity inherent in capitalist development. It was rather a political problem, a derivation of the structure of political power in the expanding states.[192] This in turn implied that political measures could be undertaken to combat this bellicosity effectively even within the context of capitalist society.

On the basis of this analysis, Kautsky rejected the radicals' slogan, "imperialism or socialism," and formulated a more moderate alternative, "world war or disarmament." He admitted thereby that it was possible to reform international relations among capitalist states and to prevent, or at least to delay, the outbreak of war with political measures short of socialist revolution. Specifically, he called upon the party to take the lead in combating the militarist compo-

Parallel Theories of Imperialism," *Midwest Journal of Political Science* v (May 1961), 101–28.

[191] Kautsky, "Nochmals die Abrüstung," p. 850.

[192] Groh, *Negative Integration*, pp. 219–23; Haupt, *Socialism and the Great War*, p. 150.

nent of capitalist expansion, not only by continuing to refuse to vote for defense appropriations in the Reichstag, but now, more constructively, by fostering the peaceful expansion of capitalism in free trade and promoting international agreements on disarmament and arbitration.

Just how much Kautsky's theory represented a compromise may be judged by the vehemence with which the radicals denounced it and the fact that it seemed indistinguishable from the position that revisionists such as Bernstein, Gerhart Hildebrand, and Ludwig Quessel had been defending in the *Sozialistische Monatshefte*.[193] Nevertheless, it became clear in the course of debate in 1911 and 1912 that Kautsky's position had taken on the status of party orthodoxy and that it enjoyed the support of major figures in the party central and Reichstag *Fraktion*, including Hugo Haase, Georg Ledebour, and August Bebel.[194] In his comments on the Agadir crisis at the party's congress in 1911 in Jena, Bebel proclaimed: "German industry and German commerce have expanded enormously; great amounts of French, English, and American capital have been invested in Germany. I openly admit that perhaps the greatest guarantee of world peace lies in this international export of capital."[195] At the party congress the next year in Chemnitz imperialism was the subject of a long debate, during

[193] Eduard Bernstein, "Die internationale Politik der Sozialdemokratie," *Sozialistische Monatshefte* XIII, 2 (1909), 613–24; Ludwig Quessel, "Imperialismus und Verständigung," *ibid.*, XIX (1913), 333–39; Mandelbaum, "Die Erörterungen," pp. 28–30, 44–46; Schulz, "Die deutsche Sozialdemokratie," p. 110.

[194] Bebel had always been less opposed to proposals for disarmament and arbitration than most other party leaders: NL Wehberg (43), Untersuchungsausschuss Protokoll, 15 March 1922, p. 22; HB (1), p. 302; Bebel, "Das Wettrüsten der Nationen," DWN, VII (1898), 129–39. On Ledebour see Ursula Ratz, *Georg Ledebour (1850–1947): Weg und Wirken eines sozialistischen Politikers* (Berlin, 1969), pp. 114–15.

[195] *Protokoll über die Verhandlungen des Parteitages der Sozialdemokratischen Partei Deutschlands* (Jena, 10–16 September 1911) (Berlin, 1911), p. 345; cf. "Das Kapital als Friedensgarantie," FW, XIII (1911), 304.

which it was apparent that despite the objections of the radicals, most of the party agreed with Bebel and Kautsky. After Haase, the principal speaker, had noted that "economic interdependence constitutes a force that restricts belligerent agitators," Bernstein called for a "protest against protectionism, a demonstration in favor of peace, freedom, and free trade."[196] The resolution adopted by the congress endorsed Kautsky's views by declaring that although imperialism would definitively end only with the demise of capitalism, "nothing must be overlooked in alleviating those of its effects that are dangerous for everyone."[197]

There is much to support the claim that with the debate over imperialism the party central began openly to espouse revisionism. Here it is germane only to point out that Kautsky's theory of imperialism bore a remarkable resemblance to Alfred Fried's scientific pacifism. Both pointed to commercial and industrial expansion, growing international organization, and interdependence as natural patterns of capitalist development that would promote peace among the nations by binding them closer together.[198] Both alluded to the dangers of militarism, but rejected the proposition that these were irremediable products of the capitalist system. And both called for promoting the peaceful tendencies in capitalist expansion with agitation in favor of arbitration and arms limitation.

This ideological convergence attested to the relevance of the imperialism debate to the SPD's view of the bourgeois peace movement. Kautsky's analysis of imperialism implied

---

[196] *Protokoll über die Verhandlungen des Parteitages der Sozialdemokratischen Partei Deutschlands* (Chemnitz, 15–21 September 1912) (Berlin, 1912), pp. 411–12, 420.

[197] *Ibid.*, p. 529; cf. Ratz, "Abrüstungskontroverse," p. 225; Drachkovitch, *Les socialismes français et allemand*, pp. 281–86.

[198] They disagreed on the role of finance capital; Fried held it to be a pacifistic factor, while Kautsky drew from Rudolf Hilferding (and Marx) in identifying it as a baleful influence. This disagreement was, however, of peripheral significance.

that the bourgeoisie was itself split between those industrial and commercial sectors whose inclinations were peaceful, and those that had come under the influence of militarism. It consequently behooved the SPD, as Kautsky wrote in 1913, "to utilize every opportunity afforded us to strengthen the forces that promote international understanding."[199] This in turn led the party's leadership to view the peace movement in a much more favorable light. As early as November 1910 Ledebour had noted in the Reichstag that "far beyond our [socialist] ranks people are working in bourgeois circles with great resolve and passion for the idea of peace."[200] In April 1911 Kautsky, too, called favorable attention to the work of the bourgeois pacifists: "The most immediate [way for the SPD to work against war] is to support and strengthen the movement against war and the arms race that is rooted in the bourgeoisie. We must not underestimate this movement. The factors that give rise to it are as real as those that nurture the movement that opposes it, and we have every reason to strengthen it against these opponents."[201] Vorwärts began at the same time to treat the pacifists with more respect and printed appeals and resolutions passed by the German Peace Society.[202]

The pacifists watched the transformation of the party's attitude with great interest. Fried in particular was impressed by the SPD's apparent endorsement of his theories, and in order to encourage the tendencies that had appeared, he began to supply the party leadership with copies of his journal and other pacifist literature, at least some of which the socialists read.[203] If Bebel's remarks on the

[199] Kautsky, "Die Berner Konferenz," NZ, XXXI, 2 (1913), 267–68.
[200] StBR, xx L.P., 2 Session (26 November 1910), CCLXII, 3169; cf. FW, XII (1910), 233.
[201] Kautsky, "Krieg und Frieden," p. 101; cf. Goldscheid, Fried Gedenkblätter, p. 14.
[202] Vorwärts, 22 April 1913, 10 May 1913; FW, XIII (1911), 129–30.
[203] NL Fried, Fried to Kautsky, Vienna, 11 May 1912.

Agadir crisis at the party congress in Jena sounded as if they could have been inspired by a reading of *Die Friedens-Warte*, it was because, in all likelihood, they were.[204]

The principal conduit between the SPD and the peace movement was Eduard Bernstein, the man who, in a sense even more than Kautsky, was the spiritual father of the party's new orientation toward imperialism and the peace movement.[205] As early as 1908 he had anticipated the party's new attitude toward the pacifists, and his subsequent pronouncements on international policy were entirely consistent with bourgeois pacifism.[206] "Nations are component parts of the great body of *humanity*," he wrote in 1909. "The internationalization of life in the civilized nations, especially international commercial ties and the legal relationships that grow out of such ties, have created, even today, concepts and rules for a system of international law. . . . We have entered a new epoch, the epoch of increasingly prevalent international law."[207] After he and Fried began to correspond regularly in 1911, Bernstein became the most outspoken advocate of Fried's views in socialist circles.[208] In 1912 he published an article in Fried's journal, which for a socialist, even then, was unusual.[209] In 1913 he paid Fried

[204] NL Fried, Bernstein to Fried, Berlin, 22 October 1911. Bernstein requested extra copies of an issue of Fried's journal: "I showed my copies to Bebel in Jena, before he gave his speech on Morocco, and afterwards they were damaged or had parts cut out." Bebel undoubtedly read Fried's commentary on the crisis, which emphasized the role of economic interdependence in averting war: Fried, "Betrachtungen zur Marokkocrisis," FW, XIII (1911), 217–21.

[205] Pierre Angel, *Eduard Bernstein et l'évolution du socialisme allemand* (Paris, 1961), p. 379.

[206] FW, X (1908), 177–78; FB, IX (1908), 124.

[207] Bernstein, "Die internationale Politik der Sozialdemokratie," pp. 614, 616, 623.

[208] NL Fried, Bernstein to Fried, Berlin, 19 November 1911; Goldscheid, *Fried Gedenkblätter*, pp. 14–15.

[209] Bernstein, "Wie man Kriegsstimmung erzeugt," FW, XIV (1912), 2–7.

the ultimate compliment and praised his *Handbuch der Friedensbewegung* during a debate in the Reichstag.[210] None of the revisionists was as convinced a pacifist or as favorably disposed toward the peace movement as Bernstein; indeed, some right-wing socialists endorsed German imperialism with an enthusiasm that hardly befitted Kautsky's understanding of peaceful capitalist expansion.[211] Nevertheless, several of the figures politically close to Bernstein, among them David, Max Maurenbrecher, Ewald Vogtherr, Ludwig Frank, and Lily Braun, shared his desire to cooperate with the bourgeois pacifists.[212]

The most significant sign of the SPD's new orientation toward the peace movement came in 1913, when for the first time party leaders agreed to participate in an event openly sponsored and coordinated by bourgeois pacifists. In March 1913, as the German government prepared to submit a new arms bill to the Reichstag, the socialist deputy Ludwig Frank proposed at a party rally in Mannheim that French and German socialists join in a demonstration to protest the acceleration of the arms race.[213] He first discussed his proposal with socialists in France, and when they showed an interest, he approached Robert Grimm, a socialist member of the Swiss National Council, whom he asked to suggest

[210] StBR, XIII L.P., 1 Session (14 April 1913), CCLXXXIX, 4742; cf. ibid., (14 May 1913), CCLXXXV, 1996; PM, II (1913), 225; NL Fried, Bernstein to Fried, 18 January 1913.

[211] Ascher, "Imperialists within German Social Democracy," p. 415; William Maehl, "The Triumph of Nationalism in the German Socialist Party on the Eve of the First World War," *Journal of Modern History* XXIV (1952), 15-41.

[212] NL Fried, David to Fried, Wiesbaden, 13, 19, 30 March 1913; Maurenbrecher to Fried, Mannheim, 20 February 1913; Röttcher to Vogtherr, 5 March 1914; FB, x (1908), 36; VF, XII (1911), 48.

[213] On the joint conferences in Berne and Basel see: Albert Gobat, *La conférence interparlamentaire franco-allemande de Berne* (Berne, 1913); Conciliation internationale, *Bulletin*, number 3, 1913, pp. 11–66; number 2, 1914, pp. 67–72; Wehberg, *Internationale Beschränkung*, pp. 164–67; Ziebura, *Die deutsche Frage*, pp. 141–54; Wild, *Baron d'Estournelles de Constant*, pp. 414-34.

publicly that a joint conference be held in Switzerland. Along with Friedrich Stampfer, Frank then spoke with leaders of the SPD, who agreed after considerable hesitation to participate.[214] The reservation of the German socialist leadership about the project stemmed in large part from the fact that Frank's initial proposal was already growing into something much more elaborate. On 9 April 1913 the Swiss National Council issued invitations not only to socialists in France and Germany, but to all members of the Reichstag and the French Senate and Chamber of Deputies. At the same time, Albert Gobat, a left-liberal member of the Swiss National Council, became the moving force behind the proposed conference. Gobat was also director of the International Peace Bureau, and his prominence in the affair lent it an entirely new dimension, as the bourgeois peace movement now became an active sponsor in both France and Germany. In Germany the peace society began to agitate in favor of the conference, as did the *Verband für internationale Verständigung*.[215] Ludwig Quidde worked closely with Gobat in making preparations for the meeting, and the Carnegie Endowment provided financial support.[216] The conspicuous role of the peace movement was not without its liabilities, but it unexpectedly scared off not the socialists, but the left-liberals in the Reichstag. Leaders of the German branch of the Interparliamentary Union, who were trying to cultivate their image as realists by keeping a safe distance from the pacifists, refused to participate in the conference, despite

---

[214] NL Fried, Frank to Fried, Mannheim [June 1913]; Ludwig Frank, *Aufsätze, Reden und Briefe* (Berlin, 1924), p. 251; Philipp Scheidemann, *Memoiren eines Sozialisten* (2 vols., Dresden, 1928), I, 227.

[215] NL Haussmann (1), Gobat to Haussmann, Berne, 22 December 1913; NL Haussmann (2), Aufruf [of French and German peace societies]; NL Haussmann (4), Nippold to Haussmann, Oberursel, 3 May 1913.

[216] Carnegie Endowment, *Year Book for 1913-1914*, p. 77; Wehberg, *Ludwig Quidde*, p. 37.

the urgings of the Interparliamentary Bureau.[217] Their disinclination was reinforced by their hesitancy to become involved in what looked like a largely socialist affair, as well as by the government's lack of enthusiasm for the event, and the fact that the conference was scheduled to meet during the campaign for elections to the Prussian Landtag.[218]

When the conference convened in Berne on 11 May 1913, there was an enormous and embarrassing disparity between the French and German delegations. A total of 185 French parliamentarians appeared, including over forty socialists, led by Jaurès. The German group numbered thirty-four, of whom only six, including Conrad Haussmann, Ludwig Haas, Franz von Liszt, and Friedrich Naumann, were members of the Progressive party. The most significant feature of the German delegation, in view of the role of the peace movement in arranging the conference, was the fact that its great majority, twenty-five members, were leading socialists, among them Haase, Ledebour, Bebel, Bernstein, Philipp Scheidemann, and Karl Liebknecht.[219]

After initial consternation over how few Germans had found their way to the conference had subsided, the delegates attended two days of speeches and demonstrations carefully designed to offend no one, particularly over the problem of Alsace-Lorraine.[220] In one of the highlights of the conference, Bebel, in one of his last public appearances, gave a brief speech that could only encourage those who contemplated closer cooperation between the peace movement and the SPD: "In the name of all the German dele-

[217] NL Haussmann (2), Eickhoff to Haussmann, Berlin, 15 April 1913; NL Haussmann (3), Chr. Lange to Haussmann, Brussels, 17 April 1913.

[218] NL Fried, Quidde to Fried, Munich, 24 April 1913; KVfiV, II (20 June 1913), 3; ER, II (1913), 115–16; Romberg to Bethmann Hollweg, Berne, 19 April 1913, GP, XXXIX, 307–309, number 15,704.

[219] Wild, *Baron d'Estournelles de Constant*, pp. 405–406; cf. Wehberg, *Internationale Beschränkung*, pp. 164–67; Haupt, *Socialism and the Great War*, p. 117.

[220] NL Gothein (28), Quidde to Gothein, Munich, 15 May 1913.

gates, without respect to party, I have the honor to express our warmest and most heartfelt thanks to those [who] have called and organized this conference. . . . We [i.e., all of us] represent justice, we represent peace, humanity, and the welfare of nations."[221] At the end of the proceedings a resolution was passed condemning "reprehensible chauvinistic agitation" in both countries and calling for submission to the Hague court of disputes that could not be settled diplomatically.[222]

By the conclusion of the conference the mood had become almost euphoric, and the delegates returned home in the hope that they had laid the foundation for a genuine *rapprochement* between the two countries. In Germany the reaction of socialists was tempered, but in general quite favorable. Kautsky concluded that the experiment had "succeeded beyond all expectation," while Frank called the conference "a good beginning."[223] The report submitted by the party central to the *Parteitag* in September 1913 was skeptical over the failure of many bourgeois politicians to attend, but cautioned against underestimating the results of the conference, pointing in particular to the "unconditional recognition of the principle of arbitration" contained in the conference resolution.[224]

Socialist involvement in the affair continued to be a source of complications. When Conrad Haussmann attempted to put together a permanent committee to coordinate future joint activities with the French, he discovered that only socialists were willing to serve on it. Finally, after an embarrassing delay, he managed in November 1913 to

[221] Quoted in PM, II (1913), 212.
[222] Full text of the resolution is in GP, xxxix, 316–18, number 15,707.
[223] Kautsky, "Die Berner Konferenz," p. 265; Frank, *Aufsätze*, pp. 266–67.
[224] *Protokoll über die Verhandlungen des Parteitages der Sozial-demokratischen Partei Deutschlands* (Jena, 14–20 September 1913) (Berlin, 1913), pp. 7, 370; Scheidemann, *Memoiren*, I, 230; *Vorwärts*, 13 May 1913.

find enough Progressives and liberal Catholics in the Reichstag to balance the socialists.[225] The reluctance of bourgeois deputies to participate dictated the character of the Franco-German venture for the remaining few months before the war. In order not to embarrass the Germans again, a second joint conference, held in Basel in May 1914, was restricted to members of the French and German permanent committees.[226] In Basel the delegates agreed to continue a program of regular joint conferences, to be held now in French and German cities, and to establish a correspondence sheet for distribution to newspapers in both countries.

Although the outbreak of war cut short any further activities, the joint conferences of French and German parliamentarians were important, less in terms of their impact on the conduct of foreign policy than because of what they revealed about the changing position of the German socialists toward the peace movement. As their participation in Berne and their continued willingness to cooperate in the joint venture indicated, the German socialists had by the eve of the war articulated a role for themselves in working within the framework of capitalist society for reforms that bourgeois pacifists had long advocated. The pacifists were elated over the events in Switzerland, as well they might have been, for the support given by the SPD to their program, when taken in conjunction with the party's apparent willingess to collaborate with left-liberals, represented the most promising sign that the movement in favor of arbitration and arms limitation might acquire real popular support in Germany.[227]

Still, the possibility that the peace movement could ever have become a factor of any political significance in imperial

[225] NL Haussmann (3), Chr. Lange to Haussmann, Brussels, 2 June 1913; NL Haussmann (2), Haussmann to d'Estournelles, Stuttgart, 23 September 1913; Wild, *Baron d'Estournelles de Constant*, pp. 413–14.

[226] NL Fried, Frank to Fried, Berlin, 29 April 1914.

[227] VF, xiv (1913), 73; FW, xv (1913), 231.

Germany was extremely remote, given the social, political, and constitutional obstacles it faced. In the first place, the social gulf that separated the various groups advocating arbitration and arms limitation remained very wide, and cooperation between the SPD and the bourgeois peace movement was strictly limited, as was cooperation between socialists and left-liberals generally. For all the similarities it displayed with bourgeois pacifism, Kautsky's theory of imperialism was still basically a doctrine of utopian pacifism, although it did introduce certain themes drawn from the ideological pacifist tradition. In fact, Kautsky's new doctrine was not at all inconsistent with the strategy he had long defended. Far from representing a renunciation of socialist revolution, his call for strengthening the peaceful tendencies that he admitted existed in capitalism was designed to enhance the electoral appeal of the SPD and to delay the outbreak of war until socialists could, as he believed they must, grow strong enough to enact the fundamental social changes necessary to eliminate warfare altogether.[228] The growing threat of war and leftist radicalism convinced him that the party's cause would be better served by limited cooperation with bourgeois pacifists than by continued isolation. But he remained profoundly at odds with the pacifists in his belief that a really stable international peace was inconceivable as long as a social system marked by class conflict survived. Although Kautsky and other party leaders accepted much of the bourgeois pacifists' analysis of international tension, they could not conclude along with the pacifists that class conflict was in the final analysis merely a product of international political problems. Nor were the pacifists, for all their satisfaction over the socialists' new benevolence, prepared to compromise their own views and admit the primacy of class conflict in capitalism. In arbitration and arms limitation the bourgeois pacifists saw a panacea, where the socialists saw a tactical device with which to

[228] Groh, *Negative Integration*, pp. 291, 353–54.

avert a general war, which they foresaw as a disaster to their own cause.

Even tentative cooperation with the socialists was not an unmixed blessing for the bourgeois pacifists. It was indicative of the enormous political obstacles faced by the German peace movement that open endorsement of arbitration and arms limitation by the socialists probably did as much to discredit these reforms as it did to promote them. Arbitration and arms limitation were politically unacceptable to all but the socialists and left-liberals, groups that had been branded *Reichsfeinde* by Bismarck and remained the most isolated from the real centers of power in Germany. Their identification with arbitration and arms limitation did nothing to dispel the impression left by agencies of political socialization that advocacy of these reforms was unpatriotic.

Finally, the German peace movement, and whatever allies it might have found, faced constitutional barriers that were probably insurmountable. Control over foreign and military policy, which was essential for the implementation of the peace movement's proposals, lay beyond the competence of even a unanimous Reichstag. The elites who did control these critical aspects of German policy were inalterably opposed to arbitration and arms limitation, for they well recognized the potential threat these reforms posed to their power. They had little cause for alarm, however. The character of prevailing attitudes about international relations in Germany ensured that arbitration and arms limitation remained politically innocuous.

7

The German Peace Movement and International Politics

THE PEACE movement was severely at odds with the German political system. Leaders of the movement were critical of attitudes that formed the German political culture, while the elites who ruled the country were resolutely opposed to the reforms and the orientations toward international affairs which the peace movement sought to promote. In view of this discordance between the peace movement and the political system it hoped to reform, it is a paradox that the pacifists enthusiastically accepted the system's most fundamental values—the legitimacy of the German nation-state itself and its claim to preeminence in Europe. Indeed, given the categories in which they analyzed international politics, the German pacifists were outspoken patriots. Nowhere was this more evident than in their efforts to promote international community by resolving the major international issues of the day.

To view international events of the prewar period through the eyes of the German pacifists is to see them in an unusual, sometimes bizarre perspective. In 1896, for instance, Bertha von Suttner hailed the negotiation of an arbitration treaty between England and the United States as "the greatest triumph which the cause of civilization has hitherto attained."[1] An international meeting of gynecologists in Berlin in 1912 impressed the pacifists as an event of major significance.[2] According to the pacifists, military alliances, a form of international cooperation, provided an index to the progress of pacifism; thus, when the heads of

[1] DWN, v (1896), 465.
[2] "Pazifistische Gedanke am Gynekologenkongress," FW, xiv (1912), 391–92.

state of the Triple Alliance met in 1908, it conjured up visions of a *Menschheitsfamilie*.[3]

This eccentric sense of proportion derived from the pacifists' understanding of international affairs. They believed that they were witnessing the playing out of a great confrontation between two antithetical systems of international politics, the one emphasizing armed force, the balance of power, and secret diplomacy, the other based upon international community, law, and morality. Since they believed that the triumph of the latter system was inevitable, pacifists were especially sensitive to evidence that seemed to confirm their expectations. Their analysis of international affairs was thus governed more by anticipation of an international community than by an effort to understand the workings of a system they held to be bankrupt. As Umfrid explained it in 1912, "We attempt to remain true to our principles by judging current questions in the light of justice and morality."[4]

The pacifists believed that the community of nations prescribed normative principles of international conduct and that these could be translated into statutory law. International politics would be transformed into a *Rechtssystem* founded upon a comprehensive code of international law, appeal to which would bring the just resolution of all disputes. Conflict resolution (to use the modern term) would thus become a question of determining objectively where justice resided in any given dispute—a procedure for which a disinterested court of arbitration would be best qualified.

Difficulties, the implications of which they did not appreciate, arose as soon as the pacifists attempted to add substance to their concept of justice by defining it more precisely. Some of the most unedifying episodes in the history of the prewar peace movement were occasioned by disagreements among irate men of peace over interpretations of international justice. One incident, which illustrated with particular clarity the problems inherent in the pacifists' ap-

[3] FB, IX (1908), 77.   [4] VF, XIII (1912), 125.

proach to international politics, occurred in 1910 when the French pacifist Émile Arnaud presented the Universal Peace Congress in Stockholm with a specific proposal for a code of international law.[5] The Germans immediately objected to it. Nippold, no doubt offended by Arnaud's lack of academic credentials, called the proposal "a disgrace."[6] Although Umfrid hailed it as a "standard work" for the peace movement, he disagreed strenuously with some of Arnaud's ideas about international justice. He was particularly alarmed over the guidelines in the code that denied the validity of past conquests and called for the independence of "subjugated" territories, for he detected here an attempt to establish a French claim on Alsace-Lorraine.[7]

Such disagreements were frequent within the international movement, for pacifists in all countries were patriots. The result was a remarkable coincidence in pacifist commentary between national interest and international morality. In 1907, for example, the English pacifist William Stead defended the justice of expanding the British navy.[8] In 1911 Italian pacifists proclaimed their approval of the Italian invasion of Libya, and when Italian parliamentarians were faced with censure over their support of the Libyan war, they withdrew from the Interparliamentary Union.[9]

The Germans were quick to condemn such behavior, but

[5] *XVIIIᵉ Congrès universel de la paix à Stockholm, du 1ᵉʳ au 5 août 1910* (Stockholm, 1911), pp. 46–52, 287–312.

[6] NL Fried, Nippold to Fried, Schwanden ob Sigriswil, 3 September 1910.

[7] Umfrid, "Der Kodex des internationalen Rechts," VF, XII (1911), 91–92. Article 29 read: "The right of sovereignty over an inhabited territory cannot result from peaceful occupation, nor from conquest, nor from a cession of title of any kind." Article 44 provided that "The inhabitants of a subjugated territory have the right to invoke the benefits of the clauses of this code and to demand their autonomy and constitute themselves as an independent nation": *XVIIIᵉ Congrès universel*, pp. 291–94.

[8] "Die Affäre Stead," FW, X (1908), 10–11.

[9] Fried, "Das Versagen der italienischen Pazifisten," FW, XIII (1911), 281.

they themselves were as patriotic as any contingent in the international peace movement. Indeed, the fact that pacifists throughout the western world regarded Germany as the main disruptive force in international politics probably made the German pacifists more sensitive to the interests of their country.[10] This was especially evident in the persistent claim made by German pacifists, from Eugen Schlief to Otto Umfrid, that a cardinal tenet of international justice was the validity of the European *status quo*.[11] Ironically, in this one respect the German pacifists were heirs of Bismarck, the man whose *Machtpolitik* epitomized the system they proposed to eliminate. Like Bismarck, they believed that Germany was satiated in Europe, the most powerful country on the continent. As disciples of Ivan Bloch, they could harbor no illusions about the impact of even a victorious war on their country. Thus, from the standpoint of national interest, they advocated that Germany promote an international federation, which would peacefully guarantee the country's continued preeminence by lending moral authority to the *status quo*.[12]

Yet it would be both inaccurate and unfair to dismiss the pacifists as hypocrites who tried to cloak national interest in morality, for they could not admit any divorce between politics and morality. They owed far more to Herder and Kant than to Bismarck; their concept of the nation, as well as their pride in their country, was cultural and ethical. They welcomed international competition and deplored only that it had to be played out in military rivalries rather than in cultural interchange or economic competition. In

[10] See for instance Ernst Richard, "The Peace Movement and Germany," *Advocate of Peace* LXVIII (1906), 12; G. H. Perris, "The Paragon of Militarism," *Concord* (April–August 1903), pp. 49–51, 72, 93–94, 125–26.

[11] Wehberg, *Führer*, pp. 16–18; FW, III (1901), 144; FB, VIII (1907), 29; VF, XI (1910), 55; VF, XII (1911), 91–92; FW, XXVI (1926), 326.

[12] See Otto Umfrid, *Bismarcks Gedanken und Erinnerungen im Lichte der Friedensidee und Anderes zur Kritik nationalsozialer Afterpolitik* (Esslingen, 1905), pp. 8, 13.

the final analysis, it was their patriotism that made them pacifists; they believed that Germany's ethical mission was to lead the nations of the world into political federation and a higher stage of civilization.[13] In order to facilitate this they were prepared to renounce any German territorial aggrandizement in Europe and asked pacifists in other countries to make the same pledge.

The "international dimension" of the German pacifists' campaign, like their work with influential sectors of German society, was designed to facilitate the transition from the old to the new system of international politics by promoting attitudes conducive to international community. In this case the pacifists hoped to demonstrate through their own actions that international community was an emerging reality. In addition to drawing attention to the arms race, secret diplomacy, and other perversities of the *Machtsystem*, they founded and participated in organizations to encourage contacts and more cordial relations among different countries.[14] They also attempted with their commentary to facilitate the just and peaceful settlement of international disputes, which they thought were based only on misunderstandings. Although the hostility of the German government toward the peace movement dictated that most of this activity be confined to nonofficial channels, the persistence of rivalries and disputes between the German government and other powers exerted an overbearing influence on the pacifists' work.

Alsace-Lorraine and Rapprochement with France

No problem plagued the international peace movement as much as Alsace-Lorraine. Long after it had ceased to be an

[13] FB, VII (1906), 74; VF, XI (1910), 98–99; VF, XV (1914), 73; CBM, XIII (1908), 94.

[14] For instance: Schlief, *Hohe Politik*, pp. 8–9; Umfrid, "Kabinetts-Diplomatie," FW, XIII (1911), 222; Fried, "Die Reform der Diplomatie," *Dokumente des Fortschritts* I (1908), 489–91; R. Gädke, "Die neue Wehrvorlage," VF, XIV (1913), 27.

active issue among the powers at an official level it continued to be a source of acute dissension among the pacifists, the most hotly debated topic at Universal Peace Congresses.[15] The pacifists were convinced that Alsace-Lorraine lay at the root of all the international crises of the prewar period and that international tension would persist until the issue was solved.[16]

The overriding importance pacifists attached to this problem reflected their moralistic appreciation of international politics. French pacifists—and many others—believed that the Treaty of Frankfurt was unjust and thus that German possession of Alsace-Lorraine was immoral; and because silence on the issue might imply acquiescence in immorality, they were unable to let the Germans forget it.[17] The Germans, however, though they occasionally had qualms about the justice of the Treaty of Frankfurt, could hardly admit the legitimacy of the French claim without sacrificing whatever little appeal the peace movement enjoyed in Germany.[18] Their response to the French was to insist that recognition of the European *status quo* was the indispensable basis for a just world order and, therefore, that the Alsace-Lorraine problem did not exist at all, or that it would disappear naturally once justice reigned and national antagonisms ceased to figure in international affairs.[19]

Alsace-Lorraine became a source of tension as soon as a peace movement appeared in Germany, and the peace so-

[15] See Heinz-Otto Sieburg, "Die Elsass-Lothringen-Frage in der Deutsch-Französischen Diskussion von 1871 bis 1914," *Zeitschrift für die Geschichte der Saargegend* xvii/xviii (1969/70), 9–37.

[16] "The ten thousand who have today been slaughtered to death in the Balkans are in the final analysis nothing but victims of the Franco-German antagonism." NL Wehberg (59a), Fried to Wehberg, Vienna, 6 November 1912; cf. FW, xxv (1925), 49.

[17] Abrams, "European Peace Societies," pp. 280–82, 296–97.

[18] Otto Umfrid, *Anti-Treitschke* (Esslingen, n.d.), p. 9; DWN, v (1896), 63; FW, xiii (1911), 213.

[19] MFK, iii (December 1895), 3.

cieties of the 1880s in south Germany were casualties of this problem. In the early 1890s it continued to provoke dissension despite pleas by Germans for "abstinence from meddling with actual [*sic*] political questions, which, particularly in [Germany], lead to suspicion and injury to our cause."[20] In the interest of comity, the issue was banned from the agenda at Universal Peace Congresses, so most Germans in the peace movement were content to counsel postponement of all discussion of the problem until the establishment of a durable *Rechtsordnung*.[21] Yet criticism of the German position continued in the pacifist press in France and elsewhere, until it provoked a major incident. Early in 1895 Franz Wirth, whose energy in founding peace societies was matched only by his inability to tolerate criticism from the French, removed all constraints on the debate when he published an unfortunate article advising the French to reconcile themselves to the loss of the provinces for the simple reason that they lacked the military power to retake them.[22] The article, which was widely reprinted in the French press, outraged the French peace movement. Gaston Moch, one of the leading French pacifists, who was also an Alsatian Jew, led the French counterattack, calling for debate of the issue at a Universal Peace Congress, a plebiscite in the provinces, and the expulsion of Wirth from the peace movement.[23] Bertha von Suttner and the International Peace Bureau were appalled at the tone of the recriminations, but not even their mediation could bring an

[20] *Proceedings of [II] Universal Peace Congress*, p. 19.

[21] Fried, *Elsass-Lothringen und der Friede* (Leipzig, 1895); Suttner, "Aphoristisches zu dem Thema: 'Elsass-Lothringen und die Friedensbewegung,'" DWN, IV (1895), 161.

[22] MFK, II (March 1895); BIP (vB6), Wirth to Ducommun, Frankfurt, 29 April/4 May 1894.

[23] NL Fried, Moch to Fried, 16 August 1896; BIP (vIA1b), Moch, "Revision du Traité de Francefort: La paix par la justice," May 1895; BIP (vIA1b), Émile Arnaud to Peace Bureau, March 1895; PD, VI (1896), 207-13.

end to the debate, which ceased, without resolution, only when Wirth died in 1897.[24]

At the turn of the century an uneasy truce prevailed among the proponents of two hopelessly incompatible viewpoints. Citing their slogan, *"La paix par le droit,"* French pacifists argued that peace could only come with the triumph of justice in international affairs—specifically, the retrocession of Alsace-Lorraine. The Germans replied by inverting the French slogan, insisting that the reign of justice would perforce await the establishment of a durable peace, which in turn required general acceptance of the *status quo* in Europe. But despite the suggestion of French pacifists that the issue might appropriately be discussed at the Hague conference in 1899, the problem of the provinces remained more or less dormant until 1903, when the Franco-German antagonism erupted in the most vituperative exchange of the whole prewar period.[25]

Heinrich Molenaar was one of the well-meaning eccentrics who, like Eduard Löwenthal and Moritz von Egidy, operated on the periphery of the German peace movement. A teacher of French in a *Gymnasium* in Munich, he has the distinction of being the "only active disciple" of August Comte whom Professor Simon could unearth in Germany.[26] His devotion to Comte's philosophy led him first into the *Münchner Freidenker-Vereinigung*, but he soon fell out with its leaders and founded his own group, the *Deutsche Positivistische Vereinigung*, under whose aegis he published a series of newsletters about the practical application

[24] DWN, IV (1895), 101; DWN, V (1896), 89–99, 100–104, 315.

[25] PD, VIII (1898), 232; cf. Liedtke, "Die Entwicklung des Pazifismus," pp. 49–51, 86; Fried, "Die Haager Konferenz und Elsass-Lothringen," FW, I (1899), 81–84; AA, Eur. Gen. 37 number 1, Bd. 2, A10537 (ACP 102), Derenthall to William II, Berlin, 13 September 1898.

[26] Simon, *European Positivism*, pp. 253–55. On the Molenaar episode see Wild, *Baron d'Estournelles de Constant*, pp. 197–202.

of Positivism.[27] Most of his acquaintances regarded him as a harmless idealist, however, and he would no doubt have attracted little attention had he not tried to apply Comte's teachings to international politics.[28]

Early in 1903 Molenaar founded the *Deutsch-französische Liga* to promote what Comte had foreseen as a *République occidentale*.[29] In the long run Molenaar envisaged an international alliance for the exploitation of nature; in the short run he was alarmed by an apparent Anglo-American plot to exploit European disunity and dominate the world. In order both to resist this plot and to lay the foundation for a republic of civilized nations, he called for a Franco-German alliance. To this end, he proposed what seemed to be an eminently reasonable solution to the one divisive issue between the two countries: in exchange for Luxemburg or a French colony (preferably in the Middle East), the Germans would return to France those areas in Lorraine where French was the predominant language.[30] Despite the fact that the program of the *Deutsch-französische Liga* included themes designed to appeal to both the pacifists and the Pan-German League, Molenaar's organization never had more than sixty members, and Molenaar himself was the only one who was active.[31] In France, on

[27] StOb, 24 a1 87/4097, Georg Pfretzscher to Königliche Polizeidirektion München, Munich, 20 November 1903.

[28] StOb, AR 3198/1018, Königliche Polizeidirektion München to Pourtalès, Munich, 14 May 1903.

[29] Molenaar, "August Comte et la paix," PD, XII (1902), 293–97.

[30] Molenaar, "Die Notwendigkeit der Annäherung Deutschlands und Frankreichs," *Mitteilungen über die deutsch-französische Liga,* number 3/4 (1905), pp. 33–64; Molenaar, *Metz und Strassburg: Die natürliche Lösung der elsass-lothringischen Frage* (Weissenburg a. S., n.d.).

[31] Molenaar advertised one of his lectures with the slogan: "The Pan-German League, the pacifists, and the Franco-German League—resolution of the points of disagreement." StOb, AR 3198/1018, Molenaar to Königliche Polizeidirektion München, Munich, 5 January 1905; NL Fried, Richter to Fried, Pforzheim, 20 July 1903; [Mole-

the other hand, the founding of the *Deutsch-französische Liga* attracted a great deal of attention both in parliament and the press. D'Estournelles de Constant had been in close contact with Molenaar and took him very seriously; he announced the establishment of the league in a widely reprinted letter to *Le Temps* and promoted interest in the organization among his colleagues in the Chamber of Deputies.[32] Of the major political figures whom d'Estournelles approached, only Clemenceau accurately perceived the significance of Molenaar's venture, which he dismissed as a *"plaisanterie munichoise."*[33] While the *Deutsch-französische Liga* encouraged some gullible Frenchmen, it thoroughly alarmed the German pacifists, who foresaw that it could only have unfortunate consequences. Fried quickly condemned the league, which, he pointed out, was "offering the pack of chauvinist hounds everywhere an object for attack."[34] Richter also pleaded with Molenaar to be quiet, but Molenaar, who continued to receive moral support from France, persisted in his agitation.[35]

Tensions were already high when, in September 1903, the Universal Peace Congress convened in Rouen. On the second day, when the committee on current affairs met, Umfrid found himself the only German among a hostile crowd of French pacifists and their friends, who had followed Molenaar's activities closely and were determined to bring up the issue of Alsace-Lorraine before the plenary

---

naar] "Die deutsch-französische Liga–Offener Brief an Herrn Alfred H. Fried in Berlin [*sic*]," Munich, 22 December 1903.

[32] StOb, AR 3198/1018, Abschrift aus einer Mitteilung des Vorstandes der Zentralpolizeistelle im Ministerium für Elsass-Lothringen in Strassburg von 9 Juli 1903; PD, XIII (1903), 230–32; NL Fried, Molenaar to Fried, Munich, 18 April 1903; Wild, *Baron d'Estournelles de Constant*, pp. 198–200.

[33] *Ibid.*, p. 202, n. 84.

[34] "Eine deutsch-französische Liga," FW, v (1903), 58–59.

[35] NL Fried, Richter to Fried, Pforzheim, 12 May, 20 July 1903.

session of the congress.[36] Attacked from all sides in a language he did not understand, Umfrid finally succeeded in replacing the French motion to consider the issue with an innocuous resolution that postponed debate until the next congress and called upon the International Peace Bureau to study the whole problem.[37]

Umfrid won a tactical victory in Rouen, but the Franco-German debate had begun anew in public. In November 1903 the Frenchman Alphonse Jouet published a bitter article in the leading French pacifist journal in which he condemned the "brutal" German empire and called for the return of both provinces in exchange for a colony.[38] Molenaar joined the French in attacking the German pacifists, even taking his case to the nationalist *Münchner Neueste Nachrichten*.[39] In April 1904 the French peace societies officially called for a plebiscite in the provinces, resolving that the Treaty of Frankfurt was a violation of justice and that Frenchmen were morally obligated to seek retribution.[40] This resolution drew the intemperate rejoinder from Umfrid, "As if our emperor would not sooner wage ten wars than let those jewels be broken from his crown by a plebiscite."[41] Indeed, as the debate raged on, Umfrid emerged as the heir to Wirth's impetuosity in dealing with the French. Determined to have done with the issue by establishing a German moral claim to the provinces, he pointed out that the annexation of Alsace-Lorraine had taken place at a time

[36] FB, IV (1903), 140, 146.

[37] *Bulletin du XII⁰ Congrès universel*, pp. 119–20; FB, IV (1903), 146–47, 151.

[38] Jouet, "La question d'Alsace-Lorraine et le XIIme Congrès de la paix," PD, XIII (1903), 417–25.

[39] NL Fried, Molenaar to Fried, Munich, 11 December 1903; FB, V (1904), 1–6; FW, V (1903), 164–65, 180–85; FW, VI (1904), 6–7, 52–53, 79; PD, XIV (1904), 49–54, 63–64.

[40] *Déclaration de la Délégation permanente des sociétés de la paix sur l'attitude du parti pacifique dans la question d'Alsace-Lorraine. Deuxième Congrès national de la paix, Nîmes, 7–10 avril 1904* (Paris, 1904), pp. 9–15; FB, V (1904), 76.

[41] FB, V (1904), 78.

when there was no recognized international law to be violated and, therefore, that it was fatuous to claim that the Treaty of Frankfurt was unjust; removed from the realm of moral considerations, German possession of the provinces was justified in Umfrid's eyes by historical necessity.[42] He also noted that if the French had won the war of 1870, they would doubtlessly have done something similar.[43] The position officially adopted by the German Peace Society was more moderate, but it too urged an end to all debate on the issue.[44]

Fortunately, the Universal Peace Congress met in Boston in 1904, and few French or German pacifists could afford to attend. There the delegates decided to devote another year to studying the problem and appointed a commission to report to the next congress, which was to meet in Lucerne. While the tone of the debate became more subdued, the problem remained the focus of great concern, and tensions were very high when, in September 1905, the pacifists congregated in Lucerne. The commission appointed in Boston submitted its report, which consisted of a survey of proposals it had received but contained no explicit recommendations.[45] The scene in the committee on current affairs again became heated when Jouet and Molenaar (who had arrived in Lucerne with a Dutch mandate) attempted to push through a resolution repudiating the German position. Finally, through the mediation of the Belgian delegate Henri La Fontaine, the committee agreed to submit a compromise resolution to the plenary session of the congress.

[42] NL Fried, Umfrid to Fried, Stuttgart, 29 January 1904; FB, v (1904), 1-2; cf. Umfrid, *Friede auf Erden*, p. 83.

[43] FB, v (1904), 6; cf. VF, XIII (1912), 131; PM, II (1913), 35-36.

[44] BIP (vA1b), Mémoire approuvé par la Société allemande de la paix sur la question du rapprochement franco-allemand dans l'assemblée de ses délégués réunié à Cassel le 26 mars 1904 (Pforzheim, 1904).

[45] BIP (viA1b), Rapport sur un rapprochement franco-allemand (Berne, 1905); Propositons soumises au XIVe Congrès universel de la paix par la commission d'étude pour le rapprochement franco-allemand (9 May 1905).

Largely the work of Ludwig Quidde, the resolution involved major concessions on both sides. Acknowledging the German position, it called for the postponement of a final solution of the problem until the establishment of a system of international justice; but it also stated explicitly that the "results of former conquests" would then be subject to revision according to the principles of justice "if the injustice and violence of these results are still strongly felt."[46] At the plenary session Quidde pleaded with the Germans to accept the compromise, after which Frédéric Passy, the dean of the French pacifists, urged his colleagues to do the same. Then, in a dramatic gesture in front of all the delegates, Quidde and Passy extended hands to one another, symbolizing their desire to end the antagonism. The congress thereupon approved the compromise resoultion by acclamation.[47]

Quidde later recalled the emotional scene in Lucerne as one of the proudest moments in his life, but many in the German delegation had approved the resolution only with great misgiving.[48] Their worst fears were confirmed immediately after the congress, when an article, first published in the *Neue Züricher Zeitung* (ordinarily a friend of the peace movement), made the rounds of the German press, castigating the German pacifists for having allowed the issue to be debated at all, and for then approving a resolution that seemed to concede the legitimacy of the French claim to the provinces.[49] Umfrid in particular returned from Lucerne with second thoughts and tried to have the resolution repudiated, threatening his own resignation

[46] *Bulletin officiel du XIVe Congrès universel de la paix tenu à Lucerne du 19 au 23 septembre 1905* (Berne, 1905), p. 38.

[47] *Ibid.*, pp. 37–40; FW, VII (1905), 191–92; FB, VI (1905), 113–14; Quidde, "Meine letzte Begegnung mit Frédéric Passy," FW, XXXVIII (1938), 93–95.

[48] NL L. Quidde, Quidde, "Aus den Erinnerungen eines alten Pazifisten."

[49] *Ibid.*; PD, XVI (1906), 207–209.

should the peace society ratify it.[50] In October 1905 the *Landesverein Württemberg*, which was large enough to speak for the whole peace society, did endorse the resolution, but in a manner equivocal enough to satisfy Umfrid and other reluctant German pacifists. According to the official German interpretation, "The resolution limits the retroactive application of the . . . [principles] of justice expressly to the future, when the system of justice advocated by the pacifists will be firmly established; the resolution consequently denies that this can be done in connection with the contemporary situation [*gegenwärtige Verhältnisse*]."[51] With this, the Germans emasculated all the concessions Quidde had made in Lucerne, for they could contend that the issue of Alsace-Lorraine, since it was an aspect of the "contemporary situation," could not under any circumstances be scrutinized in the light of *Rechtsnormen*; such scrutiny would be limited to conquests made after the triumph of a system of justice. This was, of course, absurd, for in the world the pacifists envisaged conquest was presumably to have no place.

Nonetheless, the Lucerne congress and its aftermath did bring an end to the most intense phase of the Franco-German dispute. The French pacifists viewed the Lucerne resolution as vindication of their position and looked aside as the Germans watered it down to the point where they could live with it. Since everyone was anxious to avoid further controversy, Heinrich Molenaar was no longer in a position to cause much trouble. Shortly after the Lucerene congress he moved to Bayreuth, where he continued to promote assorted progressive causes, including an international insurance fund, the antivaccination crusade, and an international language he contrived as an alternative to Esperanto.

In succeeding years the dialogue became more construc-

---

[50] NL Fried, Umfrid to Fried, Stuttgart, 13 October 1905; Max Hoeltzel to Fried, Stuttgart, 15 October 1905.

[51] FB, VI (1905), 130.

tive, as pacifists in both France and Germany found some areas in which they could agree. After Lucerne all admitted that the solution of the problem would have to await establishment of a *Rechtssystem*, and all pacifists, including the Germans, supported full autonomy for Alsace-Lorraine within the German empire as an interim compromise.[52] But tensions remained just beneath the surface. The revival of interest in Alsace-Lorraine in 1911, which accompanied the second Moroccan crisis and the promulgation of a constitution for the *Reichsländer*, threatened once more to split the peace movement.[53] The French again denounced the injustice of German rule and Umfrid rushed to the defense of the German position.[54] It seemed likely that the stormy scenes in Rouen in 1903 would be repeated when, in September 1912, delegates to the Universal Peace Congress convened in Geneva. When the issue of Alsace-Lorraine arose in the committee on current affairs, Quidde was able to avert a crisis with another compromise resolution that reaffirmed the Lucerne resolution and called for full autonomy for the provinces.[55] Thereafter the debate quieted down again. It was in part an indication of how weary pacifists in both countries had become that the Zabern incident in late 1913 did not bring about a renewal of the conflict; this was also because the German pacifists condemned the

[52] NL Wehberg (59a), Fried to Wehberg, Vienna, 30 October, 6 November, 21 November 1912; cf. FW, xxv (1925), 49; Wild, *Baron d'Estournelles de Constant*, p. 197; Umfrid, "Los von Berlin," FB, vi (1905), 8; Albert Gobat, "An Autonomous Alsace-Lorraine the Necessary Preliminary to Franco-German Rapprochement," PM, iii (1914), 7–10.

[53] See Ziebura, *Die deutsche Frage*, p. 23.

[54] D'Estournelles de Constant, "Das Mittel gegen den bewaffneten Frieden," FW, xiii (1911), 68; PD, xxii (1912), 753; NL Fried, Umfrid to Fried, Stuttgart, 11 April 1911; Umfrid, "Die Aussöhnung zwischen Deutschland und Frankreich," FW, xiii (1911), 102–104.

[55] NL M. Quidde (354/59), L. Quidde to M. Quidde, Geneva, 20, 22 September 1912; *Bulletin officiel du XIXᵉ Congrès universel de la paix tenu à Genève du 22 au 28 Septembre 1912* (Berne, n.d.), pp. 128–29; FW, xiv (1912), 419–20.

German government's handling of the incident no less than did the French.[56]

Any agreement between French and German pacifists on the problem of Alsace-Lorraine could only be provisional, for in view of the categories in which the peace movement analyzed international politics, the conflict was basically insoluble; each side held the claims of the other to be immoral, and neither was prepared to sacrifice any essential points of its own position. The pacifists themselves were reluctant to admit the insolubility of the problem and created several committees in an attempt to promote a Franco-German *rapprochement*. The experience of these organizations demonstrated, however, that it was impossible to do more than reduce the stridency of the debate.

In an effort to capitalize on the good will created by the Lucerne congress, the pacifists set up a "Permanent Committee for Franco-German Conciliation" (*Ständiges Comitee für deutsch-französische Verständigung*), composed of leaders of the peace movement in both countries. They rapidly forgot about the committee, however, until the recurrence of trouble in 1911/12 prompted them to reconstitute it.[57] Quidde, who among the German pacifists was the most consistent advocate of an understanding with the French, thereupon began to recruit notables for a new "Franco-German League" to promote better relations by granting genuine autonomy for Alsace-Lorraine.[58] A French section was founded in May 1913. By September the German organizers had found some three hundred persons who were willing to join, most of whom were familiar faces from the German Peace Society or *Verband für internationale*

---

[56] VF, xv (1914), 1, 5–6; PD, xxiii (1913), 753–54; PD, xxiv (1914), 48–53.

[57] BIP (viK8), Comité d'entente franco-allemand; FW, vii (1905), 192; CBM, xiii (1908), 41.

[58] *Bulletin officiel du XIXe Congrès universel*, pp. 128–31; VF, xiv (1913), 19–20. Quidde's group was in no way related to Molenaar's earlier league, though they went by the same name.

Verständigung—people such as Haeckel, Umfrid, Neufville, Adolf Richter, Gothein, Lamprecht, Liszt, Maurenbrecher, Müller-Meiningen, Piloty, and Schücking.[59] Many others whom Quidde approached, including Brentano, Schönaich-Carolath, Haussmann, and Eickhoff, refused to join or joined only with reservations. Some refused to sign the league's manifesto, which included the objectionable statement that "It is impossible for the French to renounce the just claim of every people to self-determination."[60] When the war broke out, the Franco-German League, like its predecessor, existed on paper only.[61]

More successful than the committees in which pacifists played the leading role was the Franco-German Reconciliation Committee (*Deutsch-französisches Annäherungskomitee*), which was founded in 1908 in order to promote a *rapprochement* between the two countries "in the areas of politics, economics, science, art, and sport."[62] Fried was so impressed by the new organization that he suggested that the pacifists dissolve their own Franco-German committee and join forces with it.[63] But despite the presence on the committee of men whom the pacifists respected, such as Zorn, Eickhoff, and Ludwig Fulda, both the composition of the new group and the character of its leadership suggested that it was a dubious ally. The committee was the creation

[59] NL Haussmann (1), Deutsch-Französische Liga, Deutsche Abteilung, Beitrittserklärungen bis zum 25. September 1913.

[60] NL Brentano (49), Brentano to Quidde, Munich, 21 May 1913; NL Haussmann (4), Quidde to Haussmann, Ammerland, 30 June 1913; NL M. Quidde (355/59), L. Quidde to M. Quidde, Bad Kreuth, 28 May 1913; VF, XIV (1913), 19–20.

[61] The organization did, however, bring together many of the people who emerged during the war as leaders of the German peace movement, including Anita Augspurg, Gertrud Bäumer, Martin Barkowsky, and Kurt von Tepper-Laski: cf. Lehmann-Russbüldt, *Der Kampf der deutschen Liga für Menschenrechte*, pp. 9–12; Deak, *Left-Wing Intellectuals*, p. 67.

[62] AA, Deutschland 141 number 8a, Bd. 2, A3482, Carl René to Schoen, Berlin, 6 March 1908.

[63] "Zur deutsch-französischen Annäherung," FW, X (1908), 86.

of Carl René, whose background was as shady as it was cosmopolitan. Of French ancestry, he held both German and Hungarian citizenship, was well known in official circles in St. Petersburg and Paris, and served as consul both for the Republic of Guatemala in Stettin and for Paraguay in Budapest. Based in Stettin, where he operated a firm that made pianos, he utilized his many contacts to buy into a consortium that invested in railway construction in the Cameroons. René was a man of great resourcefulness, whose techniques for serving his business interests ranged from embezzlement to founding the Franco-German Reconciliation Committee with an eye to its impact on the extension of his railroad into the French Congo.[64] Nor were the motives of other members of the committee above suspicion. In addition to René's close friend Hermann Paasche, who was no friend of the peace movement, and Otto von Manteuffel, the nominal president of the committee, the most promiment members were representatives of big industrial interests—men not noted for their progressive social or political views. Included were Conrad von Schubert and Bogdan von Hutten-Czapski of the Stumm concern, Victor von Ratibor, C. A. von Martius, Rudolf Koch, Emil Jacob, and Paul von Roëll.[65] The committee had ties to the foreign office, which made possible its only significant achievement.[66] In April 1909 it sponsored a tour by d'Estournelles de Constant to Berlin, where he spoke in the *Herrenhaus* on the subject of "Franco-German Conciliation as a Precondition for World Peace." At the urging of the committee, four hun-

[64] AA, Deutschland 141 number 8a, Bd. 2, A 14496 (ACP 415), Miquel to Bülow, St. Petersburg, 21 August 1906; Wild, *Baron d'Estournelles de Constant*, pp. 327-28.

[65] AA, Deutschland 141 number 8a, Bd. 2, A3482, René to Schoen, Berlin, 6 March 1908; Charles René, "Les essais de rapprochement franco-allemand avant la guerre et le rôle de Clemenceau," *L'Europe Nouvelle*, number 636 (19 April 1930), pp. 631-33; FW, x (1908), 73.

[66] AA, Deutschland 141 number 8a, Bd. 2, zu A6782, Schoen Notiz, 3 May 1908. Schoen complained of being "flooded with letters and other material" from René.

dred business and political leaders attended the lecture, and it was covered extensively in the press. Afterwards both Bülow and the German foreign secretary, Wilhelm von Schoen, held cordial interviews with the visiting Frenchman.[67] René's committee undertook no subsequent activity of any importance, apart from an abortive attempt on René's initiative (and without the knowledge of the foreign office) to begin negotiations with the French government "on the basis of extensive autonomy for Alsace-Lorraine."[68] Other members of the committee evidently did not know of his solicitude for the autonomy of the provinces either. Early in 1914 Paasche, who probably spoke for many of the others, warned that "Alsace-Lorraine is on the way to becoming French again. . . . This internal peril, which together with ever-growing individualist tendencies, would ultimately threaten the integrity of the German empire, must be combated."[69]

On 31 May 1914 Quidde spoke in Lyon before the national congress of the French peace society, the *Association de la paix par le droit*. On the subject of Alsace-Lorraine, he noted progress toward full autonomy but cautioned the French not to interfere: "It would be a dangerous illusion for people in France to think that the improvement of conditions in Alsace-Lorraine could be a prerequisite of Franco-German conciliation; this improvement will rather be one of the most certain results of conciliation."[70] The fact that the French pacifists applauded Quidde's remarks was a hopeful sign that the French and German pacifists were

[67] Wild, *Baron d'Estournelles de Constant*, pp. 328–37; Bülow, *Memoirs*, II, 562–63.

[68] AA, Deutschland 141 number 8a, A3494, René to Kiderlen-Wächter, Stettin, 21 February 1912; NL Fried, René to Fried, Gravenhage, 28 August 1913; GP, XXXI, 381–82, n.

[69] PM, III (1914), 124.

[70] PD, XXIV (1914), 389–91; FW, XXXVIII (1938), 38, 66; BA, R 45 III/62, Quidde, "Im Kampf gegen Verleumdung: Eine Erklärung" (16 October 1914); NL L. Quidde, Quidde, "Der deutsche Pazifismus während des Weltkrieges," pp. 5–7.

reaching a viable agreement on a problem that had poisoned relations between them. Such an agreement, if it was in fact emerging, was more the product of the pacifists' fatigue over the issue than the work of the various shortlived Franco-German friendship committees, which, if honest, quickly found themselves debilitated by the contradictions inherent in the rival positions.[71] In any event, the conflict with the French over Alsace-Lorraine had had important effects on the German peace movement's approach to other international problems.

Colonialism and Conciliation with England

The dispute over Alsace-Lorraine forced the German pacifists to insist that the *status quo* in Europe was inviolable and that the *Rechtsnormen* of the future recognize and sanction it. This was a difficult position to defend. Apart from the criticism it drew from the French, it seemed to deny the dynamism of international relations by endowing the map as it was then drawn with eternal validity. But the German pacifists did not think that relations among nations could be frozen at any point in time; they merely thought that all changes would take place outside Europe. As Otto Umfrid, the German Peace Society's spokesman on colonial affairs and self-styled expert on the subject, wrote in 1903:

> Everything on earth is in a state of flux. Some nations are on the rise, and others are in decline. There are countries whose populations are increasing in geometric proportion and others whose population seems to have reached a

[71] In 1912 another short-lived committee was founded by the Frenchman Jacques Grand-Carteret and a retired railway official in Stuttgart, Adolf Schleicher. The German members of this *Comité de rapprochement intellectuel franco-allemand* included Fried, Suttner, Max Liebermann, Haeckel, Fulda, Gerhart and Carl Hauptmann, Eduard Bernstein, Richard Dehmel, Ludwig Stein, Stefan Zweig, and Walther Rathenau: BIP (viK8), Le Comité de rapprochement intellectuel franco-allemand; PD, xxii (1912), 472–73; cf. FW, x (1908), 85–86.

standstill, or even entered a decline. It goes without saying that the overflow from the densely populated countries will spill over into the broad expanses of the sparsely populated areas; and those dynamic nations, which by emigration and colonization are bringing the blood of life to other stagnating areas for the first time, will naturally want in the course of time to exercise political influence in the areas their comrades have built up. But by no means can one proceed from these basic premises to advocate a policy of brutal conquest.[72]

This assertion, which but for the last sentence might have come from the Pan-German League, well reflected both the pacifists' understanding of the dynamics of international relations and the problematic conclusions they drew from it. In their analysis, the primary index of a nation's power and vitality, the most important variable in international relations, was population growth. They reasoned further that the pressure of population growth, which had occasioned wars in the past, was a legitimate reason for a country to claim more territory. In order to prevent this pressure from again causing a war, outlets had to be found where densely populated nations might settle their excess population. And since they ruled out any territorial changes in Europe, the German pacifists looked to Latin America, Asia, and Africa. They argued that a system of international justice would provide for the moral right of densely populated nations to expand peacefully and establish colonies in sparsely settled areas outside Europe.[73] To the objection that colonies could

[72] Umfrid, "Unkriegerische Landerwerbungen," FB, IV (1903), 93. For other statements on the colonial problem see: Umfrid, "Kolonisation und Auswanderung," FB, IX (1908), 117–21, 129–32; Der deutsche Friedenskongress in Jena, 1908 (n.p., 1908), pp. 38–43; R. L. Berendsohn, "Kolonialpolitik und Friedensbewegung," FB, VII (1906), 79; NL Wehberg (88), Umfrid to Wehberg, Stuttgart, 10 June 1913.

[73] Umfrid, "Die Grenzen des Schiedsgerichtsgedankens," DWN, VII (1898), 339–44, 390–94; Umfrid, Anti-Treitschke, p. 4; VF, XIII (1912), 61.

only be acquired by force, they replied that once morality governed international relations, it would be possible to negotiate an international treaty of population resettlement (*Niederlassungsvertrag*), which would adjust colonial holdings to conform to the relative population densities of European countries.[74]

The logic of the pacifists' position on the European *status quo* and their emphasis on the demographic foundations of international political change compelled them to endorse colonial expansion in principle; there was simply no other way to divert from Europe the tension that inevitably accompanied transformations in the pattern of population density.[75] But they approved of colonialism for other reasons as well. Since they believed that their own mission was to educate the unenlightened, the pacifists were attracted to arguments that justified colonial expansion in terms of bringing the blessings of civilization to the savages. They were particularly interested in ridding backward areas of warfare and thus preparing them for eventual inclusion in the international political community.[76] Appeals to economic considerations to justify colonial acquisitions the pacifists found less convincing; they believed that colonies cost more than they brought in and that the commercial interests of all states would best be served by an international agreement to open all colonial areas to unrestricted trade.[77] Finally, the German pacifists endorsed colonial activity be-

[74] FB, ix (1908), 76; Umfrid, *Europa den Europäern*, pp. 68–69.

[75] The resolution opposing the *Wehrvorlage*, which leaders of the peace society submitted in 1913, read in part: "an effort should be made to conclude an international agreement, in which states mutually guarantee their possessions and make overseas expansion possible in case of emergency." Quoted in Wehberg, *Internationale Beschränkung*, pp. 411–12.

[76] Kohler, "Die Friedensbewegung und das Völkerrecht," pp. 136–37; HB (1), 24; FB, vii (1906), 97; FB, viii (1907), 45; VF, xiv (1913), 55.

[77] Umfrid, "Deutsch-englische Interessensphäre," FW, xiv (1912), 328; FB, ix (1908), 129–30.

cause they believed that Germany had been sold short in the race for colonies and that the country had, by virtue of its growing population density, a moral claim to more.[78] Thus, while the pacifists could not emphasize strongly enough the sanctity of the *status quo* in Europe, they were nearly as emphatic in pointing out the injustice of the colonial *status quo*. They anticipated that the *Rechtssystem* of the future would bring about a more equitable distribution of colonies and award Germany with areas for peaceful settlement, most appropriately, Umfrid believed, in eastern Brazil, Asia Minor, and the Middle East.[79]

This favorable orientation toward German colonialism made the peace society a consistent supporter of the German foreign office during disputes that involved colonial issues, notably in the two Moroccan crises. In both instances the pacifists were concerned chiefly with finding a peaceful settlement, but they concluded that justice resided with Germany. In the first crisis they admitted that the French were justified in claiming a special interest in Morocco; but under Delcassé, whom the German pacifists called an "ambitious adventurer," French policy had clearly exceeded the bounds of morality in trying to monopolize Moroccan commerce and reduce the country to the status of a colony.[80] By defending free trade and the sovereignty of the Moroccan sultan, the German government was, in the pacifists' opinion, acting as the champion of justice and "the international principle."[81] Believing that arbitration would be more likely than an international conference to produce a settlement

[78] *Der Friedenskongress in Jena*, pp. 42–43; cf. Umfrid, "Kolonisation und Expansionspolitik," FB, VIII (1907), 52–56; FB, VII (1906), 79.

[79] FB, IX (1908), 118; FB, VIII (1907), 55; VF, XV (1914), 13; Umfrid, "Die Zukunft der Türkei," in *Bismarcks Gedanken und Erinnerungen*, pp. 36–37.

[80] Umfrid, "Die marokkanische Frage," FB, VI (1905), 49–50; FW, VIII (1906), 56–57; CBM, XI (1906), 25–26, 37. Pacifists in France likewise defended the position of their government as just: Liedtke, "Die Entwicklung des Pazifismus," pp. 393–94.

[81] FB, VI (1905), 50, 79; FW, VIII (1906), 56; FB, IX (1908), 78.

that acknowledged the justice of the German position, the pacifists petitioned Bülow to submit the dispute to the Hague court.[82] Despite Bülow's failure to follow their advice, they rejoiced when the Algeciras conference settled the dispute and hailed the peaceful *dénouement* of the crisis as a victory for the "pacifistically influenced *Zeitgeist*."[83] When Morocco again became the focal point of an international crisis in 1911, the German pacifists again rallied to the support of German policy, though not with the assurance they had displayed in 1905. Umfrid admitted that all the powers seemed to be guided more by profit and power than by justice, and he regretted that the German government had not made use of its most defensible argument, population growth, to justify its interest in North Africa.[84] Other pacifists alluded to Germany's defense of the open door in Morocco as evidence of the justice of the country's foreign policy.[85]

The pacifists reacted with alarm to both Moroccan crises, not only because of the threat to European peace. Almost as disturbing was the fact that despite its constant advocacy of international justice, Germany was becoming diplomatically isolated. The only way the pacifists could explain this anomaly was to cite the tactless methods with which German statesmen were trying to promote their just cause. Thus the pacifists' commentary, which was invariably favorable to the general thrust of German foreign policy, was quite critical of the country's diplomatic style. Surveying the European situation in the aftermath of the second Moroccan crisis, Umfrid touched upon the problem: "We have not managed to make moral conquests; we have underestimated the imponderables in politics, and since we have not

[82] FB, VII (1906), 34; CBM, XI (1906), 29-30.
[83] FB, VII (1906), 49; CBM, XI (1906), 10 July annex; HB (2), II, 164.
[84] Umfrid, "Aktive Politik," VF, XII (1911), 57-58; FW, XIII (1911), 222.
[85] Ernst Lang, "Schiedsgerichtliche Möglichkeiten," VF, XII (1911), 86-87; VF, XII (1911), 71; VF, XIII (1912), 130-31.

understood how to make any friends, our great armaments appear more threatening than in the case of other great powers. As paradoxical as it may sound, our power is an obstacle to the development of our power."[86] If a critical note appeared in the pacifists' remarks on the Moroccan crises, it was the complaint that German diplomats had not been very adroit in arguing a good case; the dispatch of the *Panther* to Agadir, for instance, was ill-advised and obscured the fact that German interests would have been much better served by peaceful negotiations.[87] The pacifists also believed that the German government's rejection of the peace movement and its goals was not only morally reprehensible, but a tactical mistake. German policy at The Hague, the country's refusal to negotiate general treaties of arbitration, and the plight of German pacifists at home were all contributing to Germany's diplomatic isolation.[88] "We are isolating ourselves," Walther Schücking wrote in 1908, "for the people of poets and thinkers has no understanding for the great idea of the future—the organization of the world."[89]

The pacifists accepted fatalistically certain aspects of Germany's growing isolation. Many of them concluded that the problem of Alsace-Lorraine might well be insoluble, and they were not surprised or overly disturbed to find France among the emerging anti-German *entente*. Much more alarming was the increasing antagonism between Germany and England; for one of the results of the dispute with the French over Alsace-Lorraine had been to make the German pacifists inveterate Anglophiles. To rationalize

[86] Umfrid, "Europäisches Unbehagen," VF, XIII (1912), 2.

[87] FW, VII (1905), 127–28; VF, XIII (1912), 16.

[88] Umfrid, "Die Schiedsgerichtsverträge und Deutschlands Isolierung," FB, V (1904), 78–79; C. Simon, "Die Rückständigkeit der deutschen Reichsregierung und des deutschen Reichstages," VF, XI (1910), 35; FB, VII (1906), 79; FW, VII (1905), 127–28; FW, XI (1909), 128, 183; VF, XI (1910), 8, 97.

[89] Quoted in FW, X (1908), 102.

their views they cited a close racial tie and commercial interdependence between the two countries.[90] They also admired British democracy, a political tradition devoid of revolution, and the British peace movement, which by common agreement was the strongest in Europe.[91] Like the churchmen in the Associated Councils of Churches, the German pacifists were convinced that the special community of interests between the two countries could become the foundation for the international organization of the future. They were not impressed by the possibility that German colonial pretensions, which they themselves shared, might become the source of a conflict with England as insoluble as the dispute with the French over Alsace-Lorraine. Instead they insisted that, unlike the problem with the French, all controversies with England were of secondary significance.[92]

In the pacifists' estimation, the basic cause of all Anglo-German tension was the German navy. They did not, however, regard this as a symptom of any fundamental conflict of interest, but rather a remediable tactical error on Germany's part. Nowhere, indeed, was the pacifists' criticism of the ineptitude of German statecraft more pronounced than on the subject of the navy, which they held to be of questionable military value, financially indefensible, and a grave political liability.[93] They viewed the British claim to naval supremacy as just, because of the country's location and defense needs. Thus, they called on their own country to stop contesting this supremacy, and to negotiate an

[90] FB, VII (1906), 76; FB, IX (1908), 59; VF, XI (1910), 62–63; FW, XIV (1912), 327.

[91] A. Bürk, "Die tieferen Gründe der englischen Friedensliebe," VF, XIII (1912), 71; VF, XI (1910), 57; FB, IV (1903), 140; FW, XI (1909), 188.

[92] NL Wehberg (59a), Fried to Wehberg, Vienna, 21 November 1912; cf. FW, XXV (1925), 49.

[93] Umfrid, "Flottenschwärmerei und Erfahrungen im ostasiatischen Seekriege," FB, VI (1905), 73–75; FB, VI (1905), 117–18; FB, VII (1906), 74; VF, XI (1910), 13–15; VF, XII (1911), 61–62.

agreement with England exchanging a halt in German naval construction for British support for Germany's just claim to colonial expansion.[94] This, they believed, was an eminently feasible arrangement because the English, unlike the French, were sincerely committed to peace and justice.

The German pacifists did not hesitate to criticize aspects of English policy, but on the whole they actively defended it. The German Peace Society did, to be sure, play a role in the protests against the Boer War in Germany, and in fact capitalized on them to attract new members. But when, in the course of these protests, they found themselves in the unlikely company of nationalists, who were more interested in embarrassing the English than in speaking out against the war, the pacifists anounced that they wanted not to antagonize England, but rather to give expression to the "outraged conscience of an international system of justice."[95] When the deterioration of Anglo-German relations became more acute after 1904, the alarmed pacifists began a campaign to defend British policy in Germany, particularly the British proposals for a limitation of the naval race.

The preference of German pacifists for England was also reflected in the vitality of the committee they formed to work for Anglo-German friendship, which provided a contrast to the uninspiring records of the various Franco-German committees in which pacifists were active. In 1905, at the Universal Peace Congress in Lucerne, pacifists from Germany and England established the Anglo-German Conciliation Committee (*Deutsch-Englisches Verständigungs-*

[94] Richter, "Freundschaft zwischen England und Deutschland," FB, IX (1908), 142; Umfrid, "Rede zur deutsch-englischen Verständigung," VF, XIII (1912), 61–62; VF, XIII (1912), 3–4; PM, I (1912), 246.

[95] One committee organized to protest the war included Adolf Stroecker, Ernst Hasse, Max Hugo Liebermann von Sonnenberg— and Wilhelm Foerster: NL Fried, A. Schowalter to Fried, Munich, 16 February 1901. Foerster admitted that it was possible he was being used: NL Suttner (LsI5), Foerster to Suttner, 5 February 1900. See also HB (2), II, 149; Reuter, "Die falsche Taktik der Burenfreunde in Deutschland," FW, III (1901), 35; CBM, V (1900), 39, 52, 140.

komitee), which was founded on the conviction that "there is no rational basis of either an economic or political nature for unfriendly feelings between the two nations."[96] The crisis over Morocco later that year, which seemed to belie this confidence, prompted the branches of the committee in both countries to organize demonstrations of friendship. In Germany public meetings in Berlin, Munich, Stuttgart, Cologne, and Dresden drew a response that far exceeded the pacifists' expectations, and by 1907 over eight hundred persons had endorsed the appeal the committee had issued at its founding.[97] In the list of endorsements were some of the most socially and politically prominent people in the country, as well as a number of mayors and chambers of commerce.[98] The committee had originally been set up with headquarters in Stuttgart under the direction of two pacifists, Eduard de Neufville and Max Hoeltzel. The widespread interest in the undertaking made it necessary to recast the committee on a new basis in order to tone down the role of pacifists in it.[99] In June 1908 it was officially recon-

[96] HStASt, E 151c/II, Bü 238 (2), Deutsch-Englisches Verständigungskomitee, Aufruf.

[97] *Ibid.*; HStASt, E 151c/II, Bü 238 (5), Deutsch-Englisches Verständigungskomitee, Stuttgart, January 1907; NL Brentano (49), Quidde to Brentano, Bad Kreuth, 20 May 1913; NL Fried, Hoeltzel to Fried, Stuttgart, 5 December 1905. On these attempts to improve Anglo-German relations see Gerald Deckart, "Deutsch-englische Verständigung: Eine Darstellung der nichtoffiziellen Bemühungen um eine Wiederannäherung der beiden Länder zwischen 1905 und 1914" (Inaugural dissertation, Munich, 1967).

[98] HStASt, E 151c/II, Bü 238 (2), Deutsch-Englisches Verständigungskomitee. Included in the list were Theodor Barth, Hermann von Bernstorff, Lujo Brentano, Wilhelm Faber, Heinrich Flinsch, Ernst von Heydebrand und der Lasa, Robert Lucius von Ballhausen, Albrecht Mendelssohn-Bartholdy, Christian Meurer, Wilhelm von Pechmann, Karl Schrader, Adolf Stoecker, and an imposing array of nobility—Princes zu Erbach-Schöneberg, Carl zu Salm-Horstmar, Schönaich-Carolath, Emich zu Leiningen-Amorbach, and Immenhausen und Knyphausen.

[99] NL Fried, Neufville to Fried, Frankfurt a. M., 9 March 1910.

stituted in Berlin with Theodor von Holleben, the secretary of the *Deutsche Kolonialgesellschaft* and former German ambassador to Washington, as president. Neufville, who remained the driving force in the organization, was included in the executive, but was surrounded by safe people, such as Felix Dahn, Hans Delbrück, and Heinrich Wiegand, the director of *Norddeutscher Lloyd*.[100] Not all those who had endorsed the committee's appeal formally joined the group, but by 1911 it had a membership of over two hundred in Germany.[101]

Like the German Peace Society and *Verband für internationale Verständigung*, the Anglo-German committee conceived of itself as an agency of popular enlightenment and attempted to improve relations between the two countries through exchanges, public meetings, and a campaign of pro-English publicity. In 1911 it began to publish its own *Nachrichten*. The German government viewed the committee's work with interest and, if the number of its members from the Prussian *Herrenhaus* is an indication, mild approval.[102] The government's help figured in some of the committee's major activities. In 1906 Hoeltzel and Neufville arranged through the English branch of the committee for a visit to England by leading editors and journalists, most of whom were known not to think much of the peace movement.[103] The visit was a great success, and the following year the Germans, having been assured that the government viewed the undertaking "most benevolently," hosted

[100] HStASt, E 151c/II, Bü 238 (7), Deutsch-Englisches Verständigungskomitee, "An die verehrl. Mitglieder," 1 July 1908.

[101] NL Siegmund-Schultze (B IV d 4 c), Mitglieder-Verzeichnis des Deutsch-Englischen Verständigungskomitees pro 1911.

[102] NL Fried, Neufville to Fried, London, 23 March 1906. The foreign office refused, however, to give anything that might be construed as official endorsement to the committee: HStASt, E 151c/II, Bü 238 (2), Rundschreiben des k. Minist. der ausw. Angelegenheiten vom 17 Januar 1908, number 398.

[103] NL Fried, W. Hartmann to Fried, Stuttgart, 17 July 1906; cf. above, chapter 5, pp. 188–89, 191.

a return visit for English journalists, who were wined and dined by Bülow and other government officials.[104]

Late in 1911, in the aftermath of the Agadir crisis, the English branches of the Associated Councils of Churches and the Anglo-German Conciliation Committee, together with leaders of the British peace societies, suggested that an Anglo-German conference be organized to counteract the growing hostility between the two countries. Their proposal was enthusiastically received by the peace-oriented groups in Germany, which had themselves become very alarmed during the crisis. Indeed, so great was their concern over the possibility of war that they agreed to a project long advocated by the peace society but resisted by the other organizations. In the spring of 1912 representatives of the German Peace Society, the *Verband für internationale Verständigung*, the Anglo-German Conciliation Committee, and the German branch of the Associated Councils of Churches established a joint committee to promote an Anglo-German conciliation conference, to be held in the summer of 1912.[105] Led by Walter Lübke, the mayor of Bad Homburg, the joint committee began to enlist support among German political leaders. In the foreign office Kiderlen-Wächter and Wilhelm von Stumm gave encouragement to the committee, as did Bethmann Hollweg and Marschall von Bieberstein, who was now the German ambassador to England.[106] Neither their support nor several postponements of the conference, however, enabled the German organizers to find much support beyond the active-

104 NL Fried, Protokoll der Sitzung vom 17. Februar [1907] . . . um über den Gegenbesuch der englischen Journalisten in Deutschland zu beraten; Whyte, *Stead*, ii, 285–86.

105 NL Haussmann (1), Vorschläge betreffend die Konferenz in London, [Frankfurt] 12 May 1912; NL Siegmund-Schultze (B iv d 4 b), Lübke to Siegmund-Schultze, Homburg v.d. Höhe, 13 May 1912.

106 NL Siegmund-Schultze (B iv d 4 b), Spiecker to Baker, Berlin, 17 April 1912; Spiecker to Heinecken, Berlin, 29 May 1912; Lübke to Siegmund-Schultze, Homburg, 9 June 1912; *ibid.* (B iv d 4 c), Spiecker to Lübke, Berlin, 9 October 1912.

ly participating groups. The committee found that aside from a handful of Progressives, no one in the Reichstag was very interested in the conference.[107]

The conference finally convened in London between 30 October and 1 November 1912, attended by several hundred persons. Speakers from both countries touched upon various problems of Anglo-German conciliation, including colonial disputes, the intemperate tone of newspapers, and the issue of private property at sea in wartime.[108] The press in both England and Germany covered the conference extensively, and the delegates dispersed in the hope that they had cleared the air at least a little. But the conference had virtually no impact on relations between the two countries. Most of those who attended, including the prominent members of the German delegation—Kasimir von Leyden, Schönaich-Carolath, Holleben, Harnack, Dryander, and Foerster—had long been active in the campaign to improve Anglo-German relations and needed no further convincing. Even within the peace movement the conference failed to have the lasting effect the pacifists had hoped for. The German Peace Society's proposal that the joint committee to coordinate the conference be made into a permanent agency was turned down by the other groups.[109]

The efforts of the committees to improve Anglo-German relations were little more successful than the work of the Franco-German groups. The factors that led to the failure of the Anglo-German campaign, however, were somewhat different. The attempt at Franco-German conciliation was handicapped by the minimal conviction with which the pacifists themselves approached it. The efforts on behalf of Anglo-German friendship were more the casualties of grow-

[107] *Ibid.* (B IV d 4 b), Spiecker to Lübke, Berlin, 20 May 1912; Siegmund-Schultze to Richter, Berlin, 11 June 1912.

[108] NL M. Quidde, Program of the Anglo-German Understanding Conference, London, 30 October–1 November 1912.

[109] NL Siegmund-Schultze (B IV d 4 c), Joint German Committee, Protocol, Berlin, 19 May 1913; Kirchliches Komitee to Lübke, Berlin, 14 June 1913.

ing antagonism between the two countries, which reached a peak after the second Moroccan crisis, and did not abate in spite of the efforts of the peace society and the other friendship groups. Indeed, in the aftermath of Agadir even pacifists who had consistently worked for Anglo-German conciliation began to suspect that there might be grave differences between the two countries. And the disillusionment born of this suspicion colored the German peace movement's reaction to the outbreak of war in 1914.

War, 1914

"What was this, then, that was in the air? A rising temper. Acute irritability. A nameless rancour. A universal tendency to envenomed exchange of words, to outbursts of rage—yes even to fisticuffs."[110] Although it did not actually lead to fisticuffs, the mood in the German peace movement in the years just before the war partook of the same kind of irascibility that Thomas Mann described on the Magic Mountain. The pacifists' commentary on international politics became bitter and cynical, and the leaders of the peace society had to contend with the prospect of open rebellion within their ranks.

In the revival of the question of Alsace-Lorraine after 1911 the German pacifists did little to disguise their hostility toward the French. Indeed, their writings on the threat from France began to smack a little of the paranoia found in the writings of extreme nationalists. In 1913 Umfrid felt compelled to admonish those of his colleagues who believed that Germany should take the initiative in disarming. "Were we to disarm," he predicted, "the chances are a hundred to one that the French . . . would attack."[111] While the tone of these recriminations against the French might have been more strident in the years after 1911, the hostility itself was

[110] Thomas Mann, *The Magic Mountain*, translated by H. T. Lowe-Porter (New York, 1966), p. 682.
[111] Umfrid, "Volksthümliches über Krieg und Frieden," VF, xiv (1913), 38; VF, xiii (1912), 42, 131; FW, xiii (1911), 102.

hardly new. Much more startling were the attacks on the English that began to emanate from the German peace movement after 1911. The Agadir crisis raised serious doubts in the minds of many about the benevolence of British intentions—particularly in the light of revelations in the German press that the British fleet had been ready to strike in the summer of 1911. "You cannot imagine," Siegmund-Schultze wrote to Allen Baker in November 1911, "how deeply the nation feels that there is one other nation which will not allow any advantage or enlargement of Germany."[112] Schücking complained that the "immoderate position of England" and its readiness for war had "set our good cause back decades."[113]

At first it seemed that not even the Agadir crisis could shake the confidence of the German Peace Society in England. Umfrid, Quidde, and other spokesmen defended British behavior, even Lloyd George's provocative speech at the Mansion House, as a justified response to Germany's tactical ineptitude.[114] It soon became clear, however, that the rank and file no longer shared this confidence, and the fact that a leader of the peace society who tried to defend England was heckled by his colleagues at a peace congress late in 1911 was but one indication of the growing unrest in the organization.[115] Then, in October 1912, a major dispute broke out, when Johannes Tiedje, the leader of the local group in Königsberg, published a sharp critique directed at Umfrid and others who had spoken out in favor of England. Such an uncritical endorsement of England would, he predicted, only damage the cause of pacifism in Ger-

[112] NL Siegmund-Schultze (B 1 c), Siegmund-Schultze to Baker, 26 November 1911; Nieders to Baker, Königsberg, 1 December 1911; *ibid.* (B iv b 4), Harnack to Sir John Kennaway, Berlin, 28 December 1911.

[113] NL Fried, Schücking to Fried, Marburg, 10 November 1911.

[114] Quidde, "Ein wenig Gerechtigkeit gegenüber England," FW, xiv (1912), 8; VF, xiii (1912), 51, 62–64, 71; FW, xiii (1911), 380.

[115] NL Fried, Richter to Fried, Pforzheim, 27 November 1911.

many: "Even today, at a time when we Germans are justly on guard against England, to mix our work with such a heterogeneous faith in England's pacifistic intentions is to lead pacifism up a blind alley. . . . The German psyche perceives clearly that between our two countries there is not only the naval question . . . but that England is threatening the vital security of our national growth."[116] Criticism of Umfrid and other leaders became more general and high-pitched in succeeding months. The opposition, which was centered in the *Ortsgruppen* in Königsberg, Cronberg, Frankfurt, and Marburg, called for the removal of Umfrid and all other devotees of what it called *Suttnerei*, and it even proposed to dissolve the peace society into the *Verband für internationale Verständigung*, whose leaders seemed to have a keener appreciation for the realities of international politics.[117] Tension within the peace society had clearly been exacerbated by the frustrations born of the feud with the *Verband*; and these frustrations were not allayed when in 1913 the Carnegie Endowment snubbed the German Peace Society by refusing to subsidize its activities. Nor was the atmosphere made more conciliatory by the controversy in 1913 over the *Wehrvorlage*, which found the peace society deeply divided.[118]

Throughout the attacks on his person and his policy, Umfrid insisted that the English sincerely wanted an understanding with Germany. Yet even he had begun to have doubts. In March 1912 he reviewed Paul Rohrbach's *Deutschland unter den Weltvölkern* and was forced into an admission that, coming from one of Germany's most devout Anglophiles, was not without significance. "I must admit," he wrote, "that although I followed the[se] parts of his

---

[116] Tiedje, "Vaterland oder Staat," VF, XIII (1912), 99-100.

[117] *Ibid.*; NL Fried, Wehberg to Fried, Düsseldorf, 28 January 1914; Tiedje to Fried, Königsberg, 11, 17 March 1914; Tiedje to Fried, Tegenersee's Hof, 29 June 1914.

[118] "Eine Korrespondenz über did Milliardenrüstung," VF, XIV (1913), 94.

book with reluctance, Rohrbach has convinced me of the reality of King Edward's attempts to encircle us."[119]

The years immediately prior to the war were thus a period of serious unrest in the German peace movement. The growing discontent was reflected in the pacifists' recriminations against France, England, the leadership in Stuttgart, the Carnegie Endowment, and in resignations from the peace society.[120] The intervention of Fried in 1913 in the uncharacteristic role of peacemaker alleviated the tension somewhat, as did the firing of Nippold and the election of Quidde to the presidency of the German Peace Society in June 1914.[121] Nevertheless, the situation in the peace movement was agitated when the July crisis erupted into war.

The international peace movement had long been divided about the permissibility of defensive wars. In those sectors of the movement where the Quaker impulse was dominant, chiefly in England and the United States, pacifists rejected all forms of war, regardless of their origin. But aside from a handful of Tolstoy's disciples, unconditional repudiation of war did not find much support on the European continent, where pacifists recognized the validity of both defensive wars and armed sanctions undertaken by an international organization.[122]

The German peace movement admitted the probity not only of defensive war and armed sanctions, but any war waged in the name of a just cause. Umfrid once condemned wars undertaken for material interests, but went on to pro-

---

[119] Umfrid, "Deutschland unter den Weltvölkern," VF, XIII (1912), 26; cf. VF, XIII (1912), 43.

[120] VF, XIII (1912), 30, 132; VF, XV (1914), 21; FW, XIII (1911), 369.

[121] NL Fried, Tiedje to Fried, Königsberg, 19 June 1913, Anlage; Fried to Tiedje, Vienna, 21 June 1913.

[122] Wehberg, "Das Problem der Kriegsdienstverweigerung auf den Weltfriedenskongressen der Vorkriegszeit," FW, XXIV (1924), 290-92; Wehberg, "Der Verteidigungskrieg auf den Weltfriedenskongressen der Vorkriegszeit," FW, XXIV (1924), 330-33; Carl Ludwig Siemering, "Tolstoi und der Pazifismus," FB, V (1904), 110; FW, XII (1910), 221-22; VF, XIV (1913), 38.

claim: "How much different it would be if the trumpets were to blare for war in support of justice and freedom, or for the restoration of order."[123] Beyond this, the pacifists' rather liberal definition of a just war comprehended international police actions, wars of intervention to save victims of persecution, and wars of liberation.[124] It was thus extremely unlikely, given the facility with which they identified German policy with justice, that the German pacifists would find their country fighting an unjust war. But Umfrid even provided for this eventuality. More limited by the Lutheran political tradition than he realized, he denied the right of selective resistance to wars that the pacifist—or anyone else—might hold to be unjust: "Even if a war undertaken [only] for national interests—something we [pacifists] condemn—should break out, our exhortation to the individual soldier would still be: 'You are fighting for a good [and] holy cause; you are bleeding and dying for your fatherland; the responsibility belongs not with you, but rather with those who unleashed the war.' "[125]

Since most of the professors in the *Verband für internationale Verständigung* did not recognize the category of justice in international politics, they approached the problem of war more openly from the standpoint of national interest. They, too, admitted that the nation could legitimately resort to arms under certain conditions, most notably to defend itself. Friedrich Curtius, the chairman of the organization at the outbreak of the war, even implied that preventive wars fell into this category. Early in 1914 he an-

123 Umfrid, *Anti-Stengel* (Esslingen, 1909), p. 37; see also Köhler, "Die deutsche Friedensgesellschaft," p. 366.

124 FB, VII (1906), 97; CW, XX (1906), 869. A remark Löwenthal once made provides insight into the pacifists' appreciation of war: "*A peace without truth and justice* is in no way preferable *to war*." NL Fried, Löwenthal to Fried, Berlin, 29 December 1909 (italics his); cf. Dr. H., "Die Friedensgesellschaften," *Die Kritik* 1 (1894), 35.

125 Umfrid, "Die theologische Gegnerschaft gegen die Friedensbewegung und die Rechtswidrigkeit des heutigen Krieges," CW, XX (1906), 869.

nounced that "A state can be compelled to attack if it would otherwise be abandoning its future."[126] Thus, it was very unlikely that anyone in the German peace movement would withhold his support for the country in the event it became involved in a war.

The abrupt development of the final diplomatic crisis of 1914 left leaders of the peace movement with little opportunity to comment on the events in search of justice. From the pacifists' standpoint the most significant event of the early summer of 1914 was the death of Bertha von Suttner, and their activities were devoted to arranging memorials to the great lady. Fried included only a short notice in his journal on the assassination of the archduke, blaming it on nationalist emotions and international anarchy.[127] As war became imminent, leaders of the peace society dispatched appeals for moderation to their Russian friends in the peace movement. On 30 July Quidde and Neufville travelled to Brussels for a meeting of representatives of peace societies throughout Europe, but the German Peace Society, fearing that antiwar demonstrations would be misconstrued as non-support for the German government, declined to take any formal action during the last hours of peace.[128]

Once the armies began to march, the German Peace Society quickly endorsed the war effort. Its official statement announced that "There can be no doubt about the duties of the pacifists during the war. We German pacifists have always recognized the right and obligation of national self-defense. Each pacifist must fulfill his common responsibilities to the fatherland just like any other German."[129] The

[126] Curtius, "Krieg und internationale Verständigung," KVfiV, III (1914), 1-4; NL Fried, G. Grosch to Fried, Stuttgart, 9 June 1914; Curtius to Fried, Strassburg, 11 December 1913.

[127] "Die Bluttat von Sarajevo," FW, XVI (1914), 269.

[128] Hoover Institution, Fried Collection, "An die Ortsgruppen der Deutschen Friedensgesellschaft, Stuttgart," 1 August 1914.

[129] Hoover Institution, Fried Collection, Deutsche Friedensgesellschaft, "Nach Ausbruch des europäischen Krieges," Stuttgart, 15 August 1914.

professors in the *Verband* likewise rallied to the cause.[130] In fact, the German peace movement supported the war with as much conviction, if not as much enthusiasm, as other Germans. Fried announced that pacifists ought not to cease being patriots and that every pacifist could fulfill his duties toward his country in battle "without being untrue to his obligation to humanity."[131] Umfrid, as he said he would, exhorted the departing German troops: "Go with God. You are fighting for a holy cause; you are suffering and bleeding for your fatherland."[132]

Umfrid's response to the outbreak of war was automatic, but this did not mean that he believed Germany was fighting an unjust war; on the contrary, all German pacifists were convinced that their country was fighting in the name of humanity, justice, and international law. The German government's attempt to portray the war as a defensive struggle against a Russian invasion convinced the pacifists, perhaps even more than the Social Democrats. Pacifists blamed the war on the irresponsible men around Nicholas II who had somehow prevailed upon the *Friedensczar* to let loose the Slavic hordes on Germany.[133] But the western powers also shared much of the responsibility in the pacifists' eyes, as the tension that had been building up in the German peace movement found an outlet in the hostilities of war. Umfrid castigated the French government for stirring up a frenzy of anti-German sentiment. Even more bitter were his attacks on England, the country for whose defense he had been reproached. Ascribing the origins of English foreign policy to a "phenomenal world-egoism," he concluded that British imperialism was Germany's most dangerous enemy. "England," he observed, "is obviously in-

---

[130] Nippold, *Erlebnisse*, pp. 18–19; cf. Klaus Schwabe, *Wissenschaft und Kriegsmoral: Die deutschen Hochschullehrer und die politischen Grundfragen des Ersten Weltkrieges* (Göttingen, 1969).

[131] "Der Krieg," FW, XVI (1914), 281.

[132] Umfrid, "Der Weltbrand," VF, XV (1914), 99.

[133] Fried, *Kriegstagebuch*, I, 8–9; FW, XVI (1914), 284–85, 324; VF, XV (1914), 100.

tent upon first crushing the German empire with the aid of Russia and France, in order then perhaps to create a unified western Europe under its own hegemony as a front against Russia."[134] Quidde was more moderate in his judgment, but he too believed that the balance of justice lay with Germany, and he attempted, with little success, to plead the German case among his French and English colleagues.[135]

The vitriol in the pacifists' reaction stemmed no doubt, in part, from the realization that the war represented the ultimate failure of their campaign—although, to be sure, they hesitated to admit this. Fried, for instance, predicted that the war would do away definitively with the old system of international anarchy and bring on international organization. "War," as this perpetual optimist put it, "is the continuation of pacifism's work, only by other means."[136] But behind their forced optimism and their endorsement of the war, pacifists—including people such as Umfrid and Curtius who had sometimes loudly justified war in the past —felt acute dismay at the bloodshed and mindless passion, which they had foreseen and tried to prevent.[137] In the first week of the war Fried made one of the most accurate predictions of his career: "I can see it all coming, all the suffering of this war, which is going to go on interminably."[138]

The accuracy of such predictions underscores the difficulty of analyzing a phenomenon as paradoxical as the German peace movement. The campaign to bring about a world without war was characterized by both remarkable

[134] Umfrid, "Imperialismus," FW, XVI (1914), 324-25; see also Umfrid, "Der Egoismus in der Politik," VF, XV (1914), 118.

[135] Fried, Kriegstagebuch, I, 19; FW, XVI (1914), 289, 325-27; Wehberg, Führer, p. 29.

[136] FW, XVI (1914), 281; cf. Umfrid, "Ein Denkmal für die Gefallenen," VF, XV (1914), 112.

[137] NL Fried, Quidde to Fried, Munich, 13 August 1914; Umfrid, Zum Gedächtnis von Otto Umfrid, p. 35; NL Rade, Curtius to Rade, Strassburg, 25 August 1914; NL Schücking (58), Verband für internationale Verständigung, Zirkular für Nichtmitglieder.

[138] Fried, Kriegstagebuch, I, 2; FW, XVI (1914), 282.

insight and political fantasies, critical awareness and colossal gullibility. The pacifists' criticism of the maladroit tactics of German statesmen was perceptive, as was their diagnosis of the ominous features of political socialization in Germany. Yet despite the great friction between them and the political system within which they operated, the pacifists consistently defended Germany's claims in Europe and abroad, and in 1914 they went willingly to war in the belief that their country was fighting in the name of international justice.

One possible way to resolve this paradox would be to emphasize the pacifists' astute grasp of politics, the fact that they criticized those aspects of German society and politics that they believed were in fact detrimental to Germany's power and interests. In this interpretation, the pacifists' campaign was ultimately an attempt to promote "an *Ersatzmodell* for aggressive imperialism," for they perceived "that it was possible to reach the same goals through peaceful means."[139] There is considerable evidence in the pacifists' commentary on international politics to support this view, but it introduces an element of cynicism that was completely alien to the peace movement. Indeed, a more compelling explanation for the paradox of the peace movement lies in the very guilelessness and naiveté of its adherents. Attributing the most noble motives to statesmen, especially to German statesmen, most of them simply failed to see that their criticism touched the very core of the imperial political system. While they believed a policy of conciliation and justice would indeed contribute to the country's welfare, they were oblivious of the problems raised by the attempt to regulate international politics by morality; the implications of their repeated quarrels with the French pacifists were completely lost on them.

Emphasizing the pacifists' naiveté also suggests an obvious explanation for the overwhelming rejection of the peace

[139] See Stiewe, "Die bürgerliche deutsche Friedensbewegung," pp. 107, 218.

movement in Germany: the pacifists' program was so hope-lessly out of touch with political reality that it might be more appropriate to ask why they found any sympathy at all. This hypothesis would point to the peace movement's own failings as a sufficient cause of its weakness in imperial Germany and minimize the importance of inimical factors in the political culture. This hypothesis can now be tested.

8

Excursus:
The Peace Movement in France

In 1919, in an effort to refute allegations that Germany bore exclusive guilt for unleashing the world war and to defend the new German republic from domestic attack, the National Constituent Assembly in Weimar commissioned a parliamentary committee to investigate the outbreak of the war and the German collapse at its conclusion. One of the members of this committee, which deliberated until 1930, was Walther Schücking, who sat in the Reichstag between 1919 and 1928 as a member of the *Deutsche Demokratische Partei*. Convinced that the hostility of the German empire toward the peace movement and its goals had been a major factor in causing the war, Schücking succeeded in placing this problem on the committee's agenda. Sessions devoted to the topic were sometimes the scene of heated debate, as Schücking attempted to expose the shortcomings of German policy by parading like-minded witnesses before the committee, including his close friend Hans Wehberg.[1] At one session in June 1923 the accusations provoked old Hans Delbrück to point out that the peace movement was itself to blame for the hostility that it had encountered in Germany: "it can be shown that advocacy of pacifism in Germany was so colossally inadequate and absurd, that the arguments propounded by the most prominent, best, and most cheerful pacifists—not only by Frau von Suttner but also by the gentlemen who have been participating here in our committee—were so palpably in contradiction with the facts, so utterly impossible to subscribe to, that it was very

[1] Wehberg, *Gutachten, passim*; cf. Acker, *Schücking*, pp. 137-45.

327

difficult to enter into a positive discussion with them."[2] Delbrück was no friend of the peace movement (he had in fact been one of its most astute critics), so his testimony was not unbiased. Nonetheless, his thesis has a great deal to recommend it. As the pacifists' commentary on international affairs made painfully clear, the level of their political intelligence and sophistication was not high. Their conception of international relations was legalistic and moralistic, and a community of nations seemed to have little relevance in a world agitated by a series of grave diplomatic crises, in which power and interest were clearly the determinants of national policy. It is thus tempting to join Delbrück in arguing that one need look no further than to the eccentricity of the peace movement itself for the causes of the great resistance it found in Germany.

The implications of this argument ought to be pursued. It implies that a movement whose program was "so palpably in contradiction with the facts" must have been rejected everywhere as it was in Germany. Or, if the peace movement was in fact stronger in other countries, this must have been because advocacy of pacifism elsewhere was less inadequate and absurd than it was in Germany. It would seem possible to test the validity of these implications with an analysis of the experience of the peace movement in other countries prior to the First World War. If these implications were to prove unfounded, it would suggest that one should look beyond the admitted failings of the peace movement in explaining its overwhelming rejection in Germany.

The body of literature on the history of the peace movement is rapidly growing.[3] As yet, however, there has been no study devoted to a systematic comparison of the movement—its social recruitment, organization, program, activi-

[2] NL Wehberg (44), Untersuchungsausschuss Protokoll, 13 June 1923, p. 21.

[3] See Blanche Wiesen Cook, ed., *Bibliography on Peace Research in History* (Santa Barbara, Calif., 1969).

ties, and impact—in different countries. The existing literature does seem to indicate that the peace movement was internationally a relatively homogeneous phenomenon, that it was drawn everywhere from the middle classes, and that it sought in all countries to popularize arbitration and arms limitation through a campaign of popular enlightenment. Moreover, studies of the movement in Belgium,[4] Norway,[5] the United States,[6] and England[7] suggest that it was considerably larger, stronger, and more effective in these countries than in Germany.

Conclusions based upon this literature cannot really challenge the argument that the peace movement was responsi-

[4] Robert Parsons Baker, "The Belgians and the European Peace Movement, 1889–1914" (Master's thesis, Stanford University, 1962).

[5] Oscar J. Falnes, *Norway and the Nobel Peace Prize* (New York, 1967); Halvdan Koht, *Histoire du mouvement de la paix en Norvège* (Kristiania, 1900).

[6] Peter Brock, *Pacifism in the United States: From the Colonial Era to the First World War* (Princeton, 1968); Merle Curti, *Peace or War: The American Struggle, 1636–1936* (New York, 1936); Warren F. Kuehl, *Seeking World Order: The United States and International Organization to 1920* (Nashville, Tenn., 1969); Michael Latzker, "The 'Practical' Peace Advocates: An Interpretation of the American Peace Movement, 1898–1917" (Ph.D. dissertation, Rutgers University, 1969); C. Roland Marchand, *The American Peace Movement and Social Reform, 1898–1918* (Princeton, 1972); David Sands Patterson, "The Travail of the American Peace Movement, 1887–1914" (Ph.D. dissertation, University of California, Berkeley, 1968); Patterson, "An Interpretation of the American Peace Movement, 1898–1914," *American Studies* XIII (1972), 31–49.

[7] A. J. A. Morris, *Radicalism against War, 1906–1914: The Advocacy of Peace and Retrenchment* (London, 1972); Morris, "The English Radicals' Campaign for Disarmament and the Hague Conference of 1907," *Journal of Modern History* XLIII (1971), 367–93; Hines, "Norman Angell"; Howard Weinroth, "Norman Angell and *The Great Illusion:* An Episode in Pre-1914 Pacifism," *Historical Journal* XVII (1974), 551–74; Joyce Arrech Berkman, "Pacifism in England, 1914–1939" (Ph.D. dissertation, Yale University, 1967); the dissertation of Eric W. Sager of the University of British Columbia has just been completed: "Pacifism and the Victorians: A Social History of the English Peace Movement, 1816–1873."

ble for its own weakness in Germany. The evidence for other countries is still insufficient, particularly since most of the research has concentrated on developments internal to the peace movement and has largely avoided the problem of how much influence it actually exerted in society and politics. In addition, most of the existing literature has dealt with countries whose geopolitical situation diminishes the significance of the peace movement's comparative vitality. The size and modest political aspirations of countries such as Norway and Belgium—the fact that they were not directly involved in international political rivalries—no doubt made arbitration and arms limitation more attractive there than in Germany. The relative isolation of the United States from the tensions of European rivalries surely accounts for much of the peace movement's success in this country; and, to a lesser extent, the same is true of England, at least until the first decade of the twentieth century.

Of the larger countries on the European continent, whose circumstances more closely approximated Germany's, France offers probably the most enlightening case for comparison. France was certainly caught up in the tensions of great power rivalry. Both France and Germany had relatively high levels of ethnic homogeneity and formal political participation, so these factors would not account for significant differences in the experience of the peace movement, as they would if the German movement were being compared with the Russian or Austrian.[8]

In order to put the plight of the German peace movement into perspective, I propose now to examine briefly the history of its counterpart in France. Unfortunately, apart from the general surveys there is very little literature on the history of the French peace movement. My conclusions are

[8] See Josef Bauer, "Die österreichische Friedensbewegung" (Inaugural dissertation, Vienna, 1949); and especially Richard Robert Laurence, "The Problem of Peace and Austrian Society, 1889–1914: A Study in the Cultural Origins of the First World War" (Ph.D. dissertation, Stanford University, 1968).

thus based largely on my own limited research, and they must be regarded as tentative. I shall argue that the French and German peace movements were alike insofar as both were recruited from a socially conservative middle-class constituency and attempted to win support for a world organization in which disputes would be settled by arbitration rather than by armed force. I shall argue further that the similarity between the two ended here, that the French peace movement was far more extensive than the German, and that it was far more successful in winning support for its program among important political groups and agencies of political education.

The Contours of the French Peace Movement

Like their German counterparts, the French pacifists could find a tradition of opposition to war in their nation's past. Just as German pacifists claimed Kant as their precursor, the French regarded themselves as the heirs of Sully, St. Pierre, and the Enlightenment. In France, however, this tradition found expression in an organized peace movement much earlier than it did in Germany. The first French peace society on record was the *Société de morale chrétienne*, which was founded in Paris in 1821 by the duc de La Rochefoucauld-Liancourt.[9] Like the Anglo-American societies that had been founded shortly before, the French organization emphasized the religious aspect of the problem of peace, and its program called for the reform of international relations according to Christian principles. In fact, however, the society became a center of liberal opposition to the restored monarchy, and its membership included Benjamin Constant, Guizot, Lamartine, and the duc de Broglie. The interests of these and other members waned during the July Monarchy, and the peace society continued only a nominal existence. In the 1840s the growing con-

---

[9] *Premier Congrès national des sociétés françaises de la paix [Toulouse], Octobre 1902* (Toulouse, 1903), p. 32; Beales, *A History of Peace*, p. 54.

servatism of the regime placed legal obstacles in the way of its activity. The opposition of the regime likewise obstructed the work of a new peace society which was founded in the early 1840s by a number of liberal economists, including Frédéric Bastiat, Joseph Garnier, and Francisque Bouvet, in order to promote peace through free trade.[10]

During this period the most outspoken and famous pacifist in the world was a Frenchman, Victor Hugo. His activities, however, were perforce restricted to oratory at peace congresses held outside France. The revolutionary events of 1848 brought a brief resurgence to the peace movement in France and enabled him to return home. In August 1849 an international peace congress convened in Paris with the blessings of the republican government; indeed, among the French delegates were Lamartine and Tocqueville. Hugo was the man of the hour, and his opening address to the congress became one of the highlights in the annals of the peace movement: "A day will come when the bullets and bombshells will be replaced by votes, by the universal suffrage of nations, by the venerable arbitration of a great sovereign senate, which will be to Europe what the Parliament is to England, what the Diet is to Germany, what the Legislative Assembly is to France."[11]

In the first half of the nineteenth century the French peace movement was held together more by this kind of eloquent idealism than by any organizational ties or coherent program. Yet certain of the characteristics that were to mark the movement down to the First World War were already in evidence. Pacifism was closely tied to French liberalism, an outgrowth of its political and, in the early phases, even more of its economic demands. International peace, these early French pacifists argued, would be the natural condition of a world in which constitutional govern-

[10] *Premier Congrès national*, pp. 32–33; Silberner, *Problem of War*, pp. 100–104.

[11] Quoted in Beales, *A History of Peace*, p. 79.

ment and free trade had been instituted. French pacifism also reflected the influence of Mazzini in its belief that the nations of the world constituted harmonious subgroupings of humanity. It called for the political organization of this sisterhood of nations in order to guarantee lasting peace.

To advocate such views in public was difficult during the second empire, particularly in the 1850s, when there was virtually no organized pacifist activity in France. The imperial dictatorship kept the peace movement quiet, but in so doing, it radicalized the pacifist credo politically; henceforth pacifists would be, almost without exception, outspoken republicans. At the same time, they retained their faith in free trade, encouraged by the negotiation of the Cobden-Chevalier treaty in 1860. The liberalization of the empire in the 1860s made possible the reappearance of peace societies. In 1863 Edmund Potonié-Pierre established the *Ligue du bien public* in Paris with a program that called for achieving peace by removing every manner of restriction on personal liberty, particularly monopolies and trade barriers.[12] Though based in France, Potonié's organization soon gained an international following, which included Richard Cobden and some of the most prominent republicans in Europe, among them the exiled Victor Hugo and Giuseppe Garibaldi. To popularize his ideas, which entailed ultimately establishing a world republic, Potonié issued a series of newsletters: *Le cosmopolite, Petits plaidoyers contre la guerre*, and, from London, where he found the political atmosphere more cordial, *Le courrier international*. After the Franco-Prussian War his society became dormant, though he himself continued to agitate in the service of his cause.

The period of the liberal empire also saw the establishment of two organizations that were to remain centers of the peace movement until the First World War. The first appeared in the spring of 1867, in response to the war scare between France and the North German Confederation over

12 *Ibid.*, pp. 102–103; *Premier Congrès national*, pp. 33–34.

Luxemburg. A series of letters in *Le Temps* urged moderation on all parties involved in the crisis and called for the creation of a peace society. The authors of the letters, Gustave d'Eichtal, Martin Paschoud, and Frédéric Passy, thereupon founded the *Ligue internationale et permanente de la paix* in May 1867.[13] Less outspoken in its republicanism than Potonié's organization, the *Ligue internationale* sought, by emphasizing free trade, to attract members of all political persuasions, as well as to avoid the harassment that might accompany overt political agitation. Among the figures who joined the organization were Jean Dolfuss, who became president, Michel Chevalier, Joseph Garnier, and the abbé Gratry.

The second of the organizations founded in this period was limited by no such inhibitions about political action; as a result, though its inspiration and membership were predominantly French, it had to be established in Switzerland. The creation of Charles Lemonnier, a flamboyant and uncompromising benefactor of mankind, the *Ligue internationale de la paix et de la liberté* was founded in Geneva in September 1867 at an international congress presided over by Garibaldi.[14] Its program called for world peace through universal substitution of democracy for monarchy, separation of church and state, abolition of standing armies, and establishment of a United States of Europe. Branches of Lemonnier's group soon appeared in Italy and France, where it became a center of republican opposition to the empire, and counted Léon Gambetta, Gustave Vogt, and Jules Barni among its members.[15] Lemonnier's aggressive

[13] *Premier Congrès national*, pp. 34–35; Beales, *A History of Peace*, p. 119. On the French peace movement between 1867 and 1899 see especially Abrams, "European Peace Societies"; Schou, *Histoire de l'internationalisme*, pp. 338–55; and Liedtke, "Die Entwicklung des Pazifismus," pp. 9–12.

[14] Beales, *A History of Peace*, pp. 120–21; *Premier Congrès national*, pp. 40–41.

[15] Abrams, "European Peace Societies," p. 132.

appeal to the masses was a source of embarrassment and concern to the *Ligue internationale et permanente de la paix*, whose leaders emphasized free trade, both for fear of antagonizing the authorities and because of their more conservative political and social views. Consequently, relations between these two peace societies remained cool prior to the Franco-Prussian War.

The outbreak of war in 1870 and its disastrous outcome had significant ramifications for the French peace movement, and indeed continued to affect it until 1914. The Treaty of Frankfurt made it difficult for anyone in France to renounce war when this could be construed as acquiescence in the loss of Alsace-Lorraine. Throughout the period prior to the First World War, French pacifists encountered the reproach that it was singularly inappropriate for France, a country that had suffered injustice at the hands of Germany, now to offer the hand of justice and conciliation.[16] Yet, paradoxically, the loss of the provinces also brought a kind of patriotic appeal to the French peace movement that it might otherwise have lacked. To those who despaired of France's ever being able to reconquer Alsace-Lorraine, the peace movement's program seemed no less unrealistic than resort to armed force. By calling for the reform of international relations in the light of justice and law, pacifism took on the character of a *revanchisme légal*.[17] At the very least, pacifists could persuasively parry the charge that they were unconcerned about the honor of their country; there is little

---

[16] *Ibid.*, p. 296; cf. [Kloss] *Das Friedensjahrbuch 1913*, pp. 53–54. Ironically, the same argument was mustered against the German peace movement after the First World War. In 1924 Hans von Seeckt wrote to the *Deutsches Friedenskartell*: "The train of thought in international pacifism is intrinsically difficult to comprehend for a people that has been internationally mistreated the way the Germans have." Hellmut von Gerlach, "Seeckt und die deutschen Pazifisten," *Neue Züricher Zeitung*, 18 March 1924. This did not mean, of course, that people such as Seeckt had been supporters of pacifism when the Treaty of Frankfurt, rather than the Treaty of Versailles, was operative.

[17] Abrams, "European Peace Societies," p. 297.

doubt, however, that they believed that the international organization of the future would indeed vindicate the French claim to the provinces and return them in the only feasible way.

In the immediate aftermath of the war such calculations were overwhelmed in national outrage, and the French peace movement entered what one commentator referred to as a "veritable *moyen-âge*."[18] Potonié's society disappeared. The *Ligue internationale et permanente*, which was transformed under Passy's direction into the *Société française des amis de la paix*, continued to exist, at least on paper. Its membership consisted of some six hundred intellectuals, philanthropists, and businessmen devoted to free trade; but, in fact, only a handful around Passy and Adolphe Frank, who was president of the organization, were at all active. The most striking aspect of their campaign was its timidity. Still afraid of provoking an angry public with open propaganda, the society was content with quiet academic discussions of aspects of the peace problem.[19] Lemonnier, less reticent as always, continued to convoke international congresses in the 1870s and founded some short-lived peace societies.[20]

It should be pointed out that however anemic the French peace movement was in the aftermath of the Franco-Prussian War, it far exceeded in extent and enthusiasm anything comparable in Germany. And as resentment over the Treaty of Frankfurt became less politically acute in France, the peace movement began to grow significantly. The decade of the 1880s saw the appearance of peace societies in Clermont-Ferrand and Guise, which between them had a membership of close to two thousand.[21] Hodgson Pratt also travelled repeatedly to France in the 1880s in an effort to set up peace societies and bring some cohesion to the

---

[18] *Premier Congrès national*, p. 31.
[19] Abrams, "European Peace Societies," pp. 126–29, 199–200.
[20] *Ibid.*, pp. 194–95; *Premier Congrès national*, p. 40.
[21] *Ibid.*, pp. 41–42.

French peace movement. Convinced that the movement could find support among the working classes, he negotiated with numerous socialists before he discovered that the social tensions born of the Commune were still too strong for them to support a "bourgeois" cause.[22] Pratt's only real accomplishment came in 1888, when he brought about the consolidation of Passy's society with most of the other existing peace groups in France. The new organization, called the *Société française pour l'arbitrage entre nations*, was led by Passy, now a member of the Chamber of Deputies. Its executive committee of forty comprised most of the pacifist leaders in France on the eve of the first Universal Peace Congress.

Just as this consolidation was being negotiated, the peace society that would shortly become the most important and influential in France was being organized, inauspiciously, by a handful of teenagers. In April 1887 the *Association des jeunes amis de la paix* was created by a group of eighty students at a *lycée* in Nîmes, with a program that advocated a court of international arbitration and the abolition of standing armies. From this improbable beginning the organization, originally conceived as a youth group, expanded as the students graduated and dispersed. It was held together by a journal, *La paix par le droit*; in 1895 the society changed its name to *Association de la paix par le droit* and dropped all age restrictions on its members. The growth of the organization reflected the social and professional advancement of the young men who had founded it, such as Charles Brunet, Jacques Dumas, Théodore Ruyssen, and Jules Prudhommeaux. By 1902 there were twelve hundred members, of whom three hundred were university students. As the society grew, so did the stature of its journal. With a subscription of three thousand in 1899, it became the focus of the French peace movement, carrying articles by leading intellectuals and political figures, including Charles

22 Abrams, "European Peace Societies," pp. 194–99.

Beauquier, Léon Bourgeois, Charles Gide, Yves Guyot, Ernest Lavisse, and Émile Worms.[23]

The growth of the *Association de la paix par le droit* in the 1890s was but one aspect of the expansion of the French peace movement. In part this expansion was the result of the international attention, cohesion, and direction the peace movement acquired after 1889; it was even more a by-product of an important transition in French politics. The growing ascendency of Radical republicanism, which culminated in the aftermath of the Dreyfus affair, converted the peace movement from a protest movement lost in a flood of national indignation into a force much closer to the center of French political life. Radicalism and pacifism were closely related phenomena. Like the peace movement, Radicals advocated the rigorous application of democratic principles, distrusted soldiers, renounced all but defensive wars, and called for arms limitation and arbitration of international disputes.

The decade of the 1890s was marked by the proliferation of new peace societies in France and the growth of those that had already been established. By 1899 there were twenty different peace societies at work in France, many of which had several local branches.[24] In 1896 a central agency, the *Bureau français de la paix*, was set up by Gas-

[23] *Ibid.*, pp. 206–11; *Premier Congrès national*, pp. 42–43.

[24] *Ibid.*, pp. 44–49, 81. French peace societies in 1899 included: the Société française pour l'arbitrage entre nations (Passy's group), with branches in Nice and Le Havre; the Ligue internationale de la paix et de la liberté (led after Lemonnier's death by Émile Arnaud), with French branches in Paris, Sarthe, Drôme, Ardêche, Lens, and a "section departmentale du Nord"; the Association de la paix par le droit (led by Ruyssen), with branch groups in Montpellier and Paris; the Alliance universelle in Saint-Raphaël (Var); the Société de la paix d'Abbeville et du Ponthieu; the Société de la paix de Felletin et Aubisson; the Alliance universelle des femmes pour la paix par l'éducation; L'Égalité; le Comité de défense des indigènes; the Société Gratry de la paix; the Association "La paix et le désarmement par les femmes"; the Association internationale des journalistes amis de la paix; the Société chrétienne des amis de la paix.

ton Moch to coordinate the French peace societies and to serve as an intermediary between them and the International Peace Bureau in Berne. The events of the end of the decade—the Hague conference and the Dreyfus affair—added momentum to the growth of the French peace movement. Although French peace societies remained officially neutral during *l'affaire*, most sympathized with the Dreyfusard cause and clearly profited from the Radical counteroffensive in the aftermath.[25] Indeed, the years between 1899 and 1906 represented the period of the peace movement's greatest influence in France. Between 1898 and 1902 alone, twenty-seven new peace societies were formed, and in 1902 the French peace societies began to hold regular national congresses.[26] In addition, many other organizations, which were not strictly speaking peace societies, began to affiliate corporately with the *Bureau français de la paix* and to send representatives to national peace congresses. In 1900 Moch announced that some four hundred different organizations had sent their *adhésions* to his *bureau*.[27] After 1905, with the onset of what Eugen Weber has described as the "nationalist revival"—a phenomenon the pacifists were among the first to perceive—the rate of the peace movement's progress declined, but the movement continued to expand nonetheless.[28] As elsewhere, the intervention of the Carnegie Endowment eased its financial plight in the last years of peace.[29]

On the eve of the war the French peace movement was, organizationally at least, an impressive phenomenon. It included in 1913 twenty-eight different societies devoted to

[25] BIP (vB1), Moch to Ducommun, Paris, 11 February 1898; Passy to Ducommun, Neuilly, 28 February 1898.

[26] *Premier Congrès national*, p. 81.

[27] CBM, v (1900), 142.

[28] Ruyssen, "La crise du pacifisme," PD, xv (1905), 481–85; see also PD, xvi (1906), 12–24; Eugen Weber, *The Nationalist Revival in France, 1905–1914* (Berkeley and Los Angeles, 1959).

[29] Carnegie Endowment, *Year-Book for 1913–1914*, p. 66.

popularizing arms limitation and arbitration.[30] Of these, many also had local branches. The *Association de la paix par le droit* included twenty local groups in 1913, the *Société française pour l'arbitrage entre nations* had seven, and the *Société de l'éducation pacifique* had twenty-one. The French peace movement also comprehended a large number of sympathetic organizations, which had affiliated with one of the peace societies, the national bureau, or the International Peace Bureau.[31] Among these were the *Ligue française pour la défense des droits de l'homme et du citoyen* and the *Fédération des universités populaires de France*, as well as numerous Masonic lodges, *bourses du travail*, and cooperative societies.

The French peace movement was much more dispersed than its German counterpart. The various peace societies continued to enjoy complete autonomy, unhindered by any administrative or financial obligations to one another. This situation gave rise to a great deal of competition and duplication of effort among the societies, many of which could ill afford it. In 1896, for instance, there were fifteen separate peace societies in France, and among them they published nine different journals.[32] In an effort to reduce the liabilities of this dispersion, leaders of the larger societies pressed repeatedly for some kind of administrative consolidation, be it full fusion into a national peace society on the German model, or a looser form of federation. To their dismay, they discovered that the independent little groups jealously guarded their independence, so that it was impossible to create more than a loose confederative agency in Moch's *bureau* (which in 1902 was renamed the *Délégation per-*

---

[30] *Annuaire du mouvement pacifiste pour l'année 1913 publié par le Bureau international de la paix à Berne* (Berne, 1913), pp. 111–41.

[31] BIP (vA5), Adhésions au Bureau international permanent de la paix de Berne adressées par M. Henry Casevitz, 22 May 1906.

[32] Gaston Moch, "De l'organisation du mouvement pacifique en France," PD, VI (1896), 229–41; *Premier Congrès national*, pp. 52–54.

manente des sociétés françaises de la paix).[33] On paper an impressive organization composed of the leading pacifists in France, the agency had no power over the independent locals, many of which refused even to affiliate, and it succeeded mainly in creating a forum in which local rivalries could receive national attention.[34]

The absence of central coordination also affected the geographical distribution of the French peace societies (see map). For much of the prewar period there was a surfeit of them in Paris, but none in other major urban centers such as Marseilles or Bordeaux, or in the provincial west.[35] By the eve of the war many of the gaps had been filled, chiefly through the establishment of local branches by the larger societies, but the distribution of peace societies still showed a lack of direction. Orléans, which had no peace society in 1902, had three in 1913; Toulouse had five, and several other localities, including some small towns such as Angoulême and Sète, were the sites of more than one. Paris remained the geographical center of the peace movement, as no fewer than twenty peace groups had headquarters or branches in the French capital or its immediate environs. Peace societies appeared in cities and towns of all sizes, but a significant proportion of them were located in towns that were very small. Many peace societies were situated in coastal areas, particularly those affiliated with Passy's organization, which continued to emphasize the importance of "commercial liberty" in bringing world peace.[36]

Although adequate statistical evidence is lacking, membership recruitment in the French peace movement seems

[33] *Premier Congrès national*, pp. 52–54; BIP (vB1), Moch to Ducommun, Paris, 25 November 1896, 8 June 1897; BIP (vIIIA1), Moch to Docummun, Paris, 16 May 1901.

[34] BIP (vB1), Moch to Ducommun, Paris, 29 November 1896; cf. PD, xxiii (1913), 332, 359.

[35] *Premier Congrès national*, p. 53.

[36] BIP (vB1), Passy to Ducommun, Neuilly, 12 July 1896. Source for map of France: *Annuaire du mouvement pacifiste*, pp. 111–41.

FRENCH PEACE SOCIETIES IN 1913

• Boulogne

• Bully
• Lens

• Abbeville (Ponthieu)
Luneray • • Blangy
• St. Lucien
Le Havre (2) • Amiens (2)
Trouville- Rouen (2) • Guise
Deauville
• Bernay • St. Quentin
Condé - sur - Noireau • Chauny

• Heusse
• Reims (2)

• Luzarches • Nancy
Brest • PARIS (20) • Vitry - le - François
Rennes • St. Barthélémy

• Chartres Troyes
• Essoyes
• St. Pierre-les-Corps • Sougy • Mélisay - Tomlay
St. Nazaire Orléans (3)
• Blois
Nantes • St. Maur sur Indre

• Blan
Fontenay- • St. Laurs • Selancour
le-Comte • Aziré
• Dun sur Auron • Besançon
• La Rochelle • St. Jean-de-Losne
• Chaumecy Lons - le - Saunier
• Pionsat • Bourg
• Angoulême • Cusset
• Ile de Ré Limoges (2) • Clermont-Ferrand
Lyons
Bordeaux • St. Rambert • Artemare
• Eymet • Valence • Guâ
• G3
Soumensac
• Cajarc • Gap
• Villeneuve • Columbier- le - Jeune
• Laffite
• Montauban
• Dax Nîmes (2)
Toulouse (5) Montpellier Nice
• Castres
• Pau Sète (2) • Istres
• Pamiers
• Armisson Marseilles Toulon

to have been comparable to the German. Both were drawn from a middle-class constituency, though judging from a comparison of their local and national leaderships, the French movement was possibly somewhat less *petit bourgeois* in character.[37] Occupations listed by some one hundred fifty local and national leaders of the French peace societies in 1913 showed a predominance of four broad categories: academic, public administration, professional, and commercial or manufacturing.[38] Like the peace societies in Germany, those in France were staffed by large numbers of educators, both teachers and school officials; but in contrast to Germany, this category was not limited to those at the primary school level, although, to be sure, *instituteurs* were probably the single most important occupational group in the French peace movement. Professors, both at universities and *lycées*, were much more conspicuous in peace societies in France. Even more remarkable, by comparison, was the prominence in the French peace societies of people other than school teachers who were employed by, or dealt professionally with, the state. In Germany, with the exception of low-level officials in municipal bureaucracies in the south and west, very few people directly or indirectly involved with public administration were members of the peace society. In France public officials on all levels of administration composed an important segment of the peace societies. Deputies and senators, members of departmental General Councils, and judges and justices of the peace were all well represented; so were members of the legal profession who had frequent contact with the government, such as notaries and *avocats*. Other professional people were also prominent in the French peace movement; there was even an international physicians' peace society which had its headquarters in Paris. Commercial and manufacturing occupations were also important, although small businessmen do not seem to have predominated to the ex-

[37] See above, chapter 2, p. 74.
[38] *Annuaire du mouvement pacifiste*, pp. 111–41.

tent they did in the German movement. As in Germany, women represented a significant sector of the French peace movement; women appeared frequently on boards of directors of peace societies, and several feminist organizations were set up primarily to agitate for peace.

The problem of ascertaining the numerical extent of the French peace movement is far more complex than it is for the German. The German movement was more centralized and represented a much more discrete—or isolated—organization within the fabric of German society and politics; and, in an attempt to impress the international movement with their progress, the Germans became obsessed with the statistics of their organization. In France, on the other hand, the peace movement did not have the national organization that might have enabled it to keep detailed statistics; nor did the French pacifists care much about their statistics —a measure of their confidence (and of French statistics). In addition, the character of the French movement was such that there was often no clear distinction between the peace societies, whose principal aim was to popularize arbitration and arms limitation, and the many other organizations, such as the *Office central des nationalités*, which officially endorsed the goals of the peace movement but were primarily interested in other things. Any estimate of the numbers involved in the French peace movement is, therefore, rough at best, and must be based on the scanty figures that exist. Individual peace societies, and the local branches of the major ones, seem to have averaged several hundred members. For example, the twenty sections of the *Association de la paix par le droit*, which appear to have been fairly typical, had a membership of about four thousand in 1912.[39] If one calculates an average of about two hundred for each society or local branch, there were roughly twenty to twenty-five thousand people who belonged to peace societies in France. When the membership of groups corporately affiliated with the movement is taken into consid-

[39] PD, XXII (1912), 321.

eration, this figure rises appreciably. There were about eight thousand members in the *Fédération des universités populaires*, and some forty thousand in groups associated with the *Société de l'éducation pacifique*; membership in the *Ligue française pour la défense des droits de l'homme et du citoyen* exceeded one hundred thousand, and many of the other affiliated societies, such as the *Association nationale des libres penseurs*, the Masonic lodges, and the co-operatives, counted their members in the thousands.[40] Taking all these organizations into account, and even providing for the likelihood that many Frenchmen belonged to more than one such group, the estimate of Alfred Fried that there were three hundred thousand people in France involved in the peace movement is probably reasonable.[41]

One must exercise caution in interpreting these statistics, not only because of their imprecision. Just as official membership figures presented with pride by the German Peace Society belied the actual state of affairs, it would be mistaken to conclude from the statistical picture that there were several hundred thousand devoted and active pacifists in France. It is obviously difficult to interpret the significance of the corporate *adhésions* that swelled the ranks of the peace movement. It is significant, by comparison, that aside from a few Masonic lodges and other groups, no organizations in Germany were willing to affiliate in this way with the peace movement. But while such affiliations no doubt reflected a general sense of sympathy or approval within the organization for the peace movement's goals, they did not imply unanimity, nor did they commit the members of the organization in question to participate in the activities of the peace movement.

[40] BIP (vA5), Adhésions au Bureau, number 91; *Annuaire du mouvement pacifiste*, pp. 127–29.

[41] Fried, "Etwas von der Friedensbewegung und ihren Organen," *Westermanns Illustrierte Deutsche Monatshefte* CI, 2 (February 1907), 749; Fried, *Die moderne Friedensbewegung*, p. 79; Fried, "Die moderne Friedensbewegung in Deutschland und Frankreich, II: Die Bewegung in Frankreich," *Der Continent* I (1907), 1078.

There is, in addition, evidence that the core of the French peace movement, the societies devoted primarily to peace propaganda, suffered from many of the same problems that the Germans encountered. As in Germany, a good proportion of the peace societies existed on paper only. Once founded by a local notable or philanthropist, a peace society would typically recruit a few hundred members from the locality, hold several meetings, and perhaps even begin to publish a newsletter. At this point, with its diminutive treasury exhausted, it would relapse into dormancy, to be awakened occasionally on the urgings of some local activist.[42] Leaders of the French movement were probably right when they argued that such conditions at the local level were fostered by decentralization, but the experience of the more centralized German movement would suggest that organizations of this kind were bound to encounter indifference among their nominal members. The result of this situation was that the French peace movement very much resembled the German, inasmuch as the bulk of the work at the national level was carried on by a group of dedicated activists, and the movement was supported on the local level by a few notables in a given locality.[43]

In France, however, this elite was considerably larger than in Germany. French national peace congresses were attended as a rule by several hundred people, including representatives from affiliated organizations; French delegations to Universal Peace Congresses were nearly always much larger than the German.[44] The group of active pacifists in France probably numbered several thousand, while it is doubtful that this figure exceeded five hundred in Germany. But the difference lay in more than numbers. In

[42] BIP (viiiA1), Moch to Ducommun, Paris, 26 January 1897, 27 February 1900; BIP (vB1), Passy to Ducommun, Neuilly, 26 November 1904; *Premier Congrès national*, p. 52.

[43] BIP (viB), Passy to Ducommun, Paris, 21 October 1902.

[44] See, for instance, ii. Congrès national des sociétés françaises de la paix, Nîmes, 7–10 avril 1904, *Compte-rendu des séances* (Nîmes, 1904), pp. 109–16.

Germany these men and women were isolated individuals, who suffered ostracism because of their pacifism, commanded very little social respect, and even less political power. In France such people were better situated and more highly regarded. People who could be described as dedicated pacifists, such as Léon Bourgeois and d'Estournelles de Constant, were major political figures in the French republic. Active pacifists, including Gaston Moch and Frédéric Passy, wore the Legion of Honor. Charles Richet, president of the *Société française pour l'arbitrage entre nations*, was a renowned professor of physiology at the University of Paris. Many of the young men who founded the *Association de la paix par le droit* rose to positions of professional and social prominence. Théodore Ruyssen, whose study of Kant received an award from the *Académie française*, was a professor at the university in Aix-en-Provence. Jules Prudhommeaux became a professor in Nîmes, while Lucien Le Foyer rose to prominence in the Radical party and served briefly in the Chamber of Deputies. Because they enjoyed greater respect and were more in the mainstream of French society and politics, the activists in the French peace movement were better able than their German counterparts to agitate effectively.

The credo and program of the French peace movement were substantially the same as the German. The French also subscribed to a "scientific" pacifism, which held that the natural and predictable evolution of society was toward an international community. On the foundation of social, economic, and cultural solidarity, which the pacifists believed was already being laid, a political organization would be established to make possible the regulation of international relations by law. The chief ideologue of the French movement was the man who had inspired Fried, Jacob Novikow; his positivistic theories exerted considerable influence in France.[45] Within the sociological framework supplied by

[45] Ruyssen's judgment on Novikow's *La fédération de l'Europe* was: "This book ought to be for many years the *vade mecum* of those who

Novikow, the French tended to emphasize somewhat different aspects of the problem of establishing a political organization. The Germans speculated a great deal about the character of the world federation and its institutions, but paid relatively little attention to the process by which such a federation would emerge out of the existing structure of international relations. Only with the founding of the *Verband für internationale Verständigung* did the German peace movement begin to deal systematically with the juridical complexities of the transition to international organization. In France, the peace movement began much earlier to adopt a juridical approach, and the pacifist credo tended as a result to be less speculative, although the goals were, to be sure, the same; French pacifists called instead for the extension of international law on the foundation of the Hague convention of 1899. The early prominence of jurists such as Jacques Dumas and Émile Arnaud in the movement set the tone of French pacifism, and French pacifists spoke less in terms of moral enlightenment or the progress of civilized culture, emphasizing instead the importance of practical, politically oriented agitation on behalf of arbitration.[46]

Since French pacifists were not as inclined to speculation, they were also less disturbed than the Germans about the apparent conflict between scientific and idealist motifs in pacifism—a conflict that existed potentially in the French credo since many pacifists did believe that the forces at work

popularize the idea of peace." PD, xi (1901), 174; cf. Wild, *Baron d'Estournelles de Constant*, pp. 192–93.

[46] By the logic of Delbrück's argument one would have to ascribe the comparative success of the French peace movement to this difference of emphasis. This is just the thesis propounded by Marianne Liedtke in her dissertation: Liedtke, "Die Entwicklung des Pazifismus," esp. pp. 6–7, 46, 156–57, 210–21. Significantly, Delbrück's indictment of the German pacifists extended to Schücking and Wehberg, who were the foremost advocates of a less speculative, more practical and juridical approach.

in society were making the victory of their cause inevitable.[47] That the problem did not become acute in France was at least partially because the idealist motif in the French credo was clothed in political garb. It emerged as a form of latter-day Jacobin nationalism, according to which the destiny of France in the twentieth century was to lead the nations of the world into political federation, just as revolutionary France had brought the ideas of political liberty and equality to the rest of Europe at the end of the eighteenth century.[48] "We are ready," wrote Théodore Ruyssen in 1908, "for our profit just as much as for our glory, to become the principal motor and one of the associates of a federation of nations."[49] Although the German pacifists attempted to define a similar role for their own country, the revolutionary heritage made it more plausible to argue this way in France. Moreover, as Ruyssen's claim suggested, there were considerations of a more practical nature that also made this role more fitting for France than Germany. French pacifists were troubled over the discrepancy between their country's declining power and resources, on the one hand, and, on the other, its inflated international aspirations, which included playing the role of a great power, fulfilling a *mission civilisatrice* in a far-flung empire, and the reacquisition of Alsace-Lorraine. The pacifists seized upon what appeared to be a logical and compelling solution to this problem. By championing the substitution of law and justice for armed power in international politics, France could both pave the way for the return of

[47] Liedtke, "Die Entwicklung des Pazifismus," pp. 210–11.

[48] On this phenomenon see Carlton J. H. Hayes, *The Historical Evolution of Modern Nationalism* (New York, 1931), pp. 43–83. The idealist motif also surfaced with a Bergsonian flare: "In fact as well as in principle, there remain so many reasons to believe in the certain, if not the immediate victory of spirit over matter, and of ideas over brute force." BIP (vIB), Jacques Dumas to Ducommun, Rethel, 24 July 1900.

[49] Ruyssen, "La mission de la France," PD, xviii (1908), 193–201; cf. Liedtke, "Die Entwicklung des Pazifismus," pp. 9, 31, 88–89.

the provinces through arbitral decree and unburden itself of the costs of an armed peace, thereby freeing the country to accomplish its mission overseas.

Like the Germans, the French pacifists perceived no conflict between their patriotism and their pacifism. They emphasized that they would obey the laws of the land, specifically with regard to military service, and that they would defend *la patrie* in the event of attack.[50] And, as the German pacifists were reminded whenever the Franco-German dialogue became heated, French pacifists championed tenaciously what they held to be the welfare of their country, be it in the case of Alsace-Lorraine, Morocco, or war with Germany in 1914.[51]

Differences in programmatic emphasis or nuance should not obscure the fact that in terms of the character (if not the extent) of their memberships and the goals they pursued, the French and German peace movements were basically alike. Both believed that the evolution of society toward international federation ought to be promoted for the benefit of mankind and their respective nations. Moreover, both proposed to go about this in the same way, by educating public opinion through a campaign of propaganda in the press, schools, political parties, and other agencies of attitude and opinion formation.[52] Like the Germans, the French pacifists believed that the power of an enlightened public opinion would compel statesmen to establish an international organization.

Within the context of this campaign, though, there was a significant difference of emphasis between the way the German and French peace movements operated. This owed less to differing philosophies on how best to proceed, however, than to differences in the two political systems. The campaign of the German peace movement was diffuse; it

[50] Ruyssen, "Le refus du service militaire," PD, XII (1902), 330–34.
[51] Liedtke, "Die Entwicklung des Pazifismus," pp. 393–94; PD, XXIV (1914), 441.
[52] See *Premier Congrès national*, pp. 54–56.

was aimed at all the agencies that could be identified as important in the socialization process. Because of their own fear of being labeled a political cause and because they found very little support among the country's political leaders, the German pacifists saw no reason to concentrate their campaign in the political sector at the expense of the others. In France, the peace movement's campaign was oriented much more directly toward politics. This was because pacifism found appreciable support among French political parties, and because the parties themselves, unlike their German counterparts, did enjoy direct access to power over foreign and military policy.

The Peace Movement and French Politics

In the political vocabulary of the third French republic, probably no word is so important, or so notoriously ambiguous, as "Radicalism." At one level, Radicalism represented an ethos, "*un état d'esprit très fluide,*" to use Jacques Kayser's expression, based upon a small-town, socially conservative, petty bourgeois constituency, and marked by a militant commitment to defend the republic against its enemies, who were typically defined as royalists, reactionary soldiers, and especially clerics.[53] At the level of parliamentary politics, Radicalism connoted a "cluster" of political groupings, which could only be brought together into a single party in 1901, after the Dreyfus affair had revealed the magnitude of the danger the republic faced.[54] At this level, the militance and whatever consistency the ethos possessed gave way to ideological incoherence, as an abiding suspicion of authority and the blandishments of political power made deputies who called themselves Radicals resistant to parliamentary discipline.

[53] Jacques Kayser, *Les grandes batailles du radicalisme 1820–1901* (Paris, 1962), p. 2.

[54] *Ibid.*, pp. 290–310. The term "cluster" is Leo Loubère's: "Left-Wing Radicals, Strikes, and the Military, 1880–1907," *French Historical Studies* III (1963), 93.

The real basis of Radicalism, however, lay in the myriad of local committees and associations which transformed the ethos into an effective political program and which collectively made up what might be called the Radical movement. Foremost among them were the electoral committees, composed of local notables, which recruited and promoted candidates for local and national office. Beyond these committees, numerous other organizations, closely if unofficially linked to the party, worked to mobilize wider sectors of the populace for the Radical cause. The most prominent were the Masonic lodges (and the organizations affiliated with them), the *Ligue pour la défense des droits de l'homme*, and the free-thought movement. It would hardly be inaccurate to characterize all these various groups as facets of the same movement, for not only were they linked by a common anticlerical and antiauthoritarian program, but they were tied together by a widespread interconnection of leadership on both the local and national levels. The notable who chaired the local Radical committee was frequently a Mason, a member of the local group of *libres penseurs*, and on the board of directors of the local branch of the League of the Rights of Man. Similarly, on the national level many of the most important Radical politicians were Masons, who had founded and continued to be active in the League of the Rights of Man.

The political significance of the French peace movement was that it was one of the components of the Radical movement. Both locally and nationally there was widespread interpenetration between the two movements. The leader of the local peace society was often the same Mason who presided over the local Radical committee or the branch of the League of the Rights of Man. There was also a significant overlap in the membership of the peace societies and the other local Radical organizations. National leaders of the Radical party were active in the peace movement, and pacifists were prominent in the national party organization.

The ideological juncture between pacifism and Radicalism lay in a common faith in democracy and progress, but more directly in the fear, born of the Boulanger and Dreyfus crises, that a powerful professional army was a threat to the republic. This fear informed the program of the Radical party on the subject of national defense and international relations, and it made Radicals responsive to arrangements, such as arbitration, which would minimize the influence of soldiers in political councils. The party's program condemned "the abuses and prejudices of the military spirit" and "any adventurous [foreign] policy," calling instead for "democratic recruitment of an officer corps," an "*entente cordiale* among the nations," and the "extension of the application of international arbitration in serious disputes."[55] The significance of pious affirmations such as these, which could also be found in the programs of left-liberal parties in Germany, ought of course not to be overestimated; many Radical politicians regarded foreign affairs with only peripheral interest prior to 1905 and found arbitration one of the easier points in their party's program to abandon, particularly with growing international tension after 1905.[56] Nevertheless, major figures in the Radical party did favor the advancement of arbitration to a degree few German leaders would have found politically possible. Léon Bourgeois, one of the most eminent Radical politicians of the prewar period, and a man who held nearly every conceivable national office, was an outspoken pacifist.[57] His work in this area extended beyond his continuing defense of arbitration within the Radical party organization, his honorary membership in peace societies, and his participa-

[55] Ferdinand Buisson, *La politique radicale: Étude sur les doctrines du parti radical et radical-socialiste* (Paris, 1908), pp. 256–57.

[56] Bertha R. Leaman, "The Influence of Domestic Policy on Foreign Affairs in France, 1898–1905," *Journal of Modern History* XIV (1942), 450–51.

[57] Maurice Hamburger, *Léon Bourgeois (1851–1925): La politique radicale socialiste, la doctrine de la solidarité, l'arbitrage international et la Société des Nations* (Paris, 1932), esp. pp. 213–38.

tion at peace congresses.[58] As chief French delegate to both Hague conferences, he was principally responsible for salvaging from German attacks whatever little remained of an arbitral agency.

Bourgeois was hardly an isolated figure in his party; numerous other important Radicals were directly involved in the peace movement. Ferdinand Buisson, Charles Beauquier, and Yves Guyot were members of the executive committee of the French section of the *Ligue internationale de la paix et de la liberté*. Beauquier was a vice-president and Hippolyte Laroche a member of the executive committee of the *Société française pour l'arbitrage entre nations*. Lucien Le Foyer, a secretary on the executive committee of the Radical party and a member of the Chamber of Deputies, was the secretary-general of the *Délégation permanente des sociétés françaises de la paix*. Under his influence the executive committee of the party sent its *adhésion* to national peace congresses.[59] Radicals, including Bourgeois, Beauquier, Buisson, Berteaux Maurice, and Jules Pams, were prominent in the French branch of the Interparliamentary Union, and after d'Estournelles de Constant reorganized the group in 1903, virtually every Radical in the French parliament became a member.[60]

The connections were also close between the peace movement and the other organizations that served as auxiliaries of the Radical party. French Freemasonry was decidedly more political than its German counterpart; indeed, its ties to the Radical party were so undisguised that one authority has spoken of the lodges as "little more than political societies."[61] This political orientation made French Masons much less hesitant than Germans to endorse the peace movement, which shared their confidence in science, reason, and prog-

[58] *Ibid.*, pp. 231, 240; PD, XI (1901), 290–91.
[59] PD, XV (1905), 206.
[60] Wild, *Baron d'Estournelles de Constant*, p. 148.
[61] Mildred J. Headings, *French Freemasonry under the Third Republic* (Baltimore, 1949), p. 282.

ress. Numerous local lodges sent delegates to national peace congresses, and several, including "Cosmos"—probably the most pacifistic lodge in the country—were actually affiliated with the International Peace Bureau.[62] The Masonic-controlled *Ligue d'Enseignement* likewise sent delegates to peace congresses. Masonic organizations sought to promote international arbitration and conciliation through public manifestoes (which were often identical with resolutions passed at peace congresses), by utilizing their ties to the Radical party in order to sponsor legislation in the Chamber of Deputies, and by fostering closer ties to Masonic organizations in other countries.[63] Most of the leading French pacifists, from Lemonnier to Charles Richet, were Masons. In sum, both the commitment of Masons to pacifism and their willingness to translate this into political action were considerably more pronounced in France than in Germany.

The distinction between Freemasonry and the freethought movement in France was often unclear. Many of the same people were active in both, and their programs were alike insofar as they both styled themselves champions of science and reason, identifying clericalism as the primary threat to the French republic. Moreover, like the Masonic lodges, *libres penseurs* in France viewed war as an outrage to reason and progress, with the result that they too were closely allied with the peace movement.[64] Local freethought organizations and laic societies sent delegates to national peace congresses. Victor Charbonnel, who in 1902 founded the *Association nationale des libres penseurs de France*, and Charles Beauquier, who became its president,

[62] See II. Congrès national, *Compte-rendu*, p. 114; *Annuaire du mouvement pacifiste*, p. 133.

[63] PD, XI (1901), 169; PD, XXII (1912), 807–808; Headings, *French Freemasonry*, pp. 224–36.

[64] See Pierre Lévêque, "Libre pensée et socialisme (1889–1939): Quelques points de repère," *Le mouvement social*, number 57 (October/December 1966), p. 112; cf. PD, XV (1905), 410.

were both pacifists. Under their leadership the organization affiliated with the International Peace Bureau.[65]

Although founded by a Moderate republican, and later led by a socialist, the *Ligue pour la défense des droits de l'homme et du citoyen* became another Radical stronghold, as its program of republican defense corresponded to that of the Radical party. The league was also closely tied to the peace movement. Both prewar presidents of the organization, Ludovic Trarieux (the Moderate) and Francis de Pressensé (the socialist), were pacifists, as were several members of the league's central committee, including Charles Richet and Lucien Le Foyer.[66] Both the national organization and local branches regularly sent delegates to national peace congresses, and in 1906 the entire organization affiliated with the International Peace Bureau.[67]

There was thus extensive interpenetration and cooperation between the peace movement and the Radical movement. On the national level this was perhaps best illustrated in the career of Charles Beauquier, who was simultaneously a Radical member of the Chamber of Deputies, a member of the Masonic lodge "Cosmos," president of the *Association nationale des libres penseurs*, a major figure in the *Ligue des droits de l'homme*, and president or leading member in half a dozen peace societies. Beauquier's example was extreme in degree, but it exemplified a tendency on both the national and local levels toward multiple affiliations in these organizations. Théodore Ruyssen was president of the *Association de la paix par le droit*, a leader of the local *Union démocratique* in Aix-en-Provence, and active in the local laic society. Delegates frequently arrived at national peace congresses with mandates from several different organizations, such as a local committee of the league, a Masonic lodge, and a local peace society.

[65] BIP (vA7–8), Charbonnel to Peace Bureau, 1 August 1907.

[66] MFK, II (February 1895); PD, XX (1910), 239; see also Henri Sée, *Histoire de la ligue des droits de l'homme, 1898–1926* (Paris, 1927).

[67] BIP (vA5), Henry Casevitz to Ducommun, Paris, 5 June, 25 June 1906.

While pacifism in France was in large part a facet of the Radical movement, it was not exclusively so. To the right of the Radicals, Moderate republicans, the most prominent of whom were Trarieux and d'Estournelles de Constant, were active in the peace movement. Further to the right, though, among conservatives, monarchists, and clericals, there was virtually no sympathy for the peace movement. To the left of the Radicals, however, in sectors of the labor movement, the peace movement found important allies.

It is more difficult to generalize about the attitude of the labor movement toward the bourgeois peace movement in France than in Germany. For most of the prewar period the discipline of the German labor movement stifled, ideologically at least, the forces within it that favored cooperation with the bourgeois pacifists. In France, although socialists came together in a unified party in 1905, conflicting currents remained and surfaced more readily. The fact that the relationship between the socialist party and the trade union movement was less clearly defined than in Germany only made the picture more clouded. In these circumstances sympathy for the peace movement could be more freely expressed both within the socialist party and the wider sectors of the labor movement.

In France, as in Germany, the relationship between socialists and pacifists was governed by the ideological debate over the capacity of capitalist society for peaceful reform, specifically the problem of whether international conflict could be eliminated prior to the realization of socialism. At the risk of considerable oversimplification, it is possible to discern in this debate two opposing tendencies within the French labor movement. One held that the interests of the working class were completely opposed to the prevailing norms of bourgeois society, that *la patrie*—itself a bourgeois institution—was not worth fighting for in any circumstances, and that workers should refuse military service and respond to the outbreak of war with a general strike in order to destroy capitalism. Only this would bring lasting peace.

357

This position, which was generally referred to as "antimilitarism" (as opposed to pacifism), found its most articulate spokesman in Gustave Hervé, a school teacher in Yonne whose views became increasingly radical after the turn of the century, until just before the war, when he began to turn toward militant patriotism. After its endorsement by the congresses of the *Confédération générale du Travail* in Amiens in 1906 and Marseilles in 1908, antimilitarism became the official doctrine of this organization on the problem of war and capitalist society.[68] Within the French socialist parties the groups that inclined toward orthodox Marxism, which in 1902 coalesced under the leadership of Jules Guesde and Paul Lafargue into the *Parti socialiste de France*, agreed with the antimilitarists insofar as they too emphasized the antagonism between the worker and capitalist society and insisted that only the revolutionary overthrow of capitalism would bring the end of war (though they objected to the general strike as a tactic).

Among socialist and labor organizations that shared this outlook, the French pacifists found no more support than German pacifists found in the SPD while party orthodoxy remained intransigent.[69] Another sector of the French labor movement, however, was receptive to the idea that arbitration and disarmament represented feasible alternatives to warfare, even within the context of capitalist society. The most prominent representative of this tendency was Jean Jaurès, whose ideas on war and capitalism anticipated the views articulated by Kautsky during the imperialism debate. Although he believed that only socialism would guarantee a world without war, he was convinced that there were peaceful tendencies inherent in capitalist development

[68] See Jacques Julliard, "La CGT devant la guerre (1900–1914)," *Le mouvement social*, number 49 (October/December 1964), pp. 47–62; Drachkovitch, *Les socialismes*, pp. 87–92, 131–55.

[69] "L'internationalisme au congrès socialiste de Limoges," PD, xvi (1906), 438–40; Wild, *Baron d'Estournelles de Constant*, p. 105; Drachkovitch, *Les socialismes*, pp. 93–95.

and that measures short of socialist revolution could and should be undertaken to promote them.[70] He thus abandoned the skepticism he had shown about arbitration early in his career and, after the turn of the century, became an outspoken proponent of both international arbitration and socialist cooperation with the bourgeois peace movement. Indeed, Jaurès's conceptions of international politics were in many respects much the same as the bourgeois pacifists'; he emphasized the division of mankind into fundamentally harmonious national units, whose preservation was necessary and desirable, even in a socialist world.[71] Both his humanism and his concern for the welfare of the working class led him to devote much of his career to averting war, but his belief in the validity of the nation made it impossible for him to accept Hervé's radical doctrines. Instead, he found in disarmament and arbitration the keys to the nonviolent realization of lasting peace. He believed that these reforms could be made effective once they were supported by a determined coalition of the labor movement and the progressive bourgeoisie.[72]

The amalgamation of Guesde's party and Jaurès's *Parti socialiste français* into the *Section française de l'internationale ouvrière* compelled Jaurès to abandon his views on the desirability of socialist participation in bourgeois governments, but he continued to advocate international arbitration and disarmament. Indeed, Jaurès's views on these matters became dominant in the unified party, both because he was the party's principal spokesman on international affairs and because most of the others in the party's "foreign policy cabinet"—men such as Pressensé, Édouard Vaillant,

---

[70] Haupt, *Socialism and the Great War*, pp. 152–53.

[71] Harold R. Weinstein, *Jean Jaurès: A Study of Patriotism in the French Socialist Movement* (New York, 1936), esp. pp. 132–55; Drachkovitch, *Les socialismes*, pp. 101–14.

[72] Elizabeth M. Garber, "L'arbitrage international devant le mouvement socialiste français 1890–1914," *La revue socialiste* (New Series) number 105 (March 1957), pp. 298–304; cf. Jaurès, "Sozialdemokratie und Pacifismus," FW, x (1908), 204–205.

Marcel Sembat, and Maurice Allard—were of the same persuasion.[73] Under the influence of these leaders, the SFIO's position increasingly resembled that of the bourgeois pacifists. As a gesture to Hervé and his supporters, party resolutions ritually made mention of the general strike, but it was clear that Jaurès, Vaillant, and a majority of the party held the general strike to be permissible only in certain well defined circumstances, and then less as a device to bring down capitalism than as one of the many tools available to the working class to prevent the outbreak of an aggressive war—for most regarded defensive wars as legitimate—or to force the arbitration of disputes that might lead to war.[74] At party congresses and in the Chamber of Deputies, socialist leaders emphasized arbitration as the principal means to prevent war, and they called upon the working-class movement to force the implementation of effective arbitration. At the SFIO congress in 1910 in Nîmes, for instance, the delegates approved by an overwhelming majority a resolution introduced by Sembat, which urged the Socialist International "to make sure that the courts of arbitration, which the capitalist bourgeoisie has been compelled to institute, function on as regular and general a basis as possible."[75]

This of course had a direct bearing on the socialists' appreciation of the bourgeois peace movement. Relations between pacifists and the socialists who followed Jaurès were generally quite cordial. Jaurès and Passy were on terms of mutual esteem.[76] In 1904 L'Humanité, which Jaurès edited,

[73] PD, xx (1910), 178; PD, xxiv (1914), 62; see Jack D. Ellis, *The French Socialists and the Problem of the Peace, 1904-1914* (Chicago, 1967), pp. 9-10, 26-27, 100.

[74] Ellis, *The French Socialists*, pp. 18-32; Haupt, *Socialism and the Great War*, pp. 174-75; Garber, "L'arbitrage international," pp. 301-302.

[75] Quoted in Garber, "L'arbitrage international," p. 305; see also Ellis, *The French Socialists*, p. 23; Drachkovitch, *Les socialismes*, pp. 95-101.

[76] BIP (viB), Passy to Ducommun, Neuilly, 29 October 1903.

submitted its *adhésion* to the International Peace Bureau.[77] When the French branch of the Interparliamentary Union was reorganized in 1903, Jaurès became a vice-president, and many French socialists followed him into the organization; in 1912 fifty-five of the seventy-six socialists in the Chamber of Deputies belonged.[78] Socialists also belonged to peace societies. Alexandre Millerand, though no longer officially a socialist after 1905, was a member of the central committee of the *Ligue internationale de la paix et de la liberté*. The president of the Ardennes section of the *Association de la paix par le droit* was a socialist, Henri Louis Doizy, who in 1910 was elected to the Chamber of Deputies.[79] Several local socialist federations, including the *Fédération des travailleurs socialistes de l'Yonne* before it came under Hervé's influence, gave their *adhésions* to bourgeois peace societies or to national peace congresses.[80]

The tendency that Jaurès represented was stronger within the socialist party than in the CGT and other organizations of the wider labor movement, where antimilitarism was ideologically predominant. Yet here, too, there were pockets of support for the bourgeois peace movement, in organizations where, for one reason or another, reformist influence was strong. Foremost in this regard were the *universités populaires*, institutions founded during the Dreyfus affair to educate workers in republican virtues by exposing them to instruction in history, science, economics, and other disciplines through lectures delivered by academicians recruited from local *lycées* or universities.[81] Predictably, the

---

[77] BIP (vA5), Casevitz to Ducommun, Paris, 4 November 1904.

[78] Garber, "L'arbitrage international," p. 305, n. 35.

[79] PD, XXIV (1914), 269.

[80] BIP (vQ2h), Rapport sur l'exécution des résolutions des congrès de la paix relatives à la propagande (Berne, 30 August 1903), p. 25; BIP (vA5), Madeleine Carlier to Ducommun, Croisilles, 14 May 1903.

[81] See Daniel Halévy, "Coopératives et universités populaires en France," *Essais sur le mouvement ouvrier en France* (Paris, 1901), pp. 136–99.

spectacle of workers' being educated by bourgeois intellectuals provoked the opposition of Guesde and Lafargue, but Jaurès endorsed them warmly, for they corroborated his belief in the possibility of working within capitalist society for the edification of the working class.[82] People's universities in turn endorsed Jaurès's views on arbitration and disarmament. By 1906 over one hundred of them had submitted their official *adhésions* to the International Peace Bureau, largely because of a campaign undertaken by Henry Casevitz, the business manager of *L'Humanité*, who was also a member of the *Délégation permanente des sociétés françaises de la paix*.[83]

Among the trade unions and *bourses du travail*, support for the peace movement was less widespread. The reformist miners' federation sent a delegate, Claude Gignoux, to Universal Peace Congresses in Boston and London, and Louis Niel, a reformist leader in the CGT, spoke at the national peace congress in 1908.[84] But this was unusual. Prior to 1914 only about two dozen *bourses du travail* had affiliated with a peace society or sent their *adhésions* to national peace congresses. In most cases these *bourses* were in localities, such as Nîmes or Toulouse, where there were active peace societies, or they were closely connected to the local *université populaire*, in some cases, as in Agen, Narbonne, and Clermont-Ferrand, actually having their headquarters in the same building.[85]

Finally, sympathy for the peace movement was strong in the cooperative movement, particularly in the nonsocialist segment of the *Union des sociétés coopératives de consom-*

[82] Harvey Goldberg, *The Life of Jean Jaurès* (Madison, 1962), pp. 269–70.

[83] BIP (vA5), Adhésions au Bureau international permanent de la paix de Berne adressées par M. Henry Casevitz, 22 May 1906.

[84] *Official Report of the Thirteenth Universal Peace Congress*, pp. 144–45; CBM, XIII (1908), 117; II. Congrès national, *Compte-rendu*, p. 66.

[85] *Annuaire du mouvement pacifiste*, pp. 139–40; cf. Halévy, "Coopératives et universités," p. 185.

mation, whose leader, Charles Gide, was a pacifist.[86] Both the central committee of the cooperatives' union and local cooperatives regularly sent representatives to peace congresses.[87] Gide was also instrumental in persuading the International Cooperative Alliance to affiliate with the International Peace Bureau in 1902.[88] The same close ties existed between the peace movement and the producer-cooperative movement, which, to be sure, could hardly be called a working-class phenomenon after the turn of the century, so individualistic and middle class had it become. But like the consumer cooperatives, producer organizations cultivated close relations with the peace movement, sending representatives regularly to peace congresses.[89]

French pacifists were thus more successful than their German colleagues in dealing with the labor movement in their country. This was largely because support for the pacifists was not muzzled in the French labor movement by ideological intransigence and party discipline. A significant segment of the socialist party was prepared to collaborate with progressive bourgeois politicians from the Radical party on a wide range of issues, including arbitration and arms limitation. At the same time, the French pacifists were themselves, at least in a small way, responsible for the more cordial relations they enjoyed with working-class organizations. Although they supported private property and condemned social revolution with as much conviction as the

[86] Jean Gaumont, *Histoire générale de la coopération en France* (2 vols., Paris, 1923–24), II, 662; A. Lavondès, *Charles Gide, un apôtre de la coopération entre les hommes, un précurseur de l'Europe unie et de l'U.N.O.* (Uzès, 1953); cf. David J. Saposs, *The Labor Movement in Post-War France* (New York, 1931), pp. 366–75; PD, XXIII (1913), 20.

[87] BIP (vA5), A. Daudé-Bancel to Peace Bureau, Paris, 4 July 1901; Moch, "Le VIIIe Congrès universel," p. 346.

[88] *Bulletin officiel du XIIe Congrès universel*, p. 228; Gaumont, *Coopération en France*, II, 662.

[89] "La coopération et la paix," PD, XIII (1903), 197–98; CBM, XIII (1908), 117.

Germans, their approach to the labor movement was more imaginative and accommodating. They clearly perceived the tensions within the movement and threw their moral support to Jaurès and his allies in their conflict with Hervé. Not only did they recognize an ally in Jaurès, but they saw that Hervé's antimilitarism threatened to discredit all forms of antiwar activity; the reproach directed by *Le Temps* at the peace movement, that "pacifism is the preface to Hervé-ism," was one the pacifists frequently heard.[90] French pacifists were also prepared to concede to socialists that "the principal causes of war reside in the economic inequality of men in all countries," which "gives rise to the feelings of egotism in individuals and, thus, the savage instinct of combat and war."[91] To be sure, not all French pacifists were willing to go this far, and none of them was willing to countenance the socialists' solution to the problem of inequality. But as disciples of Léon Bourgeois's *solidarisme*, they were prepared to accept a considerable amount of public intervention in the economy and society, including factory legislation, social insurance, and even "obligatory arbitration of labor conflicts."[92] French pacifists, in short, acknowledged that the economic and social inequalities that inhered in capitalism were in large measure responsible for international tension. This was an acknowledgment that German pacifists, whose confidence in capitalism was more doctrinaire, were less willing to make.

Even had the German pacifists found more support among the labor movement and political parties, it would have been quite irrelevant to the formulation of German foreign policy. In France, where foreign policy was subject to parliamentary control and hence more sensitive to public opinion, political support for the peace movement was

[90] PD, xv (1905), 409, 430; PD, xvii (1907), 13–14.

[91] ii. Congrès national, *Compte-rendu*, p. 68.

[92] PD, xix (1909), 333. On *solidarisme* see John A. Scott, *Republican Ideas and the Liberal Tradition in France, 1870–1914* (New York, 1951), pp. 157–86; Hamburger, *Léon Bourgeois*, pp. 45–66.

translated into modest attempts on the part of the government to put arbitration into general practice.

In Germany the peace movement enjoyed virtually no access to persons in positions of political power; with a handful of exceptions, all Germans of any official importance regarded it with great distaste. The French peace movement, on the other hand, was treated well on all levels of government. City councils and departmental *Conseils généraux* responded to the pacifists' appeals by passing resolutions urging the extension of international arbitration—innocuous gestures, perhaps, but more than any similar institutions were willing to undertake in Germany.[93] On the national level, too, French leaders were more willing than their German counterparts to treat the pacifists with civility, and some went considerably further than that.[94] Pacifist leaders also had regular access to officials in the foreign office.[95]

Far more important than all this, in translating the sentiments articulated by the peace movement into policy, was the presence in French politics of a mediator between pacifists and politicians, a man who devoted his career to promoting arbitration and who possessed considerable political power and influence. There was no figure comparable to Paul Henri d'Estournelles de Constant in Germany; indeed, given the realities of German politics, it is difficult to conceive of how there could have been.[96] Having spent his

[93] BIP (vBɪ), Ville de Bourges, Extrait du registre des délibérations du conseil municipal, 21 February 1903; MFK, 1 (March 1894); PD, x (1900), 28; PD, xɪɪɪ (1903), 253, 362–64; PD, xxɪ (1911), 84.

[94] For example, Baron de Courcel, who in 1894 became French ambassador to England, was a member of the central committee of Passy's peace society: BIP (vɪB), Passy to Ducommun, Neuilly, 11 October 1894.

[95] BIP (vBɪ), Passy to Ducommun, Neuilly, 26 October 1896; BIP (vɪB), Passy to Ducommun, Neuilly, 29 October 1903; PD, xɪɪɪ (1903), 132.

[96] For an exhaustive study of d'Estournelles de Constant see Wild, *Baron d'Estournelles de Constant*.

early career in the diplomatic service, he entered the Chamber of Deputies in 1895 and was elected to the Senate in 1904. A member of the Moderate republican *Union républicaine*, he rapidly gained a reputation as a convinced yet realistic champion of arbitration, and he succeeded in organizing political support for it among Moderates, Radicals, and reformist socialists alike. He served on the French delegations at both Hague conferences. In 1909 he received the Nobel Peace Prize. Although he failed to hold a ministerial position, he was frequently mentioned as a likely candidate for the ministry of foreign affairs.

Early in 1903 d'Estournelles reorganized and reinvigorated the French section of the Interparliamentary Union by establishing the *Groupe de l'arbitrage international*. At its founding the group consisted of some two hundred deputies and senators, among them some of the most important figures of the republican left.[97] With succeeding elections it grew, until by 1914, 168 of 300 senators and 344 of 584 deputies belonged.[98] The impact of the organization was soon felt. Within two years of its founding it had successfully sponsored general treaties of arbitration with England, Italy, Spain, Holland, Sweden, Norway, and Switzerland.[99] Typically these obligated the contracting states to arbitrate disputes arising out of the interpretation of existing treaties between them. Although matters affecting a country's vital interests and national honor were carefully excluded, d'Estournelles regarded these treaties as a promising beginning, and his group sponsored fourteen of them before the war. The Germans, parenthetically, concluded only the one with England.

Relations between the *Groupe de l'arbitrage* and the peace societies were not completely without friction, for

[97] *Ibid.*, pp. 148–50; "Le groupe de l'arbitrage international," PD, XIII (1903), 125–30. Included were Aristide Briand, Ferdinand Buisson, Joseph Caillaux, Alexandre Millerand, Jaurès, Bourgeois, Vaillant, Marcellin Berthelot, Alphonse de Courcel, and René Waldeck-Rousseau.

[98] VF, XV (1914), 15; cf. PD, XVI (1906), 253.

[99] HB (2), I, 185–88.

many French politicians feared too close an identification with a group of people accused by conservatives and nationalists of political naiveté and insufficient patriotism.[100] Nonetheless, the relationship between the two camps was much more cordial than in Germany, both because the *Groupe de l'arbitrage* was more genuinely interested in arbitration than were the German parliamentarians, and because d'Estournelles was not prepared to use the pacifists as whipping boys. While he did, for tactical reasons, maintain a certain distance from the peace societies, he was a member of the administrative council of Passy's society and participated in several peace congresses.[101]

D'Estournelles quickly became aware, though, of the need for an organization more attractive to men of prominence than the existing peace societies. Accordingly, in 1905 he founded *Conciliation internationale*, a group designed to bring together political, cultural, and business leaders in order to promote arbitration while adding prestige to the concept through the very eminence of its membership.[102] He was able to recruit several hundred notables, including such politicians as Bourgeois, Beauquier, and Marcellin Berthelot, scholars such as Henri Bergson, Ernest Lavisse, and Henri Poincaré, and the members of some forty chambers of commerce. So great was his success in France that he began to recruit members abroad. In the United States, the American Association for International Conciliation was set up as a branch of d'Estournelles' organization, as was the *Verband für internationale Verständigung* in Germany.

D'Estournelles de Constant also played an important role at the Hague conferences, where the French showed that, unlike the Germans, they were prepared to make important concessions to the peace movement. The tsar's proposal for a disarmament conference caused as much consternation

---

[100] Passy, "Congrès et conférence," *L'arbitrage entre nations* III (July 1899), 153–55.
[101] BIP (vBI), Passy to Ducommun, Paris, 29 May 1901.
[102] Wild, *Baron d'Estournelles de Constant*, pp. 220–40.

in the French foreign office as it did in Berlin.[103] The French foreign minister, Théophile Delcassé, did not hold the peace movement or its program in high regard, and like the German diplomats, he was principally concerned over the practical implications of the tsar's proposal.[104] He was especially worried that the conference might guarantee the European *status quo* and undermine the French claim to Alsace-Lorraine.[105] From the beginning, however, the French government was unable to treat the project with the sovereign contempt of the Germans. More than the Germans, the French feared lest the Russians, their allies, be humiliated by the failure of the conference.[106] In addition, the pressure of public opinion, which had been mobilized by the peace movement, was a factor French statesmen could not ignore. Accordingly, French officials responded publicly in a most accommodating way to the Russian proposal and took pains, in a series of interviews with leading pacifists, to assure the peace movement that the French government was seriously interested in limiting the arms race.[107] More significantly, there was less disparity in France than in Germany between what officials said in public and what they did in private. Although they were cer-

[103] Moulin to Chanoine, Paris, 28 September 1898, DDF (1), xiv, 581, number 274.

[104] BIP (vBi), Passy to Ducommun, Paris, 27 November 1903; Wild, *Baron d'Estournelles de Constant*, p. 103; PD, xii (1902), 432-33.

[105] Christopher Andrew, *Théophile Delcassé and the Making of the Entente Cordiale: A Reappraisal of French Foreign Policy, 1898-1905* (London, 1968), pp. 121-22.

[106] Delcassé to Vauvineaux, Paris, 23 September 1898, DDF (1), xiv, 576-77, number 369; AA, Eur. Gen. 37 number 1, Bd. 9, A4820 (ACP 103), Münster to Hohenlohe, Paris, 21 April 1899 (GP, xv, 186-87, number 4253).

[107] BIP (vBi), Paul-Edouard Decharme to Ducommun, Paris [December 1898]; Le Foyer, "Chez MM. Depuy et Delcassé," PD, viii (1898), 319-20; Le Foyer, "La 'Paix par le droit' chez M. Léon Bourgeois," PD, ix (1899), 263-64; Delcassé to Représentants diplomatiques de France . . . Paris, 8 September 1898, DDF (1), xiv, 521-22, number 332.

tainly skeptical, officials in the French foreign office concluded that certain concessions to public opinion could and should be made in the matter of arms limitation and, after the Russians proposed its inclusion on the conference agenda, international arbitration.[108]

The delegation sent by the French government to The Hague in May 1899 consisted of Léon Bourgeois as chief, d'Estournelles de Constant, and Louis Renault, a respected international lawyer in charge of legal affairs in the foreign office. Renault, who was well aware of the technical complexities of arbitration, held views comparable to those of Philipp Zorn, his German counterpart; but beyond that, the French delegation provided a striking contrast to the German team of Münster and Stengel, for both Bourgeois and d'Estournelles strongly favored arbitration and an agreement on arms limitation. The instructions they received consisted only of broad guidelines—a measure of Delcassé's trust and willingness to make concessions. On the subject of arms limitation the French were prepared to agree to a five-year moratorium on all extensions of land and sea forces, provided (and this they knew was unlikely) that such an agreement had the support of a majority of the delegates. The French team was also given great latitude to pursue an arbitration agreement, subject to the limitation that any such agreement be explicitly worded as to procedures and jurisdiction.[109]

[108] Freycinet to Delcassé, Paris, 7 February 1899, DDF (1), xv, 113–15, number 69; Note de M. Louis Renault sur la circulaire du Comte Mouravieff en date du 11 janvier 1899, 8 February 1899, DDF (1), xv, 116–17, number 71; Delcassé to Montebello, Paris, 10 February 1899, DDF (1), xv, 120–21, number 75; AA, Eur. Gen. 37 number 1, Bd. 9, A4820 (ACP 103), Münster to Hohenlohe, Paris, 21 April 1899 (GP, xv, 186–87, number 4253).

[109] Delcassé to Délégation française à la conférence de La Haye, Paris, 15 May 1899, DDF (1), xv, 284–86, number 175; cf. Delcassé to Délégation française . . . Paris, 10 June 1899, DDF (1), xv, 363–64, number 212. Münster reported to Bülow that the French delegation had been instructed not to enter into any obligatory agreements on

Once the conference convened, the behavior of the Germans made the French delegation's instructions on arms limitation irrelevant. The fact that the conference was even able to proclaim that "the limitation of military expenses . . . is extremely desirable for the growth of the material and moral well-being of humanity" was owing to the initiative of Bourgeois.[110] The Germans also caused considerable anxiety among the French delegates over the arbitration problem. The commission charged with drawing up an arbitration proposal was chaired by Bourgeois, who was anxious to achieve something substantial. For the French themselves, it was not a question of whether to agree to the principle of obligatory arbitration, but rather which kinds of disputes were admissible. Like everyone else, the French insisted that questions involving a nation's vital interests or honor be exempt, but beyond this they were prepared to be "very liberal" in defining the categories of disputes they would accept for obligatory arbitration: the list drawn up by the foreign office comprised twenty-six categories, including disputes arising over tariffs and other trade restrictions, international waterways, monetary problems, patents and copyrights, the return of naval deserters, and consular immunities.[111] To the dismay of Bourgeois and d'Estournelles, however, the Germans' refusal to countenance even the principle of obligatory arbitration made all French con-

---

either arbitration or arms limitation. He was mistaken: AA, Eur. Gen. 37 number 2, Bd. 2, A7858 (ACP 104), Münster to Bülow, Scheveningen, 26 June 1899 (GP, xv, 312–14, number 4327). On d'Estournelles' role at the Hague conferences see Wild, *Baron d'Estournelles de Constant*, pp. 69–93, 297–321.

[110] Délégation française . . . to Delcassé, The Hague, 2 July 1899, DDF (1), xv, 384–86, number 228.

[111] Délégation française . . . to Delcassé, Annex: Note de M. Louis Renault, The Hague, 29 May 1899, DDF (1), xv, 319–23, number 192; Note de M. Léon Bourgeois, Paris, 3 June 1899, DDF (1), xv, 330–31, number 199; Delcassé to Délégation française . . . Paris, 7 June 1899, DDF (1), xv, 347–51, number 205.

cessions unnecessary. The watered-down compromise the Germans reluctantly endorsed was thus far less than the French were willing to accept.

The scenario was the same at the second Hague conference. The French delegation, once again led by Bourgeois and d'Estournelles, arrived at The Hague, much to the incomprehension of the Germans, seriously interested in negotiating an international treaty of arbitration with certain obligatory provisions.[112] Once again Bourgeois presided over the commission on arbitration, where the Germans killed all hopes of setting up some form of agency with obligatory jurisdiction.

The French were no more willing than the Germans to compromise really important interests at The Hague. Indeed, the French foreign office was relieved that the Germans had taken it upon themselves to sabotage obligatory arbitration. Yet, in terms of both style and substance, the contrast between French and German policy at The Hague was glaring. For all its skepticism, the French government was prepared to make concessions to public opinion on obligatory arbitration, and these concessions were not altogether insubstantial. In the final analysis, though, the significance of this contrast lay not so much in what did or did not happen at The Hague, as in the fact that it reflected the workings of two different political systems. The peace movement was a far more potent political force in France than in Germany. In Germany, both the constitution and the character of prevailing political attitudes militated against international arbitration. In France, pacifism was politically far more viable; the movement that championed arbitration was well entrenched in French politics, and the French government could not disregard the sentiments it mobilized.

[112] Pichon to Bompard, Paris, 16 August 1907, DDF (2), XI, 225–26, number 199; AA, Eur. Gen. 37 number 6, Bd. 1, A16840 (ACP 106), Marschall to Bülow, Neuershausen, 28 October 1907, p. 12 (GP, XXIII, 281–89, number 7964).

Agencies of Political Education:
Schools, the Press, Churches

French pacifists, like the Germans, insisted that their movement and its goals were nonpartisan. This claim had even less credibility in France than in Germany, for the French peace movement was more politically active, in a way that could only with the greatest difficulty be styled nonpartisan. But in the belief that their cause transcended political divisions, the French pacifists also engaged in the same kinds of "nonpolitical" educational activities that occupied the Germans, sending petitions, appeals, and literature to schools, newspapers, and churches. And on the whole, the French found significantly more resonance and support among these important agencies of political education than did their German counterparts.

In 1904, amidst a general furor in the press, the *Union des instituteurs patriotiques* was founded. The organization represented the response of nationalists, led by the historian Georges Goyau, to what they perceived as the increasing subversion of primary education by pacifists.[113] The episode, and the heated debate it unleashed in the press, were reminiscent of the uproar occasioned by the Baden diet's decision in 1898 to examine the state's schoolbooks. But there was one important difference. In Germany the threat of pacifists' exercising any influence in primary education was very small, and the nationalist reaction to the action of the Landtag was preposterous. In France, on the other hand, the pacifist "threat" to the educational establishment was very real indeed, for there were few places in French society where the peace movement enjoyed such support.[114] Devoted to science, reason, and progress, *instituteurs* and

[113] A. Jouet, "Le parti pacifique et la Revue des deux mondes," PD, XI (1901), 362–67; cf. PD, XVII (1907), 262–70; Weber, *Nationalist Revival*, p. 23.

[114] BIP (vBI), Passy to Ducommun, Neuilly, 19 April 1901; PD, XV (1905), 422–23; cf. Reinhold Lehmann, *Die französischen Volksschullehrer als Schrittmacher der Friedensbewegung* (Stuttgart, 1920).

institutrices were, as a rule, strong defenders of the republic and were prominent in the Radical movement.[115] They were also responsive to the theories of scientific pacifism and constituted probably the most numerous occupational group in the French peace movement. In view of this, it is hardly surprising that Ferdinand Buisson, the man who, probably more than anyone else, shaped the character of primary education under the republic, was a pacifist.

In 1901 two teachers, Madeleine Carlier and Marguerite Bodin, founded the *Société de l'éducation pacifique*, with Passy as its honorary president, in order to promote peace and arbitration among primary school teachers. Immediately the organization found an enthusiastic response among the *amicales*, the departmental federations of primary school teachers.[116] By the eve of the First World War, thirty-nine such organizations, representing over forty thousand teachers, were affiliated with Carlier's society. Moreover, national congresses of the *amicales*, which altogether comprised well over one hundred thousand teachers, regularly voted resolutions condemning war.[117] The pacifism of the primary school teachers was also reflected in the pedagogical press in France. Among their supporters pacifists counted such journals as *L'école nouvelle*, *Journal des instituteurs*, *L'instituteur républicain*, and *L'éducation*.[118]

From the pacifists' standpoint, school books in France were clearly superior to those in Germany. While they did not deprecate patriotism or the obligation of all Frenchmen to defend the country from attack, most books in use in French primary schools made a concerted attempt to dissociate patriotism and war, to suggest that other cultures

[115] See Antoine Prost, *Histoire de l'enseignement en France 1800–1967* (Paris, 1968), pp. 384–86; Georges Duveau, *Les instituteurs* (Paris, 1957).

[116] BIP (vQ3a), Madeleine Carlier.

[117] *Ibid.*; PD, xv (1905), 407–408.

[118] BIP (vB1), Passy to Ducommun, Neuilly, 2 December 1901; PD, xii (1902), 320; PD, xiii (1903), 36–37.

had inherent virtues, and to demonstrate that arbitration was much preferable to war.[119] On the whole, the tenor of the French textbooks differed significantly from the German, and it is difficult to imagine how an explicitly pacifistic text, such as Carlier's *Pour la paix*, which was approved for use in French schools, could have found its way into the primary school curriculum in Germany.[120]

French universities were also more cordial to the peace movement. Many noted university scholars were members of peace societies—men such as André Weiss, Ferdinand Faure, the economist Anatole Leroy-Beaulieu, Marcellin Berthelot, Théodore Ruyssen, and Alexandre Mérignhac. Many more belonged to *Conciliation internationale*. Pacifist speakers encountered none of the harassment at French universities that they could expect in Germany. Indeed, French universities were most receptive to pacifist lecturers. In 1902, for instance, Passy, d'Estournelles de Constant, Weiss, Charles Richet, and several others held a series of lectures on pacifism at the *École des hautes études sociales* and the *École de morale* at the Sorbonne.[121] The participation of French university students in pacifistic international student organizations, such as *Corda fratres*, was far less extensive than that of English and American students, who were the real carriers of the international student movement; but French students were more in evidence than Germans, and they also made up a much greater proportion of the membership in peace societies than did their German counterparts.

[119] Jacques and Mona Ozouf, "Le thème du patriotisme dans les manuels primaires," *Le mouvement social*, number 49 (October/December 1964), 3–31; cf. Prost, *L'enseignement en France*, pp. 335–36.

[120] Liedtke, "Die Entwicklung des Pazifismus," p. 430. It was a history text written by Gustave Hervé that touched off the creation of the *Union des instituteurs patriotiques: see* PD, XIV (1904), 229–35.

[121] BIP (vB1), Passy to Ducommun, Paris, 12 January 1903; PD, XII (1902), 483; VIIe Congrès national des sociétés françaises de la paix, Clermont-Ferrand, 4–7 juin 1911, *Compte-rendu du congrès* (Clermont-Ferrand, 1911), p. 179.

Though unquestionably more favorable than the German press toward the pacifists, French newspapers were not, as a rule, enthusiastic supporters of the peace movement. As in Germany, the root of the problem lay in the nationalist bias of the press and scant reader interest in peace congresses. In 1909 the *Association de la paix par le droit* sent questionnaires to two hundred provincial papers, asking them for their opinions about the peace movement. Only seventeen announced themselves "devoted" (*acquis*) to arbitration, though an additional sixty were "favorable"; forty-two were "approachable," sixty-eight were "indifferent" or did not bother to respond, and thirty-five admitted that they were hostile.[122] If French pacifists found these statistics "far from discouraging," they were forced to admit that the situation was far worse in Paris, where the press treated them with "almost universal hostility."[123] Of the more than one hundred fifty dailies published in Paris at the turn of the century, the pacifists counted only seven among their allies; of the four mass circulation dailies, *Le Petit Journal*, *Le Petit Parisien*, *Le Journal*, and *Le Matin*, only *Le Matin* was occasionally favorable to the peace movement.[124]

Papers that were cordial to the peace movement generally had strong republican and anticlerical leanings. Thus, Yves Guyot's *Le Siècle* and Gérault-Richard's *La Petite République*, as well as *Le Radical, Le Rappel*, and the feminist daily, *La Fronde*, were the most important pro-pacifist papers in Paris.[125] Of the major provincial dailies, the Radical *Dépêche de Toulouse* was the warmest friend of the peace movement. Conversely, the papers most op-

122 Sixième Congrès national des sociétés françaises de la paix, Reims, 30 mai–2 juin 1909, *Compte-rendu des séances* (Reims, 1909), p. 64.
123 PD, XIX (1909), 365.
124 Passy, "L'arbitrage et la presse," PD, XI (1901), 52; PD, XIII (1903), 405; cf. Charles Ledré, *Histoire de la presse* (Paris, 1958), pp. 309, 325.
125 BIP (vB1), Passy to Ducommun, Neuilly, 10 March 1893; Moch to Ducommun, Paris, 30 April 1898; PD, XI (1901), 52; Garber, "L'arbitrage international," p. 297.

posed to the pacifists' campaign were those with rightist, clerical leanings, such as *La Croix*, *L'Univers*, and *Nouvellistes*. More distressing to the pacifists was the fact that the semiofficial *Le Temps* regarded the peace movement with "cool reserve" and refused to print material submitted to it by pacifists.[126]

Like the German pacifists, the French attempted to popularize their ideas in the press by organizing journalists known to be sympathetic and by creating agencies to keep newspapers informed about the peace movement. And like the German pacifists, they did not experience a great deal of success. In 1897 Émile Arnaud, together with the omnipresent Beauquier, established the *Association internationale des journalistes amis de la paix*. Designed to coordinate the efforts of pacifist journalists throughout the world, the organization did attract some personalities in France from beyond the hard core of pacifist sympathizers, including Maurice Lendet of *Figaro*, Hector Depasse of *L'Écho de Paris*, and Gaston Morin of the *Revue libérale*.[127] But the group was never able to mobilize, and in 1902 Beauquier was forced to confess that it was dormant.[128] In 1903 Beauquier tried again, this time by founding a *Syndicat de journalistes français s'occupant spécialement de la politique extérieure*, to be affiliated with d'Estournelles de Constant's *Groupe de l'arbitrage*.[129] This shared the fate of his earlier organization.

---

[126] Schoen to Bethmann Hollweg, Paris, 28 April 1913, GP, xxxix, 309–11, number 15,701; BIP (viB), Passy to Ducommun, Neuilly, 11 October 1894; BIP (vB1), Passy to Ducommun, Paris, 28 October 1898; Passy to Ducommun, Neuilly, 21 December 1898; cf. *Schulthess' Europäischer Geschichtskalender, 1907*, p. 85.

[127] BIP (vA2), Adresses des journalistes de l'agence en projet de la paix [1897]; MFK, v (January/February 1898), 30; *Bulletin officiel du XIIe Congrès universel*, p. 211.

[128] *Premier Congrès national*, pp. 121–22.

[129] BIP (vQ2h), Rapport sur l'exécution des résolutions des congrès de la paix relatives à la propagande, Berne, 1903; *Bulletin officiel du XIIe Congrès universel*, p. 211.

The French pacifists also took pains to keep the press informed about events of significance for the peace movement. The *Association de la paix par le droit* regularly sent out a bulletin, *Correspondance de la paix*, with peace news.[130] Disseminating information was made much easier when, in 1900, the principal French wire service, Havas, offered to distribute pacifist bulletins at a nominal charge.[131] In addition, minor wire services, such as Fournier, *Correspondance de la presse*, and *La Presse associée*, placed themselves at the pacifists' disposal.[132] The problem was not that French newspapers had insufficient access to information about the peace movement, but rather that they were indifferent to such information and chose not to print it.[133] In this respect the plight of the French and German pacifists was similar, as both discovered that news about reason and progress was not at a premium in an age of mass circulation. The French pacifists did, however, find one way to ensure that a major newspaper printed everything they wanted. *L'Indépendance belge*, though published in Brussels, had an international circulation. Its views were unconditionally pacifist. Indeed, it became the mouthpiece of the peace movement after a consortium of French pacifists, including Moch, Richet, and Arnaud, bought it in 1895.[134]

The press was not an area in which the French peace movement was strong. Yet even here, despite the similarity of the problems they faced, French pacifists found a more favorable reception than their German colleagues. French newspapers that were friends of the peace movement were few, though not so few as in Germany. But the papers that were inveterate critics of the peace movement were less numerous, and far less vocal than in Germany.

[130] Sixième Congrès national, *Compte-rendu*, p. 64.

[131] *Premier Congrès national*, p. 123.

[132] BIP (vB1), Moch to Ducommun, Paris, 23 May 1897, 30 April 1898; BIP (vA2), Arnaud to Gobat, Luzarches, 3 October 1909.

[133] *Premier Congrès national*, p. 122.

[134] BIP (vA7), Arnaud to Ducommun, Luzarches, 7 November 1895.

In Germany both Catholic and Protestant churches were hostile to the peace movement, for reasons that were in large part political. In France, too, political considerations figured prominently in determining the attitude of the churches toward pacifism, but while Catholics were very ill-disposed toward the peace movement, Protestants were generally quite favorable.

The political tradition of French Protestantism was very different from that of the German churches; indeed, it was almost the opposite. Although Protestant churches were state-supported in France throughout the nineteenth century, they did not have the Erastian tradition of the German Evangelical churches. Their exclusion from political power in a series of authoritarian regimes dominated by Catholics made French Protestants suspicious of political authority. The establishment of the anticlerical third republic enabled Protestants to play a much more significant role in political life, but the French Protestant remained, in Adrien Dansette's words, theologically and politically "a liberal who seeks his inspiration within his own conscience without referring to any outside authority."[135] Consequently, Protestants numbered among the more progressive supporters of the republic, and were active in causes that were allied with the Radical movement, including pacifism. While admittedly patriotic and prepared to defend the country, French Protestant churches publicly advocated arbitration as a means to lasting peace.[136] At synodal congresses and on other occasions they endorsed arbitration and called for the celebration of an annual peace Sunday.[137] In 1911 the executive council of the *Fédération protestante*

[135] Adrien Dansette, *Histoire religieuse de la France contemporaine* (2 vols., Paris, 1948–51), II, 52.

[136] BIP (vQ7–8), J. Laurent-Haintz to Gobat, Le Havre, 12 April 1912; A. Weber to Peace Bureau, Paris, 28 November 1906; PD, XXII (1912), 471.

[137] BIP (vA7), Allégret to Gobat, Le Havre, 23 April 1909; PD, X (1900), 501–502; PD, XII (1902), 75.

de France issued a circular calling on all member churches to devote services on the Sunday before Christmas to peace.[138] The campaign in favor of a peace Sunday was also promoted by a small peace society led by Protestant clergymen. Founded in 1899 in Le Havre by Paul Allégret, a pastor in the Reformed church and the editor of *L'Universel,* the *Société chrétienne des amis de la paix* took on branches in Rouen, Limoges, and several small towns, where pastors recruited members from their parishes.[139]

The Catholic church in France was opposed to the peace movement for many of the same reasons Protestants supported it. Despite the *Ralliement* of the 1890s, many Catholics were not fully reconciled to the republic—and certainly not to the libertarianism and anticlericalism of some of its champions. These considerations were critical in determining the attitude of Catholics toward the peace movement, which was a haven for just the kinds of people they found most objectionable: free-thinkers, Masons, outspoken republicans, and Protestants. Catholic thinking on the subject of war still reflected the influence of Joseph de Maistre. Like German Protestantism, it accepted international violence as an aspect of a secular order bestowed by God on sinful men; war was, accordingly, a phenomenon to be endured, not to be rejected as a remediable evil.[140] In consequence, Catholic priests in France distinguished themselves in much the same way as Protestant clergymen in Germany. As one pacifist noted in 1900, "Our most impassioned opponents [are] Catholic priests."[141]

There was one notable attempt to propagate a Catholic pacifism in France. Encouraged by papal pronouncements that urged Catholics to work for world peace, a group of

138 PD, xxi (1911), 707.

139 BIP (vBi), Allégret to Ducommun, Le Havre, 2 May 1903; *Bulletin officiel du XIIe Congrès universel,* p. 240.

140 Chénon, "Les Catholiques et la paix," *Bulletin de la Société Gratry,* number 1 (July 1907), p. 2.

141 PD, x (1900), 106.

French Catholics in 1899 founded the Gratry Society, named after a nineteenth century liberal Catholic, Alphonse Gratry, who had been active in Passy's *Ligue internationale et permanente de la paix*. In the aftermath of the Dreyfus affair this peace society collapsed and remained dormant for several years. In 1906 interest was rekindled by a letter Pius X sent to the Universal Peace Congress in Milan, which seemed to remove all theological objections to Catholics participating in the peace movement. Among other things, the pope announced his approval for the proposition that working to avoid war "only conforms to the precepts of the Gospel."[142] While this made very little impression on most of the French church, it did stimulate a small but important group of clergymen who had been calling for an accommodation between the church and modern, democratic society. In 1906 several leading "democratic priests" and members of Marc Sangnier's reform movement, *Le Sillon*, reconstituted the Gratry Society. Among the committee that presided over the reestablishment of the group were Marc Sangnier himself, Georges Fonsegrive, Émile Chénon, Paul Gemähling, and the abbés Gayraud, Lemire (who was also a deputy), and Pichot.[143] But the real inspiration behind the Gratry Society was Alfred Vanderpol, an engineer in Lyons and a member of *Le Sillon*, whose pacifism was inhibited by none of the skepticism of Marc Sangnier, the abbé Lemire, and some of the other members of the society.[144]

The mission undertaken by the pacifists in the Gratry Society was not unlike that of liberal Protestants in Germany, who sought to replace a fatalistic theological acceptance of war with an active commitment to putting Christian prin-

[142] PD, XVII (1907), 293.

[143] *Ibid.*, p. 294. On the Gratry Society see also A. Vanderpol, "Les sociétés catholiques de la paix," *Almanach de la paix* (1911), pp. 61–64; PD, XXII (1912), 508–11.

[144] See Jeanne Caron, *Le Sillon et la démocratie chrétienne 1894–1910* (Paris, 1967), pp. 433–35; Jean-Marie Mayeur, *Un prêtre démocrate: L'abbé Lemire 1853–1928* (Paris, 1968), pp. 524–26.

ciples to work in international politics. In the words of the
society's "Appeal to Catholics," "the principles of Christian
morality apply as much to relations among peoples as to relations among individuals."[145] Accordingly, the society proposed that "governments institute juridical interrelations
like those that exist among civilized men."[146] In practice, the
organization worked as a pressure group within the church,
attempting to win the support of Catholic clergymen for the
peace movement. But the political and theological obstacles
that it faced were considerable, and it never succeeded in
expanding beyond a small group of liberal Catholics. In
1910, when the organization changed its name to the *Ligue
des Catholiques français pour la paix*, it had a membership
of seven hundred, of whom about two hundred were priests;
it also had branch groups in Amiens, Rouen, Marseilles,
Toulouse, and Orléans.[147] Although several bishops sent
their encouragement, the society did not find much support
in the hierarchy of the French church. Sympathy for the
pacifism it espoused remained by and large restricted to the
pages of liberal Catholic journals, such as *L'Éveil démocratique* and *La France catholique*, and the circles in which
these journals were read.[148]

Despite the general hostility of French Catholics toward
the peace movement, churches in France were more receptive to pacifism than they were in Germany. This was particularly true in the case of Protestant churches, for reasons
that involved important differences in the political orientations of the two Protestant traditions. But it was also true,
if to a lesser extent, of Catholicism. The fact remains that

[145] PD, XVII (1907), 293; see also Chénon, "Les Catholiques et la paix," pp. 1–8.

[146] PD, XVII (1907), 293.

[147] PD, XX (1910), 231; cf. Renouvin and Duroselle, *History of International Relations*, p. 210.

[148] BIP (vQ7–8), Abbé Toiton to Gobat, Paris, 25 March 1911; *Bulletin de la Société Gratry*, number 2 (October 1907), p. 12; number 3
(1908), pp. 15–17; number 8 (1909), p. 14.

no Catholic peace society could take hold in Germany, in spite of the efforts by Vanderpol and others to set one up. The concern of German Catholics that they be counted as good patriots was thus even more effective in inhibiting support for arbitration than was the reactionary tradition of the French church.

Although the evidence that supports this survey of the French peace movement is thin, it does invite at least some tentative conclusions. By whatever comparative indices one uses, the French peace movement appears to have been significantly stronger and more successful than its German counterpart. French peace societies were more numerous and extensive. The peace movement was much closer to the mainstream of French politics and to the centers of power. French statesmen, though skeptical, were much less afraid of arbitration than were Germans; they were prepared to submit certain kinds of disputes to obligatory arbitration, and they entered into a series of general arbitration agreements with other countries. Finally, important agencies of political education—churches, the press, and the educational system—were more receptive in France to pacifism than in Germany; the French schools in particular provided a marked contrast in their deprecation of warfare and affirmation of international arbitration.

It is difficult to believe that the disparity in the experiences of the French and German peace movements was caused alone—or even primarily—by the fact that French pacifists were more sophisticated or employed more effective methods in winning converts. This argument undoubtedly overestimates the capacity of the French peace movement—or any peace movement—to intervene consciously and effectively in the process of attitude formation. And, in fact, French and German pacifists shared substantially the same expectations and operated in much the same fashion. The explanation for the disparity lies far less in the character of the peace movement's campaign than in the cultural context of this campaign in the two countries. The pacifists in France and Germany encountered significantly different political cultures. The comparative success of the French peace movement, the resonance it found in French politics, reflected the prevalence of political attitudes and traditions more receptive to the concept of international community. To claim that international disputes could and should be resolved by law rather than force was not politically imprudent in France; it assuredly was in Germany.

The comparative weakness of the German peace movement was due largely to social and political conditions in Germany. Here, to a greater extent than elsewhere, the political culture militated against pacifism. The experience of the peace movement not only documented the character and dissemination of prevailing attitudes toward international politics in Germany; it suggested why these attitudes were so incompatible with international community.

9

The Peace Movement in Imperial Germany: The Nature of the Opposition

"Forgive my candor," Eduard Bernstein wrote in 1911 to Alfred Fried. "Pacifism is really an unfortunate word—it seems too foreign to Germans."[1] That Germans should reject as foreign even the word "pacifism" was only fitting, since they proved so resistant to the political orientations the word implied. As the peace movement's campaign showed, the groups and agencies that shaped political attitudes in Germany repudiated the proposition that the nations of the world constituted—or could constitute—a harmonious community, in which arbitration was the appropriate avenue for resolving disputes. And the experience of the French peace movement suggests that resistance to this proposition was greater in Germany than elsewhere.

If someone were to undertake a comparative history of the peace movement prior to the First World War, he would surely discover that pacifism was strongest in countries where congenial traditions colored the political culture. In France the strength of the peace movement derived from Radical republicanism, the positivism and Jacobin nationalism that underlay it, and the fact that there was an articulate reformist tradition in the labor movement. In England pacifism was strong because of the Quaker impulse, the prominence of reformist socialism, and the continuing vitality of free-trade liberalism. In the United States, the country that Bertha von Suttner called "the cradle and shelter of the peace movement," pacifism was based on Quaker-

[1] NL Fried, Bernstein to Fried, Berlin, 1 December 1911. Eugen Schlief said the same thing: NL Fried, Schlief to Fried, Strassburg, 4 March 1902.

ism and a traditionally moralistic view of international affairs.[2] In addition, the fact that these countries were all political democracies no doubt contributed to the comparative success of the peace movement, since the implications of prewar pacifism were clearly democratic.

In the semiauthoritarian German empire all these traditions were either weak or nonexistent. After the disasters of 1866 and 1879 the elements in the German liberal tradition that were sympathetic or conducive to pacifism were shattered. The positivist tradition was weak in Germany, so scientific pacifism did not hold much appeal; nor did progressive movements, such as that of the free-thinkers, who in France were both politically powerful and strongly supportive of the peace movement. The ideological repudiation of reformist socialism in Germany prevented the pacifists from enlisting working-class support throughout most of the prewar period. An alliance with religious organizations, particularly important in England and the United States, was also unavailable to the German pacifists; indeed, the influence of the German churches was almost wholly detrimental to the peace movement. Finally, German idealism, an indigenous tradition on which the pacifists hoped to capitalize, also worked to impair the peace movement; for most Germans, the road back to Kant led through Treitschke and Hegel.

In imperial Germany the dominant traditions militated against the peace movement. The most directly injurious was the tradition of militarism, whose vitality was, to be sure, related to the weakness of German liberalism, the transformation of German idealism, and the Erastianism of the Protestant churches. Militarism, which Gerhard Ritter has defned as "an exaggeration and overestimation of the importance of the military," has been one of the most thoroughly studied problems of German history.[3] Historical

[2] Suttner, *Memoirs*, II, 177; cf. DWN, VII (1898), 169.

[3] Gerhard Ritter, *Staatskunst und Kriegshandwerk: Das Problem des "Militarismus" in Deutschland* (4 vols., Munich, 1954–67), I, 13.

research has corroborated the judgment of contemporary observers that in Wilhelmine Germany the influence and prestige of the military were immense.[4] Not only were soldiers conspicuous in high political circles, but the respect they commanded on all levels of society fostered popular attitudes that put a premium on military virtues such as valor, discipline, obedience to authority, and vigilance. Beyond the general incompatibility between an emphasis on such virtues and a credo that aspired to do away with war, the specific problem that militarism posed for the peace movement involved contradictory orientations toward international relations. The soldier's very *raison d'être* is the possibility of armed international conflict; he must, by virtue of his profession and role in society, be sensitive to potential dangers from abroad. This sensitivity has historically colored soldiers' perceptions of international relations, in a way that Lord Salisbury noted in his famous maxim that "If you believe the doctors, nothing is wholesome; if you believe the theologians, nothing is innocent; if you believe the soldiers, nothing is safe."[5] The political prominence of soldiers and the pervasiveness of their attitudes in society have tended to promote the view that international relations are by their very nature governed by armed conflict and that war is always likely, if not desirable. This view, of course, represented the direct negation of prewar pacifism,

[4] In addition to Ritter's *Staatskunst*, standard works on the problem of German militarism include Heinz Fick, *Der deutsche Militarismus der Vorkriegszeit: Ein Beitrag zur Soziologie des Militarismus* (Potsdam, 1932); Alfred Vagts, *A History of Militarism* (New York, 1959); Gordon A. Craig, *The Politics of the Prussian Army, 1640–1945* (New York, 1956); Gerhard Ritter, "Das Problem des Militarismus in Deutschland," *Historische Zeitschrift* CLXXVII (1954), 21–48; Hans Herzfeld, "Der Militarismus als Problem der neueren Geschichte," *Schola* I (1946), 41–67.

[5] Quoted in Michael Howard, "Introduction: The Armed Forces as a Political Problem," in Michael Howard, ed., *Soldiers and Governments: Nine Studies in Civil-Military Relations* (London, 1957), p. 24.

which postulated the basic harmony of international relations and the feasibility of eliminating warfare.[6]

Prewar pacifism and militarism were thus converse aspects of the same problem, which centered upon conflicting orientations toward international relations. As facets of the same problem, they are analytically complementary and throw considerable light on one another. While militarism was the most significant factor underlying the weakness of the peace movement in Germany, the ordeal of the movement exposed a great deal about the problem of German militarism—its character, diffusion, and the role it played in the German political system.

By way of analyzing in greater depth the impotence of the German peace movement, I propose to conclude with an examination of "antipacifism" in Germany, drawing together the disparate antagonistic currents and themes the peace movement encountered during its campaign. Once systematized, they reveal two rather distinct patterns of articulate resistance to pacifism. Although these differed in their perception of the ultimate significance of the peace movement, both were militaristic in the sense that they reflected a view of international relations that rationalized and supported the continuing prominence of the military in society. Together they were so firmly entrenched in the agencies of attitude and opinion formation that resistance to the peace movement was axiomatic in the orientations toward war and international relations that were dominant in the political culture of imperial Germany.

The Feasibility of War: The Confutation of Bloch

The German pacifists spent a great deal of time studying their opponents and replying to their criticisms. At times the pacifists actually welcomed the abuse showered on them by critics, since they believed that this clearly focused the issues and drew attention to the work of the peace move-

[6] Cf. Vagts, *History of Militarism*, p. 17.

ment.[7] They also believed in the desirability of engaging their detractors in rational debate, in order to demonstrate that criticism of the peace movement rested upon remediable misunderstandings or logical fallacies. They pointed out, for example, that contrary to common allegations, pacifists were not calling for the immediate, unilateral disarmament of Germany, nor did they oppose national defense, nor were they in alliance with international socialism.[8] They soon discovered that such reasoned replies fell on deaf ears, for there was no real basis for dialogue between them and their antagonists.

Most of those who vocally and systematically criticized the peace movement repudiated all the pacifists' assumptions about the nature of international politics. In the first place, they refused to admit that war had become unfeasible as an instrument of policy. The pacifists insisted that the same social and economic developments that were forging a community of nations were also making war impossible. Modern technology had rendered nations so interdependent and their armies capable of such destruction that warfare would bring catastrophe to all involved. To support this claim they appealed to the work of Ivan Bloch.

When Bloch's massive study of war appeared in Germany in 1899, it aroused interest in circles far beyond the peace movement.[9] While soldiers attended lectures by Feldhaus on the subject, military analysts, who well recognized the dangerous implications of Bloch's work, subjected his findings and conclusions to intense scrutiny. The controversy made it apparent that many other writers had been studying the technological advances that seemed to revolutionize

[7] NL Fried, Fried Notiz, Vienna, 30 June 1909; cf. Umfrid, *Anti-Stengel*, p. 4; VF, XI (1910), 33, 97; FW, XI (1909), 233.

[8] Alfred H. Fried, *Die hauptsächlichsten Missverständnisse über die Friedensbewegung* (Berlin, 1903); Adolf Richter, "Die Einwendungen gegen die Friedensbewegung," in Grosch, *Deutsche Pazifisten*, pp. 18–26.

[9] E.g., NL Fried, Westarp to Fried, Berlin, 6 January 1902.

the art of warfare. Unhappily for the pacifists, who regarded Bloch's study as a Bible, military writers, whose credentials were far superior to Bloch's, uniformly rejected his
conclusions and pronounced warfare entirely feasible.

In the most devastating of all the attacks on Bloch's work,
Hans Delbrück summarized his failings as if commenting
upon a dull student's thesis: "From a scientific standpoint the
work does not have much to recommend it. It is a rather
uncritical and poorly arranged collection of material; and
although it is embellished with illustrations, the treatment
is amateurish and overburdened with vast amounts of detail
that have nothing to do with the actual problem. Moreover,
the conclusions are extremely faulty and hastily drawn."[10]
Delbrück was pointing to what was, by common agreement, Bloch's most serious limitation: he was a dilettante,
whose evident lack of first-hand military experience severely impaired the value of his work. His conclusions could
thus be no more than fanciful speculations, for they were
underlain on all levels of analysis by misconceptions no seasoned soldier would make.[11] Most importantly, Bloch's
critics found fault with him for portraying the war of the
future as an impersonal, mechanized encounter whose character and eventual outcome would be determined primarily
by material forces. Thus, Bloch consistently disregarded
the importance of the human and moral factors in warfare.
At the tactical level, for instance, critics noted that he overestimated the significance of rapid-firing, small-caliber
weapons, overlooking the fact that human error would
diminish their effectiveness.[12] An unfamiliarity with actual

[10] Delbrück, "Zukunftskrieg und Zukunftsfriede," *Preussische
Jahrbücher* XCVI (1899), 208.

[11] Ulrich Wille, "Der Krieg," *Zeitschrift für Sozialwissenschaft* II
(1899), 326–27; Major Heilmann, "Der zukünftige Krieg," *Allgemeine
Zeitung*, 26 May 1899, Beilage, p. 1; Major L., "Der zukünftige Krieg,"
Die Umschau, 11 February 1899, pp. 121–25.

[12] Delbrück, "Zukunftskrieg," pp. 208–11; Wille, "Der Krieg," pp.
340–49; Generalmajor Zepelin, "Der 'Zukunftskrieg' in russischer, fach-

battle conditions also caused Bloch to jump mechanically from the tactical to the strategic level; he assumed that the same tactical situation would recur uniformly throughout the front and that losses that might accompany a single tactical encounter were indicative of casualties to be sustained by entire armies.[13] In fact, some critics suggested, new weapons, together with improvements in logistics and sanitation, might actually reduce the losses sustained in modern war; small-caliber weapons, for example, could send a bullet cleanly through a man.[14] Bloch's emphasis on the advantages of defensive warfare likewise derived, in the opinion of his critics, from his overestimation of the importance of material factors. He failed to see that the offensive was morally the superior mode of warfare on both the tactical and strategic levels; in addition to demonstrable tactical advantages, attacking troops possessed the initiative and a sense of emotional superiority.[15]

The publication of Bloch's study found opinions divided in Germany about the probable duration of a future war. Many analysts believed that the new weapons, the enormous strains imposed by combat among mass armies, and the democratization of Europe would combine to make wars of the future very short.[16] Others agreed with Bloch

---

männischer Beurteilung," *Jahrbücher für die deutsche Armee und Marine* cx (1899), 59.

[13] Major L., "Der zukünftige Krieg," pp. 124, 151–52 (18 February 1899).

[14] Mtz., "Das Verlustertragen im Zukunftskrieg," *Neue militärische Blätter* LVI (1900), 181–84.

[15] W. von Blume, "Staat und Gesellschaft in einem grossen Krieg unserer Zeit," *Deutsche Rundschau* CXXII (1905), 52, 54–55; Karl von Bruchhausen, *Der kommende Krieg: Eine Studie über die militärische Lage Deutschlands* (Berlin, n.d.), pp. 38, 50–52; Wille, "Der Krieg," pp. 329, 341, 351–55; Zepelin, "Der 'Zukunftskrieg,'" p. 60; Mtz., "Das Verlustertragen," p. 184.

[16] Major L., "Der 'zukünftige Krieg,'" p. 152; Bruchhausen, *Der kommende Krieg*, pp. 49–50; Glatzel, "Ueber den Einfluss der Friedensbewegung auf die europäischen Rüstungsverhältnisse," *Deutsche Revue* XXXVI (1911), 228.

that war would become a protracted ordeal, but they hardly agreed that it had become impossible; they predicted that war would only be a more vast and extended test of a nation's resolve.[17] Here again, Bloch's critics claimed that his concentration on the material side of warfare had led him astray. He failed to account for the ability of an inspired nation to sustain sacrifice. He overlooked human flexibility and ingenuity, which could overcome any economic dislocation a long war might bring. Indeed, many commentators welcomed the prospect of a long war, arguing that the strength and elasticity of the German economy, as well as the Germans' proven ability to endure the burdens of a modern war machine, would ultimately be the deciding factors.[18]

In view of the character of military operations in the First World War, this confutation of Bloch's predictions makes one wonder who was more naive, the pacifists or their critics.[19] For the pacifists' campaign in Germany, however, the significance of the controversy over Bloch's work was that despite any concessions they might have made to the accuracy of his predictions, Bloch's critics rejected his general characterization of warfare as too materialistic, and they emphatically denied that war had become unfeasible as an instrument of policy. In the words of one writer: "As long as in . . . civilized states two 'modern' men still fight with one another for any reason . . . war between states will not be in the realm of the impossible, in spite of perhaps still unforeseen technological progress, in spite of all the social and economic dangers, and in spite of all the calcula-

[17] See Colmar von der Goltz, *Das Volk in Waffen: Ein Buch über Heerwesen und Kriegführung unserer Zeit* (5th ed., Berlin, 1899).

[18] Blume in *Deutsche Rundschau*, CXXI, 371, 382; CXXII, 229; Delbrück, "Zukunftskrieg," pp. 216–18; Otto Neurath, "Die Kriegswirtschaftslehre als Sonderdiziplin," *Weltwirtschaftliches Archiv* I, 2 (April 1913), 346–48.

[19] See Alexander Prinz von Hohenlohe-Schillingsfürst, "Herr von Bloch und der gegenwärtige Krieg," FW, XVIII (1916), 39–41; H. G. Wells, "Der Krieg Blochs," FW, XVIII (1916), 147–49.

tions of this ignorant theoretician."[20] The results of the controversy undermined the pacifists' claim that war had become impossible in the modern world and that this fact could be documented with scientific certainty. Thus, antipacifists of all persuasions could dismiss this aspect of the pacifist credo as uninformed speculation.

While all shades of opposition to the peace movement affirmed the feasibility of warfare, the antipacifist camp was split into two groups, which concentrated on different aspects of the pacifist credo in their attack.[21] One variety of antipacifism repudiated the idea of an international community, postulating instead the necessary and constructive role of warfare in international relations. Those of this persuasion became the pacifists' most outspoken adversaries. Another, moderate variety of antipacifist thought was more equivocal about the role of war in international affairs but rejected the pacifists' claim that arbitration and arms limitation were the proper means to ensure international peace.[22]

The Indispensability of War: Extreme Antipacifism

In 1880 the jurist Johann Caspar Bluntschli wrote to Count Moltke to solicit the great soldier's opinion about a manual on the rules of war that the *Institut de droit international* had just published. Moltke's reply included a passage that would become the bane of pacifists once the letter was made public in the 1890s: "Perpetual peace is a dream, and not a pleasant one at that; and war is part of God's ordering of the world. In war the most noble human virtues develop—courage and self-deprivation [*Entsagung*], faithfulness to duty and the willingness to sacrifice one's life. Without

[20] Major L., "Der 'zukünftige Krieg,'" p. 150.

[21] Fried, *Missverständnisse*, p. 5; "Zusammenbruch der Kriegsanhänger," FW, XII (1910), 34; cf. Gobat, "The Newer Civilization," PM, I (1912), 285.

[22] The distinction between the two varieties of antipacifism is related to the distinction Max Scheler has drawn between *Gesinnungsmilitarismus* and *Instrumentalmilitarismus*: Scheler, *Die Idee des ewigen Friedens*, p. 12.

war, the world would wallow in materialism."[23] After Moltke's death a dedicated group of men, many of whom were themselves officers or exofficers, elaborated, systematized, and propagated this unabashed defense of war and became ideologues for the most intense and vitriolic opponents of the peace movement. Prominent among this group were Max Jähns (Moltke's biographer and former aide), August Keim, Conrad Bornhak, Albrecht von Boguslawski, Ernst von Reichenau, Rudolf Steinmetz, Philipp Stauff, Ernst Reventlow, and Friedrich von Bernhardi.[24] Ironically, however, the principal advocate of such views, particularly as they related to the peace movement, was Karl von Stengel, the man who served as legal consultant to the German delegation at the first Hague conference.[25] By virtue of his first-hand contact with the problems of arbitration and arms limitation, Stengel became known as the foremost authority in Germany on all aspects of the peace movement, with the result that editors and officials regularly solicited his views on the "peace problem."[26]

[23] *Gesammelte Schriften und Denkwürdigkeiten des General-Feldmarschalls Grafen Helmuth von Moltke* (8 vols., Berlin, 1891–93), V, 193–97.

[24] Albrecht von Boguslawski, *Der Krieg in seiner wahren Bedeutung für Staat und Volk* (Berlin, 1892); Max Jähns, *Ueber Krieg und Frieden: Eine Umschau* (2d ed., Berlin, 1893); Ernst von Reichenau, *Einfluss der Kultur auf Krieg und Kriegsrüstung* (Berlin, 1897); Philipp Stauff, *Der Krieg und die Friedensbestrebungen unserer Zeit* (n.p., 1907); Rudolf Steinmetz, *Die Philosophie des Krieges* (Leipzig, 1907); Ernst Reventlow, *Holder Friede, Süsse Eintracht: Eine politische Satire* (Leipzig, 1906); Friedrich von Bernhardi, *Deutschland und der nächste Krieg* (Stuttgart and Berlin, 1912); HB (2), II, 240–41; DWN, IV (1895), 100, 140.

[25] Stengel, *Der ewige Friede* (3d ed., Munich, 1899); Stengel, *Weltstaat und Friedensproblem* (Berlin, 1909).

[26] See Karl von Stengel, "Die Idee des ewigen Friedens und die sogenannten Friedenskonferenzen," *Die Umschau* XI (1907), 321–23, 381–84, 472–74; *National-Zeitung*, 31 August 1909. When in 1910 the Staatswissenschaftliche Fortbildungskurse für preussische Verwaltungsbeamte offered a lecture on the problem of peace, Stengel was

Drawing principally from Heraclitus, Hegel, Darwin, and Treitschke, Stengel and the others of his persuasion denied flatly that the nations of the world could ever constitute a harmonious community, sharing common values and peacefully settling disputes among its members. In their view international relations had always been, and would continue to be, characterized by violent conflict among states which embodied competing cultures; insoluble antagonisms constituted the very stuff of international relations. The mechanism of historical change, they believed, was the progressive rise and decline of states and cultures. Young, vibrant cultures expanded and grew. As they did, they came into contact, and then conflict, with other cultures which were already ascendant and attempting to prevent their own decline into historical obscurity. Eventually such confrontations developed to the point at which only violence could resolve the antagonism. But far from deploring this ultimate resort to arms, Stengel and the others regarded it as inevitable, natural, and indeed indispensable. By governing competition among cultures and dictating that the most powerful survive to absorb and carry on the best elements of decadent cultures, war was the essential agency of historical change.

Seen in this light, war took on aesthetic and ethical qualities. By eliminating atrophied cultures and replacing them with more dynamic successors, war ensured optimum cultural vitality for mankind at all times. Shortly before he was named to represent Germany at the Hague conference, Stengel extolled the benefits of war: "Just as storms cleanse the air and throw decayed and putrid trees to the ground, while the robust and sturdy oak perseveres through the most powerful storm, so is war the test for the political, physical, and spiritual value of a people and state."[27] Or, as

chosen to deliver it: Hans Wehberg, "Der erste pazifistische Lehrauftrag," *Vossische Zeitung*, 27 August 1926.

[27] Stengel, *Der ewige Friede*, p. 15.

one like-minded writer put it, with an impassioned and turgid eloquence: "War is the great chiming of the world clock . . . the opening of new paths for human culture; the expulsion of stagnation by progress; the struggle of the stronger and more vigorous, with the chance to create new cultural values of a richer existence; a necessity that cannot be eliminated."[28] It was not merely a question of cultural competition or antagonism; there was something ennobling about the fact that this competition involved violent conflict. War occasioned man's greatest exertion and self-fulfillment. It fostered the most admirable individual virtues—comradeship, heroism, idealism, self-sacrifice, and the realization of one's manhood. Engaged in a struggle for its very survival, the state, too, underwent galvanization and spiritual sublimation. War worked as well to the benefit of civilization as a whole by promoting art, science, medicine, and industry. In the eyes of people such as Stengel war was, in sum, a noble and uplifting experience, which lent meaning, purpose, and value to human existence.

Just as these antipacifists idealized warfare, they deprecated what Treitschke once referred to as "the corroding influence of peace."[29] If war exercised a therapeutic and purgative influence on civilization, protracted periods of peace threatened to stifle the process; they promoted materialism, excessive individualism, eroticism, feminism, and the decline of religion—all of which were signs of cultural stagnation.[30]

When Stengel and the others spoke of the indispensability of war, they did so with a sense of almost frantic urgency. This derived from their perception of Germany's own position in the panorama of world history. In their view the German empire was the political embodiment of

[28] Stauff, *Der Krieg und die Friedensbestrebungen*, pp. 24–25.

[29] Heinrich von Treitschke, *Politics* (2 vols., New York, 1916), I, 50; see also I, 65–67; II, 599.

[30] Stauff, *Der Krieg und die Friedensbestrebungen*, p. 64; FW, VIII (1906), 96–97; CBM, XV (1910), 10–11; PM, II (1913), 217.

a dynamic, young, ascending culture. England and France represented cultures that had already passed through their dominant phases and had begun to decline. The stage was thus set for a titanic confrontation among these powers, which would revolve around the issue of Germany's securing more territory to correspond to the nation's growing population, cultural awareness, and political power. Since the countries directly challenged by German growth would soon be compelled to defend themselves, war seemed imminent. Indeed, as they surveyed the world situation, Stengel and the others concluded that Germany faced extreme danger. England and France, in league with Russia (which these writers identified as another aspiring young culture), were already preparing for a violent confrontation and had joined in a conspiracy to annihilate Germany as a world power. Since these enemies were prepared to strike at the first opportunity, it behooved Germany to arm to the hilt, both morally and militarily.

This extreme variety of antipacifist thinking was a peculiar, often inconsistent and irrational amalgam of themes.[31] The most prominent characteristic of this "style"—to use the expression of Richard Hofstadter, who tried to analyze this kind of phenomenon with psychological concepts—was its obsession with the danger that lurked all around Germany in the international arena.[32] Thus, these antipacifists felt compelled to alert Germans to the threats they faced and to exhort them to make ready for a war that was both imminent and necessary.

Curiously, there were a number of remarkable similarities between the pacifists and these, their most dedicated opponents. Not the least was the crusading intensity with

[31] See Robert Clark Stevenson, "Pacifism and Militarism: A History and Analysis of Ideas" (Ph.D. dissertation, University of California, Berkeley, 1929).

[32] Richard Hofstadter, "The Paranoid Style in American Politics," in *The Paranoid Style in American Politics and Other Essays* (New York, 1967), pp. 3-40.

which both approached politics, a process they perceived in moralistic terms.[33] Beyond this, the pacifists and their opponents agreed that the violent conflict of competing cultures had been the driving force of history; the pacifists, however, believed that in the modern, interdependent world such conflict would be sublimated into nonviolent economic and cultural competition. In addition, the pacifists and these critics agreed that Germany would have to expand territorially; the pacifists, Umfrid in particular, believed that such growth could take place peacefully, while the antipacifists were convinced it could not.

Any such similarities were altogether obscured in the virulent attack these nationalists delivered against the peace movement. They believed the pacifists were threatening the country's survival by eroding its will to fight. Indeed, they attributed far more power and influence to the peace movement than it really enjoyed. Despite all the objective evidence to the contrary, they viewed the movement as an extensive, well financed organization, which had acquired a wide popular following and had seized control of most of the German press.[34] In fact, they were convinced that pacifists exerted more influence in Germany than anywhere else.[35] In other respects, too, their perception of the peace movement was grounded in their fears and vivid imagination. Although very few Jews were active in the German movement—only Fried and Heilberg were conspicuous—extreme antipacifists adduced the whole range of standard

[33] One who perceived this early was Heinrich Molenaar: "Pacifismus und Militarismus," *Positive Weltanschauung* v (1906), 39.

[34] NL Fried, A. Flemmich to Fried, Freiburg, 4 December 1912; Alexander Grabowski to Fried, Berlin, 20 February 1913; *Ostdeutsche Rundschau*, 17 March 1914; Deutscher Wehrverein, *Die Friedensbewegung*, pp. 20–21; Stauff, *Der Krieg und die Friedensbestrebungen*, foreword.

[35] Stengel, *Der ewige Friede*, p. 25; Stengel, *Weltstaat*, p. 28; Deutscher Wehrverein, *Die Friedensbewegung*, p. 4; Stauff, *Der Krieg und die Friedensbestrebungen*, pp. 63–64.

anti-Semitic arguments in attacking it.[36] Nor did it matter to these critics that Social Democrats were as abusive of the pacifists as were nationalists themselves; they were convinced that the peace movement and the socialists were in an active alliance.[37]

In league with international socialism and Jewry, the haven for irreligious Masons and free-thinkers, and the champion of democracy and feminism, the peace movement impressed these militant nationalists as both a cause and symptom of the materialistic decadence that had begun to threaten German culture. As one nationalist warned: "When a nation opens the flood-gates to cosmopolitanism, it signifies that it does not want to elevate its culture, but that it is instead about to undergo a cultural decline. The peace movement is thus ultimately working also for the downfall of German culture."[38] Preaching world peace would lead to a "lackadaisical spirit, cowardice [*Unmännlichkeit*], and a prejudice against military activity which must inevitably do harm to the military excellence of the German people."[39] In spite of the pacifists' protests, nationalists condemned

[36] NL Fried, Umfrid to Fried, Stuttgart, 21 May 1905; Fried to Umfrid, Vienna, 24 May 1909; Edward Kowalek, "Kritik des 'gebildeten' Antisemitismus in seinem Verhältniss zur Friedensidee," DWN, III (1894), 60–65, 103–108; *Tägliche Rundschau*, 10 June 1893; DWN, III (1894), 300–301; DWN, VI (1897), 110; see also Kurd von Strantz, "Gefährliche Friedensseligkeit," *Politisch-anthropologische Revue* XI (1912/13), 474; Otto Schmidt-Gibichenfels, "Der Krieg als Kulturfactor," *ibid.*, pp. 453–54; Erich Ludendorff, *Kriegführung und Politik* (Berlin, 1922), pp. 42–43. On this general problem see the instructive dissertation of Klemens Felden, "Die Uebernahme des antisemitischen Stereotyps als soziale Norm durch die bürgerliche Gesellschaft Deutschlands (1875–1900)" (Inaugural dissertation, Heidelberg, 1963), esp. pp. 55–64.

[37] NL Fried, Alexander Grabowski to Fried, Berlin, 20 February 1913; DWN, III (1894), 148–49; DWN, VIII (1899), 127; Suttner, *Randglossen*, II, 499.

[38] Müller-Brandenburg, "Eine falsche Rechnung," in Deutscher Wehrverein, *Die Friedensbewegung*, p. 20.

[39] *Ibid.*, pp. 2–4, 19–20; see also FB, IX (1908), 26–27.

them for opposing national defense and advocating Germany's immediate and unilateral disarmament. They believed further that the pacifists' calls for arbitration misrepresented the very nature of international relations and threatened to lull Germans into a false sense of security. The concept of international law was also dangerous because it was static; it would freeze the political *status quo* and artificially preserve cultures otherwise destined to decline.[40]

These antipacifists then reached the most ominous conclusion of all about the peace movement, as they asked why the pacifists were engaged in such perverse activity. While it seemed clear that many pacifists, perhaps even most of them, were naive idealists seduced by a noble-sounding cause, nationalists suspected that the driving forces behind the peace movement were in the service of Germany's enemies. These they variously defined. Among the more frequently mentioned beneficiaries, and hence benefactors, of the peace movement were the Russians (because they had called the Hague conferences and because of Bloch—a Jew), the Americans (because of Andrew Carnegie), high finance (because of Andrew Carnegie), and ultramontanism (the reason for this is somewhat obscure—perhaps it was because the pope had been suggested as a possible arbitrator).[41] The principal instigator of the peace movement, however, was unquestionably England, the country these nationalists viewed as the gravest threat to Germany. It was hardly a coincidence, they believed, that peace societies were more numerous in England than anywhere else in Europe, or that German pacifists were Anglophiles, or

[40] Stauff, *Der Krieg und die Friedensbestrebungen*, pp. 13–16.
[41] Fried, "Der deutschfeindliche Hintergedanke bei den amerikanischen Schiedsverträgen," FW, XIV (1912), 48; see also David Starr Jordan, *The Days of a Man: Being Memories of a Naturalist, Teacher and Minor Prophet of Democracy* (2 vols., Yonkers-on-Hudson, 1922), II, 539; VF, XI (1910), 80; FW, XII (1911), 23; Deutscher Wehrverein, *Die Friedensbewegung*, p. 20.

that the English were the most consistent advocates of arbitration and arms limitation. Enlarging upon Friedrich Naumann's half-facetious remark that "international means English," these antipacifists predicted that the realization of the peace movement's goals would guarantee English supremacy in the world and consign Germany to the rank of a second-rate power.[42]

It was a mark of extreme antipacifism that those who espoused it were inclined to take action against the peace movement. A number of the nationalist tracts that appeared in Germany before the war, like Bernhardi's infamous *Germany and the Next War*, were designed to counteract the spread of pacifism.[43] Other concerned nationalists found in the press an accessible forum, where they could proclaim their fears about the peace movement. Leading pacifists, Umfrid and Schücking in particular, learned to endure every manner of personal abuse from these critics, most of which arrived in the form of anonymous letters.[44] Occasionally, outraged nationalists even broke into peace meetings and threw them into confusion by taunting the speakers.[45] Public officials also joined in the harassment. The careers of Quidde and Schücking were severely impaired by the official opprobrium they suffered. And, like Fried, whose request for naturalization was rejected in 1900 by the *Regierungspräsident* of Brandenburg, many pacifists had

[42] Reventlow, *Holder Friede*, esp. pp. 10, 25, 28; Stengel, *Weltstaat*, p. 130; see also W. von Bremen, "Friedenskonferenz und englischer Abrüstungsscherz," *Daheim* XLIII (1907), 12–13; Umfrid, *Bismarcks Gedanken und Erinnerungen*, pp. 31–32; FB, IV (1903), 69; FW, VIII (1906), 217–18; cf. Treitschke, *Politics*, I, 65.

[43] Friedrich von Bernhardi, *Denkwürdigkeiten aus meinem Leben, nach gleichzeitigen Aufzeichnungen und im Lichte der Erinnerung* (Berlin, 1927), p. 350; cf. Ritter, *Staatskunst*, II, 143–46.

[44] Fried, *German Emperor*, p. vi; Wehberg, *Führer*, p. 54; VF, XI (1910), 98.

[45] JPC, Mez to Jordan, Munich, 19 June 1914; NL Fried, Quidde to Ruyssen, Kreuth, 28 August 1911.

to contend with ill-willed police inspectors and local officials.[46]

Nowhere in Germany was the reception of the peace movement more actively hostile than in Hamburg. The fact that pacifists should be so tormented in a great port city was in itself an interesting comment on Fried's theory that international contacts would breed pacifism. The local branch of the German Peace Society was one of the most vigorous in the country, but its opponents were numerous and dedicated. Nationalists disrupted peace meetings and complained to the city government about the peace society's subversive activities.[47] Their concern was shared by two of the city's leading newspapers, the *Neue Hamburger Zeitung* and especially the *Hamburger Nachrichten*, whose slanderous derision of the pacifists was unexcelled anywhere in Germany.[48] Public officials also participated in the campaign against the pacifists. The police made life difficult for them with supervision of their activities.[49] When the pacifists brought libel proceedings against the *Nachrichten* in 1907, after a particularly scurrilous attack, the judge who presided at the trial reproached them for advocating foreign interests.[50] When one teacher who was a member of the peace society requested a leave of absence from his *Volksschule* in order to attend a Universal Peace Congress, his superiors denied it to him, pointing out that pacifism conflicted with the state's military policy.[51] School officials

[46] NL Fried, Feldhaus to Fried, Bottm. Muble, 22 March 1905; Fried to Schwonder, Vienna, 22 May 1911; Fried to W. Foerster, Vienna, 12 March 1912; Tiedje to Fried, Königsberg, 11 March 1914; cf. AStA, MH 11561, Verbot gegen Einführung der in Brüssels erschienenen Drückschrift, "Die Frauen und der Krieg," 1910–1911.

[47] NL Fried, Bloh to Fried, Hamburg, 9 May 1913; VF, XIV (1913), 78; PM, II (1913), 336; PD, XXIII (1913), 340–41.

[48] FW, XI (1909), 57.

[49] FW, IX (1907), 97; cf. FB, VIII (1907), 59.

[50] FW, IX (1907), 97; FW, X (1908), 53; FB, IX (1908), 51, 66, 90.

[51] NL Fried, Harder to Fried, Hamburg, 19, 21 October 1906; FW, VIII (1906), 198.

suspended another pacifist from his job after he published a vivid description of the horrors of modern war.[52]

Because this kind of opposition was extravagant, its origins and sources of support were easy to identify. Those in Hamburg and elsewhere who denounced and harassed the pacifists were usually zealous patriots active in *vaterländische* organizations such as the Pan-German League, the *Deutscher Wehrverein*, and the *Reichsverband gegen die Sozialdemokratie*.[53] Numerically they were not a very extensive group, although they far outnumbered those involved in the German peace movement. But by virtue of their vehemence and the fact that they had friends in important places, these people exerted an influence out of proportion to their numbers. Included in their ranks were many public officials and leaders in agencies of opinion formation—newspaper editors, professors, Protestant clergymen, as well as important political figures, such as the crown prince.

The conspicuousness of these extreme antipacifists also makes it easy to overestimate their importance. The experience of the pacifists themselves suggested that most Germans were not very alarmed by the activities of the peace movement. The situation in Hamburg was unusual, and on the whole there was no coherent pattern of harassment of the pacifists—certainly nothing to indicate a systematic campaign to persecute them. For the most part, the pacifists had to contend with a more moderate, subtle, and effective kind of opposition.

[52] NL Fried, Lamszus to Fried, Hamburg, 20 October 1912; FW, XIV (1912), 391; VF, XIV (1913), 9.

[53] NL Fried, Schwonder to Fried, Königsberg, 21 December 1913; Deutscher Wehrverein, *Die Friedensbewegung*; Barkeley, *Die deutsche Friedensbewegung*, p. 17; cf. Konrad Schilling, "Beiträge zu einer Geschichte des radikalen Nationalismus in der Wilhelminischen Aera 1890–1909: Die Entstehung des radikalen Nationalismus, seine Einflussnahme auf die innere und äussere Politik des Deutschen Reiches und die Stellung von Regierung und Reichstag zu seiner politischen und publizistischen Aktivität" (Inaugural dissertation, Cologne, 1968).

The Likelihood of War: Moderate Antipacifism

In the extreme variety of antipacifism war itself had positive connotations; to advocate its abolition was hence perverse and dangerous. However, the peace movement's campaign suggested that, publicly at least, most Germans did not share this view. Like the pacifists, they regarded war as bad, but they disagreed with the pacifists over how best to prevent it, if indeed they believed prevention of war to be at all possible. Germans who held these views espoused, in one form or another, a less extravagant, but far more pervasive form of antipacifism.

Of all the attacks on Bloch's work, none so deeply troubled the pacifists as Hans Delbrück's.[54] This was not only because of Delbrück's prestige, but because he proceeded from his critique of Bloch to a general theory of international relations, which claimed to serve the pacifists' ultimate goal of world peace while it dismissed as utopian their views on the nature of international politics.[55] He thus emerged as the most formidable and articulate spokesman for the pacifists' moderate opponents.

Delbrück began by affirming the preferability of peace. Whatever the limitations of Bloch's study, Delbrück conceded that it had demonstrated how destructive the tools of war had become. The prevention of war was thus a legitimate and desirable undertaking, but one that would have to proceed from the realities of international relations. These Delbrück characterized entirely differently from the

[54] NL Fried, Fried to Delbrück, Vienna, 31 March 1909; Delbrück to Fried, Berlin, 13, 19 November 1909; CBM, XI (1906), 127.

[55] Hans Delbrück, "Zukunftskrieg und Zukunftsfriede," *Preussische Jahrbücher* XCVI (1899), 220–29; Delbrück, "Der Abrüstungs-Gedanke, England und Deutschland," *ibid.*, CXXVIII (1907), 369–81; Delbrück, "Weshalb baut Deutschland Kriegsschiffe? Beantwortung der Frage eines Engländers," *ibid.*, CXXXVIII (1909), 149–61. The last two of these are reprinted in Hans Delbrück, *Vor und nach dem Weltkrieg: Politische und historische Aufsätze 1902–1925* (Berlin, 1926), pp. 177–95, 297–311. See also Annelise Thimme, *Hans Delbrück als Kritiker der Wilhelminischen Epoche* (Düsseldorf, 1955), pp. 105, 115.

pacifists. Where they foresaw the progressive development of an international community, which would enable nations to dispense with power in their dealings with one another, he asserted that although arbitration might be feasible in certain minor disputes, military power had always been, and would continue to be, the basic factor in international relations. No amount of economic or cultural solidarity could eradicate international political antagonisms, which were ultimately so profound that they could not admit of juridical settlement. Rather than drawing the conclusion that the persistence of these antagonisms would make war forever necessary, however, Delbrück suggested that they represented the surest guarantee of peace. As he surveyed the international situation at the turn of the century, he descried in the clash of conflicting interests the emergence of a delicate balance of tension among the powers, as each armed to hold the others in check. Through the careful manipulation of this balance—notably by such means as expanding the German navy as a check on English arrogance—Delbrück was confident that peace could be maintained indefinitely. Indeed, he believed that peace would actually become more secure, because as the general level and destructive capability of armaments rose, the powers would be increasingly reluctant to run the risk of war.

Thus, Delbrück concluded that the only realistic way to ensure the peace was to act according to the formula, *si vis pacem, para bellum.* Pacifism, while praiseworthy in its conceptions and goals, rested upon illusions about the nature of international relations. The regulation of international politics by law and arbitration required trust and consensus among the powers and presupposed the basic compatibility of their interests. The character of international antagonisms contradicted these assumptions. Disarmament likewise presupposed a world that could not exist, and was in fact even more foolhardy than arbitration, because it would dismantle the very mechanism that was preserving the peace. In this connection Delbrück pointed out the fallacy that underlay Bloch's work and the conclusions the pacifists drew from it: having shown that modern weaponry had made war prohibitively destructive, Bloch called for disarmament, despite the fact that this would logically make warfare less destructive, less hazardous, and hence more likely. Beyond this, disarmament was technically unfeasible. So complex had modern military establishments become that the suspicion and antagonism that would accompany negotiations on an arms agreement, to say nothing of an attempt to implement and supervise it, would pose far graver threats to the peace than a high level of armaments.

Delbrück was an optimist—more so, in this respect, than the pacifists, who insisted that the armed peace Delbrück justified was inherently unstable and would not effectively prevent war. But in affirming the desirability of peace while characterizing international relations as a system dominated by antagonism and conflict, Delbrück articulated the sentiments of most Germans, many of whom were less optimistic than he about the prospects for a durable peace. Indeed, if in the course of their campaign the pacifists encountered one clearly dominant attitude, it was that conflict was inevitable in international politics, that peace, while desirable, was always tenuous, and that it could be secured only through the deterrent effect of a strong military force.[56]

This moderate antipacifism involved one other motif. To affirm that peace, arbitration, and disarmament were laudable goals, yet impractical in the real world, created a certain tension between precept and reality. The effort to resolve this tension led only a few Germans into the peace movement. Much more common was an attempt to project its resolution into the indefinite future, by alluding to a time

[56] See Fürst Lichnowsky, "Die Friedensfrage in militärischer und politischer Beleuchtung," *Deutsche Revue* xxxiv (1909), 165–68; Émile Flourens, "Die Kehrseite der pazifistischen Medaille," *ibid.*, xxxviii (1912), 73–87; Kattenbusch, *Das sittliche Recht des Krieges*, pp. 14–15; Curtius, "Ueber militärische Suggestion," KVfiV, ii (6 December 1913), 5; ER, i (1912), 146.

in which either human nature or the character of international relations would change in such a basic way that perpetual peace could become reality. Moderate antipacifism was thus more equivocal about the peace movement than was the extreme variety. The pacifists' goals were noble and could perhaps in the distant future be realized; for the present, though, in the harsh realities of international politics, they were utopian, naive, and ill-advised.

This theme, which coupled an affirmation of peace with a grave "*noch nicht*" in response to the reforms advocated by the pacifists, surfaced in several interesting variations throughout articulate sectors of German society. Most importantly, it was the official position of the German government and served as the rationale for German opposition to proposals for arms limitation. Speaking to the Reichstag in March 1911, Bethmann Hollweg presented a concise statement of the theme: "Whoever reflects impartially and earnestly upon the question of general disarmament, and follows it through to its ultimate consequences, must conclude that it is insoluble as long as men are men and states are states."[57] It was also a theme pacifists heard frequently from German politicians. During the Reichstag debate in 1913 on the new arms bill, Georg Oertel, a Conservative, spoke for many delegates—not only those on the right—when he announced his support for the bill because he thought a strong army was the best guarantee of peace in a threatening international situation: "Whoever dreams of world peace will also have to admit that humanity still has a powerfully long way to go before reaching this goal."[58] In its religious variation, the theme informed the thinking of many Protestant theologians on the problems of war and peace. In response to the pacifists' appeals, pastors emphasized that violent international conflict was a burden man was destined to endure until the Kingdom of Heaven brought perpetual

---

[57] StBR, xii L.P., 2 Session (30 March 1911), cclxvi, 6002; cf. VF, xii (1911), 26–28.

[58] StBR, xiii L.P., 1 Session (15 April 1913), cclxxxix, 4765.

peace. And it was a measure of their "negative integration" into German politics that the Social Democrats, too, appropriated a variation of the theme in rejecting the peace movement.[59] They insisted that war represented an intrinsic aspect of capitalism and would persist until the fundamental reconstitution of politics in the wake of socialist revolution.

In all its variations this theme condemned the pacifists to the role of well-intentioned people who were playing in dreamland. Their advocacy of arbitration and arms limitation as practical reforms betrayed their basic misunderstanding of the nature of international politics. They were dangerous only to the extent that they obscured the likelihood of war and the need for a vigilant army.[60] However, it was a mark of this moderate form of antipacifism that those who espoused it did not take this danger very seriously. Unlike the extreme antipacifists, they saw the peace movement for what it really was: a small group of well-meaning but ineffectual men and women. If the belief that the pacifists were dangerous led extreme opponents to harass and denounce them, the realization that they were harmless led rather to indifference spiced with waggish ridicule.

The patterns of opposition the pacifists encountered suggested that the latter view was overwhelmingly prevalent in Germany. Indeed, a subtle resistance to the peace movement, based upon moderate antipacifism, was in a sense built into the German political system. Pacifism rested upon an orientation toward international affairs that denied or minimized the role of political conflict. However, the institutions and agencies that shaped orientations toward inter-

[59] On the problem of "negative integration" see Guenther Roth, *The Social Democrats in Imperial Germany: A Study in Working Class Isolation and National Integration* (Totowa, New Jersey, 1963); and Groh, *Negative Integration*.

[60] Lichnowsky, "Die Friedensfrage," p. 166; Glatzel, "Ueber den Einfluss der Friedensbewegung," pp. 228–29; cf. Nippold, *Chauvinismus*, p. 118.

national affairs in Germany actively cultivated a view that emphasized the inevitability of such conflict. The result was to cast the pacifists in the popular image of foolish people who had failed utterly to adjust to the hard realities of international politics.[61] The pervasiveness of such an orientation toward international affairs made active persecution of the peace movement unnecessary, as it produced a climate of opinion that effectively stifled it.[62]

To be a pacifist in such a climate entailed liabilities beyond harassment at the hands of concerned patriots. Association with the peace movement was not conducive to social or professional advancement, and it made a successful political career next to impossible.[63] The most pervasive manifestation of this hostile climate was massive indifference to the peace movement's campaign. To an extent, one can ascribe this to a general indifference to politics among many Germans, for even the Pan-Germans complained of it.[64] Yet in the case of the peace movement this indifference far exceeded anything nationalists had to face. The market for pacifist literature, which was one good index, was minuscule in comparison with the market for nationalist tracts.[65] Few people beyond the circles of the peace movement itself bothered to buy or read anything written by a pacifist. Most newspapers and publishing houses avoided pacifist material altogether, and much of their literature appeared in print only by the grace of generous progressive

[61] See PM, II (1913), 441; FB, V (1904), 98; PD, XX (1910), 408–409; FW, XIV (1912), 347–48; Fried, *German Emperor*, pp. 189–90.

[62] See Buchanan and Cantril, *How Nations See Each Other*, p. 60.

[63] Wehberg, *Gutachten*, p. 87; cf. FW, II (1900), 172; FW, XIII (1911), 274, 311–12; FW, XIV (1912), 391; Deak, *Left-Wing Intellectuals*, p. 115.

[64] VF, XI (1910), 3; Schilling, "Geschichte des radikalen Nationalismus," pp. 181–85.

[65] NL Fried, Moritz Busch to Fried, Leipzig, 17 May 1893; Hartmann to Fried, Stuttgart, 30 June 1900; Wilhelm Langguth to Fried, Esslingen, 1 February 1906; "Die Pazifisten und ihre Literatur," FW, X (1908), 72.

publishers.[66] In these circumstances prevailing opinions about the peace movement were uninformed or based upon a reading of Stengel or some other outspoken critic.[67]

Indifference was even more disturbing to the pacifists than the abuse they received, for they could not understand how anyone could remain unmoved by their message. On occasion it led even these inveterate optimists to despair. Umfrid's lament in 1909 can stand as a reasonably accurate summary of the German peace movement's entire experience: "We answer in our writings and lectures the objections that result from patent misconceptions and are repeated a thousand times over. . . . People do not read our writings; they do not listen to our lectures. We are prejudged before we are given a chance to plead our case. We send appeals, but people neither read nor distribute them, all the while maintaining an innocent pose as if to say they know nothing about us."[68]

Indifference was the lot of pacifists in all countries. It stemmed from a number of factors, including the charged international atmosphere, which made the pacifists' claims sound naive, the limited means at their disposal, and the extravagance of their goals. In Germany, though, the situation was clearly worse than elsewhere. The hostile climate was more pervasive, the indifference was more paralyzing, and the articulate opposition was more centrally placed. In

[66] The peace society's official publisher was Wilhelm Langguth in Esslingen. The firm of E. Pierson in Dresden also published a great deal of the pacifists' literature.

[67] In 1910 Umfrid complained to Fried: "Do you not find, too, that every announcement by Stengel or now even reproductions of that nonsense from Moltke are taken up in hundreds of newspapers, while pacifists' rebuttals are simply hushed up? You place an article here and there, even in a larger paper, but what does that mean among so many? At most, I place my articles in the [Stuttgart] *Beobachter*, but nobody else wants them. Aside from our pacifist press no single paper has taken notice of my [book] *Anti-Stengel*." NL Fried, Umfrid to Fried, Stuttgart, 5 March 1910.

[68] FW, XI (1909), 184.

the final analysis this was in part because pacifism was fundamentally incompatible with the imperial German political system.

The Indispensability of the Likelihood of War

The pacifists denied vigorously that their program was subversive. In support of this claim they could point to a great deal of evidence. Their patriotism was indisputable. They emphasized the continuity of their program with important aspects of the national tradition, and they defended German interests within the international peace movement. They assuredly did not wish to challenge the foundations of capitalist society in Germany. Their respect for the laws of the land was profound; they conscientiously complied with the provisions of the various state *Vereinsgesetze* and made great efforts not to antagonize the authorities.[69] The only thing they wished to revolutionize was the structure of international politics, and they insisted that this could be done without drawing into question the social or political order in Germany, or the country's international preeminence. Thus, the German pacifists viewed their movement and its goals as unambiguously *staatserhaltend*, and they dismissed as ignorant or perverse the accusations of their critics that pacifism was dangerous.

Ironically, their critics were right, but generally for the wrong reasons. They claimed that the peace movement was dangerous because, by advocating disarmament and questioning the role of the army, it undermined the country's will to fight. This claim had no basis in fact; and, even if it had, the peace movement would logically have worked to the relative advantage of Germany, since it exercised far more influence in France, England, and the United States.[70]

[69] The striking thing about the peace societies' relationship with the police was how infrequently, compared to other "political organizations," the pacifists were in trouble: cf. AStA, MInn 66308, Statistik der politischen Vereine: Gerichtliche Einschreitungen, 1887–1899.

[70] See Émile Arnaud, *Le pacifisme et ses détracteurs* (Paris and Berne, 1906).

Yet pacifism was subversive in Germany, in a way it was not in these other countries. The reasons for this were more subtle than those cited by most antipacifists, and they had to do with the nature of the German political system. Ultimately, the comparative weakness of the peace movement in Germany was a result of the structural peculiarities of the German empire.

In order to pursue this argument, it is necessary to reconstruct briefly the picture of the German empire that has emerged out of the intense historiographical controversy which was prompted in large part by the publication, in 1961, of Fritz Fischer's *Griff nach der Weltmacht*.[71] While many of Fischer's provocative claims remain in dispute, most historians now agree with him that the German empire, which in the 1920s seemed in retrospect to have been a bastion of political stability, was in reality a very troubled system, plagued by deep social cleavages and political antagonisms.[72] The constitutional structure of the state which Bismarck created in 1871 ensured the social and political preeminence of the Prussian aristocracy; in significant respects, however, the unification of the German states on the map failed to produce a unified political system, as many important social groups did not acknowledge the legitimacy of the new state or the claim to rule of those who dominated it. Liberal democrats, Catholics, workers, Poles, Frenchmen, Danes, and assorted other groups within the empire found that the state failed, in one way or another, to conform to their expectations about how a political system should be constituted. The dominant elites in the new state in turn regarded these various antagonists with fear and scarcely veiled hostility.

[71] Fritz Fischer, *Griff nach der Weltmacht* (Düsseldorf, 1961); American edition, *Germany's Aims in the First World War* (New York, 1967). See James J. Sheehan, "Germany, 1890–1918: A Survey of Recent Research," *Central European History* 1 (1968), 345–72.

[72] For a sampling of recent historical thinking on the problem of the empire see Michael Stürmer, ed., *Das kaiserliche Deutschland: Politik und Gesellschaft 1870–1918* (Düsseldorf, 1970).

Because of these antagonisms the German empire remained into the twentieth century a basically unintegrated political system.[73] It lacked a consensus among its constituent groups about the ground rules of politics, with the result that political debate routinely drew into question the legitimacy of the Bismarckian system itself. The hotly debated problem of the Prussian suffrage, for instance, touched upon the very foundations of the imperial system by challenging one of the constitutional devices that made possible the rule of the aristocracy. The "social question" likewise implied a visceral threat to the imperial system and its dominant elites—one that became more acute with the growth of a militant working class movement in the wake of Germany's prodigious industrialization at the end of the century. Thus, on the eve of the First World War, the largest single political organization in the country, the Social Democratic party, was ideologically opposed to the constitutional system.

In the view of many scholars, the history of the German empire can be written largely in terms of the efforts made by the traditional elites, threatened by social and political modernization, to deal with the problems of an unintegrated society. Specifically, these elite groups faced the problem of neutralizing the forces that challenged their preeminence and creating a new consensus or set of common orientations with which to stabilize the system. In their efforts they displayed considerable imagination and versatility. Among the techniques they employed were the political and social cooptation of the industrial bourgeoisie, parliamentary manipulation, a remarkably progressive program of social insurance, and outright repression of Catholics, socialists, and ethnic minorities; they were also prepared,

[73] M. Rainer Lepsius, "Parteiensystem und Sozialstruktur: Zum Problem der Demokratisierung der deutschen Gesellschaft," in Wilhelm Abel, et al., eds., *Wirtschaft, Geschichte und Wirtschaftsgeschichte: Festschrift zum 65. Geburtstag von Friedrich Lütge* (Stuttgart, 1966), pp. 371–93.

in the last resort, to undertake a *coup d'état* against the Reichstag.[74]

The character of German foreign policy also reflected the problems of an unintegrated political system. Recent studies have shown persuasively that Bismarck and those who succeeded him as planners of German foreign policy actively contemplated the likely impact of their policies on domestic tensions. Since the Bismarckian system itself failed to generate a consensus, leaders hoped to foster a common set of political orientations among Germans *vis-à-vis* the rest of the world. One aspect of this was the pursuit of an "active" foreign policy, by which the government attempted to sublimate domestic antagonisms into a new national consensus born of a sense of pride in Germany's international stature and power. Bismarck's decision to embark upon a path of colonialism was thus dictated in part at least by his calculation that the step would, to quote Hans-Ulrich Wehler, "produce an integrating effect and conceal grave internal social and political tensions."[75] Bismarck relied chiefly, however, on his ability to manipulate conflicting domestic forces in order to control them; with his departure resort to foreign policy grew in importance as a device for promoting domestic integration. The attempt to diminish internal tensions and reinforce the monarch's prerogatives in foreign and military policy figured prominently in the decision to embark upon a *Weltpolitik* and to construct the battle fleet which such a policy seemed to require.[76] And,

[74] See Hans Rosenberg, *Grosse Depression und Bismarckzeit: Wirtschaftsablauf, Gesellschaft und Politik in Mitteleuropa* (Berlin, 1967), esp. pp. 118–68, 192–257; Stürmer, "Staatsstreichgedanken," pp. 566–615; Wolfgang Sauer, "Das Problem des deutschen Nationalstaates," in Hans-Ulrich Wehler, ed., *Moderne deutsche Sozialgeschichte* (Cologne and Berlin, 1970), pp. 428–36.

[75] Hans-Ulrich Wehler, *Bismarck und der Imperialismus* (Cologne and Berlin, 1969), p. 454.

[76] Volker Berghahn, *Der Tirpitz-Plan: Genesis und Verfall einer innenpolitischen Krisenstrategie unter Wilhelm II* (Düsseldorf, 1971); cf. Eckart Kehr, *Schlachtflottenbau und Parteipolitik 1894–1901:*

while historians continue to debate over whether German policy makers decided to go to war in 1914 in the hope that a "grasp at world power" would shore up the monarchy, it seems clear that domestic problems were central in their calculations during the final diplomatic crisis.[77] At the very least, the evidence suggests that Bethmann Hollweg operated during the July crisis in a deep sense of malaise over the domestic situation in Germany. The chancellor thus took a "calculated risk" and gave the Austrians the blank check on 5 July, because, in the words of one recent biographer, he had "fatalistically decided to try to reverse the diplomatic, political, and cultural deterioration of Germany in one bold stroke."[78]

Pursuing an active foreign policy was one aspect of the attempt to promote domestic integration by invoking Germany's relations with the rest of the world. The other was the systematic exploitation of what one political scientist has recently called "one of the most venerable hypotheses in the social sciences: *an external threat or danger will submerge internal conflicts.*"[79] It was in this connection that the role of militarism was crucial in the imperial political sys-

---

Versuch eines Querschnitts durch die innenpolitischen, sozialen und ideologischen Voraussetzungen des deutschen Imperialismus (Lübeck, 1930).

[77] See the recent discussions of this by Wolfgang J. Mommsen, "Die latente Krise des Wilhelminischen Reiches. Staat und Gesellschaft in Deutschland 1890–1914," *Militärgeschichtliche Mitteilungen*, number 1, 1974, esp. pp. 24–28; and Michael R. Gordon, "Domestic Conflict and the Origins of the First World War: The British and German Cases," *Journal of Modern History* XLVI (1974), 191–226.

[78] Konrad H. Jarausch, *The Enigmatic Chancellor: Bethmann Hollweg and the Hubris of Imperial Germany* (New Haven and London, 1973), p. 158; cf. *Kurt Riezler: Tagebücher, Aufsätze, Dokumente*, edited by Karl Dietrich Erdmann (Göttingen, 1973), pp. 181–84.

[79] Eric A. Nordlinger, *Conflict Regulation in Divided Societies* (Cambridge, Mass., 1972), pp. 43–44 (italics his); cf. Otto Kimminich, *Rüstung und politische Spannung: Studien zum Problem der internationalen Sicherheit* (Gütersloh, 1964), pp. 145–52.

tem. The pervasiveness of military attitudes in German society went hand in hand with a perception of international affairs that justified the army's preeminence by emphasizing external threats to German security. The ramifications of this situation in domestic politics were direct and effective. On the basis of the purported threat from abroad the regime clung to its prerogatives in foreign and military policy, which were cornerstones of the imperial constitution. In the face of demands that the Reichstag's competence be extended into these areas, the emperor and his cabinet argued that the Reichstag was too fractious and inefficient a body to control these vital matters in such troubled times.[80] "My reply to naive theoreticians," Bethmann Hollweg told the Reichstag in 1912 during a debate on this problem, "is that Germany's position in the world is not secure enough for us to dispense with our disciplined organization."[81]

Resort to an active foreign policy and an emphasis on external dangers were based upon a common view of international relations. They both assumed that power, competition, antagonism, and violent conflict were integral features of the process by which nations interacted. Both implied the need for a strong military establishment, national cohesion and resolve, and the curtailment of domestic strife. There was thus a direct link between domestic stability, or rather resistance to reform, in the German political system and the

[80] That the principle involved here has general application is evident from a recent report from the United States Senate on the president's war-making powers. If the United States, the report reads, "is to be continually at war, or in crisis, or on the verge of war, or in small-scale, partial or surrogate war, the force of events must lead inevitably toward executive domination despite any legislative roadblocks that may be placed in the Executive's way": quoted in I. F. Stone, "Can Congress Stop the President?" *New York Review of Books* xx (19 April 1973), p. 20.

[81] StBR, XIII L.P., 1 Session (16 February 1912), CCLXXXIII, 67; cf. Wernecke, *Der wille zur Weltgeltung*, p. 288.

perception of conflict in international relations. Historians continue to argue about the extent to which Germany's leaders were actually willing to engage in such conflict. Beyond dispute, however, is the fact that the regime actively cultivated a vision of international relations that stressed antagonism and the likelihood of violent conflict. And it was to this vision that the regime appealed in parrying demands for democratic reform.

Herein was the real source of the tension between the peace movement and the imperial political system. The pacifists denied the utility, desirability, and necessity of international political conflict, and they claimed that the implementation of their program would eliminate definitively the need to fear external dangers. Potentially at least, these were subversive ideas, inasmuch as they threatened to eliminate the specter of international conflict as a source of domestic integration. That they posed no practical threat to the Bismarckian system was a reflection of how effectively the agencies of attitude and opinion formation fostered the view that armed conflict in international relations was desirable or very likely.

This the pacifists discovered first hand. As they attempted to win acceptance for the concept of international community, they discovered that schools and universities, youth groups, the army, the press, churches, political parties, and the government itself repudiated their assumptions about the nature of international politics. The result was that an overwhelming majority of Germans subscribed to one variety or the other of antipacifism and regarded the pacifists either as dangerous or, more commonly, ridiculous. In this situation the peace movement played the convenient role of bugbear in the German political system. To the extent that it injected its ideas into political discussion, it succeeded only in exposing them to discredit and ridicule as products of *schwärmerische Duselei*. In this way, the peace movement probably served more to reinforce prevailing orientations toward international conflict than to weaken them.

The peace movement's more perceptive critics recognized the true character of the threat the pacifists posed to the imperial political system.[82] Certainly the German government itself was aware of the potential danger, and this explains its singularly obdurate resistance to the innocuous projects debated at the Hague conferences. Oddly, many of the pacifists themselves failed to see the source of their problems in Germany, even though their campaign laid bare the connection between parliamentary impotence and the perception of international conflict. Other pacifists, especially Quidde and Schücking (and Fried on occasion) harbored no illusions about the domestic implications of their program. One of the most acute observers of all was Eugen Schlief. Writing in 1898 on the impact of the peace movement in Germany, he pointed out that the movement's ideals clashed with the interests of the most important people in the country: "One can easily imagine how certain people are going to feel driven into a corner. Specifically, it will be those who call for the strengthening of 'throne and altar' as security against 'the party of revolution.' These people believe that the best way to do this is to keep international affairs basically in a condition of anarchy, since such a situation offers the pretext for constantly increasing and modernizing what is said to be the effective pillar of the throne—the standing army."[83] Schlief's perception of the obstacles faced by the peace movement in Germany drove him out of the movement rather early. Those

[82] NL Fried, Fried to Redaktion der "Neuen Preussischen Zeitung," Vienna, 27 January 1913; Boutiron to Delcassé, Berlin, 3 September 1898, DDF (1), XIV, 505–509, number 322; Naumann, "Der Krieg in der Zukunft," pp. 4–5; Stauff, *Der Krieg und die Friedensbestrebungen*, p. 43.

[83] Schlief, *Hohe Politik*, p. 8; see also the perceptive analyses of Richard Reuter: FW, VI (1904), 27–29; FW, VII (1905), 179; FW, VIII (1906), 67.

who remained active in it were sustained by their idealism and their illusions.

These illusions were no doubt great. Even today the pacifists' vision of an international community, in which all disputes can be settled by law, seems badly out of touch with political reality. But this says as much about our own cynicism as it does about the peace movement's goals. The extravagance of the pacifists' expectations is not enough to explain the overwhelming rejection of the peace movement in imperial Germany; nor is the atmosphere of international tension early in the century, which admittedly did nothing to enhance the appeal of the pacifists' program. The fact remains that a movement operating in the same strained international atmosphere and sharing the same vision of an international community found significantly more support and resonance in France than in Germany.

The reasons for the comparative weakness of the peace movement in Germany lie ultimately in the character of prevailing orientations toward international relations and in the political system that fostered these orientations. The peace movement advocated more than a set of specific international political reforms; it represented a general view of international affairs, which emphasized the community of nations and denied the validity of violent international conflict. The political culture of imperial Germany was hostile to this vision of a world without war, in part because the perception of international conflict was vital to the preservation of the domestic *status quo*. Agencies that shaped attitudes about international politics systematically repudiated not only the peace movement and its specific proposals, but its assumptions about the very nature of international affairs. In this situation, the peace movement remained pathetically weak—far weaker than in other countries—and it exercised no political influence, except perhaps to reinforce prevailing attitudes. Thus the threat which the pacifists' vision potentially posed to the elites who dominated the imperial system never materialized.

Whether or not the peace movement, had its influence been greater, could have prevented the outbreak of the First World War can be left to speculation, although the failure of the far stronger socialist movement to prevent it raises serious doubts. In any event, the dimensions of the peace movement's failure in Germany reflected a dangerous state of affairs, in which the expectation of international conflict permeated the political culture and extended into the highest councils of government. To the extent that it revealed the existence and underlying causes of this state of affairs, the plight of the German peace movement represents an important chapter in the story of the origins of the war.

Bibliography

Bibliographical Aids

American Historical Association. Committee for the Study of War Documents. *A Catalogue of Files and Microfilms of the German Foreign Ministry Archives, 1867–1920.* [Washington, D. C.], 1959.

Breycha-Vauthier, Arthur Carl de. "Dokumente um ein Leben: Die 'Bertha-von-Suttner Sammlung' der Bibliothek der Vereinten Nationen," *Festschrift des Haus- Hof- und Staatsarchivs* I (1949), 9–12.

Bureau international de la paix, Bibliotheque du Bureau international de la paix, *Cahiers d'inventaire.* [Berne], 1933.

Cook, Blanche Wiesen, ed. *Bibliography on Peace Research in History.* Santa Barbara, Calif., 1969.

La Fontaine, Henri. *Bibliographie de la paix et de l'arbitrage international.* Monaco, 1904.

Milatz, Alfred. *Friedrich Naumann Bibliographie.* Düsseldorf, 1957.

Sheehan, James J. "Germany, 1890–1918: A Survey of Recent Research," *Central European History* I (1968), 345–72.

Siegmund-Schultze, D. F., ed. *Inventarverzeichnis des Oekumenischen Archivs in Soest (Westfalen).* Soest, 1962.

Snell, John L. "Imperial Germany's Tragic Era, 1888–1918: Threshold to Democracy or Foreground of Nazism?" *Journal of Central European Affairs* XVIII (1958/59), 380–95; XIX (1959/60), 57–75.

Stanford University Archives/National Historical Publications Commission. *Guide to the Microfilm Edition of the David Starr Jordan Papers, 1861–1964.* Stanford, 1964.

Verzeichnis von 1000 Zeitungs-Artikeln Alfred H. Frieds zur Friedensbewegung (Bis März 1908). Berlin, 1908.

Winnacker, R. A. "The Third Republic, 1870–1914," *Journal of Modern History* X (1938), 372–409.

Unpublished Sources

Ball State University, Muncie, Indiana: Norman Angell Papers, A5–2, C78–13.

Bayerisches Hauptstaatsarchiv, Munich; Allgemeines Staatsarchiv: MInn 66306, 66308, 66321, 73536, 73551; MH 11561.

Bayerisches Hauptstaatsarchiv, Munich; Geheimes Staatsarchiv: MA 93657 (1, 2, 4, 5, 6).

Bayerisches Hauptstaatsarchiv, Munich; Kriegsarchiv: MKr 228, 11521.

Bayerisches Hauptstaatsarchiv, Munich; Staatsarchiv für Oberbayern (now Staatsarchiv München): AR 3186/384, 3187/401, 3198/1018; RA 3784/57791, 3785/57794; 24 aI 79/4299, 105/4250, 87/4097.

Bundesarchiv, Coblenz: NL Lujo Brentano; NL Hans Delbrück; NL Georg Gothein; NL Maximilian Harden; NL Ludwig Quidde; NL Walther Schücking; NL Hans Wehberg; NL Philipp Zorn; Kleine Erwerbungen, number 80, number 311; R 45 III/62.

Evangelische Kirche in Deutschland Archiv, Berlin: NL Friedrich Siegmund-Schultze (formerly located in the Oekumenisches Archiv, Soest).

Hauptstaatsarchiv Stuttgart: NL Conrad Haussmann (Q 1/2); E 130 I, Bü 457; E 151C/II, Bü 238.

Hessisches Staatsarchiv, Marburg: Univ. Marburg/L. Rektor u. Senat. Acc. 1950/9, number 192.

Hoover Institution, Stanford University: Alfred Fried Collection, Manuscript Materials; David Starr Jordan Collection, Peace Correspondence.

Politisches Archiv des Auswärtigen Amtes, Bonn: Eur. Generalia 37 number 1, Bd. 1–13; 37 number 2, Bd. 1–9; 37 number 2a, Bd. 1–6; 37 number 3, number 3c, Bd. 1–3; 37 number 4, Bd. 1–6; 37 number 5, Bd. 1–9; 37 number 5 secr.; 37 number 6, Bd. 1–2; 37 number 6a; 37 number 7; 37 number 7 secr.; Deutschland 141 number 8a, Bd. 2.

Staatsarchiv, Hamburg: Polizeibehörde (Politische Polizei), S4930, Deutsche Friedensgesellschaft.

Stadtbibliothek München, Handschriftenabteilung: NL
Margarethe Quidde.

United Nations Library, Geneva: NL Alfred Fried; NL
Bertha von Suttner; Suttner-Fried Correspondence;
Archives of the Bureau international permanent de la
paix; Manuscript Collection.

Universitätsbibliothek, Marburg: NL Martin Rade.

Published Sources

DOCUMENTS

*Déclaration de la Délégation permanente des sociétés de
la paix sur l'attitude du parti pacifique dans la question
d'Alsace-Lorraine. Deuxième Congrès national de la paix.
Nîmes, 7–10 avril 1904.* Paris, 1904.

Deutsche Friedensgesellschaft, Ortsgruppe Königsberg.
*Auf dem Weg zum Weltfrieden in Ostpreussen (Dritter
Jahresbericht 1912–Februar 1913).* Königsberg, 1913.

————. *Jahresbericht 1910.* Königsberg, 1910.

————. *Jahresbericht Februar 1911–1912.* Königsberg, 1912.

Documents diplomatiques français (1871–1914). First and
Second Series. 29 vols. Paris, 1929–55.

Dotation Carnegie pour la paix internationale, Centre européen. Procès-verbal des séances de la commission de la
presse, 22–23 janvier 1914.

Gooch, G. P., and Harold Temperley, eds. *British Documents on the Origins of the War.* 11 vols. London,
1926–38.

Lepsius, Johannes; Mendelssohn-Bartholdy, Albrecht; and
Thimme, Friedrich, eds. *Die Grosse Politik der europäischen Kabinette 1871–1914: Sammlung der Diplomati-
schen Akten des Auswärtigen Amtes.* 40 vols. Berlin,
1926–27.

*Liste des organes du mouvement pacifiste au 1er janvier
1907.* Berne, 1907.

Mommsen, Wilhelm. *Deutsche Parteiprogramme: Eine
Auswahl vom Vormärz bis zur Gegenwart.* Munich, 1952.

[Neufville, Eduard de]. *Concerning a Good Understanding between England and Germany*. Munich, 1906.

Programm und Satzung der Deutschen Friedensgesellschaft. Esslingen, n.d.

Rich, Norman, and Fisher, M. H., eds. *The Holstein Papers*. 4 vols. Cambridge, 1963.

Schulthess' Europäischer Geschichtskalender, 1900–1914. Munich, 1901–15.

Statut und Programm der Deutschen Friedensgesellschaft. N.p., [1897].

Statuten des Verbandes für internationale Verständigung. Frankfurt, n.d.

Wehberg, Hans. *Gutachten. Deutschland und die Friedensbewegung. Sonderabdruck aus Das Werk des Untersuchungsausschusses der Verfassungsgebenden Deutschen Nationalversammlung und des Deutschen Reichtages 1919–1930. Erste Reihe. Die Vorgeschichte des Weltkrieges*, Band v, 1. Berlin, n.d.

JOURNALS, NEWSPAPERS, AND YEARBOOKS

The Advocate of Peace.

Almanach de la paix.

Annuaire de l'Union interparlementaire. Brussels and Leipzig, 1911–19.

Annuaire de la vie internationale. Brussels and Monaco, 1905–11.

Annuaire du mouvement pacifiste pour l'année 1913 publié par le Bureau international de la paix à Berne. Berne, 1913.

Bulletin de la Société Gratry pour le maintien de la paix entre les nations (Ligue des Catholiques français pour la paix).

Bulletin de l'Union internationale de la presse pour la paix.

Carnegie Endowment for International Peace. *Year Book for 1912*. Washington, D. C., 1913.

———. *Year Book for 1913–14*. Washington, D. C., 1914.

Christliche Welt.

Conciliation internationale. *Bulletin*.

Concord.

Correspondance bi-mensuelle.

Correspondenz für die Friedensbewegung.

Deutsche Friedensgesellschaft, Frauenbund. *Flugblatt.*

Dokumente des Fortschritts.

Die Eiche.

Ethische Rundschau.

Die Friedens-Blätter.

Friedens-Correspondenz.

Die Friedens-Warte.

The Herald of Peace and International Arbitration.

[Kloss, Walter]. *Das Friedensjahrbuch 1911.* Stuttgart, 1911.

―――. *Das Friedensjahrbuch 1913.* Stuttgart, 1913.

Korrespondenz des Verbandes für internationale Verständigung.

Mitteilungen der Deutschen Friedensgesellschaft.

Mitteilungen des Verbandes für internationale Verständigung.

Monatliche Friedenskorrespondenz.

Nachrichten des Deutsch-Englischen Verständigungskomitees.

Neue Zeit.

La paix par le droit.

The Peace Movement.

Der Völker-Friede.

Die Waffen nieder!

PROTOCOLS

Anglo-German Understanding Conference. *Report of the Proceedings.* . . . London, 1912.

Bulletin du Ier Congrès universel de la paix, Paris 1889. Berne, 1901.

Bulletin officiel du IVme Congrès universel de la paix tenu à Berne du 22 au 27 août 1892. Berne, 1892.

Bulletin du VIme Congrès de la paix, Anvers 1894. Antwerp, 1895.

Bulletin officiel du VIIe Congrès universel de la paix tenu à Budapest du 17 à 22 septembre 1896. Berne, 1896.

Bulletin officiel du VIIIe Congrès universel de la paix tenu à Hambourg du 12 au 16 août 1897. Berne, 1897.

Bulletin officiel du IXe Congrès universel de la paix tenu à Paris du 30 septembre au 5 octobre 1900. Berne, 1901.

Bulletin officiel du XIe Congrès universel de la paix tenu à Monaco du 2 au 6 avril 1902. Berne, 1902.

Bulletin officiel du XIIe Congrès universel de la paix tenu à Rouen et Le Havre, 1903. Berne, 1903.

Bulletin officiel du XIVe Congrès universel de la paix tenu à Lucerne du 19 au 23 septembre 1905. Berne, 1905.

Bulletin officiel du XVme Congrès universel de la paix tenu à Milan du 15 au 22 septembre 1906. Berne, 1906.

Bulletin officiel du XVIe Congrès universel de la paix tenu à Munich du 9 au 14 septembre 1907. Berne, 1908.

Bulletin officiel du XIXe Congrès universel de la paix tenu à Genève du 22 au 28 septembre 1912. Berne, n.d.

Bulletin officiel du XXme Congrès universel de la paix tenu à La Haye du 18 août au 23 août 1913. Berne, n.d.

Cinquième Congrès national de la paix, La Rochelle, 7–9 juin 1908. *Compte-rendu des séances.* La Rochelle, 1908.

Der deutsche Friedenskongress in Jena, 1908. N.p., 1908.

Der deutsche Friedenskongress in Wiesbaden, 1910. N.p., 1910.

II. Congrès national des sociétés françaises de la paix, Nîmes, 7–10 avril 1904. *Compte-rendu des séances.* Nîmes, 1904.

V. Deutscher Friedenskongress am 26. und 27. Oktober 1912 in Berlin. N.p., n.d.

XVIIIe Congrès universel de la paix à Stockholm. Du 1er au 5 août 1910. Stockholm, 1911.

Official Report of the Fifth Universal Peace Congress, Chicago, August 14–20, 1893. Boston, n.d.

Official Report of the Seventeenth Universal Congress of Peace. . . . London, July 27 to August 1, 1908. London, 1908.

Official Report of the Thirteenth Universal Peace Congress, Boston, Massachusetts, October 3–8, 1904. Boston, 1904.

Premier Congrès national des sociétés françaises de la paix [Toulouse], Octobre 1902. Toulouse, 1903.

Proceedings of the Universal Peace Congress . . . London, July 14–19, 1890. London, 1890.

Proceedings of the Tenth Universal Peace Congress, Glasgow, September 10–13, 1901. London, 1902.

Protokoll über die Verhandlungen des Parteitages der Sozialdemokratischen Partei Deutschlands (Jena, 17–23 September 1905). Berlin, 1905.

Protokoll über die Verhandlungen des Parteitages der Sozialdemokratischen Partei Deutschlands (Jena, 10–16 September 1911). Berlin, 1911.

Protokoll über die Verhandlungen des Parteitages der Sozialdemokratischen Partei Deutschlands (Chemnitz, 15–21 September 1912). Berlin, 1912.

Protokoll über die Verhandlungen des Parteitages der Sozialdemokratischen Partei Deutschlands (Jena, 14–20 September 1913). Berlin, 1913.

viie Congrès national des sociétés françaises de la paix, Clermont-Ferrand, 4–7 juin 1911. *Compte-rendu du congrès.* Clermont-Ferrand, 1911.

Sixième Congrès national des sociétés françaises de la paix, Reims, 30 mai–2 juin 1909. *Compte-rendu des séances.* Reims, 1909.

Stenographische Berichte über die Verhandlungen des Reichstages. Berlin, 1871–1933.

Troisième Congrès international de la paix, Rome, Novembre 1891. Rome, 1892.

Pacifist Literature

Arnaud, Émile. *Le pacifisme et ses détracteurs.* Paris and Berne, 1906.

Berendsohn, Robert L. *Krieg oder Frieden? Deutsches Volk —Entscheide!* Hamburg, 1907.

Bloch, Jean de. *The Future of War: In Its Technical, Economic, and Political Relations.* Boston, 1914.

Bloch, Johann von. *Der Krieg: Uebersetzung des russischen Werkes des Autors: Der zukünftige Krieg in seiner technischen, volkswirthschaftlichen und politischen Bedeutung.* 6 vols. Berlin, 1899.

———. "Die Lehren des Transvaalkriegs für Deutschland," *Deutsche Revue* XXVI (1901), 257–78.

Böhme, Ernst. *Friedensbewegung und Lebenserziehung.* Gautzsch b. Leipzig, 1913.

———. *Die Unterlassungssünde der Kirche vor dem Kriege.* Stuttgart, 1919.

Bönninger, Arthur. *Die Presse und die internationale Verständigung.* Munich, 1911.

Bräutigam, Ludwig. "Die Kriegsdichtung in den Schulen," *Pädagogisches Wochenblatt* VIII (1898/99), 187–89.

Brück, H., and Triebel, E. *Erziehe zum Frieden! Eine ernste Mahnung an Eltern und Lehrer.* Frankfurt a. M., 1905.

Dietz, Alexander. *Franz Wirth und der Frankfurter Friedensverein.* Frankfurt, a. M., 1911.

Flügge, C. A. *Gegenwartsnöte: Aus dem Zeitenspiegel der Tagespresse.* Kassel, n.d.

Fried, Alfred H. *Die Ausgestaltung der Friedensaktion in Deutschland.* Berlin, 1903.

———. *Bertha von Suttner.* Charlottenburg, n.d.

———. *Elsass-Lothringen und der Friede.* Leipzig, 1895.

———. "Etwas von der Friedensbewegung und ihren Organen," *Westermanns Illustrierte Deutsche Monatshefte* CI, 2 (1907), 742–50.

———. "Freimaurerei und Friedensfrage," *Zwanglose Mitteilungen aus dem Verein Deutscher Freimaurer* II (June 1914), 272–74.

———. "Die Friedensbewegung im Berichtsjahr 1912," *Jahrbuch des Völkerrechts* I (1911–12), 1303–12.

———. "Friedensbewegung und Freimaurerei," *Zwanglose Mitteilungen aus dem Verein Deutscher Freimaurer* II (June 1914), 275–76.

———. *Friedens-Katechismus: Ein Compendium der Friedenslehre.* Dresden and Leipzig, 1894.

———. *Der gegenwärtige Krieg und die Friedensbewegung.* Vienna, 1904.

———. *The German Emperor and the Peace of the World.* London, 1912.

———. *Die Grundlagen des revolutionären Pacifismus.* Tübingen, 1908.

———. *Handbuch der Friedensbewegung.* Vienna and Leipzig, 1905.

———. *Handbuch der Friedensbewegung.* 2d ed. 2 vols. Berlin and Leipzig, 1911–13.

———. *Die hauptsächlichsten Missverständnisse über die Friedensbewegung.* Berlin, 1903.

———. *Der Kaiser und der Weltfriede.* Berlin, 1910.

———. *Kaiser werde modern!* Berlin, 1905.

———. *Kleine Anzeigen: Sociale Streifbilder vom Jahrmarkt des Lebens.* Berlin, 1900.

———. *Kurze Aufklärungen über Wesen und Ziel des Pazifismus.* Berlin and Leipzig, 1914.

———. *Die Lasten des bewaffneten Friedens und der Zukunftskrieg.* Esslingen, n.d.

———. *Die moderne Friedensbewegung.* Leipzig, 1907.

———. *Die moderne Friedensbewegung in Deutschland und Frankreich.* Gautzsch b. Leipzig, 1908.

———. "Die moderne Friedensbewegung in Deutschland und Frankreich," *Der Continent* 1 (1907), 696–704, 1076–87.

———. *Pan-Amerika: Entwicklung, Umfang und Bedeutung der pan-amerikanischen Bewegung.* Berlin, 1910.

———. *The Peace Movement and the Press.* Berne, 1913.

———. "Pro Domo," *Der Friede* (February 1895).

———. *Unter der weissen Fahne: Aus der Mappe eines Friedensjournalisten.* Berlin, 1901.

———. *Die zweite Haager Konferenz: Ihre Arbeiten, ihre Ergebnisse und ihre Bedeutung.* Leipzig, n.d.

Das Friedenswerk. Von einem Menschenfreund der Tat. Altona, n.d.

Friedrichs, Elsbeth, and Friedrichs, Friedrich M. *Der Völkerfriede und die Religion.* Gautzsch b. Leipzig, 1910.

Giesswein, Alexander. *Der Friede Christi: Christentum und Friedensbewegung.* Vienna, 1913.

Gobat, Albert. *Le cauchemar de l'Europe.* Strassburg and Paris, n.d.

——. *La conférence interparlamentaire franco-allemande de Berne.* Berne, 1913.

Goldscheid, Rudolf. *Friedensbewegung und Menschenökonomie.* Berlin and Leipzig, 1912.

Grosch, Georg, ed. *Deutsche Pazifisten: Eine Sammlung von Vorkämpfern der Friedensbewegung in Deutschland.* Stuttgart, 1920.

——. "Völkerrecht und die Weltfriedensbewegung," *Zeitschrift für die gesamte Staatswissenschaft* LXVII (1911), 179–217.

Jordan, David Starr. *Krieg und Menschheit.* Berlin and Leipzig, 1912.

Katscher, Leopold. *Bertha von Suttner, die "Schwärmerin" für Güte.* Dresden, 1903.

Koester, Otto. "Theologische Gegner der Friedensbewegung," *Nord und Süd* XXXVIII (August 1914), 157–66.

Koht, Halvdan. *Histoire du mouvement de la paix en Norvège.* Kristiania, 1900.

Lamprecht, Karl. *Der Kaiser: Versuch einer Charakteristik.* 2d ed. Berlin, 1916.

——. *Die Nation und die Friedensbewegung.* Berlin, 1914.

Lehmann, Reinhold. *Die französischen Volksschullehrer als Schrittmacher der Friedensbewegung.* Stuttgart, 1920.

Lenz, Kurt, and Fabian, Walter, eds. *Die Friedensbewegung: Ein Handbuch der Weltfriedensströmungen der Gegenwart.* Berlin, 1922.

Löwenthal, Eduard. *Geschichte der Friedensbewegung: Mit Berücksichtigung der zweiten Haager Friedenskonferenz.* 2d ed. Berlin, 1907.

Lucht, J. *40 Erwägungen über Religion und Weltfrieden.* Berlin, 1908.

Michelis, H. *Geschichte und Ziele der modernen internationalen Friedensbewegung.* Königsberg, 1906.

Moch, Gaston. "Le viiie Congrès universel de la paix," *Questions diplomatiques et coloniales* I (1897), 345–55.

Molenaar, H. *Metz und Strassburg: Die natürliche Lösung der elsass-lothringischen Frage.* Weissenburg a. S., n.d.

————. "Die Notwendigkeit der Annäherung Deutschlands und Frankreichs," *Mitteilungen über die deutsch-französische Liga,* No. 3/4 (1905), pp. 33–64.

————. "Pacifismus und Militarismus," *Positive Weltanschauung,* v (1906), 39–43.

————. "Zur Friedensbewegung," *Positive Weltanschauung,* v (1906), 192–96.

Nippold, Otfried. *Der deutsche Chauvinismus.* Stuttgart, 1913.

————. "Die deutsche Regierung und die 2. Haager Friedenskonferenz," *Deutsche Revue* XXXIII (1908), 169–74.

————. *Durch Wahrheit zum Recht: Kriegsaufsätze.* Berne, 1919.

————. "Eine Anregung zum internationalen Zusammenschluss der Völkerrechtsgelehrten," *Zeitschrift für Völkerrecht und Bundesstaatsrecht* III (1908), 217–20.

————. *Die Fortbildung des Verfahrens in völkerrechtlichen Streitigkeiten: Ein völkerrechtliches Problem der Gegenwart speziell im Hinblick auf die Haager Friedenskonferenzen.* Leipzig, 1907.

————. "Kulturentwicklung und Weltpolitik," *Deutsche Revue* XXXV (1910), 190–202.

————. "Vorfragen des Völkerrechts," *Jahrbuch des öffentlichen Rechts* VII (1913), 20–48.

————. *Ziele und Aufgaben des Verbandes für internationale Verständigung.* Stuttgart, 1913.

Nithack-Stahn, Walther. *Kirche und Krieg.* Halle, n.d.

————. *Kirche und Vaterland.* Berlin-Schöneberg, 1914.

————. *Völkerfriede? Ein Streit-Gespräch.* Stuttgart, n.d.

Novikow, J. *Die Föderation Europas*. Berlin and Berne, 1901.

———. *Der Krieg und seine angeblichen Wohlthaten*. Leipzig, 1896.

Passy, Frédéric. "Congrès et conférence," *L'arbitrage entre nations* III (1899), 153–55.

———. *Historique du mouvement de la paix*. Paris, 1904.

———. "Les origines et le but de la Ligue internationale de la paix, selon M. de Bismarck," *Revue de la paix* (December 1902), pp. 392–93.

Paszkowski, Wilhelm. *German International Progress in 1913*. Washington, D. C., 1914.

Pazifismus und Internationalismus (Veröffentlichungen des Freimaurerbundes "Zur Aufgehenden Sonne," No. 1). Nuremberg, 1911.

Quidde, Ludwig. *Caligula: Eine Studie über römischen Cäsarenwahnsinn*. Leipzig, 1894.

———. *Der Militarismus im heutigen deutschen Reich: Eine Anklageschrift*. Stuttgart, 1893.

———. *Studien zur Geschichte des Rheinischen Landfriedensbundes von 1259*. Frankfurt a. M., 1885.

Rade, Martin. *Der Beitrag der christlichen Kirchen zur internationalen Verständigung*. Stuttgart, 1912.

Schücking, Walther. "Modernes Weltbürgertum," *Die Zukunft* LX (1907), 244–45.

———. *Das Nationalitätenproblem: Eine politische Studie über die Polenfrage und die Zukunft Oesterreich-Ungarns*. Dresden, 1908.

———. *Neue Ziele der staatlichen Entwicklung*. 2d and 3d eds. Marburg, 1913.

———. *Die Organisation der Welt*. Leipzig, 1909.

Siegmund-Schultze, F. "Religion und Friede," *Monatsschrift für Pastoraltheologie* VII (1910–11), 101–106.

Siemering, Carl Ludwig [Oskar Schwonder]. *Von der ersten deutschen Friedensgesellschaft*. Frankfurt a. M., 1909.

Stein, Ludwig. *Die Philosophie des Friedens*. Berne, 1899.

Suttner, Bertha von. *Die Waffen nieder! Eine Lebensge-schichte.* 38th ed. 2 vols. Dresden, n.d.

Tiedje, Johannes. "Die Friedensfrage: Eine Gewissensfrage für die deutschen Freimaurer," *Zwanglose Mitteilungen aus dem Verein Deutscher Freimaurer* II (June 1914), 265–72.

Umfrid, Otto. *Anti-Stengel.* Esslingen, 1909.

———. *Anti-Treitschke.* Esslingen, n.d.

———. *Bismarcks Gedanken und Erinnerungen im Lichte der Friedensidee und Anderes zur Kritik nationalsozialer Afterpolitik.* Esslingen, 1905.

———. "Die Bitte der Deutschen Friedensgesellschaft um eine Subvention vor der württembergischen Kammer der Standesherren," *Der Beobachter* (Stuttgart), 11 May 1909.

———. *Europa den Europäern: Politische Ketzereien.* Esslingen, 1913.

———. *Die Formel der Abrüstung mit besonderer Berück-sichtigung des englischen Abrüstungsvorschlags.* Stuttgart, n.d.

———. *Friede auf Erden! Betrachtungen über den Völker-frieden.* Esslingen, 1897.

———. *Vaterlandsliebe und Menschheitsliebe.* Esslingen, n.d.

———. *Völkerevangelium.* Esslingen, 1913.

———, ed. *Der Wehrverein eine Gefahr für das deutsche Volk: Polemisches und Irenisches.* Esslingen, 1914.

Wagner, Ludwig. *Warum muss der Lehrer Stellung zur heutigen Friedensbewegung nehmen?* Stuttgart, 1914.

Wehberg, Hans. "Friedensbewegung, Völkerrechtswissen-schaft, Haager Friedenskonferenz," *Deutsche Revue* XXXV (1910), 349–54.

———. *Die internationale Friedensbewegung.* Moenchen Gladbach, 1911.

———. *Neue Weltprobleme: Gesammelte Aufsätze über Weltwirtschaft und Völkerorganisation.* Munich and Leipzig, 1914.

Wirth, Franz. "Die soziale Bedeutung des internationalen Friedensbewegung," *Berichte des Freien Deutschen Hochstiftes zu Frankfurt* XI (1895), 185–88.

Other Contemporary Literature

Bernhardi, Friedrich von. *Deutschland und der nächste Krieg.* Stuttgart and Berlin, 1912.

———. *Unsere Zukunft: Ein Mahnwort an das deutsche Volk.* Stuttgart and Berlin, 1912.

Bernstein, Eduard. "Die internationale Politik der Sozial-demokratie," *Sozialistische Monatshefte* XIII, 2 (1909), 613–24.

Biermer, M. *Die finanzielle Mobilmachung.* Giessen, 1913.

Bleibtreu, Karl. "Der falsche Friedenspreis der Nobel-stiftung," *Die Gegenwart* LXXIV (1908), 418–19.

Blume, W. von. "Staat und Gesellschaft in einem grossen Krieg unserer Zeit," *Deutsche Rundschau* CXXI (1904), 365–84; CXXII (1905), 45–63, 220–33.

Boeck, Chr. de. "Ludwig von Bars Lebenswerk," *Zeitschrift für Völkerrecht* VIII (1914), 420–36.

Boguslawski, Albrecht von. *Der Krieg in seiner wahren Bedeutung für Staat und Volk.* Berlin, 1892.

Bourdon, Georges. *L'énigme allemande: Une enquête chez les Allemands.* Paris, 1913.

Bremen, W. von. "Friedenskonferenz und englischer Abrü-stungsscherz," *Daheim* XLIII (1907), 12–13.

Bruchhausen, Karl von. *Der kommende Krieg: Eine Studie über die militärische Lage Deutschlands.* Berlin, n.d.

Buisson, Ferdinand. *La politique radicale: Étude sur les doctrines du parti radical et radical-socialiste.* Paris, 1908.

Dehn, Paul. "Für internationale Verständigung," *Alldeutsche Blätter* XXII (1912), 217–18.

Delbrück, Hans. "Der Abrüstungs-Gedanke, England und Deutschland," *Preussische Jahrbücher* CXXVIII (1907), 369–81.

———. *Vor und nach dem Weltkrieg: Politische und his-torische Aufsätze 1902–1925.* Berlin, 1926.

————. "Weshalb baut Deutschland Kriegsschiffe? Beantwortung der Frage eines Engländers," *Preussische Jahrbücher* CXXXVIII, I (1909), 149–61.

————. "Zukunftskrieg und Zukunftsfriede," *Preussische Jahrbücher* XCVI (1899), 203–229.

Deutscher Wehrverein. *Die Friedensbewegung und ihre Gefahren für das deutsche Volk.* Berlin, 1914.

Driesmans, Heinrich, ed. *M. von Egidy: Sein Leben und Wirken.* Dresden, 1900.

Eberle, Franz Xaver. *Krieg und Frieden im Urteile christlicher Moral.* Stuttgart, 1914.

Egidy, Moritz von. *Ernste Gedanken.* Leipzig, 1890.

Eickhoff, Richard. "Die interparlamentarische Union (1889–1914)," *Zeitschrift für Politik* VIII (1915), 452–93.

Eigenbrodt, August. *"Berliner Tageblatt" und "Frankfurter Zeitung" in ihrem Verhalten zu den nationalen Fragen 1887–1914.* Berlin, 1917.

Flourens, Émile. "Die Kehrseite der pazifistischen Medaille," *Deutsche Revue* XXXVIII (1912), 73–87.

Foerster, Wilhelm. *Die ethische Bewegung in Deutschland.* Berlin, 1903.

Fruhstorfer, Karl. "Treibende Kräfte und Charakter der Friedensbewegung," *Theologisch-praktische Quartalsshrift* LXIV (1911), 84–90.

Glatzel. "Ueber den Einfluss der Friedensbewegung auf die europäischen Rüstungsverhältnisse," *Deutsche Revue* XXXVI (1911), 226–32.

Goltz, Colmar von der. *Das Volk in Waffen: Ein Buch über Heerwesen und Kriegführung unserer Zeit.* 5th ed. Berlin, 1899.

H., Dr. "Friedensgesellschaften," *Die Kritik* I (1894), 34–35.

Hagen, E. "Ist der Krieg unabänderliches Völkergeschick?" *Militär-Wochenblatt* LXXIX (1894), 2075–78, 2095–99.

Harms, Bernhard. *Volkswirtschaft und Weltwirtschaft: Versuch der Begründung einer Weltwirtschaftslehre.* Jena, 1912.

Harnack, Adolf. *Militia Christi: Die christliche Religion und der Soldatenstand in den ersten drei Jahrhunderten.* Tübingen, 1905.

Heilmann, Major. "Der zukünftige Krieg," *Allgemeine Zeitung,* 26 May 1899, Beilage.

Horneffer, August. *Deutsche und ausländische Freimaurerei.* Munich, 1915.

Huber, Max. "Beiträge zur Kenntnis der sozialen Grundlagen des Völkerrechts und der Gesellschaft," *Jahrbuch des öffentlichen Rechts* IV (1910), 56–134.

———. *Die soziologischen Grundlagen des Völkerrechts.* Berlin, 1928.

"Internationale Verständigung," *Kölnische Zeitung,* 9 October 1912.

"Zur internationalen Verständigung," *Kölnische Zeitung,* 12 June 1911.

Jähns, Max. *Ueber Krieg und Frieden: Eine Umschau.* 2d ed. Berlin, 1893.

Jellinek, Georg. *Der Kampf des alten mit dem neuen Recht.* Heidelberg, 1907.

Karski, J. "Das Urtheil eines bürgerlichen Ideologen über den Militarismus," *Neue Zeit* XVII, 2 (1898/99), 171-74.

Kattenbusch, Ferdinand. *Das sittliche Recht des Krieges.* Giessen, 1906.

Kautsky, Karl. "Die Berner Konferenz," *Neue Zeit* XXXI, 2 (1913), 265–69.

———. "Der erste Mai und der Kampf gegen den Militarismus," *Neue Zeit* XXX, 2 (1912), 97–109.

———. "Krieg und Frieden: Betrachtungen zur Maifeier," *Neue Zeit* XXIX, 2 (1911), 97–107.

———. "Nochmals die Abrüstung," *Neue Zeit* XXX, 2 (1912), 841–54.

Kirchhoff, Arthur, ed. *Männer der Wissenschaft über die Friedenskonferenz.* Berlin, 1899.

Kohler, Josef. "Die Friedensbewegung und das Völkerrecht," *Zeitschrift für Völkerrecht und Bundesstaatsrecht* IV (1909–10), 129–40.

L., Major. "Der zukünftige Krieg," *Die Umschau*, 11 February 1899, pp. 121–25; 18 February 1899, pp. 149–52.

Lamprecht, Karl. *Europäische Expansion.* Ullsteins Weltgeschichte, Vol. 6. Berlin, 1908.

Landmann, Karl Ritter von. "Die heutige Friedensbewegung," *Hochland* v (1908), 465–75.

Lehmann-Russbüldt, Otto. *Der geistige Befreiungskrieg durch Kirchenaustritt.* Berlin, 1914.

———. "Der kirchliche Liberalismus und die Kirchenaustrittsbewegung," *Das Monistische Jahrhundert* 1 (1912/13), 641–44.

Leuthner, Karl. "Allgemeine Friedensbürgschaft," *Sozialistische Monatshefte* XIV, 2 (1910), 1017–20.

Lichnowsky, Fürst. "Die Friedensfrage in militärischer und politischer Beleuchtung," *Deutsche Revue* XXXIV (1909), 165–68.

Lifschitz, F. *Deutschlands Stellung zu der Friedensidee und der internationalen Schiedsgerichtsbarkeit.* Berlin, 1917.

Marcks, Erich. "Die imperialistische Idee in der Gegenwart," *Männer und Zeiten.* 2 vols. Leipzig, 1911, II, 265–91.

Meurer, Christian. *Das Friedensrecht der Haager Konferenz.* Munich, 1905.

———. *Das Kriegsrecht der Haager Konferenz.* Munich, 1907.

Mtz. "Das Verlustertragen im Zukunftskrieg," *Neue militärische Blätter* LVI (1900), 181–84.

Müller, Ed. *Der Friedensvereine Heil und Haken.* Berlin, 1892.

Naumann, Friedrich. "Der Krieg in der Zukunft," *Die Hilfe* v (1899), 4–5.

———. "Was ist der Friede?" *Süddeutsche Monatshefte* 1 (1904), 453–59.

Naumann, Friedrich. "Der Zwang zum Frieden," *Die Hilfe* XVIII (1912), 258–59.

Neurath, Otto. "Die Kriegswirtschaftslehre als Sonderdizi-plin," *Weltwirtschaftliches Archiv* I, 2 (April 1913), 342–48.

Niemeyer, Theodor. *Internationales Recht und nationales Interesse*. Kiel, 1907.

————. "Vom Wesen des internationalen Rechtes," *Zeitschrift für internationales Recht* XX (1910), 1–15.

Quessel, Ludwig. "Imperialismus und Verständigung," *Sozialistische Monatshefte* XIX (1913), 333–39.

Reichenau, Ernst August Ludwig. *Einfluss der Kultur auf Krieg und Kriegsrüstung*. Berlin, 1897.

Reventlow, Ernst. *Holder Friede, Süsse Eintracht: Eine politische Satire*. Leipzig, 1906.

Saenger, Samuel. "Pazifistische Illusionen," *Neue Rundschau* XXII, 1 (1911), 737–44.

Schlief, Eugen [pseud. B.O.T. Schafter]. *Der Friede in Europa: Eine völkerrechtlich-politische Studie*. Leipzig, 1892.

————. *Hohe Politik: Kritische Randbemerkungen zum internationalen Leben der Gegenwart*. 2d ed. Berlin, 1902.

Schmidt-Gibichenfels, Otto. "Der Krieg als Kulturfactor," *Politisch-anthropologische Revue* XI (1912/13), 393–407, 449–61.

————. "Uralte Herrschaftsorganisationen in moderner Beleuchtung," *Politisch-anthropologische Revue* XI (1912/13), 281–93.

Spahn, Martin. *Der Friedensgedanke in der Entwicklung des deutschen Volkes zur Nation*. Stuttgart, 1913.

Stauff, Philipp. *Der Krieg und die Friedensbestrebungen unserer Zeit*. N.p., 1907.

Steinmetz, Rudolf. *Die Philosophie des Krieges*. Leipzig, 1907.

Stengel, Karl Freiherr von. *Der ewige Friede*. 3d ed. Munich, 1899.

―――. "Die Frage der internationalen Schiedsgerichte," *Münchner Neueste Nachrichten*, 2 August, 4 August, 5 August 1899.

―――. "Die Friedensidee in Deutschland," *Die Zukunft* LXVIII (1909), 309–14.

―――. "Die Idee des ewigen Friedens und die Friedensbewegung," *Deutsche Revue* XXXV (1910), 203–31.

―――. "Die Idee des ewigen Friedens und die sogenannten Friedenskonferenzen," *Die Umschau* XI (1907), 321–23, 381–84, 472–74.

―――. *Weltstaat und Friedensproblem*. Berlin, 1909.

Strantz, Kurd von. "Gefährliche Friedensseligkeit," *Politisch-anthropologische Revue* XI (1912/13), 469–80.

Tiedje, Johannes. *Die deutsche Freimaurerei*. Marburg, 1913.

Traub, Gottfried. "Friedensbewegung," *Die Zeit* II (1902/1903), 752–55.

Treitschke, Heinrich von. *Politics*. 2 vols. New York, 1916.

"Die Waffen nieder!" *Neue Zeit* XXXII, 2 (1914), 601–604.

Wille, Ulrich. "Der Krieg," *Zeitschrift für Sozialwissenschaft* II (1899), 325–61.

Zepelin, Generalmajor. "Der 'Zukunftskrieg' in russischer, fachmännischer Beurteilung," *Jahrbücher für die deutsche Armee und Marine* CX (1899), 56–67.

Zorn, Philipp. *Das Deutsche Reich und die internationale Schiedsgerichtsbarkeit*. Berlin and Leipzig, 1911.

―――. *Deutschland und die beiden Haager Friedenskonferenzen*. Stuttgart and Berlin, 1920.

Memoirs and Diaries

Angell, Norman. *After All: The Autobiography of Norman Angell*. London, 1952.

Baker, Elizabeth Balmer, and Baker, P. J. Noel. *J. Allen Baker, M.P.: A Memoir*. London, 1927.

Bernhardi, Friedrich von. *Denkwürdigkeiten aus meinem Leben, nach gleichzeitigen Aufzeichnungen und im Lichte der Erinnerung*. Berlin, 1927.

Braun, Lily. *Memoiren einer Sozialistin.* Munich, 1909.

Bülow, Bernhard von. *Memoirs of Prince von Bülow.* 4 vols. Boston, 1931.

Curtius, Friedrich. *Deutsche Briefe und elsässische Erinnerungen.* Frauenfeld, 1920.

Eickhoff, Richard. *Politische Profile: Erinnerungen aus vier Jahrzehnten an Eugen Richter, Carl Schurz und Virchow, Werner Siemens und Bassermann, Fürst Bülow, Hohenlohe u.a.* Dresden, 1927.

Foerster, Wilhelm. *Lebenserinnerungen und Lebenshoffnungen (1832 bis 1910).* Berlin, 1911.

Frank, Ludwig. *Aufsätze, Reden und Briefe.* Berlin, 1924.

Fried, Alfred H. *Jugenderinnerungen.* Berlin, 1925.

———. *Mein Kriegs-Tagebuch.* 4 vols. Zurich, 1918–20.

Gerard, James W. *My Four Years in Germany.* New York, 1917.

Gerlach, Hellmut von. *Von Rechts nach Links.* Zürich, 1937.

Gesammelte Schriften und Denkwürdigkeiten des General-Feldmarschalls Grafen Helmuth von Moltke. 8 vols. Berlin, 1891–93.

Goldscheid, Rudolf, ed. *Alfred H. Fried: Eine Sammlung von Gedenkblättern.* Leipzig, 1922.

Guttmann, Bernhard. *Schattenriss einer Generation, 1888–1919.* Stuttgart, 1950.

Heuss, Theodor. *Erinnerungen 1905–1933.* Tübingen, 1963.

Hiller, Kurt. *Leben gegen die Zeit [Logos].* Reinbek, 1969.

Hohenlohe-Schillingsfürst, Chlodwig zu. *Denkwürdigkeiten der Kanzlerzeit.* Osnabrück, 1967.

Jäckh, Ernst. *Der goldene Pflug: Lebensernte eines Weltbürgers.* Stuttgart, 1954.

Jordan, David Starr. *The Days of a Man: Being Memories of a Naturalist, Teacher and Minor Prophet of Democracy.* 2 vols. Yonkers-on-Hudson, 1922.

Lamprecht, Karl. *Rektoratserinnerungen.* Edited by Arthur Köhler. Gotha, 1917.

Lehmann-Russbüldt, Otto. *Der Kampf der Deutschen Liga für Menschenrechte,* . . . *1914–1927.* Berlin, 1927.

Löwenthal, Eduard. *Mein Lebenswerk auf sozialpolitischem, neu-religiösem, philosophischem und naturwissenschaftlichem Gebiete.* 2d ed. Berlin, 1912.

Ludendorff, Erich. *Kriegführung und Politik.* Berlin, 1922.

Niemeyer, Theodor. *Erinnerungen und Betrachtungen aus drei Menschenaltern.* Kiel, 1963.

Nippold, Otfried. *Meine Erlebnisse in Deutschland vor dem Weltkriege (1909–1914).* Berne, 1918.

Ostwald, Grete. *Wilhelm Ostwald: Mein Vater.* Stuttgart, 1953.

Ostwald, Wilhelm. *Lebenslinien: Eine Selbstbiographie.* 3 vols. Berlin, 1926–27.

Quidde, Ludwig. "Wie ich zur Demokratie und zum Pazifismus kam," *Frankfurter Zeitung,* 4 January 1928.

René, Charles. "Les essais de rapprochement franco-allemand avant la guerre et le rôle de Clemenceau," *L'Europe nouvelle,* number 636 (19 April 1930), pp. 631–33.

[Riezler, Kurt]. *Kurt Riezler: Tagebücher, Aufsätze, Dokumente.* Edited by Karl Dietrich Erdmann, Göttingen, 1973.

Rittelmayer, Friedrich. *Aus meinem Leben.* Stuttgart, 1937.

Scheidemann, Philipp. *Memoiren eines Sozialdemokraten.* 2 vols. Dresden, 1928.

Spahn, Martin. "Selbstbiographie," in Hans von Arnim and Georg von Below, eds., *Deutscher Aufstieg: Bilder aus der Vergangenheit und Gegenwart der rechtsstehenden Parteien.* Berlin, 1925, pp. 479–88.

Stampfer, Friedrich. *Erfahrungen und Erkenntnisse: Aufzeichnungen aus meinem Leben.* Cologne, 1957.

Stein, Ludwig. *Aus dem Leben eines Optimisten.* Berlin, 1930.

Suttner, Bertha von. *Aus der Werkstatt des Pazifismus.* Leipzig and Vienna, 1912.

———. *Der Kampf um die Vermeidung des Weltkrieges: Randglossen aus zwei Jahrzehnten zu den Zeitereignissen vor der Katastrophe (1892–1900 und 1907–1914) von Bertha von Suttner.* Edited by Alfred H. Fried, 2 vols. Zurich, 1917.

———. *Lebenserinnerungen.* Edited with an introduction by Fritz Böttger. Berlin, 1968.

———. *Memoirs of Bertha von Suttner: The Records of an Eventful Life.* 2 vols. Boston and London, 1910.

Umfrid, Grete, ed. *Zum Gedächtnis von Otto Umfrid.* Stuttgart, n.d.

Weber, Marianne. *Max Weber: Ein Lebensbild.* Tübingen, 1926.

White, Andrew Dickson. *Autobiography of Andrew Dickson White.* 2 vols. New York, 1905–1907.

Wiese, Leopold von. "Die deutsche Gesellschaft für Soziologie: Persönliche Eindrücke in den ersten fünfzig Jahren (1909 bis 1959)," *Kölner Zeitschrift für Soziologie* XI (1959), 11–20.

Zorn, Philipp. *Aus einem deutschen Universitätsleben.* Bonn, 1927.

Zweig, Stefan. *Die Welt von gestern: Erinnerungen eines Europäers.* 2d ed. Berlin, 1962.

Secondary Studies

Abrams, Irwin. "Bertha von Suttner and the Nobel Peace Prize," *Journal of Central European Affairs* XXII (1962–63), 286–307.

———. "A History of European Peace Societies, 1867–1899." Ph.D. dissertation, Harvard University, 1938.

Acker, Detlev. *Walther Schücking (1875–1935).* Münster, 1970.

Almond, Gabriel. "Comparative Political Systems," *Journal of Politics* XVIII (1956), 391–409.

Almond, Gabriel, and Powell, G. Bingham, Jr. *Comparative Politics: A Developmental Approach*. Boston and Toronto, 1966.

Almond, Gabriel, and Verba, Sidney. *The Civic Culture: Political Attitudes and Democracy in Five Nations*. Boston and Toronto, 1965.

Andrew, Christopher. *Théophile Delcassé and the Making of the Entente Cordiale: A Reappraisal of French Foreign Policy, 1898–1905*. London, 1968.

Angel, Pierre. *Eduard Bernstein et l'évolution du socialisme allemand*. Paris, 1961.

Angell, Norman. "Pacifism," *Encyclopedia of the Social Sciences*. New York, 1933, XI, 527–28.

Ascher, Abraham. "Imperialists within German Social Democracy prior to 1914," *Journal of Central European Affairs* XX (1961), 397–422.

Baasch, E. *Geschichte des Hamburgischen Zeitungswesens vom Anfang bis 1914*. Hamburg, 1930.

Bainton, Roland H. *Christian Attitudes toward War and Peace: A Historical Survey and Critical Reevaluation*. New York and Nashville, Tenn., 1960.

Baker, Robert Parsons. "The Belgians and the European Peace Movement, 1889–1914." Master's thesis, Stanford University, 1962.

Barkeley, Richard. *Die deutsche Friedensbewegung 1870–1933*. Hamburg, 1948.

Barkin, Kenneth D. *The Controversy over German Industrialization, 1890–1902*. Chicago and London, 1970.

Bauer, Josef. "Die österreichische Friedensbewegung." Inaugural dissertation, Vienna, 1949.

Beales, A. C. F. *The History of Peace: A Short Account of the Organized Movements for International Peace*. London, 1931.

Benson, Lee. "An Approach to the Scientific Study of Past Public Opinion," *Public Opinion Quarterly* XXXI (1967/68), 522–67.

Berghahn, Volker. *Der Tirpitz-Plan: Genesis und Verfall einer innenpolitischen Krisenstrategie unter Wilhelm II.* Düsseldorf, 1971.

Berkman, Joyce Arrech. "Pacifism in England, 1914–1939." Ph.D. dissertation, Yale University, 1967.

Binder, Leonard, *et al. Crises and Sequences in Political Development.* Princeton, 1971.

Bosanquet, Helen. *Free Trade and Peace in the Nineteenth Century.* Kristiania, 1924.

Bosl, Karl, ed. *Bayern im Umbruch: Die Revolution von 1918, ihre Voraussetzungen, ihr Verlauf und ihre Folgen.* Munich and Vienna, 1969.

Bozeman, Adda B. *Politics and Culture in International History.* Princeton, 1960.

Bredendiek, Walter. *Der ewige Friede—Traum, Hoffnung, Möglichkeit: Friedensideen und Friedensbewegungen der Vergangenheit.* [Berlin] 1960.

————. *Irrwege und Warnlichter: Anmerkungen zur Kirchengeschichte der neueren Zeit.* Hamburg, 1966.

————. "Otto Umfrid—ein vergessener Vorkämpfer für eine Welt ohne Krieg: Zu seinem fünfzigsten Todestag," *Stimme* (Stimme der Gemeinde zum kirchlichen Leben, zur Politik, Wirtschaft und Kultur, 13) XXII (1970), 394–402.

Brim, Orville G., Jr., and Wheeler, Stanton. *Socialization after Childhood: Two Essays.* New York, 1966.

Brock, Peter. *Pacifism in Europe to 1914.* Princeton, 1972.

————. *Pacifism in the United States: From the Colonial Era to the First World War.* Princeton, 1968.

Bry, Gerhard. *Wages in Germany, 1871–1945.* Princeton, 1960.

Buchanan, William, and Cantril, Hadley. *How Nations See Each Other: A Study in Public Opinion.* Urbana, 1953.

Bühler, Andreas. *Kirche und Staat bei Rudolf Sohm.* Zurich, 1965.

Burgelin, Henri. "Le mouvement pacifiste dans l'Allemagne de Weimar," *Cahiers de l'Association interuniversitaire* (Strassbourg, 1961), pp. 57–88.

Carnegie Endowment for International Peace. *Perspectives on Peace, 1910–1960.* London, 1960.

Caron, Jeanne. *Le Sillon et la démocratie chrétienne 1894–1910.* Paris, 1967.

Carroll, E. Malcolm. *Germany and the Great Powers, 1866–1914: A Study in Public Opinion and Foreign Policy.* New York, 1938.

Chickering, Roger. "The Peace Movement and the Religious Community in Germany, 1900–1914," *Church History* XXXVIII (1969), 300–11.

———. "A Voice of Moderation in Imperial Germany: The 'Verband für internationale Verständigung,' 1911–1914," *Journal of Contemporary History* VIII (1973), 147–64.

Clarke, I. F. *Voices Prophesying War, 1763–1984.* London, 1966.

Cohn, Norman. *The Pursuit of the Millennium: Revolutionary Messianism in Medieval and Reformation Europe and Its Bearing on Modern Totalitarian Movements.* New York, 1961.

Coleman, James S., ed. *Education and Political Development.* Princeton, 1965.

Cooper, Sandi E. "Liberal Internationalists before World War I," *Peace and Change* I (1973), 11–19.

———. "Peace and Internationalism: European Ideological Movements behind the Two Hague Conferences (1899 to 1907)." Ph.D. dissertation, New York University, 1967.

Craig, Gordon A. *The Politics of the Prussian Army, 1640–1945.* New York, 1956.

Curti, Merle. *Peace or War: The American Struggle, 1636–1936.* New York, 1936.

Dansette, Adrien. *Histoire religieuse de la France contemporaine.* 2 vols. Paris, 1948–51.

Dauber, Doris. "A. H. Fried und sein Pazifismus." Inaugural dissertation, Leipzig, 1923.

445

Dawson, Richard E., and Prewitt, Kenneth. *Political Socialization: An Analytic Study*. Boston, 1969.

Deak, Istvan. *Weimar Germany's Left-Wing Intellectuals: A Political History of the Weltbühne and Its Circle*. Berkeley and Los Angeles, 1968.

Deckart, Gerald. "Deutsch-englische Verständigung: Eine Darstellung der nichtoffiziellen Bemühungen um eine Wiederannäherung der beiden Länder zwischen 1905 und 1914." Inaugural dissertation, Munich, 1967.

Dörpinghaus, Hermann Josef. *Darwins Theorie und der deutsche Vulgärmaterialismus im Urteil deutscher katholischer Zeitschriften zwischen 1854 und 1914*. Freiburg, 1969.

Dörzbacher, Erwin. *Die deutsche Sozialdemokratie und die nationale Machtpolitik bis 1914*. Gotha, 1920.

Doob, Leonard W. *Public Opinion and Propaganda*. 2d ed. Hamden, Conn., 1966.

Drachkovitch, Milorad M. *Les socialismes français et allemand et le problème de la guerre 1870–1914*. Geneva, 1953.

Duveau, Georges. *Les instituteurs*. Paris, 1957.

Ellis, Jack D. *The French Socialists and the Problem of the Peace, 1904–1914*. Chicago, 1967.

Elm, Ludwig. *Zwischen Fortschritt und Reaktion: Geschichte der Parteien der liberalen Bourgeoisie in Deutschland 1893–1918*. Berlin, 1968.

Epstein, Klaus. *Matthias Erzberger and the Dilemma of German Democracy*. Princeton, 1959.

Fagen, Richard R. *Politics and Communication*. Boston, 1966.

Falnes, Oscar J. *Norway and the Nobel Peace Prize*. New York, 1967.

Felden, Klemens. "Die Uebernahme des antisemitischen Stereotyps als soziale Norm durch die bürgerliche Gesellschaft Deutschlands (1875–1900)." Inaugural dissertation, Heidelberg, 1963.

446

Fick, Heinz. *Der deutsche Militarismus der Vorkriegszeit: Ein Beitrag zur Soziologie des Militarismus.* Potsdam, 1932.

Fischer, Fritz. "Der deutsche Protestantismus und die Politik im 19. Jahrhundert," *Historische Zeitschrift* CLXXI (1951), 473–518.

———. *Germany's Aims in the First World War.* New York, 1967.

———. *Griff nach der Weltmacht.* Düsseldorf, 1961.

———. *Krieg der Illusionen: Die deutsche Politik von 1911 bis 1914.* Düsseldorf, 1969.

Fonck, A. "Deutschlands Haltung zur Abrüstungsfrage auf der Friedenskonferenz im Haag 1899," *Berliner Monatshefte* VII (1929), 1091–95.

Fortuna, Ursula. *Der Völkerbundsgedanke in Deutschland während des Ersten Weltkrieges.* Zurich, 1974.

Fraenkel, Ernst. "Idee und Realität des Völkerbundes im deutschen politischen Denken," *Vierteljahrshefte für Zeitgeschichte* XVI (1968), 1–14.

Fricke, Dieter, *et al. Die bürgerlichen Parteien in Deutschland: Handbuch der Geschichte der bürgerlichen Parteien und anderer bürgerlicher Interessenorganisationen vom Vormärz bis zum Jahre 1945.* 2 vols. Leipzig, 1968–70.

Friedrich, Carl Joachim. *Inevitable Peace.* Cambridge, Mass., 1948.

Fuchs, Gustav. *Der deutsche Pazifismus im Weltkrieg.* Stuttgart, 1928.

Garber, Elizabeth M. "L'arbitrage international devant le mouvement socialiste français 1890–1914," *La revue socialiste* (New Series), number 105 (March 1957), pp. 293–313.

Gasman, Daniel. *The Scientific Origins of National Socialism: Social Darwinism in Ernst Haeckel and the German Monist League.* London and New York, 1971.

Gaumont, Jean. *Histoire générale de la coopération en France.* 2 vols. Paris, 1923–24.

Gilg, Peter. *Die Erneuerung des demokratischen Denkens im Wilhelminischen Deutschland: Eine ideengeschichtliche Studie zur Wende vom 19. zum 20. Jahrhundert.* Wiesbaden, 1965.

Goldberg, Harvey. *The Life of Jean Jaurès.* Madison, 1962.

Gordon, Michael R. "Domestic Conflict and the Origins of the First World War: The British and German Cases," *Journal of Modern History* XLVI (1974), 191–226.

Gregor, Josef. *Gerhart Hauptmann: Das Werk und unsere Zeit.* Vienna, n.d.

Greuner, Ruth. *Wandlungen eines Aufrechten: Lebensbild Hellmut von Gerlachs.* Berlin, 1965.

Groh, Dieter. *Negative Integration und revolutionärer Attentismus: Die deutsche Sozialdemokratie am Vorabend des Ersten Weltkrieges.* Frankfurt, 1973.

Gross, David. "Heinrich Mann and the Politics of Reaction," *Journal of Contemporary History* VIII (1973), 125–45.

Gross, Leo. *Pazifismus und Imperialismus: Eine kritische Untersuchung ihrer theoretischen Begründungen.* Leipzig and Vienna, 1931.

Grünberg, Carl. *Die Internationale und der Weltkrieg.* 2 vols. Leipzig, 1916–28.

Gülzow, Erwin. "Der Bund 'Neues Vaterland': Probleme der bürgerlich-pazifistischen Demokratie im Ersten Weltkrieg (1914–1918)." Inaugural dissertation, Berlin, 1969.

Hackett, Amy. "The German Women's Movement and Suffrage, 1890–1914: A Study of National Feminism," in Robert J. Bezucha, ed., *Modern European Social History.* Lexington, Mass., 1972, pp. 354–86.

Hale, Oron J. *The Great Illusion, 1900–1914.* New York, 1971.

———. *Publicity and Diplomacy, with Special Reference to England and Germany, 1890–1914.* New York, 1940.

Halévy, Daniel. *Essais sur le mouvement ouvrier en France.* Paris, 1901.

Hallgarten, George W. F. *Imperialismus vor 1914.* 2d ed. 2 vols. Munich, 1963.

448

Hamburger, Maurice. *Léon Bourgeois (1851–1924): La politique radicale socialiste, la doctrine de la solidarité, l'arbitrage international et la Société des Nations.* Paris, 1932.

Hamerow, Theodore S. *The Social Foundations of German Unification, 1858–1871: Ideas and Institutions.* Princeton, 1969.

Haupt, Georges. *Socialism and the Great War: The Collapse of the Second International.* Oxford, 1972.

Hayes, Carlton, J. H. *France: A Nation of Patriots.* New York, 1930.

——. *A Generation of Materialism, 1871–1900.* 2d ed. New York, 1963.

——. *The Historical Evolution of Modern Nationalism.* New York, 1931.

Headings, Mildred J. *French Freemasonry under the Third Republic.* Baltimore, 1949.

Heberle, Rudolf. *Hauptprobleme der politischen Soziologie.* Stuttgart, 1967.

Heinel, Jürgen. *Die deutsche Sozialpolitik des 19. Jahrhunderts im Spiegel der Schulgeschichtsbücher.* Braunschweig, 1962.

Hemleben, Sylvester John. *Plans for World Peace through Six Centuries.* Chicago, 1943.

Henderson, Gavin B. "The Pacifists of the Fifties," *Journal of Modern History* IX (1937), 314–41.

Henning, Hansjoachim. "Kriegervereine in den preussischen Westprovinzen: Ein Beitrag zur preussischen Innenpolitik zwischen 1860 und 1914," *Rheinische Vierteljahrsblätter* XXXII (1968), 430–75.

Herz, Heinz. *Alleingang wider die Mächtigen: Ein Bild vom Leben und Kämpfen Moritz von Egidys.* Leipzig, [1970].

Herzfeld, Hans. "Der Militarismus als Problem der neueren Geschichte," *Schola* I (1946), 41–67.

Heuss, Theodor. *Friedrich Naumann: Der Mann, das Werk, die Zeit.* Stuttgart and Tübingen, 1949.

Hines, Paul David. "Norman Angell: Peace Movement, 1911–1915." Ed.D. dissertation, Ball State Teachers' College, 1964.

Hinsley, F. H. *Power and the Pursuit of Peace: Theory and Practice in the History of Relations between States.* Cambridge, 1963.

Höfele, Karl Heinrich. "Selbstverständnis und Zeitkritik des deutschen Bürgertums vor dem ersten Weltkrieg," *Zeitschrift für Religions- und Geistesgeschichte* VIII (1956), 40–56.

Höhn, Reinhard. *Die Armee als Erziehungsschule der Nation.* Bad Harzburg, 1963.

Hoffmann, Stanley. *The State of War: Essays on the Theory and Practice of International Politics.* New York, 1965.

Hofstadter, Richard. *The Paranoid Style in American Politics and Other Essays.* New York, 1967.

Holl, Karl. "Europapolitik im Vorfeld der deutschen Regierungspolitik: Zur Tätigkeit proeuropäischer Organisationen in der Weimarer Republik," *Historische Zeitschrift* CCXIX (1974), 33–94.

———. "Ludwig Quidde," *Liberal* XIII (1971), 224–29.

———. "Die 'Vereinigung Gleichgesinnter': Ein Berliner Kreis pazifistischer Intellektueller im Ersten Weltkrieg," *Archiv für Kulturgeschichte* LIV (1972), 364–84.

Holt, Niles Robert. "Ernst Haeckel's Monistic Religion," *Journal of the History of Ideas* XXXII (1971), 265–80.

———. "The Social and Political Ideas of the German Monist Movement, 1871–1914." Ph.D. dissertation, Yale University, 1967.

Honigsheim, Paul. "Die Gründung der deutschen Gesellschaft für Soziologie in ihren geistesgeschichtlichen Zusammenhängen," *Kölner Zeitschrift für Soziologie* XI (1959), 3–10.

———. *On Max Weber.* New York and East Lansing, 1968.

Howard, Michael. "The Armed Forces," *The New Cambridge Modern History,* XI: *Material Progress and World-Wide Problems, 1870–1898.* Cambridge, 1967, pp. 204–42.

————, ed. *Soldiers and Governments: Nine Studies in Civil-Military Relations*. London, 1957.

Huber, Wolfgang. "Evangelische Theologie und Kirche beim Ausbruch des Ersten Weltkrieges," in Huber, ed., *Historische Beiträge zur Friedensforschung*. Stuttgart and Munich, 1970, pp. 134–215.

Hudson, Daril. "The Ecumenical Movement and World Order." Ph.D. dissertation, London School of Economics and Political Science, University of London, 1965.

Hughes, H. Stuart. *Consciousness and Society: The Reorientation of European Social Thought, 1890–1930*. New York, 1958.

Hyman, Herbert H. *Political Socialization: A Study in the Psychology of Human Behavior*. New York, 1959.

Iggers, George C. *The German Conception of History: The National Tradition of Historical Thought from Herder to the Present*. Middletown, Conn., 1968.

Internationales Institut für den Frieden. *Vermächtnis und Mahnung zum 50. Todestag Bertha von Suttners*. Vienna, 1964.

Irrlitz, Gerd. "Bemerkungen über die Einheit politischer und theoretischer Wesenzüge des Zentrismus in der deutschen Sozialdemokratie," *Beiträge zur Geschichte der deutschen Arbeiterbewegung* VIII (1966), 43–59.

Jäckh, Ernst. *Der Völkerbundgedanke in Deutschland während des Weltkrieges*. Berlin, 1929.

Jaeger, Hans. *Unternehmer in der deutschen Politik (1890–1918)*. Bonn, 1967.

Jahn, Georg. "Karl Lamprecht als Wirtschafts- und Kulturhistoriker . . ." *Schmollers Jahrbuch* LXXVI (1956), 129–42.

Jarausch, Konrad H. *The Enigmatic Chancellor: Bethmann Hollweg and the Hubris of Imperial Germany*. New Haven and London, 1973.

Joll, James, *The Second International, 1889–1914*. New York, 1966.

Julliard, Jacques. "La CGT devant la guerre (1900–1914)," *Le mouvement social*, number 49 (October/December 1964), pp. 47–62.

Kaelble, Hartmut. *Industrielle Interessenpolitik in der Wilhelminischen Gesellschaft: Centralverband Deutscher Industrieller 1895–1914*. Berlin, 1967.

Kamiński, Andrej Józef. *Stanowisko Niemiec na pierwszej Konferencji Haskiej 1899*. Poznan, 1962.

Kann, Robert A. "Public Opinion Research: A Contribution to Historical Method," *Political Science Quarterly* LXXIII (1968), 374–96.

Kantzenbach, Friedrich Wilhelm. *Der Weg der evangelischen Kirche vom 19. zum 20. Jahrhundert*. Gütersloh, 1968.

Kautsky, John H. "J. A. Schumpeter and Karl Kautsky: Parallel Theories of Imperialism," *Midwest Journal of Political Science* v (1961), 101–28.

Kautksy, Karl. *Krieg und Demokratie: Eine historische Untersuchung und Darstellung ihrer Wechselwirkungen in der Neuzeit*. Berlin, 1932.

———. *Sozialisten und Krieg: Ein Beitrag zur Ideengeschichte des Sozialismus von den Hussiten bis zum Völkerbund*. Prague, 1937.

Kayser, Jacques. *Les grandes batailles du radicalisme 1820–1901*. Paris, 1962.

Kedourie, Elie. *Nationalism*. New York, 1960.

Kehr, Eckart. *Schlachtflottenbau und Parteipolitik 1894–1901: Versuch eines Querschnitts durch die innenpolitischen, sozialen und ideologischen Voraussetzungen des deutschen Imperialismus*. Lübeck, 1930.

Kelman, Herbert C., ed. *International Behavior: A Social-Psychological Analysis*. New York, 1965.

Kempf, Beatrix. *Bertha von Suttner: Das Lebensbild einer grossen Frau*. Vienna, 1964.

Kimminich, Otto. *Rüstung und politische Spannung: Studien zum Problem der internationalen Sicherheit*. Gütersloh, 1964.

Klein, Fritz, *et al. Deutschland im ersten Weltkrieg*. 3 vols. Berlin, 1968–70.

Köhler, Fritz. "Deutsche Friedensgesellschaft (DFG) seit 1892," in Dieter Fricke, *et al.*, *Die bürgerlichen Parteien in Deutschland: Handbuch der Geschichte der bürgerlichen Parteien und anderer bürgerlicher Interessenorganisationen vom Vormärz bis zum Jahre 1945*. 2 vols. Leipzig, 1968–70, I, 364–77.

Kohn, Hans. "Nationalism and Internationalism in the Nineteenth and Twentieth Centuries," XIIᵉ *Congrès international des sciences historiques, Vienne, 29 août–5 septembre 1965, Rapports*. Horn and Vienna, n.d., I, 191–240.

Kruck, Alfred. *Geschichte des Alldeutschen Verbandes 1890–1939*. Wiesbaden, 1954.

Kuehl, Warren F. *Seeking World Order: The United States and International Organization to 1920*. Nashville, Tenn., 1969.

Kuhnert, Adolf. *Der Streit um die geschichtswissenschaftlichen Theorien Karl Lamprechts*. Gütersloh, 1906.

Kulemann, W. *Die Berufsvereine*. Erste Abteilung: *Geschichtliche Entwicklung der Berufsorganisationen der Arbeitnehmer und Arbeitgeber aller Länder*, II. Jena, 1908.

Kupisch, Karl. *Der deutsche CVJM: Aus der Geschichte der Christlichen Vereine Junger Männer Deutschlands*. Kassel-Wilhelmshöhe, 1968.

———. *Studenten entdecken die Bibel: Die Geschichte der Deutschen Christlichen Studenten-Vereinigung (DCSV)*. Hamburg, 1964.

Kurzweil, Zwi Erich. "Gustav Wynecken, sein Werk und seine Auseinandersetzung mit Hermann Lietz," *Paedagogica historica* XI (1971), 31–59.

Lange, Chr., *et al. The Interparliamentary Union from 1889 to 1939*. Lausanne, 1939.

Langer, William L. *The Diplomacy of Imperialism, 1890–1902*. 2d ed. New York, 1965.

Langsam, Walter Consuelo. "Nationalism and History in the Prussian Elementary Schools under William II," in Edward Mead Earle, ed., *Nationalism and Internationalism: Essays Inscribed to Carlton J. H. Hayes.* New York, 1950, pp. 241-60.

Laqueur, Walter Z. *Young Germany: A History of the German Youth Movement.* London, 1962.

Laschitza, Annelies. "Karl Liebknecht und Rosa Luxemburg über die Dialektik von Frieden und Sozialismus," *Zeitschrift für Geschichtswissenschaft* XIX (1971), 1117-38.

Latzker, Michael. "The 'Practical' Peace Advocates: An Interpretation of the American Peace Movement, 1898-1917." Ph.D. dissertation, Rutgers University, 1969.

Laurence, Richard Robert. "The Problem of Peace and Austrian Society, 1889-1914: A Study in the Cultural Origins of the First World War." Ph.D. dissertation, Stanford University, 1968.

Lavondès, A. *Charles Gide, un apôtre de la coopération entre les hommes, un précurseur de l'Europe unie et de l'U.N.O.* Uzès, 1953.

Leaman, Bertha R. "The Influence of Domestic Policy on Foreign Affairs in France, 1898-1905," *Journal of Modern History* XIV (1942), 449-79.

Ledré, Charles. *Histoire de la presse.* Paris, 1958.

Lehmann, Johannes. *Die Aussenpolitik und die "Kölnische Zeitung" während der Bülow-Zeit (1897-1909).* Bleicherode am Harz, 1937.

Leitich, Ann Tizia. "Bertha von Suttner," *Grosse Oesterreicher.* Vienna, 1957, X, 66-75.

Lepsius, M. Rainer. "Parteiensystem und Sozialstruktur: Zum Problem der Demokratisierung der deutschen Gesellschaft," in Wilhelm Abel, *et al.*, eds., *Wirtschaft, Geschichte und Wirtschaftsgeschichte: Festschrift zum 65. Geburtstag von Friedrich Lütge.* Stuttgart, 1966, pp. 371-93.

Lévêque, Pierre. "Libre pensée et socialisme (1889–1939): Quelques points de repère," *Le mouvement social*, number 57 (October/December 1966), pp. 101–41.

LeVine, Robert. "Political Socialization and Culture Change," in Clifford Geertz, ed., *Old Societies and New States: The Quest for Modernity in Asia and Africa*. New York, 1963, pp. 280–303.

Liedtke, Marianne. "Die Entwicklung des Pazifismus in Deutschland und Frankreich von der Ersten Haager Friedenskonferenz (1899) bis zur Zweiten Haager Friedenskonferenz (1907)." Inaugural dissertation, Cologne, 1953.

Loubère, Leo A. "Left-Wing Radicals, Strikes, and the Military, 1880–1907," *French Historical Studies* III (1963), 93–105.

Lübbe, Hermann. *Politische Philosophie in Deutschland: Studien zu ihrer Geschichte*. Basel and Stuttgart, 1963.

Lutz, Heinrich. *Demokratie im Zwielicht: Der Weg der deutschen Katholiken aus dem Kaiserreich in die Republik 1914–1925*. Munich, 1963.

Lyons, F. S. L. *Internationalism in Europe, 1815–1914*. Leyden, 1963.

Maehl, William. "The Triumph of Nationalism in the German Socialist Party on the Eve of the First World War," *Journal of Modern History* XXIV (1952), 15–41.

Maenner, Ludwig. *Prinz Heinrich zu Schönaich-Carolath: Ein parlamentarisches Leben der wilhelminischen Zeit (1852–1920)*. Stuttgart and Berlin, 1931.

Mandelbaum, Kurt. "Die Erörterungen innerhalb der deutschen Sozialdemokratie über das Problem des Imperialismus (1895–1914)." Inaugural dissertation, Frankfurt a. M., 1926.

Mann, Thomas. *The Magic Mountain*. Translated by H. T. Lowe-Porter. New York, 1966.

Mannheim, Karl. *Ideology and Utopia: An Introduction to the Sociology of Knowledge*. New York, 1936.

Marchand, C. Roland. *The American Peace Movement and Social Reform, 1898–1918.* Princeton, 1972.

Martin, David A. *Pacifism: An Historical and Sociological Study.* New York, 1966.

Matthias, Erich. "Kautsky und der Kautskyanismus: Die Funktion der Ideologie in der deutschen Sozialdemokratie vor dem ersten Weltkrieg," in Iring Fetscher, ed., *Marxismusstudien.* 2 Folge. Tübingen, 1957, pp. 151–97.

Mayeur, Jean-Marie. *Un prêtre démocrate: L'abbé Lemire 1853–1928.* Paris, 1968.

Meinecke, Friedrich. *Weltbürgertum und Nationalstaat.* Munich, 1962.

Melamed, Samuel Max. *Theorie, Ursprung und Geschichte der Friedensidee: Kulturphilosophische Wanderungen.* Stuttgart, 1909.

Merle, Marcel, ed. *Pacifisme et internationalisme, XVIIe–XXe siècles.* Paris, 1966.

Meulen, Jacob ter. *Der Gedanke der internationalen Organisation in seiner Entwicklung.* 2 vols. The Hague, 1929–40.

Missala, Heinrich. *Gott mit uns: Die deutsche katholische Kriegspredigt 1914–1918.* Munich, 1968.

Mitzman, Arthur. "Tönnies and German Society, 1887–1914: From Cultural Pessimism to the Celebration of the *Volksgemeinschaft*," *Journal of the History of Ideas* XXXII (1971), 507–24.

Moe, R. *Le prix Nobel de la paix et l'institut Nobel norvégien: Rapport historique et descriptif accompagné d'une histoire du mouvement pacifiste de 1896 à 1930.* 2 vols. Oslo, 1932.

Mommsen, Wolfgang J. "Die latente Krise des Wilhelminischen Reiches. Staat und Gesellschaft in Deutschland 1890–1914," *Militärgeschichtliche Mitteilungen,* number 1 (1974), pp. 7–28.

———. *Max Weber und die deutsche Politik 1890–1920.* Tübingen, 1959.

Morgenthau, Hans J. *Politics among Nations: The Struggle for Power and Peace.* 4th ed. New York, 1967.

Morrill, Dan L. "Nicholas II and the Call for the First Hague Conference," *Journal of Modern History* XLVI (1974), 296–313.

Morris, A. J. A. "The English Radicals' Campaign for Disarmament and the Hague Conference of 1907," *Journal of Modern History* XLIII (1971), 367–93.

―――. *Radicalism against War, 1906–1914: The Advocacy of Peace and Retrenchment.* London, 1972.

Morsey, Rudolf. "Die deutschen Katholiken und der Nationalstaat zwischen Kulturkampf und Erstem Weltkrieg," *Historisches Jahrbuch* XC (1970), 31–64.

Mühlmann, Wilhelm, ed. *Chiliasmus und Nativismus: Studien zur Psychologie, Soziologie und historische Kasuistik der Umsturzbewegungen.* Berlin, 1961.

Mulert, Hermann, ed. *Vierzig Jahre "Christliche Welt": Festgabe für Martin Rade.* Gotha, 1927.

Muller, Joseph. *L'oeuvre de toutes les confessions chrétiennes (églises) pour la paix internationale.* Paris, 1931.

Nettl, Peter. "The German Social Democratic Party 1890–1914 as a Political Model," *Past and Present*, number 30 (April 1965), pp. 65–95.

―――. *Political Mobilization: A Sociological Analysis of Methods and Concepts.* New York, 1967.

Nettl, J. P., and Robertson, Roland. "Industrialization, Development or Modernization," *British Journal of Sociology* XVII (1966), 274–91.

―――. *International Systems and the Modernization of Societies: The Formation of National Goals and Attitudes.* New York, 1968.

Nipperdey, Thomas. *Die Organisation der deutschen Parteien vor 1918.* Düsseldorf, 1961.

Nisbet, Robert A. *Social Change and History: Aspects of the Western Theory of Development.* New York, 1969.

Nordlinger, Eric A. *Conflict Resolution in Divided Societies.* Cambridge, Mass., 1972.

Nürnberger, Richard. "Imperialismus, Sozialismus und Christentum bei Friedrich Naumann," *Historische Zeitschrift* CLXX (1950), 525–48.

Oberschall, Anthony R. *Empirical Social Research in Germany, 1848–1914.* The Hague, 1965.

Ozouf, Jacques and Mona. "Le thème du patriotisme dans les manuels primaires," *Le mouvement social,* number 49 (October/December 1964), pp. 3–31.

Patterson, David Sands. "Andrew Carnegie's Quest for World Peace," *Proceedings of the American Philosophical Society* CXIV (1970), 371–83.

———. "An Interpretation of the American Peace Movement, 1898–1914," *American Studies* XIII (1972), 31–49.

———. "The Travail of the American Peace Movement, 1887–1914." Ph.D. dissertation, University of California, Berkeley, 1968.

Pauli, Hertha. *Nur eine Frau: Biographischer Roman.* Vienna, 1937.

Playne, Caroline E. *Bertha von Suttner and the Struggle to Avert the World War.* London, 1936.

———. *The Neuroses of the Nations.* London, 1925.

Prawer, Siegbert S., *et al. Essays in German Language, Culture and Society.* London, 1969.

Pross, Harry. *Jugend, Eros, Politik: Die Geschichte der deutschen Jugendverbände.* Berne, Munich, Vienna, 1964.

Prost, Antoine. *Histoire de l'enseignement en France 1800–1967.* Paris, 1968.

Pye, Lucian W., and Verba, Sidney, eds. *Political Culture and Political Development.* Princeton, 1965.

Randall, John Herman, Jr. *The Career of Philosophy,* II: *From the German Enlightenment to the Age of Darwin.* New York and London, 1965.

Rathje, Johannes. *Die Welt des freien Protestantismus: Ein Beitrag zur deutsch-evangelischen Geistesgeschichte. Dargestellt an Leben und Werk von Martin Rade.* Stuttgart, 1952.

Ratz, Ursula. "Briefe zum Erscheinen von Karl Kautskys 'Weg zur Macht,' " *International Review of Social History* XII (1967), 432–77.

———. *Georg Ledebour (1850–1947): Weg und Wirken eines sozialistischen Politikers.* Berlin, 1969.

———. "Karl Kautsky und die Abrüstungskontroverse in der deutschen Sozialdemokratie," *International Review of Social History* XI (1966), 197–227.

Raumer, Kurt von. *Ewiger Friede: Friedensrufe und Friedenspläne seit der Renaissance.* Freiburg and Munich, 1953.

Reichel, K. F. *Die pazifistische Presse.* Würzburg, 1938.

Reicke, Ilsa. *Bertha von Suttner: Ein Lebensbild.* Bonn, 1952.

Renouvin, Pierre, and Duroselle, Jean-Baptiste. *Introduction to the History of International Relations.* New York, 1967.

Rich, Norman. *Friedrich von Holstein: Politics and Diplomacy in the Era of Bismarck and Wilhelm II.* 2 vols. Cambridge, 1965.

Ridley, F. F. *Revolutionary Syndicalism in France: The Direct Action of Its Time.* Cambridge, 1970.

Rieger, Isolde. *Die wilhelminische Presse im Ueberblick, 1888–1918.* Munich, 1957.

Ringer, Fritz. *The Decline of the German Mandarins: The German Academic Community, 1890–1933.* Cambridge, Mass., 1969.

Ritter, Gerhard. *Europa und die deutsche Frage: Betrachtungen über die geschichtliche Eigenart des deutschen Staatsdenkens.* Munich, 1948.

———. "The Military and Politics in Germany," *Journal of Central European Affairs* XVII (1957), 260–65.

———. "Das Problem des Militarismus in Deutschland," *Historische Zeitschrift* CLXXVII (1954), 21–48.

———. *Staatskunst und Kriegshandwerk: Das Problem des "Militarismus" in Deutschland.* 4 vols. Munich, 1954–67.

Rogge, Heinrich. *Nationale Friedenspolitik: Handbuch des Friedensproblems und seiner Wissenschaft.* Berlin, 1934.

Rosenberg, Hans. *Grosse Depression und Bismarckzeit: Wirtschaftsablauf, Gesellschaft und Politik in Mitteleuropa.* Berlin, 1967.

Roth, Guenther. "Max Weber's Empirical Sociology in Germany and the United States: Tensions between Partisanship and Scholarship," *Central European History* II (1969), 196–215.

———. *The Social Democrats in Imperial Germany: A Study in Working-Class Isolation and National Integration.* Totowa, New Jersey, 1963.

Rouse, Ruth, and Neill, Stephen Charles, eds. *A History of the Ecumenical Movement, 1517–1948.* Philadelphia, 1954.

Samuel, Richard, and Thomas, R. Hinton. *Education and Society in Modern Germany.* London, 1949.

Saposs, David J. *The Labor Movement in Post-War France.* New York, 1931.

Sauer, Wolfgang. "Das Problem des deutschen Nationalstaates," in Hans-Ulrich Wehler, ed., *Moderne deutsche Sozialgeschichte.* Cologne and Berlin, 1970, pp. 407–36.

Saul, Klaus. "Der 'Deutsche Kriegerbund': Zur innenpolitischen Funktion eines 'nationalen' Verbandes im kaiserlichen Deutschland," *Militärgeschichtliche Mitteilungen*, number 2 (1969), pp. 95–159.

———. "Der Kampf um die Jugend zwischen Volksschule und Kaserne: Ein Beitrag zur 'Jugendpflege' im Wilhelminischen Reich, 1890–1914," *Militärgeschichtliche Mitteilungen*, number 1 (1971), pp. 97–143.

Schätzel, Walther, and Schlochauer, Hans-Jürgen, eds. *Rechtsfragen der internationalen Organisation: Festschrift für Hans Wehberg zu seinem 70. Geburtstag.* Frankfurt a. M., 1956.

Schallenberger, Horst. *Untersuchungen zum Geschichtsbild der Wilhelminischen Aera und der Weimarer Zeit: Eine vergleichende Schulbuchanalyse deutscher Schul-*

geschichtsbücher aus der Zeit von 1888 bis 1933. Ratingen bei Düsseldorf, 1964.

Scheer, Friedrich-Karl. "Die Anfänge der Friedensforschung in der historischen Friedensbewegung Deutschlands," *Jahrbuch für Friedens- und Konfliktsforschung* II (1972), 173–82.

Scheler, Max. *Die Idee des Friedens und der Pazifismus.* Berlin, 1931.

Schiffer, Walter. *The Legal Community of Mankind: A Critical Analysis of the Modern Concept of World Organization.* New York, 1954.

Schilling, Konrad. "Beiträge zu einer Geschichte des radikalen Nationalismus in der Wilhelminischen Aera 1890–1909: Die Entstehung des radikalen Nationalismus, seine Einflussnahme auf die innere und äussere Politik des Deutschen Reiches und die Stellung von Regierung und Reichstag zu seiner politischen und publizistischen Aktivität." Inaugural dissertation, Cologne, 1968.

Schönebaum, Herbert. "Karl Lamprecht," *Archiv für Kulturgeschichte* XXXVII (1955), 269–305.

————. "Karl Lamprechts Mühen um innere und äussere Kulturpolitik," *Die Welt als Geschichte* XV (1955), 137–52.

Schoeps, Hans-Joachim, ed. *Zeitgeist im Wandel,* I: *Das Wilhelminische Zeitalter.* Stuttgart, 1967.

Schorske, Carl E. *German Social Democracy, 1905–1917: The Development of the Great Schism.* New York, 1955.

Schou, August. *Histoire de l'internationalisme,* III: *Du Congrès de Vienne jusqu'à la première guerre mondiale (1914).* Oslo, 1963.

Schröder, Hans-Christoph. *Sozialismus und Imperialismus: Die Auseinandersetzung der deutschen Sozialdemokratie mit dem Imperialismusproblem und der "Weltpolitik" vor 1914,* I. Hannover, 1968.

Schulz, Gerhard. "Die deutsche Sozialdemokratie und die Idee des internationalen Ausgleichs," in Alfred Hermann, ed., *Aus Geschichte und Politik: Festschrift zum 70. Ge-*

burtstag von Ludwig Bergsträsser. Düsseldorf, 1954, pp. 89–116.

Schwabe, Klaus. "Ursprung und Verbreitung des all-deutschen Annexionismus in der deutschen Professoren-schaft im I. Weltkrieg," *Vierteljahrshefte für Zeitge-schichte* XIV (1966), 105–38.

———. *Wissenschaft und Kriegsmoral: Die deutschen Hochschullehrer und die politischen Grundfragen des Ersten Weltkrieges*. Göttingen, 1969.

———. "Zur politischen Haltung der deutschen Professoren im Ersten Weltkrieg," *Historische Zeitschrift* CXCIII (1961), 601–34.

Schwarz, Gotthard. *Theodor Wolff und das "Berliner Tage-blatt": Eine liberale Stimme in der deutschen Politik 1906 bis 1933*. Tübingen, 1969.

Scott, John A. *Republican Ideas and the Liberal Tradition in France, 1870–1914*. New York, 1951.

Sée, Henri. *Histoire de la ligue des droits de l'homme, 1898–1926*. Paris, 1927.

Shanahan, William O. "Friedrich Naumann: A Mirror of Wilhelminian Germany," *Review of Politics* XIII (1951), 267–301.

———. "Liberalism and Foreign Affairs: Naumann and the Pre-War German View," *Review of Politics* XXI (1959), 188–223.

Sheehan, James J. *The Career of Lujo Brentano: A Study of Liberalism and Social Reform in Imperial Germany*. Chicago and London, 1966.

Sibley, Mulford Q. "Pacifism," *International Encyclopedia of the Social Sciences*. New York, 1968, XI, 353.

———. *The Political Theories of Modern Pacifism*. Phila-delphia, 1944.

Sieburg, Heinz-Otto. "Die Elsass-Lothringen-Frage in der Deutsch-Französischen Diskussion von 1871 bis 1914," *Zeitschrift für die Geschichte der Saargegend* XVII/XVIII (1969/70), 9–37.

Silberner, Edmund. *The Problem of War in Nineteenth Century Economic Thought.* Princeton, 1946.

Simon, Klaus. *Die württembergischen Demokraten: Ihre Stellung und Arbeit im Parteien- und Verfassungssystem in Württemberg und im Deutschen Reich 1890–1920.* Stuttgart, 1969.

Simon, W. M. *European Positivism in the Nineteenth Century: An Essay in Intellectual History.* Ithaca, 1963.

Singer, J. David. "International Conflict: Three Levels of Analysis," *World Politics,* XII (1959/60), 453–61.

————. "The Level-of-Analysis Problem in International Relations," *World Politics,* XIV (1961/62), 77–92.

Smekal, Ferdinand G., ed. *Oesterreichs Nobelpreisträger.* Vienna, Stuttgart, Zurich, 1961.

Smelser, Neil J. *Theory of Collective Behavior.* New York, 1963.

Smith, Rennie. *Peace Verboten.* London, 1943.

Soltau, Roger H. *French Parties and Politics, 1871–1930.* London, 1930.

Souleyman, Elizabeth V. *The Vision of World Peace in Seventeenth and Eighteenth Century France.* New York, 1941.

Starke, J. G. *An Introduction to the Science of Peace (Irenology).* Leyden, 1968.

Starker, Greta. "Die geschichtliche Entwicklung des deutschen Pazifismus seit 1900: Ein Beitrag zum Zusammenbruch Deutschlands im Weltkrieg." Inaugural dissertation, Heidelberg, 1935.

Stegmann, Dirk. *Die Erben Bismarcks: Parteien und Verbände in der Spätphase des Wilhelminischen Deutschlands.* Cologne and Berlin, 1970.

Steinberg, Hans-Josef. *Sozialismus und deutsche Sozialdemokratie: Zur Ideologie der Partei vor dem I. Weltkrieg.* Hannover, 1967.

————. *Die Stellung der II. Internationale zu Krieg und Frieden.* Trier, 1972.

Stenkewitz, Kurt, *Gegen Bajonett und Dividende: Die politische Krise in Deutschland am Vorabend des ersten Weltkrieges.* Berlin, 1960.

Stevenson, Robert Clark. "The Evolution of Pacifism," *International Journal of Ethics* XLIV (1934), 437–51.

———. "Pacifism and Militarism: A History and Analysis of Ideas." Ph.D. dissertation, University of California, Berkeley, 1929.

Stiewe, Dorothee. "Die bürgerliche deutsche Friedensbewegung als soziale Bewegung bis zum Ende des Ersten Weltkrieges." Inaugural dissertation, Freiburg, 1972.

Stürmer, Michael, ed. *Das kaiserliche Deutschland: Politik und Gesellschaft 1870–1918.* Düsseldorf, 1970.

———. "Staatsstreichgedanke im Bismarckreich," *Historische Zeitschrift* CCIX (1969), 566–615.

Sumler, David E. "Domestic Influences on the Nationalist Revival in France," *French Historical Studies* VI (1970), 517–37.

Tate, Merze. *The Disarmament Illusion: The Movement for a Limitation of Armaments to 1907.* New York, 1942.

Taube, Utz-Friedebert. *Ludwig Quidde: Ein Beitrag zur Geschichte des demokratischen Gedankens in Deutschland.* Kallmünz, 1963.

Taylor, A. J. P. *The Trouble Makers: Dissent over Foreign Policy, 1792–1939.* London, 1957.

Thimme, Annelise. *Hans Delbrück als Kritiker der Wilhelminischen Epoche.* Düsseldorf, 1955.

Tompert, Helene. *Lebensformen und Denkweisen der akademischen Welt Heidelbergs im Wilhelminischen Zeitalter: Vornehmlich im Spiegel zeitgenössischer Selbstzeugnisse.* Lübeck, 1969.

Vagts, Alfred. *A History of Militarism.* New York, 1959.

Valentin, Veit. *Geschichte des Völkerbundgedankens in Deutschland: Ein geistesgeschichtlicher Versuch.* Berlin, 1920.

Victor, Max. "Die Stellung der deutschen Sozialdemokratie zu den Fragen der auswärtigen Politik," *Archiv für Sozialwissenschaft und Sozialpolitik* LX (1928), 147–79.

Waltz, Kenneth N. *Man, the State, and War.* New York, 1959.

Weber, Eugen. *The Nationalist Revival in France, 1905–1914.* Berkeley and Los Angeles. 1959.

Wegner, Konstanze. *Theodor Barth und die Freisinnige Vereinigung: Studien zur Geschichte des Linksliberalismus im Wilhelminischen Deutschland (1893–1910).* Tübingen, 1968.

Wehberg, Hans. "Alfred Fried," *Deutsches Biographisches Jahrbuch.* 11 vols. Berlin, 1914–29, III, 105–106.

———. "Alfred Hermann Fried," *Neue Deutsche Biographie.* Berlin, 1961, V, 441–42.

———. *Die Führer der deutschen Friedensbewegung (1890 bis 1923).* Leipzig, 1923.

———. *Die internationale Beschränkung der Rüstungen.* Stuttgart and Berlin, n.d.

———, ed. *Ludwig Quidde: Ein deutscher Demokrat und Vorkämpfer der Völkerverständigung.* Offenbach a. M., 1948.

———. "Ludwig Quidde, ein deutscher Pazifist," *Die Wage* XXV (1922), 61–63.

Wehler, Hans-Ulrich. *Bismarck und der Imperialismus.* Cologne and Berlin, 1969.

Weinstein, Harold R. *Jean Jaurès: A Study of Patriotism in the French Socialist Movement.* New York, 1936.

Weintraub, Karl J. *Visions of Culture: Voltaire, Guizot, Burckhardt, Lamprecht, Huizinga, Ortega y Gasset.* Chicago and London, 1966.

Wernecke, Klaus. *Der Wille zur Weltgeltung: Aussenpolitik und Oeffentlichkeit im Kaiserreich am Vorabend des Ersten Weltkrieges.* Düsseldorf, 1970.

Wette, Wolfram. *Kriegstheorien deutscher Sozialisten— Marx, Engels, Lassalle, Bernstein, Kautsky, Luxemburg: Ein Beitrag zur Friedensforschung.* Stuttgart, 1971.

Whyte, Frederic. *The Life of W. T. Stead.* 2 vols. New York and Boston, 1925.

Wiener, P. B. "Bertha von Suttner and the Political Novel," in Siegbert S. Prawer; R. Hinton Thomas; and Leonard Foster, eds., *Essays in German Language, Culture and Society.* London, 1969, pp. 160–76.

Weinroth, Howard. "Norman Angell and *The Great Illusion*: An Episode in Pre-1914 Pacifism," *Historical Journal* XVII (1974), 551–74.

Wiese, Leopold von. "Die deutsche Gesellschaft für Soziologie: Politische Eindrücke in den ersten fünfzig Jahren (1909 bis 1959)," *Kölner Zeitschrift für Soziologie* XI (1959), 11–20.

Wild, Adolf. *Baron d'Estournelles de Constant (1852–1924): Das Wirken eines Friedensnobelpreisträgers für die deutsch-französische Verständigung und die europäische Einigung.* Hamburg, 1973.

Wittwer, Walter. *Streit um Schicksalsfragen: Die deutsche Sozialdemokratie zu Krieg und Vaterlandsverteidigung 1907–1914.* Berlin, 1964.

Ziebura, Gilbert. *Die deutsche Frage in der öffentlichen Meinung Frankreichs von 1911–1914.* Berlin, 1955.

Zmarzlik, Hans-Günter. "Der Sozialdarwinismus in Deutschland als geschichtliches Problem," *Vierteljahrshefte für Zeitgeschichte* XI (1963), 246–73.

Index

Académie française, 347
Agadir, *see* Moroccan crises
Alber, Paul, 62, 67
Albert, King of Monaco, 234
Algeciras conference, 309
Allard, Maurice, 360
Allégret, Paul, 379
*Allgemeine Evangelische-Luthe-
ranische Kirchenzeitung*,
196–97
Alliance universelle, 338n
*Alliance universelle des femmes
pour la paix par l'éducation*,
338n
Almond, Gabriel A., 30
Alsace-Lorraine, dispute over,
43–44, 281, 288, 290–301, 310–
11, 317, 350; peace movement
strong in, 59, 205–206
Alsatian (political party), 258n
American Association for Inter-
national Conciliation, 27, 367
American Civil War, 8
amicales, 373
Amira, Karl von, 151
anarchism, 20, 125, 209
Angell, Norman (*né* Ralph
Norman Angell Lane) 107, 123,
180–81, 246
Anglo-German Conciliation
Committee, 232, 312–16
Anglo-German conciliation conference, 157, 315–16
Anglo-German relations, peace
movement and, 211–14, 312–17
Anti-Corn Law League, 149
antimilitarism, 358, 364
antipacifism, 387, 392, 392n, 416;
extreme, 392–402; moderate,
403–409
anti-Semitism, 127, 397–98

arbitration, international, 4, 28,
30, 33, 121, 308, 330, 375, 378,
382; and Hague conferences,
13, 56–57, 211, 257, 369–71,
370n; German government and,
219–30, 235, 238, 257, 310; opposition to, in Germany, 130,
136, 174, 188, 190, 201, 244, 285,
382, 384, 392–93, 399–400, 404–
405, 407; peace movement and,
7, 12, 14–15, 22, 24–28, 41, 45,
48, 88, 91–94, 99, 110, 113–14,
149, 151, 158, 194, 209, 214, 253,
255, 258, 263, 284, 287, 329;
socialists and, 28, 260–61, 267–
68, 271, 275–76, 275n, 283–85,
358–63; support for, in France,
332, 337–38, 340, 344, 350, 353–
55, 358–63, 365–67, 373–74; support for, in Germany, 131, 145–
47, 167, 171, 184, 243, 246–48,
252–53; treaties of, 12, 45, 48,
113, 149, 179, 229, 238, 286, 310,
366
*Archiv für die Geschichte der
Philosophie*, 140
arms bill, of 1887, 133; of 1893,
47, 49, 85, 246; of 1912, 237; of
1913, 240, 279, 307n, 319
arms limitation, 121, 330; German
socialists and, 260, 268–69, 271,
273–76, 275n, 283–85; as goal of
German peace movement, 14,
88, 91, 94, 110, 113, 129, 284, 329;
and Hague conferences, 56–57,
219–20, 223–26, 228–30, 236, 367,
369–70, 370n; opposition to, in
Germany, 130, 159, 201, 244,
285, 388, 392–93, 400, 404–407,
410; support for, in France, 338,
340, 344, 358–59, 362–63; sup-

arms limitation (*cont.*)
port for, in Germany, 42, 131,
246, 248, 250, 253, 258
army, 181–84, 193, 416
Arnaud, Émile, 14, 288, 288n,
338n, 348, 376–77
Arndt, Ernst Moritz, 171
Arnhold, Georg, 68, 188
Associated Councils of Churches
in the British and German
Empires for Fostering Friendly
Relations between the Two
Peoples, 212–14, 232, 242n, 311,
315–16
Association de la paix par le droit,
304, 337–38, 338n, 340, 344, 347,
356, 361, 375, 377
*Association des jeunes amis de la
paix*, 337
*Association internationale des
journalistes amis de la paix*,
338n, 376
*Association "La paix et la désar-
mement par les femmes,"* 338n
*Association nationale des libres
penseurs de France*, 345, 355–56
Auer, Fritz, 190
Aufklärung, see Enlightenment
Augspurg, Anita, 302n
Austrian Peace Society, 46, 78–80

B. Z. am Mittag, 191
Bachem, Julius, 152n, 191, 203
Bachem, Karl, 245
Baden, state government, 173–74
Bajer, Frederik, 43, 263n
Baker, J. Allen, 211–12, 214, 318
Bamberger, Ludwig, 45
Baptists, 197
Bar, Ludwig von, 45, 145, 147,
155, 155n
Barkowsky, Martin, 302n
Barni, Jules, 334

Barth, Theodor, 45, 47, 56, 245–
47, 250, 253–54, 313n
Bassermann, Ernst, 242
Bastiat, Frédéric, 7, 332
Baumbach, Karl, 45, 245
Bäumer, Gertrud, 302n
Baumgarten, Hermann, 85
Bavaria, state government, 69–70,
225, 231, 239
Bavarian Academy of Sciences, 85
Beales, A.C.F., 16
Beauquier, Charles, 337–38, 354–
56, 367, 376
Bebel, August, 259, 269, 275–78,
275n, 278n, 281–82
Bellers, John, 6
Bennigsen, Rudolf von, 153n, 243n
Beobachter (Stuttgart), 84, 409n
Bergson, Henri, 349n, 367
Berliner Börsen-Zeitung, 186
Berliner Lokal-Anzeiger, 186
Berliner Morgenpost, 190–91
Berliner Neueste Nachrichten,
186
Berliner Tageblatt, 79, 188, 190,
192
Berliner Zeitung, 80, 190, 247
Bernhardi, Friedrich von, 183,
393, 400
Bernhardt, Sarah, 79
Bernstein, Eduard, 267, 271, 275–
76, 278, 278n, 281, 305n, 384;
pacifism of, 278–79
Bernstorff, Hermann von, 313n
Bernstorff, Johann von, 238
Berthelot, Marcellin, 366n, 367,
374
Bethmann Hollweg, Theobald
von, 140, 214, 234, 236–38, 315,
414–15
Biberpelz, Der, 133
Bismarck, Otto von, 121, 285,
411–13, 416; and peace move-
ment, 42, 46–47, 289

Bloch, Ivan, 67, 101, 182, 184, 192, 230, 289, 399; on war, 97–99, 99n, 388–91, 403, 405
Bloh, Friedrich, 65
Blücher, Gebhard von, 133
Bluntschli, Johann Caspar, 392
Bodin, Marguerite, 373
Boer War, 233, 312
Boguslawski, Albrecht von, 183, 393
Bornhak, Conrad, 393
Bothmer, Count, 65
Boulanger, Georges, 353
Bourdon, Georges, 176
Bourgeois, Léon, 338, 347, 353–54, 364, 366n, 367; at Hague conferences, 369–70
bourses du travail, 340, 362
Bousset, Wilhelm, 207
Bouvet, Francisque, 332
Braun, Lily, 279. See also Gizycki, Lily von
Bredendiek, Walter, 216–17
Breitscheid, Rudolf, 154, 246
Brentano, Lujo, 70, 139, 156n, 302, 313
Breslauer Zeitung, 191
Briand, Aristide, 366n
Bright, John, 6
Broglie, duc de, 331
Brunet, Charles, 337
Buckle, Henry Thomas, 92
Büchner, Ludwig, 43, 124, 126
Bülow, Bernhard von, 230, 234, 255–56, 304, 309, 315, 369n; and first Hague conference, 218–21, 223, 227–28, 231
Bülow bloc, 246
Buisson, Ferdinand, 354, 366n, 373
Bund Deutscher Frauenvereine, 166–67
Bund Neues Vaterland, 129
Bureau français de la paix, 338–40

Burschenschaften, 154, 154n, 178–79

Caillaux, Joseph, 366n
Caligula, 86
Calker, Wilhelm van, 152n
Calwer, Richard, 267
Canterbury, Archbishop of, 212
Caprivi, Leo von, 45, 47, 49, 85, 234, 246
Carlier, Madeleine, 373–74
Carnegie, Andrew, 131n, 235, 238, 399
Carnegie Endowment for International Peace, 137n, 319–20; subsidizes peace movement, 13, 67, 69, 80, 155–56, 177, 213, 280, 339
Casevitz, Henry, 362
Cassirer, Eduard, 154
Catholic Center party, 174, 283; and peace movement, 154, 241, 243–45, 255, 258, 258n
Catholicism, French, and peace movement, 378–82; German, and peace movement, 186, 195–97, 202–204, 213, 381
Cauer, Minna, 167–68
Centrists (SPD), 272
Chamber of Deputies, Denmark, 257
Chamber of Deputies, France, 280, 295; deputies in, and peace movement, 257, 262, 337, 347, 354–56, 360–61, 366
chambers of commerce, 75, 154–55, 313, 367
Charbonnel, Victor, 355–56
Chénon, Émile, 380
Chevalier, Michel, 334
Christian churches, 195–96; in France, and peace movement, 378–82; in Germany, and peace movement, 164, 195–217, 385,

Christian churches (*cont.*)
416. *See also* Catholicism,
Protestant churches
Christian ecumenicism, 211
Christianity, 125, 192–93, 195, 202,
204, 206–208, 216, 251; and
pacifism, 18, 20, 196, 200, 208–
209. *See also* Catholicism,
Protestantism
Christliche Welt, 188, 207–208,
210; Friends of the, 207, 210
Class, Heinrich, 132
Clemenceau, Georges, 295
Cobden, Richard, 6, 95, 333. *See
also* Cobdenism
Cobden-Chevalier treaty, 333
Cobdenism, 102
Cohen, Hermann, 139–40, 151, 178
Comité de défense des indigènes,
338n
*Comité de rapprochement intel-
lectuel franco-allemand*, 305n
Comte, Auguste, 92, 96, 123, 293–
94
Conciliation internationale, 155,
367, 374
*Confédération générale du Tra-
vail* (CGT), 358, 361–62
Conseils généraux, 343, 365
Conservative party, 186, 230, 240–
42, 242n, 244, 256, 258n
Constant, Benjamin, 331
Constantine, Emperor, 208
cooperative movement, 362–63
Corda fratres, 374
Correspondance de la paix, 377
Correspondance de la presse, 377
Cosmopolitan Clubs, 179
cosmopolite, Le, 333
Cosmos, 355–56
Courcel, Alphonse de, 365n, 366n
courrier international, Le, 333
Crimean War, 8
Croix, La, 376

Crucé, Émeric, 5, 21
Curti, Theodor, 189
Curtius, Friedrich, 155n, 205n,
210, 321, 324

Dahn, Felix, 134, 314
Danish Peace Society, 263n
Dansette, Adrien, 378
Darwin, Charles, 92, 123, 140, 394
Darwinism, 127
David, Eduard, 271, 279
Dehmel, Richard, 305n
Dehn, Paul, 159
Delbrück, Hans, 136, 314; as
critic of peace movement, 327–
28, 348n, 398, 403–405
Delcassé, Théophile, 308, 368–69
*Délégation permanente des so-
ciétés françaises de la paix*, 340–
41, 354, 362
Demokratie und Kaisertum, 249
Demokratische Vereinigung, 246
Demokratischer Verein, 50
Depasse, Hector, 376
Dépêche de Toulouse, 375
Dernburg, Bernhard, 238
*Deutsch-Englisches Verständi-
gungskomitee*, see Anglo-
German Conciliation Com-
mittee
Deutsch-Evangelische Blätter,
197
Deutsch-französische Liga
(Molenaar), 294–95, 294n
*Deutsch-französisches Annähe-
rungskomitee*, 242n, 302–304
Deutsche Bank, 152
*Deutsche-Christliche Studenten-
Vereinigung*, 214
Deutsche Demokratische Partei,
71n, 327
Deutsche Freisinnige Partei, 45.
See also Progressive parties
Deutsche Gewerkvereine, 264–65

Deutsche Kolonialgesellschaft, 68, 127, 314
Deutsche Positivistische Vereinigung, 125, 293
Deutsche Revue, 151, 191
Deutsche Tageszeitung, 158, 173, 186
Deutsche Volkspartei, *see* Süddeutsche Volkspartei
Deutsche Zeitschrift für Geschichtswissenschaft, 85
Deutscher Flottenverein, 127, 255
Deutscher Freidenkerbund, 124–26. *See also* free-thought movement
Deutscher Grosslogenbund, 130
Deutscher Lehrerverein, 172
Deutscher Monistenbund, 125, 127–28
Deutscher Verein für Frauenstimmrecht, 167
Deutscher Verein für internationale Friedenspropaganda, 41, 239
Deutscher Verein für obligatorische Friedensjustiz, 41
Deutscher Wehrverein, 402
Deutsches Friedenskartell, 335n
Deutschland unter den Weltvölkern, 319
Dickinson, Willoughby, 212
Dietz, Alexander, 189
Dilthey, Wilhelm, 140
disarmament, *see* arms limitation
Dix, Arthur, 188
documents du progrès, Les, 123
Dohrn, Heinrich, 45
Doizy, Henri Louis, 361
Dokumente des Fortschritts, 123
Dolfuss, Jean, 334
Doob, Leonard, 33
Dove, Heinrich von, 245
Dresdner Bank, 68

Dreyfus affair, 338–39, 351, 353, 361, 380
Dryander, Ernst, 212, 316
Dumas, Jacques, 337, 348
Duncker, Franz, 264
Durkheim, Émile, 123
Duse, Eleonora, 79

Eberle, Cyprian, 51
Echo de Paris, L', 376
école nouvelle, L', 373
economics, academic, and pacifism, 139
éducation, L', 373
Edward VII, King of England, 320
Égalité, L', 338n
Egidy, Moritz von, 193–95, 207, 293
Eiche, Die, 213
Eichtal, Gustave d', 334
Eickhoff, Richard, 152, 255, 258, 302
Einem, Karl von, 234
Enlightenment, 38, 122, 331
Erastianism, 378, 385
Erbach-Schöneberg, Prince zu, 313n
Erfurt program, 268
Ernste Gedanken, 192–93
Erzberger, Matthias, 244
Esperanto, 129–30, 299
Estournelles de Constant, Paul Henri de, 161; delegate to Hague peace conferences, 367, 369–71; and French peace movement, 347, 354, 357, 365–66, 374, 376; and Germany, 155, 160, 234, 257, 295, 303–304
ethical culture movement, 124–26, 141, 194
Ethical Culture Society, 124–26, 167
Europäischer Unionsverein, 41

Evangelical churches, *see* Protestant churches
Evangelical-Social congress, 215
Evangelical-Social movement, 207
Éveil démocratique, L', 381
ewige Friede, Der, 225

Faber, Wilhelm, 212, 313n
Faure, Ferdinand, 374
fédération de l'Europe, La, 347n
Fédération des travailleurs socialistes de l'Yonne, 361
Fédération des universités populaires de France, 340, 345
Fédération protestante de France, 378–79
Feldhaus, Richard, 51–52, 62–63, 65, 68, 388
feminism, 27, 344, 375, 398
feminist movement, 165–68, 166n
Festspiel in deutschen Reimen, 133
Figaro, 376
Finkenschaften, see Freie Studentenschaften
First World War, 71, 71n; peace movement after, 88, 335n; peace movement and outbreak of, 320, 322–24, 350, 419; peace movement during, 84–85, 87–88, 107, 129, 137n, 150n, 252n, 302n
Fischer, Fritz, 157n, 411
Fleischmann, Max, 151
Flinsch, Heinrich, 132, 313n
Foerster, Wilhelm, 76, 76n, 124, 126, 128; activities in peace movement, 47, 152n, 155, 312n, 316
Fonsegrive, Georges, 380
foreign office, France, 365–66, 368–71
foreign office, Germany, and Hague conferences, 219–20, 225–26, 228–29; and peace

movement, 69, 86, 150, 232, 235, 256, 303–304, 314n, 315; supported by pacifists, 308
Fortschrittliche Volkspartei, 154, 248. *See also* Progressive parties
Fortschrittlicher Verein, Munich, 253
Fournier, 377
Fowler, H. W., 15n
France catholique, La, 381
Franco-German joint parliamentary conferences (Berne and Basel, 1913–1914), 279–83
Franco-German League (Molenaar), *see Deutsch-französische Liga*
Franco-German League (Quidde), 301–302, 302n
Franco-German *rapprochement*, peace movement and, 301–305, 305n, 312, 316
Franco-German Reconciliation Committee, *see Deutsch-französisches Annäherungskomitee*
Franco-Prussian War, 8, 10–11, 98, 297; French peace movement and, 333, 335–36
Frank, Adolphe, 336
Frank, Ludwig, 279–80, 282
Frankfurter Friedensverein, 43–44, 52–53, 61n, 67, 72, 174; membership in, 64 (fig. 2), 72, 73 (fig. 3), 75
Frankfurter Zeitung, 44, 150, 188–89, 191–92
Franz Ferdinand, Archduke, 80, 322
Frau der Gegenwart, 167
Frauen-Tageszeitung, 167
Die Frauenbewegung (journal), 167
Free Conservative party, 174, 258n

free religious communities, 125
free-thought movement, in
France, 352, 355–56, 379, 385; in
Germany, 124–26, 385, 398
free-trade groups, 131–32
Free Trade Unions, 269
Freemasonry, in France, 340, 345,
352, 354–56, 379; in Germany,
130–31, 203, 345, 354, 398
Freie Studentenschaften, 179–80
*Freimaurerbund "Zur Aufgehen-
den Sonne,"* 131
Freisinnige Vereinigung, 246. See
also Progressive parties
Freisinnige Volkspartei, 247. See
also Progressive parties
French Revolution, 117, 349
Freytag, Gustav, 46
Fried, Alfred Hermann, 55–56,
68, 128–29, 133–34, 138, 140, 142,
168, 230, 322–24, 384, 397, 400,
417; career of, 80–82, 82n; and
France, 295, 302, 305n, 345, 347;
and German government, 235–
37, 235n; and German Peace
Society, 46–47, 49–50, 54, 57–58,
63, 88, 320; and other pacifists,
48, 52, 58, 77–78, 84–85, 89n, 93,
255, 406n; and political parties,
240–43, 247, 251–52; and press,
187–89, 190–92; and socialists,
80, 269, 276–78, 276n, 278n; and
universities, 176–78, 177n; and
*Verband für internationale
Verständigung,* 148–51, 158,
160; theories of, 94–112, 98n,
108n, 114–15, 116n, 118, 120,
122–23, 146–48, 401
Friedens-Blätter, Die, 62, 67
Friedens-Warte, Die, 68, 79–82,
322; distributed, 177, 177n, 240,
277–78, 278n
Friedensblatt, 42

Friedensvereinigung München,
53, 61n
Friedrichs, Elsbeth, 65
Friedrichs, Friedrich, 65
Friends of the *Christliche Welt,*
see *Christliche Welt*
Fronde, La, 375
Fulda, Ludwig, 134, 302, 305n

Gambetta, Léon, 334
Garibaldi, Giuseppe, 333–34
Garnier, Joseph, 7, 332, 334
Gasman, Daniel, 127n
Gayraud, abbé, 380
Gemähling, Paul, 380
General-Anzeiger, 186
General Councils, *see Conseils
généraux*
General Peace Convention
(1843), 7–8
Geneva convention (1864), 226
Gérault-Richard, Alfred, 375
Gerlach, Hellmut von, 190, 246–
47
German Peace Society, 45–88,
71n, 148, 233, 250, 345; campaign in Germany, 173, 175,
177, 187, 205, 211, 260, 262,
263n, 266, 268, 277, 280; founding, 46–47, 53, 77, 243, 245; program and goals, 93, 103, 105,
107, 163–64, 218, 235, 239–40;
and international politics, 297,
299, 301, 305, 307n, 308, 312,
314–19, 322–23; leaders, 76–88,
94, 201; membership, 59–60, 62–
67, 64 (fig. 2), 71–72, 75–76,
75n, 126–28, 131, 134, 172, 182–
83, 197, 202, 215, 238, 244–45,
247, 265; and other peace
groups 122, 148–49, 156–60, 162,
214, 254, 258, 316; structure, 57,
60 (map), 61–62, 67–69, 71–72,
121, 167, 317–19, 401

German People's party, *see Süd-deutsche Volkspartei*
German Sociological Association, 141–43
Germany and the Next War, 400
Gesellschaft für ethische Kultur, see Ethical Culture Society
Gide, Charles, 338, 363
Gignoux, Claude, 362
Gizycki, Georg von, 124, 126, 167
Gizycki, Lily von, 167. *See also* Braun, Lily
Gobat, Albert, 13, 132, 280
Göhre, Paul, 207, 210
Goldscheid, Rudolf, 141–42
Gossler, Heinrich von, 184
Gothein, Georg, 142, 154, 245, 302
government, France, 308n, 323, 364–71
government, Germany, imperial, 164, 177n, 281, 290, 416–17; attitude toward peace movement, 230–39, 254–58, 290, 314, 406, 417; criticized by peace movement, 233, 301, 309–11; and Hague conferences, 218–30; supported by peace movement, 308–309, 322–23
government, Germany, state (Land), 239–40. *See also* Baden, Bavaria, Hamburg, Prussia, Württemberg
Goyau, Georges, 372
Grand-Carteret, Jacques, 305n
Gratry, Alphonse, 334, 380
Gratry Society, 338n, 380–81
Griff nach der Weltmacht, 411
Grimm, Robert, 279
Groh, Dieter, 265
Groupe de l'arbitrage interna-tional, 366–67, 376
Guesde, Jules, 358–59, 362
Guizot, François, 331

Guyot, Yves, 338, 354, 375
Gwinner, Arthur von, 153n, 155
Gyssling, Robert, 153n

Haas, Ludwig, 281
Haase, Hugo, 275–76, 281
Haberland, Georg, 244
Haeckel, Ernst, 124, 127n, 137, 170; and peace movement, 127, 151, 155, 302, 305n
Hague convention, 228, 262, 348
Hague, The, international tribu-nal, 3–4, 35, 113, 282, 309
Hague, The, peace conferences, 136, 273, 310, 366–67, 371, 399, 410, 417; German government and, 218–30; peace movement and, 13, 55–57, 148
—of 1899, 69, 98, 175, 261, 293, 393–94; and France, 339, 369–71; German policy at, 177, 218–29, 231; response to, in Germany, 99, 105, 135, 145–47, 208, 244, 246n, 254, 267–68
—of 1907, 211, 221, 371; Ger-man policy at, 229–30, 257; response to, in Germany, 147, 242, 244
Haldane, Richard, 140
Hallgarten, George W. F., 161
Hamburg, state government, 55, 231, 401
Hamburger Nachrichten, 186, 401
Handbuch der Friedensbewe-gung, 100, 103, 110, 115, 146, 279
Handelsvertragsverein, 132
Hansabund, 132
Harburger, Heinrich, 70
Harmening, Ernst, 245
Harms, Bernhard, 139, 154
Harnack, Adolf, 151, 193, 210,

215, 316; liberal Protestantism of, 206–209, 215–16
Hartmann, Wilhelm, 62
Hasse, Ernst, 312n
Hauptmann, Carl, 133–34, 305n
Hauptmann, Gerhart, 133–34, 170, 305n
Haussmann, Conrad, 153n, 154, 245, 247–48, 255, 281–82, 302
Havas, 377
Hayes, Carlton, J. H., 122
Heberle, Rudolf, 34
Hegel, G.W.F., 83, 385, 394
Heilberg, Adolf, 62, 65, 397
Heraclitus, 394
Herder, J. G., 39, 289
Herold, Der, 131
Herrenhaus, Prussian, 303, 314
Hertling, Georg von, 244
Hervé, Gustave, 358–61, 364, 374n
Hesse, Hermann, 134
Heuss, Theodor, 77
Heydebrand und der Lasa, Ernst von, 258, 313n
Hildebrand, Gerhart, 275
Hilferding, Rudolf, 276n
Hirsch-Duncker unions, see Deutsche Gewerkvereine
Hirsch, Max, 45, 47, 56–57, 174, 254–55, 264
history, academic, and pacifism, 136–39
Hobbes, Thomas, 100, 115
Hoeltzel, Max, 313–14
Hoffmann, Leonhard, 245
Hofstadter, Richard, 396
Hohe Meissner, 170
Holleben, Theodor von, 314, 316
Holstein, Friedrich von, 220–21, 227, 254n
Hörth, Otto, 188
"Hottentott" elections, 270
House of Commons, 257

Huber, Max, 148
Hughes, H. Stuart, 122
Hugo, Victor, 332–33
Humanité, L', 360, 362
Hutten-Czapski, Bogdan von, 303

Idea for a Universal History, 38
Immenhausen und Knyphausen, Prince, 313n
imperialism, debate over, in SPD, 270–76, 273n, 278–79
Indépendance belge, L', 377
Institut de droit international, 9, 392
instituteur républicain, Le, 373
International, The, 123
International Arbitration and Peace Association of Great Britain and Ireland, 11, 43
International Catholic Peace League, 195, 197, 204
International Cooperative Alliance, 363
International Council of Women, 166
international language, 27, 129–30. See also Esperanto
international law, 9, 156, 323; academic, and pacifism, 143–48; attitudes toward, in Germany, 222, 232, 247–48, 253, 278, 399, 404; French peace movement and, 348; pacifists and, 22–23, 48, 93, 97, 111, 114, 150, 287–88, 288n; Verband für internationale Verständigung and, 151–53, 160–61
International Law Association, 9
"international movement," 9
International Peace Bureau, 13, 61, 66–67, 140, 173, 262, 280, 292, 295; and French peace movement, 339–40, 355–56, 361–63;

International Peace Bureau
(*cont.*)
and German peace movement,
54, 62, 87, 159
International Socialist Bureau,
262, 262n
International Union of the Pacifist Press, 189
International Women's Union,
166
Internationale Handels-Union,
131, 131n
Internationale Studentenvereine,
179–80
internationalism, 137, 196, 245;
defined, 25; liberal political,
25–27, 162
internationalization, 8–9, 9n, 183,
234–35, 252, 278; and internationalism, 25–26; and pacifism,
24, 101–102, 118, 122
Interparliamentary Bureau, 13,
281
Interparliamentary Conferences,
13–14, 14n, 78, 257, 262, 269;
Germans at, 44–45, 254; Paris,
1889, 12; London, 1890, 44–45;
Rome, 1891, 45; Christiania,
1899, 58; London, 1906, 255;
Berlin, 1908, 255–57
Interparliamentary Union, 12n,
27–28, 41, 253, 254n, 256–59,
261, 288; French branch, 262,
354, 361, 366–67 (*see also*
Groupe de l'arbitrage interna-
tional); German branch, 242n,
243–44, 250, 253–59, 258n, 280–
81 (*see also* Parliamentary
Committee for Peace and Arbitration); German government and, 236, 254–57; German
socialists and, 259, 262, 262n,
269

Jacob, Emil, 303
Jacobinism, 349, 384
Jacobsen, Adolf, 56
Jäckh, Ernst, 252n
Jähns, Max, 393
Jatho, Karl, 210
Jaurès, Jean, 261, 281, 358–62,
364, 366n
Jellinek, Georg, 145, 151, 178
Jodl, Friedrich, 124, 126, 170
Joll, James, 260
Jouet, Alphonse, 296–97
Journal, Le, 375
Journal des instituteurs, 373
Jugendbewegung, see youth
groups
July crisis, 3–4, 320, 322, 414
July Monarchy, 331
Jungdeutschlandbund, 168
Junker, 120

Kaiser und der Weltfriede, Der,
235
Kaiser werde modern!, 235
Kant, Immanuel, 5, 21, 40, 115,
117, 139–40, 140n, 347, 385;
German pacifists and, 38, 105–
108, 106n, 117, 289, 331
Kattenbusch, Ferdinand, 216
Kautsky, Karl, 266–67, 277, 282,
358; theory of imperialism,
272–76, 273n, 276n, 278–79, 284
Kayser, Jacques, 351
Keim, August, 255, 393
Kiderlen-Wächter, Alfred von,
234, 315
Kieler Zeitung, 191
Kinsky, Bertha von, *see* Suttner,
Bertha von
Kirchliche Komitee zur Pflege
freundschaftlicher Beziehungen
zwischen Grossbritannien und
Deutschland, Das, see Asso-
ciated Councils of Churches in

the British and German Empires for Fostering Friendly Relations between the Two Peoples

Koch, Rudolf, 303

Köhnische Zeitung, 191

Kölnische Volkszeitung, 191, 203

Königsberger Hartungsche Zeitung, 191

Körner, Theodor, 171

Kohler, Josef, 47, 49, 49n, 148

Kohler, Martin, 62

Komitee "Konfessionslos," 201

Kopp, Georg Cardinal, 202

Krause, Karl Christian Friedrich, 39

Kreuzzeitung, 184, 186

Krieg, 133–34

Krupp, Friedrich, 47

Kulturkampf, 202

Laband, Paul, 154

labor movement, French, and peace movement, 357–64, 384; German, and peace movement, 357. *See also* Social Democratic Party of Germany

Lafargue, Paul, 358, 362

La Fontaine, Henri, 13, 70, 297

Lahusen, Dieter, 212

Lamartine, Alphonse de, 331–32

Lamprecht, Karl, 137–39, 151–52, 170, 236–38, 302

Landesverein Württemberg, 59, 299

Landtag, 51, 175, 240, 245, 254; Baden, 173–74, 242, 372; Bavaria, 87, 258; Prussia, 174, 254, 281; Württemberg, 68

Langguth, Wilhelm, 409n

Laroche, Hippolyte, 354

La Rochefoucauld-Liancourt, duc de, 331

Lassalle, Ferdinand, 40–41

Lavisse, Ernest, 338, 367

League of Nations, 35

Ledebour, Georg, 275, 277, 281

Le Foyer, Lucien, 347, 354, 356

Legien, Carl, 269–70

Legion of Honor, 347

Lehmann, Max, 136, 154

Lehrervereine, 172

Leibnitz, G. W. von, 38

Leiningen-Amorbach, Emrich zu, 313n

Leipziger Volkszeitung, 271

Lemire, abbé, 380

Lemonnier, Charles, 11, 82, 334, 336, 338n, 355

Lendet, Maurice, 376

Lensch, Paul, 271

Leo XIII, 195

Leroy-Beaulieu, Anatole, 374

Levysohn, Arthur, 188, 190

Leyden, Kasimir von, 316

Libyan war, 288

Lieber, Ernst, 243

Liebermann, Max, 305n

Liebermann von Sonnenberg, Max Hugo, 312n

Liebknecht, Karl, 281

Liebknecht, Wilhelm, 263n, 269

Liedtke, Marianne, 348n

Ligue d'Enseignement, 355

Ligue des Catholiques français pour la paix, 381

Ligue du bien public, 333–34, 336

Ligue française pour la défense des droits de l'homme et du citoyen, 340, 345, 352, 356

Ligue internationale de la paix et de la liberté, 11, 82–83, 334–35, 338n, 354, 361

Ligue internationale et permanente de la paix, 10–11, 334–37, 380

Lilienkron, Detlev von, 134

Lindau, Paul, 140

Lipps, Theodor, 152n
Liszt, Franz von, 145, 151–52, 281, 302
Lloyd George, David, 318
Löwenthal, Eduard, 40–42, 41n, 55, 58, 239, 293, 321n
Lucius von Ballhausen, Robert, 313n
Lübbe, Hermann, 124
Lübke, Walter, 315
Luther, Martin, 199–200
Lutheranism, 206, 208, 321. See also Protestantism
Luxemburg, Rosa, 271

MacDonald, Ramsay, 123
Magdeburgische Zeitung, 186
Maier, Hermann, 152
Maistre, Joseph de, 379
Mann, Heinrich, 134
Mann, Thomas, 317
Mannheim, Karl, 18
Mansion House, 318
Manteuffel, Otto von, 303
Marburg school, 140
Marcks, Erich, 136
Marschall von Bieberstein, Alfred, 221, 229–30, 315
Martius, C. A. von, 303
Marx, Karl, 42, 95, 104, 276n
Marxism, 25, 28, 96, 104, 358
März, 191
Maschinenzeitalter, Das, 92
Matin, Le, 375
Maurenbrecher, Max, 279, 302
Maurice, Berteaux, 354
May, Karl, 134
Mazzini, Giuseppe, 7, 11, 333
Meinecke, Friedrich, 39, 136
Mendelssohn-Bartholdy, Albrecht, 313n
Mérignhac, Alexandre, 374
Methodenstreit, 137
Methodists, 197

Meurer, Christian, 146–47, 152, 313n
Meyer, Alexander, 188, 245
Michels, Robert, 142
Middle Ages, 97
militarism, 133–34, 247; peace movement and, 92, 112–13, 163, 173, 263, 276; and resistance to peace movement, 385–87, 392n, 414; German socialists and, 261, 268, 276–77
Militia Christi, 208, 216
Mill, James, 6
Millerand, Alexandre, 361, 366n
Mitteleuropäischer Wirtschaftsverein, 132
Moch, Gaston, 292, 338–40, 347, 377
Moderate republicans, 356–57, 366
Molenaar, Heinrich, 293–97, 299, 301n, 397n
Moltke, Helmuth von (the Elder), 392–93, 409n
Mommsen, Theodor, 135
Monatliche Friedenskorrespondenz, 57–58
monism, 125–29, 135, 201, 215
monist movement, 124–29. See also monism
Monistenbund, Austrian, 141
Monistische Jahrhundert, Das, 128
Montesquieu, Charles de, 96
Moravian Brethren, 197
Morgenstern, Lina, 103, 167–68
Morgenthau, Hans, 23
Morin, Gaston, 376
Moroccan crises, 208–10, 350; of 1905–1906, 117, 308–309, 313; of 1911, 153, 278, 300, 309–10, 315, 317–18
Mosse, Rudolf, 56, 190, 190n
Motherby, Robert, 40
Müller, Richard, 245

Müller-Lyer, Franz, 143
Müller-Meiningen, Ernst, 70, 87,
    153n, 302
Münchner Allgemeine Zeitung,
    191
Münchner Freidenker-Vereini-
    gung, 293
Münchner Neueste Nachrichten,
    186, 296
Münster, Georg zu, 225, 227, 229-
    30, 369, 369n

Nachrichten (Anglo-German
    Conciliation Committee), 314
Napoleon, 200
Napoleonic wars, 5
Nation, Die, 245
National Constituent Assembly
    (Weimar), 327
National Council, Switzerland,
    279-80
National Liberal party, 174, 186,
    230, 242-44, 258n
National Socialist (Naumann),
    see National-Sozialer Verein
National-Sozialer Verein, 249-51
national unification, wars of, 8,
    40, 89
National-Zeitung, 188
Nationalverein, 152n
Natorp, Paul, 139-40, 151, 178
naturalism, 133
Naumann, Friedrich, 207, 247,
    400; and peace movement, 151,
    161, 248-52, 281
navy, German, 127, 246, 311-12,
    404, 413
Navy League, see Deutscher Flot-
    tenverein
Nazism, 88n, 127n
neo-Kantianism, 139-40, 140n.
    See also Kant
Neue Hamburger Zeitung, 401
Neue Zeit, 273

Neue Züricher Zeitung, 298
Neufville, Eduard de, 62, 68, 211,
    213, 302, 313-14, 322
New York Times, 238
New York World, 238
Nicholas II, 55, 98, 105, 219, 223n,
    268, 273, 323
Niemeyer, Theodor, 146, 160
Nippold, Otfried, 147-48, 179,
    183, 189, 232, 242, 288; as head
    of Verband für internationale
    Verständigung, 150-53, 150n,
    155-56, 156n, 157n, 158-60, 162,
    320
Nisbet, Robert, 108
Nithack-Stahn, Walther, 210
Nobel, Alfred, 78-79
Nobel Committee, 84
Nobel Peace Prize, 42, 67n, 78-
    79, 81, 84, 88, 366
Nobel prizes, 133
Nord und Süd, 140
Nordau, Max, 123
Norddeutsche Allgemeine Zei-
    tung, 174, 186
Norddeutscher Lloyd, 154-55,
    314
North German Confederation,
    41, 333
Nouvellistes, 376
Novalis, 39
Novikow, Jacob, 98n, 106, 123,
    132; and Fried's theories, 96,
    100, 102; ideologist of French
    peace movement, 347-48, 347n
Nürnberger, Richard, 251

Oertel, Georg, 241, 406
Oeser, Rudolf, 153n, 245
Office central des nationalités,
    344
Oncken, Hermann, 136
Ossietsky, Carl von, 92

Ostwald, Wilhelm, 124–25, 127–
28, 138, 142, 170, 201, 215

Paasche, Hermann, 132, 258, 303–
304
Pachnicke, Hermann, 47, 153n
pacifists, 15, 15n
pacifism, 38–39, 47, 84, 132–33,
149, 286, 318–19, 324, 327, 335n,
411; academic interest in, in
Germany, 135–48, 162; of
Bertha von Suttner, 79, 90–95,
109–10; and Christian churches
in Germany, 204, 208–209, 214–
15, 244; definition and scope of
term, 14–27; in France, 332–33,
335, 338, 347–51, 353, 355, 357–
58, 364, 373, 378–81; German
socialists and, 267, 276, 276n,
278, 284; history of term, 14–
16; ideological and utopian
traditions, 17–22, 25–26, 34, 38,
72, 76, 209, 266, 270; implications of, 116–21, 263; liberal
Protestant, 208–209, 214; opposition to, in Germany, 42, 60,
384–85, 392, 401, 403, 407, 410;
and political parties in Germany, 245–46, 249–51; scientific,
94–112, 108n, 122, 160, 200, 247,
276, 276n; and sympathetic
groups in Germany, 123, 125–
30, 132, 167–68; in various
countries, compared, 120, 371,
382–85; and *Verband für internationale Verständigung*, 158,
160
Pädagogisches Wochenblatt, 172
paix par le droit, La, 296, 337
Pams, Jules, 354
Pan-German League, 127, 137,
153, 159, 232, 294, 294n, 306, 402,
408
Panther, see Moroccan crises

Paris Commune, 337
Parliamentary Committee for
Peace and Arbitration, 45; in
1890s, 253–55; under Eickhoff,
255–59
Parti socialiste de France, 358–59
Parti socialiste français, 359
Paschoud, Martin, 334
Passy, Frédéric, 10, 13, 298, 334,
336–37, 338n, 341, 347, 360, 365n,
367, 373–74, 380
Payer, Friedrich von, 153n, 245,
247–48
peace movement, 35, 37, 328–30;
comparative success of, 330–31,
382–85, 410; defined, 15–16, 22,
26–28; program and goals, 28–
30, 32–37, 163–64; in Austria,
38–39, 330; in Belgium, 70, 262;
in England, 204, 261, 311, 320,
384
—in France, 36–37, 280; and
Alsace-Lorraine, 292–301,
350; character of, 378–82;
compared to German, 342–48,
348n, 350–51, 365, 372, 378,
382–85; development of, 331–
39; and education, 372–74;
and labor movement, 261–62,
357–64; and politics, 352–67;
and press, 375–77
—in Germany, 37, 194–95, 302n,
305–10, 324–25; and academic
community, 74, 135–48; and
Alsace-Lorraine, 291–301;
and army, 182–84; and business organizations, 74, 131–32;
and Christian churches, 195–
217; compared to French,
335n, 342–48, 350–51, 365, 372,
378, 382–83; and education,
170–81; and England, 310–18;
and Freemasonry, 130–31;
German government and,

219, 230–39; ideology of, 38–39, 90, 93–94, 102–109; internal aspects, 40–43, 49–59, 50n, 67–68, 70–71, 71n, 77–78, 122, 148–49, 162, 317–20, 323; opposition to, 42, 88, 121, 218, 225, 286, 325–28, 384–419; and politicians, 241–59; and press, 184–92; program and goals, 36, 109–16, 164–65, 218; socialists and, 259–85; and sympathetic groups, 125–29, 167–68; on war, 317, 322–24; writers and, 132–35; and youth groups, 168–70
—international, 67, 96, 123, 130, 166, 219, 234, 320, 332; development of, 4–14, 44, 338; disputes in, 287–300; and Germany, 47, 53–54, 62, 78–82, 289, 344, 410; socialists and, 259–62, 260n; in Russia, 322, 330; in United States, 320, 384–85
Peace of God movement, 96
Peasant War, 200
Pechmann, Wilhelm von, 313n
Penn, William, 6
Penzig, Rudolf, 126
Permanent Committee for Franco-German Conciliation, 301–302
Perpetual Peace, 38, 106, 106n
Peter the Hermit, 52
petit Journal, Le, 375
petit Parisien, Le, 375
petite République, La, 375
Petits plaidoyers contre la guerre, 333
Pflüger, Georg, 245
philosophy, academic, and pacifism, 139–40
Pichot, abbé, 380
Pierson, E., 409n

Piloty, Robert, 151–52, 302
Pius x, 195, 380
Planck, Karl Christian, 83, 85, 209
Podewils, Clemens von, 70
Poincaré, Henri, 367
Poles (political party), 258n
positivism, 123–24, 135, 141, 294, 384–85; legal, 97, 143–44, 147, 160–61
Posse, Ernst, 191
Potonié-Pierre, Edmund, 333–34, 336
Pratt, Hodgson, 11, 42–43, 89, 126, 336–37
press, French and German compared, 375; French, and peace movement, 292, 295, 372, 375–77; German, and peace movement, 70, 164, 184–92, 230, 256, 298, 316, 397, 416
presse associée, La, 377
Pressensé, Francis de, 356, 359
Preuss, Hugo, 154, 245
Preussische Lehrerzeitung, 174
Progressive parties, 50, 245–48, 252–53; and Interparliamentary Union, 45, 253, 258, 258n; and other peace groups, 154, 245, 281, 283, 316
Protestant churches, in France, 378–79, 381–82; in Germany, 125, 155n, 196–97, 204–205, 205n, 212–16, 378, 385. See also Protestantism
Protestantism, 193, 207, 209, 267, 379; French and German compared, 381; French, and peace movement, 378–79, 381; German, and peace movement, 196–202, 204–205, 212–13, 216; liberal, 206–10, 214–16, 248, 380
Prudhommeaux, Jules, 337, 347
Prussia, state government, 231

Quakerism, 6–8, 11, 22, 211, 320, 384–85
Quessel, Ludwig, 275
Quidde, Ludwig, 56, 129, 136, 137n, 176, 235n, 318, 322, 324, 400, 417; career, 85–88, 88n; and France, 280, 298–302, 301n, 304; in German Peace Society, 62, 66, 69–71, 320; pacifism of, 96–97, 102, 106–109, 114, 117; and politics, 247–48, 252–53, 258; and *Verband für internationale Verständigung*, 152, 158

Rade, Martin, 129, 178, 193, 200, 211, 250; and liberal Protestantism, 207, 209, 215–16, 248; and peace movement, 151, 157n, 188, 210, 213
Radical, Le, 375
Radical party, 347, 352–54, 356, 363, 366. See also Radical republicanism
Radical republicanism, 338–39, 351–57, 373, 375, 378, 384
Radicalism, *see* Radical republicanism
Ralliement, 379
Rappel, Le, 375
Rathenau, Walther, 305n
Ratibor, Victor von, 303
Reformed church (France), 379. *See also* Protestant churches
Reichenau, Ernst von, 393
Reichsbote, Der, 196
Reichspartei, see Free Conservative party
Reichstag, Catholics in, and peace movement, 202, 244; deputies in, and peace movement, 42, 44–45, 51, 152, 154, 156, 242–43, 255, 257–58, 280, 283, 316; and German Peace Society, 49, 56, 68, 240; pacifism and, 223–24, 228, 241, 243, 285, 415; Progressives in, and peace movement, 245, 250, 253–54; socialists in, and peace movement, 262, 269, 273, 275, 277, 279–80
Reichsverband gegen die Sozialdemokratie, 402
Reinhardt, Max, 133–34
Renault, Louis, 369
René, Carl, 303–304, 303n
Reuter, Richard, 51–52, 417n
Reventlow, Ernst, 393
Revue libérale, 376
Rheinisch-Westfälische Zeitung, 186
Richet, Charles, 347, 355–56, 374, 377
Richter, Adolf, 44, 103, 247, 252, 295, 302; career, 82–83, 82n; and German Peace Society, 47, 50–52, 54, 61–62, 66, 71, 86–88
Richter, Eugen, 44, 247, 252, 255
Rickert, Heinrich, 45, 245, 246n, 250
Riesser, Jakob, 132
Rippler, Heinrich, 191n
Ritschl, Albrecht, 216
Ritter, Gerhard, 385
Roëll, Paul von, 303
Rogalla von Bieberstein, Ferdinand, 184
Rohrbach, Paul, 319–20
Rössler, Heinrich, 68, 128, 152, 158, 175, 247
Röttcher, Fritz, 126
Royal Prussian Historical Institute (Rome), 85
Rupp, Julius, 40
Russo-Japanese War, 270
Ruyssen, Théodore, 337, 338n, 347, 347n, 349, 356, 374

Saint-Pierre, Charles François, abbé de, 5, 21, 331
Salisbury, Lord, 386
Salm-Horstmar, Prince Carl zu, 313n
Sangnier, Marc, 380
Sarbonne, 374
Scheidemann, Philipp, 281
Scheler, Max, 16n, 392n
Schelling, Friedrich von, 39
Schiemann, Theodor, 137n
Schippel, Max, 267
Schlegel, Friedrich, 39
Schleicher, Adolf, 305n
Schleiermacher, Friedrich, 200
Schlief, Eugen, 48, 93, 97, 149–50, 289, 384n, 417
Schmoller, Gustav, 85
Schoen, Wilhelm von, 303n, 304
Schönaich-Carolath, Prince Heinrich zu, 56, 152, 155, 242–43, 302, 313n, 316
schools, German, and peace movement, 170–75
Schrader, Karl, 47, 245, 250, 313n
Schubert, Conrad von, 303
Schücking, Walther, 77, 136, 176, 246, 250, 302, 310, 318, 327, 348n, 400, 417; career, 147–48, 177–78, 177n; and *Verband für internationale Verständigung*, 150, 152, 160
Schumpeter, Joseph, 119, 273, 273n
Schwäbischer Merkur, 186
Schwartzhoff, Gros von, 176, 225–26
second empire (French), 333
Second International, *see* Socialist International
Section française de l'internationale ouvrière (SFIO), 357, 359–60
Sedanfeier, 175

Seeckt, Hans von, 335n
Sembat, Marcel, 123, 360
Senate, France, 280, 366
Septennat, 1887, *see* arms bill
Siècle, Le, 375
Siegmund-Schultze, Friedrich, 210–11, 213–15, 318
Sieveking, Heinrich, 152n
Sillon, Le, 380
Simmel, Georg, 123, 141–42, 154
Simon, W. M., 293
Sir, Michael, 245
Smelser, Neil, 34
Smith, Adam, 96
Social Democratic Party of Germany (SPD), 71n, 323, 358, 398, 412; change of attitude toward peace movement, 270, 272–85
—congresses: Jena, 1911, 275, 278, 278n; Chemnitz, 1912, 272, 275; Jena, 1913, 282
Fried and, 80, 95, 240, 269; hostility toward peace movement, 186, 259–70; 407; and Interparliamentary Union, 258n, 259, 262, 262n, 269
Social Democratic Party of Switzerland, 262
socialism, 20, 76, 95, 124–25, 265, 385, 388, 398
Socialist International, 9, 22, 104, 360; and peace movement, 260–62, 260n, 266, 266n, 273n
socialist movement, 28, 40, 259–62, 260n, 269, 419
socialists, 28, 166n, 119, 230, 412; French, and peace movement, 356–66. *See also* Social Democratic Party of Germany
Société chrétienne des amis de la paix, 338n, 379
Société de la paix d'Abbeville et du Ponthieu, 338n

Société de la paix de Felletin et Aubisson, 338n
Société de l'éducation pacifique, 340, 345, 373
Société de morale chrétienne, 331–32
Société française des amis de la paix, 336–37
Société française pour l'arbitrage entre nations, 337, 338n, 340–41, 347, 354, 365n, 367
Société Gratry de la paix, see Gratry Society
Society for the Promotion of Permanent and Universal Peace, 5
sociology, and pacifism, 141–43
Sohm, Rudolf, 198–99, 209, 249, 251
Solf, Wilhelm, 232
solidarisme, 364
Sombart, Werner, 123, 141
Sozialistische Monatshefte, 275
Spahn, Martin, 136, 157n
Spahn, Peter, 153n, 244
Spencer, Herbert, 92, 96, 123
Spiecker, Albert, 212
Spielhagen, Friedrich, 46–47, 134
Ständiges Comitee für deutsch-französische Verständigung, see Permanent Committee for Franco-German Conciliation
Stampfer, Friedrich, 280
state diets, *see* Landtag
Stauff, Philipp, 393
Stead, William, 13, 123, 230, 288
Stein, Ludwig, 140, 305n
Steinmetz, Rudolf, 393
Stengel, Karl von, 225, 228, 369, 393–96, 393n, 409, 409n
Stevenson, R. C., 16
Stöcker, Adolf, 193, 312n, 313n
Stöcker, Helene, 167
Strupp, Karl, 148

Stumm, Wilhelm von, 315
Stumm-Halberg, Carl Ferdinand von, 303
Süddeutsche Volkspartei, 42, 82, 86–87, 247–48, 252. *See also* Progressive parties
Südekum, Albert, 263n
Sully, Maximilien de Béthume, duc de, 5, 21, 331
Suttner, Arthur von, 78
Suttner, Bertha von (*née* Kinsky), 13, 44, 68, 132–33, 167, 176, 253, 269, 286, 292, 305n, 322, 384; career, 46, 78–80, 78n; criticized and mocked, 93, 230–31, 249, 257, 261–62, 319, 327; and Fried, 49, 77–78, 81, 89n, 94, 103, 116n, 122; and German peace movement, 46–47, 70, 88; as novelist, 12, 89, 89n; and other pacifists, 48, 67n, 85, 128, 138, 142, 194; pacifism of, 79, 90–95, 103–104, 108–10, 122
Sybel, Heinrich von, 85
Sylva, Carmen, 79
Syndicat de journalistes français s'occupant spécialement de la politique extérieure, 376

Tägliche Rundschau, 186, 191n, 196
Taft, William Howard, 238
Telegraphic Union, 8
Temps, Le, 295, 334, 364, 376
Tepper-Laski, Kurt von, 302n
Thibault, Narcissus, 67
Tiedje, Johannes, 318
Tirpitz, Alfred von, 163
Tocqueville, Alexis de, 332
Tönnies, Ferdinand, 123, 141-42
Tolstoy, Leo, 209, 320
trade unions, French, and peace

movement, 362. *See also* Free
Trade Unions
Trarieux, Ludovic, 356–57
Traub, Gottfried, 210
Treaty of Frankfurt, 291, 296–97,
335–36, 335n
Treaty of Versailles, 335n
Treitschke, Heinrich von, 385,
394–95
Trendel, August, 245
Trimborn, Karl, 154, 245
Triple Alliance, 287
Troeltsch, Ernst, 151, 207, 210,
215–16
Tschirsky, Heinrich von, 223
Tzschoppe, Walter von, 174

Ullmann, Emmanuel von, 152,
155n, 164
Ullstein, Hans, 56, 80, 190–91,
190n
Umfrid, Otto, 175, 185, 187, 259,
287, 289, 309, 400, 409, 409n;
career, 83–85, 85n; and
churches, 196, 201, 204–206,
209, 211, 213; and colonialism,
305, 308–309, 397; and England,
318–20; and France, 288, 295–
300, 302, 317, 323; and German
Peace Society, 51–52, 59, 61–
63, 67, 67n, 71–72, 88; pacifism
of, 77, 103, 114, 117–18, 209,
320–21, 323–24
Uncle Tom's Cabin, 12
Union démocratique (Aix-en-
Provence), 356
*Union des instituteurs patrio-
tiques*, 372, 374n
*Union des sociétés coopératives
de consommation*, 362–63
Union of International Associations, 9
Union of the German Press
Friendly to Arbitration, 188

Union républicaine, 366
United Nations, 35
Univers, L', 376
Universal Peace Congresses, 13–
14, 14n, 29, 195, 231, 262, 291–
92, 346, 401; Germans at, 44, 66,
78, 87; Paris, 1889, 11, 44, 337;
Rome, 1891, 127, 245; Berne,
1892, 46; Hamburg, 1897, 54–55,
69, 70n, 167–68, 194; Glasgow,
1901, 15; Rouen/Le Havre,
295–96, 300; Boston, 1904, 297,
362; Lucerne, 1905, 297–301,
312; Milan, 1906, 380; Munich,
1907, 69–70, 69n, 86, 139; London, 1908, 362; Stockholm,
1910, 288; Geneva, 1912, 300
Universal Postal Union, 8
Universel, L', 379
universités populaires, 361–62
universities, French, and peace
movement, 374; German, and
peace movement, 176–81, 177n,
416

Vaihinger, Hans, 153n
Vaillant, Édouard, 359–60, 366n
Valentin, Veit, 137n
Vanderpol, Alfred, 380, 382
Vandervelde, Émile, 262
Vereshchagin, V. V., 80
Verba, Sidney, 30
*Verband für internationale Ver-
ständigung*, 151–62, 152n, 153n,
182–84, 188, 191, 205n, 321, 323,
348, 367; background and
founding, 148–52; churchmen
and, 210–11, 214; and England,
314–16; and France, 280, 301–
302; and German Peace So-
ciety, 157–60, 319; government
and, 232–33; politicians and,
154, 156, 242–43, 243n, 245, 247,

Verband für int. Verständ.
(*cont.*)
250–51; program and goals,
152–53, 163–64, 218; and uni-
versities, 176–80
Verband reisender Kaufleute,
131
Verein Berliner Presse, 46
Verein Deutscher Freimaurer, 131
Verein für Sozialpolitik, 152
Vereinsgesetz, imperial, 240; of
states, 410
Versöhnung, Die, 194
Vierkandt, Alfred, 142, 154
Virchow, Rudolf, 42–43, 45, 56
Völker-Friede, Der, 62, 67
Völkerschlacht, 133
Vogt, Gustave, 334
Vogtherr, Ewald, 279
Voigts, Bodo, 212
Volksschule, Die, 172
Vorwärts, 95, 262, 268, 272, 277
Vossische Zeitung, 186, 188

Waffen nieder!, Die, journal, 46,
49, 78–79; novel, 12, 46, 52, 78,
89–90, 92, 261–62
Wagner, Jacob, 39
Waldeck-Rousseau, René, 366n
Wandervögel, 169–70
War of the Future in Its Tech-
nical, Economic and Political
Significance, The, 97–99, 97n.
See also Bloch, Ivan
Wars of Liberation, 133, 170
Weber, Alfred, 154
Weber, Eugen, 339
Weber, Max, 141–42, 151, 161,
249, 251
Weg zur Macht, Der, 272
Wehberg, Hans, 77, 147–48, 160,
176, 178–79, 327, 348n; and
Fried, 82, 99, 109–10

Wehler, Hans-Ulrich, 413
Wehrkraftvereine, 168
Wehrvorlage, see arms bill
Weimar Cartel, 125
Weinel, Heinrich, 77, 152n, 210
Weiss, André, 374
Weizsäcker, Julius, 85
Welt am Montag, 80, 190
Weltbürgertum und National-
staat, 39, 136
Weltpolitik, 413
Welträtsel, Die, 124, 127
Weltwirtschaftliches Archiv, 139
Wendt, Hans, 210
Wesen des Christentums, Das, 206
Weser-Zeitung, 191
Westphal, Arthur, 126, 201
Wiegand, Heinrich, 314
Wiesbadener Friedensgesell-
schaft, 47, 61n
Wiese, Benno von, 89
Wille, Bruno, 123
William, Crown Prince, 234, 402
William II, 55, 70n, 86, 91, 202–
203, 253, 296; and Hague con-
ference, 1899, 219, 221, 223,
223n, 224n, 225–28; and peace
movement, 214, 231, 233–35,
235n, 238–39, 256
Windelband, Wilhelm, 140n
Wirth, Franz, 43–44, 67, 247; and
France, 292–93, 296; and Ger-
man Peace Society, 47, 50–54,
51n, 57
Wirth, J.A.G., 43
Wirth, Max, 44
Wolf, Julius, 132
Wolff, Christian, 38
Wolff Telegraphic Bureau, 187,
189
Wolff, Theodor, 190
Wolff-Metternich, Count Paul,
255–56

Worms, Émile, 338
Württemberg, state government, 233
Wynecken, Gustav, 169–70

Y.M.C.A. movement, German, 214
youth groups, 168–70, 210, 217, 416

Zabern incident, 300–301
Zeitschrift für Völkerrecht und Bundesstaatsrecht, 148
Zeller, Eduard, 140
Zorn, Philipp, 146–47, 225–27, 232, 302, 369
Zukunft, Die, 147
Zwanzigste Jahrhundert, Das, 134
Zweig, Stefan, 305n

Library of Congress Cataloging in Publication Data

Chickering, Roger, 1942-
    Imperial Germany and a world without war.

    Bibliography: p.
    1. Peace—History.   2. Germany—History—1871-1918.
3. Germany—Politics and government—1871-1918.   I. Title.
JX1961.G3C47   943.08'4   75-2983
ISBN 0-691-05228-X